Legal Ethics
Text and Materials

Law in Context

Editors: William Twining (University College, London) and
Christopher McCrudden (Lincoln College, Oxford)

Legal Ethics
Text and Materials

Richard O'Dair

Senior Lecturer, University College, London

CAMBRIDGE
UNIVERSITY PRESS

CAMBRIDGE UNIVERSITY PRESS
Cambridge, New York, Melbourne, Madrid, Cape Town, Singapore, São Paulo

Cambridge University Press
The Edinburgh Building, Cambridge CB2 8RU, UK

Published in the United States of America by Cambridge University Press, New York

www.cambridge.org
Information on this title: www.cambridge.org/9780521606004

© Reed Elsevier (UK) Ltd 2001

First published by Butterworths 2001
Published in Malaysia by Malayan Law Journal Sdn Bhd 2001
Published in the United States of America by Lexis Law Publishing 2001
Digitally reprinted by Cambridge University Press 2007

A catalogue record for this publication is available from the British Library

ISBN 978-0-521-60600-4 paperback

Preface

This book is the result of the writer's observation early in 1994 that while some legal subjects benefited from numerous textbooks and considerable critical commentary, others seemed by comparison to be bereft. Legal Ethics seemd to be in the latter category and this book was conceived as an attempt to fill the gap. The book is not intended as a comprehensive guide to any particular professional code. Therefore many of the topics covered in, for example, the *Law Society's Guide to the Professional Conduct of Solicitors*, are not covered in this book. Rather the book aims to inform and stimulate debate about fundamental questions of ethics as they relate to the practice (business?) of law at the beginning of the 21st century

Thanks are due to a great many people and institutions without whose help and support this book would not have been written. The Alexander Maxwell Law Scholarship Trust funded an extended period of study leave during which I undertook the major part of the research. Professor Deborah Rhode was my host at the Stanford Law School's Keck Center for the Study of Legal Ethics and the Legal Profession in the academic year 1995-1996. Professors Dawn Oliver and Jeffrey Jowell as successive Deans of University College London Faculty of Law gave me moral support and practical help. Professor William Twining, as general editor of this series, took the time to read the manuscript and make many helpful suggestions before it was submitted to the publishers. Stephen Guest, Kim Economides, Ian Dennis, Rodney Austin, Julian Webb and June Chapman all read and commented on individual chapters. My students on the undergraduate Legal Ethics course at UCL taught me a great deal about the strengths and weaknesses of various draft chapters. Eversheds, one of the UK's leading law firms, generously sponsored the study packs used by those students, which included much of the material now contained in this book. John Hall, head of Eversheds education department, was particularly helpful.

Finally, my wife Kathy gave me endless encouragement and helped me to persevere when my faith in the project was beginning to wane.

Richard O'Dair

February 2001

Acknowledgments

The author and publishers wish to thank the following for their permission to reproduce in this work materials from their titles. The publishers would also be pleased to her from those copyright holders from whom permission has been sought, but not yet received.

CHAPTER 1

- University of Chicago Law Review

CHAPTER 2

- Capital University Law Review
- Columbia Law Review
- Duke Law Journal
- Georgetown Law Journal
- Maryland Law Review

CHAPTER 3

- Professor Richard L Abel
- Blackwell Publishers Ltd
- International Journal of the Legal Profession

CHAPTER 4

- Dartmouth Publishing Company Ltd
- Harvard Law Review
- Adrienne Stone

CHAPTER 5

- American Bar Association
- American Bar Foundation Research Journal
- Capital University Law Review
- Columbia Law Review
- Harvard Law Review
- Maryland Law Review
- Michigan Law Review
- Professor Stephen L Pepper
- Princeton University Press
- Wisconsin Law Review
- Yale Law Journal

CHAPTER 6

- Crown Prosecution Service
- Harvard Law Review
- Legal Research Institute, Warwick University
- London School of Economics and Political Science
- Michigan Law Review
- Oxford University Press

CHAPTER 7

- Law Society Publishing

CHAPTER 8

- California Law Review
- Iowa Law Review
- Journal of Legal Education
- Lloyd's of London Press Limited

CHAPTER 9

* Maryland Law Review
* Texas Law Review
* Wisconsin Law Review
* Yale Law Journal

CHAPTER 10

* Blackwell Publishers Ltd
* Civil Justice Quarterly
* Her Majesty's Stationary Office
* International Journal of the Legal Profession
* Oxford University Press
* AAS Zuckerman

CHAPTER 11

* Oxford University Press
* Stanford Law Review
* Richard Tur
* University of Pennsylvania Law Review

The Alexander Maxwell Law Scholarship Trust

Maurice W Maxwell, whose family founded Sweet & Maxwell the law publishers, by his Will established a charitable trust to be known as the Alexander Maxwell Law Scholarship Trust in memory of both his great-great-grandfather and his great-grandfather.

The Trust is committed to promoting legal research and writing at various levels by providing financial assistance to authors whether they be experienced legal practitioners or those in the early years of practice. (The Trust does not assist towards the cost of any course or post-graduate work.)

The author of this book received financial assistance from the Trust to undertake the work.

The Trust calls for applications for awards from time to time (usually awards are made in the early part of each calendar year, with a deadline for applications on the preceding August 31). Anyone interested in the work of the Trust or wishing to discuss a possible application should contact:

The Clerk to the Trustees
Alexander Maxwell Law Scholarship Trust
c/o Sweet & Maxwell Limited
100 Avenue Road
London NW3 3PF

The Trust now has a website: http://www.amlst.org.uk and can be reached by e-mail: clerk@amlst.org.uk

Contents

CHAPTER TEN

Lawyers, ethics and access to justice   365

CHAPTER ELEVEN

Conflicts of interest   435

Abbreviations

ABA	American Bar Association
ACLEC	Lord Chancellor's Advisory Committee on Legal Education and Conduct
CCB	Code of Conduct of the Bar in England and Wales
CPS	Crown Prosecution Service (UK)
LAB	Legal Aid Board (UK)
LSC	Legal Services Commission (UK)
LSGPC	Law Society Guide to the Professional Conduct of Solicitors
LSO	Legal Services Ombudsman (UK)
MCPR	ABA Model Code of Professional Responsibility (US)
MRPC	ABA Model Rules of Professional Conduct (US)
SCB	Solicitors Complaints Bureau (UK)
OSS	Office for the Supervision of Solicitors (UK)
RCCJ	The Royal Commission on Criminal Justice (the Runciman Commission) Cmnd 2263 (London, HMSO, 1993)

PART I

Pervasive issues in legal ethics

CHAPTER ONE

Introduction to legal ethics

Q: Should solicitors be able to trust what other solicitors say?

A: It depends on the circumstances, the conversation they are having.[1]

As the new millennium dawns, professional lawyers face a number of challenging problems. Not the least of these is the willingness of government and consumers to take a skeptical approach to their claim to be ethical professionals. Consequently, there could hardly be a better time to be involved in serious debate about the ethics of professional lawyers ('legal ethics') and this book attempts to be part of that debate. Of course, there is likely to be fundamental disagreement about what constitutes appropriate responses to the ethical problems which are currently facing legal practitioners but that only makes informed debate all the more important. In this introduction, I elaborate upon the importance of legal ethics and more generally set out the scope and aims of the book. The chapter concludes with a case study which illustrates some of the points made. The remaining four chapters in Part I deal with some of the major pervasive issues of legal ethics which impact upon the specific topics considered in Part II.

1 The importance of legal ethics

Legal ethics have both a private and a public importance. As to the former, legal ethics are closely related to occupational satisfaction. As Thomas Shaffer says:

> People become lawyers for many reasons. For some it is the money; for some it is the thrill of competition and a desire for success; for others it is the status that comes

1 Exchange between counsel and a solicitor witness in *Ernst and Young v Butte Mining plc* [1996] 1 WLR 1605, which is extracted in chapter 8 at pp 318-323.

from being in a profession. But the big desk, the plaques on the walls, and the things that one can purchase with a large income can only carry a person so far. We suspect that part of the reason that many lawyers are disenchanted with the practice of law is that these things are not inherently satisfying.[2]

In other words, if the motivation and commitment necessary to sustain a career in the law are to be sustained over a lifetime, there needs to be a goal other than self-advancement. Practitioners need to be engaged in something which they believe to be of enduring value, something which justifies the often onerous demands of modern legal practice. Another critic of the view that legal practice is simply an instrument for the attainment of personal wealth and satisfaction is Anthony Kronman. In the following extract he considers what good reasons there might be for pursuing a career in the law.

It is best, perhaps, to begin with the answer that many will think the least respectable, even if they also consider it the most honest. A large number of lawyers undoubtedly believe that the life they have chosen is a desirable one because it offers great opportunities for wealth and prestige, for a disproportionate share of society's material resources and high professional status. Lawyers are generally well-compensated for their work and, though as a group they are often the object of popular vilification they tend, individually, to occupy positions of distinction in their communities. This, one might think, is reason enough to choose a career in the law, and other explanations can easily seem by comparison either unnecessary or disingenuous. Many, of course, will find this view repellent and judge the lawyer who candidly admits that his or her professional goal is money and honour and nothing else irresponsibly selfish. I, too, think that this conception of the worth or value of law practice deficient, but would place the deficiency at a different point.

To enter the practice of law for money and honour alone is, at bottom, to view one's professional career as a vehicle for accumulating those things that are needed in other areas of life in order to acquire or accomplish what seems intrinsically important – important, that is, for its own sake and not as a means of some yet further end. The lawyer who takes this view of his practice treats it as a means to the things he truly cares about, the things that claim his attention, so to speak, at the end of the working day. In this general respect, however, he is no different from the rest of us, for we all do certain things not because we enjoy them or find them rewarding on their own terms but because they enable us to engage in other activities that do have these characteristics. Whether the lawyer who cares only about the pecuniary and honorific benefits of his professional work, who treats his profession as an instrumental good with no intrinsic value of its own, leads a life that in an overall sense is to be admired or regarded with pity and contempt, is a question that ultimately turns on the nature of the ends he uses the external rewards of his work to pursue. The corporate lawyer, for example, who works twelve hours a day at tasks he finds dull and unchallenging may nevertheless be leading a life that no only makes sense as a whole but even has appeal or a measure of nobility. Everything depends on what happens after hours and on whether this way of accumulating the instrumental goods needed to do the important things in life is preferable to the alternatives, both in terms of what it yields and what

2   Thomas L Shaffer *Lawyers Clients and Moral Responsibility* (Minnesota, St Paul, 1994) at p 135.

it takes. So a lawyer should not feel deeply ashamed to say that he is in it just for the money and prestige, though, to be sure, he must give us some account of what these things are for before we can decide whether his life is one we can admire. The question of whether he has reason to care about his professional career merges, at this point, into the larger and less focused question of whether he has reason to care about the things that give his life its meaning as a whole. He may or may not; what I want to stress is that this question is an open one even for the lawyer who values his profession not for what it is but for what it brings.

Still, as I have said, there is something deficient in this view. The deficiency lies, I think, in the breadth of the instrumental attitude that it endorses. No doubt, we must all take an instrumental attitude toward some of the things we do and even, in certain circumstances, toward other people (though our treatment of others as means – in the process of contractual exchange, for example – is usually circumscribed by obligations that reflect what might be called a non-instrumental conception of the other person). What makes the nakedly instrumental view of law practice that I have just described so unattractive is that it takes in too much of life, or more exactly, too much of what is important in life. This should first be understood in a purely quantitative sense. The lawyer who works the kind of hours at the kind of pace necessary to achieve great wealth or fame is likely to discover he has little time or energy left in which to pursue the things for whose sake he has made his professional career the instrument or vehicle. Faulkner, it is true, wrote *As I Lay Dying* in six weeks while working the night shift in a boiler room, but his tasks were intermittent and mindlessly physical and, in any case, he was a genius. No matter how humdrum, the practice of law is always a mental exercise and often an emotional one, and the intellectual and spiritual resources that a lawyer has available for his extra vocational pursuits, whatever they may be, are bound to be depleted in the course of his work itself – significantly so if the work is as long and as demanding of careful attention as it often is.

There is a second, non-quantitative sense in which the instrumental view is deficient and this, it seems to me, is more important still. The deficiency I have in mind can best be brought out if we begin by taking note of a basic fact about the nature of personal identity. Of the various things a person does, many have no bearing on who he is, on his character or personality; he would be the same person and have the same identity whether he happened to do them or not. I myself feel this way, for example, about washing the dishes and commuting to work. There are good reasons, of course, why I do these things but I am quite confident that I would be the same person if I had never done them or never did them again. To be sure, others may view these particular activities in a different light and think of them as being more directly connected with their own distinctive identities (though I must admit that I find this difficult to imagine). What seems to me indisputable, however, is the presence in every person's life of some rough division between those involvements and activities that constitute his character or personality, on the one hand, and those, on the other, that do not, between those that make someone the person he or she *is* and those one merely *has* or *does*.

Now the whole of a person's professional life can, in theory at least, be placed on either side of this line. There is nothing, in the nature of things, that absolutely requires that the various activities of which one's professional existence is composed be character-forming in the sense I have suggested. I believe, however, that the practice of law exerts a very strong pull in this direction. To practice law well requires not only a formal knowledge of the law (a knowledge of what the legal realists termed the 'paper' rules or rules 'on the books') but certain qualities of mind and temperament as well. Most lawyers recognise this and recognise, too, that the qualities in question are also the ones that experience in law practice tends to encourage and confirm[3].

Kronman argues that the problem of professional satisfaction remains even if legal practice can be seen as a way of serving the public interest. There remains 'the risk that [the lawyer] will fail to give due weight to the character-forming consequences of law practice, to the fact that by living in the law one not only accomplishes certain things but tends to become a certain person as well.'[4] His view is that legal practice will be intrinsically satisfying to the extent that it offers the opportunity to develop good judgment, ie to become a person characterised by the ability to make wise choices.

Whatever the potential satisfaction to be derived from legal practice, there is a growing body of evidence that many practitioners are extremely dissatisfied with their experience: one survey of assistant solicitors found large numbers of them expressing a desire to leave the profession.[5] Similarly a recent study by a leading UK expert on occupational stress of the incidence of stress across a range of professional groups concluded that

> Compared with other professional groups, the lawyers studied have the highest levels of occupational stress. They have low levels of job and organisational satisfaction and are the least committed to their organisations. They report the worst levels of mental and physical health.[6]

And the US literature of the legal profession displays a recurrent concern with professional dissatisfaction. Whilst arguing that life in the law has in the past been intrinsically satisfying Anthony Kronman is pessimistic about the prospects under modern conditions. The title of his book *The Lost Lawyer: Failing Ideals of the Legal Profession*[7] tells its own story.

Legal ethics are also of immense public importance. The legal systems of most developed nations may usefully be seen as complex machines with lots of flashing dials and levers whose actual operation will depend upon which levers are pulled in which order. Clients on the whole lack the expertise or the time to pull these levers themselves and employ lawyers to do it for them, though an image of lawyers work which portrayed them solely as technicians would be to beg a host of important questions. Speaking very broadly, the basic orientations of lawyers may be said to be

3   A T Kronman 'Living in the Law' 54 University of Chicago Law Review 835 (1987) at pp 838-841.
4   Ibid at p 845.
5   By the recruitment consultants Zarak MaCrae Brenner: see (1997) *The Lawyer*, 11 November.
6   Stephen Williams and Lesley Cooper *Stress in the Professions: Law Society and Young Solicitor Group Analysis* (Resource Systems, 1998) p 7.
7   A T Kronman *The Lost Lawyer: Failing Ideals of the Legal Profession* (Cambridge, Harvard, 1993). Kronman's views are extremely controversial. See David Wilkins 'Practical Wisdom for Practising Lawyers: Separating Ideals from Ideology in Legal Ethics' [1994] 108 HL 458 and James Altoona 'Modern Litigates and Lawyer Statesmen' [1994] 103 Yale LJ 1031.

either libertarian or communitarian. That is they may perceive their role as being the maximisation of their clients freedom from the restraints of the law; or they may see their role as being to assist their clients in adjusting their affairs to ensure the realisation of the community's purposes as embodied in the substantive law. The latter view is strongest when it can draw upon the moral claims of democratic government and so it is sometimes referred to as the democratic view[8].

The choice made by lawyers between these two approaches either generally or on particular occasions is immensely importance because as explained later in the book[9], there are distinct limits to what can be achieved by regulatory control of the legal profession. Put another way, rules accompanied by the threat of sanctions are likely to be relatively ineffective as a means of controlling unethical behaviour. One reason for this is that so much of the work done by lawyers takes place in private settings and is thus unobservable by regulators. This is particularly true of advisory work. Consider for example a question which arises in relation to client interviewing. Should the client be told the applicable law before s/he is asked to give an account of the facts? The danger is that a client informed of the applicable law will face an irresistible temptation to embroider the truth. The contrary view is that memory is sensitive to assumptions about relevance and that clients may well omit to mention important facts unless their importance is made clear. However we define the range of defensible responses to this dilemma, it will usually arise in the privacy of the lawyer's office. As a result everything will depend on the ethical sensitivity and commitment of the practitioners involved.

2   Legal ethics: something old or something new?

What is legal ethics?

The claim that legal ethics has been neglected as a subject of serious study requires more precision about what we mean by legal ethics, the study of legal ethics and the stage of legal education at which the neglect is said to have occurred. I take legal ethics to be

The *critical* consideration of
1.   the arrangements made by society for the delivery of legal services and in particular of the legal profession, its structures, roles and responsibilities (sometimes termed macro legal ethics); and
2.   the roles and responsibilities of individual lawyers in the provision of legal services together with the ethical implications of those roles (sometimes termed micro legal ethics); and
3.   the wider social context, especially the philosophical economic and sociological context in which lawyers work,

8   Charles Sampford and Stephen Parker 'Legal Regulation, Ethical Standard Setting and Institutional Design' in *Legal Ethics and Legal Practice - Contemporary Issues* (Parker and Sampford (ed) Oxford, OUP, 1995) pp 20-24.
9   See especially chapters 4 and 10.

with a view to identifying and , if possible, resolving the ethical difficulties which face professional lawyers so to enable them to view legal practice as morally defensible and therefore personally satisfying.[10]

It is levels 1 and 3 which make this conception of legal ethics novel. The ethical choices with which individual lawyers are presented (level 2) are significantly influenced by and can only be understood in relation to the context in which legal practice takes place.

As an example consider whether an advocate for the defendant in a rape trial is morally justified in cross-examining the complainant about her prior sexual history[11]. Let us suppose too that the advocate believes that (i). such evidence would be admitted by the trial judge; (ii) may lead to an unjustified acquittal; (iii) is of little relevance to the issue; and (iv). will cause great stress to the complainant. This difficult question most obviously presents itself as a question of micro legal ethics (level 2) but can only be understood in the light of the role of the advocate in an adversarial system of justice (level 1). Moreover, the urgency with which many advocates would now feel the difficulty (and the indignation which they would arouse if they did not) can only be understood in the light of changing assumptions about sexual relations (level 3). The importance of these contextual elements is that changes in context can change the nature of the ethical problems which face individual practitioners at the 2nd level. This is why chapter 2, 'Philosophical foundations of legal ethics', conducts a broad ranging, if selective, survey of some current issues in moral philosophy. These developments may assist us in understanding the ethical problems faced by lawyers.

The same approach is adopted in the discussion of access to justice in chapter 10. The chapter considers the ethical implications of the problem of ensuring access to legal services for those of modest means. Since the Second World War, this problem has been addressed primarily through the judicare legal aid scheme, the essence of which has been that persons with legal problems of a type covered by the scheme and of insufficient means are able to choose and employ a private practitioner at the state's expense. Since the mid 1990s, all the major political parties have agreed that public expenditure must be strictly limited and, consequently, the judicare scheme has all but disappeared. In this context, it is not surprising that there has been renewed debate about whether and if so why lawyers should do pro-bono work. Thus changes in social context (the retreat of the welfare state) can be seen as contributing to a change in the legal context (the contraction of the legal aid scheme) and hence to renewed discussion of pro-bono work at the 2nd level. This conception of what is involved in the study of legal ethics necessitates an interdisciplinary approach and the book draws upon and/or refers to philosophical, economic, sociological and theological perspectives upon the work of lawyers.

---

10   For a different view of the major questions of legal ethics see William H Simon *The Practice of Justice: A Theory of Lawyer's Ethics* (Harvard, HUP, 1998). Simon sees the major questions facing lawyers as raising not a tension between the law and morality but rather the issue of what is required by fidelity to law. Simon's views are considered in detail in chapter 5.

11   See further chapter 6.

Legal ethics and legal education

This book is aimed primarily at undergraduate students of law and their teachers. It was inspired by the perception, shared by the First Report of the Lord Chancellors Advisory Committee on Legal Education and Conduct, that first degrees in law had much to offer in relation to ethics but had hitherto failed to make a real contribution[12]. This position was in stark contrast to the position in the US, where following the involvement of a number of lawyers in the Watergate scandal the ABA imposed upon American law schools an obligation to teach legal ethics. As a result those taking first degrees in law in US law schools have available to them a rich literature on the subject. The continuing neglect in the UK was the result of an approach to the curriculum which resulted in a narrow range of subjects being regarded as academic and therefore within the province of an undergraduate degree in law. Contract fell within the academic field, ethics, like procedure, did not. For much of the 20th century, ethics were taught during articles or pupillage rather than being formally taught. Following the report of the Ormrod committee, subjects regarded as non academic were left to the one year vocational courses which graduates must take before entering pupillage or training contracts. This approach is flawed because it fails to see that legal education is a continuum with each of the differing elements (undergraduate, vocational, in-house pre-qualification and continuing professional development) having important things to contribute to the same subject. In relation to ethics, the opportunity has been lost to encourage students to think critically about legal ethics in an educational context where the pressures to conform to established patterns of behaviour are much lower than they will be in the work place. Indeed there is a sense in which academic law teachers may have been failing vocational law teachers and others whose efforts come later in the educational continuum. Vocational education in the UK has in recent years come to lay heavy emphasis on the teaching of legal skills such as advocacy, drafting and conference skills. This is a development which has been widely welcomed[13] but there are dangers involved in teaching 'how to' if there is insufficient thought about 'whether to'. As Karl Llewellyn once put it 'Technique without ideals is a menace; ideals without technique are a mess'.[14] Ideally, undergraduate legal education ought to be refining and focusing student ideals so to guard against the dangers identified by Karl Llewellyn.

Legal ethics and the liberal legal education

If first degree legal education has much to offer tomorrow's practitioners, what does legal ethics have to offer to a liberal legal education? After all, given the steep rise in

12   Lord Chancellor's Advisory Committee on Legal Education and Conduct *First Report on Legal Education and Training* (London, HMSO, 1996) para 2.11.
13   See for example Joanna Shapland, Valerie Johnson and Richard Wild *Studying for the Bar: The Students Evaluation of the New Vocational Training Course at the Council of Legal Education* (Sheffield, Institute for the Study of Legal Practice, 1998).
14   'The Adventures of Rollo' 2 University of Chicago Law School Record 3 [1952] p 23.

undergraduate law degree places in recent years, it is likely that large numbers of graduates in law will need to find careers outside legal practice. Consequently, it can be argued that the undergraduate degree must remain a broad ranging education in law for citizens ('the liberal law degree') so that legal ethics has a limited claim to space within a crowded curriculum. In my view, the argument misconceives the nature of the liberal law degree on which it purports to be based. Most fundamentally, as Professor Hepple, one of the academic representatives on ACLEC has argued, this dichotomy is false, unhelpful and a deviation from the historic bases of the liberal law degree.[15] The liberal law degree cannot afford to ignore the insights arising from the law as practised. Similarly, the practice of the law is enriched when its practitioners have benefited from a liberal law degree. Indeed, no legal subject can properly be labelled exclusively vocational or exclusively academic. Professor Hepple has said of the founders of the liberal law degree that

> what is common to Blackstone, Amos and Maitland (and to Dicey in his celebrated inaugural as Vinerian Professor in 1883) is that they draw no distinction between a 'liberal' or 'academic' legal education and a 'professional' or 'vocational' one. As Professor Kahn Freund commented in 1966 (in relation to Blackstone and Dicey): [There is] 'not a trace of the thought or superstition that only that which is of practical importance is worthy to be taught or of the perhaps even more pernicious superstition that the less a thing has to do with practice the better it is for the so-called training of the mind.'[16]

Furthermore, legal ethics responds to two of the recurring concerns of the liberal law degree: namely perspective and skills. As to the former, every law school will seek to develop its students' understanding of the basic principles of its domestic law and of its' domestic legal system. If so, legal ethics must form part of the curriculum because the development of legal institutions depends upon, and can only be understood in the light of assumptions about the ethics of the legal profession. It is thus an important perspective on the legal system.

Two examples will serve to illustrate the point, the first being drawn from contract law. Oral contracts are now commonly enforced but this has not always been the case due, it is said, to the courts' earlier lack of confidence in their ability to depend upon oral testimony. The modern position does not only depend upon the assumption that cross-examination will expose false testimony. It also assumes that legal practitioners will not assist in the creation by their clients of perjured evidence. The importance of professional responsibility has recently been re-emphasised by the practice of allowing a witness statement prepared by a solicitor to stand in place of evidence in chief. This practice saves costs for all concerned, but is acceptable only in so far as the legal profession can be trusted to stay on the right side of the line between drafting witness statements and creating them.[17]

---

15   B A Hepple 'The Renewal of the Liberal Law Degree' [1996] 55 CLJ 470.
16   Ibid at p 474 (original footnotes omitted).
17   See *Access to Justice - Final Report* by the Right Honourable the Lord Woolf (London, HMSO, 1996) paras 53-60 at pp 128-130.

The second example is the Family Law Act 1996. Many of its reforming provisions were based on the government's assumption that divorce lawyers will inevitably behave in an adversarial unhelpful fashion. This was particularly true of the shift to mediation rather than litigation as the preferred dispute resolution procedure[18]. Family law is therefore an area where an understanding of lawyers' ethics and of common perceptions about legal ethics are necessary for an adequate understanding of some important substantive reforms.[19]

With respect to skills,[20] the relationship is more complicated. On the one hand, it can be argued that ethical judgment is a skill in the sense that it cannot be reduced to a rule so as to eliminate the need for judgment or in Aristotelian terminology practical wisdom.[1] On the other hand, ethics represents a counterpoint to a concern with skills. Underlying ACLEC's vision for the future of legal education[2] was the view that the law school of the future must attempt to ensure that those trained in the discipline of law should be persons endowed not only with intellectual and technical skills but also with the ethical judgment necessary to ensure that the power which comes with skill and knowledge is used responsibly. Karl Llewellyn's dictum applies whether the skills being taught are general intellectual skills or the more specific skills and techniques relevant to legal practice.

Finally, there is also Anthony Kronman's point that legal practice may effect the characters of practitioners. Kronman argues that practice will be attractive to the extent that it leads to the development of judgment. In the following extract, he elaborates upon the notion of good judgment using as one of his examples career choices:

> I propose to begin by examining more closely what a philosopher might call the 'phenomenology' of judgment, the felt experience of judging itself. I mean to explore, more exactly, the experience of a certain sort of judging, the sort that we engage in when trying to make an important personal decision about our lives – the decision, for example, to get married, have a child, or pursue a particular career. First-personal decisions of this sort are not, of course, the only ones in which judgment plays a role; we must also exercise judgment in the advice we give to others and in the political choices that we make. It is difficult, in fact, to identify an area of our private or public lives that does not provide a theatre for the exercise of judgment or depend upon its proper use. ...
>
> We must all, from time to time, make hard personal choices – to get married or divorced, go to law school or drop out, support a parent or renounce a friend. If we find such choices difficult, it is usually because the alternatives seem in some fashion incommensurable. Each has its own balance of advantages and disadvantages and there is no common metric that permits us to assess their relative attractiveness in a decisive and unambiguous way. The choice that we must make cannot, therefore, simply be a

18   See Family Law Act 1996, ss 13,14 and 29.
19   See generally, *Looking to the Future - Mediation and the Grounds for Divorce* (Cmnd 2799) (Lord Chancellor's Department London, HMSO, 1995).
20   See generally, William Twining 'Legal Skills and Legal Education' (1998) 3 Law Teacher p 7.
1   See generally David Luban 'Epistemology and Moral Education' [1983] 33 J Legal Ed 636 .
2   Report supra note 12 at para 2.4.

matter of deduction or calculation, as utilitarians sometimes suggest. Nor is it a matter merely of waiting for the appropriate intuition, the one that will tell us what to do. We tend to deal with our personal dilemmas, even the intractable ones, in a more active and methodical way than that. Choices of the sort I have in mind call not for deduction or intuition but deliberation, which is another name for judgment. Indeed, it is precisely in situations of this kind, where the choice to be made is between alternatives not easily compared, that our reliance upon the faculty of judgment is most evident. In exercising this faculty, what exactly is it that we do?

The answer, I think, is something like the following. When faced with an important personal decision, I am frequently required to make what amounts to a choice among competing ways of life – different ways of life that might be mine though none of them, by assumption, yet is, at least in its fully developed form. To make such a choice, I must explore the alternatives in my imagination. That is to say, I must make the effort to see and feel, from within, what each would be like were I to choose *it* rather than the others. The effort to do this is not unlike the everyday attempts we make to understand the experience of other people, and it resembles, too, the attempt that historians and anthropologists make to understand those who are remote from them in time and cultural attitude. In these latter cases, of course, it is other people and not ourselves that we are struggling to understand. But the self I will become if I embrace a certain way of life may very well seem, at the moment of decision, something of a stranger too, a person both familiar and remote in the way that other people often are. So to grasp the possibilities before me, even where they are only different ways of living my own life, I need the same sort of imaginative powers that are required to make sense of someone else's situation or experience. What is needed, above all else, is a certain measure of compassion, in the literal sense of 'feeling with.' I must make the effort, in choosing a life for myself, to feel along with each of the persons I might become the special cares and concerns, the risks and opportunities, that give the experience of that possible future self its own distinctive shape.

This is not always easy to do. Much in the experience of my imaginary future selves is bound to remain opaque to me, so opaque, in fact, that I fail even to notice how little I understand. And though I may have an abstract conviction that a particular way of life would be the best one for me, all things considered, my present affections may pull so strongly in another direction that I am unable to feel any genuine compassion for the person I believe I ought to be. Still, even with these qualifications, our powers of compassionate understanding seem sufficiently robust to carry us across the distances that separate us from others and from our own future selves and to permit us to take up – only partially, perhaps, but in a spirit of fellow-feeling – their preoccupations and concerns.

If a person who is faced, say, with a choice between alternative careers must make an effort to grasp in imagination each of the different ways of life these alternatives represent, if it is essential to his deliberations that he entertain their claims sympathetically and see each in the best possible light (the light in which one devoted to that way of life would see it), it is also necessary that he maintain a certain distance or detachment from the points of view he is attempting to understand. From each imaginative foray into a possible future career, he must be able to withdraw to the standpoint of decision, which is the standpoint he occupies at present. At least he must be able to do this if he is genuinely to make a decision among the alternatives rather than merely be swept along by the tide of feeling that any sympathetic association with a particular way of life – even if it is only an imagined way of life – can easily arouse. To ensure that this does not happen, to ensure that he remains sufficiently detached to survey all the alternatives from a vantage point different from any of their own internal points of view, it is necessary that he hold something in reserve even while making a maximum effort at imaginative understanding. The person faced with a hard choice must given each alternative its due; he must entertain all the possibilities by feeling for himself what is most attractive in each. But he must do this while withholding his commitment to any.

One way of expressing this idea is to say that the process of deliberation is peculiarly bifocal. Through one lens, the alternatives are seen not merely at close range but actually from within; through the other, all the alternatives are held at an identical distance. As anyone who has ever put on a pair of bifocal glasses knows, it takes time to learn to shift smoothly between perspectives and the effort to do so can easily give one a headache. The same is true of deliberation: it is difficult to be sympathetic, and difficult to be detached, but what is most difficult of all is to be both at once. Yet it is in just this combination of opposite-seeming attributes that the process of deliberation consists. Deliberation is neither deduction nor intuition. It is the compassionate survey of alternatives viewed simultaneously from a distance, and those who show excellence in deliberation and whose judgement we value are the men and women best able to meet these conflicting requirements and to endure the often considerable tension between them.

DELIBERATION AND CHOICE

To this last proposition, it may be objected that in ascribing sound judgment to a person we mean not only to imply that he or she is able to entertain an especially wide range of alternatives but able, as well, to make the proper choice among them. A person of sound judgment, it will be said, is one who regularly makes the right decision, a fact that my 'procedural' account of judgment appears to ignore. I do of course agree that in attributing sound judgment to a person we are saying something about the sorts of decisions he makes as well as the deliberative procedures he employs in making them. I also believe, however, that these two aspects of judgment are connected and that the choices of a person who deliberates well – with sympathy and detachment – are themselves likely to be sound or practically wise in a sense that I shall now explain.

Someone faced with a difficult personal decision must make an effort, as I have said, to entertain the competing concerns that the possibilities before him represent; he must make an effort to enter, in imagination, each of the ways of life between which he will eventually have to choose. Now the critical term here is 'entertain.' What exactly do I mean by it? By entertain, I mean something different from and *less than* complete endorsement. To entertain a set of values is not to make them one's own without condition or reservation, but to take them up with a measure of detachment that sets these values apart from those to which one is at present actually committed. By the same token, however, I also mean something different from and *more than* a mere knowledge of the fact that the values in question happen to be the ones associated with a particular way of life. I may be said to have entertained a set of values, rather than simply taken account of their existence, only when I have succeeded in seeing them in a sympathetic light and have experienced for myself something of their power and appeal. Entertaining a value or concern, then, is an attitude midway between adopting it and merely acknowledging its existence. Though familiar to us all, this midway attitude is surprisingly difficult to describe. Perhaps the best we can do is say that it is the attitude of fellow-feeling, a term that suggests the combination of compassion and detachment I mean to emphasise.

It is helpful to think of the different ways of life that a person confronts when required to make an important decision about his future as representing different parts or aspects of himself, each part being developed in a way that requires the neglect or subordination of certain others. Choices of this sort are inevitable in any moderately complicated human existence, and one of the great challenges of personal life is to discover the way of living that best accommodates all the different things one wishes to do and be. Since it is impossible to be them all, however, it is even more important to discover which way of life is most likely to preserve a relation of fellow-feeling or friendship, as Aristotle calls it, among the different parts of one's own self, some of which must necessarily be subordinated for the sake of others. A person whose soul has, in Aristotle's phrase, 'friendly feelings' toward itself, a person whose parts are not openly at war or engaged in subtler contests of repression and revenge, possesses a quality of wholeness that is best described by the simple term 'integrity.' Most often, of course, we use this term to describe the steadiness of action and purpose, the reliability of character, the dignity of self-respect that a person shows in relations with others and in his or her conduct generally. It is difficult, however, – if, indeed, it is possible at all – to sustain an outward constancy of this sort without the inward friendship of which Aristotle speaks. If a person's soul is divided against itself the pressures of the world are likely, in time to explode whatever fragile truce has been established among its parts. The alternative is not the elimination of all conflict the soul – after Freud we cannot hope or even wish for a psychic unity of this sort. Nor is it the kind of harmonic ordering of higher and lower parts that Plato proposes in the *Republic*, an ordering that no longer has for us the naturalness it had for him. The alternative is sympathy toward oneself and to a large degree it is on this attitude that the basic good of integrity depends.

Though the measure of integrity that a person achieves is in part, like most things, a matter of luck (including the luck of his original endowment of feeling and intelligence), it is also a function of the various choices that he makes, for these are likely, over time, either to strengthen the friendly attitude that Aristotle describes or to encourage its opposite – self-hatred and a spirit of regret. It is this difference, a difference in the consequences that important choices have for the achievement or preservation of integrity, that marks the line, in personal matters at least, between those decisions that show good judgment and those that do not. If we say, for example, that someone has shown good judgment in his choice of a career, it is not because the particular career he has chosen – the career, say, of a scholar, artist, athlete, or entrepreneur – is intrinsically superior to the others he might have pursued instead. We have no basis for making such comparisons, at least with regard to those ways of life that have a prima facie claim to worthiness (of which the number is large even if it is not infinite). There is, however, another way of understanding what is meant by the claim that a person has shown good judgment in making the decisions that have turned his life in one direction rather than another. To assert this is to claim that he has chosen a life which allows him the reasonable hope of a stable friendship among his different parts, among the interests he has had to abandon or subordinate and those at the centre of his life (a condition of the soul which, though often associated with some rough match up between a person's career and his abilities, may be present where the match up is absent and missing where it exists). When we call a personal decision wise or say that it shows good judgment, what we mean is that it promotes integrity by increasing the chances that the person who has made it will be able to live with himself on amicable terms. In the domain of personal life, wise judgments lead to integrity and unwise ones to disintegration and regret. This is the only meaning these terms can have, in this domain at least, so long as we lack a scale along which to rank the worthiness of the different ways of life to which human beings may reasonably and responsibly devote themselves.[3]

If career decisions can be life changing in this sense, the ethical demands of legal practice need to be considered before irrevocable career choices are made, which means that legal ethics should form part of the undergraduate curriculum.

Legal ethics, judicial ethics and legislative ethics

We need to consider the relationship between, on the one hand, legal ethics and, on the other, legislative and judicial ethics. Many legal educators would argue that there is nothing new in the argument that ethics should be a serious part of legal education. One of the central arguments in jurisprudential debate concerns whether propositions of law (especially judicial propositions of law) are also ethical or moral statements. Those taking the view that legal reasoning is a form of moral reasoning might say that to study law at all is to study ethics. Legal positivists generally insist that the law can and should be discernible without the making of moral judgments. Equally however, they have usually insisted on the separation of law and morals as a precursor to the making of a moral evaluation. On this view, the study of law does not by logical necessity involve the study of ethics, but it has been the aim of many of those writing in the positivist tradition to facilitate ethical critique.

However, it is all too easy for legal educators on both sides of this debate to assume that ethical evaluation be restricted to the decisions of judges and legislators.[4] The common error is to assume that the central question in relation to any rule of law is whether the reasons given by judge or legislator for the rule are adequate. The problem is that such reasons only establish the appropriate scope for regulation by the state. It is one of the central premises of political liberalism that conduct may be morally wrong but nevertheless permitted by the State. It follows from this however that further arguments must be made by the citizen and the lawyer whom s/he consults before it can be concluded that what is legal is also ethical. And it is important that such arguments are made because the need for the state to interfere in and regulate the

---

3   Kronman, supra p 4 note 3 at pp 850-856.
4   See Simon supra note 10 at p 127 for a critique of this tendency.

lives of its citizens will be diminished to the extent that the informal norms we normally call morality operate to prevent the freedom allowed by the law from being abused.

These points are strikingly illustrated by the debates surrounding privacy and the press. Few observers of the UK scene would doubt that in recent years, the press has on many occasions committed serious breaches of a moral right to privacy. Equally however, most people have serious reservations about introducing comprehensive *legal* protection for privacy. The reason is simply that it would be difficult to frame the legislation or common law principles in terms sufficiently precise as to eliminate the risk of restricting the sort of investigative journalism required by a healthy democracy. Reliance is therefore placed on the self-restraint, the professional ethics, indeed, of journalists and their editors.

Again, few would doubt that a developed legal system needs a statute of limitations. Such statutes rescue the judiciary from the need to adjudicate upon disputes where the facts have become unclear due to the passage of time. For a judge therefore no great issues of conscience arise in holding a claim to be barred by a statute of limitation. But what of the individual lawyer whose client says that the debt for which he is being sued is indeed owed but discloses to the lawyer facts sufficient to set up a cast iron limitation defence. The problem is that the debt is owed under a valid contract – which is one reason why the client, had he paid the debt in ignorance of the statute, would be unable to reclaim it[5]. Nevertheless, the statute makes the debt unenforceable in order to protect the court from adjudicating upon debts the existence of which is the subject of unreliable oral evidence. From the Court's perspective, this makes sense but the lawyer has no problem about deciding whether or not the debt is owed. The lawyer knows that the debt is owed because the client has admitted the fact. So for the lawyer there is a real ethical problem.

Consider finally an example drawn from company law. Few would doubt the functional utility of the limited liability principle or, from a different ethical standpoint, argue that the principle necessarily infringes the rights of each and every creditor. Consider however the position of the lawyer whose client is about to market a new product which inevitably carries some risk of product liability. Should the lawyer, as one leading UK practitioner text recommends[6], advise the setting up of a shell company so that anyone wrongfully injured by the product will be left with a worthless claim? The legislator may perhaps have an easy conscience; even if such conduct is widely recognised as morally wrong, legislation may not be able to distinguish such practices from other more acceptable uses of limited liability with sufficient precision or at acceptable cost so as to permit regulatory control. The lawyer however cannot plead in moral defence that what the law allows must be ethical. For the lawyer knows a great deal about the way in which this particular client intends to exploit the limited liability principle. S/he is therefore the best placed of all the law's agents to discern that this represents an abuse. Accordingly there is a profound moral problem. And for the

5   See *Moses v Macferlan* (1760) 2 Burr 1005 at 1007 per Lord Mansfield.
6   See Jane Stapleton 'Product Liability' (London, Butterworths, 1993) p 356 note 26 citing M Thornton and T Ellis ' The United Kingdom' in 'European Product Liability' (ed P Kelly and R Attree) (London, Butterworths, 1992) pp 429, 470, 471.

teacher, the message is the same as it is for the practising lawyer. The ethical evaluation of a rule of law should not cease merely because we have accepted that the executive or the judiciary was fully justified in adopting it.

This suggests that the clients on whom lawyers depend for a living cannot assume that what is legal is necessarily ethical. It would seem to follow that lawyers cannot deflect charges that they have behaved unethically simply by reference to the fact that they have fulfilled their clients' lawful goals. This is however a controversial proposition for it raises important questions about the respective roles and responsibilities of the individual lawyer, professional association and client for deciding on the appropriate limits for the exercise of legal freedom. Indeed it raises metaethical questions about the nature and force of ethical claims which are considered further in chapter 2. Depending on how these questions are answered it is possible to end up affirming that ethics requires lawyers to facilitate the exercise by their clients of their legal rights. I happen to disagree with this argument but the controversy which surrounds it clearly illustrates that legal ethics concerns issues beyond those raised by legislative and judicial ethics.

Legal ethics and codes of conduct

Lawyers' work is regulated by the 'Law on Lawyering'. This consists in part of the provisions of substantive and procedural law which apply to their work. The law of contract for example governs the relationship between solicitor and client. But the law of lawyering also includes the professional codes formulated by the Bar and the Law Society. Serious breaches of these bodies of law will lead to the imposition of sanctions which are ultimately backed by the power of the state. We need to consider therefore the relationship between professional codes of conduct and legal ethics.

Anyone who wishes to be an ethical lawyer or to evaluate the ethics of lawyers needs to be aware of the provisions of any applicable code of conduct. Hence this book cites at various points relevant provisions of the Law Society's *Guide to the Professional Conduct of Solicitors*[7] and *the Code of Conduct of the Bar in England and Wales*[8]. For comparative purposes, reference is also made to the Model Code of Professional Responsibility and the Model Rules of Professional Conduct formulated by the American Bar Association[9].

It is sometimes assumed however that all the ethical difficulties facing lawyers can be settled solely by reference to their codes of conduct. For a number of reasons, this is not the case. To begin with, it is doubtful whether social life can be governed by rules which, once formulated, require no further exercise of judgment by those to

---

7   *The Guide to the Professional Conduct of Solicitors* (8th ed) (London, Law Society, 1999).
8   *The Code of Conduct of the Bar of England and Wales* (7th ed) (London, General Council of the Bar, 2000).
9   Neither the Model Code of Professional Responsibility ('the Model Code') , formulated in 1969 nor the Model Rules of Professional Conduct ('the Model Rules') formulated in 1985 are directly binding on lawyers. The disciplinary bodies in each State may however choose to promulgate one or other of these two codifications with or without modifications and most do so.

whom they are addressed. Even if social life could be organised in this way, there would remain the question of why lawyers should obey the relevant code when it conflicts with their own moral convictions: if the applicable rules of professional ethics require a criminal defense barrister representing a rapist to exploit the complainant's sexual history in order to obtain an acquittal, is the barrister *morally required* to put aside her own view that this evidence is irrelevant? Thus we must ask whether it would ever be right to disobey the Code of Conduct. This is a particularly pressing point for lawyers in a jurisdiction like that in England and Wales where the codes are for the most part drawn up by lawyers for lawyers[10]. Those sceptical about the value of self-regulation may fear that the professional codes are determined more by self-interest than by genuinely ethical considerations. In addition, law students not yet subject to the obligations of the code and lawyers with an opportunity to influence the policy of the professional association, will need to consider whether the codes are in need of reform.

In any case, there are good reasons to think that whatever the content of a given professional code, it is likely to represent a minimal standard with which lawyers must comply rather than a comprehensive definition. Professional codes are usually drafted by the elected leaders of the profession and will rarely be backed by the comprehensive enforcement apparatus upon which the drafter of a criminal law statute can hope to rely. Consequently, the norms which it endorses must be such as commend the active assent of a large majority. Otherwise they will be widely ignored. Therefore, the standards endorsed will tend to have the character of a lowest common denominator. As a result, the demands of ethics are likely to be considerably more exacting than those of the professional code. In the US, this possibility was given institutional form by the Model Code of Professional Responsibility which distinguished between disciplinary rules, breach of which was subject to sanction and 'ethical considerations' which being aspirational were not. The English codes do not have the same formal structure. However, the same effect will be achieved whenever an ethical problem is either ignored or dealt with by granting practitioners a discretion, as typically occurs for example in relation to the permitted exceptions to the professional duty to keep a client's affairs confidential.[11]

For all of the above reasons, professional codes are *inherently* likely to be no more than a starting point in the study of legal ethics. In addition, even if it is technically possible to formulate a code with such detail that ethical discretion is squeezed out of the lives of ordinary practitioners and into the domain of professional conduct committees, the fact remains that the UK codes are a long way from this particular promised land. Many of their provisions are so open textured as to confer upon lawyers a broad discretion the exercise of which will require ethical judgment. This is pre-eminently the case for example of Solicitors Practice Rule 1 which is described in the *Guide to Professional Conduct of Solicitors* as the bedrock of ethical practice:

10   Note however inroads on this principle made by the Courts and Legal Services Act 1990, s 29 which have the effect of making *changes* to rules of conduct subject to approval by the Lord Chancellor. See further chapter 4, text to notes 8-13.

11   See further chapter 7.

A solicitor shall not do anything in the course of practising as a solicitor, or permit another person to do anything on his or her behalf which compromises or impairs or is likely to compromise or impair any of the following:

a)   the solicitor's independence or integrity;
b)   a person's freedom to instruct a solicitor of his or her choice;
c)   the solicitor's duty to act in the best interests of the client;
d)   the solicitor's proper standard of work;
e)   the solicitor's duty to the court.

On a host of difficult issues, such as the ethics of negotiation, the UK codes say virtually nothing and the existence of gaps such as these reinforces the need for ethical sensitivity and commitment. For all of these reasons, the ethical codes currently governing the UK legal profession can only be the starting point for the study of legal ethics.[12]

3   United Kingdom and United States

This book draws extensively on the voluminous American literature on the topic. This is partly because the under-development of the subject almost everywhere else[13] means that anyone in the UK seeking to begin working in the field has little choice but to start across the Atlantic. This literature began to emerge in the late 1970s and early 1980s as the American academy began to respond to the alarm expressed by the leaders of the American Bar about the misdeeds of the lawyers involved in the Watergate scandal. There emerged the impressive body of scholarship which has been described by David Luban as 'the New Legal Ethics scholarship'.[14] The sheer quality of the work which has been done is one reason why those grappling with the problems of legal ethics in the UK context need to look west.

There is however a problem, which David Luban has himself set out in graphic terms.

> ... the exclusively American development of the New Legal Ethics has had a pernicious effect.... American scholars often forget that the rest of the world exists, or at any rate assume that propositions about America are propositions about reality as such. The New Legal Ethics is no exception. Its practitioners grapple with exclusively American examples – examples which presuppose American regulations, American constitutionalism, the American version of the adversary system, the unified Bar and a legal culture that everyone recognises in other contexts is quite exceptional.

12   This assumption is reflected in the terminology used, particularly when considering problem questions. Responses to problem questions will be referred to as *misconduct* if they involve a breach of the LSGPC or the CCB and as *unethical*, if whilst not being misconduct they are nevertheless unethical.

13   For recent contributions in the UK see Andrew Boon and Jennifer Levin *The Ethics and Conduct of Lawyers in England and Wales* (Oxford, Hart, 1999) and Donald Nicholson and Julian Webb *Professional Legal Ethics: Critical Interrogations* (Oxford, OUP, 1999).

14   David Luban 'Introduction: A New Canadian Legal Ethics' IX Canadian Journal of Law and Jurisprudence Vol 1 [1996].

> This is unfortunate in two ways. First, it casts doubt on whether the insights of the New Legal Ethics are true at the level of philosophical generality. Perhaps their supporting arguments conceal illicit generalizations from a uniquely American phenomenon. Secondly, scholars in other countries who wish to participate in the exciting research and reform programmes of the New Legal Ethics confront a literature that focuses entirely on American law and American practices. (Other) scholars must treat the New Legal Ethics cautiously, asking of virtually every proposition whether it is true in their own culture.[15]

This warning must be taken seriously. Nevertheless, I would contend that quite apart from the pragmatic point (where else can one go?), it is important not to exaggerate the problem. For one thing, there are important similarities between the US and UK systems, most obviously the adversary system and common law reasoning, as well as important differences. Moreover, globalisation generally, and the influence of US legal firms on certain sections of the UK legal services market in particular may be working to reduce the differences between the two cultures. Indeed, there is a danger that unease about some of the perceived excesses of the American legal profession may induce UK commentators to discard too easily the insights of the New Legal Ethics scholarship on the grounds of its' cultural context. This would allow the evasion of some genuine and uncomfortable questions. So while writers from other jurisdictions should 'treat the New Legal Ethics cautiously', their reservation must be measured. The approach taken in this book is to attempt to draw on the US literature whilst remaining aware that there are undoubted differences in legal culture and legal system.

4   Legal profession(s): barristers and solicitors

One of the differences between the US and the UK to which Luban points is that the UK legal profession is divided into the two sub-professions[16] of barristers and solicitors. Whether this arrangement is in the public interest is a question which has been much debated but that debate is not rehearsed in this book partly because recent legislative reforms have eroded many of the distinguishing features of the two professions. In particular solicitors may now exercise higher court rights of audience and be appointed to senior judicial office. More importantly, it is generally assumed that the major ethical questions are the same for each of the two professions. That assumption is facilitated by the brevity of most of the provisions of the CCB which as a consequence rarely requires conduct different from that required of solicitors by the LSGPC. Thus from the perspective of legal ethics, it is assumed that it does not matter very much whether a given problem is being faced by a barrister or a solicitor. For the most part, questions are posed in the text for a reader who is assumed only to be (acting as) a member of the legal profession. Where, as in the following case study, the assumption does not hold, this is made clear in the text.

15   Ibid.
16   One of the features of the legal landscape of the last two decades has been the emergence of new sub-professions such as licensed conveyancers. For reasons of space however these new sub-professions are not considered in this book.

Case study: Khan's case

Stephen Smith, aged 28, is a solicitor in the property department in the firm of Knapp Somes and Co, a medium-sized firm of provincial solicitors with 10 partners. Under normal circumstances, he could expect to be considered for partnership within the next year. However, due to a downturn in the property market income from conveyancing has been declining and some within the firm feel that the property department is not pulling its weight. There have even been rumours of redundancy. Early in May 1997, Stephen is consulted by Amaar Khan, a well-known and successful businessman for whom the firm's company and commercial department has done a great deal of work. Mr Khan asks Stephen to deal with the conveyancing aspects of a forthcoming transaction and Stephen agrees. Mr Khan tells him that he wishes to take out a second mortgage on the family home in order to raise money to pay off an earlier loan which he and his wife used to purchase a yacht for their private use. He shows him an application to the Midwest Building Society requesting a loan of £60,000 for this purpose. Mr Khan tells Stephen that the house was purchased five years ago and is currently worth £120,000, with the existing mortgage being £40,000. The house is in his wife's name but Mr Khan says there will be no problem with obtaining his wife's signature to the guarantee and legal charge required by the Society. Three weeks later, Stephen receives a letter from the Midwest asking him to act also for them in the proposed transaction. This causes Stephen no surprise – the firm is on a list of firms approved by the Society to act for them in its lending transactions.

Three weeks later, Stephen goes out for a drink after work with Karen, an assistant solicitor in the company and commercial department with whom he has recently become friendly. Later that evening, conversation turns to the office and Karen says that one of her biggest clients, Amaar Khan has suffered a catastrophic downturn in his mail order business and that unless he obtains refinancing in the near future, his company is likely to be put into liquidation. Indeed it is most likely doomed in any case.

In July, Stephen meets with Mr and Mrs Khan for the formal signature of the documents. Mrs Khan, who is dressed in traditional Islamic dress, is in her late 30s and seems very much steeped in the culture of the Indian subcontinent from which she and her husband emigrated to England 10 years previously. Stephen asks Mrs Khan if she is happy with the proposed arrangement and she replies that if her husband is happy with the arrangement then so is she. Mr Khan adds that Mrs Khan knows little about finance since she is occupied full time in caring for their three children all of whom are under five. Stephen presents the Khans with a series of documents: a loan agreement under which Amaar Khan borrows £60,000 repayable with interest over five years; a corresponding charge over his interest in the matrimonial home; a guarantee of his indebtedness by Mrs Khan and a corresponding charge over her interest in the matrimonial home. These are signed and transmitted to the Building Society and the formalities of the transaction are duly completed. The Khans fail almost immediately to make the necessary payments. In January 1998, having negotiated unsuccessfully with the Khans for some time, the Midwest Building Society starts possession proceedings in the county court. At this point, taking into account unpaid interest, the

Khan's owe £66,000. Mrs Khan makes an appointment with Sarah Wise, a partner in the firm of Lovell Smythe and Couts, another medium-sized firm in the same area. The relevant parts of the conversation are as follows.

Sarah Wise: Now Mrs Khan, how can I help you?

Mrs Khan (agitated): My husband has received a letter from the bank saying that they are going to take our house away because we have not paid our debts. (She shows Sarah the loan documentation.)

Sarah Wise: Could you tell me how these debts were incurred?

Mrs. Khan: But can we stop them? Just tell me whether we can save our home. Does the law allow them to do this?

Sarah Wise: That depends. If you knew what you were doing when you signed these documents then I'm afraid they can. But if your husband lied to you or bullied you in order to get the money for himself, then the bank can't throw you out unless you had advice from a solicitor.

Mrs Khan: Yes, yes that's it. He lied to me. He said the money was to be used to pay the loan on the boat, but he used it to pay off his company's debts. I never saw a solicitor – only my husband's lawyer.

Sarah then asks Mrs Khan if she is able to pay to have the claim defended and Mrs Khan produces a document under which she and her husband are entitled to legal expenses insurance up to a limit of £20,000 which she estimates will be (just) sufficient to pay her firms costs, though not those of the Society.[17]

Following their meeting, Sarah does some further research on the law and drafts a witness statement[18] describing how Mr Khan had lied to Mrs Khan and how she trusted his judgment without question throughout the transaction. At their next meeting, Sarah reads the statement which is then signed by Mrs Khan. At the request of the legal expenses insurers, Sarah then sends this statement together with relevant documentation to Mr Mark Hughes an experienced member of the local Bar for an opinion on the merits of the proposed defence. Mr Hughes' opinion is that the defence is clearly arguable and may well succeed. On this basis, the legal expenses insurers agree to pay for Mrs Khan's defence.

In July 1998, the case comes on for hearing before Judge Snout QC (who has a reputation for being extremely conservative in his outlook and sympathetic towards lenders seeking possession of mortgaged property.) Three days before the hearing, Sarah receives a phone call from Mr Hughes' clerk. He says that unfortunately Mr

17   In civil litigation, the normal rule is that costs follow the event meaning that the loser will be ordered to pay the winners legal costs as well as its own. Where one of the party's has legal expenses insurance the insurers will normally pay that party's lawyers in advance and be repaid by the other side in the event of its' client succeeding.

18   A written document in which a witness in a forthcoming trial sets out what he/she would say if called to the witness stand. In most cases, the witness is never called to give evidence by her own lawyer, instead this statement is read by the court and the other side, which then cross-examines the witness on the truth of the statement.

Hughes is currently away on holiday. At the Clerk's suggestion, the brief is passed to Ms Indira Gundhi, the most junior member of Mr Hughes' chambers. Later the same evening, Sarah attends a reception given by her firm for local businessmen and overhears two prominent members of the local community discussing Mr Khan's troubles. One of them comments that he is not surprised since Mr Khan has never had a head for business. Indeed his business ventures have always been built upon the success of his wife's business dealings in the local Asian community. Sarah is somewhat shocked and unsure how to respond to this news.

On the day of the hearing Sarah, attends at court with Mr and Mrs Khan and Ms Gundhi. Ms Gundhi is nervous. On the one hand she is excited at the prospect of what would be her first court appearance and the size of the brief fee (£2000) is a welcome boost for her overdraft. On the other hand, she is only too aware of her inexperience. She was not taught advocacy at University and she considers the tuition she received on the Bar vocational course and during pupillage to be good in quality but insufficient in its extent. She also feels underprepared because she has recently been given a huge amount of work by the Clerk due to more senior members of chambers being on holiday. The building society is represented by Mr John Brilliant, an experienced London barrister. He has seen Mrs Khan's witness statement and has come to court feeling that his client's case is a weak one. He has instructions to settle if at all possible. The client is desperate to avoid the adverse publicity which would result from a hearing in open court. In addition, it fears the creation of an adverse precedent which might adversely effect its chances in a number of other cases which are pending against Asian business men and their wives. Finally, it knows that Mrs Khan's legal expenses cover is likely to be swallowed up by the defendant's lawyers expenses so that even if it wins the case it is likely to have to pay its' own lawyers costs.

Mr Brilliant is surprised and indeed pleased to be faced by Ms Gundhi rather than Mr Hughes and the two of them withdraw to a conference room to discuss the case. The Khans and Sarah Miles wait outside. During the negotiations, Mr Brilliant takes a strong stand, stating inter alia:

Your clients' defence is desperately weak.

My clients are determined to obtain possession... it's a matter of principle.

If the case comes to court, I would have to subject your client to the sternest cross-examination..

Judge Snout is known to have little sympathy for ignorant wives' defences.

(However) neither you nor I stand to gain from wasting our time in court on a case which can only have one result when we could be back in chambers doing some really useful work. Surely we can settle this out of court.

Ms Gundhi presents her case (as contained in Mrs Khan's witness statement) as forcefully as possible but with little conviction. Moreover she is so flustered that she forgets to play what she had previously regarded as one of her strong points ie that whatever the outcome of the hearing the bank is in any case likely to end up paying its' own costs. Eventually, Mr Brilliant proposes an agreement whereby

i. the Building Society will not seek an order for possession and will not enforce such rights as it may have under the documents signed in July 1997.

ii. Mrs Khan agrees to pay the Building Society £55,000 within six months and to enter into a legally effective mortgage document such that the Building Society will have a legally effective security for this sum.

iii. the terms of the settlement are to remain confidential.

Ms Gundhi goes back to the Khans and explains the terms of the proposed settlement to them. She says that while she is confident in the strength of their case, Judge Snout is known to be unsympathetic to defendants in cases of this kind. Her advice is to accept the settlement which will after all leave them with sufficient funds to pay the deposit on another home. After considering for a moment Mr Khan says that they will accept the terms being offered. Minutes later the settlement is signed.

Notes

1. The law of undue influence:

The dispute between the Khans and the Midwest which forms the background to this case is governed by the law of undue influence. Any transaction may be set aside if it has been procured by the undue influence (whether actual or presumed) of one party upon the other. Undue influence will be found wherever one party has come to trust the other so completely that they have ceased to exercise independent judgment.

Undue influence may be presumed from the type of relationship (eg doctor-patient) in which the parties find themselves ('Category 2A relationships'). Alternatively it may be presumed upon proof of the history of the actual relationship between the particular parties. ('Category 2B relationships'[19]). The difference is well illustrated by the treatment of the marriage relationship. A husband is not presumed merely because of the fact of marriage to be exercising undue influence over his wife, so the relationship as such is not within Category 2A. On the other hand, a particular married relationship may have a history such that undue influence is presumed generally to infect mutual dealings of husband and wife. Once the presumption is found to operate the transaction will be set aside unless it is rebutted by the other side, usually by showing that the alleged victim had the benefit of independent advice, for example from a solicitor.[20]

In practice, the important question has been that of when third parties are effected by the exercise by a husband of undue influence upon his wife. The context is normally the giving of a guarantee by a wife of her husbands borrowings, backed by a charge over the matrimonial home. When the husband defaults and the lender seeks possession, it is claimed that the husband procured the giving of the guarantee by the exercise of undue influence. In *Barclay's Bank* v *O'Brien*[1], it was held that the guarantee would be set aside against the third party only when it could be said to have constructive

19   This classification was set out by the Court of Appeal in *BCCI v Aboody* [1990] 1 QB 923 CA and has been approved on several occasions.
20   It is disputed whether in addition, the victim must prove that the transaction is manifestly disadvantageous: See *CICB v Pitt.* [1994]1 AC 200 per Lord Brown-Wilkinson at pp 209E-H.
1   [1994] 1 AC 180 HL.

notice of the undue influence. This however could arise relatively easy upon proof that the matrimonial relationship existed and that the wife, as guarantor, did not stand to benefit from the transaction. In such circumstances a finding of constructive notice will be avoided only if the third party asked the wife to seek independent legal advice. Once she is urged to do so however the lender is usually[2] protected. This is so even if the wife refuses to seek independent advice or if the advice given by the independent legal adviser is clearly defective[3].

2. The law on lawyering:

(A)   Contract tort and agency law
i) The legal basis of the lawyer-client relationship is provided by principles drawn from the law of tort, the law of contract and the law of agency. The term 'retainer' has historically used to denote the existence of a contractual relationship between solicitor and client.

ii) Barristers are not generally in a contractual relationship with either solicitor or client. However both solicitors and barristers, like other providers of professional services, may come under a duty of care arising in the law of tort even in the absence of an enforceable contract.[4] In the case of *Henderson v Merrett Syndicates Ltd*[5], the House of Lords held that such a duty will be owed whenever there has been an undertaking to carry out a task with care and skill or, alternatively behaviour such as might reasonably be viewed as constituting such an undertaking.

iii) As a matter of law, a lawyer is a fiduciary agent and owes the client (ie the principal) a duty of undivided loyalty[6]. Hence, s/he must not agree to act for two principals whose interests conflict. As a matter of law, clients may agree to waive this duty[7] but it is open to professional bodies to impose stricter duties.

(B)   Relevant principles of the Law Society's Guide to the Professional Conduct of Solicitors and The Code of Conduct of the Bar in England and Wales

I. THE LSGPC

12.02   When Instructions Must Be Refused

A solicitor must not act, or where relevant, must stop acting, where the instructions would involve the solicitor in a breach of the law or a breach of the principles of professional conduct, unless the client is prepared to change his or her instructions.

2   For an exceptional contrary instance see *Credit Lyonnais Bank Nederland NV v Burch* [1997] 1 All ER 144
3   See *Royal Bank of Scotland v Etridge (No 2)* [1998] 4 All ER 705 CA.
4   *Hedley Byrne v Heller* [1964] AC 465.
5   [1995] 2 AC 145.
6   See generally the judgment of Millet LJ in *Bristol and West Building Society v Mothew* [1998] Ch 1.
7   See *Clarke Boyce v Mouat* [1994] 1 AC 428.

12.04   Duress or Undue Influence

A solicitor must not accept instructions which he or she suspects have been given by a client under duress or undue influence.

15.01   Conflict of Interest

A solicitor or firm of solicitors should not accept instructions to act for two or more clients where there is a conflict or a significant risk of conflict of interest between the interests of those clients

....
2.   Even if an actual conflict of interests exists and is disclosed to the client and the client consents to the solicitor acting, the solicitor must not accept the instructions.

15.03

A solicitor or firm of solicitors must not continue to act for two or more clients where a conflict of interest arises between those clients.

1.   If a solicitor has already accepted instructions from two clients in a matter... and a conflict subsequently arises between the interests of the clients, the firm must usually cease to act for both parties. A solicitor may only continue to act for one client of not in possession of relevant confidential information concerning the other...

16.01   General Duty of Confidentiality

A solicitor is under a duty to keep confidential to his or her firm the affairs of clients and to ensure that the staff do the same.

16.02   Circumstances which override confidentiality

The duty to keep a client's confidences can be overridden in certain exceptional circumstances.

1.   The duty of confidentiality does not apply to information acquired by a solicitor where he or she is being used by the client to facilitate the commission of a crime or fraud because that is not within the scope of the professional retainer.

3.   A solicitor may reveal confidential information to the extent that he or she believes necessary to prevent the client or a third party committing a criminal act that the solicitor believes on reasonable grounds is likely to result in serious bodily harm.

17.01   Fairness

Solicitors must not act ... towards anyone in a way which is fraudulent deceitful or otherwise contrary to their position as solicitors. Nor must solicitors use their position to take unfair advantage either for themselves or another person.

1.   A solicitor must not deceive anyone; however any information disclosed must be consistent with the solicitors duty of confidentiality.

2.   When dealing with an unrepresented third party, a solicitor must take care to ensure that no retainer arises by implication between the solicitor and the third party.

19.01   Duty of Good Faith

A solicitor must act towards other solicitors with frankness and good faith consistent with his or her overriding duty to the client.

21.01   Duty Not to Mislead the Court

Solicitors who act in litigation, whilst under a duty to do their best for their client must never deceive or mislead the Court.

II.   THE CCB

301 A barrister...must not;
(a)   engage in conduct whether in pursuit of his profession or otherwise which is
   (i)   dishonest or otherwise discreditable to a barrister;
   (ii)   prejudicial to the administration of justice; or
   (iii)   likely to diminish public confidence in the legal profession or the administration of justice or otherwise bring the profession into disrepute.

Questions

1. A lawyer is required to carry out a great many tasks in the course of his/her professional work each of which requires a different skill or mixture of skills. Identify and label all the different task you observe being carried out by the lawyers in this problem? Are there any tasks which you regard as typical of lawyers work which you do not in fact observe being carried out?

2. To what extent is the behaviour of lawyers in carrying out these tasks open to scrutiny by those charged with enforcing professional codes? What is the significance of your answer for legal ethics?

3. Identify Stephen's client(s).

4. Is it misconduct for Stephen to agree to represent both the Midwest and the Khans? Is it unethical? What would be the advantages and disadvantages of a new rule of conduct stating that

   A solicitor shall under no circumstances represent both the borrower and the lender in a mortgage transaction.

5. What is the significance in terms of professional conduct of Stephen's conversation with Karen? See principles 16.01, 16.02, 15.01 and 15.03. Was Stephen's actual response ethically justifiable?

6. What action should Stephen have taken as a matter of conduct and/or ethics as a result of what he learns of Mrs Khan during their first meeting (See principle 12.04.)

7. Suppose Stephen *had* perceived himself to be facing one or more ethical dilemmas during the course of his representation of the Khans. Where might he have sought help in his attempt to resolve them? Does he face any and if so what pressures to behave unethically or to breach the LSGPC?

8. Do you think Sarah's conduct of the interview with Mrs Khan is in any way problematic? If so, in what way?

9. What issues of conduct and/or ethics arise from Sarah's drafting of Mrs Khan's witness statement?

10. Why is Sarah concerned about what she learns at the reception? What action do you think she should have taken, if any? (See principles 12.02, 16.01, 17.01,19.01 and 21.01.)

11. Which of the circumstances surrounding the negotiations at the door of the court were influential (and in what way) upon the final outcome?

12. Evaluate the conduct of Mr Brilliant in the light of paragraph 301 of the CCB.

13. We are told that

> Ms Gundhi ....presents her case (as contained in Mrs Khan's witness statement) as forcefully as possible but... is so flustered that she forgets to point out that whatever the outcome of the hearing the bank is in any case likely to end up paying its own costs.

Explain why the terms of the legal expenses insurance might have strengthened Ms Gundhi's bargaining position. Would she have been behaving ethically in making this point?

14. Why does Mr Brilliant insist upon clause iii of the settlement? Was Ms Gundhi right to accept it?

15. Was justice done in this case? Why is this such a difficult question to answer? What implications does this difficulty have for lawyers as they approach issues of conduct/ethics?

CHAPTER TWO

Philosophical foundations of legal ethics

God is dead and
Everything is Relative...

Nevertheless

Napalming babies is bad.
Starving the poor is wicked.
Buying and selling each other is depraved.
Those who stood up to and died resisting
Hitler, Stalin, Amin, and Pol Pot-
And General Custer too – have earned salvation.
Those who acquiesced deserve to be damned.
There is in the world such a thing as evil.

[All together now:]

SEZ WHO?

Debates about legal ethics cannot be insulated from the philosophical context in which they occur. We must therefore consider some of the debates within moral philosophy which are likely to impact upon lawyers ethical problems. These wider debates may assist in the resolution of the problems, or, alternatively may turn out to be part of the problem. We begin with the question of the nature and status of ethical claims. Since the Enlightenment, one of the major problems has been that of whether in the absence of divine revelation ethical claims are anything other than a statement of the speakers personal preferences. Philosophers have attempted to explore the limits of rational argument as a means of 'grounding' morality in something other than the

---

1   Adapted from Arthur Allen Leff 'Unspeakable Law, Unnatural Ethics' Duke Law Journal 1229 [1979].

individual will. The question has been whether in the word of one commentator 'ethical reasoning is conceptually autonomous from more conventionally held beliefs, affording an impartial point of view from which people rise above and critically assess the ethical validity of the beliefs of their state, society, ethnic or religious or racial group.[2] As a reaction against the limited success of this exercise, there has emerged in recent years a stress on the importance of character and community in understanding ethical behaviour. The implications of this body of thought are considered before we turn finally to consider whether feminism and the 'ethics of care' offer an alternative approach to legal ethics.

1   Ethics – a house on firm foundations?

In the following extract, Rob Atkinson reviews some of the questions about the status of moral statements (which he calls questions of metaethics) prior to his consideration of the work of William H Simon and David Luban, two of the leading writers of the leading theorists of legal ethics...

> [an] insistence that lawyers conform to publicly defined role obligations is a statement of what moral philosophers call normative, or first-order, ethics, a statement about the content of ethical norms. Such statements tell us what we ought to do, or what is good. A set of second-order moral questions, questions of what ethical philosophers call metaethics, deals with the status of first-order statements. In this Part, we will explore one such question, that of the foundation of first-order statements: whether and in what sense they can be said to be objective, to rest on something other than individual human wills.
>
> A.   THREE POSITIONS
>
> There are three basic positions on that issue that are relevant to our purposes, if not exhaustive of the possibilities: realism, interpretivism, and scepticism. Once we have examined these positions, we will be better able both to assess Luban and Simon's alternative to the old role morality and to understand why they have rejected other alternatives, including the one that I prefer. We will see some general problems with realism and interpretivism, the positions they implicitly adopt, and some of the reasons they and others find the sceptical position unappealing, and even a bit appalling.
>
> *1.   Realism* – Realism maintains that binding ethical norms or values are 'out there,' objective and identifiable, both external to individual human wills and binding upon them. Furthermore, realism maintains that these norms or values are knowable by human reason. Realism is the metaethical position that best comports with our ordinary moral language, taking it at nearest to face value. When we say that something is right or good, on this view, we mean precisely what those words ordinarily imply: that the something in question 'really' is right or good, right or good for all times and places, at least for those similarly situated. And not only do we mean this; according to the realists,

2   D Richard 'Moral Theory, The Developmental Psychology of Ethical Autonomy and Professionalism' (1981) 31 Journal of Legal Education 359 at 365.

we are also correct. In a phrase more popular among critics of this approach than defenders, moral values are 'part of the furniture of the universe,' at least in the sense that statements about moral values are no less true or objectively verifiable than statements of scientific or historical fact.

But what are these objective moral values like, and how do we have access to them? David Hume noted a fundamental problem in this regard:

> I cannot forbear adding to these reasonings an observation, which may, perhaps, be found of some importance. In every system of morality... I have always remarked, that the author proceeds for some time in the ordinary way of reasoning, and establishes the being of a God, or makes observations concerning human affairs; when of a sudden I am surprised to find, that instead of the usual copulations of propositions, is, and is not, I meet with no proposition that is not connected with an ought, or an ought not. This change is imperceptible; but is, however, of the last consequence. For as an ought, or ought not, expresses some new relation or affirmation, 'tis necessary that it should be observed and explained; and at the same time a reason should be given, for what seems altogether inconceivable, how this new relation can be deduced from others, which are entirely different from it... [T]his small attention would subvert all the vulgar systems of morality, and let us see, that the distinction of vice and virtue is not founded merely on the relation of things, nor is perceived by reason.

The question Hume raised is phrased variously – whether an 'ought' can ever be derived from an 'is'; whether prescription can ever be fully reduced to description; whether reason can bridge the gap between facts and values. The debate on these points is still open (and vigorous), and I cannot close it definitively here. Nevertheless, we should note briefly two fairly common forms of response, and the issues they in turn raise.

In the first place, some realists themselves conceded that the gap between is and ought cannot be filled, that moral principles cannot rationally be derived from matters of nonmoral fact. For them, the objective values are out there to be discovered, but not by inference from nonmoral facts. Rather, they are to be perceived directly, by intuition or by reason acting in a special mode distinct from its ordinary empirical methods.

Thus, according to John Finnis, a leading exponent of this school,

> When discerning what is good, to be pursued (prosequendum), intelligence, is operating in a different way, yielding a different logic, from when it is discerning what is the case (historically, scientifically, or metaphysically); but there is no good reason for asserting that the latter operations of intelligence are more rational than the former.

Thinkers of this school quite rightly point out that, even if Hume is correct that an 'is' cannot be derived from an 'ought', it does not follow, as he seems to have thought, that moral values are not directly apprehended by reason. It is one thing to say that 'the distinction of vice and virtue is not founded on the relations of things'; it is quite another to add 'nor is perceived by reason'.

Yet thought this is logically true, it is not without problems of its own, most particularly, how reason works in this distinctive mode. Consider Finnis's account:

> At this point in our discourse (or private mediation) [the point at which we are discovering the basic forms of human good], inference and proof are left behind (or left until later [when moral laws are derived from basic human goods]), and the proper form of discourse is: '... [a candidate for basic human good] is a good, in itself, don't you think?'

As in instantiation of this approach, Finnis discusses in detail one particular putative basic good, knowledge. According to him, we move in the following way from the desire or felt inclination for particular knowledge – from what Hume and his sceptical successors would call a fact – to grasping that knowledge in general is inherently valuable:

> Commonly one's interest in knowledge, in getting to the truth of the matter, is not bounded by the particular questions that first aroused one's desire to find out. So readily that one notices the transition only by an effort of reflection, it becomes clear that knowledge is a good thing to have (and not merely for its utility), without restriction to the subject-matters that up to now have aroused one's curiosity.

This process crosses the gap between is and ought without a logical inference; the objective and intrinsical value of what you are in fact inclined to pursue (knowledge, in the example) simply 'become clear'.

Such insights logically divide the world into two classes, those who have had them and those who have not. Those who have seen the light need no further proof; the insight is, as Finnis describes it, as irreducible as a sense perception. The problem, however, is not that they have seen something, but whether what they have seen is the kind of externally existing moral value they claim. How can they know that their perception of intrinsic goodness corresponds to something in an external world of moral values any more than, say, an alcoholic's pink elephants correspond to something in the external world of sensory objects? One answer is to import God as the guarantor of the moral vision. This way, however, only moves the problem back a step: How do you know that it is God who guarantees that your moral vision is clear? Mystics tell us that direct contact with the Ultimate is unmistakable. But it tends to be ineffable as well. Again, they can only point us in the right direction and, in their own darker moments, wonder not whether they have really touched the Ultimate, but what the Ultimate really is.

Another answer is to insist that I have placed too great a burden of validation on the realists and their moral perceptions, that I am trading at their expense on an unwarranted distinction between the 'hardness' of physical facts and 'softness' of values. This distinction, so the argument runs, rests on a naïve, and erroneous, understanding of what physical phenomena are and how they are perceived. This response has an appealing symmetry about it. Against the objection that the perception of values is peculiar, the response is that, on close analysis, the perception of facts becomes equally peculiar. In a world of quarks and quantum mechanics, things may well not be quite what they seem.

Even so, however, the question remains: are things as they are in the realms of physics, history, and the like, of the same order, and knowable in the same way, as the values that realists purport to find in the world? To show that they are, realists must disabuse us of 'the stubborn intuition that particular non moral judgments are 'given' by observation in a way that particular moral judgments are not[3].' Claims in the factual

---

3   Michael S Moore 'Moral Reality' (1982) Wisc L Reve 1061 at 1113.

realm, after all, are submitted both in principle and in practice to the judgment of the conscientiously sceptical.

But on the other hand, what are the conscientiously sceptical to make of these facts: first, that our ordinary moral language bristles with implications of objective morality; and, second, that Finnis and others report rational contact with real values in the world? To take the latter first, it will hardly do to deny the data, particularly in light of the notorious difficulty of proving a negative. In the absence of disproof, perhaps the best we can do is offer a plausible alternative account. Perhaps what realists see – and really see – is not a realm of moral values outside themselves, but a projection of their own or others' values outside themselves, a projection of their own or others' values upon the world, a projection induced not by the effects of drugs on the brain, but by the effects of social conditioning upon the conscience. Ordinary language simply reflects the fact that we have long mistaken this projection of ourselves for a discovery of something other, just as it reflects our more readily discredited geocentricism in expressions like 'sunrise' and 'sunset'. On this view, it comes as no surprise, nor any metaethical problem, that when we stare down into the inky waters of morality, we see what seems a familiar face. The problem only arises when we are moved to declare the face ideal, or when we become convinced it has an existence apart from our own.

Once again, I am not asserting that the position of the realists has been, or even can be, disproved. But we are on notice that these claims are problematic, and we are entitled to wonder whether the realists' efforts to defend them are worth the energy. In particular, we may legitimately question whether morality cannot be built on another foundation.

2.   *Skepticism* – One response to the claims of moral realism is scepticism, of either a more or a less thorough-going sort. In its more aggressive mode, scepticism denies in principle the possibility of moral truths. The claims of the realists are to be not just doubted, but denied; they are not just unproved, but false. In its milder form, moral scepticism implicitly adopts the logic of what in law is known as the Scottish verdict – to show that someone's case is not proved is not to have disproved it. As we have seen, the realists' claims that rest on special forms of knowing are especially difficult to disprove in principle. After all, the more modest sceptic admits, some day the scales may fall from my eyes, allowing me, too, to see the ineffable and underived light of moral truth. Until then, however, we must live by our own lights, even if they fail to reveal a moral code in the order of the cosmos. The common element in these two forms of moral scepticism, the mild and the aggressive, is the rejection, tentatively or tenaciously, of an objective moral realm external to the human will.

So stated, scepticism has not only a negative, but also a positive, or at least potentially positive, aspect. Denying moral standards external to the human will leaves open the logical possibility of grounding morality in the will itself. Yet this is only a potentially positive aspect; it is only to say that if moral values exist at all, they are grounded in the will.

To affirm the position that moral values do exist, grounded in the will, is to move beyond scepticism to what I will call fideism, a kind of Cartesian ethical system. I may (and I do) doubt that things come with value attached or built-in and that, as Art Leff puts it, an Unevaluated Evaluator confers it upon them. But I cannot doubt that I myself evaluate things, in the sense of judging them worthy of my time and talents. My very belief in their worth, not in the sense of acknowledging their objective value, but in the sense of committing myself to their realisation, gives them their worth in the minimal, Cartesian sense that fideism requires. I put forward the possibility here not to defend it in detail, but to anticipate the objection that scepticism logically leads to either of two very different metaethical positions.

Some, lapsing in their logic, suggest that scepticism leads to the first of these other positions, relativism, the notion that one first-order moral position or system is just as good (or right or true) as any other. To say that all values are groundless (or, more precisely, grounded only on human will), however, is not to say that all things capable of being valued should be valued equally. Indeed, to make the latter claim is implicitly to deny the sceptical premise, for that claim implies a position of moral certitude, a 'midair' position morally superior to the contending moral claims, from which perspective each is declared good. The central tenet of scepticism, by contrast, denies or at least calls into fundamental question, the very existence of any such metaethical high ground.

Just as fideism must be distinguished from its logically illegitimate sibling, relativism, so it must be distinguished from its suicidal twin, nihilism. To draw the latter distinction we must backtrack a bit. Recall that, although the derivation of relativism from scepticism is logically flawed, the derivation of fideism from scepticism is not logically compelled. Relativism wrongly suggests that from scepticism necessarily follows the conclusion that one substantive moral position is as good as any other. Nihilism rightly points out that from scepticism precisely nothing positive necessarily follows. Skepticism is a necessary, but not a sufficient, condition of fideism. The next move, on the very premises of scepticism, is not a matter of logic, but of choice. Fideism's move is affirmative; it chooses to believe in, in the sense of being committed to, something.

But there is another, negative, possibility, and that is to deny that anything matters. This is the turn that nihilism takes. As Yoda and the Prince of Denmark will tell you, the pull of this, the Dark Side, is strong. Yet you do not necessarily ally yourself with the Dark Side when you begin to wonder whether there is any moral Force out there to be with. From the position that 'there are no moral absolutes, no objective measures of the right and the good', it does not follow that 'nothing matters,' that 'all is vanity and a striving after wind.' Indeed, implicit in the position I have described as fideism is the affirmation that something does matter – what you are committed to. At that most minimal level, for example, this discussion matters to me, who wrote it, and to you, who are reading it. (And beyond that, it is but a short step for what I say to matter to you, and for what you say to matter to me.)

With this distinction between nihilism and fideism in mind, I can correct a possible misunderstanding ... I [have] referred repeatedly, and with at least implicit acquiescence, to the claims of ordinary morality, its goods and its goals; I have [now] suggested that those goods and goals are without any external foundation. These two positions are discordant, but they can be harmonised. Even if the moral sceptics are right on the metaethical issue, and the moral score is not to be transcribed from the music of the spheres, it does not follow that every note sounded by ordinary morality over the centuries is sour.

You could, of course, opt for the self-induced moral tone deafness of the nihilists, or you could follow Nietzsche's invitation to compose on a value scale of your own creation, perhaps with particular emphasis on percussion. But you could also follow fideism in a different direction. You could compose a moral score of your own with not just notes, but phrases and leitmotifs, borrowed from ordinary morality but transposed into a sceptical key and recombined into a new song, a song to which no one but you (and perhaps your friends) need march – or dance.

3.   *Interpretivism* – Realists, we have seen, insist on a world of hard moral reality outside human will; sceptics doubt, or even deny, the existence of such an external moral world. Interpretivists try to have the best – and avoid the worst – of both positions. From their perspective, they have transcended a tired old philosophical dualism and salvaged a binding, public, and objective morality from the bleak conclusions of sceptics without resort to the metaphysical and epistemological oddities of the realists.

It is in this metaethical middle ground that Simon and Luban have chosen to erect their new role morality. If it is fairly easy to define interpretivism in relation to realism and scepticism, it is virtually impossible to give a positive, descriptive account of interpretivism in its own right. If the interpretivists are united in what they want to avoid and, at least in broad outline, in what they want to achieve, they are deeply divided on how they propose to go about it.

For our purpose, however, defining them in terms of what they try to do will suffice; our purpose is to see the difficulties they have in meeting the task they have set for themselves. Trying to prove that this middle ground is a mirage would take us beyond my present purpose, and beyond the mild form of scepticism I identified and espoused above. What I mean to do here is show how unstable this middle ground is.

The middle ground of interpretivism is a continental divide that slopes steeply down to realism on one side and to fideism on the other; walking the dividing line makes extreme demands on interpretivists' intellectual equilibrium. On the one hand, interpretivists tend to fall into realism, in any one of several related ways. They may assume or suggest that our 'shared' values are as they should be, or at least are not subject to further analysis. Similarly, they may maintain or imply that considered opinions about moral matters, the perspective of 'reflective equilibrium', is objectively superior to other perspectives, or that matters as to which some (or most, or all) members of a community agree are morally binding. In all of these ways, they risk implicitly elevating an 'is' to an 'ought', importing a judgment that a particular state of affairs not only is the case, but also is good. In so doing, they invite Hume's polite puzzlement and Leff's insistent 'Sez who?'

Interpretivists may answer by asserting that 'we say', where 'we' are those who share a set of common convictions about values. Interpretivism, then, becomes a process of revealing and systematising common moral convictions, a process of organising the data of our shared moral experience into a more coherent whole. But if interpretivists take this tack, they run a dual risk. The first risk is that of leaving the path of ethics for a special branch of cultural anthropology, a purely descriptive exercise that recounts the shared views of a particular community without claiming any normative force for those views. On the other hand, if they stay on the path of interpretivist ethics and try to give those views any normative weight, they run the risk of falling into the fideist form of scepticism. By focusing on moral common ground, they tacitly admit that their moral system binds only those who find themselves in agreement with it, and binds them only on the basis of their individual assent. This is a viable alternative for interpretivists, as it is for others, but it returns them to the problem with which we began. If they abandon an objective basis for morality by tacitly admitting that their conclusions rest only on their own individual commitments to them, then on what grounds can they claim that those who disagree are morally bound?[4]

Notes and questions

1. As an example of interpretivism consider Ronald Dworkin's approach to abortion[5]. Dworkin argues that most of those who are party to the abortion debate feel that they hold irreconcilable views. In reality, however, the only way to make sense of the many of convictions of those involved about particular sub-issues is to conclude that in fact all concerned **agree** that the main issue is about how to honour the importance of the sacredness (in the special non-religious way Dworkin defines the term) of human life. Why otherwise would the pro-choice lobby accept the need for serious consideration before termination? This would not make sense if the foetus were merely human tissue similar to a cyst. Nor on Dworkin's account do the pro-life group really think that the foetus is a person with the same right not to be killed as any other person. If they did, they would not be able to believe as many do that if the life of the mother were under imminent threat it would be right to intervene to save the mother at the expense of the life of the child. The disagreements are about competing interpretations of what it means to honor the sacredness of human life. This is a religious issue and everyone agrees that each individual is entitled to freedom of conscience. It follows that after further thought all concerned ought to agree that legislative restrictions on abortion are an infringement of religious freedom and be able to live together in mutual toleration.

Is this is a useful way of thinking about differences of opinion over abortion?

2. Under British Rule in India various attempts were made to stamp out the practices of widow burning and exposing new born baby girls thus allowing them to die so as to prevent the need to find a dowry becoming a burden on the family. Was it right to do so? If so why? What are the implications for this question of moral realism, skepticism and interpretivism?

3. In part IV of his article (which is not extracted here) Atkinson outlines a more appealing response to skepticism than nihilism which he calls fideism. Atkinson considers fideism to be a secular analogue to some forms of religious faith. Fideism consists for Atkinson in a decision to live ones life by certain values whilst

4   R Atkinson 'Beyond the New Morality for Lawyers' 51 Maryland Law Review 852 [1992] pp 872-889.
5   Ronald Dworkin *Life's Dominion – An Argument About Euthanasia* (London, Harper Collins 1993) especially chapter 2.

acknowledging that they cannot be shown rationally to have any foundation in the sense claimed by moral realists. To the moral realist's question 'Surely you believe, don't you, that Nazism was *really* wrong,' the fideist replies 'Whether or not, it is really wrong, I will give my life to defeat it'. Is this a satisfactory alternative to realism?

One of the most memorable reflections upon the attempt to construct a moral code through rational analysis has been penned by Arthur Leff....

> I want to believe – and so do you – in a complete, transcendent and immanent set of propositions about right and wrong, findable rules that authoritatively and unambiguously direct us how to live righteously. I also want to believe – and so do you – in no such thing, but rather that we are wholly free, not only to choose for ourselves what we ought to do, but to decide for ourselves, individually and as a species what we ought to be. What we want, Heaven help us, is simultaneously to be perfectly ruled and perfectly free, that is, at the same time to discover the right and the good and to create it.
>
> I mention the matter here only because I think that the two contradictory impulses which together form that paradox do not exist only some high abstract level of arcane *angst.* In fact, it is my central claim that much that is mysterious about much that is written about law today is understandable only in the context of this tension between the ideas of found law and made law: a tension particularly evident in the growing, though desperately resisted, awareness that there may be, in fact, nothing to be found – that whenever we set out to find 'the law' we are able to locate nothing more attractive, or more final, than ourselves.
>
> My plan for this Article, then, is as follows. I shall first try prove to your satisfaction that there cannot be any normative system ultimately based on anything except human will. I shall then try to trace some of the scars left on recent jurisprudential writings by this growing, and apparently terrifying, realisation. Finally, I shall say a few things about – of all things – law and the way in which the impossibility of normative grounding necessarily shapes attitudes toward constitutional interpretations.
>
> Consider what a 'finder' of law must do. He must reach for a set of normative propositions in the form 'one ought to do X,' or 'it is right to do X,' that will serve in, indeed serve as the foundation for, a legal system. Once found, these propositions must themselves be immune from further criticism. Of course, once the finder finds what it is he is looking for, his work is not necessarily over. He may still work with the propositions, show their interactions, argue about their reach and implications, rationalise, restate, and reflect. But the propositions he has found are the premises of his system, and once found they cannot just be dispensed with. That which is found becomes a given for the system, however the system may be systematically manipulated. It is not created by the finder, and therefore it cannot be changed by him, or even challenged.
>
> Imagine, now, a legal system based upon perceived normative propositions – *oughts – which* are absolutely binding, wholly unquestionable, once found. Consider the normative proposition, 'Thou shalt not commit adultery.' Under what circumstances, if any, would one conclude that it is *wrong* to commit adultery? Maybe it helps to put the question another way: when would it be impermissible to make the formal intellectual

equivalent of what is known in barrooms and school yards as 'the grand sez who'? Putting it that way makes it clear that if we are looking for an evaluation, we must actually be looking for an *evaluator:* some machine for the generation of judgments on states of affairs. If the evaluation is to be beyond question, then the evaluator and its evaluative processes must be similarly insulated. If it is to fulfil its role, the evaluator must be the unjudged judge, the un-ruled legislator, the premise maker who rests on no premises, the uncreated creator of values. Now, what would you call such a thing if it existed? You would call it Him.

There is then, this one longstanding, widely accepted ethical legal system that is based upon the edicts of an unchallengeable creator, of the right and the good, in which the only job of the person who would do right is *to find* what the evaluator said. Assuming that I know what the command 'Thou shalt not commit adultery' means, then it' (and only if) the speaker is God, I ought not commit adultery. I ought not because He said I ought not, and why He said that is none of my business. And it is none of *my* business because it is a premise of *His* system that what He says I ought not to do, I ought not to do.

It is of the utmost importance to see why a God-grounded system has no analogues. Either God exists or He does not, but if He does not, nothing and no one else can take His place. Anything that took His place would also be Him. For in a God-based system, we do not define God's utterances as unquestionable, the way we might state that a triangle has three sides and go on from there and only from there. We are not doing the defining. Our relationship to God's moral order is the triangle's relationship to the order of Euclidean plane geometry, not the mathematician's. We are defined, constituted, as beings whose adultery is wrong, bad, unlawful. Thus, committing adultery in such a system is 'naturally' bad only because the system is supernaturally constituted.

Put another way, God, for philosophical purposes, is uniquely in the universe that being whose every pronouncement, including evaluative ones, is a 'Performative utterance.' A 'performative' is a statement that does not describe facts or conform to them but instead constitutes them, creates them, 'performs' them. When I say, 'I am taking a walk,' I am describing what I am doing. When I say, 'I apologise,' or 'I swear,' I am *doing* it. There is no question whether I am accurately reporting on the world, because I am in the process of constituting it.' Especially for lawyers, the realm of the performative utterance is not arcane. It is one of the things we deeply understand, often without knowing it. Important performatives, after all, include 'I promise......' I now pronounce you man and wife,' and 'This watch that I now give you, my son, is yours.'

We also understand that what a performative performs is not some mysterious emanation of magic words, but the product of certain rules and laws. Therefore, a performative utterance may not have, under all circumstances, the effect it has under some. 'I promise' is a promise, but it may not result in a contract unless the promisor has capacity, there is no fraud in the inducement, consideration is present, and so on. 'I now pronounce you man and wife' will not necessarily create the status of marriage if, for instance, the speaker is an imposter cleric, and at least one of the putative spouses knows it at the time.

This is why there can ordinarily or 'naturally' be no such thing as a normative performative utterance. A statement in the form 'you ought to do X.....' it is right to do X,' or 'X is good' will establish oughtness, rightness, or goodness only if there is a set of rules that gives the speaker the power totally to determine the question. But it is precisely the question of who has the power to set such rules for validating evaluations that is the central problem of ethics and, as we shall see, of legal theory. There is no one who can be said a priori to have that power unless the question being posed is also being begged.

Except, as noted, God. It *necessarily* follows that the pronouncements of an omniscient, omnipotent, and infinitely good being are always true and effectual. When God says, 'Let there be light,' there **is** light. And when He sees that it is good, good is what it is.

Now I certainly have not gone on at such a length to clarify the special status of God as the foundation of an ethical or legal system because I intend to discuss whether or not He exists and can ground such a system for us. That, obviously, is not something that can be decided here. I have pursued this discussion for so long because it will make it much easier to understand why there is discontent verging on despair whenever some theorist tries to develop a system in which 'found' ethical or legal propositions are to be treated as binding, but for which there is no supernatural grounding. God's will is binding because it is His will that it be. Under what other circumstances can the unexamined will of anyone else withstand the cosmic 'says who' and come out similarly dispositive?

There are no such circumstances. We are never going to get anywhere (assuming for the moment that there is somewhere to get) in ethical or legal theory unless we finally face the fact that, in the Psalmist's words, there is no one like unto the Lord. If He does not exist, there is no metaphoric equivalent. No person, no combination of people, no document however hallowed by time, no process, no premise, nothing is equivalent to an actual God in this central function as the unexaminable examiner of good and evil. The so-called death of God turns out not to have been just *His* funeral; it also seems to have effected the total elimination of any coherent, or even more-than-momentarily convincing, ethical or legal system dependent upon finally authoritative extra systemic premises. What Kurt Godel did for systems deicide has done for normative systems, including legal systems. Put briefly, if the law is 'not a brooding omnipresence in the sky,' then it can be only one place: in us. If we are trying to find a substitute final evaluator, it must be one of us, some of us, all of us but It cannot be anything else. The result of that realisation is what might be called an exhilarated vertigo, a simultaneous combination of an exultant 'We're free of God' and a despairing 'Oh God, we're free.'

Thus, once it is accepted that (a) all normative statements are evaluations of actions and other states of the world; (b) an evaluation entails an evaluator; and (c) in the presumed absence of God, the only available evaluators are people, then only a determinate, and reasonably small, number of kinds of ethical and legal systems can be generated. Each such system will be strongly differentiated by the axiomatic answer it chooses to give to one key question: *who* ultimately gets to play the role of ultimately unquestionable evaluator, a role played in supernaturally based systems by God? Who among us, that is, *ought to* be able to declare 'law' that *ought* to be obeyed?

Stated that baldly, the question is so intellectually unsettling that one would expect to find a noticeable number of legal and ethical thinkers trying not to come to grips with it, if its avoidance were at all possible. And of course it turns out that it is possible, at least as a desperate temporary matter, and that the impulse has been actualised in an enormous body of modern writing.

The most popular of those moves may be called 'Descriptivism'. It goes like this: it is not at all necessary to specify *who* is generating the legal system, much less to describe how that generation is being effected. A legal system is a fact. It is something (including processes) that exists. The way to identify its existence is to discover what rules are in fact obeyed. Once you have made that identification, it is possible, at least in theory, to describe how the rules originated, and accurately to describe them as the product of certain people using certain processes.

That is, you can say if you wish that the law is 'the command of the sovereign,' but that is only to say that law is the result of that of which it is the result. If law is defined as the command of the sovereign, then the sovereign is defined as whatever it is the commands of which are obeyed. Any sovereign is 'as good as,' that is, validates the law to the same degree as, any other. The term 'the law' describes not *good* behaviour or *right* behaviour, but behaviour. It is not that whatever is is right, but that whatever is *as* right as anything else that might be.

I found it enormously interesting that this approach to finding a replacement for a transcendent source of values involves, in effect, a redirection of metaphorical energy: to find a human equivalent for God, there is a focus not on God's goodness, but on His power. It makes sense. For this too may be predicated of God: whether or not it is ever coherent to question if His will ought to be done, one way or another His will *is* done. All of His 'statements,' evaluative and other, are performatives: when God says, 'Let there be light,' light there is. It may, of course, be His will *that your* will is free to do or not to do one thing or another, but His response is inexorable – not to mention infinite and eternal.

The central difficulty with the Descriptivist position, then, for all the subtlety and intelligence with which various adherents have elaborated it, is that it 'validates' every legal system equally. If a valid system is one that is in fact in place, then anything that is in fact in place is the legal system. No particular characteristic of or procedure employed by the 'sovereign' is necessary to validate the system except its power to generate something that is in fact obeyed. The basic engine of law is nowhere – or, rather, it is anywhere at any moment it happens to be – and that robs Descriptivism of any *critical* capacity. Under Descriptivism, it is impossible to say that anything ought or ought not to be.

A critical jurisprudence is impossible when one gives God's place to anyone who happens to be conventionally obeyed, with nothing turning on who that is. If that seems unsatisfactory, then one must finally face the question of who *ought* to have God's validating power. That is, one will have to seek out some way to validate a particular legal system without thereby necessarily validating *every* legal system.

Since we are talking about people, the question really is whether there is any person or set of persons whose generation of law is entitled to final respect. The obvious first move is to decide whether one can found a system on the premise that each person is his *own* ultimate evaluative authority. In this approach, God is not only dead, but He has been ingested seriatim at a universal feast. Everyone can declare what ought to be for himself, and no one can legitimately criticise anyone else's values-what they are or how they came to be-because everyone has equal ethical dignity. In this approach everything that was true of God's evaluations is true of each person's evaluations. Each individual's normative statements are, for him, performative utterances: what is said to be bad or good, wrong or right, is just that for each person, solely by reason of its having been uttered.

In the absence of a supernatural validator, what could be more natural' than that? Alas, there is a problem: who validates the rules *for interactions* when there is a multiplicity of Gods, all of identical rank? The whole point of God, after all, is that there is none **like** unto Him. But the whole point of turning people into Gods is to make every one like every other one. It is totally impermissible under such a conception for there to be, so to speak, interpersonal comparisons of normativity: there is literally no one in a position to evaluate them against each other.

I have been told that the ancient Babylonians, possessed of (or by) a multiplicity of Gods and therefore faced with similar problems, concluded that in cases of conflict the big Gods ate the little ones. That sort of move here, however, would serve only to collapse this 'God-is me' solution into the 'whoever-wins-is-God' approach of Descriptivism. If the difficulty with Descriptivism is that it validates any normative system, the problem with the 'God-is-me' approach – call it 'Personalism' – is that it validates everyone's individual normative system, while giving no instruction in, or warrant for, choosing among them.

This feature of the Personalist ethical system is something of a hindrance if one wants to found a legal system on it, that is, a system designed to govern interactions among people. It constitutes humanity as a series of autonomous monads, each of identical 'dignity,' each entitled to exactly the same respect. As long as they remain the ethical equivalent of the atoms of Lucretius raining down from some indescribable noplace, running immovably parallel, eternally untouching and untouchable, there is, of course, no problem. A universe of ethical solipsism is perfectly adequate. But what happens if, again like Lucretius' atoms, they enter a world where they cannot continue on their hermetic courses, but have to bang into each other? If they in fact clash, that is, if people actually do affect each other when their autonomous, equally valid value sets are translated into actions, what happens? When these individual moral monads leave the world of definition and entailment for the world of existence and causality, the world in which legal systems operate, the Personalist has one hell of a problem: who *ought* to give way?

Note that this is not the same question as who *will* give way. Picture two of these monstrous monads simultaneously coming upon something that they both want (and that, by the way, they are by definition equally 'right' to want). One of them shoulders the other aside and appropriates the object, or maybe he just gets there first. One could say it 'ought' to be his because he got it: a single-instance equivalent of Descriptivism. The key question, however, is whether, using the assumptions of Personalism, one can say anything else. If the impulses to possess are, by definition, equally 'valid,' is not the result equally acceptable whichever way it comes out? Is there any ground from which to criticise the *method* by which a monad fulfils its unchallengeable desires?

The answer is no, not at least within the confines of Personalism. If some methods of actualising desires in contest with other desires are to be forbidden, the forbidding will have to be done on some basis not entailed by the tenets of the Personalist ethic. By definition, one who considers force an appropriate way to deal with conflicting desires is just as justified as one who feels otherwise, for the propriety of activities in the world is no different from any other subject of evaluation.

That does not mean that one cannot generate and seek to defend a system that provides, for instance, that the little Gods may not use force or fraud on each other when they fall into conflict over aims. One could indeed defend a system that says that all conflicts have to be settled somehow to the satisfaction of both contending parties. One could say that such a rule for interdivinity transactions will produce more health or wealth or wisdom, and that health, wealth, and wisdom are good. What one cannot do is defend it on the basis of Godlet preference. Hence it should come as no surprise that a system of 'each-God-for-himself' is not, by itself, much of a solution to any basic problem of *human society*. Nor is there any way out for a Personalist via 'agreement,' real or hypothetical. Absolutely nothing is gained by hypothesising or even bringing about some 'contract' or treaty among the monads about what they are permitted to do with or to each other. Under the Personalist view, a promise ought to be kept only if each promisor thinks it ought to be kept; the value of promise-keeping is no different from any other.

What then is left? Pure Descriptivism is exactly what it purports to be: a description of a state of affairs with no normative content at all. The Personalist, internalising God on a one-man-one-God basis, leaves evaluations of interactions between the Godlets formally impossible. If the receptacle for God's evaluative role cannot therefore be either 'wherever it is' or 'equally in everyone,' then where *can* it be?

The next move, one would guess, would be to find some way to distinguish among the individuals either quantitatively through some aggregation principle, or qualitatively. One might choose to stand, that is, on the most evaluations or the best ones.

Over the first alternative, counting noses, we need not linger long. If we assume that it is impermissible to distinguish qualitatively among the entities being counted – if by stipulation we are not allowed to look inside the heads from which the noses protrude, and if each individual is by definition as 'right' and 'good' as every other – then all our count tells us is that a multiplicity of perfectly virtuous monads are not necessarily also identical. If we are to cope with the matter through a vote, it must be because of some *rule* that itself cannot be derived from any monad or combination thereof. All one has is the assumed conclusion that in cases of conflicting perfections, the largest number wins.

Can we then get out of our bind by deciding after all to pay attention to the quality of the ethical boxes? No, we cannot. The shortest way to put the reason is this: a fundamental *assumption* of the perfect monad Personalist view is that no inquiry can be made of the quality of any ethical position held by a monad. Each one is his own God. That is the whole purpose of the Personalist view, to insulate fundamental ethical conclusions from any further examination. If monad A believes X, and monad B believes Y, it is central to the system that there is *no* criterion for choosing between X *and* Y. The moment one suggests a criterion, then individual men have ceased to be the measure of all things, and something else-and that necessarily means someone else has been promoted to the (formally impossible) position of evaluator-in-chief

Nonetheless, this impulse to give different weights to different positions based on their 'quality' is so common in modern ethical discourse that it deserves further consideration. After all, very rarely do modern moralists actually give the ethical positions of the people on the Clapham Omnibus equal weight. Notably preferred to them are the people in the professorial Volvo, ostensibly because they do not have just any old view of an ethical question, but a 'considered' view, or a 'serious and reflective' view, or may even have reached the enviable state of being in 'reflective equilibrium.'

I am making fun of all this, but I should not. Underlying this impulse to rate certain positions over others is the understandable and perhaps unavoidable human desire to give human reason some role in ethical theory. One would think that a fully considered moral position, the product of deep and thorough intellectual activity, one that fits together into a fairly consistent whole, would deserve more respect than shallow, expletive, internally inconsistent ethical decisions. Alas, to think that would be to think wrong: labour and logic have no *necessary* connection to ethical truth.

Let us say that person A decides that one ought to do X under particular circumstances. Person B believes that under those circumstances one ought to do Y. Person A's conclusion is based upon deep and mature thought and comes out of an intellectual structure such that doing X will work no discernible contradiction with anything else he might think one ought to do. Not so Person B. He thinks one ought to do Y, but he has not thought about it, and if he did think about it he would recognise that doing Y is totally, flagrantly inconsistent with a host of other things he thinks one ought to do. Should one not in such a situation give more weight to A's position than to B's? Only if *someone* has the power to declare careful, consistent, coherent ethical propositions 'better' than the sloppier, more impulsive kinds. Who has that power and how did he get it?

Of course, B himself might concur. If A shows B that B's decision grows out of or into a logical muddle, B may decide to go along with A. Monads are not *necessarily* sealed off from each other. But what if B does not care, that is, what if his own evaluation system does not require logical consistency, let alone elegance? Can A (or we) say that B *is ethically* mistaken? If B will not be persuaded, can he be threatened into changing his views, or physically forced? *Where* do we get that power? Bluntly, intellectual beauty is not a necessary prerequisite to ethical adequacy unless someone declares it to be.

Of course, if ethical propositions are made subject to intellectual criteria, ethical discourse is made more interesting, not to mention possible. Once certain intellectual canons are accepted, one can criticise another's conclusion with respect to those canons. The argument

(1) $p = q$;
(2)   if p, *then* x;
(3)   if q, *then* not x

doubtless can be described as lousy argument, whether the letters p, q, and x stand for propositions of mathematics or of ethics. But so what? The aim of ethical discourse is ethics, not discourse, and a piece of lousy thinking is not necessarily 'immoral.'

And with the elimination of any requirement that ethical statements be coherent goes any requirement for any particular process leading to more intelligent and intelligible decisions. It would be surprising, after all, if a system based upon the existence of ethical monads whose normative premises are by definition beyond inquiry were also to incorporate some *necessary,* and necessarily normative, rule about communicating them, for instance, that they explain themselves to each other. Gods have their own individual rules for chatting, even with each other. No one else can say that a certain process – free speech, for instance, or equal access to each other-is required, unless there is a super-God who can insist.

There remains, then, only one considerable approach to the validation of ethical systems. Under it no search is made for any evaluator, but rather some state of the world is declared to be good, and acts which effect that state are ethical acts. Merely to express this approach is, of course, to refute it, for a good state of the world must be good *to someone.* One cannot escape from the fact that a normative statement is an evaluation merely by dispensing with any mention of who is making it. Hence the description of a particular end state eg human happiness is just another evaluator centred approach, but with blinkers added. Wealth is good and, makes our acts good, if someone, or some collection of someones says so. But *which* someone or someones count still has to be accounted for.

I have gone through the preceding elaborate discussion because it leads to an important assertion about legal Systems in general and ours in particular. *There is no such thing as an unchallengeable evaluative system.* There is no way to prove one ethical or legal system superior to any other, unless at some point an evaluator is asserted to have the final, uncontradictable, unexaminable word. That choice of unjudged judge, whoever is given the role, is itself, strictly speaking, arbitrary.

But if the system in addition presumes to coherence, then once the final – evaluator role is distributed, almost all questions must be answered determinatively in a manner characteristic of, and in all important ways predictable from, the original assignment of final evaluative power. It is thus the first assumption, combined with simple canons of intellectual coherence (the need for which is itself an undefendable assumption), that determines the legal result in any particular instance.

One methodological consequence of the unprovability of the bases of any legal or ethical system is that it makes one particular kind of scholarly work attractively easy to write. If a series of values is set forth to be justified – 'proved' in the strong sense used here – all attempts will necessarily fail. On the other hand, if the set includes a value that is to prevail *unless* some other contradictory value is 'proved,' then the value not requiring proof will always win. That is, an argument in the form 'A, *unless p, q, or r'* will always generate 'therefore A,' if the system makes it impossible to establish *p, q, or r.*

A splendid example of that scholarly move is Robert Nozick's book, *Anarchy, State, and Utopia* which opens: 'Individuals have rights, and there are things no person or group may do to them (without violating their rights).' Nozick devotes much of the rest of the book to showing how no contrary position-for instance, that the poor as a class, have rights against the rich or that the sick have rights against the well can be established. But obviously each of those positions (and alas, an infinity of others too) could be established the same way 'Individuals have rights.....' was established, by simple declarative assertion.

I certainly do not want to suggest that Nozick is unique in this mode of argument. It is hard to know, in fact, how else one could proceed, given the proven unprovability of normative propositions. At some point in every sustained argument about what is right or wrong, or what ought or ought not to be done, some normative proposition about who has the final power over normative propositions will have to be asserted. It may be veiled or open, but it will have to be there. And once it is there, whatever it is, it will determine the form of the system that emerges.

That is why works that seem so different in surface detail turn out to have so surprisingly much in common. For example, any system the central premise of which is that individuals may not morally be dominated by other individuals, no matter how many of them there are, will encounter identical problems and not surprisingly will tend to come up with similar 'solutions.' As we have seen, the problem with turning each person into an evaluative Godlet is that it is then impossible to ground rules for how the individuals ought to deal with each other. To put it another way, if the individuals are assumed to be simultaneously equal and nonidentical, there must be conflict, and that conflict cannot be adjudicated by any extra-individual evaluation system.

As suggested earlier, however, that fatal weakness in the radical individualist position would melt away if, in some mysterious way, equal dignity could be joined to identical evaluation; if everyone believed the same thing were right, there would be no conflict. But there is a strong empirical implausibility to the existence of identical evaluative criteria, at any level above triviality, for any collection of real individuals. Thus, we find two scholars as different in approach as Nozick and Roberto Unger both committed to a no-domination constraint on interpersonal behaviour, making almost identical moves. What they both do is hypothesise some process that would lead to geographic concentrations of the like-minded, which grouplets would then coexist, but at a spatial remove, with other concentrations of otherminded individuals. The processes leading to the creation of these mini-societies, insofar as they are described at all, are vastly different in the two works, but the result is the same: conflict among the individuals within the sub groups, while not treated as technically impossible, is treated, implicitly, as vastly less important once the individual members have found each other. Individuality, that is, is seen as being retained at relatively low individual cost.

The conceptual difficulty with this solution (leaving totally aside the practical implausibilities of the processes envisioned) is that conflict necessitated by a system of equally 'right' monads is merely transferred to the level, so to speak, of international law. Each little cluster of individuals may have become normatively homogeneous, but the world now consists of heterogeneous clusters, and by hypothesis the beliefs of no one of them are entitled to more respect than those of any other. All that has been achieved is the creation of corporative, agglutinative, nonbiological 'individuals' whose evaluations are to remain unquestionable. But which rules ought to govern *their* interactions is a question that, necessarily, still has no answer.

Interestingly enough, the same basic move — generating a process that will produce identical biological individuals so as to eliminate conflict over values — is typical of some forms of neo-Marxism, which is moderately resurgent of late in (of all places) legal scholarship. This 'Marxist' move is to make the winnowing and duplicating process temporal rather than, like Unger's and Nozick's, spatial. The Marxist utopia is located in a blessed future when there will be only one class that, at least impliedly, will have no evaluative conflict. The vision is a powerful one because it does not leave the landscape dotted with presumably antagonistic agglutinations of the militantly like-minded. There will be no need for any 'international law' governing interclass conflicts of morality because all the other 'classes' will be gone...

I have told these too-brief-for-fairness tales about various currently popular ethical approaches concretely to illustrate what is, I think, already obvious: not only will the choice of any nonsupernatural source of ethical premises be arbitrary, but choosing either 'natural' alternative locus – the individual or society – will lead to either individual or social implausibilities. If each person is a Godlet, there is no room for a valid society; if each society is God, there is no space for individual freedom. And if the two approaches are mixed-society can insist on X, but the individual has a right to Y – there is no way, except by deception or bluster, to ground all the divers X's *and Y's*.

Which brings me, at last, to the lawyer's dog to be wagged by the enormous preceding tail of this Article. I would suggest that the United States Constitution, and many of our legal problems with it, can be illuminated by the foregoing analysis. None of the problems can, as you might have guessed, be solved that way, but that is the whole point: all of our problems of constitutional interpretation arise because it is most likely impossible to write a constitution, or create one by interpretation, that does not simultaneously invoke more than one theory as to where ultimate, unchallengeable normative power is to be placed. Or, at any rate, that seems to be the case with respect to the real Constitution we have.

Assume for the moment that the Constitution can be treated as God, and that it is not only transcendent but immanent, that there is a way in which, when it speaks to us, we can hear it. If one looks at it for its message about who has final evaluative power under its aegis, it becomes plain that its most important element is a structurally basic equivocation. 'The people' have the ultimate normative word, of course, but it is ostentatiously unclear whether that God – like role is lodged in 'the people' as a category or in each constituent person of 'the people.' Or, in the language of traditional constitutional analysis, along with a structure setting up checks and balances between state and national power, and among executive, legislative, and judicial powers, and between 'the people' and each foregoing instantiation of 'government,' ultimate normative power is divided between two fundamentally different conceptions of personhood: person as fundamental moral building block of 'people,' and person as mere constituent cell of the fundamental moral entity known as 'the people.' In short, the Constitution simultaneously establishes rights and democracy.

It may by now be obvious why it could not be otherwise. As we have seen, if total, final normative authority were assigned to each biological individual, and he were made morally autonomous, no rules to govern the interaction between those individuals – the Godlets, as I have called them, could be justified under the assumption of moral autonomy. There would be *nothing but* rights. If, on the other extreme, moral finality were lodged in 'the people' as a class, then no claim for moral breathing space could be upheld for any atom out of which the class was constituted. If 'the people' decided, by whatever process it validated, what was right, it would be unchallengeably right for each person: there could be *no* rights. Thus, under the second collectivist conception, individual evaluations would be morally impossible. But if I am correct that people rightly see themselves simultaneously as part of 'the people' and as autonomous persons, neither of the these results is attractive. Nor was it attractive to the drafters of the Constitution, nor is it, to many subsequent interpreters. It is thus with respect to this dual self-image that the Constitution really plays God. It commands that *both* of these conceptions of the final lodging place of evaluative power be simultaneously reflected in the operation of the American polity; that is, it attempts to do something that can be done *by neither* an individually nor a collectively grounded system.

Since the Constitution is not God, its case-by-case allocations of Godship are, in the sense I have used the term, 'arbitrary.' But that does not mean that those allocations do not exist: that clipping should nullify a touchdown pass is also arbitrary in that sense, but that does not mean there is no such rule or result. With respect to the collectivist aspects of the Constitution, there are side-bar restrictions on how the collectivity can make its decisions (notably various aggregation rules, like majoritarianism), rules on who counts as part of the group, and most important, restrictions upon the way in which collective determinations can be enforced against individuals in the collective (notably the detailed regulations constituting due process, and, indeed, the institution of the judicial branch itself). Moreover, certain areas of individual activity are withdrawn from collective interference-religious beliefs, for example.

At the same time, however, the very existence of these collective powers acts as a restriction upon individual evaluative autonomy. To put it very briefly, if you do not want to be taxed for the common good as the common good is defined by the group, tough.

As long as the Constitution is accepted, or at least not overthrown, it successfully functions as a God would in a valid ethical system: *its* restrictions and accommodations govern. They could be other than they are, but they are what they are, and that is that. There will be, as with all divine pronouncements, a continuous controversy over what God says, but whatever the practical importance of the power to determine those questions, they are theoretically unthreatening. It is only when the Constitution ceases to be seen as fulfilling God's normative role, ceases, that is, to be outside the normative system it totally constitutes, or when, as is impossible with a real God, it is seen to have 'gaps,' that a crisis comes to exist. What 'wins' when the Constitution will not say, or says two things at the same time?

At that point, you see, we are really forced to see ourselves as lawmakers rather than law finders, and we are immediately led into a regress that is, fatally, not infinite. We can *say* that a valid legal system must have some minimum process for rational determination and operation. We can *say* that the majority cannot consistently disadvantage any minority. We can *say* that, whatever else a majority can do, it cannot systematically prevent a minority from seeking to become a majority. We can *say* all sorts of things, but what we cannot say is why one say is better than any other, unless we state some standard by which it definedly is. To put it as bluntly as possible, if we go to find what law ought to govern us, and if what we find is not an authoritative Holy Writ but just ourselves, just people, making that law, how can we be governed by what we have found?

Naturally, one need not be on crisis alert all the time. Even if it is hard to come up with any convincing reason why a two-hundred-year old document ought to be given final respect, indeed to be given any respect, on some current question about the allocation of power and freedom in America, it is awfully hard to be a credible constitutional thinker by treating the Constitution as irrelevant. It is, therefore, a convention of constitutional law, and may be of American society, that (a) the Constitution does speak to our problems; (b) it can, much of the time, be heard and understood; and (c) when you do hear and understand it, that's it. That is, much of the time one can act as if there is, for constitutional determinations, a God, though He may occasionally mumble.

Hence it is possible to 'handle' any number of questions by trying *to understand* what the Constitution says. It is possible to say that such and such is a problem of equal protection, ie, that 'the God' accords all people equal dignity and will not allow mere people to do otherwise. It is possible to say that such – and – other is a question of due process, *ie,* that 'the God' treats all people as rational, and communication channels for the determination of truth must be kept open. It is not possible, however, forever to avoid having to ask whether, in a particular instance, the individual with a 'right' or the collectivity with its 'power' is to govern. For the Constitution clearly says that there are circumstances in which the collective may override the normative beliefs of a bare numerical minority, and other circumstances in which one biological individual is entitled to withstand everyone else, but the Constitution does not exhaustively specify which circumstances are which. The Constitution as God says, in effect, that one wins out over the other when it, the Constitution, says so, and not when the individual or the group says so. But what then can one do when the Constitution, quite obviously, says nothing at all?....

All I can say is this: it looks as if we are all we have. Given what we know about ourselves and each other, this is an extraordinarily unappetising prospect; looking around the world, it appears that if men are brothers, the ruling model is Cain and Abel. Neither reason, nor love, nor even terror, seems to have worked to make us ' good,' and worse than that, there is no reason why anything should. Only if ethics were something unspeakable by us, could law be unnatural, and therefore unchallengeable. As things now stand, everything is up for grabs.[6]

Note

Arthur Leff did not take the fideist alternative. A brilliant man who was widely admired by colleagues at the Yale Law School, Leff concluded that broad ranging philosophical inquiry was futile and devoted himself instead to writing a legal dictionary which was so detailed that he estimated it would not be concluded before 2075[7]. Only the letters A, B and C had been finished before his own early death from cancer.[8]

Questions

1. Arthur Leff comments that 'The so-called death of God turns out not to have been just *His Funeral,* it also seems to have effected the total elimination of any coherent,

---

6   Arthur Leff 'Unspeakable Law, Unnatural Ethics' [1979] 85 Duke Law Journal at 129-145.
7   Susan Z Leff [1984] 94 Yale LJ 1850.
8   The finished sections where printed in a special edition of the Yale Law Journal: ibid at 1853.

or even more than momentarily convincing, ethical or legal system dependent upon finally authoritative extra systematic premises?'.[9]

What does this mean?

2. What according to Arthur Leff would the relationship between God and mankind have to be like if (contrary to his assumption) there did exist a set of unchallengeable moral principles. If it is a premise of God's system that 'adultery is wrong?' why should we obey him? What is the importance of power?

3. Is there such a thing as evil? What are the implications of your answer?

4. What are the implications of Arthur Leff's argument for a) democracy and b) individual rights? What are its implications for the Human Rights Act 1998?

5. Why should lawyers obey the code of conduct governing their profession? Consider the views
i)   that they implicitly promise to do so when they are admitted to the profession; and
ii)   that it is in their interests to do so because society entrusts the legal professions with various functions (eg advocacy) on the basis that its members can be trusted to observe certain standards?

2   Character and community

Arthur Leff is concerned to question the plausibility of the attempt to ground morality solely in rational analysis. A related question is whether the analytical frameworks on offer bear any relation to the way in which individuals actually make decisions; one of the paradoxes of utilitarianism in most of its forms is that it is difficult to see how anyone could hope to act upon it in daily life. Similarly, even if particular rational frameworks are viewed as helpful by those having a prior commitment to living a moral life, what do they have to say to those lacking such commitment? It is commonly observed that many of those involved in Nazism were people of considerable intellectual gifts which raises a doubt is to whether evil has its roots in intellectual error.

By way of reaction to these problems, the last 20 years have seen moral philosophers take a renewed interest in virtue ethics. Though its adherents are diverse, they tend to stress that moral life cannot be seen as a matter of applying abstract rules to fact situations by a process of rational analysis. Conduct in fact flows from character. What matters are the habitual patterns of conduct (be they good (virtues) or bad (vices)) you have acquired particularly in the family and the community of your youth. These will determine what you are. Who you are determines what you do. This line of

9   Supra note 6 at p 1232.

thinking is Aristotelian in origins and also influenced the writers of the New Testament. St Paul writes,

> I find this law at work; when I want to do what is good what is evil is the only choice I have . My inner being delights in the law of God . But I see a different law at work in my body- a law that fights against the law my mind approves of. It make me a prisoner to the law of sin which is at work in my body. What an unhappy man I am! Who will rescue me from this body that is taking me to death?[10]

Closely related to this has been a stress on the importance of community for it is within community that character and identify are formed. On this view, moral growth may be a matter of realising who you are rather than analysing what you ought to be doing. This in turn calls into question the desirability of organising your social life so as to maximise individual freedom which has been a common response to the limits of rational analysis of moral values. Many of these themes have been taken up in relation to lawyers' ethics by Professor Thomas Shaffer. Shaffer notes critically that the provisions of the Model Code relating to conflict of interest assume that lawyers will normally represent and seek to maximise the interests of individuals rather than collective entities such as the family. He comments that

> The moral premise... is, I think, that the truly important and deep things in human life are individual and singular; they are matters of autonomy. To put it another way, the highest good I can seek for a person on whom I focus my beneficence is that he be free -- and free here means self-ruling and radically not committed. The things that people share under this logic are relatively superficial; they are the harmonies that radically autonomous individuals choose to have. Employment by a group of persons is possible only if the lawyer stays with chosen harmonies. The employment is imperilled if the lawyer intrudes on these individualistic choices. If the employment will necessarily intrude on these choices, then the radically individualistic nature of the persons who are client(s) requires separate lawyers for each individual.
>
>> The competing premise... is that human harmonies do not rest on the choices of autonomous individuals; they rest instead on communities. Human harmonies are not chosen but given. As Abraham Joshua Heschel put it,
>>
>>> [T]he self is a monstrous deceit . . . something transcendent in disguise . . . . I am endowed with a will but the will is not mine; I am endowed with freedom, but it is a freedom imposed on the will. Life is something that visits my body . . . . The essence of what I am is not mine. [11]
>
> Organic communities such as families are prior to individuals[12].

Shaffer describes 'radical individualism' as 'the philosophy of the adolescent who says he had no parents.'[13] In the following extract, Stephen Peppe,r one of the foremost

---

10   Romans 7:21-24 (GNB).

11   Citing A Herschel *Between God and Man: An Interpretation of Judiasm* (1959) at 62.

12   Thomas L Shaffer 'The Legal Ethics of Radical Individualism' [1987] 65 Texas Law Review 963 at p 975.

13   Supra note 12 at p 977.

defenders of individual autonomy as the central value of law and legal practice considers the claims of communitarianism and comments on the work of Professor Shaffer.

There is a widely shared perception that our law and politics emphasise individualism too much and support community too little. It is this recognition and the movement to provide a remedy that I refer to here as 'communitarian'. This point of view starts with the simple fact that human beings do not, and cannot, exist in isolation, as atoms. We come to be physically, psychologically , and socially, through others. It emphasises the socially embedded and connected nature of human life, the fact that we are necessarily and basically connected to others: first to families; later to larger intermediate groups; ultimately, and pervasively, a large part of our 'selves' is determined by and part of the culture and society in which we are raised. The individual under this understanding is an 'implicated self', one whose 'deepest and most important obligations flow from identity and relatedness, rather than from consent'. The message is that belonging is as significant in our lives as freedom and independence, in fact more significant because prior to, and a necessary basis for, freedom and independence: connection and community come first, freedom and independence must be partial and secondary.

Michael Sandel[14] is one of the leading examples, emphasising in his writing the fact that the individual does not stand separate and alone, an isolated chooser; but is in large part constituted by the community. The community comes first, and in forming us is fundamentally implicated in our identities, including our individual commitments, goals, and vision of what is good and worth pursuing in life. Congruent with Sandel's view of the community as constitutive of the individual is the movement toward a neo-Aristotelian view of ethics. Identified primarily with Alasdair MacIntyre,[15] this understanding asserts that ethics is not essentially about rules or principles which guide individual behaviour. To the contrary, a person's character – the virtues that a person habitually exemplifies – is the proper concern of ethics; character and the presence or absence of virtues determine moral behaviour. And both character and the virtues derive from community, from a tradition and practices which can only exist within an ongoing group. Thus an individual's moral life is inextricably bound up with that person's character; and that person's character is in turn inextricably bound up with the community of which she is a part. Ethics is thus coherent only in the context of a community and its traditions...

This is a perception which I share. The problem is that even agreeing with it, it is very difficult to figure out what to do with it.

II. WHAT TO DO WITH THE COMMUNITARIAN VIEW?

A. The Tension Between Individual and Community

Even if the group comes first, and is constitutive of the individual, the individual does exist and is separate from the group. We are at the same time fundamentally separate from and fundamentally connected to others. The structure of our lives and our greatest joys and meaning come from our connections to others. But others also are the source of some of our greatest fears; others are often the source of oppression, pain, and

14   Michael Sandel *Liberalism and the Limits of Justice* (2nd ed) (Cambridge, CUP, 1998).
15   Alasdair MacIntyre *After Virtue: a study in moral theory* (London, Duckworth, 1981).

much that is the worst in life. We need and it is good to be connected, but we need and it is good to be separate. Much of our lives, including our moral and political lives, is involved in working out this tension.

Few of us would want to return to a legal regime where the group subsumes the individual, where the individual was in some sense the property of the group. Individual rights – the legal protection of the individual from groups, particularly from that larger political group which is the government – is a great achievement, one not lightly abandoned. And it is an achievement which few of the new communitarians wish to undo. Few emphasise a desire to strengthen community at the large scale level of federal or state government; few wish to significantly cut back on individual rights in relation to those manifestations of community. Freedom is 'perhaps the most important value' for Americans, and it is an achievement which few of the new communitarians wish to cede back to the government.

Strengthening community can be seen as a threat to the legal recognition of and protection for the individual and, more specifically, as a threat to legal protections for individual freedom. But strengthening community can also be seen as the crucial contemporary need in relation to individual freedom. Few of us wish to be alone or isolated, and those who are alone and isolated are relatively powerless. Community and connection enhance our individual freedom at least as much as they threaten it. If one has on the one side very large governmental institutions and very large corporate entities and on the other side isolated individuals, freedom for the individuals is not likely to mean a lot; single individuals are not likely to have much power to exercise their freedom in relation to those vastly larger corporate and governmental entities. Thus the importance of intermediate communities to the individual, an importance which the new communitarians remind us is not solely instrumental but also inherent; necessary both for our individual identities to be effective (our freedom) and necessary as constituent parts of those identities (what it is we perceive ourselves to be and what it is we want). And thus arises the communitarian project of developing the concepts, laws, and institutions to support intermediate communities without sacrificing legal protection for the individual.

B. The Opposite of Autonomy

If the lawyer's ethic is premised upon the value of the autonomy of the client, what does that mean? Does 'autonomy' in this context mean or imply isolation and disconnection for the client? Or does it mean and relate to the client's freedom and liberty? Or is there no difference between these meanings: are freedom and disconnection the same? In suggesting autonomy as one of the base values that support the contemporary lawyer ethic, the cluster of meanings I intended was the 'liberty, freedom, autonomy' group. The opposite of autonomy in this sense of the concept is domination and oppression; it is not connection or relation. To value autonomy in the political and legal context is not to assume or suggest that the self is either totally or naturally free. Obviously it is neither. Rather, it is to appreciate that we ought to be very limited and careful in deciding by whom, when, and how the self is to be *legally* constrained. Likewise, to value autonomy in the political and legal context is not to assume that the individual is isolated and disconnected. Obviously he is not. It is, again, to be limited and careful in deciding what *legal* powers those connections or communities are to have over the individual.

And this is where the lawyer comes in. The law both limits and empowers. Theft is prohibited; so is dumping your garbage on your neighbour's front lawn. The corporate form of enterprise, the contract and the will, on the other hand, all allow one to reach results otherwise unattainable. These enabling forms of law obviously facilitate and empower connection at least as much as they facilitate separation, including the kind of extended basic connections we identify as communities. The lawyer serves the client's freedom and power (autonomy) through providing both knowledge of the limits of the law and access to the law's instruments and possibilities. The lawyer transmits both the limits and the powers of the law.

Another way to focus on the meaning of autonomy in relation to connection and community is to consider a category of restraint and limit aside from the law. This second category includes those restraints we choose, or that we recognise as part of our selves. Consider some examples: We choose to get married and consider it a commitment of serious dimension which significantly limits our range of permissible options and actions. Or we perceive that speaking derisively to our children is simply not part of the person we are. Or we choose to run three miles regularly, and may after time see this activity no longer as chosen but as part of who we are. Many of us think of ourselves as Italian or Jewish or Mormon in a way that has consequences for conduct. Or we buy a house assuming that we will maintain it in a way that will consume resources of time and money, thereby significantly restraining our future conduct. And so on. These choices and these aspects of our selves are part of our autonomy, part of who we are and what we want to be (or see no choice about being). Often restraints and limits of this sort are a large part of what we mean by community and connection. And it is in this sense that community and connection enhance autonomy rather than impinge upon it. Connection and community are part of what we all want, they are part both of what we *are* and of what we *choose,* and the combination is what we usually mean when we speak of 'autonomy'.

These commitments or limits are relevant to the lawyer's ethical role as well: the lawyer serves and honours the client's autonomy by serving and honouring these restraints. Thus, the lawyer in serving the client's autonomy also serves the client's chosen or accepted connections and communities. In this way it should be clear that the opposite of autonomy is not connection, relation or community. The opposite of autonomy is unchosen or unaccepted restraint: domination and oppression by others. Thus, it should also be clear that the lawyer need not be an agent of disconnection or isolation, that this is not the meaning of serving the client's freedom and autonomy. The absence of domination and oppression is not the absence of influence and connection. The lawyer in serving the client can remind the client of his or her connections and can suggest how those connections matter in whatever it is the lawyer and client are working on. Not just 'can' but probably should; for to emphasise the client's isolation and interests aside from others at the expense of the client's connections and interests in relationships and community is probably to dishonour the client's autonomy, both what the client is and wants.

And one of those influences and connections is with the lawyer himself or herself. Lawyer and client need not be disconnected, even if the purpose of the relationship is the instrumental one of access to the law for the client. The lawyer need not create a discipline which denies his humanity, which renders him an abstract, neutral 'voice of the law', unwilling to influence the client beyond educating her as to her options under the law and assisting her in using the law. It is the obligation of the lawyer to do *at least* that, to provide the client with full access to the law 'as it is,' to present it in as objective and accurate a way as the lawyer is able. But in addition the lawyer ought to bring with him his full humanity, including his own connections, relations and values; and should be able and willing to influence the client in her decisions.

C. Serving the Client's Connections and the Client's Autonomy

One crucial distinction is between 'influence', on the one had, and 'domination' and 'oppression' on the other. The one can well be seen as consonant with a full understanding of autonomy, the other is autonomy's opposite. In applying this distinction, one must keep in mind the significant difference between influences which are chosen – or accepted – and those which are imposed. There is, of course, a continuum from the chosen to the unchosen, the accepted to the unaccepted. Seeking the difference is not easy and involves us in the difficulties inherent in the complexities of free will, coercion, identity and choice. Nonetheless, as persons and as professionals concerned with the law, we constantly act with these difficulties at least in the background, and not infrequently with them in the foreground. Those connections or relations or communities which the lawyer assists in influencing the client should be those chosen by the client or acknowledged by the client as being his part of his identity, chosen or not. This includes the relation with the lawyer herself. If the client chooses access to the law without the influence of the lawyer's character, if the client prefers the services of a lawyer without a connection to the lawyer's full person, then the client should have it, at least to the degree it is possible. Access to the law is sufficiently basic and important that it should not come at the cost of a connection (and restraint) which the client explicitly does not want.

A second necessary distinction is between influence and authority. Who has the authority to impose connections upon the individual; who has the authority to dominate? The government has that authority when it acts through the law; and parents have that authority over their children when they do not go beyond the limits of the law. Beyond that, our society is wary about delegating the legal authority to coerce, and part of the communitarian project must be building genuine (therefore authoritative?) communities in the shadow of that (legitimate) wariness. In short, authority to impose upon the individual in our system comes through the law. And the law has not, at least to date, delegated that authority to the lawyer. The lawyer simply has no warrant to exercise authority over the client. Influence, yes; authority, no..............

While each of us is formed and constituted by our groups – our families, religious and ethnic communities, neighbourhoods and so on – each of us must make choices as well. And whether those choices are to follow where those communities point, or to go in some other direction, is our decision. It is appropriate for the lawyer to remind the client of his or her connections, of his or her family and his or her ethnic or religious values; it is appropriate for the lawyer to help the client find out – or remember – who he or she *is*. It is also appropriate for the lawyer to speak from who he or she *is*, to take part in the moral dialogue as a member and part of the lawyer's connections and community. But it is for the client to decide how all of that connects to who the client is and who the client will become. Thus, for me, the client's connections and community are served through service to the client's autonomy, and are indeed part of the client's autonomy as it is properly conceived....

With much of 'Legal Ethics After Babel'[16] I agree, including the general direction of its argument. From my perspective, however, several of its insights are drawn too broadly, resulting in the exclusion of a foundation I believe essential for lawyers' ethics. A passage from his essay will move us into the discussion.

It has been a mistake for us to write, study, and teach about the acts of abstract, depersonalised, inevitably male lawyers. It has been a mistake for us to ask whether certain hypothetical actions are right or wrong and to neglect to ask about the people who perform the acts. It has been a mistake for us to think of people as if they had no personalities and then to discuss them as we learned to discuss landowners in the law of property ('A conveys Blackacre to B who leases to C').

Professor Shaffer is right; it has been a mistake to think only of depersonalised lawyers and clients. His point is the communitarian point: who we are is to a large extent determined by our connections and our communities, and who we are matters. To a large extent our ethics are not chosen; they are determined by who we are. But with this important truth as a foundation, he reaches a conclusion that seems quite overdrawn and misleading: because much of what we are and much of what we are presented with is not chosen, choice itself is somehow unimportant or uninteresting. Consider Professor Shaffer's use of the movie 'Crimes and Misdemeanours'[17] as illustration, and his conclusion: 'The old philosopher says of us human beings that each of us is the sum of his choices, but: *the doctor did not choose to be a Jew*. What is special – and therefore, interesting – in his guilt is not something he chose'. This is to take an important insight and hold it so close that it obscures one's vision of everything else.

Indeed, it is important, perhaps crucial, to know who we are and where we come from in order to be good people. But that is only the beginning, in both art and life. 'A storyteller cannot do anything with choosers', assets Professor Shaffer, but is it not at least as true that a storyteller cannot do anything with people who have no choice? Who the doctor *is* (his personhood, where he has come from) is basic (and necessary to the story), but it is only one of the three elements which make up the drama. The second element is what the world presents to the doctor, the position he finds himself in. And the third, that which makes for drama and narrative, is the choice presented by the combination of the first two. The doctor is certainly not an interchangeable cipher; he is a particular person who has been constituted by a particular tradition and community (or communities); but life has now presented a situation that calls for choice. The doctor must decide not just what he is but also what he is to become.

Here I think Professor Shaffer is mistaking an important part for the whole: the interesting part is not *only* who we are, with the choice somehow boring or irrelevant. That is a surprisingly static view of life and personality and character. The interesting part is at least as much: who are we to become? And who we are to become is the

16   Stephen Pepper's article emerged from a symposium at which Professor Shaffer gave a paper. entitled 'Legal Ethics After Babel' [1990] 19 Cap UL Rev 989 in which he considered the implications for legal ethics of communitarianism.

17   Shaffer ibid at pp 999-1001.

combination of all three elements: who we are (or, perhaps where we have come from), the situation life presents us with, and the choices we make. And, of course, each makes and remakes us as life goes on: the choices we make and the person we have been become, and both together then take part in creating the situations which present further choice, and the choices made continue the process by which who we are changes into who we become.

To be fair, Professor Shaffer perhaps believes that somehow the first element – who we are – subsumes the other two, or at least subsumes and determines who we are to become. But I believe that this belies the reality we each experience. We experience choice as important; we experience some sense of control over who we are to become. Even those of us lucky enough to have a firm sense of where we have come from (and hence, who we are) experience choice as significant, as something we must do and decide in order to forge a connection between who we are now and who we will become, or in order to continue being who we are. We cannot avoid who we are, and perhaps we cannot stray too far from it – that may be Professor Shaffer's point – but we also cannot avoid choices that are important. The doctor chose to become a murderer; it was not his Jewish communal identity that did that. And his guilt may have been Jewish guilt – that surely was part of who he was – but he still could not avoid the choice of how to deal with that guilt: turn himself in, deny the guilt, find a way to live with it.

Professor Shaffer is right that '[s]eeing is a moral art.' In fact, seeing may be *the* moral art. But the art is in the ability to see all three elements: who you are, what life is presenting you with, and that you have a choice which will implicate who you are to become. 'Choice' may be 'secondary' – that is, the person and the situation come first – but choice is what we can do something about, and choice is what we experience every day. '[O]ur moral quality . . . functions in what we see and remember and know . . .', but all of that comes to fruition in the choices we experience every day, and those daily choices both embody what we already are and what we are becoming. The moral art is to see that, all of that; and much of the moral art is to see that we have *moral* choices every day in our own mundane lives; to see that moral choices are not special or unusual, but part of the fabric of life.

Professor Shaffer wants us to see that moral choice is most often 'coming home', a recognition of where we belong. And this is an important insight. But here again the vision is too unitary, for many of us perceive that we can't go home again. We may carry with us a 'community of memory' if we are lucky, and that community is part of us, but only part. My father was part of a small, primarily immigrant, ethnic and religious community which embraced and surrounded his life. He was surer of who he was than anyone else I have known. And that is part of me, through and through. But I don't live in that community or even in that city. I have become a member of the legal professions and of the academic community, which are quite different and less solid connections than those of my father; and my connections by marriage and friendship diffuse from any single community, where his concentrated and focused upon one community. So, even knowing – at least a little – where I come from, I cannot go home to that community, even though remnants of it do exist. And this situation is not unusual in a nation characterised by both geographic and social mobility, by homogenising public education, by urbanisation, and by the weakening of traditional communal ties. Turning our attention to facts such as these, of course, circles us back to some of the primary motive forces for the communitarian vision, back to the problem which it reaches to remedy.[18]

Questions

1. What according to Pepper is the relationship between the insights of communitarianism and ethical choices? Think of a decision which you have recently had to make which you regarded as raising questions of an ethical nature. Which of the following do you think most influenced you in the choices you made about these ethical questions: family primary and secondary education; university education; role models; the media?

2. How might the insights of communitarianism be relevant to the recruitment policies of a) a large corporate law firm and b) of a four partner firm in general practice in a working class coal mining community?

3. In what sort of practice settings might the insights of communitarianism be most relevant? Are there any settings where they would not be relevant?

4. What are the implications of the communitarian ethic for the role of professional codes of conduct? Consider once again Khan's Case[19] and the various influences acting upon Stephen as he responds to the choices before him.

5. In what ways does Pepper disagree with Shaffer?

Is he correct to do so?

6. In his article *Living in the Law*[20], Dean Anthony Kronman argues that a life lived in the law is likely to have an impact upon the lawyer's personality, that is upon who s/he is. Consider your current career ambitions. How might they alter who you are? If you have already made career choices, what impact have those choices had upon who you are?

7. What might be distinctive about the approach to clients of a lawyer convinced of the value of communitarianism?

---

18   Stephen Pepper 'Autonomy, Community and Lawyers' Ethics' [1990] 19 Capital University Law Review 939 at pp 940-948 and 950-954.
19   Supra chapter 1.
20   [1987] 54 University of Chicago Law Review 835.

3   Feminism and the ethic of care

The view that the client must be understood in terms of the community and therefore the relationships of which s/he is a part addresses concerns raised by a number of leading feminists. A central figure is the psychologist Carol Gilligan[1] who has claimed that men and women address moral problems in very different ways. Gilligan's claim was based upon the analysis of the differing responses of boys and girls to moral problems such as Heinz's dilemma: Heinz's dilemma is that his wife is ill but he cannot afford to buy from the chemist the medicine she needs. When asked what Heinz should do, the male response is to interpret the question as a request for a hierarchical ranking of moral principles relating to the protection of life and property. This has been called the ethics of justice. The contrasting female response is to seek to open channels of communication between Heinz and the chemist such that each can come to recognise the concerns of the other and to come to an accommodation. This alternative approach, often termed the ethics of care, refuses to solve moral problems by accurately applying abstract, hierarchically related moral principles for this is to treat human problems as mathematical puzzles. Instead, it seeks to care for all those involved in a way which honours their existing relationships and creates the possibilities for new ones, with the implications of caring in any given case being highly dependent on context. One useful way of thinking of the difference between two approaches is to think of different dispute resolution processes. Litigation on this view asks a court to decide that one of the other of the opposing parties is 'right' and to justify this conclusion by reference to an abstract principle. Negotiation by contrast can, depending on how the negotiation is conducted[2] lead to an accommodation between apparently opposing interests. Mediation would also seem to be a hospitable process for lawyers seeking to live out an ethic of care. Whether or not caring in this sense is a peculiarly female trait has been controversial amongst feminist thinkers[3] who have been wary of its potential as an argument for excluding women from high ranking positions in the legal system. Nevertheless, there remains the question of whether this alternative mode of reasoning has the potential to transform legal practice[4]. In the following extract, Stephen Ellman begins by considering whether caring is a rational process before going onto consider how an ethic of care might affect a lawyer's choice of client.

> Can we reason in terms of the ethic of care? Choosing to do so may be controversial, for Gilligan herself insists that the ethic of justice is incomplete because it places too much emphasis on reasoning from abstract principles and not enough on the concrete, practical assessment of particular situations. Gilligan has even been seen as rejecting the idea of 'rationality' altogether. I do not take this to be her intention, however, nor the necessary content of an ethic of care. Though there may be moral problems for

1   Carol Gilligan *In a Different Voice: Psychological Theory and Womens Development* (Cambridge, Harvard University Press, 1982).
2   See further chapter 8.
3   Carrie Menkel Meadow 'Portia Redux: Another Look at Gender, Feminism and Legal Ethics' in Charles Sampford and Stephen Porter (eds) Legal Ethics and Legal Practice – Contemporary Issues (Oxford, OUP, 1995) p 32ff.
4   See generally, Carrie Menkel Meadow 'Portia in A Different Voice – Speculations on a Women's Lawyering Process' Berkley Women's Law Journal 1 (1985).

which the care perspective offers no demonstrably 'right' answer, the same is true of other moral frameworks as well. To acknowledge uncertainty, even to disparage the notion of the ineluctable power of particular frameworks of argument to generate convincing answers, is not to abandon reason. Nor is an emphasis on the role of emotion in human decision making an abandonment of reason; no one's reasoning is truly bloodless, and acknowledging the emotional commitments that influence our efforts to make moral judgment does not require us to believe that moral judgment consists of nothing but blind or intuitive leaps of faith. As Gilligan has commented, care, like justice, is a 'moral perspective...that organise[s] both thinking and feelings.'

At the same time, I want to emphasise the range of conclusions that can be reached when reasoning within this framework. I do not claim that all conclusions are equally plausible, and I will offer my own judgements about the implications of care reasoning, but the ethic of care does not generate one and only one set of guidelines for lawyers or anyone else. Unitary conclusions would be inconsistent with the contextual character of care reasoning, in which the details of particular situations are central to the identification of the nature of moral responsibility. Demanding only one possible outcome would also be inconsistent with the idea of the ethic of care as a *framework* for moral judgement. Other moral frameworks, such as theories of natural rights or of utilitarian calculation or of biblical mandate, do not produce any such unitary set of approved conclusions. Nor, as we will see, does the ethic of care.

One illustration will demonstrate this ambiguity in the implications for lawyers of the ethic of care. Consider the case of rape. This is a terrible crime, and it is entirely appropriate to feel a great deal of sympathy for the rape victim. Feeling such sympathy, a lawyer might have no hesitation in concluding that her responsibility lay in prosecuting rape cases so as to compensate in some measure for the harm done to the victim and to protect future victims from such harm. At the same time, another lawyer might feel sympathy for the defendant, whether because he came from a troubled or disadvantaged background or simply because she empathised with the fear and trembling that anyone facing the power of the state and the prospect of prison might experience. This lawyer might see it as her responsibility to provide the defendant with all the personal support and legal zeal that the law allows. She might feel this even while believing her client to be guilty; of course, her determination to fight on his behalf might be even more intense if she also doubted the accuracy of the case against him.

These polar positions by no means exhaust the range of possibilities. Not every criminal defence lawyer necessarily would feel so committed to her client; less moved by her client's plight and more incensed by the victim's suffering, a defence lawyer might believe that her obligation of care for the victim required her to limit the vigour of her defence, either with or without the client's consent. A different lawyer, either prosecutor or defence counsel, might look for a way to bridge the distance between alleged rapist and rape victim, out of a feeling that the worst moral error is a denial of connection and that the ideal resolution of differences lies in a restoration or establishment of relationship. It may be hard for most readers as it is for me, to accept such a response to rape as an alternative to punishment, but Gilligan's account of the ethic of care strongly suggest that she sees such responses as appropriate in at least some contexts. Yet another lawyer, say a lawyer appointed to represent the defendant, might see the most important object of her caring as neither the defendant nor the victim, but rather her own family. For example, if her children were shunned at school or her family's income were seriously reduced as a result of her taking the case, she might seek to withdraw out of care for her loved ones. One more lawyer, remembering her own experience as a victim of rape, might find the case impossible to handle; she might see herself as the one most in need of her own care. Every one of these lawyers would be approaching moral problems through the ethic of care – yet their conclusions about the implications of that ethic for their behaviour as lawyers would be radically different.....

II. THE JUSTIFICATION OF LEGAL REPRESENTATION – OF CARING MORE FOR CLIENTS THAN FOR OTHERS.

For whom should the caring lawyer care? One answer to this question might be that the caring lawyer – that is, the lawyer for whom considerations of care are central to moral judgment – should care for everyone involved in a situation. This answer is entirely consistent with Gilligan's account of the approach Amy takes to the dilemma of 'Heinz and the druggist'. Faced with a situation in which a druggist is charging so high a price for a life-saving drug that Heinz's wife will die if the price must be paid, Amy urges that the druggist and Heinz discuss the matter together. Amy sees Heinz and the druggist as people in connection, and she seeks to bring the druggist to recognise their connection. She does not choose to punish the druggist for his or her past indifference to this connection; instead, the druggist also is apparently entitled to the care implied in seeking to rebuild connection rather than in seeking to override the druggist's wishes through theft. Generalised, Amy's response could suggest that everyone in a situation is entitled to the lawyer's care, regardless of how uncaringly he or she may be acting. The next step – a discussion of which I will postpone for a moment – would be to say that everyone is also entitled to *equal* care from the lawyer.

Gilligan seems to believe that the ethic of care generates a caring attitude towards everyone. She writes, for example, that 'an ethic of care rests on the premise of non-violence – that *no one* should be hurt.' Similarly, Robin West, in her account of 'cultural feminism', sees the caring qualities of women as the source of a caring approach to all of human life. She and others find this caring stance exemplified in the care given by mothers to their children, but they maintain that women's care is not merely for their own children, but for all children and all people everywhere.

The idea that everyone is entitled to the lawyer's care is problematic within the framework of care, however, because it is so universalistic and so indifferent to context. If everyone is entitled to the lawyer's care, this must be because lawyers have an obligation to care that is completely indifferent to the actual personalities or behaviours of the people to whom the obligation is owed. The lawyer must care for every member of the community, each person in the web of interconnection, including those people who have manifested indifference or antagonism toward this very idea of mutual responsibility – manifested it, perhaps, by frauds, or crimes, or simple lack of caring for their fellow community members. To say that the lawyer should care for everyone regardless of character or conduct is rather like saying that everyone is entitled to exercise his or her legal rights regardless of character or other conduct – a quintessential claim of rights morality.

Even if Gilligan and others are correct that an ethic of care extends care to everyone, it is surely not the case that those who follow an ethic of care must care for all people *equally*. The ethic of care is a contextual form of moral judgment, in which the actor seeks to discern her moral responsibilities through a detailed understanding of the situation in which she finds herself. 'Equal care for all' is a demand that is on its face indifferent to context.

Moreover, the notion of equal care for all is psychologically implausible. Ordinary people, women and men, do not feel equal care for all. Saints may offer such love to all, but the ethic of care is not an ethic of saints. On the contrary, Gilligan is at pains to chart the path of maturation in care reasoning, a path on which women come to see themselves as proper objects of their own care and so to reject an equation of responsibility with selflessness. Ordinary people are not selfless, nor do they view all those with whom they come into contact with equal amounts of care. On the contrary, we care for our family and for our friends more than we care for strangers and those whom we dislike, to say nothing of our enemies. The classic, indeed stereotypical, example of the inequality of caring feelings is an example of particular relevance to a feminist ethic of care – a mother's care for her children, a feeling that hardly conforms to a notion that caring people care for all others equally.

More prosaically, the ability to feel another's experience as if it were one's own – to empathise – is very much a part of caring, and we do not empathise equally with everyone. Instead, empathy seems to be decidedly parochial; we empathise most with those most like us. Presumably we also empathise more with those whom we know better, and so with those with whom we have had longer, and closer, associations.

What is true for people in general should be true for lawyers in particular: caring lawyers, like other caring people, need not care equally for all involved in any given situation. This proposition is important because it allows us to conclude that the idea, that lawyers should have clients to whom they owe special responsibilities, is consistent with the ethic of care. If responsibilities are derived from care, and if care is greater towards some than towards others, then caring people have greater responsibilities towards some than towards others. If so, then caring lawyers can represent particular clients, to whom these lawyers will acknowledge greater responsibilities than they owe to anyone else in a situation. As long as the measure of the responsibilities imposed by the law governing the lawyer-client relationship does not exceed what can be justified by considerations of care, the attorney-client relationship is consistent with the ethic of care. It remains to be seen, however, which potential clients a caring lawyer should represent, how she should act towards those she accepts as clients, and how she should act on her clients' behalf.

III. WHICH CLIENTS SHOULD A CARING LAWYER REPRESENT?

If the appropriateness of entering into lawyer-client relations rests on the consistency of those relations with the responsibilities of care, the choice of clients should also be consistent with those responsibilities. Hence, the caring lawyer should not represent someone for whom care does not justify, or permit, taking on responsibility. Moreover, it follows that lawyers should not decline those cases in which care does call for them to take on responsibility. It might be thought, then, that the freedom lawyers currently enjoy[5], to take on any case they can competently handle – or reject it – must entirely

---

5   Pepper is speaking here of American lawyers. In the UK barristers (though not solicitor advocates) are bound by a 'Cab Rank Rule' which requires them to accept any brief appropriate for a lawyer of their knowledge and seniority regardless of their opinion of the client or the clients cause.

fall away if care becomes the central consideration in lawyers' ethics. Perhaps surprisingly, however, this inference is mistaken. As we will see, the ethic of care recognises the lawyer herself as a proper object of her own care, and thus permits her to take or reject cases when, if her own interests were ignored, care would call for a different course of action. Yet, it would also be mistaken to assume that the ethic of care leaves lawyers wholly free to pick and choose among potential cases. Unless care for herself justifies her advancing an uncaring cause, we will find, the responsibilities of care will significantly guide the lawyer's choices of clients and causes to represent.

To understand the extent to which the ethic of care would permit the lawyer to take her own interests into account, we must consider an aspect of Gilligan's explication of the ethic of care that has received less attention than other elements of her work: her account of women's moral decisions about abortion. Based on interviews with twenty-nine women in the first trimester of their pregnancies, as well as on follow-up interviews conducted approximately a year later, Gilligan's 'abortion decision study' illuminates the process by which some caring women decided to abort their pregnancies. The women Gilligan studied did not necessarily take the view, adopted by the United States Supreme Court in *Roe v Wade*, that foetuses were not 'persons' and therefore had no constitutional rights – or, in care terms, were not entitled to consideration in weighing the obligations of care. Instead, it appears that in some cases women chose abortions despite seeing their foetuses as unborn children for whom they *did care.*

Caring for their unborn children, these women nevertheless terminated their pregnancies. How they reached this decision no doubt varied from woman to woman. Some may have understood their decision as based only on care for the unborn baby, who might face a difficult life if brought into the world, for example because mother and child would be mired in poverty. But Gilligan hears in the words of the women she studies evidence of 'a sequence in the development of the ethic of care', whose highest stage entails more care for the self than an exclusive focus on the unborn baby would allow. In this three-stage sequence, 'an initial focus on caring for the self' gives way to a second stage, in which 'the good is equated with caring for others'. But the highest stage of care reasoning rejects this 'inequality between other and self', and from a recognition that 'self and other are interdependent' draws the conclusion that both are the proper objects of care. At this most mature stage of care reasoning, the caring person recognises herself as one of the legitimate objects of her care, and weights her needs in the balance with those of others. On the basis of her needs, then, a caring person – a person who wishes to avoid hurting others when possible – will sometimes, deliberately, hurt them. Such hurt is sometimes unavoidable; to try to deny that, as Gilligan rightly argues, is not so much caring as it is immature.

This understanding of mature care reasoning implies that the caring lawyer is also a proper object of her own care. Perhaps this lawyer needs to pay debts, or to cover the cost of educating her children. Perhaps she hopes for a decisive step forward in her career, or fears the retribution of uncaring superiors at her law firm. She can properly weigh these needs and responsibilities in deciding whether to undertake a representation that would otherwise not be sustainable on the basis of care, or in deciding whether to pass up a case that would be valuable in care terms. A lawyer faced with sufficiently demanding responsibilities in other facets of her life could even vigorously represent a client whom she believed to be engaged in deeply harmful and uncaring activities. In these circumstances, the difference between her and a lawyer who simply maintained that his choice of clients presented no moral questions, so long as what he did for his clients was lawful, is precisely that the caring lawyer would see a moral conflict and would recognise and regret – though she would also accept – the moral cost involved in meeting one caring responsibility while failing to meet another.

Although the ethic of care thus imposes no hard and fast rules for choosing clients, this ethic does affect the lawyer's choices. As the analysis just presented suggests, the lawyer may take on a case in which her victory would advance a cause that denies connection and responsibility – one that is, in a word, uncaring – but she will only do so when other considerations of care justify this decision. Put more affirmatively, the ethic of care indicates that the lawyer should seek to shape a legal practice in which her actions will further the caring values she endorses. Unless care for herself justifies her taking a different course, she should seek to vindicate the ethic of care in the choices she makes of clients and causes to represent.

As we will see, vindicating the ethic of care in the choice of clients entails the lawyer's taking account of at least three features of the case she is considering, the import of which will sometimes coincide but sometimes conflict. First, the lawyer will want to consider the extent of client need, for caring lawyers will seek to respond to need when they recognise it. Second, she will want to listen to her own feelings of care for her potential client (or her lack of them), not only because her feelings can affect the quality of her work but also, and perhaps more fundamentally, because actually caring is part of honouring the ethic of care. Third, she will look to the caring, or uncaring, quality of her client and of the tasks he wishes her to perform, for helping another to act uncaringly is a blow to the values of care.

Perhaps the first of these factors, however, makes the others irrelevant. It might be argued that vindicating the ethic of care imposes no restriction on the choice of clients or cases at all, because the caring lawyer will see a moral connection in expressing care in every lawyer-client relationship she forms. As a psychological assertion, this suggestion has a measure of truth to it. Lawyers and clients *are* thrown together by the client need that generates the relationship. From this more or less intimate encounter can come strong feelings, particularly from the client for his lawyer, on whom the client may be dependent for emotional sustenance and legal aid, in contexts ranging from criminal defence to estate planning. The lawyer who decides to represent a client may be unable to avoid such client need; by moral disposition, the caring lawyer will not be inclined to avoid it, for she will acknowledge a responsibility to meet needs that she has helped to generate, and her contact with the client will make her especially aware of his particular set of needs. With clients in such need, in short, the lawyer will have reason to feel that her response to her clients is itself a caring act – regardless of how little her clients' aspirations or personalities themselves embody caring values. Like Charles Fried's 'lawyer as friend', the 'lawyer as caregiver', on this account, acts morally no matter whom she chooses to support with her representation and her care.

But the lawyer as caregiver does not inhabit precisely the same moral universe as Fried's lawyer as friend. Many clients need their lawyers' personal support – but not all. Some clients may need no personal sustenance from their lawyers, because they use the lawyers' services for entirely routine and unemotional transactions or projects; many probably need only limited emotional connection. Rather than being dependent on their lawyers, moreover, some clients may wield such power or act with such insistence that they dominate and intimidate their legal agents. The caring lawyer would no doubt acknowledge that even these clients may 'need' her legal services, but she will not see in her relationship with them the same intensity of connection as she will find with clients who in fact look to her to satisfy a wider and more personal range of needs. She also will not be indifferent to the likelihood that such commanding clients have only limited need even for her legal services – unless those services are somehow unique – because they will often (though not always) be well able to afford alternative counsel. By contrast, she will properly be responsive to the needs of some clients whom she does not ever expect even to meet – such as the members of a class of mentally retarded people, few of whom she will personally encounter, but all of whom she may believe need her legal assistance urgently. Need comes in many guises, but the caring lawyer will, and should, seek to represent those who need her most.

Important as it is, though, client need is not the only criterion on which caring lawyers should choose their clients. We do not always care for those who need us; sometimes we find their need frightening or simply unappealing. A child molester, for example, may feel ashamed of his crime and terrified at the thought of imprisonment, and yet some lawyers' sympathetic identification with the molester's victim or with the victim's parents may preclude their actually experiencing much care for the molester. This possibility is already recognised in existing principles of legal ethics, especially in those cases when the lawyer's revulsion is so acute that it may impair her ability to effectively carry out the representation.

For the caring lawyer, however, the significance of her personal inability to care may echo particularly widely. She may believe that an inability to care impairs her representation in ways that a different attorney might discount but that for her are nonetheless troubling. For example, she may fear that her *inability* to care will interfere with her ability to offer her client the empathetic responses that might win her client's trust and co-operation, and so enable her to provide him with effective and committed representation.

From the perspective of the ethic of care, moreover, the fact that the lawyer cares little for the client will still argue against her taking the case, even if she believes that her ability to handle it is entirely unimpaired. To be sure, one may claim that the lawyer's personal disaffection for a potential client is irrelevant in assessing how acute the client's needs are and thus how caring an act the representation of this person will be. But the ethic of care, as Gilligan describes it, is chary of abstractions, and it is a drastic abstraction from concrete context to find care equally expressed in opposite situations: in a representation that on the lawyer's part is unfeeling, and in another representation in which the lawyer feels her own deepest sympathies engaged. Actually caring is part of honouring the value of care. For this reason, the caring lawyer will consider not only the would-be client's need, but also the nature of her own response to that need, in deciding which cases to take.

The nature of the lawyer's response is important in itself, but I do not mean to suggest that the caring lawyer will automatically accept her own responses as definitive. On the contrary, she will need to consider whether her own responses comport with her commitment to an ethic of care. If she feels that her initial failure to care for a potential client is the product of bias on her part, she may be obliged to try to overcome this failing, and to recapture within herself an aspect of care that she has lost. If she cannot succeed, she may recognise, regretfully, that she cannot yet fully express care in this potential case. Her assessment of her own responses, however, may lead to quite different conclusions. In particular, she may come to feel that the reason she does not care for a particular person is that what he is or what he seeks is itself uncaring.

The conclusion that the would-be client does not honour the ethic of care would provide a further reason for rejecting his case – indeed, a reason that would weigh in the lawyer's thinking even if she found that she did care for this uncaring client. Consider again a familiar, and familiarly troubling, example: representing a guilty rapist at his trial. Suppose that this potential client confesses his guilt to his lawyer, but makes clear that he wants her to cross-examine the victim ruthlessly in order to make her truthful accusations look like lies. The lawyer senses real terror under the client's bravado and recognises that in some parts of his life this man does act in a caring fashion. At the same time, however, she judges him to be without remorse for his act of rape and as indifferent to his victim's potential suffering in court as he was to her suffering during the crime itself. This lawyer should acknowledge that her potential client has acted uncaringly (to put the point gently), and that he now wishes her to assist him in legal strategy that will amount to a further uncaring act. To assist a person in denying connection does not honour connection, and so the lawyer should take her client's lack of care as a reason not to take his case.

As I have outlined it, the caring lawyer's discretion to reject cases remains substantial, as it is under current rules of legal ethics, but is far from unlimited.[6]

Questions

1. Ellmann states in conclusion that 'these guidelines, if generally accepted, would (not) radically alter the current distribution of legal services, a distribution rooted not only in ethics but also, and perhaps primarily, in broad social and economic forces shaping our lives. But these guidelines would alter lawyers' *deliberations* about case selection substantially, and I suggest the result would be a modest, but welcome and real, increase in the social responsibility of lawyers' case decisions.'

Do you agree?

2. The Bar's 'Cab Rank Rule' would forbid an appropriately qualified Barrister to refuse to represent a client of whom s/he disapproved. Is this approach preferable to that outlined by Ellman for example when the client is a criminal defendant accused of rape?

3. Are there any other values besides care which lawyers should seek to promote? One critic has noted that unless the principle of care is modified by principles of distributive justice so as to ensure an acceptable distribution of care, the unlovely, that is those

6   Stephen Ellmann 'The Ethic of Care as an Ethic for Lawyers' [1993] 81 Georgetown Law Journal 2665 at pp 2670-2689.

whose being and situation do not naturally evoke concern from others are likely to be disregarded. [7]

4. Is it an objection to an ethic of care that it produces indeterminate solutions to problems?

5. **Where the bodies are buried**[8] : You have been asked to represent a 40-year-old man charged with murder. Your client Frank not only confesses to murdering the victim but also tells you that he has murdered two other girls who have recently been reported missing. Frank tells you where the bodies are buried and a visit to the site confirms the story. Frank suggests you use this information to broker a deal with the prosecutor under which the charge is reduced. You are visited by the parents of one of the missing girls who looks you in the face and asks if you know what has happened to his daughter. How would you approach this question as a lawyer guided by the ethic of care? Note that the LSGPC would forbid disclosure in this situation.[9]

---

7   See Louise Campbell-Browne 'Justice as Caring' (1997) UCL Jurisprudence Review p 272.

8   This account is taken from Deborah Rhode and David Luban *Legal Ethics*, (2nd ed) (New York, Foundation Press 1995) pp 225-226.

9   Principles 16.01 and 16.02 supra p 24.

CHAPTER THREE

Professionalism

Profession, business or trade: Do the professions have a future?[1]

Anyone wishing to live well in the law at the beginning of the 21st century must first consider whether the profession has a future and, if so, what that future will be. The problem arises because of the profound changes which affected the legal profession during the last two decades of the 20th century. Ironically, the period began very promisingly from the legal profession's point of view. In 1979, the Royal Commission of Inquiry into Legal Services ('the Benson Commission') set out what it regarded as the five key features of a profession namely,

A governing body (or bodies) [that] represents the profession and ... has powers of control and discipline over its members.

[mastery of] a specialised field of knowledge. This requires not only the period of education and training ...but also practical experience and continuing study of developments in theory and practice.

Admission ... is dependent upon a period of theoretical and practical training in the course of which it is necessary to pass examinations and tests of competence.

[A] measure of self-regulation so that it may require its members to observe higher standards than could be successfully imposed from without.

[1]   Title of the Law Society Research Conference, July 1994.

> A professional person's first and particular responsibility is to his client. ... The client's case should receive from the adviser the same level of care and attention as the client would himself exert if he had the knowledge and the means.[2]

The Benson Commission's understanding of professionalism was thus in harmony with the self-image prevailing within the legal profession since the Second World War. The legal profession was an occupational group which should be left free of government regulation and shielded from competitive pressures. Like other professions, lawyers could be trusted to subordinate their own interests to those of their clients, and ultimately to the public interest. The profession's sense of vocation to the service of the law – its legal ethics – was the ultimate guarantee of quality, not, as with businessmen, the discipline of the market. Consistently with its' view of professionalism, the Benson Commission accepted the profession's arguments on a number of important regulatory issues. Thus despite the arguments of consumer organisations and a number of academic critics, it agreed that the English legal profession should remain structurally divided into the sub-professions of solicitors and barristers; that it was in the public interest that solicitors retain a monopoly over conveyancing; and that barristers should similarly retain a monopoly over rights of audience in the higher courts. Nor initially did the election of the first Thatcher administration in 1979 seem to threaten the status quo. Led in relation to legal affairs by the cautious Lord Hailsham, the government announced in 1983 that it had accepted the recommendations of the Benson Commission.[3]

However, in 1984 the government introduced measures which required solicitors to share the conveyancing monopoly, on which 50% of their collective income depended, with a new profession known as licensed conveyancers[4]. The Law Society's response was that if competition was to be allowed its members would compete vigorously. The restrictions on advertising which were thought to be required by the very notion of professionalism were rapidly relaxed. In addition, the Law Society decided that if its monopoly was to be shared, then the same must apply to the Bar's monopoly over rights of audience in the higher courts. Its declared intention to campaign for a share in the Bar's monopoly provoked an intra professional war which was to last more than 10 years.

Competition and deregulation were now firmly on the political agenda as was evident from the government's ground breaking Green Paper 'The Work and Organisation of the Legal Profession' published in 1989. This consultation document began with the statement that

> The government believes that free competition between the providers of legal services will through the discipline of the market ensure that the public is provided with the most effective network of legal services at the most economic price.[5]

2   *Report of the Royal Commission on Legal Services*, ('The Benson Commission') (London. HMSO, 1979) Cmnd 7648 Vol 1:28,30.
3   *The Government Response to the Report of the Royal Commission on Legal Services* (London. HMSO, 1983) Cmnd No 9077
4   See the Administration of Justice Act 1985, Part II.
5   *The Work and Organization of the Legal Profession* (London HMSO, 1989) (Cmnd 570) para 1.2.

Armed with the ideology of the free market, the government was ready to question every aspect of the work of the legal profession in a way which the very different assumptions of the Benson Commission made impossible. Hence it was willing to consider legitimating contingency fees, previously regarded as likely to undermine the ethics of the legal profession and therefore the administration of justice. Many of the specific proposals under consideration were either modified or discarded before the Courts and Legal Services Act 1990 was passed to create a new framework for the delivery of legal services. For example, it was originally proposed that the legislation should permit solicitors and barristers to enter into partnerships with each other and with other professionals[6]. Opposition was expressed on the grounds that this would lead to a loss of professional identity and to difficulties about deciding which code of ethics would govern a multi-disciplinary partnership. Consequently, the CLSA eventually provided only that the professional bodies might permit such partnerships if they so wished. Nevertheless, this legislation established a new approach to the legal profession which rendered any form of professional privilege prima facie suspect: s 17 of the Act sets out as a general objective of the Act

the development of legal services in England and Wales ....by making provision for new or better ways of providing such services and a wider choice of persons providing them, while maintaining the proper and efficient administration of justice.

The changing face of legal practice during the last two decades cannot be attributed solely to the legal services policies of the government. For lawyers especially solicitors operating in the commercial sector, the attitudes of clients were of far more significance. Previously, many commercial clients had been content to enter into long-term and relatively undemanding relationships with their lawyers. Now however, these same clients were required to operate in highly competitive global markets and they therefore sought to gain best possible value for money from their lawyers[7]. They began to employ lawyers ('in-house lawyers') to monitor and control the work of private practitioners. Fees began to be rigorously scrutinised and work had increasingly to be won by skilful presentations in direct competition with competitors ('beauty parades'). Moreover, legal professions throughout the developed world were under similar pressures even in countries with governments with very difficult political persuasions. In America, restrictions on advertising were relaxed as a result of judicial decisions that they infringed the constitutional right to freedom of speech.

Nevertheless, one important feature of this period is that by 1990 at the latest, the legal profession seems to have lost the trust of the state. This failing faith continued during the 1990s to be an outstanding feature of Lord Chancellor Mackay's seemingly endless list of reform proposals. Consider, for example, the White Paper on family law reform[8] which led to the Family Law Act 1996. At the heart of the new regime were

6   Supra at paras 11.7, 12.8 and 12.14.
7   See generally, G Hanlon *Lawyers, the State and the Market* (Macmillan, Basingstoke, 1999) esp at pp 108-123.
8   Lord Chancellors Department *Looking to the Future – Mediation and the Grounds for Divorce,* (London, HMSO 1995) (Cmnd 2799, at paras 2.6-2.8 (p 7).

firstly a move to no-fault divorce[9] and secondly the public funding and encouragement of mediation[10]. The first change assumed that under the old system many contrived but irrefutable allegations of fault were being made by lawyers anxious to expedite their client's divorce proceedings. The second of the changes assumed that, contrary to the professed aims[11] of the Solicitors Family Law Association, the involvement of lawyers could only lead to an adversarial approach and hence to increased bitterness and hostility. All in all, this was not a very flattering picture of the legal profession. Equally unflattering assumptions about the ethics of the legal profession underpinned Lord Woolf's proposals for the reform of civil justice and the Major administration's proposals for the reform of the legal aid system (see chapter 10 below). Nor did matters improve with the election in 1997 of a Labour administration. In one of his early speeches to the Law Society, the new Lord Chancellor, Lord Irvine, declared that:

> I doubt if anyone in this Hall would seriously argue that the legal profession in recent years has done anything other than fall lower and lower in public estimation .... I want as Lord Chancellor, to preside over a legal system that is so highly respected for its speed, its economy and efficiency, that lawyers can begin to compete in public esteem with teachers and doctors and nurses in what they put into society.[12]

The Labour government's general approach to the legal professions was clearly set out in its' White Paper *Modernising Justice*[13] in which it stated:

> Most lawyers are decent and hard working people of integrity and commitment. They do not all become rich... But, in many instances, the assumptions and working practices of the legal profession are outdated and inefficient. The taxpayer often meets the cost of that inefficiency. So the Government's proposals represent a challenge to the legal profession; to adapt to a modern and rapidly changing society, in order to provide a better service and better justice for the public.[14] ...
>
> The Government is committed to safeguarding and improving a strong and independent legal profession... But the independence of the legal profession is not a justification for immunity from public scrutiny, or for preserving outmoded structures and practices. The Government also has a role: to act for the public interest in setting the framework in which a self-regulating legal profession can provide affordable, high quality and independent services to the public. Our particular objectives are to:
> *   ensure that restrictions on which lawyers can offer certain types of legal services are limited to those necessary to ensure that practitioners are properly trained and regulated; and that any restrictions operate only to serve the public interest, not the vested interests of lawyers.
> *   maintain and improve standards of service by lawyers.
> *   help make lawyers' services easier to afford, by removing unnecessary restrictions on the way they can charge for their services; and, in certain circumstances by

9   Family Law Act 1986, ss 2-9.
10   Ibid, ss 13, 14 and 29.
11   See 'The Code of Practice of the Solicitors Family Law Association' (1984) 14 Family Law 156.
12   Keynote address to the Law Society Conference Cardiff, 18 October 1997.
13   *Modernising Justice* (LCD, London, 1998) Cmnd 4155.
14   Ibid 1.4.

limiting the costs lawyers can charge their clients or pass on to the other party in litigation. It is in the interests of both consumers and taxpayers that the services provided by the legal profession are as efficient and cost effective as possible.[15]

In this spirit, the intra-professional war over rights of audience was finally resolved in the Law Society's favour by ss 36 and 37 of the Access to Justice Act 1999. Subject to compliance with the Law Society's training regulations, all solicitors whether employed (for example in the Crown Prosecution Service) or in private practice now have rights of audience. Other radical changes introduced by the Act are considered elsewhere in this book. At this point, however it is instructive to consider ss 46 and 47. Whilst the legislation was still before Parliament, the Law Society launched a massive advertising campaign with a view to rallying public opposition to the provisions in the Bill removing legal aid from personal injury litigation. Lord Irvine considered this an inappropriate use of funds earned largely from fees charged to practitioners for practising certificates. It has long been recognised that the professional bodies act partly as regulators and partly as representatives of lawyers' interests. To use practice certificate income in this way was, in Lord Irvine's view, to confuse the Law Society's regulatory and trade union functions. Consequently, s 47 of the Act gives Lord Irvine power to restrict the Law Society's use of income drawn from its regulatory functions and s 46 provides analogous powers in relation to the Bar. There could be no greater illustration of the contemporary breakdown of relations between the state and the profession.

1   Market control theory

For some observers, these changes had one particularly disturbing common feature: the professions' ethical commitment, once the guarantee of quality, was being eroded by competitive pressures. As such, the changes represent a regrettable decline of the traditional professional ideal. For Professor Richard Abel, the leading sociologist of the legal profession, events bore a different interpretation. In his view, the decline of professionalism was not something to be lamented. In the following extract[16], Professor Abel outlines the Weberian analysis of the professions on which his own work on the legal profession is based.

CONSTRUCTING THE PROFESSIONAL COMMODITY

Professions produce services rather than goods. Unlike the farmer or herder before the industrial revolution or the manufacturer of goods today, the producer of services cannot rely on consumer demand for physical objects to constitute the market. Instead, such producers confront two distinct problems in particularly acute form. First, the

15   Ibid at paras 2.21 and 2.22.
16   Richard Abel *The Legal Profession in England and Wales* (Oxford, Blackwell, 1988) pp 8-21. See further R Abel 'The Decline of Professionalism' [1986] 49 MLR 1 and 'Between Market and State: The Legal Profession in Turmoil' [1989] 52 MLR 285.

consumer must acknowledge the value of the producer's services. If we address this issue by thinking of contemporary medicine or even law, the perception of value does not seem problematic. But if we think of the sorcerer in tribal societies or the rabbinate, ministry or priesthood in most contemporary Western societies, the difficulties are immediately apparent. Second, consumers must be convinced that they cannot produce the services themselves. Once again, if we reflect on neurosurgeons or corporate lawyers, consumer incompetence may be obvious. But, in fact, we doctor and lawyer ourselves much of the time, often resisting the urgings of others that we consult an 'expert'.

The success of producers in constructing a market for their services turns on several variables. What consumers 'need' is a function of cultural beliefs over which producers have only limited control. The most they can do is amplify or dampen demand by seeking to connect their services to fundamental values: mediation between man and God with transcendental beliefs, medicine with the desire for physical wellbeing, and law with justice or the protection of political and economic stability. Structural functional theory tends to treat the demand for professional services as unproblematic – merely a rational acknowledgement by the consumer of the objective 'utility' of those services. But professions emerge and thrive with little or no evidence that their services actually benefit consumers: religion, medicine before about 1900 and psychotherapy today are vivid examples. Even established professions constantly must construct consumer confidence in the value of what they are selling. Freidson frames the question starkly: 'Is professional power the special power of knowledge or merely the ordinary power of vested economic, political and bureaucratic interests?'

Once consumers believe in the value of the services, how are they persuaded to purchase them from others rather than produce the services themselves? Part of the answer is that the division of labour compels this: as producers become specialised, consumers necessarily become generalised and thus dependent on others. But a number of other factors also shape that dependence. Perhaps the best-known formulation proposes that professional services contain an irreducible element of uncertainty or discretion, a balance between indetermination and technicality, art and science. Too much art and consumers lose confidence (as in quack medicine); too much science and consumers (or lower status producers) can provide the service themselves (do-it-yourself home repairs or conveyancing).

We can identify other ingredients in the successful construction of a professional commodity. The producer's expertise should appear to be objective, not merely the arbitrary creation of the expert. For religious believers, the warrant often is traditional – a sacred text or church hierarchy – though religion also fosters the rise of charismatic leaders. But for most contemporary professions, the strongest warrant of objectivity is connection with natural science. Despite the efforts by lawyers to make law appear to be a logico-deductive system, it is clearly man made and thus ultimately a reflection of political power. Professional knowledge must be esoteric, but legal language is just ordinary language used in strange and arbitrary ways, except for the cherished residues of Latin, French and English archaisms. Professional knowledge must reconcile stasis and change, traditional warrants of legitimacy and the novelty that ensures continuing uncertainty. But whereas scientific traditions can invoke the validation of repeated experience, ancient laws may be seen as the heavy hand of history. And whereas scientific novelty is progress and therefore good by definition, law 'reform' may be seen as a concession to some special interest. Professional knowledge is standardised; and heterodoxy threatens its very foundation – hence the difficulties that medicine encountered until the end of the nineteenth century. At least since the triumph of the nation-state, law has been the voice of a single sovereign and thus clearly unitary; but in pluralistic societies, unity may be seen as tyranny.

The construction of a marketable professional commodity also depends on variables other than the nature of professional expertise. The relation between producers and consumers clearly is critical; it can hardly be an accident that the two most successful contemporary professions, medicine and law, emerged by selling their services to individual consumers. And the failure of many latecomers to the market for services to become more than semi-professions certainly is connected to the fact that they sell their services either to existing professions (nurses, legal executives) or to large bureaucratic employers (social workers, teachers) The commodity must be packaged in units that consumers can afford, which may be one reason why physicians have been relatively more successful than lawyers. And it is very helpful to have exclusive access to a vital arena: the hospital for physicians, the courtroom for lawyers, the document registry for European notaries.

The task of constructing the professional commodity never ends, for it is constantly being undermined. Other bodies of knowledge may challenge the hegemony of professional expertise, as natural science has been eroding the authority of religion at least since the Enlightenment, and as economics may be displacing law as the foundation of government today. Expert authority also may be unmasked as political domination: the feminist critique of medicine is a contemporary example, but law is far more vulnerable to political critique. And the ratio of indetermination to technicality may become unbalanced. Art may be revealed as fakery: apricot stones as a cancer cure, for instance, or a recent finding that the intake of cholesterol is not correlated with its presence in the blood, so that dietary prescriptions for avoiding heart attacks – long a staple of modern medicine – appear to be worthless. Or, more dramatically, politicians and the public may lose faith in the ability of economists to forecast or manipulate macroeconomic trends. At the other extreme, technicality opens the professions to competition from para-professionals – dental hygienists setting up independent practices, for instance – a threat that is amplified by the rise of information technology.

PURSUING SOCIAL CLOSURE

Producers of a service who succeed in constructing a marketable commodity only become an occupation. In order to become a profession they must seek social closure. This project has two dimensions: market control and collective social mobility. Although these are inextricably linked, it is analytically useful to distinguish them, dealing with market control here and collective mobility below. All occupations are compelled by the market to compete. This may be advantageous to consumers – that is the market's fundamental justification after all – but competition is hardly pleasant for producers since it is the classic zero-sum game. Notwithstanding their ideological attachment to free markets, therefore, it is not surprising that producers energetically try to escape from that freedom.

Producers of goods can seek protection from market forces in a variety of ways: through horizontal monopolies or cartels, vertical control over raw materials and control over technology and other intellectual inputs (patent, trade mark and copyright). Because services are not embodied in a physical form, their producers have only one option: control over the production of producers. Indeed, state regulation of the markets for goods and services is roughly contemporaneous. There is nothing new about control over the production of producers, and it certainly is not limited to capitalism. Tribal societies in pre-colonial Africa often limited specialised occupations, such as blacksmith, to a particular kinship group or clan; and of course Indian castes are one of the most elaborate forms of market control. Other non-professional forms of closure include guilds, trade unions, civil service employment, academic tenure and employment within private bureaucracies. Weber suggests some of the permutations of closure:

> Both the extent and the methods of regulation and exclusion in relation to outsiders may vary widely, so that the transition from a state of openness to one of regulation and closure is gradual. Various conditions of participation may be laid down: qualifying tests, a period of probation, requirement of possession of a share which can be purchased under certain conditions, election of new members by ballot, membership or eligibility by birth or by virtue of achievements open to anyone.

Structural functionalists address this issue from a very different perspective. For them, closure is not a response to the market and certainly not a conscious, self-interested strategy by producers. It is simply the means by which society ensures that consumers receive quality services. Because it is so difficult to evaluate either the process of rendering services or the outcome, quality is maintained through input controls . Weber rejected this interpretation in the strongest terms:

> When we hear from all sides the demand for an introduction of regular curricula and special examinations, the reason behind it is, of course, not a suddenly awakened 'thirst for education' but the desire for restricting the supply of these positions and their monopolisation by the owners of educational certificates. Today the 'examination' is the universal means of this monopolisation, and therefore examinations irresistibly advance.

Parkin is equally emphatic: 'Once a professional monopoly has been established, the way then becomes clear for the elaboration of those purely ceremonial conventions by which access to specialised knowledge is carefully monitored and restricted'.

Adherents of the Weberian position can point to the lack of fit – and certainly the lack of any evidence of fit – between credentials and actual work, whether the credential is technical and the work manual or the credential is a liberal education and the work white collar. Even if there is some plausibility to the notion that education correlates with technical skill, the credentials required often far exceed the skill demanded. A telling illustration of this disjunction is the fact that the very institution responsible for producing most professionals – the university – chooses its faculty on the basis of credentials that say nothing about competence to teach. And it would be hard to make the argument that the credentials required of lawyers are necessary to the practice of law when legal education varies so greatly. Lawyers in England and the United States perform many of the same tasks, but there are substantial differences in the degree to which their education is academic or apprenticeship, through lectures or Socratic dialogue, based on treatises or casebooks, located in classrooms or clinics, and undergraduate or graduate.

Indeed, the little we know about what lawyers do suggests they make scant use of their formal legal education:

> Scottish solicitors explained that on average they would deal with the law, in the sense of technical knowledge, for something around one hour a week. The rest of their time – taken up with handling personal relationships and business negotiations, and with consultations and meetings – involved little legal skills; either they used totally routinised legal knowledge or else they moved out of, or beyond, specifically legal work. Solicitors further confirmed that in their practice, the most important factor in terms of giving clients satisfaction was not careful research, technical skills, or even (when a dispute was involved) winning a case, but rather maintaining relationships with clients on proper grounds.

And Jerome Carlin's study of solo practitioners in Chicago in the late 1950s came to similar conclusions:

> Time devoted to writing legal briefs and memoranda is at a minimum for all but a very few respondents. Reading legal material either for 'keeping up' or on research in connection with some matter at hand accounts for only a small fraction of the individual practitioner's working day – less than a half hour a day, on the average. And only 6 respondents specifically mentioned engaging in, any legal research.

> Interviewer: Do you spend any time reading legal material?

> Respondent: I'm ashamed to tell you, not even an hour a week. You can say I get by on cursory knowledge of the law. But it's mostly the same thing, not just bluffing.

> Interviewer: Do you spend any time preparing legal documents?

> Respondent: Zero. Well, pleadings, yes, but most are in subrogation cases, and I use a form, filling in the date, and so on, so it doesn't take too much time.

To the extent that mandatory education serves a purpose other than market control, it helps to confer status through association with high culture, socialises entrants to their roles as professionals and provides warrants of loyalty and discipline...

CLOSURE AS COLLECTIVE MOBILITY

The professional project is directed not only toward controlling the market but also toward enhancing professional status, an issue sociologists treat far more extensively than economists. Indeed, some sociologists define Professions as a status – a quality and degree of respect enjoyed by virtue of occupational role. This emphasis is consistent with the fact that professional elites whose economic privileges are secure energetically pursue (and often initiate) the project of raising the status of the occupational category;

and occupations with no hope of achieving market control persist in seeking professional status.

The relationship between economic privilege and social respect is very complex. Although inequality always requires justification, entrepreneurs seem to feel that success within the 'free market' is self-legitimating, whereas professionals feel compelled to offer additional explanations, since they visibly control their markets. The lengthy training professionals must complete perhaps may better be understood not as the acquisition of technical skills but as a sacrifice necessary to justify future privilege; only this can make sense of the relative poverty endured by students, their prolonged celibacy, the tedium of study, the indignities of apprenticeship, the anxiety inflicted by examinations and the lengthy postponement of adulthood.

The status of a profession is affected by two principal factors (aside from its economic standing): membership and clientele. Limitations on entry, which are the foundation of market control, inevitably influence the profession's composition as well as its numbers, whether or not this is a conscious goal. When American physicians excluded 'persons of inferior ability, questionable character and coarse and common fibre' by implementing the reforms ultimately embodied in the Flexner Report, the proportion of women medical graduates declined from 4.3 per cent between 1880 and 1904 to 3.2 per cent in 1912. Sociologists analyse entry barriers in terms of whether professional status is ascribed or achieved, the warrant is aristocratic or modern, entry is based on qualities that are particularistic or universalistic and mobility is sponsored or contested. Both the classic elite professions, such as the Bar, and those occupations that successfully professionalised during the nineteenth century, such as Scottish accountants, appear to have benefited from the fact that their members enjoyed high status by birth. Professions exhibit a movement from ascribed to achieved status during the nineteenth and twentieth centuries, as contact with higher education and the university came to confer status. But some professions resisted this transformation precisely because they feared that barriers based on achievement would admit entrants from lower social backgrounds. And many observers have noted the loss of status (and pay) within previously male occupations that were feminised during this period, such as schoolteaching and clerical work. But it is important not to allow the ideology of meritocracy to conceal the fact that all 'achieved' requirements disproportionately exclude those disadvantaged by class, race or gender. Whatever mobility does occur tends to be found within the middle class rather than between classes.

Professions also gain, and lose, status from their clients. The classic professions of law and medicine clearly benefited from their historical association with aristocratic patrons. On the other hand, the failure of other occupations to professionalise during the twentieth century may be due, in part, to their services to low-status clients. Abbott has argued, paradoxically, that professions gain public status by conferring order on disorder, though they lose intra professional status through their connection with disorder.

Although one of the defining characteristics of a profession is the fact that the status of its members is collective – conferred by entry to the profession and enhanced by mobility of the professional category – status differences inevitably persist within the profession. These, too, may be a function of the characteristics of the particular member (ascribed or achieved) or of the member's clients. But whereas collective mobility tends to solidify the professional category, intra professional mobility can impair it, as lower strata challenge higher or higher seek to immunise themselves from taint by lower.

CONTROLLING PRODUCTION BY PRODUCERS

Controlling entry – the production of producers – is only the first step in the professional project. An occupation that seeks to professionalise must also control production by producers, both for economic reasons and to enhance its status. Weber, again, surveys the range of possibilities:

> Closure within the group as between the members themselves and in their relations with each other may also assume the most varied forms. Thus a caste, a guild, or a group of stock exchange brokers, which is closed to outsiders, may allow to its members a perfectly free competition for all the advantages which the group as a whole monopolises for itself. Or it may assign every member strictly to the enjoyment of certain advantages, such as claims over customers or particular business opportunities, for life or even on a hereditary basis.

Restrictions may be formal or informal, visible or invisible. If a principal reason for adopting such restraints is to protect members from competition with each other as well as with outsiders, they also may enhance the status of the profession by conferring an aura of disinterest. The image of professionals as *honoratiores* is reinforced by such devices as the academic hood (into which students put the fees paid to professors at medieval universities), Pooh-Bah's references to bribes as 'insults' in *The Mikado* and the widespread convention that lawyers and physicians do not discuss fees in advance …

DEMAND FOR PROFESSIONAL SERVICES

The theories of professionalism as closure discussed above focus on the nature and extent of occupational control over the supply of services. This is particularly true of economic analyses, which view demand as an exogenous variable, independent of supply. Explanations of demand must be specific to the service, although demographic changes in the size of the population and its age distribution affect most services. A number of factors seem likely to influence the demand for legal services. Because law everywhere is intimately associated with the definition and transfer of property, the demand for lawyers will vary with the distribution of wealth and income. Thus, the rise of the bourgeoisie, the spread of home ownership, the growth of pension funds, the concentration of capital and the proliferation of state welfare benefits all affect that demand. Within the private sector, the mix of economic activities – between the production of goods and services, for instance – may influence the level of demand. As portions of the economy are nationalised, administration may displace law, and economists or other technocrats may be substituted for lawyers. Indeed, where the growth of the state anticipates that of private capital, lawyers become civil servants rather than private practitioners. Because law is state social control, it varies with the level of other forms of institutional control; thus, the increase in geographic mobility, the contraction of kinship bonds, the decline of ethnic communities, secularisation and other related trends may increase the demand for legal control. Whenever the state subjects new areas of social life to legal regulation the demand for lawyers will increase

– the most. notable contemporary example being laws that address the dissolution of marriage. Finally, there are differences between societies and across time in the extent to which recourse to law is culturally approved or discouraged.

But demand is not a given, which professions simply accept. Economists have argued theoretically and sought to demonstrate empirically that physicians create demand for their own services. One way professionals do this is by developing new capabilities: thus, physicians increase their ability to preserve or restore health or prolong life by expanding their scientific knowledge or technological armoury; and lawyers multiply the benefits they can confer through every legal innovation – or complication. Professions also seek to rationalise and expand their markets by using intermediaries in both the private and the public sectors. Private insurance, frequently as an adjunct of employment or union membership, has dramatically affected the markets for medical services in the United States and legal services in Germany. State subsidies have been even more important to the professions, particularly where they allow clients to obtain services from private practitioners rather than from state employees. These forms of 'demand creation' have important consequences beyond the economic benefits they confer on professionals. They introduce 'mediative' control over the production and distribution of professional services, increasing the heterogeneity of consumers, stratifying the profession and altering the relationship between producers and consumers. And they may also affect the collective status of the profession – perhaps enhancing it as a larger proportion of the population benefits from the services, but also possibly lowering it if demand creation is seen as motivated by economic self-interest.

2   Evaluating market control theory

The evidence

One question is whether Professor Abel's theory accounts successfully for the observed behaviour of the legal profession. Some aspects of its history clearly do support the theory. For example advertising and competitive behaviour were for many years regarded as unethical. Yet when the solicitors profession was threatened by the government with competition from institutional lenders for conveyancing work, the profession decided that if competition was to occur it must compete vigorously. Hence restrictions on advertising were relaxed enormously, competition flourished – and conveyancing fees fell by nearly a third. Other features of the story seem more difficult. The legal aid scheme which a market control theorist would expect lawyers to welcome as a means of creating demand was at first resisted by the Law Society on the grounds that it would lead to lawyers becoming state employees and therefore to a loss of professional independence.[17] Only when the scheme was seen as inevitable did the profession seek to use it to its advantage. Similarly, contingency fees have been

---

17   A Paterson and D Nelken 'The Evolution of Legal Services in Britain: Pragmatic Welfarism or Demand Creation?' chapter 10 of *A Reader on Resourcing Civil Justice* (Paterson and Goriely eds, Oxford, OUP, 1996).

enormously profitable for the American Bar. Yet in the UK the Bar and the Law Society, whilst being more open to conditional fees, have consistently opposed the introduction of contingency fees on ethical grounds. How is this consistent with the notion that the legal profession is engaged in the pursuit of its collective self-interest? Note too that the sociology of law is strongly influenced by the Marxist tendency to view law as superstructure and therefore subservient to underlying economic forces.[18] Consequently, it tends to struggle with the profound differences between common and civil law systems in relation to the role of lawyers. In Germany, for example lawyers far from being an independent profession have been closely associated with and subservient to the state. The 19th century revolutions were intended and have succeeded in making legal reasoning formalistic and devoid of obvious social or economic implications. The revolutionaries associated lawyer creativity and power with the ancien regime and hence imposed the new system on lawyers as a precondition of survival.[19] However this is difficult to reconcile with market control theory since the two systems have similar economic systems and hence we might expect to observe similar behaviour on the part of the legal profession.

Questions

1. How might market control theory account for the current growth[20] in pro bono work amongst both solicitors and barristers?

2. Do you find the analysis of legal education adopted by Professor Abel convincing? How could it be tested?

3. How would Professor Abel respond to the objection that in England, academic legal education aims to develop intellectual, not professional, skills?

4. Abel comments that '(o)ther bodies of knowledge may challenge the hegemony of professional expertise.'[1] Which bodies of knowledge threaten the influence of the legal profession within government? Consider the extracts from *Modernising Justice* set out above.[2]

Methodological issues

Almost any academic discipline is alive with internal methodological debates and sociology is no exception. Nevertheless, it can usefully said that sociology is closely

---

18 See Mark Osiel, 'Lawyers As Monopolists, Aristocrats and Entrepreneurs'[1989] 103 HLR 2009 at p 2053.
19 See Osiel supra at 2063 and Watson *The Making of the Civil Law* (1988) 101,103.
20 See pp 416-423 in chapter 10 infra.
1   Supra p 71 at paragraph 3.
2   See text to notes 14 and 15 supra.

associated methodologically with the natural sciences. It attempts to use these methods to produce a systematic explanation of societies' responses to two of the most important developments in European history after 1700; the industrial revolution and the French Revolution.[3] Lawyers are apt to find challenging claims that their own behaviour is governed by its own scientifically discoverable principles of behaviour rather than rules and principle of law.

More recently however there has been a growing recognition that such explanations can only ever be provisional if only because scientific method involves the construction of hypotheses sufficient to explain data followed by the search for negative cases. Consequently, scientific knowledge can only be valid 'until further notice'. This has lead one commentator to comment that

> social science cannot be powerful enough to end arguments. Yet it continues to keep alive the hope that science can serve as a tool of persuasion, albeit a limited one in a world of diverse values, perspectives and criteria for evaluation...Perhaps it can be said that knowledge relating to a certain field is provisionally valid for individuals if it explains or seems consistent with their personal experience in that field or seems consistent with data relating to that field that they accept as reliable, and accounts plausibly for other competing explanations of this data and experience by seeming to them to provide more rigorous comprehensive, or more detailed and richer explanation or elaboration of data and experience.[4]

Questions

1. As set out above, a theory must if it is truly scientific be falsifiable by contrary example. Is market control theory falsifiable in this sense?

2. What are the implications for market control theory of the claim that social science and therefore sociology is 'a tool of persuasion, albeit a limited one in a world of diverse values, perspectives and criteria for evaluation'?

3   Renegotiating professionalism

Many lawyers would vigorously and sincerely dispute the analysis of their own behaviour offered by market control theory and claim that their motives are far less self-interested. Indeed one of the problems with market control theory is that it ignores lawyers' own understanding of their motivations and thus their ideals in the interests of scientific method. Professor Alan Paterson has argued[5] that the 'traditional model

---

3   See Anthony Giddens *Sociology: A Brief But Critical Introduction* (Harcourt Brace Janovitch, 1987, 2nd ed) at p 9.

4   R Cotterrell *The Sociology of Law: An Introduction* (Butterworths, London, 1992, 2nd ed): internal citation omitted.

5   Alan A Paterson 'Professionalism and the Legal Services Market' [1996] 3 International Journal of the Legal Profession 137 at p 145.

of professionalism' described by market control theorists in fact emerged only slowly and after much debate within the professions (for example over whether advertising should be restricted). Consequently, it was not established before the early 1930s. Once established however this model became an ideological framework through which lawyers interpreted their world. This led to the illusion that a transient socially constructed model of professionalism represented an enduring ideal. In the following extract, Professor Paterson describes the renegotiation of professionalism.

What then has been happening in relation to professionalism? In a powerfully compelling piece on lawyer professionalism in the United States, Robert Nelson and David Trubek[6] argue that if we are to make sense of current changes in the profession an 'interpretative' account of professionalism is needed, linking the structural and ideological dimensions of change. Central to such an approach is an examination of the world view of lawyers, focusing on their professional ideals and practices. Professionalism is thus perceived by Nelson and Trubek as the dispositions which lawyers use to interpret their situations and orient their choices. As such it plays a crucial role in the reproduction and transformation of the legal profession. More problematic, however, is the authors' assertion that each subset of professionals will develop their own ideology or concept of professionalism. In consequence they perceive professionalism as consisting of multiple visions of what constitutes proper behaviour by lawyers, reflecting the 'arenas' or institutional settings in which the subsets or factions operate.

Such an interpretative approach highlights the dynamic and contingent aspects of professionalism which earlier writers tended to overlook. Moreover it rightly stresses the importance of the debates which take place between factions or sub-groups as to aspects of professional ideology or professionalism. However, the notion of a plurality of overlapping and interacting normative communities each with a semiautonomous approach to ethical conduct and the professional role, risks taking the insights of Bucher and Strauss to the extremes of relativism. Its value comes when used to explain the evolution of or transformations in professionalism; it is less able to account for periods of greater stability in the concept of professionalism. For example, in the United Kingdom for the fifty years prior to the recent transformation of the profession and professionalism, the core notion of professionalism remained relatively stable. This lead the bulk of the profession to assume that professionalism had always been defined in that way and it thus became thought of as the *traditional* model of professionalism. In terms of this model, professionalism contained elements which the profession expected from the state and society, namely, high status, reasonable rewards, restraints on competition and autonomy. In return the profession recognised an obligation to provide a measure of competence, access to the legal system, a service ethic and public protection.

6   Robert Nelson and David Trubeck 'Introduction: new problems and new possibilities in studies of the legal profession' in *Lawyers' Ideals/Lawyers Practices* (R Nelson, D Trubeck and R Solomon eds) (Itcha, Cornell University Press, 1990).

THE TRADITIONAL MODEL

The Clients' side	*The Lawyers' side*
COMPETENCE	HIGH STATUS
ACCESS	REASONABLE REWARDS
SERVICE ETHIC	RESTRICTED COMPETITION
PUBLIC PROTECTION	AUTONOMY

Figure 1.   *professionalism*

As can be seen, this bi-modal model of professionalism contains an implicit contractualism reflecting the enduring tension between service orientation and self-interest in the lawyer's role. In terms of this tacit concordat the profession's expectations have to be set against those of the community. There is, however, no assumption in this analysis that the balance between the two was a fair one, or that the parties to the 'contract' were equally matched or that the profession gave good measure for what it received in terms of the 'bargain'.

Indeed a analysis of the power dimension in relation to the 'contract' might suggest that for much of the heyday of the traditional model of professionalism the profession took advantage of its privileged position to extract a greater benefit from the contract than the public. It is that fact which has led to the re-negotiation of the concordat over the last decade or so, as shifting combinations of pressure groups and differing notions of the state have threatened the status (and peace of mind) of the profession.

Moreover the assertion as to the 'contractualist' nature of professionalism is ... but a heuristic device which asserts that in the era of traditional professionalism, the profession and the state behaved as if such an unwritten agreement existed. In essence it is a claim that we shall better understand the response of the profession, the state and the community to the recent changes in the profession and professionalism if we recognise that each group interprets developments in this area from a contractualist perspective. This is not a novel insight, but the argument presented here, because it emanates from an interpretative framework, places much more stress on the contingent and negotiated essence of the bargain than most previous writers.[7]

Professor Paterson's account has many advantages. It explains for example much more cogently the divisions within the professions over the last 20 years about how to respond to the changing professional environment. Similarly, it leaves open the possibility that some elements of the traditional model might be retained. For example, when seeking to extend rights of audience in the higher courts more fully to solicitors, the government affirmed that some degree of professional monopoly *is* in the public interest[8] : the legal system must be protected from the activities of unqualified persons. On the one hand, it is possible to argue that this alternative account describes the process of renegotiation but offers no guidance as to how renegotiation *ought* proceed.

7   Paterson supra note 5 at pp 139-141.
8   See *Rights of Audience and Rights to Conduct Litigation in England and Wales: The Way Ahead* (LCD Consultation Paper July 1998) at paras 2.2-2.7.

In this respect, it shares a weakness of market control theory. Both approaches show that the ideals of public service professionalism have often been betrayed but fails to provide an alternative vision.

Question

Consider the description above of sociological method. Why do you think sociological analyses struggle to offer normative prescriptions?

4 Redeeming the professional ideal

One view of the future of professionalism would be that the professions have misused the protection permitted by the state from the chill winds of competition. Therefore, the only solution is to expose them to the discipline of the marketplace. Such a policy was a central feature of the Thatcher administration's approach to the legal profession in the 1980s. Yet this is not altogether an attractive conclusion. In moral and political terms, it seems to imply that there is no such thing as a public interest for lawyers to serve, merely a series of competing individual and group interests. On a purely pragmatic level, it is not yet clear that the opening up of the market for legal services has been beneficial even for consumers. In the area of residential conveyancing for example, increased competition amongst solicitors was followed by such a steep rise in the number of professional negligence claims as to threaten the solvency of the solicitors indemnity fund. Whilst cause and effect are controversial it has been argued that this is an example of cheapest not being best leading even to a call for the reintroduction of minimum fees.[9] From the perspective of lawyers, this commodification of legal services is problematic precisely because the ideal of public service involved in the traditional notion of professionalism seems to add real meaning to working life. This theme is considered by William H Sullivan in the following extract. Sullivan writes in an American context, but his comments seem applicable to the UK.

> There is ambiguity.... in the public mind about which ... occupations are really professional. The picture is complicated by the increasing tendency of managers to seek professional status: witness the explosion of the Masters of Business Administration degree.
>
> There is a difference in status between the MBA credentialed executive of a firm and the manager of a local McDonald's. But it is noteworthy that the latter is also likely to speak of managing as an important and specific sort of art – and to carry work home in a briefcase – in other words, modern management clearly aspires toward a recognizably professional identity. Becoming professional is a key dimension of success for occupational groups as well as for individuals. The very disputes over just which occupations deserve to be called professions indicate the symbolic power of the designation 'professional.' However, the aspiration to being professional connotes

9   See the sources cited by Paterson supra note 5 at p 149.

more than a claim to higher social status. Professional work also requires the practitioner to adhere to demanding standards of competence and public service. When professional groups fail, as they often do, to hold their own members accountable to these standards, charges of malpractice can, in some fields, be taken to court.

Far more than the symbolic briefcase, then, professional work is freighted with moral weight. But this moral aspect of professionalism is also a source of ambiguity. A young beginning professional, Susan Evans, recently made this discovery. Susan takes pride in being both the first woman in her family to have graduated from college, and the first member of her family to have gone on to professional school. Following a time-honored ritual passed on through generations of students, her graduation from law school meant trading her worn, familiar student's book bag for a genuine leather briefcase. Again, following hoary tradition, Susan Evans went to a professionally recommended, and it should be noted, discount leather and luggage store downtown to select a proper case. Everything proceeded smoothly, including getting the proper monogram imprinted on the case.

As the sales clerk handed it over, he smiled, patted the case, and boomed good-naturedly, 'Hope you make lots of money with it!' Susan was stunned, looked around embarrassed, imagining, she later recalled, that 'this is how it would feel to be caught buying pornography in public view.' She made a rapid exit. Once outside, however, she began laughing nervously. 'It was a moment of truth,' she recalled. She was, after all, beginning work with a prominent law firm. And yet, somehow, the whole incident did not seem right. 'Isn't there,' she remonstrated with herself, 'more to it than that?'

That remonstrance might have been an echo of the conscience of the profession. The 'more than that' is the special dedication and clear accountability which, to common sense, distinguishes a profession from trades and businesses. A profession is 'in business' for the common good as well as for the good of its members, or it is not a profession. To demand of any occupation that its members act professionally is to appeal implicitly to the kind of social covenant which explicitly governs professional fields. As Evans realised, however, there is considerable tension between a profession as an ideal, a vocation capable of giving life meaning, and the way in which that occupation is situated – and is perceived – in contemporary society. In Evans's case, the most distressing phenomenon is what she perceives as a steady erosion in the sense of the law firm as a collegial enterprise. She notes that as the competitive pressure on the firm mounts, the partners seem to have few qualms about trying to squeeze more and more out of associates, even as they squabble among themselves over payment formulas to reflect the relative business potential of individual lawyers. What is being lost in the scramble for clients and fees, she believes, is the sense of common purpose, the satisfaction of contributing to a worthwhile public enterprise.

CALLING OR CAREER: THE TENSION WITHIN PROFESSIONALISM

Susan Evans had worked hard through professional school to become good at the craft of law, and her education would continue as she began practice. The goal of these efforts, as she saw them, was to be able to respond self-confidently to someone who had been counseled to 'get a good lawyer.' By defending and counseling those in need of justice, such a lawyer certainly performs a vital, and difficult, public office. At the same time, we can also imagine that she chose her profession in the hope that it would prove a means toward a dignified style of life. In part that means being successful in the economic sense. In America achieving economic well-being has long been a significant and honorable aspect of professional identity. But it has always meant more than that as well. A profession is understood to provide a career, an opportunity for social and economic advancement, while professionalism demands the kind of dedication to purpose characteristic of a vocation or calling. Not infrequently, these two elements of career and calling pull against each other.

An authentic profession can provide a strong sense of identity because, beyond providing a livelihood, it is a way of life with public value. It is the kind of thing one can build a life around. For the person possessing the requisite capacities and sufficient commitment, a profession can provide not only a career but a calling to useful work as well. Providing counsel and care, curing illness, bringing justice, teaching: these are activities which provide more than jobs and satisfactions for individuals. By their nature they create goods which at some time are essential for everyone, and important for society as a whole.

These functions are carried on in a commercial society in which professional skills, like others, are marketed. The labor market puts pressure on professionals to behave competitively toward their peers, and to accede to the demands of profit when these conflict with professional standards of excellence. Indeed, it is in part to combat these market pressures that professional organizations exist. The situation of professional life is farther complicated by the fact that today most professionals are no longer the solo practitioners of popular image, but parts of large bureaucratic organizations. The purposes of these organizations, like the profit motive of the market, do not always support service according to high professional standards, activities and careers to the service of public ends, ... [but] professionalism suggests how to organise the complex modern division of labor to ensure that specific functions are performed well and with a sense of responsibility for the good of the whole....

[for attorneys like Susan Evans and] many other professionals in all fields, their work is more than 'just a job,' their lives more than just a career. Professionalism remains a powerful source of moral meaning. But professional life and its institutions are far from being in the best of health. The pressures of market competition and organizational demands threaten to distort the defining purposes of professional work. Within as well as without the professions, there is unmistakable skepticism and cynicism about the whole notion of professionalism. In the face of these forces, a clear understanding of the positive meaning of professional work, and the institutional conditions needed to sustain it, are needed if the professions are to take their place as responsible occupational communities. Without such understanding, and the will to make it effective in institutional reform, the potentials of professionalism, no matter how well exemplified in individual practice, will remain largely a frustrated wish, a romantic, if noble, intention.

THE CALL TO SERVE

... there has historically been a close relationship between the learned professions and the ethic of public responsibility. Though embattled, the learned professions' sense of special responsibility persists.

The professions have long espoused an ethic of responsibility for the whole of society. The classic learned professions have traditionally served many functions for Americans, and have accordingly played public roles. The ministry, in particular, has been centrally involved with the ethic of public service. The ministry, not law or medicine, is the oldest of the learned professions in America, and the ministry has long had close connections with education. The churches were the first promoters of schools in English North America. The earliest institutions of higher learning, the colleges of Harvard and Yale, were founded expressly to train ministers. From the seventeenth century on, Americans continued to found liberal arts colleges across the continent, principally to train men and women as ministers, teachers, and missionaries.

The term profession is itself religious in origin. It derives from the act of commitment, the declaration to enter on a distinct way of life, as in the profession of monastic vows. It was, at least in theory, a response to the belief that one had received a 'call,' not an action imposed by economic or other necessity. Profession entailed a commitment to embody the virtues needed to realise the community's highest purposes. Religious institutions have perennially attended to considerably more than the individual's conscience. They have also addressed key social needs, not only in education, but by the provision of health care and social services of many kinds.[10]

In the following passage Sullivan goes on to consider the effect upon professional identity of some recent developments in urban law practice.

THE DISINTEGRATION OF PROFESSIONAL IDENTITY: A CLOSE UP

Contemporary professional life continues to be lived along parallel but unequal lines, the provincial practitioners and the metropolitan professional elites. Provincial practitioners, although usually trained at metropolitan institutions, find their most significant connections and purposes within localised settings. There, long-standing features of American civic life, especially the importance of public cooperation, moral character, and local community service, temper the allure of pure technique, the rewards of wealth, and the expanded personal options available within the metropolitan context. The vastly increased integration of national markets and aspirations has steadily overshadowed those provincial loyalties, however, creating an undertow which runs against the viability of loyalties to place and local culture.

The same dynamism of the national economy and trendsetting metropolitan organizations and opinions pull professional ambitions toward high-status national institutions. Metropolitan professionals typically work at the center of their fields and live within geographically dispersed networks of peers. They are often closely identified with the workings of national business, government, or professional organizations. They are far less tied to local civic milieus and naturally identify most closely with their careers and the settings of metropolitan life. It is not surprising, then, that it has been among metropolitan professionals that most condensed symptoms of the stresses of historical discontinuity have appeared. The yuppie syndrome is perhaps the most disturbing manifestation of tendencies which, in more buffered forms, have affected professionals, and indeed, virtually all parts of the American population.

10   William S Sullivan *Work and Integrity: The Crisis and Promise of Professionalism in Modern America* (New York, 1995) pp 4-6; 11-12.

The lifestyle adopted by the young urban professionals of the past decade compactly expresses the tensions underlying professional life. The yuppie, it should be noted, confounds much accepted cultural wisdom. Contrary to the supposed contradiction between a sturdy work ethic and hedonistic consumerism, once argued by Daniel Bell in *The Cultural Contradictions of Capitalism,* these urban professionals work very ambitiously while also consuming commodities and stimulating experiences with equal energy. The problem of the yuppie life does not seem to be conflict between work and hedonism, but the discovery that both success and pleasure are often capricious and without significance.

The ethos of yuppie life is characterised by a high level of material security and a vast number of opportunities for personal exploration and fulfillment. It is also a life of intense competitive pressure and little free time. Yuppie life is thus riven by harsh dichotomies. Competence and adaptability are the presiding values in work. This cult of competence is at the same time curiously detached, engendering few lasting ties to employers, coworkers, or organizations. The yuppie must travel light, emotionally as well as physically. The demands and stresses of highly competitive work are expected to be balanced or at least relieved in the intimate realm of personal life. Yet, even there, relationships, including marriage and family, are sources of enormous anxiety and, often, severe disappointment. The often conflicting demands of such a highly segmented life require a strategy for managing it all and, finally, soothing the hurts of an inevitably wounded self. Metropolitan professional life is therefore marked by massive consumption of professional services, from personal financial management to child care to psychotherapy. These further the fragmentation of existence, threatening to transmute the effort to live well into an exhausting battle for psychic survival.

This dichotomy between the harsh demands of the marketplace and the private sphere of personality is familiar to many of the metropolitan professionals' fellow citizens. It is rooted in the characteristically sharp differentiation Americans now experience between the public and private spheres. Our economic as well as public institutions have become increasingly governed by instrumental and utilitarian standards, pushing workers to narrow their concerns to technical competence and self-protection. In other capacities, however, as consumers, members of associations, and private persons, Americans expect a different logic to apply, one which gives expression to individual yearning and the desire for a satisfying life.

While many Americans become 'gradgrinds' at work, bent on improving efficiency and payoff, in the recesses of private life, where they believe they can be themselves, they often seek compensation as 'Bloomsburies.' They find themselves emulating the Bloomsbury set of Edwardian Britain who, finding little meaning in the public culture of their time, sought fulfillment by cultivating a romantic sensibility tinged with terminal irony. The consumer economy provides essential support for this private quest, especially in its marketing of the nostalgic delights of an upscale, autumnal hedonism. Not only metropolitan professionals, but most citizens of modern societies, even self-described post-modernists, must negotiate a compromise between these two ways of living, sometimes adopting the no-nonsense seriousness of a gradgrind, while now and again affecting a Bloomsbury style of aesthetic detachment. This division of life into contrasting spheres of value was what Max Weber identified as the modern fate. Earlier, it had seemed to G W E Hegel a description of alienation, a state of unhappy consciousness...

... achieving a meaningful, satisfying life while gripped by a devouring orientation toward career success is a very real and widespread problem in contemporary life. In the absence of an ethic of calling, the quest to 'become one's own person' though instrumental achievement cannot, for most support satisfaction in practicing a profession over time. In the absence of social confidence in the value of work done , ambition must become paranoid and self-destructive. Without shared confidence in the value of the task, there can be no secure recognition for individual achievement, leaving individuals endlessly anxious, having to validate their self-worth through comparative ranking along an infinite scale of wealth and power.

When winning isn't possible, or its personal cost becomes too high, or when one's career has plateaued, the instrumental orientation toward success reveals its poverty. It fails to provide an enduring sense that life is worth living and even, ironically, that this would – be imperial self has value. Then begins the search for authenticity in expressive identity or the secretion of a hardened shell of cynicism which are such prominent features of today's society.

By contrast, a professionalism which unfolds as part of a cooperative civic culture provides an escape from this unhappy consciousness by focusing the person's energies outward, engaging the challenges presented by social reality. But such a professionalism depends upon certain kinds of institutional development which sustain the intrinsic values of professional work while connecting professionals with other citizens. Without such institutions professional morale must wither, and with it the objective dependability of those professional functions so vital to the life of modern societies.[11]

The attractions of the traditional professional ideal have led some to ask whether it might be redeemed.[12] The major obstacle lies in the fact that increased competition in the market for legal services seems to be with us to stay. Does it not follow that in the increasingly competitive scramble for clients, lawyers will be forced into an ever more single-minded pursuit of their client's interests regardless of the ethics of the methods required and regardless of the public interest? However, in an important article Mnookin and Gilson[13] have shown that this assumption of an inevitable race to the bottom is unfounded. Under the right market conditions a reputation for fair dealing can be in the interests of the lawyer and, in the long term, its clients. Mnookin and Gilson's claim turns upon the fact that each side normally has a vast amount to gain from mutual cooperation, particularly in litigation. For example, when the Court orders discovery, the parties will be saved significant expense if they can trust each other to comply, thereby avoiding a series of expensive interlocutory battles. Such cooperation is most likely when each side is represented by a lawyer with a *reputation* for cooperative behaviour. It follows that it may be in the interests of law firms to develop a reputation for ethical behaviour. It should be noted that a reputation for ethical behaviour will

11   Supra at pp 132-136.
12   See R Gordon and W Simon 'The Redemption of Professionalism?', chapter 10 of *Lawyers Ideals and Lawyers Practices* (Nelson Trubeck and Solomon eds) (Ithaca and London, Cornell University Press, 1992).
13   Ronald J Gilson and Robert H Mnookin 'Disputing Through Agents: Cooperation and Conflict Between Lawyers in Litigation' 94 Columbia LR 458 at 571 [1994].

only be an asset in certain circumstances. In particular, the possibilities for successful marketing of a reputation for ethical behaviour are greatest in practice settings where most of the lawyers involved know each other. In one study of Chicago litigators, it was found that regulars, ie specialists in a given area who saw themselves as a loose informal fraternity of peers, were less likely to abuse the rules of discovery than the inexperienced practitioner or the newcomer.[14]

The implications of this thinking for professional organisations is the need to develop organisations that limit their membership to lawyers who specialise in cooperative representation. Such organisations might promulgate standards defining cooperative conduct and defection in various contexts. They could then certify members as adherents of these standards, but only after intensive screening and review: a number of existing members might have to vouch for the fact that the nominee had consistently behaved appropriately over an extended period of time. These organisations might also stand ready to impose sanctions – including suspension or expulsion in order to maintain such cooperative norms.

> If such an organization existed, it would obviously enhance the reputation of its members: clients and lawyers alike would be invited to rely on the organizations claim that it's members would engage only in cooperative litigation, and the organization and its members would have a powerful incentive to maintain the quality of its 'stamp of approval.[15]

Given the difficulties of working within the existing professional bodies, William Simon has suggested that ethically-motivated lawyers attempt to form their own professional associations centered on the development of ethical lawyering.

Notes

1. The argument that ethics may be a marketable asset has gone unnoticed. Early in 1999, the Law Society launched a scheme to help divorcing couples find specialist legal help by publishing a list of 4,000 firms with a track record in family law and a *'commitment to resolving matrimonial disputes peacefully'*[16] (emphasis added). The Law Society undertook to vet would-be members of the scheme.

2. Information technology is likely to be an increasingly important feature of the context in which law is practised in the 21st century. The Blair administration has proposed an extensive use of information technology and especially of the Internet as a way of distributing advice about legal problems involving for example the use of a Community Legal Service Website[17]. In this way, legal advice will be made available cheaply and from a distance. In the private sector, many law firms now use time-recording systems

---

14 See Wayne D Brazil 'Views from the Front Lines: Observations by Chicago Lawyers About the System of Civil Discovery'[1980] Am B Found Res J 217, 240.
15 Gilson and Mnookin supra note 13 at pp 561.
16 *The Times*, 28 January 1999.
17 *Modernising Justice* supra p 68 note 13 at para 2.18.

to enable clients to be billed with greater accuracy for the hours worked on their behalf. In some cases, members of the firm log-on at the start of the day and are then presented with a series of icons representing each of the clients for whom they are currently working plus icons for continuing education and administration. Clicking on an icon ensures that until it is shut down all the time worked by that lawyer will be attributed accordingly.

Questions

1. You are a partner in the company and commercial department of a large corporate law firm acting for Amex Ltd on a large take-over bid. During a long night of negotiations with lawyers for the target company, the agreement between the two sides runs through several drafts. In the early hours of the morning, one of your junior solicitors gives the other side a copy of what is meant to be the latest draft. In fact the junior solicitor has deliberately given the other side an earlier draft, which is less advantageous to them. He does this partly as a point-scoring exercise: he wants to see if the other side are sufficiently wide awake to notice what they've been given. And he does it partly on the off-chance that the other side will fail to notice the changes and actually sign the less advantageous agreement.

What is your response as supervising partner? Would you discipline the young solicitor?

Would you apologise to the other side? What difference would it make if the client had instructed the solicitor to do this?

2. What are the implications for professionalism of the developments in information technology described in note 2?

CHAPTER FOUR

Regulation and legal education

[the LSGPC is] an extremely difficult reference book to use, probably just as much for solicitors themselves as it is for outside regulators and consumer watchdogs. It runs to over 800 pages, it seeks to combine the functions of rule book and manual of good practice and it is frequently opaque and obscure. The lay user of the Guide is left with the impression that some of the principles and the commentary which accompanies them have been drafted with the intention of allowing maximum scope for interpretation.[1]

As we have seen,[2] it is widely assumed that lawyers regularly behave in ways which are unethical. In this chapter, we therefore consider a number of possible responses to unethical lawyering. In Part I, we discuss various methods of regulating lawyers' behaviour. Regulation is normally defined in terms of an interference, usually by the state, in the workings of a market so as to alter the quality and quantity of goods or services which would otherwise be produced. For our purposes however the crucial feature of regulation is that it relies for its effect on the use of incentives of various kinds so as to influence behaviour. Whether or not those regulated accept the values underlying the regulatory system is not crucial. In this sense, regulation is similar in impact to the effect of a competitive market which also relies on incentives to produce appropriate behaviour. Having considered regulation, we look in Part II at the potential of legal education to effect a different or perhaps complementary strategy, namely the internalisation of high ethical standards such that ethical behaviour will occur even in the absence of effective regulation.

---

1   Sir Michael Barnes, Fifth Annual Report of the Legal Ombudsman (London HMSO, 1996) at p 3.
2   Supra chapter 3 at pp 66-69.

1 Professional regulation

How to regulate the lawyers

Leaving aside for one moment questions about the content of professional norms and the identity of those chosen to enforce them, there are important questions about how they should be enforced. Writing in the US context, David Wilkins has usefully distinguished between four different modes of professional regulation namely,

Disciplinary procedures: these are characterised by their similarity to criminal proceedings. If an allegation of misconduct is brought against a lawyer, the complaint is investigated by officials not previously involved and if the complaint has a minimum degree of substance it is brought before a disciplinary body, with the lawyer taking the role of the defendant. It is often said to be an important and worthy characteristic of a profession that it has control over these processes and is thus self-regulating.

Institutional sanctions: the institutions within which lawyers work may themselves impose sanctions upon misconduct. A typical example is the powers, now contained within s 51 of the Supreme Court Act allowing the courts to order lawyers to pay personally any costs wasted as a result of their misconduct.

Liability rules: if a solicitor breaches a contractual duty of care to the client, the solicitor may be sued both in contract and tort by the client. A barrister may be held liable in tort. The common law of contract and tort may have an important impact upon lawyers' behaviour.

Administrative controls: the legislature may create an administrative body independent both of the courts, the legal profession and consumers of legal services charged with checking in a proactive manner the quality of legal services. An excellent example in the UK context is the work of the Legal Services Commission[3]. Under the legal services regime introduced by the Access to Justice Act 1999, only firms awarded a legal aid contract by the LSC may carry out legal aid work. Contracts are awarded only to firms, which the LSC deems capable of providing legal services of satisfactory quality. The LSC audits the work done by contractors on a regular basis regardless of whether there have been complaints by clients. The regulation is likely to be extensive[4] and detailed in order to ensure that contractors do not profit by providing low quality services.[5]

---

3   The Legal Services Commission was created by Part I of the Access to Justice Act 1999 and took over the functions of the Legal Aid Board.
4   For a critical review of the impact of the regulatory regime upon the legal profession see H Sommerlad 'Managerialism and the Legal Profession - A New Professional Paradigm' [1995] 2 International Journal of the Legal Profession 159.
5   This issue is considered further in chapter 10.

In practice, a particular institution may not fit neatly into any one of these categories. Moreover in the UK, the Law Society and the Bar are both involved in regulating the legal profession in more than one of these four ways. Most obviously, their professional bodies have disciplinary rules, breach of which may lead to formal proceedings followed, if appropriate, by the imposition of a punitive sanction. Similarly, the Law Society regulates solicitors' accounting practices and in carrying out this function has extensive powers to investigate proactively firms about which it is concerned. In this respect, it is behaving rather like an administrative regulator. Finally, both the Bar and the Law Society operate complaints procedures which allow clients to complain that a lawyer, while not guilty of misconduct, has nevertheless provided an inadequate professional service. If the complaint is upheld, the payment of limited compensation can be awarded or fees can be reduced[6]. In this respect, the professional bodies can be seen as providing low cost informal enforcement mechanisms for liability rules.[7]

Nevertheless, Wilkins' distinctions are useful in understanding the strengths and weaknesses of various procedures. The relative effectiveness and desirability of each of these models is hotly debated, with the professions generally urging the priority of the first of these models on the assumption that it will be controlled by the profession. In the following extract,[8] Wilkins urges us to remember the importance of context:

> Participants in the various enforcement debates often speak as though their compliance and independence arguments capture universal truths about lawyers, clients, and the state. For example, the American Bar Association's claim that judicially supervised disciplinary agencies should exercise 'exclusive' control over the enforcement process implicitly asserts that this form of regulation is the best system for controlling all lawyer misconduct in all contexts. Similarly, when lawyers oppose 'external' regulation on the ground that it would undermine 'professional autonomy,' they usually couch their assertions about the proper relationship between the lawyer and the state in universal terms. These universalist claims ignore relevant distinctions in both the content of professional norms and the market for legal services.
>
> I. *Acknowledging Conflict Within the Lawyer's Role.* -- It is axiomatic that lawyers are expected to be both zealous advocates for the interests of their clients and officers of the court.

6   These powers are contained in s 37A and Sch 1A to the Solicitors Act 1974. The Compensation for Inadequate Professional Services Order 2000, SI 2000/64 raised the limit on compensation to £5,000. The concept of inadequate professional service is distinct from that of breach of the contractual duty of care, covering for example failure to provide adequate information about likely costs (however justified the ultimate bill may be). Compensation is frequently paid for distress in a way which would fall outside the compensatory remedies of contract law. The Bar now has a similar procedure the upper limit for compensation being £5,000.

7   However the conceptual basis of compensation for inadequate professional services for solicitors is far from clear. One study showed that whilst the statutory context for inadequate professional services indicates that the aim should be to compensate clients for losses, the power has often been used in practice in a disciplinary way so as to penalise solicitor misconduct. See generally Moorhead Sherr and Rogers 'Compensation for Inadequate Professional Services' (London, Institute of Advanced Legal Studies, 2000) pp 26-27 and 46. Similarly the Office for the Supervision of Solicitors which exercises the power to award compensation for IPS on behalf of the Law Society sometimes declines to hear complaints on the grounds that they involve negligence and are therefore the business of the courts.

8   David B Wilkins 'Who Should Regulate Lawyers' [1992] 105 HLR 801, 814-820.

Each of these roles generates distinct professional duties. As an advocate, a lawyer is expected to keep the client informed, safeguard the client's secrets, provide competent and diligent services at a reasonable fee, and abide by the client's wishes concerning the purposes of the attorney-client relationship. As an officer of the court, however, a lawyer should not counsel or assist the client in fraudulent conduct, file frivolous claims or defences, unreasonably delay litigation, intentionally fail to follow the rules of the tribunal, or unnecessarily embarrass or burden third parties. These disparate professional duties complicate the comparative analysis of various enforcement alternatives in two respects.

First, whether the duty is owed primarily to the client or to the legal framework is likely to shape the incentives of the participants in the enforcement process. A client, for example, has an obvious and potent incentive to determine whether his lawyer is faithfully performing his duties as a zealous advocate and to seek redress when a violation occurs. The same client, however, may have no incentive to deter violations of the lawyer's duties as an officer of the court especially when these violations further the client's own interests. On the other hand, state officials charged with administering a particular legal regime often will have a strong incentive to prevent lawyer misconduct that damages the legal framework. These same officials, however, may have relatively little interest in ensuring that lawyers represent clients competently and effectively. An overall assessment of the effectiveness of any given enforcement system, therefore, must account for these differences.

Second, the coexistence of these two sets of duties suggests that the prevailing rules value two distinct kinds of professional independence. As advocates, lawyers must be independent from corrupting influences that might induce them to sacrifice their client's goals improperly. As officers of the court, they must independently assess whether the client's actions are likely to contravene the bounds of the law or otherwise improperly interfere with the lawyer's obligations to the legal framework. Independence claims, like compliance arguments, must account for this dual focus.

2. *Understanding the Role of the Market.* -- Discussions on this topic tend to assume a uniform lawyer-client relationship in which the client is incapable of understanding and evaluating lawyer conduct. This assumption fails to capture the complexity of contemporary legal practice. Clients vary widely in their experience and sophistication concerning legal practice. Some clients will hire a lawyer only once in their lifetime. For others, interacting with lawyers is a way of life. Corporations are likely to dominate this latter category. As 'repeat players,' these sophisticated consumers usually have a considerable baseline of experience from which to formulate the goals of the representation and to evaluate lawyer performance. In addition, corporations have comparatively more resources to devote to the task of understanding and evaluating lawyer conduct. Given these differences, we would expect that the average corporate client will have much greater access to information about lawyer conduct than the average individual.

This gap between corporate and individual clients is amplified by stratification and specialisation within the bar. The formal and informal relationships lawyers form with colleagues, adversaries, and state officials produce unique and effective norms, procedures, and sanctions. These embedded control systems are likely to be different for corporate and individual lawyers. Corporate lawyers tend to work in larger firms, make more money, and have greater professional status and occupational mobility than lawyers who primarily represent individuals. Similarly, corporate and individual lawyers tend to concentrate in different fields of law and interact with different state officials. These and other differences have led many to conclude that lawyers who represent corporations occupy a separate hemisphere from those who primarily represent individuals. A lawyer's hemisphere of practice plausibly will affect the operation of whatever enforcement system coexists with these embedded controls.

D. A CONTEXTUAL MODEL

Contextual differences relating to the lawyer's role and the identity of the client suggest a matrix of possible lawyer-client interactions. Figure 1 illustrates this matrix. The vertical axis charts the identity of the client, from 'individuals' to 'corporations,' as a surrogate for the range of embedded controls likely to influence the conduct of a particular lawyer. The horizontal axis delineates lawyer conduct as it relates to the two facets of the lawyer's role: 'advocacy duties' represent obligations to clients and 'officer of the court duties' symbolise responsibilities to the legal framework, identifiable third parties, and the public at large.

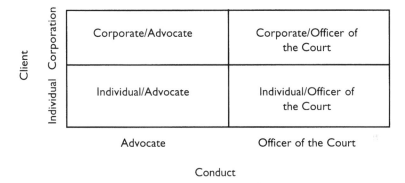

Deciding where any given case falls within this matrix will always be a matter of judgement, particularly at the margins. Certain individual clients undoubtedly will have more in common with the average corporation than with other individuals . . . Similarly, many professional duties can fairly be characterised as being owed both to clients and to the legal framework. A lawyer who knowingly files a frivolous lawsuit without informing the client of the weakness of the claim may be simultaneously violating both her duty to assist in the efficient administration of justice and her obligation to serve her client's interests competently. Nevertheless, each end of the two axes -- individual/ corporate and advocate/officer of the court -- captures something important about the context in which any enforcement system must operate. These categories therefore serve as useful reference points for the multiplicity of contextual factors that will affect the operation of any regulatory regime. The next two Parts test this claim by examining compliance and independence arguments as they relate to the categories of the matrix.....

The conduct axis of the matrix separates professional duties according to whether they are primarily directed toward serving clients or preserving the legal framework.

This distinction suggests that enforcement officials must try to prevent two categories of professional misconduct. The first, which I call 'agency problems,' involve cases in which lawyer misconduct primarily injures clients. Common examples include over-billing, allowing the statute of limitations to run, and representing conflicting interests in the same or substantially similar cases. The second, which I call 'externality problems' or 'strategic behaviour,' involve cases in which lawyers and clients together impose unjustified harms on third parties or on the legal framework. Common examples include cases in which a lawyer files frivolous pleadings during the course of litigation, knowingly allows her client to present perjured testimony, or assists the client in preparing a false or misleading proxy statement. The client axis suggests that these problems may vary according to whether the client is an individual or a corporation. As a result, each enforcement system must be evaluated in terms of its ability to control four categories of lawyer misconduct: individual/agency problems, corporate/agency problems, individual/externality problems, and corporate/externality problems. Figure 2 illustrates this matrix.

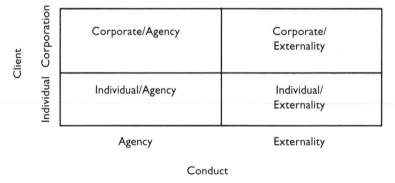

Bearing this in mind, we can evaluate the significance and potential of each of the models. At this stage, administrative systems and liability rules will be dealt with relatively quickly. Administrative systems such as that operated by the Legal Services Commission are likely to be effective particularly in relation to externality problems in that they do not rely on complaints either from lawyers or from clients.[9] The obvious drawback is the cost, for example the amount of form filling required by lawyers in order to demonstrate compliance. It is perhaps significant in this respect that under legal aid is to be delivered by via a small number of quality assured contracted suppliers. This suggests that administrative control is too costly to be an option across a wider range of legal services. The problem with liability rules is that the costs of invoking them make them unsuitable for all but large claims by well-resourced clients and in any case they are likely to deal only with agency problems. In principle, the availability of a low-cost complaints procedure which can provide compensation for inadequate professional services has great potential. However, it will be seen that this potential remains as yet unfulfilled.

9   For some of the difficulties involved in the notion of quality, see pp 383-88, chapter 10 infra.

DISCIPLINARY SYSTEMS

In the following extract, Wilkins considers the likely impact of disciplinary systems.

The Structural Limitations of Disciplinary Controls. -- I begin with disciplinary controls because this is the regulatory structure against which all others are expressly or implicitly compared. Moreover, the ABA continues to insist that a properly functioning disciplinary process can effectively control lawyer misconduct. This claim is not plausible, however, once we examine the institutional characteristics of this form of control.

(a) *Client Reporting Systems Are Unlikely to Control Externality Problems.* -- The institutional characteristics of disciplinary controls make it unlikely that this system will effectively address externality problems. Given the structural separation of the disciplinary process from the arenas in which lawyers work, disciplinary officials depend on others to generate information about lawyer misconduct. Although judges and lawyers are strongly urged to report misconduct, these knowledgeable parties rarely file complaints.

A cursory examination of the incentives facing lawyers and judges in this context reveals the causes of this deficiency. For lawyers, not only are there no tangible rewards for reporting misconduct, but adversaries who turn in their fellow lawyers also run the risk of inviting a retaliatory response. Moreover, the complex web of embedded controls surrounding many aspects of legal practice makes it possible for a lawyer wishing to sanction another member of the bar to accomplish his goal more effectively through informal controls. Although a judge does not face the same adversary system disincentives as a lawyer, she nevertheless may feel that it is not her role to interfere in the lawyer-client relationship of those who appear before her. Moreover, even if she overcomes this initial resistance, it is likely that she will, like the lawyer, prefer to use the more efficient embedded controls at her disposal to discourage the attorney conduct that most directly implicates her interests.

Given this confluence of incentives and embedded controls facing lawyers and judges, it is not surprising that the vast majority of the complaints coming to the attention of the disciplinary system are filed by clients. These clients, however, have little incentive to report strategic behaviour taken on their behalf. Despite its formal breadth, therefore, disciplinary regulation will inevitably focus on agency problems. But even in that area, the system is likely to accomplish much less than it promises.

(b) *The Paradox of Agency Problems.* -- In order to access the benefits of the disciplinary system, a client must first understand that she may have been injured by lawyer misconduct. Paradoxically, clients in the best position to make this determination are the least likely to bring their complaints to the attention of disciplinary authorities.

As frequent consumers of legal services, corporations have both the resources and the incentive to reduce the information asymmetry that usually exists between lawyers and clients. Thus, many corporations have hired 'in house' lawyers to help them identify their legal needs, hire competent outside counsel, and monitor attorney performance[10]. Others have delegated these functions to non-lawyers. Access to this kind of

10 A survey conducted by *The Lawyer* early in 1999 revealed that 70% of surveyed lawyers believed private practice fees to be excessive. Many of them were planning to seek reductions. See 'Slash your fees, say in-house to law firms' (1999) The Lawyer 11 January.

sophisticated advice will substantially reduce the incidence of certain kinds of agency problems.

Consider the frequent complaint by both individual and corporate clients that legal fees are too high relative to the real value of the services actually performed. During the decade of the seventies, a growing number of corporations began to complain about the rising cost of legal services. Although such complaints are still frequently heard, these sophisticated consumers have undertaken several cost control measures that have made it more difficult for corporate lawyers to 'run the meter.' Many corporations took a substantial portion of their legal work 'inside,' which reduces opportunistic pricing by outside firms. Moreover, when the decision is made to hire an outside lawyer, corporations can employ their legally sophisticated intermediaries to collect and evaluate reputational information about lawyer competence and trustworthiness. Outside firms may be asked to submit competitive bids, periodic budgets, detailed records, and obtain prior approval before filing documents or making major strategy decisions. Such measures will help the corporation pinpoint and eliminate lawyer incompetence or opportunistic behaviour.

Finally, these client controls are likely to be reinforced by the structure of relationships inside the corporate law firm. Corporate lawyers are generally paid according to the number of hours worked, which gives them a strong incentive to follow through on their commitments. Lawyers' incentives to keep the client happy also increase as firms move away from lock-step compensation systems toward ones that directly reward lawyers for revenue-generating activities, such as bringing in business or billing more hours. In addition, corporate firms have become increasingly rationalised and bureaucratic. Given that the heightened monitoring capabilities of corporations are likely to make the law firm as a whole more concerned with satisfying client desires, these bureaucratic controls help ensure that client directives are followed throughout the organisation.

Taken in combination, the embedded controls available to corporations make it more difficult for lawyers to overcharge these sophisticated consumers. Of course, neither corporate counsel nor senior partners are likely to invest the time that would be required to wipe out opportunistic billing in its entirety. Nevertheless, one of the most persistent agency problems for individual clients -- and one of the most frequent complaints voiced to disciplinary authorities -- is unlikely to be a significant concern in the corporate hemisphere. This is not to suggest, however, that corporate lawyers do not commit agency violations. Just as the structure of corporate law practice makes some agency problems less likely to occur, it undoubtedly increases the probability of others. Yet, corporations have little incentive to bring violations to the attention of disciplinary officials.

Conflict-of-interest problems are a typical example. The rules of professional conduct prohibit a lawyer from either simultaneously representing conflicting interests or representing a current client whose interests are adverse to those of a former client in a matter substantially related to the prior representation. The size of the average corporate law firm increases the danger of conflicts problems. Moreover, corporations are in a peculiarly difficult position to detect potential conflicts. At any given time, a large corporation often will have several law firms working on dozens of separate matters. Keeping track of their own work, let alone what other work these firms may be doing, is an extremely time consuming and difficult task. Even sophisticated clients, therefore, may be unable to protect themselves against conflicts.

Yet, when this agency problem became apparent to corporate clients in the mid-seventies, they did not invoke the protection of the disciplinary system. The disciplinary system, with its emphasis on ex post review and punitive sanctions, was not an effective means of accomplishing the objectives of corporate clients. Instead, corporations filed a wave of disqualification motions to prevent their former lawyers from representing clients with conflicting interests. This strategy proved relatively successful, as corporate law firms instituted procedures for preventing these problems from occurring in the first place. The formal disciplinary system was simply not a part of this strategy.

Corporate clients are therefore unlikely to use the disciplinary system, even when they have actually been harmed by lawyer misconduct. Individual clients do not have access to the embedded sanctions available to corporations. Although individuals have a greater incentive to invoke the disciplinary system as a protection against agency problems, they are unlikely to be able to utilise these controls effectively. As 'one-shot' participants in the legal marketplace, individual clients are subject to each of the three major information asymmetries that foster agency problems: they do not know what services they need, they do not have access to information that would allow them to predict the quality of the services that a particular lawyer is likely to render, and they do not have a sufficient baseline from which to evaluate the quality of the services performed. By relying on client complaints, disciplinary enforcement simply reproduces these market defects.

Overall, the claim that the disciplinary system will effectively enforce professional norms across the entire spectrum of lawyer-client interactions seems quite dubious. The system simply does not address externality problems. Those clients most likely to use the process to combat agency problems are the least likely to be able to do so effectively. Corporate clients that have the ability to monitor and evaluate lawyer conduct also have powerful embedded controls at their disposal that render the system largely unnecessary.

Finally, the administrative costs of achieving even this limited range of benefits can be high. Because the proceedings take place after the fact, enforcement officials must bear all of the costs of investigation, prosecution, and adjudication. Moreover, some of these agencies are chronically under-funded. As a result, many disciplinary cases take years to resolve, further adding to both participant and administrative costs.[11]

Questions

1. Wilkins suggests that disciplinary procedures are inherently likely to fail because they are unlikely to be invoked with sufficient frequency. In the UK however, the

---

11   Supra note 8 at pp 822-830. The delays of the OSS and its predecessor the SCB are one of the commonest causes of criticisms leveled at these bodies by the Legal Services Ombudsman who has recognised however that part of the problem is the sheer volume of complaints. *Legal Services Ombudsman, 7th Annual Report* (London, HMSO, 1998) at p 13.

reports of the Legal Services Ombudsman in the years 1991-1998 indicate that there has been a steep rise in the number of complaints[12]. How might this be explained? Does the rise in the number of complaints suggest a rise in the incidence of inadequate professional service? Does Professor Paterson's analysis of professionalism[13] suggest an explanation?

2. Reconsider Khan's case[14]. It is arguable that Stephen would have realised after his conversation with Karen that Amir Khan was attempting to deceive both his wife and the building society. The loan said to be necessary to pay of the loan used to purchase the boat was in fact going to be used to refinance his ailing business. According to principle 16.02 note 1 (the 'crime-fraud' exception to the duty of confidentiality), Stephen was free to communicate this information to Mrs Khan or to the building society. But should he have been under a *duty* to warn the potential victims of the client's intended fraud? If so, to what extent would compliance with the duty be more likely if breach of duty gave rise to an action for damages in tort? Such liability would be analogous to that imposed in the American case of *Tarassof v Regents of the University of California*[15]. There a psychiatric patient told the defendant psychiatrist of his intention to kill the plaintiff. The defendant did not disclose this information and the patient carried out the threat. The psychiatrist was held liable to the estate for failure to warn the victim.

3. Until the recent decision of the House of Lords in *Arthur J S Hall & Co v Simmons*[16], the common law granted barristers and solicitor advocates immunity from professional negligence claims in relation to work in court or closely connected with it. One of the common justifications for this immunity was that if advocates were to fulfil their duty to the court they needed to be freed from the possibility that they would be sued by clients. It was argued that without the immunity advocates would be prevented from fulfilling their duty to the court by the fear that a disappointed client would allege that what was from the advocates perspective fulfilling a duty to the court was in fact breach of a duty to the client.[17] A minority of their Lordships considered that this argument still carried sufficient weight in criminal proceedings as to justify the retention of the immunity.

---

12   In 1997, for example the Bar Council received 550 complaints (one complaint/25 barristers) a rise of 25% compared with 1996. The OSS received 26,445 complaints (a staggering one complaint for every three solicitors), an increase of 7% compared with 1996. *Legal Services Ombudsman, 7th Annual Report* supra note 7 at pp 11, 21.

13   Chapter 3 supra at pp 79-80.

14   Supra chapter 1 at pp 19-22.

15   551 P. 2d 334 (1976). It is highly unlikely that this decision would be followed in the UK given the recent contraction in the scope of liability in tort. See *Home Office* v *Dorset Yacht Co* [1970] AC 1004 and subsequent cases.

16   [2000] WLR 543.

17   See *Rondel v Worsley* [1967] 1QB 520, CA, especially per Salmon LJ and [1969]1 AC 191, HL, especially per Lord Reid at 227; *Saif Ali v Sydney Mitchell* [1980] AC 198.

Consider Wilkins matrix of lawyer-client interactions. Does the matrix support the argument of the minority that lawyers should be immune from suit in criminal proceedings? In what types of proceedings would the argument be strongest?

INSTITUTIONAL SANCTIONS

The key characteristic of this form of control is that they are applied by the institution within which lawyers work. In the next extract, Wilkins considers the advantages and disadvantages of this form of control taking as examples Rule 11 of the Federal Rules of Civil Procedure and the work of the Securities and Exchange Commission. The SEC regulates the US securities market and holds adjudicatory hearings at which lawyers often appear on behalf of their client. It has power to apply sanctions against lawyers found guilty of misconduct. Rule 11 gives the Federal courts a general power to punish those who abuse the civil process, for example by making frivolous arguments. The usual sanction is the award of costs to the other side.[18]

Institutional controls, such as rule II and the SEC's rule 2(e), give enforcement authority to the institutions in which lawyers work. This placement has two important consequences. First, unlike disciplinary regulation, enforcement officials do not need to rely entirely on complaints from injured parties to generate information about lawyer misconduct. Second, the actions taken by interested parties (lawyers, clients, judges, regulators, and adversaries) will be strongly influenced by the background incentives generated by the institution in which the control system is located. Independently, each of these features seems likely to expand the range of conduct coming to the attention of regulatory officials. In combination, however, they are likely to focus these regulatory regimes on certain kinds of externality problems.

(a) *Situational Monitoring and Adversary Incentives: The Information Advantages of Institutional Controls.* -- In the ordinary course of litigation, judges extensively observe the lawyers' conduct. Although the extent of judicial scrutiny should not be exaggerated, a judge will often be able to form a crude judgement about the lawyers' effort. For example, was the pleading filed? Was the attorney prepared for oral argument? A similar story can be told about enforcement officials at administrative agencies such as the SEC. In the ordinary course of business, SEC officials review formal submissions and public documents prepared by lawyers. These efforts undoubtedly provide some tentative information about lawyer conduct, such as whether the registration statement was filed on time and in the proper form or whether the information disclosed in the offering documents is consistent with the public information available to investors. Moreover, as part of their normal duties, SEC officials investigate specific market transactions to determine whether the relevant parties have complied with applicable provisions of the securities laws. These investigations also produce a significant amount of information about lawyer conduct. Simply as a result of their participation in an ongoing process, therefore, trial judges and administrative officials are likely to uncover information about lawyer misconduct that would escape the attention of disciplinary officials.

18   In the US, each side otherwise normally bears its own costs regardless of the outcome. In the UK, the winner normally has its costs paid by the other side so that costs are said to 'follow the event'.

Moreover, because of their stake in the underlying process, these officials have substantial incentives to act on this information. For example, in light of the important role that lawyers play in the administration of the securities laws, it is not surprising that the SEC has been especially vigilant in its investigation and prosecution of lawyers who have allegedly assisted their clients in circumventing relevant statutory requirements. It is also not surprising, however, that these same incentives have sometimes led the Commission to engage in what appears from a compliance perspective to be overzealous enforcement......the fact that institutional controls pose an increased danger of over deterring certain kinds of lawful conduct should be counted as a cost of the system.

The same point can be made with respect to other participants who are in a position to observe lawyer misconduct. Given the inherent limitations of independent observation and investigation, institutional regulators such as trial judges and SEC officials must rely on other knowledgeable actors to report instances of professional misconduct. By making the enforcement process a part of an ongoing system of interactions between these knowledgeable actors and the offending lawyer, institutional controls increase the incentive for these parties to participate in the regulatory process. Experience with rule II underscores this conclusion.

Rule II offers a number of formal and informal incentives to lawyers (and their clients) to report misconduct by their adversaries. Rule II specifically states that fee shifting is an appropriate sanction for violations of the rule. This alone provides substantially more incentive than the current disciplinary system. Moreover, because rule II operates during the course of litigation, adversaries may gain a number of strategic advantages from reporting lawyer misconduct. The fact that these structural differences have altered the incentives of the putative victims of strategic behaviour can be plainly seen by the number of sanctions motions that have been filed over the last eight years.

In substance, rule II does little more than spell out the traditional prohibition, contained in both the Model Code and the Model Rules, against asserting frivolous claims or defences. Not surprisingly, disciplinary action is rarely taken against a lawyer for violating this longstanding professional command. In the eight years since rule II was amended, however, there has been an explosion of activity, most of it initiated by those claiming to be the victims of conduct violating the rule. These same incentives, however, limit the overall effectiveness of this form of control.

(b) *Agency Problems and the One-Shot Player: The Danger of Reifying Institutional Power.* — Each actor in an institutional control system has an agenda. Adversaries in a litigated case want to win on the merits. Trial judges want to dispose of cases efficiently. SEC enforcement officials want to vindicate their ideas about regulatory policy. Moreover, each institution in which such a control system might be located distributes power and information among relevant participants in particular ways. Institutional controls cannot easily escape these pre-existing goals and structures. Experience with rule II is again instructive.

In theory, rule II is applicable to agency and externality problems across the entire spectrum of lawyer-client interactions. The actual reach of the rule, however, has been far more restricted. Although there is evidence that the rule has influenced the conduct of all attorneys, every study to date has concluded that plaintiffs (and their lawyers) are far more likely to be the objects of requests for sanctions and to have sanctions imposed. Moreover, it also appears that certain kinds of plaintiffs, most notably those prosecuting civil rights or employment discrimination claims, are especially likely to be disciplined under the rule.

These results are sadly predictable given the institutional dynamics of this form of control. Litigants and their lawyers file rule II motions primarily to gain some economic or strategic advantage in the litigation. Although this motivation encourages these knowledgeable actors to participate in the enforcement process, it also restricts the kind of conduct they are likely to report. Lawyers obviously have very little incentive to report pure agency violations by their adversaries. Nor are they likely to move for sanctions in cases in which the financial or strategic costs of such a move seem likely to outweigh its benefits. This strategic calculus systematically benefits institutional defendants. As sophisticated repeat players, these litigants have both a long-range view of the strategic benefits that might result from obtaining rule II sanctions in a particular case and an ability to shoulder the costs of moving for them. At the opposite end of the spectrum, a lawyer for an individual plaintiff operating under a contingent fee agreement can ill afford to invest in strategic manoeuvring that, whatever else it accomplishes, will almost certainly increase the cost of ultimately prevailing on the merits. Taken as a whole, therefore, institutional controls embedded in the litigation process tend to reify the underlying advantages already enjoyed by certain litigants.[19]

Questions

1. Reconsider Wilkins matrix of lawyer-client interactions. In what context is lawyer misconduct most likely to be controlled by institutional sanctions?

2. What are the disadvantages of these sanctions? What might be an appropriate response to the problem by judges given such powers?

In England, the courts have developed through the case law a series of duties which lawyers owe to the court. Solicitors are officers of the court and breach of one of these duties may lead the court either of its own motion or at the application of another party to invoke a summary procedure to determine whether a breach has occurred. If it has, the court has power to fine the offender or order the payment of compensation to anyone to whom loss has been caused by the breach. Barristers are not technically speaking officers of the court but judges regard barristers as being bound by the same duties and would refer any suspected breach to the Inns of Court and the Bar Council.[20] In an article published in the influential and widely read *Law Quarterly Review*, Mr Justice Ipp, an Australian Judge, has reviewed and systematised the case law in this area. He argues that the law imposes upon lawyers four general duties: a) a duty of disclosure to the court b) a duty not to abuse the court process c) a duty not to corrupt the administration of justice and d) a duty to conduct cases expeditiously and

19   Wilkins supra note 8 at pp 835-837; 838-841.
20   DA Ipp 'Lawyers Duties to the Court' [1998] 114 Law Quarterly Review 62.

efficiently[1]. The language in which these duties are described seems clearly to emphasise that the lawyers duty to the court is paramount. Indeed a fellow Australian judge is cited for the view that

> It is not that a barrister's duty to the court creates such a conflict with his duty to the client that the dividing line is unclear. The duty to the court is paramount even if the client gives instructions to the contrary.[2]

Given that this article was written against the background of Lord Woolf's plans for increased judicial management of litigation, such views may well be evidence of and a stimulus to an increased judicial activism as regulator of the work of lawyers. The profession's disciplinary procedures by contrast are described as 'relatively slow and cumbersome'.[3]

In England, the courts' power to order solicitors to compensate opposing parties for costs wasted as a result of a breach of a duty owed to the court has been codified and extended to barristers. In *Ridelhalgh v Horsefield*,[4] the Court of Appeal considered the principles relevant to the exercise of the wasted costs jurisdiction which is now contained in s 51 of the Supreme Court Act 1980. This section provides that:

> (1) Subject to the provisions of this or any other enactment and to rules of court, the costs of and incidental to all proceedings in—(a) the civil division of the Court of Appeal; (b) the High Court; and (c) any county court, shall be in the discretion of the court ...

> (6) In any proceedings mentioned in subsection (1), the court may disallow, or (as the case may be) order the legal or other representative concerned to meet, the whole of any wasted costs or such part of them as may be determined in accordance with rules of court.

> (7) In subsection (6), 'wasted costs' means any costs incurred by a party—(a) as a result of any improper, unreasonable or negligent act or omission on the part of any legal or other representative or any employee of such a representative; or (b) which, in the light of any such act or omission occurring after they were incurred, the court considers it is unreasonable to expect that party to pay ...

> (13) In this section 'legal or other representative', in relation to a party to proceedings, means any person exercising a right of audience or right to conduct litigation on his behalf.

Lord Bingham commented:

> Our legal system, developed over many centuries, rests on the principle that the interests of justice are on the whole best served if parties in dispute, each represented by solicitors and counsel, take cases incapable of compromise to court for decision by an independent and neutral judge, before whom their relationship is essentially antagonistic: each is determined to win, and prepares and presents his case so as to

---

1   Ibid at pp 103-107.
2   Ibid at p 103 citing Mason CJ in *Giannerelli v Wraith* (1988) 165 CLR 543 at p 556.
3   Ibid at p 64.
4   [1994] 3 All ER 848, CA.

defeat his opponent and achieve a favourable result. By the clash of competing evidence and argument, it is believed, the judge is best enabled to decide what happened, to formulate the relevant principles of law and to apply those principles to the facts of the case before him as he has found them.

Experience has shown that certain safeguards are needed if this system is to function fairly and effectively in the interests of parties to litigation and of the public at large. None of these safeguards is entirely straightforward, and only some of them need be mentioned here.

(1) Parties must be free to unburden themselves to their legal advisers without fearing that what they say may provide ammunition for their opponent. To this end a cloak of confidence is thrown over communications between client and lawyer, usually removable only with the consent of the client.

(2) The party who substantially loses the case is ordinarily obliged to pay the legal costs necessarily incurred by the winner. Thus hopeless claims and defences are discouraged, a willingness to compromise is induced and the winner keeps most of the fruits of victory. But the position is different where one or both parties to the case are legally aided: s 17 of the Legal Aid Act 1988[5] and Pt XIII of the Civil Legal Aid (General) Regulations 1989, SI 1989/339, restrict the liability of legally assisted parties to pay costs if they lose. And sometimes the losing party is impoverished and cannot pay.

(3) The law imposes a duty on lawyers to exercise reasonable care and skill in conducting their clients' affairs. This is a duty owed to and enforceable by the client, to protect him against loss caused by his lawyer's default. But it is not an absolute duty. Considerations of public policy have been held to require, and statute now confirms, that in relation to proceedings in court and work closely related to proceedings in court advocates should be accorded immunity from claims for negligence by their clients: Rondel v Worsley [1967] 3 All ER 993, [1969] 1 AC 191; Saif Ali v Sydney Mitchell & Co (a firm) (P, third party) [1978] 3 All ER 1033, [1980] AC 198; s 62 of the Courts and Legal Services Act 1990.[6]

(4) If solicitors or barristers fail to observe the standards of conduct required by the Law Society or the General Council of the Bar (as the case may be) they become liable to disciplinary proceedings at the suit of their professional body and to a range of penalties which include fines, suspension from practice and expulsion from their profession. Procedures have changed over the years. The role of the courts (in the case of solicitors) and the Inns of Court (in the case of barristers) has in large measure been assumed by the professional bodies themselves. But the sanctions remain, not to compensate those who have suffered loss but to compel observance of prescribed standards of professional conduct. Additional powers exist to order barristers, solicitors and those in receipt of legal aid to forgo fees or remuneration otherwise earned.

(5) Solicitors and barristers may in certain circumstances be ordered to compensate a party to litigation other than the client for whom they act for costs incurred by that

5   The relevant regulations are now those made pursuant to s 11 of the Access to Justice Act 1999. Section 11 of that Act is intended to make it easier for successful unassisted parties to recover their costs.

6   This immunity war subsequently abolished by the House of Lords in the case of Arthur J S Hall & Co v Simmons [2000] 3 WLR 543.

party as a result of acts done or omitted by the solicitors or barristers in their conduct of the litigation.

It is the scope and effect of this last safeguard, and its relation with the others briefly mentioned, which are in issue in these appeals. We shall hereafter refer to this jurisdiction, not quite accurately, as 'the wasted costs jurisdiction' and to orders made under it as 'wasted costs orders'. These appeals are not concerned with the jurisdiction to order legal representatives to compensate their own client. The questions raised are by no means academic. Material has been placed before the court which shows that the number and value of wasted costs orders applied for, and the costs of litigating them, have risen sharply. We were told of one case in which the original hearing had lasted five days; the wasted costs application had (when we were told of it) lasted seven days; it was estimated to be about half way through; at that stage one side had incurred costs of over £40,000. It almost appears that a new branch of legal activity is emerging, calling to mind Dickens's searing observation in *Bleak House*:

> 'The one great principle of English law is, to make business for itself ... Viewed by this light it becomes a coherent scheme, and not the monstrous maze the laity are apt to think it.'

The argument we have heard discloses a tension between two important public interests. One is that lawyers should not be deterred from pursuing their clients' interests by fear of incurring a personal liability to their clients' opponents; that they should not be penalised by orders to pay costs without a fair opportunity to defend themselves; that wasted costs orders should not become a back-door means of recovering costs not otherwise recoverable against a legally aided or impoverished litigant; and that the remedy should not grow unchecked to become more damaging than the disease. The other public interest, recently and clearly affirmed by Act of Parliament, is that litigants should not be financially prejudiced by the unjustifiable conduct of litigation by their or their opponents' lawyers. The reconciliation of these public interests is our task in these appeals. Full weight must be given to the first of these public interests, but the wasted costs jurisdiction must not be emasculated.

THE WASTED COSTS JURISDICTION

The wasted costs jurisdiction of the court as applied to solicitors is of long standing, but discussion of it can conveniently begin with the important and relatively recent case of *Myers v Elman* [1939] 4 All ER 484, [1940] AC 282. At the end of a five-day hearing before a jury the plaintiff obtained judgment for damages for fraudulent conspiracy against five defendants, with costs. Nothing could be recovered from any of the defendants. Nor, perhaps, was any recovery expected, for at the end of the trial the plaintiff's counsel applied for an order that the costs of the action should be paid by the solicitors who had acted for the defendants.

Notice was duly given to the solicitors and a further five-day hearing followed to decide whether the solicitors or any of them should make payment. In the case of one solicitor, Mr Elman, the trial judge (Singleton J) considered two complaints: that he had filed defences which he knew to be false; and that he had permitted the filing of an inadequate affidavit verifying his clients' list of documents. In considering these complaints the judge had before him a considerable correspondence between Mr Elman and his clients which the plaintiff's advisers had (naturally) not seen before; the reports of the case do not disclose how it came about that the clients' privilege in that correspondence was waived.

Singleton J rejected the complaint relating to the defences but upheld that based on the defective affidavit of documents. Nothing, held the judge, should be said which might prevent, or tend to prevent, either solicitor or counsel from doing his best for his client so long as the duty to the court was borne in mind, but if he were asked or required by the client to do something which was inconsistent with the duty to the court it was for him to point out that he could not do it and, if necessary, cease to act (see *Myers v Rothfield* [1939] 1 KB 109 at 115, 117). The judge ordered Mr Elman to pay one-third of the taxed costs of the action and two-thirds of the costs of the application. Mr Elman appealed, and the Court of Appeal by a majority reversed the decision of the judge. It appeared that the work in question had been very largely delegated to a well-qualified managing clerk and the conduct complained of had been his, not Mr Elman's. The majority held that to make a wasted costs order the court must find professional misconduct established against the solicitor, and such a finding could not be made where the solicitor was not personally at fault.

On further appeal to the House of Lords, Lord Russell of Killowen dissented on the facts but the House was unanimous in rejecting the Court of Appeal's majority view. While their Lordships used different language, and may to some extent have seen the issues somewhat differently, the case is authority for five fundamental propositions.

(1) The court's jurisdiction to make a wasted costs order against a solicitor is quite distinct from the disciplinary jurisdiction exercised over solicitors.

(2) Whereas a disciplinary order against a solicitor requires a finding that he has been personally guilty of serious professional misconduct, the making of a wasted costs order does not.

(3) The court's jurisdiction to make a wasted costs order against a solicitor is founded on breach of the duty owed by the solicitor to the court to perform his duty as an officer of the court in promoting within his own sphere the cause of justice.

(4) To show a breach of that duty it is not necessary to establish dishonesty, criminal conduct, personal obliquity or behaviour such as would warrant striking a solicitor off the roll. While mere mistake or error of judgment would not justify an order, misconduct, default or even negligence is enough if the negligence is serious or gross.

(5) The jurisdiction is compensatory and not merely punitive.

His Lordship then traced the evolution of the jurisdiction from its common law origins to its current statement in s 51. and continued:

There can in our view be no room for doubt about the mischief against which these new provisions were aimed: this was the causing of loss and expense to litigants by the unjustifiable conduct of litigation by their or the other side's lawyers. Where such conduct is shown, Parliament clearly intended to arm the courts with an effective remedy for the protection of those injured.

Since the Act there have been two cases which deserve mention. The first is *Re a Barrister (wasted costs order) (No 1 of 1991)* [1992] 3 All ER 429, [1993] QB 293. This arose out of an unhappy difference between counsel and a judge sitting in the Crown Court in a criminal case. It was held on appeal, in our view quite rightly, that courts should apply a three-stage test when a wasted costs order is contemplated. (1) Has the legal representative of whom complaint is made acted improperly, unreasonably or negligently? (2) If so, did such conduct cause the applicant to incur unnecessary costs? (3) If so, is it in all the circumstances just to order the legal representative to compensate the applicant for the whole or any part of the relevant costs? (If so, the costs to be met must be specified and, in a criminal case, the amount of the costs.) We have somewhat altered the wording of the court's ruling but not, we think, its effect.

The second case, *Symphony Group plc v Hodgson* [1993] 4 All ER 143, [1994] QB 179, arose out of an application for costs against a non-party and not out of a wasted costs order. An observation of Balcombe LJ is however pertinent in this context also ([1993] 4 All ER 143 at 154, [1994] QB 179 at 194):

> The judge should be alert to the possibility that an application against a non-party is motivated by resentment of an inability to obtain an effective order for costs against a legally aided litigant. The courts are well aware of the financial difficulties faced by parties who are facing legally aided litigants at first instance, where the opportunity of a claim against the Legal Aid Board under s 18 of the Legal Aid Act 1988 is very limited. Nevertheless the Civil Legal Aid (General) Regulations 1989, SI 1989/339, and in particular regs 67, 69 and 70, lay down conditions designed to ensure that there is no abuse of legal aid by a legally assisted person and these are designed to protect the other party to the litigation as well as the legal aid fund. The court will be very reluctant to infer that solicitors to a legally aided party have failed to discharge their duties under the regulations—see *Orchard v South Eastern Electricity Board* [1987] 1 All ER 95, [1987] QB 565.

[Having held that liability for wasted costs was liability for negligence his Lordship continued:]

PURSUING A HOPELESS CASE

A legal representative is not to be held to have acted improperly, unreasonably or negligently simply because he acts for a party who pursues a claim or a defence which is plainly doomed to fail. As Lord Pearce observed in *Rondel v Worsley* [1967] 3 All ER 993 at 1029, [1969] 1 AC 191 at 275:

> It is easier, pleasanter and more advantageous professionally for barristers to advise, represent or defend those who are decent and reasonable and likely to succeed in their action or their defence than those who are unpleasant, unreasonable, disreputable, and have an apparently hopeless case. Yet it would be tragic if our legal system came to provide no reputable defenders, representatives or advisers for the latter.

As is well known, barristers in independent practice are not permitted to pick and choose their clients. Paragraph 209 of the Code of Conduct of the Bar of England and Wales provides:

> 'A barrister in independent practice must comply with the 'Cab-rank rule' and accordingly except only as otherwise provided in paragraphs 501, 502 and 503

he must in any field in which he professes to practise in relation to work appropriate to his experience and seniority and irrespective of whether his client is paying privately or is legally aided or otherwise publicly funded: (a) accept any brief to appear before a court in which he professes to practise; (b) accept any instructions; (c) act for any person on whose behalf he is briefed or instructed; and do so irrespective of (i) the party on whose behalf he is briefed or instructed (ii) the nature of the case and (iii) any belief or opinion which he may have formed as to the character reputation cause conduct guilt or innocence of that person.

As is also well known, solicitors are not subject to an equivalent cab-rank rule, but many solicitors would and do respect the public policy underlying it by affording representation to the unpopular and the unmeritorious. Legal representatives will, of course, whether barristers or solicitors, advise clients of the perceived weakness of their case and of the risk of failure. But clients are free to reject advice and insist that cases be litigated. It is rarely if ever safe for a court to assume that a hopeless case is being litigated on the advice of the lawyers involved. They are there to present the case; it is (as Samuel Johnson unforgettably pointed out) for the judge and not the lawyers to judge it.

It is, however, one thing for a legal representative to present, on instructions, a case which he regards as bound to fail; it is quite another to lend his assistance to proceedings which are an abuse of the process of the court. Whether instructed or not, a legal representative is not entitled to use litigious procedures for purposes for which they were not intended, as by issuing or pursuing proceedings for reasons unconnected with success in the litigation or pursuing a case known to be dishonest, nor is he entitled to evade rules intended to safeguard the interests of justice, as by knowingly failing to make full disclosure on ex-parte application or knowingly conniving at incomplete disclosure of documents. It is not entirely easy to distinguish by definition between the hopeless case and the case which amounts to an abuse of the process, but in practice it is not hard to say which is which and if there is doubt the legal representative is entitled to the benefit of it.

LEGAL AID

Section 31(1) of the Legal Aid Act 1988[7] provides that receipt of legal aid shall not (save as expressly provided) affect the relationship between or rights of a legal representative and client or any privilege arising out of the relationship nor the rights or liabilities of other parties to the proceedings or the principles on which any discretion is exercised. (The protection given to a legally assisted party in relation to payment of costs is, of course, an obvious express exception.) This important principle has been recognised in the authorities. It is incumbent on courts to which applications for wasted costs orders are made to bear prominently in mind the peculiar vulnerability of legal representatives acting for assisted persons, to which Balcombe LJ adverted in *Symphony Group plc v Hodgson* and which recent experience abundantly confirms. It would subvert the benevolent purposes of this legislation if such representatives were subject to any unusual personal risk. They for their part must bear prominently in mind that their advice and their conduct should not be tempered by the knowledge that their client is not their paymaster and so not, in all probability, liable for the costs of the other side...

7   Now replaced (though in almost identical terms) by s 22 of the Access to Justice Act 1999.

PRIVILEGE

Where an applicant seeks a wasted costs order against the lawyers on the other side, legal professional privilege may be relevant both as between the applicant and his lawyers and as between the respondent lawyers and their client. In either case it is the client's privilege, which he alone can waive.

The first of these situations can cause little difficulty. If the applicant's privileged communications are germane to an issue in the application, to show what he would or would not have done had the other side not acted in the manner complained of, he can waive his privilege; if he declines to do so, adverse inferences can be drawn. The respondent lawyers are in a different position. The privilege is not theirs to waive. In the usual case where a waiver would not benefit their client they will be slow to advise the client to waive his privilege, and they may well feel bound to advise that the client should take independent advice before doing so. The client may be unwilling to do that, and may be unwilling to waive if he does. So the respondent lawyers may find themselves at a grave disadvantage in defending their conduct of proceedings, unable to reveal what advice and warnings they gave, what instructions they received. In some cases this potential source of injustice may be mitigated by reference to the taxing master, where different rules apply, but only in a small minority of cases can this procedure be appropriate. Judges who are invited to make or contemplate making a wasted costs order must make full allowance for the inability of respondent lawyers to tell the whole story. Where there is room for doubt, the respondent lawyers are entitled to the benefit of it. It is again only when, with all allowances made, a lawyer's conduct of proceedings is quite plainly unjustifiable that it can be appropriate to make a wasted costs order . . .

RELIANCE ON COUNSEL

We endorse the guidance given on this subject in *Locke v Camberwell Health Authority* [1991] 2 Med LR 249. A solicitor does not abdicate his professional responsibility when he seeks the advice of counsel. He must apply his mind to the advice received. But the more specialist the nature of the advice, the more reasonable is it likely to be for a solicitor to accept it and act on it.

THREATS TO APPLY FOR WASTED COSTS ORDERS

We entirely agree with the view expressed by this court in *Orchard v South Eastern Electricity Board* [1987] 1 All ER 95, [1987] QB 565, that the threat of proposed applications should not be used as a means of intimidation. On the other hand, if one side considers that the conduct of the other is improper, unreasonable or negligent and likely to cause a waste of costs we do not consider it objectionable to alert the other side to that view; the other side can then consider its position and perhaps mend its ways. Drawing the distinction between unacceptable intimidation and acceptable notice must depend on the professional judgment of those involved. [8]

---

8   Supra note 4 at pp 854E-857B; 860J-861F: 863A-864D.

Notes

1. Underlying the judgment is the English rule that costs will usually follow the event, ie be paid by the loser. This is thought likely to deter litigation that is not well grounded. Two exceptions to that general rule are plaintiffs who are legally aided (against whom costs can generally not be recovered) and plaintiffs who are insolvent. All the applications in this case fell into one or other of these two categories. As to the former, see chapter 10. Another case is where the litigation is being paid for by a third party: See the article 'Lawyers Ethics, Settlement Negotiations and the Maintainers Liability for Costs: Cases in Search of a Principle' [1997] LMCLQ 156 at p 00 an extract from which is set out in chapter 8.

2. In a number of recent cases, judges have suggested that it is a breach of the lawyer's duty to the court to argue points which are of little merit. Thus Lord Templeman has said that

> It is the duty of counsel to assist the judge by simplification and concentration and not to advance a multitude of ingenious arguments in the hope that out of ten bad points the judge will be capable of fashioning a winner. In nearly all cases, the procedure works perfectly well. But there has been a tendency in some cases for legal advisers, pressed by their clients, to make every conceivable argument without judgment or discrimination.[9]

Similarly a senior appellate court in Canada has commented that

> Counsels' duty is to do right by their clients and right by the court... In this context, 'right' includes taking all points deserving of consideration and not taking points not so deserving. The reason is simple. Counsels must assist the court in doing justice according to law.[10]

3. By far the most ambitious attempt to regulate lawyers' behaviour by means of institutional sanctions was contained in the new approach to Civil Procedure emerging from the Woolf Report. Many of Lord Woolf's proposals were put into effect with the coming into force of the new Rules of Civil Procedure in April 1999. The implications of these reforms for lawyers ethics are considered in chapter 10.

4. The new Rules of Civil Procedure contained provisions partially abrogating privilege in wasted costs applications but these provisions were declared ultra vires in the case of *General Medical Holdings v R M Patel and K K R Patel*[11] which is considered in chapter 7.

---

9   *Ashmore v Corp of Lloyds* [1992] 1 WLR 446 at p 453 cited in Ipp supra note 20 at p 100.
10 The British Columbia Court of Appeal in *Lougheed Enterprises Ltd* v *Armbruster* (1992) 63 BCLR (2d) 317 at 324-325.
11 [1999] 3 All ER 673, QBD.

Questions

1. To what extent is the court's approach to wasted costs orders influenced by the difficulties identified by Wilkins with institutional sanctions? Is the court's response satisfactory? Would its' response have been improved by considering the insights of Wilkins contextual approach?

2. Upon what basis is a lawyer supposed to decide whether proposed litigation is an abuse of the process of court? Is s 51(6) apt to regulate lawyers who bring such litigation? Consider the impact of the Master of the Rolls' comments concerning privilege.

3. Is the assertion of a duty to argue only 'deserving points' consistent with Lord Bingham's comments in *Ridelhalgh* on hopeless cases? Which approach do you think is likely to be more common in the current climate? What are the implications of these different judicial attitudes for lawyers' ethics?

4. Your client is Paula, a 21-year-old girl, who was until recently employed by Professor Smith as a research assistant/secretary. Last year, Professor Smith dismissed Paula saying she was incompetent. Paula claims that the dismissal was based on racial discrimination (Paula is of Afro-Caribbean ethnic origin) and wishes to make a claim against Professor Smith in an industrial tribunal. You have reviewed the evidence and you think Paula's case is very weak. However, Paula says that she is confident Professor Smith will cave in because he is about to resign his chair and stand for election to Parliament as a Labour MP. Any adverse publicity would seriously damage his chances. You know too that industrial tribunals award costs against unsuccessful applicants only in the case of applications which it considers to be abusive. Paula is being backed by her wealthy parents.

Should you bring the claim? What are the ethical considerations which arise? It has been said that if able lawyers are given long enough and paid enough money there is no such thing as a hopeless case. Would this tendency to rationalise be usefully checked if lawyers considering whether a claim amounted to an abuse of the process of court were to ask themselves if they would consider doing the case pro bono?

5. Your client Mr Ali is a recent immigrant to the UK. Two years ago, he started a small stationary business and obtained an order from August Ltd a nationwide chain of newsagents and stationers. Mr Ali's terms of business require payment within 30 days of delivery. Mr Ali complains to you that August like many large businesses has a practice of paying at least three months in arrears. Any complaints are met with allegations about the quality of the goods supplied which he regards as spurious. Mr Ali is fed up with what he regards as duplicity and intends to close his business. However as a matter of principle he wants prompt payment of the debts he is owed and asks for your advice. You know that the issue of proceedings in the county court

would be met by a counterclaim which would significantly delay payment. An alternative however is to issue a creditor's winding up petition in the Companies Court, a procedure designed to begin the winding up of insolvent companies which requires only that you as solicitor swear an affidavit asserting that a debt is due and unpaid for the statutory period. August is of course solvent and would ultimately succeed in having the petition dismissed. However the issuing of the petition would trigger various provisions of insolvency law which would have the effect of paralysing August's business. In addition, it would generate much adverse publicity. Should you issue the petition? [12]

Who should regulate the lawyers – the independence of lawyers

There are important questions about who is to formulate and enforce the norms governing lawyers' behaviour which are distinct from the question of process. For example we might agree that disciplinary proceedings have particular virtues as a regulatory tool but disagree about whether the applicable norms should be formulated and enforced primarily by lawyers, by government or by laymen. Similarly when the Legal Aid Board took over the administration of the legal aid scheme from the Law Society in 1988, many processes and rules remained the same. What changed was the identity of those enforcing them. For much of the 20th century, the English legal profession maintained a dominant influence over all the regulatory processes. This is most obvious with respect to disciplinary processes; the rules of professional conduct governing lawyers have been drawn up and enforced by lawyers. Less obviously, most liability rules are formulated and applied by ex barristers and solicitors (ie judges) through a process access to which is in the hands of the legal profession. Institutional sanctions are similarly lawyer dominated and, as noted, till 1988 the administration of the legal aid fund was in the hands of the Law Society.

It is often argued that the regulatory processes, particularly disciplinary mechanism, should be controlled by the professions in order to preserve the *independence* of the legal profession. However, as Wilkins points out, the independence required of lawyers is not solely a matter of independence from the state. In the case of criminal defendants menaced by the overbearing power of the state, professional independence does indeed mean independence from the State and loyalty to the client. However, in the case of very powerful clients, professional independence may require not loyalty to the client but loyalty to the legal system so as to enable the lawyer to resist client pressure to subvert the purposes of the legal system.[13]

In the UK however, the notion of an independent profession is usually understood in terms of independence from the state. This in turn is felt to be crucial to the maintenance of the rule of law within a liberal democracy. The depth of concern about this was illustrated when in 1989 the Thatcher government published its Green Paper,

---

12   See *Re a Company* [1996] 2 BCLC 49 (Hoffman J).
13   See further chapter 1 supra, text to p 5, notes 8 and 9.

'The Work and Organisation of the Legal Profession'[14], containing a proposal that the Lord Chancellors Department should take responsibility for formulating the professions' rules of professional conduct. This provoked an unprecedented outcry from the legal profession with the professional bodies and the judiciary warning that the idea carried grave constitutional dangers[15].

The case for self-regulation has always depended on the assumption that the professional bodies would be able to distinguish between the public interest and the interests of the professions. Beginning in the 1970s, this position has been the subject of growing criticism from consumer organisations, from radical critics and latterly from government. One source of dissatisfaction has been the alleged leniency with which the professional bodies respond to those of its members found guilty of professional misconduct. One study found that the Solicitors Disciplinary Tribunal persistently refused to characterise as dishonest the knowing transfer of a client's money from the solicitor's client account to the office account. Consequently, of 200 solicitors found guilty of transferring clients' money in this way, only 47% were struck off.[16] Another study found that the Office for the Supervision of Solicitors was regularly failing to recognise and investigate clear allegations of misconduct contained in clients' complaints.[17] One early result of the dissatisfaction was the setting up under the Courts and Legal Services Act 1990 of the office of Legal Services Ombudsman (The 'LSO'). The LSO is charged with general oversight of the profession's complaints and disciplinary procedures. In addition, clients who feel that their complaints have not been dealt with satisfactorily by the professional bodies can ask for their cases to be reviewed by the LSO, who has power to recommend the payment of compensation.

Public dissatisfaction has continued to grow. It has been particularly marked with regard to the professional bodies handling of complaints about inadequate service. In April 1996, a survey of 2,246 complainants carried out by the Law Society[18] showed that two thirds of those surveyed whose complaints had been dealt with by the SCB were 'very dissatisfied' with SCB's treatment of their complaint. The LSO was later to comment that :

> While only an optimist would expect most complaints about solicitors to be settled in favour of the complainant, it would be reasonable to expect that no more than 50% would remain 'very dissatisfied'. When two-thirds do so, it is clear evidence that something is fundamentally wrong.[19]

---

14   *The Work and Organization of the Legal Profession* (Cmnd 570) (London, HMSO 1989).
15   See M Zander 'The Thatcher Government's Onslaught on the Lawyers: Who Won?' [1990] 24 The International Lawyer 753.
16   See M Zander 'The talk is tough' (1998) Law Society Gazette, 5 December: of the others 19% were suspended and 34% were merely fined. For further expressions of dissatisfaction with undue leniency towards solicitors guilty of misconduct see generally *Sixth Report of the Legal Services Ombudsman* (London, HMSO, 1997) at paras 3.8 and 3.15-3.21.
17   See R Moorhead, A Sherr and S Rogers 'Willing Blindness? OSS Complaints Handling Procedures' (Law Society Research Paper No 37) (London, Law Society, 1999).
18   *Complaints against Solicitors: the complainants view* (London, Law Society, 1996).
19   *Fifth Report of the Legal Services Ombudsman* (London, HMSO, 1996) at para 3.3.

As a consequence of the perceived dissatisfaction, the SCB was replaced in the autumn of 1996 by the Office for the Supervision of Solicitors at which time the Bar also introduced a new complaints procedure. The LSO commented that these new arrangements must be regarded as the last chance for self-regulation of the English legal profession.[20] For solicitors, a major feature of the new arrangements was the composition of the adjudicatory bodies. Allegations of misconduct continued to be referred for adjudication by the Solicitors Disciplinary Tribunal which sits in panels of three, consisting of two solicitors and one lay person. However the new arrangements were different in their treatment of clients' complaints about inadequate professional service. If the client is dissatisfied with the first instance decision of the OSS official s/he may ask for it to be considered by panel having a lay majority and a lay chairperson.

At the same time, the Bar also implemented a new complaints procedure. The most common complaint about the previous procedure was that it could not offer complainants any compensation. In September 1994, the Bar's own Standards Review Body under Lord Alexander recommended the setting up of a complaints procedure with power to award compensation of up to £2,000 and/or to direct that fees be reduced. These proposals were however substantially watered down by a Bar Council Working Party. There was also opposition from the Criminal Bar which feared a flood of complaints from clients they had unsuccessfully defended. The LSO regarded this as an unreal fear since complaints rarely succeeded before him in criminal cases. Nevertheless, the Bar Council agreed in response that compensation would only be payable where actual financial loss was caused and where the inadequate professional service fell 'significantly' below the standard to be expected of a reasonably competent barrister. Even so, the new scheme was rejected by at an open meeting of members in November 1995 and was only passed after the Bar Council called a postal ballot. The LSO called this 'extremely disappointing' [1] and questioned whether the scheme was worth having at all. The Bar's procedure is in striking contrast to the new arrangements at the OSS with regard to lay involvement. The Bar's process is overseen by a Complaints Commissioner (who cannot be a barrister, solicitor or judge) appointed by the Bar Council. However, complaints about inadequate professional service are dealt with by an Adjudication Panel consisting of the Commissioner (as Chair) two barristers (including one QC) and one lay person. There is no casting vote and consequently the barrister members have a veto. When the LSO raised this with the Bar Council they said that it would not be palatable for panels with a lay majority to determine compensation levels or reduce fees.[2]

As the new millennium dawned, the professions' complaints handling procedures remained very much on trial. By 1998, the LSO was optimistic that the OSS had 'laid the foundations'[3] of an effective complaints handling system. However it still had 'some

20   Supra at para 3.7.
1   Supra para 4.32.
2   *Sixth Report* of the Legal Services Ombudsman (London, HMSO, 1997) para 3.24.
3   *Seventh Annual Report of the Legal Services Ombudsman* (London, HMSO, 1998) p.13.

way to go' not least because the volume of complaints was continuing to grow rapidly,[4] leading to significant delays. By 1999, the LSO had seen complaints handling at the OSS 'spiral out of control'[5]. The operation by solicitors of effective in-house complaints procedures has been perceived as the only solution. However, solicitors have been slow to respond to a practice rule requiring them to put such procedures in place and the LSO 'remain(s) sceptical that the Law Society has the commitment and the determination to do what is necessary to put its own house in order.'[6] The LSO has also expressed disappointment with the performance of the Bar's procedures. By 1999, only two complainants had been awarded compensation and one third of complainants were sufficiently dissatisfied with the process to refer the matter subsequently to the Legal Services Ombudsman.[7] The LSO's dissatisfaction is clearly shared by government. Sections 51-52 of the Access to Justice Act allows the Lord Chancellor to appoint a non-lawyer Legal Services Complaints Commissioner with statutory power to regulate the professions' complaints handling procedures. If they fail to meet specified complaints handling targets, they may be fined. These powers could clearly be exercised in a way which would make self-regulation merely nominal.

It is not only the professions' power to *enforce* the rules of conduct which has been questioned Their role in *formulating* their own rules of conduct has also come under pressure. We have already seen that the 1989 Green Paper originally proposed to transfer the primary responsibility for formulating codes of conduct from the professional bodies to the Lord Chancellor. Concern about the constitutional implications forced Lord Mackay to retreat. The retreat was however only partial. The Courts and Legal Services Act 1990 validated the professions' existing rules of conduct. Nevertheless, the guiding principle of the Courts and Legal Services Act was the need to expand the range of legal service providers particularly in relation to advocacy. Consequently, it was provided that any new rules of conduct which were likely to impact upon rights of audience were to require the consent of the Lord Chancellor and a committee of senior judges each of whom had a power of veto. In addition, when formulating such rules, the professions were required to seek the advice of the Lord Chancellors Advisory Committee on Legal Education and Conduct (ACLEC) an advisory body with a lay majority.[8] In this way, laymen were given a formal role in the formulation of rules of conduct for the first time.

4   In 1998, complaints to the OSS increased by 30%. In 1992, there were just under 20,000 complaints. By 1998 the figure had risen to 30,000. See Mary Seneviratne *The Legal Profession: Regulation and the Consumer* (London, Sweet and Maxwell) pp 138,159.

5   *Eighth Annual Report of the Legal Services Ombudsman* (London, HMSO, 1999) p 2. For a damning report on the competence of the OSS see Moorhead, Sherr and Rogers *Willing Blindness? OSS Complaints Handling Procedures* Law Society Research Study No 37 (Law Society, London, 1999).

6   Ibid at p 2.

7   *Seventh Report* supra note 3 at p 19. In the following year, the investigation of 638 cases led to only one payment of compensation. *Eighth Report* (supra note 44) p 21.

8   CLSA, s 19. The occupations of the first members were Law Lord (Lord Griffiths, the Chair); circuit judge; two solicitors; two QCs; law centre worker; Vice-President of Magistrates Association; director of legal services of an insurance company; head of polytechnic law school; Oxford college head (former law professor);head of London probation service; Director of National Council of Voluntary Organisations; Controller of BBC Northern Ireland; director of insurance brokers firm.

The new framework did not however produce the expansion in rights of audience desired by successive governments. By 1998, the Law Society had gained the right to grant rights of audience in the higher courts to solicitors completing the prescribed training but only 624 out of 70,000 solicitors had qualified.[9] A particular sticking point was the question of whether employed lawyers[10], whether solicitors or barristers, should be able to exercise rights of audience. A majority of ACLEC and the Bar was particularly opposed to the granting rights of audience to the Crown Prosecution Service and other government lawyers. It was feared that these lawyers would be under such pressure from their employers that they would be unable to fulfil their duties to the court, ie that they lacked professional independence.

This opposition was almost entirely successful, much to the annoyance of Lord Irvine. Consequently, the Access to Justice Act 1999 radically altered the procedures for granting rights of audience and reviewing related rules of conduct. Henceforth the ultimate decision on these issues was to be made by the Lord Chancellor in some cases following the receipt of advice from the new Legal Services Consultative Panel[11] and the Director General of Fair Trading. However, the veto formerly enjoyed by the judges under the Courts and Legal Services Act was removed. The judiciary thus lost their right to decide who should appear as advocates before them. As for the professional bodies, they were forbidden to discriminate in their rules of conduct against employed lawyers[12]. The most radical change of all however was the Lord Chancellor's new power to review any rules of conduct which might be obstructing the extension of rights of audience. After taking the advice of the senior judges, the LSCP and the DGFT, the Lord Chancellor may replace with new rules those provisions he deems to be unacceptably restrictive of rights of audience.[13]

Questions

1. Are the new arrangements for the approval of rights of audience and related rules of conduct an unacceptable restriction on the independence of the legal profession?

2. Are employed lawyers more likely than private practitioners to breach their duties to the legal system when acting as advocates because they lack independence?

---

9   See *Rights of Audience and Rights to Conduct Litigation in England and Wales: The Way Ahead* (LCD Consultation Paper July 1998) para 1.11.

10   Ie a solicitor employed by a non-solicitor or a barrister in any form of employment as opposed to practising as a self-employed professional.

11   This body was created by s 18A of the Courts and Legal Services Act 1990 (inserted by s 35 of the Access to Justice Act 1999) to replace ACLEC. Its remit was seen as essentially that of advising the Lord Chancellor rather that acting as in independent agent in the policy-making process.

12   Access to Justice Act 1999, ss 37 and 38.

13   See ss 17-24 and Sch 4 to the Courts and Legal Services Act 1990 (inserted by s 24 of the Access to Justice Act 1999). This power is exercisable by statutory instrument subject to any negative resolution of the House of Commons: See s 25 of the Access to Justice Act 1999.

2   Legal education

History and context

ACADEMIC LEGAL EDUCATION

In 1996, the Lord Chancellor's Advisory Committee on Legal Education and Conduct[14] conducted a review of legal education in England and Wales. One of the most striking features of the report was the repeated insistence that one of the central goals at every stage of legal education should be to inculcate 'legal values' meaning 'a commitment to the rule of law, to justice, fairness and *high ethical standards* (emphasis added).'[15] In particular, academic[16] law schools were invited to begin to study professional ethics, the implication being that this was something they had previously neglected.[17] This neglect was a consequence of a historically based and artificial division between academic and professional legal education. With respect to undergraduate legal education, the verdict is contained in Professor Birks comment that

> there is extraordinarily little knowledge in the (university) law school system about civil and criminal procedure or about all matters relating to legal practice, *including professional ethics*...the general neglect of the subjects assigned to the vocational phase casts a shadow over the great achievements of the university law schools in the rest of the field.[18] [emphasis added]

It is symptomatic of this neglect that UK academics have only recently began to publish in this field.[19] Consequently, the norms of professional ethics have developed without the benefit academic scrutiny. In the USA, by contrast, the deliberations of the Kutak Commission as it began to formulate the Model Rules of Professional Conduct attracted enormous academic interest.[20] It is significant that the Society of Public

14   See The Lord Chancellors Advisory Committee on Legal Education and Conduct consultation papers, the *Initial Stage* (June 1994) (*'The First Consultation Paper'*) and *The Vocational Stage and Continuing Professional Development* (June 1995) (*'The Second Consultation Paper'*) and its subsequent *First Report on Legal Education and Training* (April 1996) (*The Report*).

15   *Report* ibid para 2.4.

16   The phrase 'academic law teachers' is used here to indicate a subset of law teachers whose principal characteristics are a preoccupation with teaching undergraduate and postgraduate degrees in law, and with research. These teacher are interested in abstract theoretical rather than applied knowledge. They are to be contrasted with 'vocational law teachers' whose principal interest is in applied rather than theoretical knowledge. This definition expresses certain key features of the development of legal education in the UK between following the report of the Ormrod Committee in 1971 (*Report of the Committee on Legal Education*, 1971, Cmnd 4594). Moreover, it also corresponds with what ACLEC seems to have in mind when it speaks about university law teachers. It does not, however, assume that this is a desirable picture nor that it is unchanging.

17   *Report* Supra notes 5 para 2.11.

18   'Reviewing Legal Education' in P B H Birks (ed) (Oxford, OUP, 1994) chapter 3 at p 20. Cf *ACLEC Report* note 4 supra at para 2.11.

19   See for example Ross Cranston (ed), *Legal Ethics and Professional Responsibility* (Oxford, OUP, 1995); A Boon and J Levin *The Ethics and Conduct of Lawyers in England and Wales* (Oxford, Hart, 1999); D Nicholson and J Webb *Professional Legal Ethics Critical Interrogations* (Oxford, OUP, 1999).

20   Contrast 'A Gathering of Scholars to Discuss "Professional Responsibility and the Model Rules of Professional Conduct"' [1981] 35 *U Miami L Rev* 639.

Teachers of Law, one of the major professional associations for law teachers, whose members meet in specialised subject groups for scholarly discussion during the society's annual conference only got around to forming a subgroup on legal ethics and the professions in 1994.

VOCATIONAL LEGAL EDUCATION

In the late 1980s, vocational education at the Inns of Court School of Law and at the College of law was revolutionised. The end product was in each case a new name (The 'Bar Vocational Course' for barristers and 'Legal Practice Course' for solicitors) and more fundamentally, a revolutionary skills-based approach. These courses have as their focus the development through practice and testing of skills such as interviewing, drafting, advising, fact management and advocacy. Knowledge of and/or research into substantive law is the prerequisite for participation in simulated practice through which the skills are developed. As far as legal ethics is concerned, the new approach has involved a short introductory course setting out the ethical framework provided by the Codes, reinforced by the weaving of ethical issues into the skills exercises.

This approach has both strengths and weaknesses. The contextualising of ethical issues within simulated practice is clearly positive, making the relevance of any discussion of the issues clear to students. This ensures that the ethical frameworks developing within students take account of the real world of legal practice. The Bar Vocational Course has been greeted enthusiastically by the consumers,[1] though evaluative studies have not specifically considered ethical issues. Nevertheless, it is striking that a 1985-1986 review of the British Columbia Legal Professional Training Course (with which the BVC and the LPC have much in common) found 83% of students to be either satisfied or very satisfied with the manner in which the course dealt with professional responsibility issues.[2]

There are however two matters of concern. The first is quite simply that students engaged in the resolution of highly contextual realistic ethical problems will inevitably bring to these tasks a set of theoretical or ideological spectacles. Ideally, the academic stage of legal education ought to be concerned with the critical examination of these frameworks in the light of available data and possible alternatives. However, the neglect by UK academic lawyers of legal ethics is likely to mean that students enter vocational education with an ethical framework which, whatever its origins, owes little to the process of critical examination which is supposed to be the main virtue of academic legal education. In this sense, academic law teachers may be failing vocational law teachers.

1   See J Shapland et al *Studying for the Bar: the students evaluation of the new vocational training course at the Council of Legal Education* (Sheffield, Institute for the Study of Legal Practice, 1988).

2   *Law Society of British Canada: Curriculum Subcommittee Report on PLTC* (Cameron Committee Report 1986) Appendix 1, cited in W Brent Cotter *Professional Responsibility Instruction in Canada: A Coordinated Curriculum of Legal Education* (Federation of Law Societies of Canada, 1992) at para 6.33.

The second point is perhaps more controversial. In its Second Consultation Paper ACLEC expressed a concern that vocational legal education was perhaps too skills-orientated and lacked intellectual rigour.[3] This observation clearly provoked strong disagreement from vocational law teachers, forcing ACLEC into a hasty retreat in its subsequent report.[4] Despite this, it seems undeniable that skills-based teaching is very labour intensive and time consuming.[5] It must follow that students are unlikely to have much time for critical reflection upon the ethical premises underlying the skills they are being taught. There is therefore a danger that skills teachers will pass on implicit unexamined ethical frameworks. These frameworks will be absorbed by students lacking either the time or awareness of alternatives necessary to challenge them. More generally, it can be said that the skills movement draws heavily upon an Aristotelian moral epistemology. The ethical practitioner is one who has developed dispositions to ethical behaviour through imitation of his peers. Only after developing the necessary dispositions through practice is she in a position to give them rational exposition. The problem as Aristotle recognised is that one may be so well trained in bad habits as to become incapable of knowing better. If, as many think, the current mores of the legal profession leave much to be desired, this is profoundly worrying.[6]

A graphic illustration of the problem is found in the third edition of *Learning Lawyers Skills*[7] by Professor Philip Jones, Director of the University of Sheffield Legal Practice Course and one of the leading figures in the movement towards skills-based education. The text has much to commend it. It engages for example with the extensive US theoretical literature and an attempt is made[8] to contextualise the discussion by drawing on Professor Hazel Genn's work[9] on the negotiation of settlements to personal injury actions.

However, the choice between different methods of negotiating is presented almost exclusively in terms of effectiveness in achieving client goals.[10] Hence the writer emphasises empirical research 'proving' that competitive negotiators are unlikely to conduct successful negotiations[11] as an argument in favour of a co-operative approach. However, the only limits on behaviour are described as being 'voluntary and self-imposed'[12] for 'at the heart of negotiation there will always be opportunistic interaction

3   *Second Consultation Paper* supra note 14 at paras 3.10 and 5.8.
4   See *Report* supra note 14 paras 2.3 and 6.5.
5   Consider for example the tight time frame prescribed for the negotiations exercises used by the New Zealand Institute of Professional Legal Studies described in chapter 7 of Twining Mackie and Gold (eds) *Learning Lawyers Skills* (London, Butterworths, 1989).
6   See generally David Luban 'Epistemology and Moral Education' 33 Journal of Legal Education (1983) 636.
7   Philip A Jones (ed) (London, Blackstone Press, 1995, 3rd ed). The book is now is its 8th edition and Professor Jones is no longer one of the authors. The chapter on negotiation has now been substantially rewritten so as to deal with some of the objections I have put forward.
8   Ibid p 170 at para 24.3.1.
9   H Genn *Hard Bargaining: Out of Court Settlements in Personal Injury Actions*, (Oxford, Clarendon Press, 1987).
10   Supra note 9 p 173 at para 24.3, p 177 at para 24.4.
11   Ibid, p 170-1.
12   Ibid, p 163 at para 23.3.3.

– less than fully open motives and methods, self-interested manoeuvres.'[13] Ultimately the goals of the client seem likely to be treated as decisive.[14] This seems to accord minimal significance to paragraph 17.01 of the LSGPC which provides that

> Solicitors must not act, whether in their professional capacity or otherwise, towards anyone in a way which is fraudulent, deceitful or otherwise contrary to their position as solicitors. Nor must solicitors use their position to take unfair advantage either for themselves or another person.[15]

What matters here is not what one thinks of the approach being recommended, for there are ethical frameworks which can be called into service in its defence[16]. However there are alternative approaches which provide criteria for choosing between co-operative and competitive approaches to bargaining on grounds other than client choice[17]. The problem is that the alternatives are simply not being considered with the consequence that students are likely to accept the proffered framework in an undiscriminating manner. This unhelpful approach to professional ethics reaches its height at the end of chapter 27 where the author gives detailed guidance to the competitive negotiator on the use of threats, feigned displays of anger and evasive responses to questions before concluding

> You should never lie and you have a professional duty to act with complete frankness and good faith consistent with your overriding duty to your client. (Solicitors Practice Rules 1990, principle 16.01.)[18]

It is true that the principle cited seems itself to be guilty of self-contradiction (what if frankness is not in the interests of the client?) But it is nevertheless remarkable that no attempt is made to make sense of what is clearly intended to be a limit of some kind on what lawyers may legitimately do for their clients. At the turn of the millennium, the teaching of legal ethics seems to represent a clear example of the unhelpful disjuncture between academic and professional legal education which ACLEC was keen to end.

Academic legal education and legal ethics: possibilities and problems

If academic law schools have historically neglected legal ethics but are now to begin paying attention, there arises the question of what should be done and of their likely impact on the ethical standards of graduates. On any view, their impact is likely to be limited by the prior effect of upbringing and early education and by the subsequent impact of professional culture. Nevertheless, their positive potential can be encapsulated

---

13   Ibid, p 177 at para 24.4.
14   Ibid, p 175 at para 24.3.3.
15   *The Guide to the Professional Conduct of Solicitors* (London, Law Society, 8th ed, 1999) para 17.01.
16   See for example James J White 'Machiavelli and the Bar: Ethical Limits on Lying in Negotiations' [1980] American Bar Foundations Res Journal 926.
17   William H Simon, 'Ethical Discretion in Lawyering' [1980] 101 HLR 1083.
18   Para 27.3 at pp 195-196. The relevant paragraph is now para 19.01 of the 8th (1999) edition of the Guide.

within the notions of perspective and independence. However, as we begin to examine these notions we shall see that the impact of legal education on legal ethics may be problematic.

PERSPECTIVE

It is often said that most things in life look very different according to the perspective from which and the context in which they are viewed. So it is also with the problems of professional life. This is true of 'Standard conception of legal ethics'[19] which is considered further in chapter 5. On this view, lawyers are obliged in their professional lives to promote the interests of their clients regardless of the impact upon third parties and/or the legal system. They should disregard their own views of the merits of the client's case, the only limit on their conduct being that they should not break the law. This approach is most plausible if we assume the typical law job to be the litigation of a point of law in an appellate court, where it is the job of the bench to come to the correct conclusion assisted by the partisan arguments of opposing counsel. However, it is a fact that only a tiny proportion of litigated cases result in trials, let alone appeals. Most are settled and it is relatively easy to demonstrate that in settlement negotiations the outcome is influenced not only by the merits but inter alia by the way the law distributes liability for costs.[20] Thus a legally-aided plaintiff in a personal injury action, whose opponent is unlikely to be able to recover costs even in the event of success, is in a much stronger position than a privately paying plaintiff, regardless of the merits of the case. Considerations such as these have profound implications for lawyers' ethics. Nor is it difficult to bring them to students' attention. To put the matter another way, the acquisition of more information about an ethical difficulty may lead to an ethical judgment being changed if it can be shown to be based on a false factual premise. For example strict confidentiality obligations are usually justified on the grounds that they are necessary to engender in clients the candour necessary for effective representation. Such arguments are vulnerable to empirical demonstrations that in many cultures at different points in history professionals of all kinds have effectively represented clients without the benefit of sweeping confidentiality provisions.[1] Consequently, the comparative perspective which is most likely to be involved during initial stage legal education and which was cited by ACLEC as one of the five pillars of undergraduate legal education has significant potential as a tool for ethical education.

19   The 'standard conception of lawyer's ethics' is usually thought to contain: i) the principle of neutral partisanship requiring the lawyer do everything in his clients interests provided only that it be neither technically illegal or a clear breach of an ethical rule and ii) a principle of non accountability whereby the lawyer shifts to the client moral responsibility for any harm caused by conduct required by the first principle. The standard conception was first formulated in this way in the work of William H Simon. See 'The Ideology of the Advocacy System: Procedural Justice and Professional Ethics', [1978] *Wisconsin LR* 36.
20   See chapter 8 and Paula's case (supra p 110).
1   Deborah L Rhode 'Ethical Perspectives on Legal Practice' [1985] 37 Stan L Rev 589, 614 .

INDEPENDENCE

It is often said to be one of the virtues of higher education that it can develop in its' students the capacity for independent ethical judgment. In principle, this capacity can be developed in any legal subject provided that students are encouraged to go beyond understanding and applying the current law to a critical evaluation of whether it ought to be different. This capacity is of crucial importance for legal ethics because, as Northrop suggests, 'there are lawyers, judges and even law professors who tell us they have no legal philosophy. In law, as in other things,... the only difference between a person without a philosophy and someone with a philosophy is that the latter knows what his philosophy is.'[2] Therefore law graduates will inevitably emerge from degree level legal education with a theory of legal ethics. The theory may be caught from teachers. If for three years students are taught to explore the limits of the substantive law without any suggestion that there may be other limits on what lawyers may do for their clients, then students will be hearing the implicit message that the lawyer's job is that of the skilled technician exploiting the law to the client's best advantage[3]. In any case, those who go on to practice will quickly find themselves being trained by more senior lawyers, each of whom will have his or her theory of legal ethics. This makes it vital that the adoption of frameworks for legal ethics be conscious and critical. There is considerable evidence from the field of moral psychology, stemming principally from the work of Lawrence Kohlberg, that formal educational processes are effective in developing this capacity for independent judgment: studies of American high school students demonstrate that those who go to College show considerable development in their capacity for moral judgment as compared with their peers who choose not to do so.[4]

Whilst this would seem to represent an optimistic picture, there are some serious underlying difficulties. The more mundane one is that law teaching in the UK has been strongly influenced by legal positivism, ie the view that the describing and evaluating of the law are two fundamentally different things. Whilst many of the leading jurisprudential exponents of legal positivism have been concerned to describe the law as a preliminary to evaluating it, it is not clear that their disciples have always gone on to the second stage. More seriously, the whole notion of independent judgment is a debatable one: the Kohlbergian conception of independent judgment involves as one commentator has put it the belief that

ethical reasoning is conceptually autonomous from more conventionally held beliefs, affording an impartial point of view from which people rise above and critically assess

---

2   F Northrop *The Complexity of Legal and Ethical Experience* (1959) at p 6, cited by Twining and MacCormick in 'Theory in the Law Curriculum' chapter 13 in W Twining (ed) *Legal Theory and the Common Law* (Basil Blackwell, Oxford, 1986).

3   Carrie J Menkel-Meadow 'Can a Law Teacher Avoid Teaching Legal Ethics?' [1991] 41 Journal of Legal Education 3.

4   J D Rest 'Can Ethics Be Taught In Professional Schools? The Psychological Research' [1988] 1 Ethics Easier Said than Done 22.

the ethical validity of the beliefs of their state, society, ethnic or religious or racial group.[5]

A number of criticisms can be made. Feminists point to Kohlberg's finding that girls do not generally proceed as far along the scale as boys and suggest that Kohlberg has assumed the superiority of a particularly masculine way of responding to ethical problems. Most importantly, Kohlberg's conception of moral development makes two crucial assumptions: the first is that the only moral judgments which are valid are those which emerge from rational reflection uninfluenced by the community of which the analyst is part. The second is that such a process is capable of producing such universal principles. A critic might point out that this approach to ethics is itself the product of an intellectual consensus which took root only in the 18th century. Prior to that, at least in Christian Western Europe, the starting point for ethics was divine revelation through the Bible. Even at the end of the 20th century, these presuppositions about ethical reasoning would be fiercely disputed by thinkers from traditional Islamic cultures. The fear then is that whilst apparently liberating students from culturally determined ethical standpoints, higher education which conforms to Kohlbergian assumptions may do no more than relocate students within a different ethical community. Alternatively, if as critics like Arthur Leff suggest, the second assumption does not hold it may relocate students within an intellectual tradition which, frustrated in the search for rationally grounded universally valid statements of right and wrong becomes characterised by ethical scepticism rather than by conviction. Put at its simplest, if the evaluate tools are flawed the law teacher who teaches from within the positivist tradition may have good grounds for being reluctant to view the teaching of substantive law as an opportunity to develop independent ethical judgment.

CYNICAL LEGAL STUDIES

A disturbing challenge to the idea that academic legal education can contribute to the moral development of its students is the observation of a leading UK law teacher that legal education is often an exercise in 'Cynical Legal Studies'. Kim Economides argues[6] that the law students of the new millennium are more cynical than their more radical predecessors. This is in part due to wider social developments. Legal Aid and other sources of income for those seeking to serve the disadvantaged are ever thinner on the ground. Student debt is increasing. However, Economides argues that increased cynicism is also due in part to legal education itself. In his view, the causes of the 'Law School effect' are positivism ('law taught as a series of techniques rather than values'); the failure of radical critics to offer a positive agenda and an alleged prioritisation on the part of law schools of practice above scholarship. This admittedly personal and impressionistic account is echoed by a body of evidence from the US that many law

---

5   D Richard 'Moral Theory, The Developmental Psychology of Ethical Autonomy and Professionalism' [1981] 31 Journal of Legal Education 359 at p 365.

6   K Economides 'Cynical Legal Studies' chapter 2 of *Educating for Justice: Social Values and Legal Education* (Cooper and Trubeck eds, Aldershot, Ashgate, 1997).

students begin their studies with a commitment to public interest lawyering[7] but that this commitment is eroded during their time in law school. In the following extract, Adrienne Stone[8] considers some of accounts of law school given by students and seeks to explain this phenomenon.

> Students almost uniformly refer to the first year of law school as a difficult time. The causes of stress and tension in first year are well known (workload, Socratic method, competition between students, relocation of many students, tension in personal relations which result from separation or time spent at law school and studying) and they need not be recited in detail here. What is important to understand is that the first year of law school may wear students down in a way which affects the commitments with which they came to law school. The following comments, from Robert Stover's[9] study of the University of Denver and the panel discussion I conducted with a colleague at Columbia University, give some of the flavour of the first year experience.
>
> At the University of Denver in 1974:
>
> > The people I talk to at school – I sometimes just have to get away from them because they upset me so much. . . Sometimes I find they shake me – it's not my confidence; the competition I guess will just shake me up.
>
> At Columbia University in 1995:
>
> > It's an incredibly stressful time when you are trying to plough through and keep your head above water . . .
>
> It was not Stover's intention to focus on the experience of women nor, originally, was it mine. But in each case these comments were made by women and they are echoed clearly in major studies of the experience of women at law school. The following comments come from well-known studies of women law students at Yale and the University of Pennsylvania:
>
> At Yale University in 1985:
>
> > Law School consumes a lot of the rest of my life. It's a struggle to stay connected with [my husband] and friends.
>
> At the University of Pennsylvania in 1994:
>
> > Law School is the most bizarre place I have ever been . . . [First year] was like a frightening out of body experience.
>
> > [F]or me the damage is done; it's in me. I will never be the same. I feel so defeated.

---

7   In the US, this term denotes, positively, working for the state or for the disadvantaged and, negatively, not working for powerful corporations.

8   Adrienne Stone 'Women, Law School and Student Commitment to the Public Interest' chapter 4 of *Educating for Justice: Social Values and Legal Education* supra note 6. Much though not all of the empirical evidence supporting Stone's analysis dates from the 1980s. It is not clear to what extent US law schools have adjusted to the critique to which this evidence gave rise.

9   Robert Stover *Making It and Breaking It: The Fate of Public Interest Commitment During Law School* (University of Illinois, 1989).

Each of these comments gives support to the conclusion that 'first year students are so consumed with coping with their immediate environment, that other matters often recede from the forefront of their concerns. In this overwhelmed state, law students do appear to reassess their values. The uncertainty and loss of confidence they suffer causes them to doubt the commitments with which they came to law school. Again, this is evident both in studies of student commitment to the public interest and of women's experience at law school:

At the University of Denver:

> I'm more confused than before. It's more like I just don't think about it [a career helping others] that much. When I first started law school, I had all these ideas about what I wanted to do, and now I just think about coming here and doing the work.

At Columbia:

> Everything you think is being challenged . . . all your old opinions are being devalued. I came to doubt myself extremely in everything and not just the way I analyse a case but also . . . maybe my decision to work in public interest is wrong.

At Yale:

> [Law School] takes a bunch of people who are smart and have goals and opinions and convinces them that if they can't express themselves in a certain way, the goals are illegitimate. The place robs people of their direction and conviction.

At the University of Pennsylvania:

> [W]hatever ideals we came in with they get bashed out of us.

It is not easy, therefore, to deny the effect law school has on students by arguing that they are adults with well-formed ideals and are consequently not susceptible to the transformation law school is claimed to cause. The exhaustion and uncertainty instilled by first year leads students to reassess their views and law school, it seems, plays a role in the reformulation of these ideas....

Stone goes on to suggest that many accounts of the law school experience imply that women feel its demoralising effect most strongly. She then discusses the causes of this effect:

> ....Law teaching has long been recognised as an important factor by those who have studied the transformation of law students. Kennedy's analysis of the depoliticising nature of law teaching[10] ... is not the only critique. Robert Granfield[11] himself argues that legal analysis is partly responsible for the transformation of students which draws them away from public interest work. He focussed on three features of legal education: learning to justify opinions on 'legal grounds as opposed to ideological or substantive ones'; the ability to distinguish apparently similar cases and to draw parallels between apparently dissimilar cases and so discover a logical thread running through the law;

10   Duncan Kennedy 'Legal Education and the Reproduction of Hierarchy' 32 (1982) Journal of Legal Education 591.
11   Robert Granfield *The Making of Elite Lawyers: Visions of Harvard and Beyond.*

and the ability to argue for apparently opposing positions. These techniques dominate legal education because both students and faculty participate in establishing boundaries of acceptable argument, excluding the ideological and the emotional. Immersed in this intellectual culture, Granfield argues, 'students internalised a perspective of detached cynicism' and as a result become detached from the study of law and, importantly, do not look at involvement in the law as a way of achieving social justice.

It is important not to overstate these critiques and to appreciate that contemporary legal education has some value. First, there has been some response in legal education and law teaching to these kinds of critiques. I have already indicated my scepticism at the accuracy of the claim that law is commonly taught as if it were entirely separate from 'policy' and I am also sceptical that law is always taught as if 'legal' grounds were entirely separate from 'ideological' or 'substantive' grounds. I find it hard to believe that all law professors are utterly indifferent to the moral and ideological bases of the law and teach their students to be so. Part of legal education, I think at least in most law schools, is devoted to determining what social interests law serves, what social needs it should serve and what costs it imposes. Indeed, the understanding of the political nature of law and the interests it serves has been the contribution of first, the realists and now critical legal theorists.

Second, there is some point to traditional modes of legal thought and traditional legal education. Traditional legal skills are an essential part of legal education. All lawyers, including (and perhaps even especially) those who work in the public interest, need substantive knowledge of law, the skills of dispassionate, rational analysis, the capacity to 'think on their feet' and advance their claim in an intimidating environment.

Nevertheless, the experiences of women at law school point to an important element of those critiques which claim law teaching is hostile to public interest at law school. A theme that emerges strongly in accounts of law school focussing on the experience of women and those focussing on public interest commitment is the lack of attention to the emotional and human stories which underlie the law.

At Columbia:

> It's very dehumanised . . very much based on the theoretical as opposed to something that makes it more personal.

At Yale:

> The recklessness, the casual 'well let's look at it this way, let's spin it around and look at it from this angle' stance that others seemed to achieve – I just couldn't. So in my first few weeks it was really a shock.

> It bothers me that some professors enjoy talking about things for the hell of it . . You're taught to masturbate the ideas. You play with ideas, but you're never taught to deal with reality . . . Most lawyers are intensely talky and rational. So much of life is neither rational nor susceptible to being put into words . . . suffering for instance.

This is a valuable insight into the transformative process. Often, the impulses which have led many students to law school are emotional impulses: such as concern for the underprivileged or empathy with a social or political cause. If students are motivated to come to law school by a concern for people or a belief in a social and political cause, that is, if they came to law school because they *care* about something, it should not be surprising to us that they react poorly to large helpings of careful analytical thinking, as important and intellectually stimulating as that may be. Considering how law school comes to dominate their world, it is not surprising that law students feel that their ideas are 'devalued' or 'illegitimate' if their capacity for empathy, their concern for the state of the world is not valued in law school.

So, here the critique of law school and its effect on public interest commitment begins to sound like some feminist critiques of law school. As these students complain about their legal education, they make essentially the same point made by theorists who have argued that law school insufficiently reflects a distinctive perspective women bring to the study of law and have called for the provision of more context and reality in legal materials. These critiques stand alone, but I seek to provide an additional reason to listen to them. They give us a more subtle understanding of how law school affects public interest commitment. When read in the light of accounts of the transformative nature of law school, it becomes apparent that it is not only a matter of providing context, of presenting the law as political or ideological, or involving the students in that discovery. Although this is important, the voices of women tell us to allow for emotional response to the material.[12]

Note

In his book, *The Lost Lawyer,* Anthony Kronman takes a rather different view of the impact of the Socratic method[13]. For Kronman, this teaching methodology helps students to learn both from their peers and the judgments studied a certain wariness of sweeping statements of principle and a preference for pragmatic solutions to narrowly defined social problems. For Kronman this is one aspect of the practical wisdom which the sees as the central character trait of a good lawyer.

Questions

1. What, if anything, might be the link between the cynicism note by Stone and the assumptions about the nature of ethical reasoning discussed and criticised above? (Cf Arthur Leff supra chapter 2.)

2. In your experience is the ideology of first year law school like that attributed to (some) US Law Schools?

3. Do you think your own legal education has overvalued analysis and undervalued the importance of emotion and empathy? Stone argues that the problem might be

---

12   Supra note 8 at pp 63-65, 68-70.
13   Anthony T Kronman *The Lost Lawyer - Failing Ideals of the Legal Profession* (Harvard, Cambridge, 1994): chapter 4 esp at pp 209-225.

corrected by greater use of narrative and story telling. She cites an article about the criminal law of rape by Susan Estrich which begins

> Eleven years ago, a man held an ice pick to my throat and said:'push over, shut up. Or I'll kill you.' I did what he said , but I couldn't stop crying .A hundred years later, I jumped out of my car as he drove away.[14]

Stone comments that Estrich's account of her own rape 'gives her account an emotional bite it could not otherwise have had (without it) she would have had less of our attention... the weaving of emotion and reason give such techniques a power to persuade .... some points are best made if the reader is shown how something feels.[15] Do you agree with Stone's assessment of the value of story telling?

CLINICAL LEGAL EDUCATION[16]

Another criticism of Kohlbergian notions of ethical autonomy is that it mistakenly equates ethical behaviour with particular ways of analysing hypothetical dilemmas. On this view, the relationship between an intellectual analysis of truth telling and being truthful is like that between reading a book on tennis and learning to play. You cannot be said to really know anything about playing tennis/telling the truth until you have practised in the difficult circumstances of life, so as to make it a habit which defines who you are. Such Aristotelian criticisms of traditional classroom-centered learning have to some extent driven the development of clinical legal education, ie the provision within the curriculum of opportunities for students to advise and if appropriate represent real (usually poor) clients and then to reflect upon their experience in the classroom. Clinical courses developed rapidly in US law schools in the early 1970s and are a prominent feature of legal education in many of the newer Australian law schools. Several UK law schools (for example the University of Kent Law school) have well-established clinics, but it is generally agreed that clinical legal education is underdeveloped in the UK.[17] What is significant for present purposes is that there is some evidence that clinical legal education may ameliorate to some extent the allegedly destructive effects of non clinical legal education. In one small-scale study carried out by Sally Maresh at the University of Denver College of Law, 96% of those who prior to taking the course had had some interest in public interest practice reported that their experience in clinic had reinforced that intention. Even more significantly of those students (almost 50%) who reported prior to the course that they had no such intention, only 43% registered the same lack of interest afterwards.[18]

14   S Estrich 'Rape' [1986] 95 Yale Law Journal 1087.
15   Stone supra note 8 at pp 70-71.
16   See Julian Webb 'Inventing the Good: A Prospectus For Clinical Education and the Teaching of Legal Ethics in England'[1996] 30 *Law Teacher* 270.
17   See generally Brayne, Duncan & Grimes (eds) *Clinical Legal Education: Active Learning in Your Law School* (London, Blackstone Press, 1998).
18   Sally Maresh 'The Impact of Clinical Legal Education on the Decisions of Law Students to Practice Public Interest Law.' chapter 8 of *Educating for Justice: Social Values and Legal Education* supra note 6.

Question

Consider the following comments of Lord Bingham concerning wasted costs orders in *Ridelhagh v Horsefield* (supra)

> the threat of proposed applications should not be used as a means of intimidation. On the other hand, if one side considers that the conduct of the other is improper, unreasonable or negligent and likely to cause a waste of costs we do not consider it objectionable to alert the other side to that view; the other side can then consider its position and perhaps mend its ways. Drawing the distinction between unacceptable intimidation and acceptable notice must depend on the professional judgment of those involved. ...
>
> It is not entirely easy to distinguish by definition between the hopeless case and the case which amounts to an abuse of the process, but in practice it is not hard to say which is which.

Should the courts be setting clearer guidelines for the making of these decisions? Anthony Kronman has argued that questions such as these cannot be reduced to a formula and are matters of judgment, which is in turn a trait of character ('practical wisdom') developed through experience.[19] What are the implications of these issues for legal education?

CURRICULAR REFORM

Whilst there are doubts about whether genuine independence is possible, it is clear that there are a number of differing theoretical frameworks with which to approach legal ethics. Academic legal education offers real opportunities for students to be made aware of the differing possibilities. Moreover whatever the potential of clinical legal education within academic legal education, it could only be an effective vehicle for the teaching of legal ethics if it could build upon the work already done in non-clinical courses. Otherwise, it would reproduce the problematic features of current modes of vocational legal education. It is therefore appropriate to consider what might be needed in the way of non-clinical legal courses if ACLEC's vision is to be fulfilled. The current programme at the Stanford Law School provides one possible model. There, all students receive an introduction to the major issues of legal ethics and the profession's regulatory structure during their early weeks in law school. Thereafter, students are not required to take the specialist course in legal ethics but they are required to take at least one course which contains a substantial ethics component. This use of structured choice ensures that the major issues are considered in a context which is of interest to the student.[20] Finally, the school takes seriously the idea of 'Ethics by the Pervasive Method'[1] which rests on the argument that ethical issues

19   Kronman supra note 13.
20   See Deborah L Rhode 'Into the Valley of Ethics: Professional Responsibility and Educational Reform' [1995] 58 Law and Contemporary Problems 139.
1   See Deborah L Rhode 'Ethics by the Pervasive Method' 42 Journal of Legal Education 31 (1991).

must be addressed throughout the curriculum as they arise in substantive courses. Otherwise, the silence of teachers (other than those teaching courses which focus directly on ethics) carries an important implicit message that the ethics of lawyers are not after all terribly important. Consequently, each of the first year courses spends at least two of the available 24 hours of contact time on the ethical issues arising in that subject.

There are very real differences, between US and UK academic legal education. In the US first degrees in law are taken at the postgraduate stage. In the UK, first degrees in law may be taken as an undergraduate. Nevertheless, the Stanford model suggests a number of possibilities for UK legal education. In his 1993 survey of UK law schools[2], Professor John Wilson found that the English legal system was widely taught being compulsory in 24 of the 34 schools surveyed. On any view, such courses should be introducing students to the major questions of legal ethics. These issues, though difficult to resolve, are relatively small in number focusing largely on the validity of the standard conception of lawyers' ethics. Consequently, it should be possible to introduce them to students within the parameters of a course on the English legal system without creating enormous curriculum overload.

With regard to specialist courses, the lure of a subject that is topical, stimulating and, in the English context, unexplored is likely to make this element of the legal ethics curriculum relatively easy to provide. Moreover, jurisprudence courses have a great deal to offer to the business of teaching legal ethics, for many of the central dilemmas depend upon one's view of law and the nature of the legal system. Take the question of whether the lawyer should manipulate the legal system in the interests of the client. For many, this is a difficult dilemma. However, if you really believe along with some American legal realists that the law is what officials do about disputes, then the dilemma disappears; for, ex hypothesi, the just solution is whatever the system can be made to produce.[3] If this potential is to be fulfilled, jurisprudence courses must emphasise that questions about the nature of law have implications not only for how appellate judges decide difficult points of law but also for the every day working decisions of ordinary lawyers.

As to ethics by the pervasive method, it is striking how many of the materials particularly the cases commonly considered in substantive courses simultaneously raise ethical issues. It is symptomatic of this that in 1997 one part of the All England Reports was almost entirely taken up with reports of two hearings in the Court of Appeal in the case of *Vernon v Bosley*[4]. The plaintiff's children had drowned when the defendant, their nanny, negligently drove their car into a river. He later claimed damages for negligence for psychiatric illness allegedly suffered as a result of having witnessed the unsuccessful rescue attempts. The first hearing concerned substantive questions as to the limits of liability in negligence for psychiatric illness. This is currently one of

2   J Wilson 'A Third Survey of University Legal Education' (1993) 13 Legal Studies p 1.
3   See D Luban *Lawyers and Justice: an ethical study* (Princeton University Press, 1988) chapter 2.
4   *Vernon* v *Bosley (No 1)* [1997] 1 All ER 577; and *Vernon* v *Bosley (No 2)* [1997] 1 All ER ibid 614. This case is considered in detail in chapter 5. See below pp 176-178.

the most unsettled and controversial areas of English tort law and an area of enduring interest to undergraduate tort law teachers. The second hearing concerned the ethical obligations of the lawyers representing the plaintiff in the personal injury proceedings. Their case was that he was suffering from mental illness with a poor prognosis. They discovered, however, that he was simultaneously claiming (with the help of different lawyers but the same expert witness) in matrimonial proceedings that his mental health was rapidly improving. This would clearly assist his claim for custody of the remaining children. The question was whether the personal injury lawyers were bound to disclose what seemed to be a fraud on the tribunal.

However, there are, unfortunately, a number of practical difficulties which are likely to restrict the impact of legal ethics teaching within undergraduate law degrees in the UK. The major problem in the words of Professor Cotter, author of an exhaustive study of the optimum design for legal ethics curricula,[5] is that 'law teachers are committed to independence and autonomy at the cost of curriculum-wide structure'.[6] This is particularly likely to manifest itself in relation to the pervasive teaching of legal ethics during substantive courses. Many teachers will be loath to invest significant time in preparing to teach legal ethics pervasively if their own advancement depends primarily upon scholarly output in their own subject area. A wide-ranging interdisciplinary approach to the teaching of legal ethics will demand of law teachers a broad knowledge and a wide range of intellectual skills.

Moreover, the historic divide between academic and applied/vocational legal studies is likely to remain a prominent feature for legal education in the UK for many years to come. Consequently, an interest in legal ethics is likely to remain the interest of a committed few, for deeply ingrained attitudes cannot be changed by the reformer's prescriptive utterance. The problem also has structural features. The best way to break down the divide would be to teach an integrated four year degree encompassing both the intellectual objectives of undergraduate legal education[7] with the skills objectives of the current vocational courses.[8] However, this model, though attractive, is unlikely to be widely adopted because the Treasury has indicated that it will not provide the funding for a broad ranging extension of law degrees from three to four years.[9] Therefore, any university which seeks to adopt this model will impose upon students an unfunded fourth year, hence reducing its attraction in the market for undergraduate students.

Finally, one of the more sobering implications of the epistemology underlying clinical legal education is that law teachers may teach their students more about ethics in their general attitude to and levels of commitment towards their students than they do through formal programmes of instruction. However, the law teacher of the 21st century will be required to work in a managerialist culture and be forced to demonstrate in measurable terms his/her own performance. Unfortunately, something as intangible as

---

5   Supra p 118, note 4.
6   Ibid at 3-17 and see note 17 of that text for an amusing and illustrative account.
7   See *First Report* supra p 116, note 14 at para 4.4.
8   Ibid at pp 147 and 151.
9   Ibid at 3.19.

'care for students' is unlikely to become a major measure of academic performance and this has disturbing implications for the sorts of ethics which are likely to be taught by example.

Questions

1. To what extent are academics likely to make a significant impact on the ethics of their students? To what extent is your view related to your opinions about the nature of ethics (see chapter 2 above) ?

2. What in your view is the optimum mode of ethical education during undergraduate legal education?

3. Would you support curriculum reform in accordance with the Stanford model? What other reforms would you suggest?

4. Consider Deborah Rhode's description of the experience of US law students;

> Faced with a steady succession of hard cases and unstable distinctions, students quickly learn that there are no answers but just arguments. The result is agnosticism, relativism or cynicism.[10]

Is this an apt description of your experience of legal education?

5. Carrie Menkel Meadow has asked the question 'Can a Law Teacher Avoid Teaching Legal Ethics?'[11] How would you respond?

---

10   Deborah L Rhode 'Institutionalizing Legal Ethics' (1994) 44 Case Western Reserve Law Review 665, 775.
11   (1991) 31 Journal of Legal Education 3.

CHAPTER FIVE

The Standard Conception of legal ethics

A man and his only son were involved in an horrific road accident. The father was killed and the son, critically injured, was rushed to the nearest hospital for emergency surgery. The surgeon entered the theatre prepared for another day at the office but, on seeing the patient's terrible injuries cried out in horror 'My son... oh my only son'[1]

That many find the surgeon's tale so puzzling is an illustration of the fact that everyone wears a set of theoretical spectacles through which they view the social world. It is possible to live life unaware of one's preconceptions. Whilst this may be comfortable, it is at the same time dangerous for our theoretical spectacles to alter our perception of the real world and thus influence our behaviour. It is the job of theorists to illuminate our preconceptions and hold them up for critical scrutiny.

This chapter seeks to articulate and criticise the theoretical frameworks which lawyers may bring, consciously or otherwise to their legal work. This is a difficult task because of the neglect of legal ethics by university legal educators which was described in the previous chapter. Fortunately, the explosion of interest in legal ethics amongst US academics following the Watergate scandal has stimulated a debate about the fundamental questions of legal ethics on which we can profitably draw. After outlining the 'Standard Conception of Legal Ethics', we consider whether it represents a defensible approach to legal practice and, if so, in which practice settings. We consider in turn Stephen Pepper's libertarian defence of the Standard Conception ('the first class citizenship model'); the liberal alternative set out by David Luban[2] ('moral activism') and the radical alternative found in the work of William Simon[3] ('the contextual

---

1   Anon.
2   See in particular *Lawyers and Justice: An Ethical Study* (Princeton UP, New Jersey, 1988). Commentary upon and development of the views expressed in that book are referred to below.
3   William Simon's developed views are contained in his book *The Practice of Justice – A Theory of Lawyers Ethics* (Harvard, Cambridge Mass, 1998) and were prefigured in a number of journal articles notably 'Ethical Discretion in Lawyering' (1988) 101 Harvard Law Review 1083.

approach'). As we shall see these differing perspectives raise fundamental questions about the nature of law, the nature of morality and the relationship between the two. Also prominent is the question of the scope and extent of the moral duty to obey the law.

1   The Standard Conception of Legal Ethics

The Standard Conception described

The starting point is what is usually called the 'Standard Conception of Legal Ethics', the best know articulation being that of William Simon.[4] On this view, lawyers' ethics are based on two principles, namely

I. **The Principle of Neutrality**: the lawyer may (and if no other lawyer is willing to represent a potential client *must*) represent people who wish to employ the lawyer's services regardless of the lawyer's opinion of the justice of the cause. In so doing however, the lawyer is absolved of any moral responsibility for acts done in the name of the client,

and

II. **The Principle of Partisanship**: the lawyer is permitted and required to do everything to further the client's interests provided only that it is neither technically illegal nor a clear breach of a rule of conduct. The principle holds even when it clearly thwarts the aims of the substantive law.

Lawyers are thus subject in their professional lives to a role morality which permits and indeed often requires them to do things which they (and others) would regard as immoral in private life. Douglas Rosenthal found a striking illustration of the principle at work in a survey of US personal injury litigators. One insurance company lawyer commented:

> Frankly, we are in business to wear out plaintiffs... We're not a charity out to protect plaintiff's welfare. Take the case I was trying today. The other lawyer... doesn't know what he's doing. His client's got a good claim for a fractured skull. *I want this bastard to win* ... and I know he'll blow it. Today, I laid the foundation for contributory negligence, which is very doubtful, and the other lawyer made no attempt to knock it down. The plaintiff is a sweet gentle guy – a Puerto Rican. I met him in the john at recess and I told him that there was nothing personal in my working against him, that I was just doing my job... It's not my fault, I want him to win. It's his lawyer's fault and his own fault for not getting a better lawyer like me.[5]

---

4   See 'The Ideology of The Advocacy System: Procedural Justice and Professional Ethics' [1978] Wisconsin LR 29 at p 36.

5   Douglas E Rosenthal, *Lawyer and Client: Who's in Charge?* pp 82-83 (Sage, New York, 1974).

whilst an English counterpart commented:

> I'm acting for an insurance company. I have to use any tactic I can, to pay as little attention as possible to the plaintiff in order to pay as little as possible.[6]

How standard is the Standard Conception?

Whether the 'Standard Conception' really is 'standard' is debatable. It's influence can clearly be seen in the terms of the US Codes, particularly the Model Code which provides

CANON 7 A LAWYER SHOULD REPRESENT A CLIENT ZEALOUSLY WITHIN THE BOUNDS OF THE LAW

Ethical Considerations[6A]

EC7-1 The duty of a lawyer, both to his client and to the legal system is to represent his client zealously within the bounds of the law, which includes Disciplinary Rules and enforceable regulations. The professional responsibility of a lawyer derives from his membership of a profession which has the duty of assisting members of the public to secure and protect available legal rights and benefits... each member of our society is entitled to have his conduct judged and regulated in accordance with the law; to seek any lawful objective through legally permissible means; and to present for adjudication any lawful claim, issue or defence.

though some have argued for alternative readings[7].

In the UK, the law on lawyering[8] is even more equivocal about the 'Standard Conception'. On the one hand, professional bodies which seek authorisation from the Lord Chancellor to grant its members rights of audience must have a code of conduct which requires members to offer advocacy services regardless of the advocate's views as to the potential client's cause.[9] For the Bar, this is given effect by the 'Cab-Rank rule'. However, while barristers are thus required to observe the principle of neutrality, Principle 1 of the LSGPC sets its face firmly against the principle of partisanship. Principle 1 states that:

---

6   Insurance company (ie personal injury defence) solicitor cited in Hazel Genn, *The Central London County Court Pilot Mediation Scheme: Evaluation Report,* LCD Research Series 5/ 98.

6A   The Model Code was divided into general principles known as Canons, Ethical Considerations (which were aspirational and did not give rise , if breached, to disciplinary action) and Disciplinary Rules.

7   See Stephen Ellerman 'Lawyering for Justice in a Flawed Democracy' (1990) 90 Columbia Law Review 116 at p 120; E Chemerinsky 'Pedagogy Without Purpose: An Essay on Professional Responsibility Courses and Casebooks' (1985) Am B Found Res J 943 (1985) 189; T Schneyer Professional Responsibility Casebooks & the New Positivism: A Reply to Professor Chemerinsky' (1985) Am B Found Res J 943 (1985); and E Chemerinsky 'Training the Ethical Lawyer: A rejoinder to Schneyer' (1985) Am B Found Res J 943 (1985) at 959.

8   For the definition of this term, see chapter 1 supra at p 15.

9   S 17(3)(c)(i)-(ii) of the Courts and Legal Services Act 1990.

A solicitor shall not do anything in the course of practising as a solicitor, or permit another person to do anything on his or her behalf which compromises or impairs or is likely to compromise or impair any of the following:

a)   the solicitor's independence or integrity;

b)   a person's freedom to instruct a solicitor of his or her choice;

c)   the solicitor's duty to act in the best interests of the client;

d)   the solicitor's proper standard of work;

e)   the solicitor's duty to the court.

and adds that:

Where two or more of (the above principles) come into conflict, the determining factor in deciding which principle should take precedence must be the public interest, and especially the public interest in the administration of justice.[10]

Moreover, a number of legislative recent legislative provisions seem equally at odds with the 'Standard Conception'. Thus, s 27 of the Courts and Legal Services Act 1990[11] provides that

Every person who exercises before any court a right of audience granted by an authorised body has—

(a)   a duty to the court to act with independence in the interests of justice; and

(b)   a duty to comply with rules of conduct of the body relating to the right and approved for the purposes of this section;

and those duties shall override any obligation which the person may have (otherwise than under the criminal law) if it is inconsistent with them.

However, the informal norms of professional culture may be equally as influential as the formal statements made in the codes and by statute. From this perspective, it is striking that Lord Woolf's inquiry into civil justice, which ultimately led to fundamental reform of the rules of civil procedure, reported that the existing system was slow and unacceptably expensive because of the legal profession's excessively adversarial approach to litigation[12]. Moreover, the pages of the law reports regularly provide striking case-histories in which the 'standard conception' seems very prominent: see for example *Ernst and Young v Butte Mining PLC*[13] and *Commission for the New Towns v Cooper (Great Britain) Ltd*[14] discussed in chapter 8 and *Vernon v Bosely (No 2)* which appears at the end of this chapter. Whatever the precise position in empirical terms, it is clear that the standard conception is at least one of the available ethical frameworks. The question then is whether it is morally defensible.

---

10   Principle 1.02 Basic Principles – additional guidance, note 6.

11   Inserted by s 31 of the Access to Justice Act 1999.

12   *Access to Justice* – Final Report by the Right Honourable Lord Woolf MR (London, Lord Chancellors Department, HMSO, 1996).

13   [1996] 1 WLR 1605.

14   [1995] Ch 259, CA.

2   Stephen Pepper and first class citizenship

One of the best-known defences of the 'Standard Conception' is that of Professor Stephen Pepper and is known as the 'First Class Citizenship Model' of legal representation. In the following passage Professor Pepper sets out the main elements of the model.

The premise with which we begin is that law is a public good available to all. Society, through its 'lawmakers' – legislatures, courts, administrative agencies, and so forth – has created various mechanisms to ease and enable the private attainment of individual or group goals. The corporate form of enterprise, the contract, the trust, the will, and access to civil courts to gain the use of public force for the settlement of private grievance are all vehicles of empowerment for the individual or group; all are 'law' created by the collectivity to be generally available for private use. In addition to these structuring mechanisms are vast amounts of law, knowledge of which is tended to be generally available and is empowering: landlord/tenant law, labour law, social security – the list can be vastly extended. Access to both forms of law increases one's ability to successfully attain goals.

The second premise is a societal commitment to the principle of individual autonomy. This premise is founded on the belief that liberty and autonomy are a moral good, that free choice is better than constraint, that each of us wishes, to the extent possible, to make our own choices rather than have them made for us. This belief is incorporated into our legal system, which accommodates individual autonomy by leaving as much room as possible for liberty and diversity. Leaving regulatory law aside for the moment (and granting that it has grown immensely, contributing to the legalisation to be mentioned below), our law is designed (1) to allow the private structuring of affairs (contracts, corporations, wills, trusts, etc) and (2) to define conduct that is intolerable. The latter sets a floor below which one cannot go, but leaves as much room as possible above that floor for individual decision making. It may be morally wrong to manufacture or distribute cigarettes or alcohol, or to disinherit one's children for marrying outside the faith, but the generality of such decisions are left in the private realm. Diversity and autonomy are preferred over 'right' or 'good' conduct. The theory of our law is to leave as much room as possible for private, individual decisions concerning what is right and wrong, as opposed to public, collective decisions.

Our first premise is that law is intended to be a public good which increases autonomy. The second premise is that increasing individual autonomy is morally good. The third step is that in a highly legalised society such as ours, autonomy is often dependent upon access to the law. Put simply, first-class citizenship is dependent on access to the law. And while access to law – to the creation and use of a corporation, to knowledge of how much overtime one has to pay or is entitled to receive – is formally available to all, in reality it is available only through a lawyer. Our law is usually not simple, usually not self-executing. For most people most of the time, meaningful access to the law requires the assistance of a lawyer. Thus the resulting conclusion: first-class citizenship is frequently dependent upon the assistance of a lawyer. If the conduct which the lawyer facilitates is above the floor of the intolerable – is not unlawful – then this line of thought suggests that what the lawyer does is a social good. The lawyer is the means to first-class citizenship, to meaningful autonomy, for the client.

For the lawyer to have moral responsibility for each act he or she facilitates, for the lawyer to have a moral obligation to refuse to facilitate that which the lawyer believes to be immoral, is to substitute lawyers' beliefs for individual autonomy and diversity. Such a screening submits each to the prior restraint of the judge/facilitator and to rule by an oligarchy of lawyers. (If, in the alternative, the suggestion is that the lawyer's screening should be based not on the lawyer's personal morality, but on the lawyers assessment of society's moral views or on guidelines spelled out in a professional code of ethics, then one has substituted collective moral decision making for individual moral decision making, contrary to the principle of autonomy. Less room has been left for private decision making through a sub rosa form of lawmaking.) If the conduct is sufficiently 'bad,' it would seem that it ought to be made explicitly unlawful. If it is not that bad, why subject the citizenry to the happenstance of the moral judgment of the particular lawyer to whom each has access? If making the conduct unlawful is onerous because the law would be too vague, or it is too difficult to identify the conduct in advance, or there is not sufficient social or political concern, do we intend to delegate to the individual lawyer the authority for case-by-case legislation and policing?

An example may help. Professor Wasserstrom implies that a lawyer ought to refuse to draft a will disinheriting a child because of the child's views concerning the war in Nicaragua. 'But,' asks Professor Freedman, 'is the lawyer's paternalism toward the client preferable – morally or otherwise to the client's paternalism toward her children?' And, he asks further, is there any reason to substitute the diversity of lawyers' opinions on the issue of disinheritance based on political belief for the diversity of clients' opinions? Ought we to have a law on the issue? If not, why screen use of the legal device of testacy either through the diverse consciences of lawyers or through the collective conscience of the profession? And if the law is clear but contrary to the lawyer's moral beliefs, such as a tax loop-hole for the rich or impeachment-oriented cross-examination of the truthful witness, why allow (let alone require) that the lawyer legislate for this particular person or situation?

It is apparent that a final significant value supporting the first-class citizenship model is that of equality. If law is a public good, access to which increases autonomy, then equality of access is important. For access to the law to be filtered unequally through the disparate moral views of each individual's lawyer does not appear to be justifiable. Even given the current and perhaps permanent fact of unequal access to the law, it does not make sense to compound that inequality with another. If access to a lawyer is achieved (through private allocation of one's means, public provision, or the lawyer's – or profession's – choice to provide it), should the extent of that access depend upon individual lawyer conscience? The values of autonomy and equality suggest that it should not; the client's conscience should be superior to the lawyer's. One of the unpleasant concomitants of the view that a lawyer should be morally responsible for all that she does is the resulting inequality: unfiltered access to the law available only to those who are legally sophisticated or to those able to educate themselves sufficiently for access to the law, while those less sophisticated – usually those less educated – are left with no access or with access that subjects their use of the law to the moral judgment and veto of the lawyer.

II. THE CRITIQUE AND A RESPONSE

The Economic Inequality Criticism

The foregoing quickly leads to the observation that law is a public good in theory but not in fact, and that one of the key premises justifying the first-class citizenship model is therefore false. Like almost everything else in our society, access to law is rationed through the market – in this case, the market for lawyers' services. Thus, the rich have disproportionate access over the poor, and this is particularly unacceptable given the public nature of law and its implementing relationship to individual autonomy and first-class citizenship. This is the focus of the first criticism of the amoral role: it would be justified if everyone had access to 'first-class citizenship' through a lawyer, but everyone does not. The drastic and fundamental inequality of means in America vitiates the moral justification for an amoral professional ethic for lawyers Granting the truth of economic inequality does not, however, mean that the amoral role is a bad role, or that the lawyer currently fulfilling the role cannot be a good person. An analogous criticism might be made of the grocer and the housing contractor. Although food and shelter are (in our system) not public goods, they are more fundamentally enabling to autonomy than is law. Yet there is much less disquiet over the moral role of the grocer, housing contractor, or landlord than that of the lawyer. We live in a primarily market system, not a primarily socialist system, and the contemporary problem in defining lawyers' ethics is likely to have to be answered in this market context. Lawyers cannot magically socialise the economy or legal services.

Another way of saying this, perhaps more to the point, is that there are two issues here: the distribution of legal services and the content of what is distributed. The moral content of what is distributed – the ethical nature of the lawyer-client relationship once established – is the subject of this essay. The distribution of access to the law (legal services) is a different subject. While the effort to make law a more truly public good is under way (or assuming it fails and we are left with the status quo), the other issue remains: what is to be the moral content of the legal services that are available? To suggest that transforming the amoral facilitator role of the lawyer into the judge/facilitator role follows from the insufficient availability of legal services is a non sequitur. Such a transformation would compound inequality upon inequality – first the inequality of access to a lawyer, then the inequality of what law that particular lawyer will allow the client access to.

One can argue that the judge/facilitator role will not compound inequality but, to the contrary, will balance power because the advantage accruing to those with access to the law over those without will be balanced by the restraint of the lawyer's moral screening of access to the law. There are at least two reasons to react with scepticism to this argument. First, the inequality of distribution is neither complete nor uniform. At least some of the 'outs' have had significant access to the law through lawyers. Labour unions, criminal defendants and civil rights organisations are three prominent examples. Lawyers have played key roles in areas where many perceive gains to have been made in social justice. Second, there is little likelihood of a large difference in moral perception between lawyers and their 'in' clients. Perhaps we need more (historical? empirical?) data: Looking back, would there have been more social justice, equality, or general welfare if lawyers had altered or withheld services on the basis of their own (largely middle- or upper-class) values? How would a moralistic as opposed to an amoral role for lawyers have affected 20th-century American social history? However one is inclined to answer such questions, to the extent that the first-class citizenship argument is otherwise valid, expansion and equalisation of access to lawyers is a goal which is both consistent with and suggested by that argument. Transforming lawyers into moral screens for client access to the law, to the contrary, is a project quite problematic in its relation to equality of access to law.[15]

Questions

1. Do you agree that the question of the content of the service lawyers provide must be distinguished from the question of their distribution?

2. Professor Pepper assumes that the 'Standard Conception of Legal Ethics' would be morally justified if each citizen had access to the services of a lawyer. Do you agree? Are lawyers morally justified in taking advantage of each other's mistakes? Consider for example the conduct of the defendant's lawyers in *Commission for the New Towns v Cooper* (pp 290-291 infra). Can I justify my infringement of your rights by pointing out that you have a fully-armed body guard if all the time I have been doing my level best to evade him?

3. Do you agree with the comment that 'if ...conduct is sufficiently bad, it would seem that it ought to be made explicitly unlawful'? Consider in this respect why the press is permitted self-regulation with respect to infringements of individual privacy.

4. Professor Pepper bases himself within the liberal ethical tradition in which human autonomy is seen as an important value. However within the same tradition, one may also find a stress on equality. What argument does Pepper give for rejecting the view that the judge/facilitator role will redress the problems of unequal autonomy which arise when legal services are distributed through the market? How, rationally, could one demonstrate whether equality should be preferred to autonomy or vice versa?

As emphasised earlier, frameworks for legal ethics tend to differ in their assumptions about the nature of law and legal obligation. Professor Pepper's defence of the 'Standard Conception' is distinguished by its explicit discussion of these issues. In the following passage, he discusses the Standard Conception's limiting requirement that lawyers shall not assist clients in ways which constitute a breach of the law. This is radically affected if lawyers adopt an American legal realist perspective on the law.

We turn now to a ... rarely articulated problem presented by the first-class citizenship justification for the amoral role. Up to this point in the discussion, access to the law as

15   Stephen Pepper 'The Lawyer's Amoral Role: A Defence, a Problem and Some Possibilities' (1986) Am Bar Found Res J 613 at pp 617-623.

the primary justification for the amoral professional role has been presented with relatively little focus on what 'the law' refers to. Three different facets of law have been recognised: (1) structuring mechanisms (trusts, corporations, civil litigation), (2) definitions of intolerable conduct (criminal law and litigation), and (3) regulatory law. The implication has been that the law is existent and determinable, that there is 'something there' for the lawyer to find (or know) and communicate to the client. The 'thereness' of the law is also the assumption underlying the commonly understood limit on the amoral role: the lawyer can only assist the client 'within the bounds of the law.' This accords with the usual understanding of the law from the lay or client point of view, but not from the lawyer's point of view. The dominant view of law inculcated in (American) law schools, which will be identified here as 'legal realism,' approaches law without conceiving of it as objectively 'out there' to be discovered and applied. A relatively little explored problem is the dynamic between the amoral professional role and a sceptical attitude toward law.

By 'legal realism' I mean a view of law which stresses it's 'open-textured, vague' nature over it's precision; its manipulability over its certainty; and its 'instrumental' possibilities over its' normative content. From 'positivism' modern legal education takes the notion of the separation of law and morality: in advising the client, the lawyer is concerned with the law as an 'is,' a fact of power and limitation, more than as an 'ought.' From 'legal realism' it takes the notion of law as a prediction of what human officials will do, more than as an existent, objective, determinable limit or boundary on client behaviour. From 'process jurisprudence' it takes an emphasis on client goals and private structuring, an instrumental use of law that de-emphasises the determination of law through adjudication or the prediction of the outcome of adjudications. These three views of 'the law' are mutually reinforcing rather than conflicting. To the extent that legal education inculcates these views, 'the law' becomes a rather amorphous thing, dependent upon the client's situation, goals, and risk preferences. What is the interaction between this view of the law and the view of the lawyer as an amoral servant of the client whose assistance is limited only by 'the law'?

The apt image is that of Holmes's 'bad man.' The modern lawyer is taught to look at the law as the 'bad man' would, who cares only for the material consequences. The lawyer discovers and conveys 'the law' to his client from this perspective and then is told to limit his own assistance to the client based upon this same view of 'the law.' The modern view of contract law, for example, de-emphasises the normative obligation of promises and views breach of contract as a 'right' that is subject to the 'cost' of damages. Breach of contract is not criminal and, normally, fulfilment of a contractual obligation is not forced on a party (not 'specifically enforced,' in contract law terminology). The client who comes in with a more normative view of the obligation of contracts (whether wishing the lawyer to assist in structuring a transaction through a prospective contract or in coping with the unwelcome constraints of a past contract) will be educated by the competent lawyer as to the 'breach as cost' view of 'the law.' Similarly, modern tort law has emphasised allocation of the 'costs' of accidents, as opposed to the more normative view of 19th and early 20th century negligence law. Thus, negligence law can be characterised as establishing a right to a non-consensual taking from the injured party on the part of the tort-feasor, subject once again to the 'cost' of damages. An industrial concern assessing and planning conduct which poses risks of personal injury or death to third parties will be guided by a lawyer following this view away from perceiving the imposition of unreasonable risk as a wrong and toward perceiving it as a potential cost.

There are, of course, variations in the extent to which legal realism will be encountered in the lawyers' office. One is more likely to find the cost reductive view presented in relation to a contract problem than a tort problem, and it is more likely to come from a lawyer advising a large corporate enterprise than one advising an individual. But it is valid as a general suggestive model that most clients, most of the time, (1) will enter the lawyer's office thinking of law as more normative and more certain than does the lawyer, and (2) will go out having been influenced toward thinking of the law in terms of possible or probable costs more than they would have had they not consulted a lawyer.

From the perspective of fully informed access to the law, this modification of the client's view is good because it accords with the generally accepted understanding of the law among those who are closest to its use and administration – lawyers and judges. It is accurate; it is useful to the client. From the perspective of the ethical relationship between lawyer and client, it is far more problematic. First, the lawyer is to be an amoral technician who serves rather than judges the client. The lawyer is not the repository of moral limits on the client's behaviour. Second, the law itself, as presented by the lawyer, also is not a source of moral limits. Rather, it is presented from the lawyer's technical, manipulative stance as a potential constraint, as a problem, or as data to be factored into decisions as to future conduct. Finally, in determining how far he or she can go in helping the client, the lawyer is instructed to look to that same uncertain, manipulable source: 'the law.' 'Within the bounds of the law' sounds like an objective, knowable moral guide. Any second-year law student knows that as to any but the most obvious (and therefore uninteresting) questions, there will probably be no clear line, no boundary, but only a series of possibilities. Thus, if one combines the dominant 'legal realism' understanding of law with the traditional amoral role of the lawyer, *there is no moral input or constraint in the present model of the lawyer-client relationship.*

Again, from the premises of the first-class citizenship model, this is as it should be. The client's autonomy should be limited by the law, not by the lawyer's morality. And if 'the law' is manipulable and without clear limits on client conduct, that aspect of the law should be available to the client. If moral limits are not provided by the law and are not imposed by the lawyer, their source will be where it ought to be: the client. Morality is not to be inserted in the lawyer's office, its source either the lawyer or the law. Morality comes through the door as part of the client.

This shifts our focus from the lawyer and the law to the client. It should come as no surprise that many clients will come through the door without such internal moral guidance. Common sources of moral guidance are on the decline: religion, community, family. In a secularised society such as ours, religion no longer functions as the authoritative moral guide it once did. Geographic mobility and divorce have robbed much of the multi generational moral guidance that families can provide. Small, supportive, usually continuous and homogenous moral communities are the experience of fewer and fewer people. The rural town, the ethnic neighboured, the church attended for several generations, the local business or trade community (the chamber of commerce or the grocers' trade association) – all are the experience of a far smaller segment of the population than before. Even the role of [state schools] in inculcating values may have declined. For many, law has replaced alternative sources of moral guidance.

Our problem now posits: (1) a client seeking access to the law who frequently has only weak internal or external sources of morality; (2) a lawyer whose professional role mandates that he or she not impose moral restraint on the client's access to the law; (3) a lawyer whose understanding of the law de-emphasises its moral content and certainty, and perceives it instead as instrumental and manipulable; and (4) law designed as (a) neutral structuring mechanisms to increase individual power (contracts, the corporate form, civil litigation), (b) a floor delineating minimum tolerable behaviour rather than moral guidance, and (c) morally neutral regulation. From this perspective, access to the law through a lawyer appears to systematically screen out or de-emphasise moral considerations and moral limits. The client who consults a lawyer will be guided to maximise his autonomy through the tools of the law – tools designed and used to maximise freedom, not to provide a guide to good behaviour. If one cannot rely on the client or an alternative social institution to provide that guide, to suggest a moral restraint on that which is legally available, then what the lawyer does may be evil: lawyers in the aggregate may consistently guide clients away from moral conduct and restrain[16].

Questions

1. **Fawlty Towers**: Your client, Basil, owns a small hotel and has been informed by the heating engineers that the water boilers above the basins in the hotel rooms need replacing at a cost of £50,000. Your client says truthfully that he cannot afford to pay such a bill for at least the next three years. However the heating engineer says that there is a 20% chance that if Basil waits that long a guest will be severely burned. You research the relevant law and the factual background and you discover that:
a) to continue in business without replacing the heaters would almost certainly be a breach by Basil of his duty of care
b) if the report (hitherto verbal) was to be put in writing the rules of discovery would require it to be disclosed to the other side during any subsequent litigation
c) Basil is insured against liability in tort up to the sum of £1 million
d) to continue in business without replacing the heater would almost certainly be a breach of health and safety regulations. However prosecutions are rare and require proof of mens rea. The maximum penalty is £50,000. Imprisonment for up to one year is provided for in the relevant legislation but has almost never been imposed.

What advice should you give the client?

2. American legal realism has been described as 'the ordinary religion' of the American law school classroom. Do you consider your own legal education to have involved exposure to such a 'religion'? Consider again Deborah Rhode's comment that 'Faced with a steady succession of hard cases and unstable distinctions, students quickly

---

16   Ibid at pp 626-633.

learn that there are no answers but just arguments. The result is agnosticism, relativism or cynicism.'[17]

3   David Luban and moral activism

Lawyers and institutional excuses

At the heart of David Luban's contribution to legal ethics is his examination of one of its' most troubling features namely that lawyers are often required by their professional roles to do things which non lawyers would regard as unethical. This is graphically illustrated by two real incidents. In the case of *Spaulding v Zimmerman*[18], the plaintiff had suffered personal injuries in a motor accident and was suing the defendant for negligence. The defendants lawyer had the plaintiff examined by a doctor who discovered that the plaintiff was suffering from a latent life-threatening condition caused by the accident. However, the plaintiff's doctor and therefore the plaintiff was unaware of this. The defendant's lawyer kept this information confidential and maximised the chances of a favourable settlement but put the plaintiff's life at risk.

The second incident is the Mount Pleasant Bodies Case. In July 1973, a 17-year-old boy was murdered in Mount Pleasant a small town in New York state. Frank Garrow, a former convict was ultimately arrested and charged. Frank Armani, a local lawyer was appointed to represent him. At the same time, two girls, aged 17 and 20, had been reported missing by their parents. The police already suspected Garrow (who was in hospital having been shot trying to evade capture) but could not prove his involvement. From his hospital bed, Garrow confessed to Armani that he had killed the girls and told him where the bodies were buried.

Armani found and photographed the bodies but didn't report what he knew. Nor did he disclose when the parents of one of the girls asked him face to face if he knew what had happened. He even tried a plea bargain. At the trial a year later, Garrow confessed to all the murders in an effort to establish his insanity. Armani's knowledge of where the bodies were buried was disclosed, causing an outcry.

One of the most striking features of both episodes is that while a non-lawyer would almost certainly feel bound to disclose what s/he knew (one of Armani's friends said ' if I was the girl's father I would shoot you'), the Model Rules, the Model Code the LSGPC and the CCB all require a lawyer in such a situation to keep silent.

For Luban, this raised the question of whether morality should be regarded as universal, ie a series of duties binding on everyone regardless of their social role or as differing in its incidents according to the role occupied by the agent (role morality). On this view, it might be considered heroic for a single childless man to give up his job as an investment banker to work as an international famine relief worker. But a married man with four children who did the same might be considered immoral.

---

17   D Rhode 'Institutionalising Legal Ethics' [1994] 44 Case Western Reserve Law Review 665 at p 735.
18   116 NW 2d 704 (1962).

In the following extract, Luban considers whether morality is best thought of as being universal or particular to various social roles. He begins by noting that the apparent universality of certain moral obligations ('Thou shalt not murder') can be accounted for by a role theorist on the grounds that the same command just happened to be part of each and every role. Apparent conflicts between role morality and common morality might simply be a result of tensions between various role obligations. He continues:

> We see, then, that role theory possesses the resources to account both for universal morality and for its conflicts with role moralities. Shall we therefore allow that role theory adequately characterises our moral views? In that case, we would not deny that a role, such as that of lawyer, may contain moral conflicts. We would, however, deny that Charles Fried's question 'Can a good lawyer be a good person?' makes any sense whatsoever. For the notion of a good person *simpliciter* has been excised from the moral vocabulary.
>
> This, however, explains why the role theorist's account is not adequate. For the fact is that the notion of a good person *simpliciter* is part of our moral vocabulary, and not just as an abbreviation for 'good performer of those role obligations that happen to accrue to ones roles.' To see this clearly we must look at the way appeals to universal moral obligations work in the process of passing moral judgment.
>
> Consider once again the Talmud's role morality, consisting of ten commandments for Jews and seven for gentiles. It happens that both sets of commandments proscribe murder. The reason that such a morality would condemn murder is this: 'It is wrong for a Jew to murder and it is wrong for a gentile to murder.' But surely this misses the point.
>
> In our society, which has thousands of roles, the reason would be more complex: 'It is wrong for a lawyer to murder and it is wrong for a parent to murder and it is wrong for a bag lady to murder and it is wrong for a good 'ol boy to murder.' And this misses the point still more dramatically.
>
> The problem is not just that these reasons are needlessly ornate. The problem is that they are the wrong reasons. The fact that I must not murder has nothing to do with the fact that I am a Jew or a professor; to say that it does directs attention to irrelevancies.
>
> Now of course a role theorist will claim that reference to roles is not an irrelevancy, and that to say it is begs the question. But this underlines the problem: the role theorist is simply misdescribing the moral framework of our culture, which would in fact find it repugnant to say, for example, 'An investment banker must not murder.' (It is repugnant because it suggests that abstinence from murder is part of the special code of honour of investment bankers, that austere heroic code that sets them off from the rest of us.) But it's not that no investment banker should murder, it's that no one should murder.
>
> The point is that moral deliberation does not merely concern to whom an obligation applies – everyone, according to role theory, but only when it coincidentally turns out that way – morality concerns *in virtue of what* an obligation applies. And common moral injunctions such as the proscription of murder apply in virtue of personhood, not in virtue of investment banking. Common morality is not contingently universal: it is universal because it applies to persons *simpliciter*. It is not, therefore, merely universal

morality. It is common morality, the baseline or 'default' against which we initially assess anyone's behaviour, regardless of his or her station in society.

Common morality is morality concerned with how persons behave. Role theory cannot adequately account for this concern because it is unwilling to abstract persons from their roles. Role theory cannot, therefore, allow that being a person can provide a reason for behaving in certain ways. And so, role theory cannot account for our belief that common morality is a baseline and not just a uniformity.

As I have indicated, we can readily imagine a society that does not share this belief and in which all morality is therefore articulated as role morality. I suspect, however, that such a society seems plausible to us only if we think of its roles as given at birth-roles such as man, woman, Jew, aristocrat, and so forth. It is hard to imagine that in a society in which many roles can be assumed or discarded at will people would think that all morality is role morality. For then people would think of morality also as something that can be assumed or discarded at will.

This suggests that role theory seems plausible only when applied to pre-modern societies, that is, societies with very little social mobility and rigid caste or class structures, or (alternatively) only when applied to roles that we have little or no choice about occupying (like 'Mrs Luban's son'). Conversely, role theory seems particularly inadequate to describe a society like ours in which social and occupational mobility are fundamental facts of life. In particular, role theory does not provide a satisfactory account of professional morality. For people can discard professions, but they cannot discard moralities.

We might advance a sociological conjecture: in a society like ours with considerable social mobility and choice among social roles, it is hard to identify oneself with ones role because it is simply too obvious that the role is contingent. A related conjecture notices that modern societies are not only mobile but highly differentiated into relatively independent subsystems; since we play different roles in these various contexts, we cannot easily identify our selves with any one role. Our roles do not exhaust our selves.

Regardless of the truth of these conjectures, they highlight an important feature of our moral self-images, which we must next consider, if only to see why it is wrong. Corresponding to our view that morality is common to all persons, that is, to persons *simpliciter,* is a view of ourselves as persons first and role occupants only secondarily. The role theorist reduced us to the sum of our roles and nothing more. This, I have argued, proves to be a mistake. A first reaction to it, then, is to see ourselves as essentially free from our roles – as 'authentic' selves underlying the roles we play.

Luban goes on to consider the view that the idea of common morality requires us to see ourselves as having an existence outside our social situation and personal circumstances in the same way as actors have an identity after they have discarded their roles on stage. He points out that a similar notion was presupposed by Kantian moral theory but sees two fundamental difficulties with the idea of a 'metaphysics of the self'.

The first of these problems derives from a well-known criticism of Kant's ethics, which goes back to Hegel (and is developed very clearly by Bradley). Kant utilised our status as free and equal moral agents to derive a criterion of common morality: a moral law is one binding on all moral agents, so that the test of a maxim is its 'universalisability': 'Act only according to that maxim by which you can at the same time will that it should become a universal law.'

Hegel argued that this formula is so abstract that it is incapable of yielding any particular duties. One might, according to Hegel, be able to universalise both of two contradictory maxims without self-contradiction, and so Kant's test tells us little or nothing about our concrete obligations. What is crucial in giving content to the test is the set of mores already in place within one's society, for these give us some content to which to apply the formal test.

It is easiest to see the force of Hegel's criticism by turning to Kant's second formulation of his principle: 'Act so that you treat humanity, whether in your own person or in that of another, always as an end and never as a means only' – a principle that is sometimes paraphrased as the duty to treat people with the respect owed to persons as opposed to mere things. But there is obviously no such thing as respect in the abstract: respect is a function of the customs and practices of society, so Kant's universal moral law will have to be applied in culture-bound ways. This point is relevant to the problem of role morality, for what counts as respect will often be defined by the modes of interaction customary between persons in different roles. Treating (say) your waitress as a person and not a thing requires behaviour that, if engaged in with your children, would treat them as things and not as persons (and vice versa!).

This is one way in which the man-behind-the-social-mask view of the self simply cannot generate a common morality that is at once concrete and distinct from role morality. Another way becomes apparent when we notice that actions often cannot be described without tacit reference to roles. Consider an analogy: it is wrong to cut and maim a person, and no one can do so, not even a surgeon. But the fact that a surgeon carves you up in the course of an operation does not mean that she has done wrong, for the fact that it was surgery means that it is not correctly described as cutting and maiming. The important point is that in this case we are not faced with a conflict between role morality and common morality, because common morality does not forbid surgery: the seeming conflict arises only when we eliminate role-related terms such as 'surgery' from our moral vocabulary – a verbal confusion that forces us to misdescribe surgery as battery. When we focus exclusively on the man behind-the-social-mask, we are naturally led to impoverish our moral vocabulary in this way. What remains is a caricature of common morality. Common morality cannot be described without incorporating social roles: if it is, the result is empty and barren.

The second objection to regarding social roles as mere 'lendings' may be stated more easily. It implies that one might be able to dispense with roles, to live rolelessly and 'authentically.' But one cannot live outside social roles: to pretend to do so is merely the romantic posturing of one particular sort of social role – one so laden with self-deception that it is scarcely admirable. That role is the Bohemian, the noble savage, Mr Natural, the man or woman beyond roles. But a role it is. The rejecters of all pretence do, of course, live outside society – eight blocks outside, to be precise, in the warehouse district. Your guidebook will direct you to those famous bars where (as *Time* magazine reported) they reject social roles in never-to-be-forgotten evenings. They dress the same way and they talk the same way. And, while decade after decade it is their sense of style that makes urban culture vibrate, they are neither more authentic nor less corrupt than anyone else.

Other roles-that-reject-roles are no more attractive. Some people make a practice of denouncing hypocrisy, and by doing so they occupy the recognised (and hypocritical) role of 'moral bully.' To take another case, although it may be 'bad faith' to identify too closely with an occupational role, it is no less a distinct social role that withholds its commitment to a calling. Characteristically, that role is that of the adolescent, standing at life's crossroads with ideals too high for the compromises of professional role – as well as a belief that his own 'authenticity' is not to be sullied by the light of the public that darkens everything. Now, the adolescent's moral struggles are crucial – we've all gone through them-but someday, one way or another, they must end.... A fifty-year-old who has maintained his uncommitted authenticity may be more pathetic than pure. Nor should it be forgotten that Sartre who argued that role identification is bad faith, argued also that identification with a 'Me' that is not my role is bad faith as well.

The references to the moral bully, the Bohemian *poseur,* and the overgrown adolescent are hints that 'Me, that poor old ultimate actuality,' worthy though he (she? it?) may be in the noumenal realm, does not fare well, morally speaking, in this our vale of tears. The uncooptable twenty-year-old may claim to be purer than the rest of us, but if in fact he does no evil, it is probably because he doesn't yet have the power to do much of anything. And he frequently does more evil than he thinks: his unbendable integrity is of course highly erotic, and the moral detective might consider interviewing his sweethearts, particularly the one who became pregnant at just the moment when he could not bear to compromise his integrity by committing himself to the social roles of father or breadwinner (let alone husband). If he is forty years old, our judgment may be harsher still.

It is in the spirit of these observations that we should read Bradley's paradoxical formulation 'that to wish to be better than the world is to be already on the threshold of immorality.' Bradley says this at the conclusion of an eloquent attack on the individualistic metaphysics of 'Me, that poor old ultimate actuality' although the attack includes some unfortunate assumptions about the heritability of moral characteristics, it does not rest on these assumptions and should not be dismissed on their basis. Since, moreover, Bradley also provides a clear formulation of the Hegelian criticism of Kant, my previous arguments amount to a gloss on Bradley. This suggests giving at least an initial hearing to the solution he proposes to the problem, a solution that turns Kantian universalism on its head. Bradley's solution resolves conflicts between role morality and common morality in favour of the former: that action is justified whose justification consists in appealing to one's social role. Ultimately, I shall argue, as Bradley does later, that this too is an unacceptable moral theory; first, however, we must see how it works.

Luban argues that role morality requires consideration of the reasons which justify a social role, but that once this role been found to be generally justified, these ('exclusionary') reasons forbid reconsideration of the justification of the act required by the role. The only question for the agent is whether the act which makes him uncomfortable is required by the role. The policy justifying the role trumps worries about particular acts.

...the general argument in favour of putting policies over acts is both well-known and forceful: Policies over acts leads to greater predictability and regularity in social behaviour. If we could not count on persons occupying certain social roles (those that affect other people, us) to act according to the expectations of their roles, we would live in a very capricious society indeed. It would, furthermore, be a society in which our ability to accomplish our daily business would be delivered over to the personal discretion of many people we have no particular reason to trust. If you want to execute a will, the last thing you need is a lawyer who won't draw up the papers unless you first pass the test of a genuine I-Thou encounter, or who reserves the right to donate the funds she is managing to the charity of her choice. Finally, it is worth noting that the burden of such moral discretionary power is likely to fall most heavily upon the poor, the nonconformists, the dissidents, the *déclassé*, for they are most likely to have ends that outrage the moral sensibilities of the bureaucrats and functionaries with whom they must deal. These are strong reasons for holding role agents to the policies that define their roles...

What this amounts to is the parcelling out of moral tasks among the various social roles: it is a division of moral labour in society. Someone other than the agent – a legislator, or the famous impersonal 'they' or 'everyone'- evaluates the policies that set the perimeter to the role the agent is occupying. The agent herself, then, need not think about moral issues at all – for moral questions about acts are eliminated by the exclusionary reasons contained in the role, while moral questions about policies are someone else's concern.

The idea has its attractions. The main one, of course, is this: just as the division of labour enables economic work to be more efficiently accomplished, the division of moral labour allows moral work to be more efficiently accomplished. The tasks of each role are simplified and the roles provide checks and balances for each role's one-sidedness.

...I think that similar ideas were being expressed, albeit in a more old-fashioned terminology, by Bradley a century ago. Using the familiar metaphor that likens society to an organism, Bradley defended 'my station and its duties' by suggesting that the various stations were like organs in the body, which contribute to the life of the whole by fulfilling their preordained tasks.

OBJECTIONS TO 'MY STATION AND ITS DUTIES'

By means of these concepts – the policies over acts approach to moral evaluation, exclusionary and protected reasons, and division of moral labour – we see the structure of 'my station and its duties,' together with three reasons for adopting it: the need for social regularity, the desire for greater efficiency in 'moral work,' and of course the fact that it allows us to dispense with a dubious metaphysics of the self. Despite this, I find the picture that has emerged unsatisfactory.

First of all, there is something too neat and artificial about the way individual actions are excluded from moral assessment by second-order reasons. '*Logically* excluded only!' one reminds me: but what does that mean? In reality it can mean only one of two things: either the role agent is supposed not even to think about the excluded moral reasons that bear on her act – she is to 'think policy only!'- or else, although she may think whatever she wishes, she is not to act on those excluded thoughts. The latter is psychologically more realistic, but neither alternative is acceptable.

The problem with the first is a psychological or characterological one. A morally responsible person is a person who does not shrink from thinking in moral terms about what she does, when that is appropriate. Can we really imagine that such a person does not think in moral terms about acts, but only about policies? Moral deliberation is not a passive program that waits for whatever preselected inputs we choose to feed it: it requires first and foremost a disposition of character that is, a settled trait of personality. We must be disposed to look at ethical angles in situations we confront even though doing so is often confusing or unpleasant. Many people do not have this disposition. And if you have it, you find that it cannot be turned on or off at will, nor can it be directed with precision at only one type of logical object, a 'policy' rather than an 'act.'

If we try to imagine someone with a disposition to view the morality of all her actions from the very abstract standpoint of their underlying policies, without so much as thinking about their contingent features, we are not going to find the result attractive. Such a person would ponder the people she meets and the choices she confronts only from the viewpoint of the policies that apply to them. She is cut off from the immediate affections and tensions that are the source of the moral life. She always does the right thing, but only because one should. She is not a moral model: she is a moral prig.

It is more likely, however, that a person who does not think morally about acts does not think morally about policies either. Now we are confronted with Adolf Eichmann, rather than a moral prig. According to Hannah Arendt's memorable and unnerving analysis of the 'banality of evil,' Eichmann's evil was of a wholly different character from that of (say) Hitler or Himmler, because Eichmann had no monstrous or even malicious intentions. According to Arendt, he was quite simply incapable of thinking about what he was doing. Whether she was right or not, the picture she paints is all too plausible, and it is an important source of worry about 'my station and its duties': if one does not think about one's station because one has no disposition to think morally at all, then one never addresses the possibility that that station is evil. In that case, institutional excuses will be unavailable, or (what amounts to the same thing) come all too easily. The functionary who simply carries out his role obligations regardless of their effects on others is frightening to contemplate, and this model is uncomfortably close to 'my station and its duties.' Sometimes, Mr Bradley, you had better be better than your world.

Perhaps it will be granted that to think morally about policies, a decent person will, as a matter of psychological necessity, have to think morally about acts as well. And surely most lawyers who invoke the adversary system excuse are conscientious, morally reflective people, not Adolf Eichmanns. This brings us to the alternative interpretation of policies over acts: although one *thinks* morally about acts as well as policies, one deliberately excludes the former considerations from one's reasons for *doing* something.

But the still small voice of conscience is not so easily quieted. An agent confronts her decisions one at a time. If, after balancing the wrong done by breaking role against the wrong done by acting within a role – a 'simple' first-order balancing of the sort exclusionary reasons are supposed to exclude – one sees that the action is morally unacceptable, it cannot be correct to sweep this insight under the rug by saying that the individual act is not after all the logical subject of moral evaluation. As Bernard Williams puts it in an argument against rule-utilitarianism,

> Whatever the general utility of having a certain rule, if one has actually reached the point of seeing that the utility of breaking it on a certain occasion is greater than that of following it [and one is a utilitarian], then surely it would be pure irrationality not to break it?

The second difficulty with 'my station and its duties' is a worry about what 'my station and its duties' means in the context of modern bureaucratic organisations. The structure of bureaucratic institutions, such as those in a political system, lends itself to divided responsibility. Those who make the rules, those who give the orders, and those who carry them out each have some basis for claiming that they are not at fault for any wrong that results. Those with the authority don't know, they often tell us, what their operatives and functionaries are doing, nor are they themselves the ones who pull the triggers. And those who pull the triggers are just following orders. So it goes up and down the line, for even those who give the orders are relying on information gotten from their subordinates. They walk like angels through the moral world, surrounded by the radiant halos of their deniability. At the extremes of the hierarchy, we are left with an ignorant God who foolishly trusted his lieutenants, and innocent devils who had no authority to spare their victims. A day does not pass in which we do not read these stories in the newspapers.

This worry about large bureaucratic organisations actually breaks down into three separate though related problems. Psychologically, role players in such organisations lack the emotional sense that they are morally responsible for the consequences of organisational behaviour – they have what Eichmann called a 'Pontius Pilate feeling.' Politically, responsibility cannot be localised on the organisational chart, and thus in some real (albeit wholly artificial and self-serving) way no one – no one – ever is responsible. Morally, role players have insufficient information to be confident that they are in a position to deliberate effectively, because bureaucratic organisations parcel out information along functional lines. Put the psychological, political, and moral problems together and you have a recipe for the moral universe of Kafka's *The Trial* and *The Castle*...

It seems to me that earlier we approached our independence from roles in the wrong way. We viewed it as an indulgence we grant ourselves as moral agents, and worried that this indulgence lapses into an incoherent transcendental romanticism – into 'Me, that poor old ultimate actuality.'

A great deal of the finest recent moral philosophy has emphasised the idea that a moral theory owes us an account of the moral agent as well as the moral laws. But in the present case, I believe that such an emphasis is misplaced. Our independence from roles derives from the claim of the moral *patient*, the person affected by our actions, and not the agent. It is for the sake of you as 'poor old ultimate actuality,' and not for the sake of me, that I must be able to break loose from the duties of my station.

Recall what is attractive about the division of moral labour, its efficacy in performing what I called 'the moral work.' It involves a system of stations that interact with other stations in stereotyped or routinised patterns. And, in this Idealist dream of organic social solidarity, these routinised interactions enhance the good of each of us by enhancing the life of all. But now recall the problem with this idea, that modern bureaucracy deadens the moral life of the agent and turns the Idealist dream into a Kafkaesque nightmare – a nightmare in which the functionaries occupying society's stations indifferently go about their business regardless of the plight we are in.

We need not even bring in bureaucracy, however, because the problem was in fact pointed out by Bradley in his own remarkable criticism of 'my station and its duties':

> It is necessary to remark that the community ... may be in a confused or rotten condition, so that in it right and might do not always go together. And the very best community can only ensure that correspondence in the gross; it cannot do so in every detail.

In the details of daily life, the moral patient may be in a predicament that is not a characteristic of her station. Such a moral patient cannot be identified with a role, because human woes do not respect role boundaries. Trouble, which cuts across roles, takes us to the lowest common denominator of all roles-and that is what we call *the Person*. The moral agent, in turn, is a person because she can adopt the patient's point of view – she can recognise and acknowledge the person in trouble. But how should the agent act? Responding within the confines of the agent's role will (by hypothesis) not do the job. The duties of my station do not permit me to respond to the unusual situation, the unexpected situation, the case in which following the rules wrongs someone and a simple deviation from the rules – from the role-saves him. And so I must be prepared to break the role.[19]

Building on this position, Luban claims that role obligations are presumptions, the strength of which depends on the moral worth of the institution by which they are required. These obligations can be rebutted if the conduct required by the role obligation would be regarded as a serious infringement of common morality. Thus fatherhood is a role which carries certain obligations (for example the duty to be home in time to say good night to the children) which depend for their strength upon the importance of the institution of the family. Whilst this institution might justify a great deal (leaving work early for example throwing additional burdens on more junior colleagues), the institutional excuse has its limits. The claims of common morality would overcome the institutional excuse for example if father were to face a choice between being home in good time and stopping on the way home to call the emergency services to the scene of an accident.

Lawyers' claim to be immune from the claims of common morality is typically said to rest upon the merits of the institution known as the adversary system of trial. These have been most famously elaborated by Fuller and Randall.

> The lawyer appearing as an advocate before a tribunal presents, as persuasively as he can, the facts and the law of the case as seen from the standpoint of his client's interest. It is essential that both the lawyer and the public understand clearly the nature of the role thus discharged. Such an understanding is required not only to appreciate the need for an adversary presentation of issues, but also in order to perceive truly the limits partisan advocacy must impose on itself if it is to remain wholesome and useful.

19   *Lawyers and Justice*: supra note 2 at pp 109-111; 113-116; 118-119, 120-127.

In a very real sense it may be said that the integrity of the adjudicative process itself depends upon the participation of the advocate. This becomes apparent when we contemplate the nature of the task assumed by any arbiter who attempts to decide a dispute without the aid of partisan advocacy.

Such an arbiter must undertake, not only the role of judge, but that of representative for both of the litigants. Each of these roles must be played to the full without being muted by qualifications derived from the others. When he is developing for each side the most effective statement of its' case, the arbiter must put aside his neutrality and permit himself to be moved by a sympathetic identification sufficiently intense to draw from his mind all that it is capable of giving – in analysis, patience and creative power. When he resumes his neutral position, he must be able to view with distrust the fruits of this identification and be ready to reject the products of his own best mental efforts. The difficulties of this undertaking are obvious. If it is true that a man in his time must play many parts, it is scarcely given to him to play them all at once.

It is small wonder, then , that failure generally attends the attempt to dispense with the distinct roles traditionally implied in adjudication. What generally occurs in practice is that at some early point a familiar pattern will seem to emerge from the evidence: an accustomed label is waiting for the case and, without awaiting further proofs, this label is promptly assigned to it. It is a mistake to suppose that this premature cataloguing must necessarily result from impatience, prejudice or mental sloth. Often it proceeds from a very understandable desire to bring the hearing into some order and coherence, for without some tentative theory of the case there is no standard of relevance by which testimony may be measured. But what starts as a preliminary diagnosis designed to direct the inquiry tends quickly and imperceptibly, to become a fixed conclusion, as all that confirms the diagnosis makes a strong imprint on the mind, while all that runs counter to it is received with diverted attention.

An adversary presentation seems the only effective means for combating this natural human tendency to judge too swiftly in terms of the familiar that which is not yet fully known. The arguments of counsel hold the case, as it were, in suspension between two opposing interpretations of it. While the proper classification of the case is thus kept unresolved, there is time to explore all of its' peculiarities and nuances...

It is only through the advocate's participation that the hearing may remain in fact what it purports to be in theory: a public trial of the facts and issues. Each advocate comes to the hearing prepared to present his proofs and arguments, knowing at the same time that his arguments may fail to persuade and that his proofs may be rejected as inadequate. It is a part of his role to absorb these possible disappointments. The deciding tribunal, on the other hand, comes to the hearing uncommitted. It has not represented to the public that any fact can be proved, that any argument is sound, or that any particular way of stating a litigant's case is the most effective expression of its merits.

The matter assumes a very different aspect when the deciding tribunal is compelled to take into its own hands the preparations that must precede the public hearing. In such a case the tribunal cannot truly be said to come to the hearing uncommitted, for it has itself appointed the channels along which the public inquiry is to run. If an unexpected turn in the testimony reveals a miscalculation in the design of these channels, there is no advocate to absorb the blame. The deciding tribunal is under a strong temptation to keep the hearing moving within the boundaries originally set for it. The result may be that the hearing loses its character as an open trial of the facts and issues, and becomes instead a ritual designed to provide public confirmation for what the tribunal considers it has already established in private. When this occurs adjudication acquires the taint affecting all institutions that become subject to manipulation, presenting one aspect to the public, another to knowing participants.

These, then, are the reasons for believing that partisan advocacy plays a vital and essential role in one of the most fundamental procedures of a democratic society. But if we were to put all of these detailed considerations to one side, we should still be confronted by the fact that, in whatever form adjudication may appear, the experienced judge or arbitrator desires and actively seeks to obtain an adversary presentation of the issues. Only when he has had the benefit of intelligent and vigorous advocacy on both sides can he feel fully confident of his decision.

Viewed in this light, the role of the lawyer as a partisan advocate appears not as a regrettable necessity, but as an indispensable part of a larger ordering of affairs. The institution of advocacy is not a concession to the frailties of human nature but an expression of human insight in the design of a social framework within which man's capacity for impartial judgement can attain its fullest realisation.

When advocacy is thus viewed, it becomes clear by what principle limits must be set to partisanship. The advocate plays his role well when zeal for his client's cause promotes a wise and informed decision of the case. He plays his role badly, and trespasses against the obligations of professional responsibility, when his desire to win leads him to muddy the headwaters of decision, when instead of lending a needed perspective to the controversy he distorts and obscures its true nature.[20]

However, *Lawyers and Justice* contains a forceful and convincing attack on the alleged merits of the adversary system. Luban points out for example that when lawyers really are concerned to establish the truth (for example when researching the law prior to advising the client as to how a transaction should be structured) they almost never ask others within their office to research the law with a view to establishing diametrically opposed points of view in the faith that a clear picture of the law will somehow emerge from their adversarial efforts. Considerable faith is required if one is to believe that a system in which neither side need disclose to the other the existence of relevant witnesses is likely to establish the truth. The adversary system survives indeed only because alternative adjudicatory systems are not demonstrably better. Consequently, the adversary system generates only weak role obligations and weak excuses against the claims of common morality. Where the demands of role seriously conflict with common morality the lawyer should do what common morality requires. Sometimes this may be achieved by dialogue with the client. Sometimes it may be achieved by withdrawal from the case but in extreme cases the lawyer should betray the client.

Luban's approach can be illustrated by its impact upon *Spaulding v Zimmerman*. As noted, neither the Model Rules nor the Model Code nor the LSGPC nor the CCB would permit a lawyer in that situation to disclose. Morally however the position is

---

20   Lon L Fuller and John D Randall 'Professional Responsibility: Report of the Joint Conference of the ABA AALS' (1958) 44 American Bar Association Journal 1159, 1160-61.

different. The obligation to keep client confidences (the role obligation) is justified by the argument that confidentiality is necessary to encourage clients to be forthright with their lawyers. Such candour is necessary if the lawyer is to function as an adversarial advocate within the adversary system. However, the professional obligations of the adversarial advocate's role are as we have seen only weak presumptions about what is morally obligatory. Here the presumption is outweighed by the very serious moral wrong which will be suffered by the plaintiff if the defendant's lawyer keeps silent. Hence the lawyer should attempt to persuade the client to disclose and if persuasion fails, the lawyer should 'blow the whistle'. A lawyer who is willing to break role obligations in order to comply with common morality is in Luban's terminology a 'moral activist'.

Note

Stephen Pepper's first class citizenship model of legal representation can be seen as an attempt to respond to the weaknesses of the adversary system as a foundation for a professional role morality for lawyers. In Luban's terms, autonomous decision-making by clients within the limits of the law is an institution of such value that it demands of lawyers an amoral role. This role requires the lawyer to assist the client to achieve the clients goals even if those goals are contrary to common morality.

Question

Is 'common morality' a workable limit upon a lawyer's duty to comply with the obligations of his/her occupational role? Note Stephen Ellmann's comment that

> If Luban's references to common morality were meant to direct us to 'commonly accepted morality,' we might well respond that he had adopted a moral standard whose elements were neither necessarily valid nor even clearly defined. Whether what most people accept as moral is actually 'right' would have to be decided. What it is that most people accept would also have to be determined. I am not sure there is *any* moral common denominator. Even if there is, by the time we reach the question of the morality of particular legal tactics, the diversity of views is likely to be immense.[1]

Lawyers and institutional obligations

Luban's conclusion about the Mount Pleasant Bodies case is rather different. He argues that zealous criminal defence lawyers perform a vital role in a valuable institution (the adversarial criminal trial). Consequently, it generates strong institutional excuses against the claims of common morality, a claim we shall examine in detail in the next

1   Stephen Ellman 'Lawyering for Justice in a Flawed Democracy' [1992] 90 Columbia Law Review 116 at p122.

chapter. However even if this claim about the special qualities of criminal defence work is correct, further difficulties arise. In particular, the argument seems to show only that lawyers *may* ignore common morality not that they must do so. Let us grant that partisan criminal defence advocacy is an important bulwark against the power of the State and that it is important that criminal defendants be assured that matters disclosed to their lawyers will be kept confidential. Did that *require* Frank Armani to keep secret where the bodies were buried contrary to the promptings of those speaking for common morality? For if Armani had disclosed (and especially if he had disclosed anonymously) it is most unlikely that such disclosure would have done much long-term damage to the work of criminal defence lawyers.

The question thus raised is the surprisingly simple but often ignored, issue of why lawyers are *obliged* to obey their professional code when it conflicts with common morality and/or their own conscience. This is a vital issue. Given that much of the work of lawyers is difficult to observe[2], self-interest, especially the fear of being caught and professionally disciplined, provides very little incentive to comply. It would have been easy for Armani to disclose anonymously. If no argument can be found it may turn out that the Standard Conception which requires lawyers not to go beyond the bound of the law is too restrictive. Indeed, there follows the yet more fundamental question of why clients are obliged to obey the law. Again, if no argument can be found, the Standard Conception will turn out to have been too restrictive. In the following extract, Luban responds to an article by David Wasserman[3] in which Wasserman alleged that Luban had failed to show any reason why Armani was morally *required* to remain silent.

> In chapter three of *Lawyers and Justice*, I addressed, briefly and no doubt inadequately, one of the most ancient philosophical problems about law: the problem of determining whether laws are ever a source of moral obligation. The heart of my solution to this problem is that whenever laws amount only to a 'vertical' relation between government – 'the state' – and its subjects, they create no moral obligations. They amount to nothing more than commands. However, whenever laws can rightly be viewed as (instituting) co-operative schemes among citizens – when they establish 'horizontal' relations – the possibility of obligation arises, generated out of solidarity with our fellows and respect for them. Some laws establish horizontal relations among us, but some do not. As a result, some laws are a source of moral obligation, but some are not. To the extent that lawyers disrupt valid legal co-operative schemes, they wrong their fellows, and thus, the principle of partisanship, which requires lawyers to treat all laws as mere obstacles to or instruments of client interest, cannot be correct.

> Wasserman accepts my four basic points: (i) that 'vertical' laws – commands – are no source of moral obligations; (ii) that 'horizontal' laws – social co-operative schemes – can be a source of moral obligation; (iii) thus, that we lie under an obligation to respect some, but not all, laws; and (iv) that the principle of partisanship therefore fails. He differs from me over the exact conditions under which horizontal laws create moral obligations.

---

2   See chapter 1 supra at p 5.
3   David Wasserman 'Should a Good Lawyer Do The Right Thing? David Luban On The Morality of Adversary Representation' [1990] 49 Maryland Law Review 392 at pp 395-402.

In the subsequent discussion, I will focus on one example from *Lawyers and Justice* that Wasserman discusses at some length. 'On a trip to London, you observe people queuing up at a bus stop. How nice! you think. How unlike Manhattan! Forthwith, you cut into the front of the line.' You have done something wrong, but what? What rules out anarchy in the UK? I argue that the obligation to participate in the queuing arrangement is like the obligation to obey horizontal laws; I offer the queuing example to motivate my argument that some laws create legitimate moral obligations. Wasserman locates the source of obligation in this example elsewhere, and concludes that the example has little bearing on the obligation to obey the law. As we shall see, this difference is quite important.

I claimed in *Lawyers and Justice* that co-operative schemes create obligations when
(1) they create benefits;
(2) the benefits are general: they accrue, in a sense I shall explain subsequently, to the whole community;
(3) widespread participation in the scheme is necessary for it to succeed;
(4) the scheme actually elicits widespread participation; and
(5) the scheme is a reasonable or important one.

I should note that my argument in *Lawyers and Justice* (including the three examples to which Wasserman directs his criticism) aimed primarily at showing that (5) – the reasonableness of the co-operative scheme – should be substituted for the stronger requirement that
(5') the benefits actually are accepted by citizens (either tacitly or explicitly).

This is a highly significant substitution, for it yields a significantly more paternalistic account of legal obligation than (5'): on my view, we may lie under an obligation to participate in reasonable, generally beneficial co-operative schemes even without accepting their benefits. Many theorists, and indeed several American subcultures – the 'rugged individualists,' the libertarians, the survivalists, the Ayn Rand devotees – insist on (5') rather than (5); they view compulsory co-operative schemes with suspicion, as attempts by the collectivised multitudes to shanghai free individuals into press gangs to further alien and often stupid and unnecessary ends. In my view, by contrast, the invention of such co-operative schemes lies at the heart of the human condition. They are not merely conveniences, or merely optional; and communitarians harping on 'the social nature' of human life are not simply whistling Dixie.

Where does law fit into this picture? Co-operative schemes involving many people are hard to organise. Sometimes they require co-ordinating the behaviour of multitudes; sometimes they require breaking deadlocks; and sometimes they face collective action problems. In many such cases, people acting on their own will find it virtually impossible to achieve the optimal result – in the language of game theory, there may be no equilibrium, or the equilibrium may not be optimal – but an external authority can create a stable and optimal outcome. This the authority does through law. Strictly speaking, such laws are not themselves co-operative schemes; rather, they are instrumentally essential to co-operative schemes. Thus, still speaking strictly, laws themselves have no moral authority, though they may be necessary for the creation of schemes that possess moral authority. *In Lawyers and Justice,* I ignored this distinction, but for my purposes both there and here it is unimportant, and I happily accept it.

I argued in *Lawyers and Justice* that non-compliance with a co-operative scheme morally

> wrongs our fellows who participate in it to the extent that it expresses disrespect for them. Sometimes non-compliance expresses no such disrespect, and in that case the moral wrong of non-compliance disappears.
>
> From my point of view, the most characteristic, important, and interesting such case arises when people engage in conscientious disobedience to discriminatory laws, as was the case in the civil rights movement. Discriminatory laws fail to obligate us because they violate condition (2), the 'generality requirement,' which insists that the benefits of a law accrue to the whole community. In my characterisation of the five necessary conditions for legal obligation, the generality requirement functions as a kind of equal protection clause

Luban goes on to argue that his generality requirement (like the equal protection clause of the 14th Amendment to the US Constitution) does not require a law to benefit everyone before it can claim obedience. Indeed, a particular law may impose burdens on a particular group provided that the system of law does not regularly disadvantage that particular group. Thus, whether a law is generally beneficial requires it to be evaluated in the context of the legal system as a whole. He continues:

> The important point to take from this discussion is that a law may satisfy (1) – (5), and thus impose moral obligations upon us, even though we do not benefit from it. Wasserman errs, therefore, when he attributes to me the view that our duty of fair play rests on the benefits we receive from co-operative schemes and thus that 'our indignation at the person who cuts in front [of a queue] is aroused by her ingratitude' at the benefits conferred by the queuing arrangement. Indeed, I intended my argument as an *alternative to* the Socratic theory that we owe obligations of gratitude to the state for benefits received. The role of benefits – condition (1) above – in my argument is more indirect than Wasserman suggests. Only if a legally-created scheme creates benefits (for someone) does it make sense to regard non-compliance with the scheme as an expression of disrespect for our fellows; as I wrote in *Lawyers and Justice*, 'If the members of my community . . . choose to stand immersed up to their necks in the outhouse tank, it is hard to see why I have good reason to go along with them.' The creation of benefits is necessary for us to regard the plan as a morally significant scheme of social co-operation; but having established that it is such a scheme, the moral obligation to participate follows from the requirement to respect our fellows, regardless of the actual receipt of benefits by any particular person.
>
> It follows that when Wasserman protests that '[w]e would be equally indignant [at someone skipping in queue] even if the circumstances denied her any short- or long-term advantage from the queuing arrangement' he has not raised an objection to my view but to a gratitude-based theory of legal obligation that I reject. On my view, the short- or long-term advantage you derive from a queuing arrangement need have nothing to do with whether you lie under an obligation to wait your turn. Wasserman and I agree completely about this case.
>
> Wasserman, however, disagrees with me about the more general moral basis for queuing. I suggest that queuing establishes a co-operative scheme satisfying (1)-(5), and thus that the fairness and reasonableness of queuing obligate us to respect the arrangement, whereas Wasserman believes that the force of the example derives from 'our pre-existing duty to defer to those who have arrived first. A rule of 'first come,

first served' equalises the burden of waiting in settings in which variations in need are relatively slight and impractical to ascertain. . . .' Wasserman finds, we may say, a kind of natural law basis for the queuing arrangement: queuing is merely a scheme that 'allows us to honour our pre-existing duty to defer to those who have arrived first.'

If morality or natural law truly mandated first-come-first served, however, we ought to regard all other schemes for equalising the burden of waiting as morally objectionable. To take the most common alternative to single-line queuing, we ought to condemn the multiple queues at supermarkets and fast food outlets on moral grounds, since they do not follow the 'natural law' of first come-first-served. That seems odd to me. Suppose, moreover, that I reach the counter at Benny's Burrito Barn before a person in the next line who I observed coming in before me. If we truly recognise first-come-first-served as an antecedent duty, we ought to agree that I am obligated to offer that person the opportunity to go before me. Perhaps so; but here again my intuitions do not lead me to think anything of the sort.

Indeed, I detect an inconsistency in Wasserman's own views over just this point. Wasserman at one point likens multiple-line queuing arrangements in fast food outlets to a kind of lottery, in which customers take 'the luck of their lane.' That is precisely how it seems to me as well; but in that case he should acknowledge either that first-come-first-served is no natural law antecedent duty or else-a more complex view-that it is a peculiar sort of natural law duty that arises only when it is realised in a co-operative scheme and disintegrates when the co-operative scheme actually in place falls to institute it. I do not know exactly -what to think about the latter alternative, other than that it differs from my own view only in a rarefied and metaphysical way.

Why might Wasserman insist that queuing arrangements merely fulfil an antecedent duty of fairness rather than creating such a duty as I argue? My guess is that it is because first-come-first served seems like the only fair scheme for allocating 'the burden of waiting in settings in which variations in need are relatively slight and impractical to ascertain.' Perhaps he is right about that. Perhaps there really is something morally deficient about multiple-lane queuing in the supermarket. After all, we might reflect, the persuasive force of the queuing example lies precisely in the fact that we all agree on the intuitive moral force of queuing; if queuing were just one of many equally fair patterns for boarding a bus, we probably would not find the example compelling. When there is only one fair scheme it seems to pre-exist the practical arrangements that realise it.

In that case, however, I think that we should shake free from the example long enough to recall that the overwhelming majority of community purposes can be realised fairly in a variety of ways. Consider the income tax. Most of us agree that tax burdens ought to be distributed fairly, but what does that mean? Does it mean equal tax rates? Equal loss of utility? Equal loss of percentage of utility? Clearly, arguments can be made for various such schemes, and even after settling the general question it would be strange indeed if only one possible tax schedule filled the bill. Or consider bankruptcy. Is it really plausible that only one set of bankruptcy laws fairly distributes the losses among creditors? Indeed, even natural lawyers deny that natural law dictates uniquely justifiable solutions to legal problems. In the words of John Finnis,

> in Aquinas's view, the law consists in part ... of rules which are 'derived from natural laws like implementations [*determinationes*] of general directives.' This

notion of *determinatio* he explains on the analogy of architecture (or any other practical art), in which a general idea or 'form' (say, 'house', 'door', 'door-knob') has to be made determinate as this particular house, door, door-knob, with specifications which are certainly derived from and shaped by the general idea but which could have been more or less different in many (even in every!) particular dimension and aspect.

In the vast array of cases in which many different fair *determinationes* of the same collective end are possible, we will lie under no antecedent duty to bring our behaviour into line with any one of these *determinationes*. Only after one of them has been enacted legally will we find ourselves obligated by fairness to respect the law. In such a case, we will not be tempted to locate the obligation of fair play in antecedent duties.

Wasserman writes, 'In both the bus-queue and blocked-lane cases, the obligation we feel to comply with the co-operative scheme is contingent upon our acceptance of the priority rule it enforces.' With the above observations in mind, I would recast his point in the negative: the obligation we feel to comply with the co-operative scheme is contingent on our not finding the priority rule it enforces morally objectionable. Or, in the terminology I introduced earlier, the obligation is contingent on our not finding the priority rule unfair, unbeneficial, or unreasonable. When only one fair priority rule exists, then Wasserman's phrasing and mine coincide: if we do not find a rule unfair and only one rule is a candidate, then we morally agree with it. But in the case of real-life laws, when many reasonable schemes are possible, then Wasserman asks too much: he conditions the moral obligation to comply with a co-operative scheme on its unique suitability, rather than its generally beneficial reasonableness.

In the end, I believe that this seemingly-minor difference may run very deep. When we admit that our fellows hold the power to obligate us to participate in schemes with which we disagree schemes that may not be utterly brilliant or maximally fair – we have made an important concession of our own liberty. We acknowledge that we can be bound by social practices and histories that are imperfect and largely arbitrary. Few of us will derive comfort from this acknowledgment, for we all harbour a profound rebelliousness. The desire to restrict our obligations to those legal schemes that are uniquely reasonable may not differ much in the end from the libertarian's desire to restrict our obligations to those schemes whose benefits we have explicitly accepted. Both arise from a kind of revulsion at falling into the clutches of other people, though we recognise at the same time that 'no man is an island.'

Earlier, I argued that the dilemma between role and individuality, constraint and freedom, rule and act, amounts to an irresolvable conflict within human life. It is romantic excess to insist on absolute freedom, but every surrender to constraint is a loss of something precious. If we can find no way out of this dilemma in practice, perhaps we should not be surprised to find it recurring, in one guise or another, throughout moral and political theory.[4]

---

4   'Freedom and Constraint in Legal Ethics: Some Mid-Course Corrections to Lawyers and Justice' [1992] 49 Maryland Law Review 424 at pp 452-462 .

Questions

1. You are driving along a three-lane motorway which is suddenly reduced to one lane by road works. You wait patiently in the outside lane while a policeman directs the traffic into the remaining lane, one car advancing in succession from each of the three lanes. When you are third in line in your lane, the car which is first in line proceeds in accordance with the officer's instructions. The car which is second in line follows immediately whilst the officers attention is distracted. You feel annoyed. But is the response justified and, if so, why? What would Luban say?

2. Suppose Frank Armani had felt strongly that he was obliged by common morality to reveal where the bodies were buried. How could Luban's argument about the obligation to obey the law be reformulated as an argument for Armani's complying with the obligation imposed by his professional code to keep silent?

3. Does a lawyer have any moral obligation to obey the applicable Code of Ethics? Would it be relevant to ask whether the lawyer had sworn to obey that Code of Ethics?

4. Why does respect for others require participating in beneficial schemes of co-operation which you would not personally choose? Can you not equally show respect by refusing to join in and allowing others to do likewise? More generally, why should you respect others?

4　William Simon and ethical discretion

A contextual approach

William Simon's advice to those who would be good people and good lawyers is easy to state but difficult to follow:

> (the) basic maxim is that the lawyer should take such actions as, considering the relevant circumstances of the case, seem likely to promote justice.[5]

His approach is distinguished from most other approaches to legal ethics in that it is contextual/discretionary[6] rather than categorical. A categorical approach prescribes hard and fast rules subject to well defined exceptions and might be either the standard conception (which Simon labels 'libertarian') requiring the lawyer to do for the client anything except that which is clearly illegal; alternatively it might be what he calls the 'public interest model'[7] ie an approach which requires the lawyer to do that will resolve disputes as the institutions of the state would wish to resolve them.

5　*The Practice of Justice* supra p 133 note 3 at p 9.
6　Simon seems to have used the two terms 'contextual' and 'discretionary' to describe one and the same approach to ethical judgment at different stages in the development of his thinking.
7　This in turn corresponds to what was described in chapter 1 as the democratic model. Supra p 5.

According to Simon, all the difficult questions arise from one of three ethical tensions. The first is the tension between procedure and substance: should the lawyer use the procedural rules of the legal system so as to frustrate a valid claim eg by invoking the statute of limitations? The second is the tension between form and substance: should the lawyer frustrate the purpose of a valid legal rule by interpreting it in a way which is faithful to its' language but frustrates its' purposes. Thirdly, there is the tension between broad and narrow framing: an ethical issue is narrowly framed when it excludes from consideration issues of distributive justice which might, if considered, be thought to justify conduct which would seem unethical if these issues were ignored. For example, principle 19.01 of the LSGPC provides that it is professional misconduct for one solicitor to deceive another. This seems to prohibit lying in negotiations regardless of context, thus framing the issue narrowly. A wider perspective might say that some lies were justified for example when negotiating on behalf of a party unfairly disadvantaged in litigation by a relative lack of resources. Thus lies might sometimes be justified when acting for a privately funded personal injury claimant or a woman with dependent children in matrimonial proceedings. Categorical approaches tend to resolve these tensions in the same manner regardless of context so that the libertarian approach prefers procedure to substance, form to substance and narrow framing to broad framing. Simon's approach by contrast instructs lawyers to resolve these tensions in the way which will best promote justice. Thus, the ethical lawyer is required to engage in the complex ethical judgment which Ronald Dworkin believes is characteristic of common law adjudication. Dworkin calls his ideal judge Hercules. Simon can perhaps be regarded as describing his career prior to his or her elevation to the Bench.

In the following passage, Simon describes the discretionary approach in operation:

the lawyer's assessment of merit involves an attempt to reconcile the conflicting legal values implicated directly in the client's claim or goal. These conflicts usually arise in the form of the overlapping tensions between substance and procedure, purpose and form, and broad and narrow framing.

By tending to privilege one or the other of the conflicting elements, the conventional approaches discourage the lawyer from confronting these tensions. In doing so, they authorise or require the lawyer to act in a way that she would concede, were she encouraged to make a judgment on the issue, frustrates the most legally appropriate resolution of the matter. By contrast, the discretionary approach requires that the lawyer make her best effort to achieve the most appropriate resolution in each case.

The discretionary approach does not ignore considerations of institutional competence. It does not assume that the full responsibility for a proper resolution rests on the lawyer alone. It is compatible with the conventional understanding of the role of judicial and administrative officials in law enforcement. The discretionary approach is distinctive, first, in treating the premises of that understanding as rebuttable presumptions that do not warrant reliance when they do not apply, and second, in imposing a more flexible and demanding duty on the lawyer to facilitate an official decision when the premises do apply.

1. *Substance Versus Procedure.-* One manifestation of the substance versus procedure

tension is the lawyer's sense of the limitations both of her individual judgment of the substantive merits of the dispute on the one hand and of the established procedures for resolving it on the other. We could tell the lawyer to work only to advance claims and goals that she determined were entitled to prevail. The most important objection to this precept is not that the lawyer's decisions about the merits would be controversial -- the decisions of judges, juries, and executive officials may also be controversial. Instead, the most important objection is that judges, juries, and executive officials acting within the relevant public procedures are generally able to make more reliable determinations on the merits than the individual lawyer. But the qualification 'generally' is crucial. The lawyer will often have good reason to recognise that the standard procedure is not reliably constructed to respond to the problem at hand, and she will often be in a position to contribute to its improvement.

The basic response of the discretionary approach to the substance-procedure tension is this: the more reliable the relevant procedures and institutions, the less direct responsibility the lawyer need assume for the substantive justice of the resolution; the less reliable the procedures and institutions, the more direct responsibility she need assume for substantive justice.

This means, to begin with, that the lawyer needs to develop a style of representation that will, in the general procedural context in which she practices, best contribute to just resolutions. This will normally be the regulatory 'on the merits' style, but it may incorporate some elements of the libertarian 'arguably legal' style. The distinctive feature of the discretionary approach is that the lawyer must treat this style as a set of weak presumptions. Once the lawyer formulates her general style, she must watch for indications that some premise underlying her judgment that the style is a good one does not apply in the particular case and, when she finds them, revise the style accordingly.

The most common reasons why some premises will be inapplicable are an unusual degree of aggressiveness or vulnerability on the part of another party or an unusual incapacity on the part of official institutions. The lawyer should respond to such circumstances by taking reasonably available actions that help restore the reliability of the procedure. By directing the lawyer to attempt first to improve the reliability of the procedure, the discretionary approach respects the traditional premise that the strongest assurance of a just resolution is the soundness of the procedure that produced it. But to the extent that the lawyer cannot neutralise or repair defects in the relevant procedure, she should assume direct responsibility for the substantive validity of the decision. She should make her own judgment about the proper substantive resolution and take reasonable actions to bring it about.

Consider a well known scenario involving two lawyers negotiating a personal injury case. The plaintiff is an indigent who has suffered severe injury as a result of the undisputed negligence of the defendant, but he may have negligently contributed to his own injury. During negotiation, the insurance company lawyer conducting the defence realises that the plaintiff's lawyer is unaware that a recent statute abolishing the contributory negligence defence would apply retroactively to this case. The plaintiff's lawyer is negotiating under the assumption that there is a substantial probability that his client's negligence will entirely preclude recovery when in fact there is no such probability. The defence lawyer proceeds to conclude the negotiation without correcting the mistaken impression.

Gary Bellow and Bea Moulton, who tell this tale, incline here toward the regulatory approach. Proponents of the libertarian approach might prefer a scenario in which the victim of nondisclosure is not an indigent and the beneficiary is not an insurance company. For this purpose, we can recall Monroe Freedman's tale of a divorce lawyer opposing the 'bomber' who has no value in life other than stripping the husband of every penny and piece of property he has, at whatever cost to the personal relations and children, or anything else. The libertarian and regulatory approaches would resolve these cases through categorical rules, of nondisclosure in the libertarian approach or disclosure in the regulatory approach. The discretionary approach requires a more complex judgment.

In the personal injury case, the critical concern for the defence lawyer should be whether the settlement likely to occur in the absence of disclosure would be fair (in the sense that it reasonably vindicates the merits of the relevant claims). On the facts given, it seems probable that the settlement would not be fair. The plaintiff's lawyer probably set her bottom line well below the appropriately discounted value of the plaintiff's claims because of her mistake about the law. Here the defence counsel's responsibility is to move the case toward a fair result, and the best way to do this is probably to make the disclosure and resume the negotiation. This duty is triggered by the fact that, without some assistance from defence counsel, the procedure cannot be relied on to produce a just resolution. The plaintiff's counsel's mistake is a major breakdown in the procedure, and since the case is headed toward pretrial settlement, there will be no further opportunities for counsel, judge, or jury to remedy the breakdown.

The defence counsel should also assess the likelihood that disclosure will backfire and lead to a less fair result because the plaintiff's counsel takes this information and then tries to get more than she is entitled to through some aggressive tactic of her own. But this risk seems small if, as the scenario suggests, the defendant's lawyer is more experienced than the plaintiff's, the latter has not been aggressive, and the matter seems likely to be wound up before the plaintiff will have an opportunity to make new manoeuvres. In Freedman's divorce case, things may be different; disclosure may prompt escalation of the already unfairly high level of demands by the 'bomber.' If so, then disclosure might be deferred until future developments indicate whether the case is likely to be resolved fairly without disclosure. The lawyer's duty is not discharged, however, until she either makes disclosure or the case reaches a fair resolution without her doing so.

Now consider a case in which the breakdown arises from incapacity on the part of official institutions. Suppose an experienced tax practitioner has conceived a new tax avoidance device. She herself is convinced that it is improper, but there is a non-frivolous argument for its legality. The lawyer might believe that the Internal Revenue Service and the courts are best situated to resolve such questions. She might reason that the agency and the courts have greater expertise than she, that they are better able to resolve issues in a way that can be uniformly applied to similar cases, and that they are subject to various democratic controls. However, such arguments are plausible only to the extent that the agency and the courts will in fact make an informed decision on the matter. The arguments do not warrant the lawyer using the device in a case where the agency and the courts will never effectively review it. This might happen because the agency lacks sufficient enforcement resources to identify the issue or to take the matter to court. In such a situation, the lawyer should respond to the procedural failure.

She can do so by trying to remedy it, for example, by bringing the issue to the attention of the IRS. If that course is not possible (for example, because the client will not permit it), or if it will not be sufficient to remedy the procedural deficiencies (for example, because the agency is so strapped that it cannot even respond to such signals), then the lawyer has to assume more direct responsibility for the substantive resolution. If she thinks that the device should be held invalid, she should refuse to assist with it. In these circumstances, she is the best situated decision maker to pass on the matter.

In situations in which the procedure is sufficiently reliable that the lawyer need not assume direct responsibility for the substantive merits, she retains a duty to take reasonably available actions to make the procedure as effective as possible and to forego actions that would reduce its efficacy. When she need not consider the substantive merits herself, she should do what she can to facilitate the adjudicator in doing so.

Take an issue of deceptive impeachment tactics. Is it appropriate for the lawyer in cross-examining a handwriting expert surreptitiously to substitute a writing with a signature different from the one the witness has identified in the hope that the witness will not notice the substitution and continue to insist on what will then be a demonstrably mistaken identification? The libertarian 'arguably legal' standard tends to permit such tactics; the regulatory 'on the merits' standard tends to condemn them. Under the discretionary approach, the matter requires an inquiry into whether the tactic is likely to contribute to the adjudicator's ability to decide the case fairly. To the extent that the lawyer has no knowledge that it will not be represented at hearing, the ethical issue will not be urgent because, to the extent the tactic fails to contribute to a fair understanding of the issues, the adjudicator can discount it appropriately. But if the lawyer has knowledge or insight that will not be formulated as admissible evidence, the ethical issue may be important. Suppose that the lawyer's extra-record knowledge indicates that the witness is highly competent and the identification is correct but that the tactic might be effective because the witness is prone to nervousness and distraction in public appearances. Here the tactic is likely to detract from, rather than to enhance, the adjudicator's ability to decide fairly. On the other hand, suppose that the lawyer has extra-record knowledge suggesting that the witness is not competent and the identification is mistaken. Here she might plausibly decide that the tactic would contribute to a fair decision.

In this case, the ethical concerns arise from the fact that, even in a relatively reliable procedure, the lawyer typically has some opportunities to improve her client's chance of success in ways that, were she required to consider the matter, she would acknowledge do not facilitate a decision on the merits by the adjudicator. The libertarian approach relies on the judge to check such moves at the prompting of opposing counsel, but the judge, even after hearing from both sides, is often less well informed about specific factual issues than counsel. In such situations, counsel should not defer responsibility to the judge for tactics she does not believe contribute to a fair decision. Since she has an advantage in assessing the matter, she should exercise her own judgment and, when appropriate, self-restraint.

Thus, far from collapsing the lawyer's role into the judge's ethical discretion suggests a lawyer role that complements the generally accepted understanding of the judge's role. The lawyer assumes substantial responsibility for vindicating substantive merits to the extent that the judge cannot be expected to do so. In other situations, her responsibility is to facilitate the judicial role.

Of course, one can imagine a procedural context that is so reliable as to make superfluous the type of discretion urged here: the dispute will be determined promptly, through an adjudication by a competent decision maker able routinely to identify and neutralise obfuscation and excessive aggressiveness, after a hearing at which both sides are ably represented and adequately financed, governed by rules and procedures that ensure full development of the evidence and issues, and where effective relief is available.

It is ironic that conventional discourse about legal ethics should often treat this ideal situation as paradigmatic. Not only is the situation rare at best, but ethical issues are here unimportant. Since, by hypothesis, relevant information is fully available and each side can counter the aggression and deception of the other, ethics collapses into strategy. No ethically questionable practice would be likely to benefit the client. Ethical issues arise because actual procedures fall short of the ideal. One of the strengths of the discretionary approach is that it acknowledges and responds to procedural imperfection.

2. *Purpose Versus Form.* -- Part of the substance versus procedure tension could be considered a special variation of the purpose versus form tension. When the lawyer impeaches a witness she knows to be truthful, when she objects to hearsay she knows to be accurate, when she puts the opposing party to proof on a matter the client has no legitimate interest in disputing, she takes advantage of procedural rules designed to promote accurate, efficient decision making in a way that frustrates this purpose. When judges apply rules, we expect them to take account of the purposes underlying the rules. But the judge often lacks sufficient knowledge to determine whether the relevant purposes would be served by applying the rules. The lawyer, however, often does have sufficient knowledge to do so. Nevertheless, the libertarian approach imposes no obligation on the lawyer in such situations to see that the rules she invokes are applied in a manner that takes account of their purposes.

The argument so far suggests that a lawyer's choice between a purposive or formal approach to procedural rules should depend on which approach seems better calculated to vindicate the relevant legal merits. In most contexts, considerations of merit favour a purposive approach. Yet the discretionary approach also requires the lawyer to remain alert for indications that a purposive approach might not further consideration on the merits. This point merely summarises the substance versus procedure discussion in terms of purpose versus form. It will be useful, however, to consider the purpose versus form tension more generally because in many situations, especially those in which the lawyer must take direct responsibility for considerations of substantive merit, purpose versus form considerations are distinctively troubling.

Part of the reason for regarding law as legitimate in our culture is that it embodies the purposes adopted by authoritative lawmakers: parties to a contract, legislators enacting a statute, judges pronouncing a common law rule, the people adopting a constitution. But the legitimacy of law also depends on these intentions being embodied in the form of rules. By mediating between legislative intention and coercive application to specific cases, the rule form distinguishes law from a regime of direct personal subordination to the legislator. The rules cannot be applied sensibly without considering their underlying purposes, but the purposes can only be implemented appropriately by referring to their formal expression as rules.

In practice, such issues often arise when lawyers have an opportunity to shape an activity or a transaction in a way that seems consistent with a plausible surface interpretation of a rule but that appears to undermine its purpose. For example, a divorced husband who agreed upon separation to pay his ex-wife a percentage of his income for five years might try to save money by making arrangements with his employer to defer his income until after the alimony period expires. Or the owner of a fleet of taxicabs might attempt to shield his business assets from tort liability by holding each cab through a separate corporation.

The libertarian approach tends to license the manipulation of form to defeat purpose; the regulatory approach tends to forbid such manipulation. The discretionary approach responds to the purpose versus form tension in terms of the following maxim: the clearer and less problematic the relevant purposes, the more the lawyer should consider herself bound by them; the less clear and more problematic the relevant purposes, the more justified the lawyer is in treating the relevant norms formally. Treating them formally means understanding them to permit any client goal not plainly precluded by their language.

'Problematic' purposes are purposes that pose an especially grave threat to fundamental legal values. The discretionary maxim is grounded in the practice in our legal culture of attributing an especially high burden of formal specification to such purposes. The most well-established examples are those involving criminal penalties and civil burdens on constitutional rights. Other kinds of purposes that have been considered problematic include those of transferring wealth to or conferring economic power on powerful interest groups, and of conferring anomalous tasks on the courts.

Here is an example involving a clear, unproblematic purpose. The client is a highly paid hotel manager. The lawyer determines that the client could save a good deal in taxes by renegotiating his contract with his employer so that in return for a reduction in cash compensation he receives and agrees to reside in lodging on the hotel premises. The lawyer must decide whether to suggest this arrangement to the client, or if the client has suggested it, she must decide whether to implement it. Assume that some institutional failure makes it inappropriate to rely on the IRS to determine the case, so that the lawyer must take substantial direct responsibility for the substantive merits.

If there is any authorisation for the arrangement in the income tax laws, it lies in a statutory provision exempting lodging furnished by the employer on its premises when the arrangement is 'for the convenience of the employer' and is 'required . . . as a condition of . . . employment.' The rule arguably permits the contemplated arrangement -- the employment contract could be drafted to impose such a 'requirement.'

Suppose the lawyer interprets this provision to express a belief that when an employee receives in-kind benefits as part of his job, it would be unfair to tax him on their full market value because they are probably worth considerably less to him, both because he associates them with work and because he cannot exchange them for things he may want more, as he could with cash. The in-kind benefits probably have some value to the employee, but to estimate this value in each case would be administratively impractical, and no plausible general presumption would be accurate in a large enough percentage of cases to warrant its use. Thus, according to this theory of the statute, exempting the income is the fairest practical approach.

Suppose that the lawyer decides that it would not be consistent with the statutory purpose to apply the exemption to arrangements the taxpayer has chosen or initiated. In such situations, it is more reasonable to presume that the taxpayer does value the benefits at the amount of the agreed salary reduction or at their market value. Even if this procedure does not entirely resolve the valuation problem, the difficulty has been created by the taxpayer's own actions. Thus, the lawyer concludes that the exemption should not be available for the contemplated transaction.

Suppose further, however, that courts in the relevant jurisdiction have rejected IRS challenges to analogous in-kind arrangements initiated by taxpayers. The lawyer's theory of institutional competence suggests that the court's decisions are more authoritative than her own views on the substantive merits. Accordingly, she is inclined to decide that there is merit to the contemplated arrangement. But the analysis is not yet complete. She still ought to consider the purposive basis of the court's rulings. Suppose she concludes that the rulings are based not on a judgment that such arrangements are consistent with the substantive purposes of the statute, but on a belief that it would be too costly to determine whether each particular transaction was in fact chosen or initiated by the taxpayer. At this point, the lawyer should review her theory of institutional competence. It may be impractical for the courts and the IRS to make such determinations, but quite practical for the tax lawyer to do so, especially if the lawyer came up with the idea herself and has not yet communicated it to the client. Since the lawyer believes that the relevant purpose is clear and not problematic, she should not proceed with a plan that would frustrate the purpose.

Simon goes on to consider a case in which the lawyer has to decide whether to interpret formalistically the provisions of legislation determining the levels of deductions to be made from social security payments in the case of recipients living in accommodation provided gratis by friends. The relevant provision requires that a deduction of the full market value of the accommodation be made if the accommodation is provided gratis but makes no explicit provision for the case where a nominal rent is charged. The lawyer must therefore decide whether to advise the client to arrange to pay a token rent. Defective draftsmanship apart, the legislature's purpose seems clear; namely to ensure that recipients benefits are reduced when their needs are being met by private charity. Simon argues however that the lawyers desire to be faithful to the legal merits might entail advising the client to pay a token rent. It is true that such manipulation of the legislation frustrates its purposes . However this is justified because the purposes of the legislature are in conflict with the 'fundamental values' of the legal system, in this case the need to provide all citizens with minimal levels of income. Consequently, in the absence of explicit legislative enactment to the contrary, the lawyer must assume that there was an intention to provide minimal levels of income.

3. *Broad Versus Narrow Framing.* -- This tension arises as ethical issues are defined. If we define an issue narrowly in terms of a small number of characteristics of the parties and their dispute, it will often look different than if we define it to encompass the parties' identities, relationship, and social circumstances. On the one hand, legal ideals encourage narrow definition of legal disputes in order to limit the scope of state intrusion into the lives of private citizens and to conserve scarce legal resources. On the other hand, making rights enforcement effective and meaningful often seems to

require broadening the definition of disputes. When disputes are narrowly defined, their resolution is often influenced by factors such as wealth and power that, when we are forced to confront them, often seem arbitrary. Moreover, the growth of government regulation and civil rights enforcement has produced a large number of legal norms that regulate broadly the structures of relationships and organisations. Thus, large scale public institutional reform or antitrust litigation often challenges and seeks to transform the basic identity of the defendant.

The broad versus narrow definition tension substantially overlaps the other tensions. For example, in debates that I characterised in terms of substance versus procedure, Monroe Freedman responds to regulatory arguments by hypothesising situations in which candour and openness may impede the appropriate substantive resolution because of some procedural deficiency. A famous example concerns whether a criminal defence lawyer should cross-examine a prosecution witness who accurately places the defendant near the scene of the crime about her defective vision. In Freedman's scenario, although the testimony is accurate and thus the contemplated impeachment seems irrelevant, the defendant is in fact innocent but lacks an alibi and is the victim of some unlucky circumstantial evidence. So the proper resolution -- acquittal -- may depend on the willingness to impeach the truthful witness. Similarly, in the divorce case mentioned above, for the husband to disclose hidden income would aggravate the injustice of the probable resolution because the wife's lawyer will take advantage of the information while continuing to pursue a variety of aggressive tactics of his own. What Freedman does in these examples is to broaden the frame. The issue initially posed is one of candour about a specific piece of information. He insists that the matter be viewed in the context of the other evidence and in terms of the likely incremental influence of disclosure on the resolution. Nevertheless, broad framing has no place in Freedman's view of individual lawyer decision making. At that level, he adopts the general libertarian practice of narrow framing. He favours a categorical duty of aggressive impeachment of vulnerable witnesses regardless of the surrounding context. Freedman adopts the broader perspective only when he takes the point of view of the rulemaker deciding whether to mandate cross-examination in this context.

In contrast, the discretionary approach gives individual lawyers substantial responsibility for determining whether broad or narrow framing is appropriate in the particular case. It suggests that the lawyer should frame ethical issues in accordance with three general standards of relevance. First, a consideration is relevant if it is implicated by the most plausible interpretation of the applicable law. Issues tend to be defined more narrowly under legal norms that regulate narrowly. For example, traffic laws suggest narrower framing than family laws. Second, a consideration is relevant if it is likely to have a substantial practical influence on the resolution. Issues tend to be defined more narrowly to the extent that the parties are situated so that substantively irrelevant factors are not likely to influence the resolution. Equality of resources and of access to information are among the more important factors weighing toward narrow definition under this second standard. Third, knowledge and institutional competence will affect the appropriate framing. More broadly framed issues tend to require more knowledge and more difficult judgments. When the lawyer lacks needed knowledge or competence, narrow framing becomes more appropriate. [8]

---

8   *Ethical Discretion in Lawyering*, supra note 3 at pp 1096-1105 and 1107-1109.

Notes

1. The Human Rights Act 1998 may now allow judges and lawyers to prefer form over substance in order to protect fundamental values: s 3 of the Human Rights Act 1998 provides that '*so far as possible* primary legislation must be read and given effect in a way which is compatible with Convention Rights'. This provision may require lawyers and judges to interpret legislation formally and in a way which ignores its clear purposes in order to ensure that it does not infringe the rights conferred by the European Convention.[9]

2. For a critique of Simon's theory see Tom Campbell 'Moral Autonomy for Lawyers: A Review of William H Simon *The Practice of Justice: A Theory of Lawyers Ethics*' [1999] 1 Legal Ethics at p 56.

Questions

1. How would Stephen Pepper and David Luban expect a lawyer to advise the client in the case of the new tax avoidance device and the highly paid hotel manager? Which approach would you adopt and why?

2. You are advising a husband who has just entered into a maintenance agreement with his recently divorced wife. The agreement provides for the wife to be paid 20% of the husbands post-tax income for five years. Should you advise the husband to ask his employer to reduce his income for the next five years on the understanding that the reduction will be made good thereafter?

Does it make any difference if the settlement has been approved by the court? Does it make any difference if there are children involved and custody has been given to the wife?

Law and morality – law and legal merit

A second feature of Simon's approach is that he refuses to locate the difficulties involved in being a good lawyer and a good person in a conflict between the lawyer's professional obligations and the lawyer's private morality. Rejecting the view of legal positivism that the law is a set of rules authoritatively pronounced by recognised state officials, Simon argues that fidelity to law or legal values will sometimes require far more from lawyers than is suggested by the libertarian account of theorists like Steven Pepper. Following Dworkin, Simon argues that the citizen's, and therefore the lawyer's,

9   For discussion see M Zander *The State of Justice* (London, Sweet & Maxwell, 2000) pp 92-93.

obligation 'is to the law, and not to any particular conception of what the law requires' so that 'every citizen is a common law judge of what the law requires.'[10]

THE LIMITS OF ROLE AND LEGALITY

The discretionary approach is grounded in the lawyer's professional commitments to legal values. It rejects the common tendency to attribute the tensions of legal ethics to a conflict between the demands of legality on the one hand and those of non legal, personal or ordinary morality on the other. Although critics of conventional legal ethics discourse often adopt the law versus morality characterisation, its 'strongest influence' is to bias discussion in favour of conventional, especially libertarian, responses. Typically the conventional response is portrayed as the 'legal' one; the unconventional response is portrayed as a 'moral' alternative. This rhetoric connotes that the 'legal' option is objective and integral to the professional role, whereas the 'moral' alternative is subjective and peripheral. Even when the rhetoric expresses respect for the 'moral' alternative, it implies that the lawyer who adopts it is on her own and vulnerable both intellectually and practically. The usual effect is to make it psychologically harder for lawyers and law students to argue for the 'moral' alternative. In many such situations, however, both alternatives could readily be portrayed as competing legal values.

The specious law-versus-morality characterisation is used most frequently to privilege client loyalty. For example, in the hypothetical discussed above involving a personal injury negotiation in which the plaintiff's lawyer underestimated the value of the claim because of a mistake about the law, the defence counsel's client loyalty option is often seen as the 'legal' one and the disclosure option as a 'moral' alternative. In fact, of course, concern for the plaintiff is strongly grounded in the belief that without disclosure the plaintiff will be deprived of a substantive legal entitlement to recover for negligently inflicted losses. Thus, both options are equally 'legal' in the sense that they are grounded in important legal values.

The discretionary approach does not deny that some issues are best understood as involving conflicts between legal and non-legal moral commitments. In fact, the distinction between legal and non-legal commitments has some importance in delimiting the sphere of the discretionary approach, since the approach does not address decision making involving non-legal commitments. There are currently no generally accepted guidelines for making such distinctions, and I am not prepared to offer any here. However, it may be helpful to emphasise that such distinctions depend on important issues of legal theory that all lawyers need to resolve (though not necessarily self-consciously) in formulating their understandings of their role. In particular, such distinctions depend first on the relationship between institutional competence norms and fundamental substantive norms, and second, on the scope of lawyer discretion within the scheme of institutional competence. Whether it makes sense to view ethical conflict in terms of 'law versus morals' or the lawyer's problems as functions of 'role differentiation' depends on how these issues are resolved.

We can get some sense of the way in which theories about such issues delimit legal commitments and hence the sphere of the discretionary approach by considering two

10 *The Practice of Justice* supra p 133 note 3 at p 83 citing Dworkin *Taking Rights Seriously* (London, Duckworth, 1978) at p 274.

further cases of the sort conventionally understood in terms of conflict between law and morality.

First, recall the discussion above of financial planning, in which I argued that a lawyer might act more aggressively on behalf of the welfare recipient than on behalf of the hotel manager, largely because the relevant legislative purposes stood more clearly against the contemplated plan in the case of the manager. Many believe that there are nonlegal reasons to represent welfare recipients more aggressively than hotel managers, and some readers may suspect that such considerations motivated my argument. We can sharpen this issue by stipulating that in the welfare case the legislature has clearly indicated a purpose to preclude the proposed plan. The argument for the legality of the plan is almost (but not quite) frivolous, but because the arrangement might pass unnoticed by the welfare department, it could benefit the client.

Almost all lawyers will give weight to clear legislative expression, and many would regard it as dispositive of their obligations. However, a 'natural law lawyer' in the style of, say, Lon Fuller would have to consider whether the decisions of the legislature were so plainly wrong and the values they affronted so fundamental that the lawyer should disregard the decisions. The natural law lawyer cannot divorce 'his duty of fidelity to law' from 'his responsibility for making law what it ought to be.' Such a lawyer believes that a legal system must meet certain normative preconditions to be entitled to respect and compliance, and perhaps even to be considered a system of law. Thus, legal ideals may require that a person repudiate norms that violate such preconditions even when promulgated by otherwise legally authoritative institutions. Such repudiation is the opposite of lawlessness; it moves the system closer to being worthy of respect as lawful.

A lawyer in the welfare case who accepted this natural law theory of legal order would have to consider whether the norm of minimal subsistence income is so fundamental that it amounts to a precondition of legal legitimacy. Such a lawyer might reason that a core value of legality is the autonomy of the individual and that a person who lacked minimal material subsistence would be so dependent and debilitated that she would be incapable of exercising the autonomy that legality aspires to safeguard. In this way, the lawyer might conclude that this value is fundamental and hence that norms that violate it are not entitled to respect.

Even when a lawyer regards the decisions of authoritative institutions as conclusive, she needs to consider the scope of her own authority within the scheme of legal institutions. In particular, she needs to consider whether the lawyering role allows her nullifying powers of the sort commonly imputed to the roles of prosecutor, jury, and judge, and -- less commonly -- private citizen (to the extent that civil disobedience is justified in terms of, rather than in opposition to, legal values).

Consider another case often thought to present a conflict between legality and private moral commitment. A childless married couple have agreed on terms for an amicable divorce. The relevant state law, which has not been amended for decades, provides for divorce only on grounds of fault, such as adultery or mental cruelty, none of which is applicable to the couple's case. The lawyer must decide whether to counsel the couple to perjure themselves to get a divorce, or to risk encouraging perjury by telling them what the legally favourable circumstances would be before inviting them to describe their own. Or perhaps the clients have taken the initiative to commit perjury, and the lawyer discovers it and must decide whether to report it to the court.

In some respects, this case is an appealing one for nullification. It has some of the features on which Guido Calabresi based his defence of judicial nullification of statutes: it involves an apparently obsolescent statute that has become out of tune with majority sentiment and the surrounding legal culture, that could not be enacted today, and that survives because of legislative inertia.

Calabresi's argument raises the question of why lawyer nullification is necessary in addition to judicial nullification. Why not have the lawyer bring an action on the true facts urging the court to nullify and grant the divorce? One answer is that judicial nullification is not an option in most states. But even if it were, judges might not nullify because they would be unwilling to take the ensuing political heat from a small but energetic minority that intensely supported the statute. Or perhaps the judges would think the existence of this minority would make nullification illegitimate. It may be, however, that the statute is of large symbolic importance to this group, and that the group has no stake in low visibility enforcement decisions. Thus, while public general judicial nullification would not be feasible, low visibility ad hoc nullification at the enforcement level might be. In this respect, the divorce statute resembles statutes prohibiting fornication or soft drug possession that are routinely nullified by the exercise of prosecutorial discretion, sometimes in anticipation of jury nullification. Such low visibility nullification is unavailable here; juries rarely decide divorce cases, and the law puts the burden of initiative on private parties to file and pursue an action for divorce. But lawyer nullification seems quite practical. Perhaps it ought to be considered justified for the same reasons that justify the more commonly recognised forms of nullification.

Of course, to the extent nullification must occur through explicit lawyer assistance in perjury, most lawyers would find it unacceptable; at the regulatory level, no court or agency of the bar would justify it. Still, the nullification analogy suggests even here that some ethical dilemmas conventionally portrayed in terms of a conflict between law and morality have legal considerations that favour (as well as oppose) courses of action involving perjury. Although lawyers usually conclude that the balance should be struck against such courses, the fact remains that the conflict arises within the legal culture itself.

When the practical issue involves tacit encouragement of perjury or acquiescence in subsequently discussed client perjury, conventional professional discourse recognises (and sometimes gives dispositive weight to) only one legal value favouring acquiescence or encouragement -- confidentiality. By contrast, I believe that the significance of confidentiality concerns is overstated and that the critical legal concerns favouring acquiescence and encouragement in the divorce case involve legal merit. In the subsequent discovery case, the conventional discourse vacillates between a rule generally requiring disclosure and a rule generally forbidding it. When the issue is tacit encouragement, most (but not all) commentary disapproves, but disciplinary regimes leave lawyers a broad range of practical autonomy in such matters. The discretionary approach suggests that the lawyer's decision in all these situations should weigh all the factors that bear on legal merit, including both those that suggest that the divorce statute is obsolete and unjust and the competing factors that emphasise the presumptive validity of statutes and the presumptive wrongfulness of perjury.

The discretionary approach does not require that the issues of the relation of institutional and substantive norms and of the lawyer's range of autonomy within the scheme of institutional competence be resolved in any particular way. But how a lawyer resolves these issues will affect how she draws the distinction between professional and private ethics. In some situations, the lawyer will feel that she has a professional obligation to some legally authoritative norm that conflicts with her private, nonlegal commitments. In other situations, she may feel that her private commitment outweighs the professional one. But she will feel such a conflict only when she is reasonably certain that the legal system fails to acknowledge some value to which she is committed or that the system has conclusively rejected such a value. Only at this point is it appropriate to talk of her problem in terms of the limits of 'role morality' or 'role differentiation.' Until then, the problem remains one of the most appropriate performance of her role within the legal system. [11]

Notes

1. Nullification is a process whereby rules of law promulgated by a source of law recognised as legitimate within a particular legal system may nevertheless be effectively (though not formally) set aside by the decisions of state officials not to enforce them. In the UK, this phenomenon is most likely to occur when the Crown Prosecution Service takes a decision not to enforce a rule of criminal law (see chapter 6 infra).

2. For a critique of Simon's views on the relationship between law and morality in relation to Legal Ethics, see David Luban 'Reason and Passion in Legal Ethics' (1999) 51 Stanford Law Review 873. Luban argues that that the legal values on which Simon relies are so open-textured that conflict between them is inevitable. Consequently, choices must be made which can only be based on moral considerations.

Questions

1. Does this approach make the business of being faithful to the law stimulating, as Simon claims, or daunting – or both?

2. To what extent do the conditions of modern practice make the approach described impractical? See chapter 3 above.

3. How would a lawyer exercising ethical discretion respond to a rule of conduct requiring a client's confidence to be respected in circumstances where disclosure would avert serious harm to a third party (for example *Spaulding v Zimmermann* or the Mount Pleasant Bodies case)?

11   *Ethical Discretion in Lawyering* supra p 133 note 3 at pp 1113-1119.

4. One of the central arguments for the introduction of 'no-fault' divorce in the UK was that under the previous system (under which divorce could be obtained more quickly if one party alleged that some wrongdoing by the other had caused the breakdown of the marriage) many couples were making false and collusive allegations in order to expedite their divorce[12]. Were lawyers advising them to do so guilty of misconduct?[13] Were they being faithful to the law in Simon's sense? Alternatively, were they behaving ethically?

Like Luban's moral activist approach, this model liberates lawyers from an obligation always to do for clients whatever the letter of the law requires. Instead the obligation is an obligation to obey the spirit of the law and to be faithful to the values of the system. It might be argued that if the values of the system cannot be decisively pronounced either by court or legislature, the notion of legal values provides too insubstantial a standard for individual lawyer's judgment of legal merit. What follows is Simon's response to this objection.

> In the dominant understanding, judgments about legality and justice are grounded in the norms and practices of the surrounding legal culture. These norms and practices are objective and systematic in the sense that they have observable regularity and are mutually meaningful to those who refer to and engage in them. Even when lawyers disagree about such judgments, they usually do not regard them as subjective and arbitrary. One indication of this fact is that they do not articulate or experience their disagreement as an opposing assertion of subjective preference or arbitrary will. Rather, they oppose decisions on the ground that they are wrong -- wrong in terms of norms and practices that they plausibly believe binding on the decision maker. Moreover, they are often willing to accept a particular decision as legitimate, even when they regard it as mistaken, in part because they recognise it as a good faith attempt to apply the norms and practices of the culture.[14]

The plausibility of Simon's model thus depends on the view that the legal culture is based on agreement at a highly abstract level about values so that any apparent injustice created by a specific feature or rule of the legal system can be regarded as an intellectual mistake about the implications or requirements of values which every one accepts. In the UK a similar argument could be employed to explain disagreement about the implications for particular disputes of the Human Rights Act 1998.

Question

To what extent is Simon's model undermined by the arguments put forward by Arthur Leff? (See chapter 2 pp 35-47.)

---

12   Chapter 3 at pp 67-68.
13   See Principle 19.01 and 21.01 of the LSGPC set out in chapter 1 supra at p 25.
14   *Ethical Discretion in Lawyering* supra p 133 note 3 at p 1120.

Vernon v Bosely – a case study

Issues of legal ethics are rarely litigated in the UK but an exception to this arose in the case of *Vernon v Bosely*[15]. In 1982, Vernon witnessed unsuccessful attempts to pull his two children out of a car which their nanny had negligently driven into a river. In 1985, he issued a writ claiming damages in negligence for nervous shock against the defendant nanny. Meanwhile, his already delicate mental health deteriorated. In 1986, his business folded. Thereafter, he was unable to hold down regular work and his marriage suffered. In February 1993, his wife petitioned for divorce. In March 1993, she was granted a residence order in respect of the remaining children and during the family proceedings evidence was given by Dr Lloyd, a psychiatrist, and Mr McKay, a clinical psychologist ('LM') that Vernon might commit suicide if ordered to leave the matrimonial home.

In May (Lloyd) and November (McKay) 1993, these same experts, signed and delivered expert reports in support of Vernon's civil action for damages. That action began in January 1994 and, in April, they gave evidence in accordance with their reports to the effect that the shock of what Vernon saw was a substantial cause of serious mental illness and that his prognosis was very poor.

The defendants persisted until the close of evidence in denying that Vernon was suffering mental illness and that his prognosis was poor, a position the Court of Appeal found indefensible. This however was not their principal case. They denied causation, alleging that any mental illness was a result of the failure of his business acting upon an already vulnerable personality and was not in any way linked to the accident. Alternatively, they claimed that any mental illness caused by the accident was merely pathological grief and as such not something for which the law would give damages, compensation being limited to conditions which could be classified as post-traumatic stress syndrome.

By July, evidence had been heard and the civil proceedings were adjourned. Vernon's health had been improving since September 1993 (though in the civil proceedings his expert witnesses stressed the possibility of relapse). The improvement continued after the conclusion of the evidence in the civil case. Therefore Vernon felt able in August to apply for a residence order in respect of his children. Vernon's matrimonial solicitors instructed McKay and Lloyd as experts. On 17 November and 1 December, McKay duly reported a dramatic improvement in Vernon's health. However, this report made no reference to the possibility of relapse. The Court of Appeal subsequently thought that this was not solely the fault of the experts. Their letter of instruction, which commented that

> We need to show that his mental health has improved dramatically since .... May 1993 and moreover that it has improved again since the conclusion of his big personal injury case

was viewed by two members of the court as little more than invitation to deceive the family court

15   [1997] 1 All ER 614, CA.

Meanwhile on 24/25 October, Vernon's counsel made closing submissions in the civil proceedings relying on the expert evidence given in these proceedings by Lloyd and McKay. At this stage Vernon was aware of the evidence to be led in the matrimonial proceedings but his legal advisers were not. By 17 November however, they knew the truth. Vernon's solicitor was at first of the opinion that the changed circumstances should be communicated to Sedley J (the judge in the tort case) but counsel persuaded them there was no obligation to do so. On 6 January 1995, the family court judge dismissed Vernon's claim but found that his health had substantially improved. On 30 January 1995, Sedley J gave judgment for Vernon. in the civil proceedings for £1.3 million and commented that he had found the evidence of the experts on both sides seriously lacking in objectivity.

Between January and March 1996, the Court of Appeal heard and partly allowed the defendant Bosley's appeal with respect both to liability and to quantum of damages but at no stage did Vernon mention the change in his condition which only came to light when on 17 April Mr O'Brien QC for the defendant received anonymously copies of the proceedings and evidence in the family court. The defendant then applied to reopen the appeal.

The Court viewed the application as raising the issue: 1) of whether was the case sufficiently exceptional to justify the Court of Appeal receiving further evidence under RSC Ord 59[16] r 10(2); and 2) whether the plaintiff should have disclosed the evidence from the family proceedings either in November 1994 or before the Court of Appeal during the original hearing. As to the first issue, the Court held by a majority (Evans LJ dissenting) that the evidence should be admitted and justified a reduction in the plaintiff's damages. There follows the judgment of Stuart Smith LJ on the second issue. His Lordship began by holding that the obligation to give discovery of relevant non-privileged documents contained in RSC Ord 24 did not cease at the moment when a party provided the other side with an accurate list of documents then in its possession. The obligation continued beyond the close of evidence to the close of the case so that documents subsequently acquired had also to be disclosed. This provided one reason why the plaintiffs legal advisers ought to have disclosed to the defendants the documentary evidence in their possession of the inconsistent evidence being given by the plaintiff in the matrimonial proceedings. His Lordship continued:

DUTY NOT TO MISLEAD THE COURT

It is the duty of every litigant not to mislead the court or his opponent. He will obviously mislead the court if he gives evidence which he knows to be untrue. But he will also do so if, having led the court to believe a fact to be true, he fails to correct it when he discovers it to be false. This duty continues in my opinion until the judge has given judgment. An analogy can be drawn with the law relating to misrepresentation. A representation which induces a contract which is true at the time it is made, but is subsequently known by the representor to be false before the contract is entered into is a misrepresentation (see *With v O'Flanagan* [1936] 1 All ER 727, [1936] Ch 575).

16   The Rules of the Supreme Court referred to in this section have since been replaced (in April 1999) by new rules of civil procedure designed to implement the Woolf proposals.

Moreover, in my view the litigant does not discharge this duty simply by accepting the advice of his legal advisers. He can no doubt rely upon such advice as negativing any mens rea, so that he would not be guilty of the criminal offence of attempting to pervert the course of justice. But if the advice is incorrect, he is responsible for it vis-à-vis the other party to the civil litigation. This is the general rule where legal advisers are acting within the scope of their actual or ostensible authority.

In this case it is plain from the written submissions on general damages made to Sedley J by the plaintiff's counsel that they placed reliance on the evidence of both Mr Mackay and Dr Lloyd as to his current condition and prognosis and also on the description of the plaintiff given by Mr Moxham (a social worker employed by the Gloucestershire County Council), which was to the effect that the plaintiff was incapable of looking after himself, evidence which the judge substantially accepted. Yet at the time these submissions were made Mr Vernon knew this description did not represent the true position. And shortly afterwards his legal advisers knew the same. Unless the altered position was communicated to the judge there was clearly a risk that he would give judgment on a basis that was no longer true. And in my view that is exactly what happened.

Mr Blunt sought to rely on the distinction between actively misleading and passively standing by and watching the court be misled. This distinction was made in *Saif Ali v Sydney Mitchell & Co (a firm) (P, third party)* [1978] 3 All ER 1033, [1980] AC 198. The case concerned a barrister's duty, but the same principles apply to the litigant. Lord Diplock said ([1978] 3 All ER 1033 at 1042–1043, [1980] AC 198 at 220):

> A barrister must not wilfully mislead the court as to the law nor may he actively mislead the court as to the facts; although, consistently with the rule that the prosecution must prove its case, he may passively stand by and watch the court being misled by reason of its failure to ascertain facts that are within the barrister's knowledge.

In *Tombling v Universal Bulb Co Ltd* [1951] 2 TLR 289 at 297 Denning LJ said

> The duty of counsel to his client in a civil case—or in defending an accused person—is to make every honest endeavour to succeed. He must not, of course, knowingly mislead the Court, either on the facts or on the law, but, short of that, he may put such matters in evidence or omit such others as in his discretion he thinks will be most to the advantage of his client. So also, when it comes to his speech, he must put every fair argument which appears to him to help his client towards winning his case. The reason is because he is not the judge of the credibility of the witnesses or of the validity of the arguments. He is only the advocate employed by the client to speak for him and present his case, and he must do it to the best of his ability, without making himself the judge of its correctness, but only of its honesty.

The classic example of the distinction is the case where the barrister knows that his client has previous convictions, but the court and prosecution do not. He is not under an obligation to disclose the convictions, but he must not suggest that his client is a man of good character. Similarly, there may be several witnesses who can speak as to a certain matter of fact. Some may support one side, the others the opposite case. Neither the litigant nor his lawyers are bound to call in a civil case those witnesses who do not support their case.

But where the case has been conducted on the basis of certain material facts which are an essential part of the party's case, in this case the plaintiff's condition at trial and the prognosis, which were discovered before judgment to be significantly different, the court is not being misled by the failure of the defendant to put before it material of which she could or should have been aware, but by the failure of the plaintiff and his advisers to correct an incorrect appreciation which the court will otherwise have as a result of their conduct of this case hitherto. This can be illustrated by *Meek v Fleming* [1961] 3 All ER 148, [1961] 2 QB 366. Throughout the trial the defendant, a police officer, appeared in plain clothes and was addressed by his counsel as 'Mr'. In the ordinary way no possible objection could be taken to this; but what was known to the defence, but not known to the plaintiff or the court was that between the cause of action arising and trial, the defendant had been demoted to sergeant from chief inspector for being a party to an arrangement to practice a deception in a court of law in the course of his duty as a senior police officer. Although the matter only went to credit, the Court of Appeal ordered a retrial. The court had been misled because it was likely to have the impression, and indeed obviously did have the impression, that the defendant was still a chief inspector.

THE DUTY OF COUNSEL

Where there is a danger that the court will be misled, it is the duty of counsel to advise his client that disclosure should be made. There is no reason to suppose that if Mr Vernon had been so advised in this case, he would not have accepted that advice. If the client refuses to accept the advice, then it is not as a rule for counsel to make the disclosure himself; but he can no longer continue to act. In the unlikely event that Mr Vernon did not accept the advice, then the non-appearance of counsel and solicitors before Sedley J on 30 January and 10 May 1995 would immediately have alerted the defendant's advisers, if not also the judge, that something was afoot. I have no doubt Mr O'Brien would have smelt a rat.

In this case the position is complicated, at any rate so far as the proceedings before Judge McNaught are concerned, by r 4.23 of the Family Proceedings Rules 1991. But counsel's advice should in my view have included advice to Mr Vernon to seek the judge's leave to disclose the relevant evidence.

THE POSITION IN THE COURT OF APPEAL

Here again Mr Blunt sought to draw the distinction between not disclosing that which he asserted (wrongly in my view) he had no duty to disclose and actively misleading the court. But in attempting so to do, counsel were walking a tight-rope and in my judgment did not succeed in staying on it. As I have already pointed out, counsel sought to uphold the judge's award of £67,000 for future occupational therapy on the basis of the assessment of Mrs Waterman (an occupational therapist) of the plaintiff's condition, which was similar to that of Mr Moxham, and his needs coupled with the Mackay/Lloyd prognosis. The latter was critical to the justification of a multiplier of 13.

Similarly, so far as future domestic care and cost of gardening is concerned, counsel sought to justify the judges award of £41,000 and £3,900 on the basis of the judge's finding as to the plaintiff's present condition, as exemplified by Mr Moxham's description which was accepted by the judge, coupled with the Mackay/Lloyd prognosis. Here again the prognosis was essential in justifying a multiplier of 13 which the judge took.

In relation to future loss of earnings, I consider we were misled into thinking on the basis of the judge's findings that the plaintiff was unemployable in the future. Although there might have been argument, as there had been in the recent hearing, as to the effect the new evidence should have on his loss of earnings claim, it seems to me unarguable that it might well have some effect. And for the reasons I have given, it has.

I readily accept that the plaintiff's counsel did not deliberately intend to deceive the court and believed that the advice they gave Mr Vernon was sound. But in my judgment they made a serious error of judgment in failing to advise him on the need for disclosure. By an overtechnical construction of the rules and a failure to appreciate that their previous conduct of the case would result in the court reaching an unjust result unless disclosure was made, they found themselves in an impossible position. By the time the case came to this court they should have appreciated that they could no longer seek to uphold the judge's judgment on the four heads of future loss to which I have referred. I think it is unfortunate that counsel did not appreciate what appears to have been apparent to Mrs Vernon, Judge McNaught and apparently the plaintiff's own solicitor, Mr Bretton, until he was advised otherwise by counsel (see his affidavit of 18 November 1994, para 14). It is also unfortunate that when, towards the close of the argument before us in February 1996, Mr O'Brien, who by then had some suspicion but no tangible evidence of what had happened, applied for further discovery, we were told by the plaintiff's counsel that the defendant was on a fishing expedition and had not properly laid the foundation for further discovery, with the result that this court summarily dismissed Mr O'Brien's application.[17]

Thorpe LJ who agreed with Stuart-Smith LJ added.:

DUTY NOT TO MISLEAD THE COURT

The classic statement by Denning LJ in *Tombling v Universal Bulb Co Ltd* [1951] 2 TLR 289 at 297, cited by Stuart-Smith LJ, is clearly of enduring application. Its application to the facts of individual cases can plainly give rise to finally balanced outcomes. In that case Singleton LJ delivered what was in effect a dissenting judgment. Counsel, Mr MacDermott, had established his client's address at 96 Church Road by putting to him the leading question, 'Do you live at 96 Church Road, Stoneygate?' Like Singleton LJ I regard that as active and not passive presentation. Denning LJ was apparently reassured by the evidence of Mr MacDermott. He said:

> But after hearing Mr MacDermott I am quite satisfied that it was not done to mislead. This question was only asked so as to give the man's permanent address, without disclosing the discreditable but irrelevant fact that he was at present in prison for a motoring offence.

On the material in the report that strikes me as a charitable conclusion in the light of counsel's use of a leading question in preference to the proper form, 'Where do you live?'. . .

17   [1997] 1 All ER 614 at 629-631.

On the facts of this case I am in complete agreement with Stuart-Smith LJ that the plaintiff was under a duty to report this material development to Sedley J. As I have already pointed out, his statement of 30 September, instructions for which must have been taken from him at an earlier date, contained the claim to dramatic improvement and the letter from his solicitor in the matrimonial proceedings written on 8 August referred to significant improvement. In my judgment it is simply unconscionable for a litigant to run contradictory cases in simultaneous proceedings in the hope of gaining advantage in each. In evaluating the plaintiff's responsibility it is significant to my judgment that he was ready enough to disclose the reports prepared by Mr Mackay and Dr Lloyd in 1993 for the divorce proceedings. At that stage he had an equal aim to establish a gloomy picture in both cases.

I am equally clear that Mr Blunt's decision to withhold the material was the result of a conscientious but erroneous exercise of judgment. I have every sympathy with Mr Blunt. After some 70 days of evidence in what was unquestionably as highly charged and arduous a personal injury case as it would be possible to conceive, the prospect of reopening evidential issues must have seemed unpalatable to say the least. There is only one point that I wish to make in relation to Mr Blunt's submissions in this field. He submitted that in the dilemma of decision counsel had only to look to the authorities and apply them to the circumstances. Counsel was not to be guided by his feelings on the issue in question. I cannot accept that counsel's approach should be so strictly cerebral. There is a value in instinctive and intuitive judgment. The more difficult the decision the greater that value. The course that feels wrong is unlikely to be the safe course to follow. In general terms the balance between the advocate's duty to the client and the advocate's duty to the court must reflect evolutionary change within the civil justice system. If evolutionary shifts are necessary to match civil justice reforms they should in my judgment be towards strengthening the duty to the court. Differing practices and procedures in the family justice system, the criminal justice system, and the civil justice system must be reflected in different requirements in, for instance, a criminal trial and a Children Act hearing.

The only difference of opinion that I hold from Stuart-Smith LJ is as to counsel's obligation if his client demurs in the communication of necessary material to the judge. If counsel's duty goes no further than requiring his withdrawal from the case there seems to me to be a remaining risk of injustice. Of course such an event leads to speculation. But more than one inference is there to be drawn. I would hold that in those circumstances counsel has a duty to disclose the relevant material to his opponent and, unless there be agreement between the parties otherwise, to the judge.

EVANS LJ. Because this will be a dissenting judgment, I begin with a summary of the conclusions I have reached.

(1) I share the indignation which Stuart-Smith and Thorpe LJJ express at the conduct of the plaintiff and his expert witnesses in the Family Court proceedings, but I do not believe that it should have for these proceedings the consequences which they propose.

(2) This is not a case where the plaintiff or the expert witnesses called on his behalf gave evidence which was incorrect or expressed opinions which were unjustified at the time when their evidence was given. To suggest that he or they have 'changed their evidence' is not accurate.

(3) The further evidence which the expert witnesses gave before us in November 1996 was not such as to destroy the basic assumptions upon which their evidence was based when it was given in April 1994. That is an appropriate test for the admission of fresh evidence for the purposes of an appeal: see *Mulholland v Mitchell (by her next friend Hazel Doreen Mitchell)* [1971] 1 All ER 307, [1971] AC 666. Their prognosis at the trial was accepted then by the defendants and their expert witnesses. As the judge put it, the demands of consistency prevented the defendants from challenging it. The same restraints would have continued to operate if further evidence had been permitted before judgment was given, and in my view they continue to operate now.

(4) The case and the appeal should be decided on the evidence given at the trial, save in exceptional circumstances which do not arise here (see *Mulholland's* case). Therefore, I do not agree that any duty of disclosure continued after the close of evidence at the trial. The judge gave his judgment on the basis of the evidence given at the trial, and this court was equally concerned to decide whether his judgment was correct by reference to the evidence that was given.

(5) Neither the judge nor this court was under any illusion that the unchallenged prognosis given by the plaintiff's expert witnesses in April 1994 might already have proved to have been unduly pessimistic by the time when judgment was given, or when the appeal was heard, just as it might have been over-optimistic, in which case the defendant's representatives would certainly have objected to further evidence being introduced by the plaintiff.

(6) The fact of the plaintiff's recovery has to be distinguished from the irresponsibility shown by two of his expert witnesses, in subsequently expressing views in the family proceedings which are not easy to reconcile with their evidence in this case, whether given in April 1994 or November 1996. If the fact of improvement stood alone, I doubt whether the judge, if he had been asked, or this court, would have contemplated allowing either party to open up this issue after the original hearing. Unfortunately, the judge was already aware that the expert evidence did not achieve that standard of independence which should have characterised it. He found that the expert witnesses were parti pris, the plaintiff's and the defendant's alike.

(7) Counsel for the plaintiff were correct to advise that there was no obligation to disclose the documents in question in these proceedings, at the time when they were received by the plaintiff and by them. Moreover, the documents did not lose their privileged status in these proceedings by reason of the confidentiality given to them by statute for the purposes of the family proceedings, in which the defendant and her representatives had and have no interest.

(8) Counsel for the plaintiff did not, in my judgment, either mislead the court or act improperly in any way. The consequences of holding that they did seem to me to go far beyond the confines of the present case, particularly with regard to views expressed by expert witnesses after their evidence has been given.

(9) Certain documents were sent anonymously to leading counsel for the defendant, in breach of statutory confidence and apparently in contempt of court. I am concerned that, so far as I am aware, no steps have been taken to discover who the sender was.

(10) This case already deserved a place in the history books or in some legal museum

as an example of how costs and the length of proceedings can get entirely out of hand. Now we have a pendant to the appeal hearing, which was thought to be concluded by our judgments handed down on 29 March, and a useful reminder that interest rei publicae ut sit finis litium (it is in the public interest that proceedings should be brought to a timely end)[18]...

[in relation to whether the duty to give discovery was a continuing one, his Lordship added:]

I would hold, subject to one qualification which affects the party's representatives rather than himself, that no such duty continues after the evidence has closed. The reason essentially is one of principle. The trial process which is adversarial under our rules and traditions of procedure centres upon the evidence given at the trial itself. Only in special circumstances can evidence be given before the trial. Only in limited circumstances can a party add to, qualify or even contradict the evidence which has been given, after it has closed its case, and never without leave from the judge. When it is sought to introduce further evidence for the purposes of an appeal, the underlying principle is interest rei publicae ut sit finis litium. This is subject only to limited exceptions: the well-known three conditions in *Ladd v Marshall* [1954] 3 All ER 745, [1954] 1 WLR 1489 when the evidence existed at the time of the trial, and only in 'exceptional' circumstances when it has come into existence since the trial (see *Mulholland v Mitchell* [1971] 1 All ER 307, [1971] AC 666).

These are various practical applications, in my view, of a general principle that the judge decides the case on the evidence given at the trial. Both parties have the opportunity then to place their evidence before him, and only in special circumstances are they permitted to add to it after the stage commonly referred as the close of evidence has been reached. A general duty of disclosure continuing after that stage would be inconsistent with that general rule. One example will suffice. If the duty existed, it would extend to all relevant documents, even those which were of such trivial importance or marginal relevance that they could never be introduced in evidence, because the judge's leave would never be obtained.

The qualification I have referred to above is the duty not to mislead the court. [19]....

DUTY NOT TO MISLEAD THE COURT

This usually is identified as a professional duty owed by the party's legal representatives, and I am doubtful whether the defendant's submission that it is also owed by the party himself is necessarily correct. I do not see how the party can be expected to do more than seek and act upon the advice of his legal representatives, and if that is done in good faith, as it was here, then I would have thought that his duty was discharged, even if the advice proved to be incorrect. If it was correct, then no breach of duty has occurred.

The defendant's submission (skeleton argument para D.3) is that—

it was misleading for Sedley J to be left with the evidence of Mr Mackay and Dr Lloyd to the effect that the plaintiff was currently suffering from chronic albeit

18   [1997] 1 All ER 614 at 632-633.
19   [1997] 1 All ER 614 at 642C-E.

variable depression and that the prognosis was poor when it was known before judgment that that evidence no longer represented the opinions of those two medical experts.

This elides easily into the submission which was made orally that these two witnesses by reason of their October 1994 reports were known to have 'changed their minds' as regards the evidence they had given. That statement is not correct, except in the limited sense that by reason of the improvement in the plaintiff's condition after they gave evidence their current (October 1994) view as to (a) his condition, and (b) the prognosis for it, were different from the views which they held and expressed six months before. The evidence they gave bona fide in April 1994 was correct when it was given. It was not challenged by the defendant's experts and in large measure it was accepted by the judge. There was no reason for supposing in November 1994 that the evidence had been incorrect when it was given, and there is no basis for suggesting that now.

Their evidence in April allowed for the possibility that the improvement in the plaintiff's condition which they had observed from September 1993 would continue notwithstanding the relapse over Easter 1994, and the judge recognised and carefully analysed the likely therapeutic effect of a judgment which was in the plaintiff's favour, although not to the extent that he would have liked.

So the question becomes, was the judge misled by not being told that the plaintiff's recovery had been dramatically quicker and more complete than the expert witnesses had supposed that it would be, when they gave evidence at the trial? . . .

The extent of counsel's duty not to mislead the court is defined by the contrasting decisions in *Tombling v Universal Bulb Co Ltd* [1951] 2 TLR 289 and *Meek v Fleming* [1961] 3 All ER 148, [1961] 2 QB 366. Denning LJ said in the former case (at 297):

> The duty of counsel to his client in a civil case—or in defending an accused person—is to make every honest endeavour to succeed. He must not, of course, knowingly mislead the Court … but, short of that, he may put such matters … as in his discretion he thinks will be most to the advantage of his client.

In *Tombling*'s case the court was not misled, in *Meek v Fleming*, notoriously, it was. Both cases were concerned with the failure to put before the court evidence which was known to counsel at the trial. Neither, therefore, is directly relevant on its facts to the present case.

If material came into counsel's hands which suggested that the evidence which the witnesses gave in April 1994 was false to their knowledge when they gave it, then I would have no hesitation in holding that it was his duty so to inform the court. But that is not the present case.

Moreover, if subsequent events demonstrated that the evidence they had given could not have been correct, either factually as to the plaintiff's condition or as regards the prognosis at that time, then again, if there had been a significant inaccuracy, I would hold that the court should be told. Again, that is not this case.

The fact is that the October 1994 reports showed two things. First, that the plaintiff's recovery had been more marked than his expert witnesses had supposed that it would be, assisted in part by the fact that the long drawn-out trial was over. Secondly, it cast doubt on the reliability of Mr Mackay and Dr Lloyd as independent expert witnesses. Was the judge misled by not being informed of either of these?

I do not consider that he was. He knew that his judgment was based on the evidence given in April 1994. He knew that subsequent events might or might not have proved that the then prognosis, which was not challenged, was incorrect. Similarly, he knew that the expert witnesses whom he had heard in April/July 1994 might or might not have held the same views in January 1995 when he gave judgment as they did then. In short, his January 1995 judgment, including his assessments of future loss, was based on the prognosis as it was in, at latest, July 1994.

If he wondered whether or not the prognosis remained correct, then he would have to acknowledge that whereas one party might wish to put further evidence before him, the other would certainly object, unless it could be said that the evidence he had heard was incorrect when it was given.

In short, it seems to me that the plaintiff's counsel were entitled to take the view which they did, namely that they were under no duty to place the October 1994 reports before the judge.

What then was the extent of their duty to the Court of Appeal? In my judgment, there was no discovery obligation, for the reasons already given, and the October 1994 reports remained privileged, in the manner described above, in any event. That did not apply to the transcripts of evidence given before Judge McNaught, if the plaintiff had them, or to his judgment, but those documents were protected by the statutory requirement of confidentiality under r 4.23. Moreover, their existence was known to the defendant's representative before and during the appeal. They could have applied to the Family Court, but so far as I am aware they did not do so.

There was no mystery about the fact that family proceedings had taken place in which the plaintiff presumably was contending that he had recovered sufficiently to look after his children. His claim might be and probably was supported by expert witnesses called on his behalf. The plaintiff was in court throughout the appeal hearing and if appearances are any guide he was no longer suffering from chronic or even serious mental illness as described by the judge. He had made some degree of recovery, and it was accepted on all sides that the question for this court was whether the judge's findings were correct on the basis of the evidence he had heard in 1994. It was obvious that his condition and prognosis in January 1996 were different from, and probably better than, they had been then. There was no suggestion that fresh evidence should be called in order to assess the plaintiff's condition and prospects at the time of the appeal. There was no issue before us as to general damages or as to the plaintiff's chances of obtaining future employment if his condition should improve. In these circumstances, I do not find convincing the suggestion that we were misled by not being informed that the plaintiff's recovery had been even better than we might have supposed. I would acquit his counsel of this further charge also.[20]

---

20   [1997] 1 All ER 614 at 642-645.

Questions

1. Did Vernon and his lawyers deceive the court?

2. To what extent could the notion of broad framing set out by William Simon[1] justify the (arguably) deceptive non-disclosure of the plaintiffs lawyers? Could the same arguments be used to justify the aggressive tactics of the defendants in refusing to deny that the plaintiff was suffering any mental illness? Note that these tactics were described as 'indefensible' by the Court of Appeal.

3. What differing views of legal ethics can be seen in the behaviour and thinking of those involved in this dispute?

4. How would each of the theorists considered in this chapter view the behaviour of the plaintiff and his advisers?

5. Suppose that counsel for the plaintiff in the personal injury action had learned not that the expert had given inconsistent testimony in matrimonial proceedings but that he had written relevantly and inconsistently with his expert evidence on the nature of the medical condition afflicting the plaintiff. Would there have been a duty to disclose this?

6. Save where the lawyer acts as counsel for the prosecution, it is accepted that advocates do not have a duty to disclose the existence of witnesses whose testimony might be harmful to the client (*Re G Mayor Cooke* (1889) 5 TLR 407, 408). Is this consistent with the duty not to mislead the court as formulated in *Vernon v Bosely*?

1   Supra at pp 168-169.

PART II

Particular problems in legal ethics

CHAPTER SIX

Criminal defence and prosecution

Let Justice be done-that is for my client...though the heavens fall. This is the kind of advocacy that I would want as a client and that I feel bound to provide as an advocate.[1]

We have already discussed the dilemma faced by Frank Armani upon being informed by his client of the location of the bodies of two girls whom he had murdered. Armani defended his client diligently and his diligence was extremely costly. When the trial took place in July 1974 public feeling was running high. Armani received hate mail and on coming down to breakfast one day during the trial found a message scrawled on his napkin: 'We can take you out any time we like. That child killer better not get off.'

During the trial, Garrow confessed to all the murders in an effort to establish his insanity. Armani's knowledge of the other crimes was also revealed causing an outcry. One of Armani's friends said 'if I was the girl's father I would shoot you.' His health, marriage and law practice all suffered badly. To some, Garrow was a heroic defender of an unpopular client. To others, he was akin to an accomplice. What is clear is that Frank Armani displayed many of the characteristics of a zealous advocate practising in accordance with the 'Standard Conception of Legal Ethics'. Such a lawyer will

- attempt to ensure the best possible result for the defendant
- even if he is sure the client is guilty of the offence charged
- regardless of the damage thus caused to the State's interest in convicting the guilty
- regardless of the impact upon victims
- by any means not clearly in breach of a rule of substantive or procedural law or of a binding code of professional ethics (but interpreting any ambiguity in applicable

---

1 Monroe Freedman *Lawyers Ethics in an Adversary System* (New York, Bobs-Merrill Company, 1975) p 9.

provisions in the client's favour and assuming that restrictive provisions are significant only if they are actually enforced)
- regardless of any harm thus caused to victims, witnesses and other third parties.

We have seen that the 'Standard Conception of Legal Ethics' has been subjected to sustained criticism as a general framework for lawyers' ethics. Yet many of these critics have maintained that criminal defence work is somehow different and that in this context, zealous advocacy is ethically justified. After a brief detour into the realities of life for criminal defendants and their lawyers we consider the truth of this claim and deal also with the related question of prosecutorial ethics.

1   Criminal defence

Under and over representation

One of the paradoxes of lawyers' ethics is that whilst many would argue that the criminal defendant should be defended according to the standard conception of legal ethics, it seems clear that criminal defendants are in fact very rarely defended adequately let alone zealously. This much emerges from *Standing Accused,* an empirical study of the work of criminal defence lawyers.[2] From this study, it emerged that suspects' formal right to silence[3] was in reality of little significance during police station interviews because they lacked effective legal advice.[4] Even when a solicitor's representative did attend, the advisor was rarely legally qualified. On a significant number of occasions, the representative was a former policeman who shared the assumption of the interrogating officer that the suspect was in fact guilty and that a refusal to answer questions was illegitimate:

> I spoke to [the suspect in police custody] straight – I believe in plain speaking. I said: 'Don't mess about. If you did it, you may as well cough to it, then we can all go home'. I believe in playing by the rules – both sides. If everyone does that, there's no need to have a conscience about defending these people. I try to be fair to both sides.[5]

Often those attending were trainee solicitors with no prior training for their role and for whom survival was the immediate goal, which was achieved with some surprising strategies:

> [the police] have always been extremely courteous and very, very helpful.... I found with some of them you can say 'should I be doing this? Should I be staying for this part of the interview...' They are always very very helpful.[6]

---

2   Michael McConville, Jacqueline Hodgson, Lee Bridges and Anita Pavolovic *Standing Accused – The Organisation and Practices of Criminal Defence Lawyers In Britain* (Clarendon, Oxford, 1994).

3   The right to remain silence without adverse inferences being drawn has now been abolished. See s 34 of the Criminal Justice and Public Order Act 1994.

4   Section 58 of the Police and Criminal Evidence Act 1984 conferred upon suspects a right to free legal advice at the police station.

5   Supra note 2 at p 86.

6   Ibid p 61.

Once the client had been charged, little was done to elicit and investigate the client's version of events. Rather client interviews were conducted on the basis that the prosecution's version of events was presumed to be accurate, the main question being whether the client was willing to plead guilty. If so, this was generally accepted even if there appeared to be a defence, not least because the interviewer was often an untrained clerk who knew too little law to recognise facts amounting to a defence. Throughout the whole process, the client was almost invariably under pressure to plead guilty right up to the door of the court. In one case[7], for example, the defendant was charged with two offences, one of assaulting his wife from whom he was separated and the other of assaulting a police officer. The police were called after the wife came home with another man and found the defendant there, whereupon an argument developed. The client had admitted both offences to the police and in particular that he had started the fight with the police.

Solicitor:	You admit that you started it.
Client:	Which I didn't!
Solicitor:	Well, your wife's statement says you threw the first blow. Why did you tell the police you started it?
Client:	It was all so quick.
Solicitor:	Looking at this practically, it's a fairly soft bench today. Now, you can either plead not guilty and the case will go off for trial. [In a worried tone] It's going to be a case where, well, there's a lot of evidence and it's not going to be right to interview your wife. [More optimistically] Or, we can just...
Client:	Go guilty?
Solicitor:	[evasively] Well, let the evidence come out... Now, [more hopefully] if you plead guilty, there's a lot of mitigation. She's with another man, the police arrive, you presumably don't like them interfering and there was a fight....Now, faced with what I see as an inevitable result, I think you're better to plead guilty straight away and not dwell on all the gory details that would come out in a trial.

Having settled upon a plea, the solicitor moved to the question of mitigation, for the purposes of which she was prepared to speak to the client's wife. The wife, who was separated from the client, was asked to come into an interview room where she was seen by the solicitor alone.

Solicitor:	You don't have to talk to me if you don't want to. I'd just like to know a little of what happened.
Wife:	The police came and I said I don't want to get him into any trouble, I just want him to leave. They asked him to leave and it was just a verbal

---

7   What follows is based on a case recorded in *Standing Accused* (supra note 2) at pp 191-192 but I have omitted the authors' analysis of the significance of the words spoken.

argument really. They're saying I said I saw him throw the first punch but [emphatically] *I didn't*. When they got him on the sofa he was struggling to breathe.

Solicitor:	The police say he struck you.
Wife:	No, he didn't lay a finger on me.
Solicitor:	I think this officer got the wrong end of the stick.
Wife:	[Definitely] Yes, he did.
Solicitor:	*Did* he punch you?
Wife:	[Adamantly] *No.*
Solicitor:	Did he touch you at all?
Wife:	No, he didn't.

It was clear from this that the charge of assault on the wife had little chance of succeeding, but what of that on the police officer? There was no dispute that there had been a verbal exchange and that the client and the officers ended up on the sofa, but the crucial issue was how had this come about. Whilst the client said that he did not attack the police, his wife's version was important because, since she had little affection for him, her evidence could be presented as being almost neutral in character. The solicitor asked her about the incident in question.

Solicitor:	What about the violence between him and the police?
Wife:	He was mouthing, giving them a bit of lip. Next thing he was on the sofa.
Solicitor:	How?
Wife:	The copper pushed him.
Solicitor:	So, is it fair to say that the police came in, [your husband] got excited...
Wife:	[interrupting] Yes, he moves about a lot, waves his arms.
Solicitor:	Your husband got excited, was gesticulating.
Wife:	Yes.
Solicitor:	And the next thing he was on the sofa.
Wife:	Yes, he ended up face down with his head and neck up against the arm. I was really worried; they were on top of him.
Solicitor:	So basically, the police tried to arrest him, there was a scuffle and he got hurt.
Solicitor:	So, if I say I've spoken to you and no matter what happens between you and [your husband] you don't want to see him punished because of this, would that be fair?
Wife:	Yes.

When the wife left the interview room and returned to the court, the solicitor turned to the researcher and said:

Solicitor: I'm almost sorry it's a guilty plea now – she's such a good, strong witness.

In mitigation the solicitor said:

Solicitor: Perhaps the officer chose to deal with my client in unsympathetic tones. As I understand it, when agitated, he gesticulates... [His wife] is certain [my client] showed no direct aggression to her and the next thing she saw was her husband being pinned down on the sofa... So, there was a domestic dispute, the police were called and a scuffle – there we have it. [Emphasis supplied].

Ultimately many would argue that criminal defendants are processed by their lawyers rather than defended. Nor is this solely because criminal defence firms are insufficiently resourced by the state to enable the preparation of a proper defence (the study produced impressive though rare contrary examples of extremely diligent criminal defence work). According to Baldwin's study, a large part of the problem was that defence lawyers surveyed assumed like the police that their clients were morally guilty and therefore unworthy of effective legal defence. In private discussion, it emerged that many of the lawyers surveyed had very low views of their clients:

- He's just a dick. If he had any brains, he'd be dangerous.
- He's not telling the truth, but then which clients do?
- He's the lowest form of life; I very much doubt if he's human at all.
- Our clients don't look out of place in our shabby little offices, but in the plush surroundings of chambers you can see what we're dealing with.[8]

It seems then, that the foremost ethical problem in criminal defence work is that of the under representation of client interests and the criminal justice system's greatest need is for more advocates committed to the defence of their clients. Such commitment may be costly. Horrific crimes may generate such popular revulsion that those who defend the accused adequately let alone zealously may come to share the popular opprobrium for their clients. In addition, judges are given broad discretionary powers in relation to the conduct of a criminal trial which are capable of being abused. In 1998, the Court of Appeal allowed a posthumous appeal by Derek Bentley, who had been hanged after being found guilty of murdering a policeman. One of the successful grounds of appeal was that Lord Goddard, the Lord Chief Justice, had given a summing up which was severely and unfairly prejudicial to the defence. Parts of the summing up could not be read 'as other than a highly rhetorical and strongly-worded denunciation of both defendants and of their defences. The language used was not that of a judge but of an advocate ... (and was) such as to deny the appellant that fair trial which is the birthright of every British citizen.'[9] If counsel concludes that the client's legal and moral right to

8   Ibid at p 35.
9   *R v Bentley* (1998) Times, 31 July (citation from the Smith Bernal Transcipt).

a fair trial are being breached s/he is in an unenviable position. If a challenge is made to the judge's behaviour, then the offending conduct may be exposed thus laying the ground for an appeal. On the other hand, the judge's decisions are prima facie binding unless overturned on appeal and to challenge them may invite a report to the professional body or even in an extreme case, a use of the judge's power to fine for contempt of court those deemed to be interfering with the administration of justice. Such challenges may become more necessary as the criminal justice system like every other part of the State at the beginning of the 21st century comes under increasing pressure to use resources efficiently. Such pressure will inevitably make judges (unacceptably?) more receptive to the notion that counsel's freedom to present the case as s/he sees fit should be curtailed in the interests of speed and efficiency. Whether the advent of the Human Rights Act and the fair trial guarantees contained in Article 6 will provide sufficient contrary pressure remains to be seen.

Question

In what ways might the structure of the market for legal services influence the conduct of a defence lawyers faced with a hostile judge? Reconsider the extract from the work of David Wilkins in chapter 3.

Over representation of client interests

Whilst the empirical reality may be the under representation of client interests, over representation is also possible and we need to consider whether there is, as some have claimed, something special about criminal defence work which justifies zealous advocacy. After considering the limits imposed by the law (whether substantive or procedural) and by codes of ethics, we consider in turn arguments based on the need to contain state power and on the defendant's right to a fair trial. We then turn to consider the 'social worker's argument'. This argument is distinct in that unlike the first two arguments it does not defend the standard conception by arguing that it is inherent in the role given to defence lawyers by the criminal justice system. Such arguments assume the legitimacy of the criminal justice system. The 'social worker's argument' argues for its illegitimacy. As a consequence, it yields a more radical version of the standard conception in which all constraints on zealous advocacy are abandoned, save for the prudential. An ongoing theme within all three arguments is what may be called the social scientist's perspective ie the argument that judgments about what is ethical must take account of what we know of how the criminal justice system operates in practice.

2 Constraints on the zealous advocate

Misleading the court

Most codes of ethics impose upon advocates a duty not to mislead the court. The LSGPC provides:

> Solicitors who act in litigation, whilst under a duty to do their best for their client must never deceive or mislead the Court.[10] ... A solicitor would be guilty of professional misconduct if he or she called a witness whose evidence is untrue to the solicitor's knowledge as opposed to his or her belief.[11]

> Where a client, prior to or in the course of any proceedings, admits to his or her solicitor that the client has committed perjury or misled the court in any material matter in continuing proceedings or in relation to those proceedings, the solicitor must decline to act further in the proceedings unless the client agrees fully to disclose his or her conduct to the court.[12]

The CCB provides that:

> A practising barrister has an overriding duty to the Court ... and must not deceive or knowingly or recklessly mislead the Court.[13]

However defence lawyers are not under a duty to inform the court of facts relevant and helpful to the prosecution case if the prosecution does not prove them. Hence the defence is not obliged to notify the prosecution of the identity and whereabouts of witnesses. The crucial dividing line is between actively misleading the court and between passively acquiescing in its ignorance.

A number of factors complicate the notion of a prohibition against misleading the court. One is that the defendant is entitled to have the prosecution put to proof of its case. Thus if the defendant admits his guilt to the lawyer, the lawyer is not allowed to assist the accused in giving evidence contrary to the prosecution case. S/he may however cross-examine prosecution witnesses with a view to testing their credibility. This strategy may raise sufficient doubt in the minds of the jury about the prosecution case as to secure an acquittal in reliance on the burden of proof.[14] However, the dividing line between misleading the court and reliance on the burden of proof can be very thin and a tempting target for a truly committed zealous advocate. Indeed, it is arguable that it is virtually impossible to convince the fact finder that the burden of proof has not been satisfied without presenting, at least implicitly, an alternative account of the evidence before the court which makes better sense of that evidence than the prosecution's case.[15]

10　Principle 21.01.
11　Principle 21.07 note 5.
12　Principle 21.13.
13　Para 202.
14　See generally paras 3.1 – 3.10 of the Standards Applicable to Criminal Cases (CCB annex H).
15　See generally W Twining *Rethinking Evidence: Exploratory Essays* (Oxford, Blackwell, 1990) p 243.

A further difficulty is the interaction of the duty not to deceive the Court and the lawyer's general duty of confidentiality (which, together with its exceptions, is considered in chapter 7). The problem is that in many situations the lawyer will know that the accused (or a witness on the accused's behalf) has given false evidence or proposes to do so only because of what the client has revealed to the lawyer in confidence. Consequently, Munroe Freedman has argued that lawyers should be free to assist their clients in giving perjured evidence. The argument arises from what Freedman calls the perjury trilemma: the lawyer has the duty to discover all facts relevant to the client's case, the duty to keep secret anything disclosed in confidence by the client and the duty to be candid with the court. Freedman argues that the first of these two duties is inconsistent with the third. Lawyers will usually know that the client is deceiving the court only because of something said in confidence. Yet if clients cannot trust their lawyers to keep confidential facts disclosed in private they will be reluctant to reveal their story. Therefore, argues Freedman, the duty of candour must give way.

Most fundamentally of all however, the prohibition against misleading the court assumes that the fact finder is determining the truth about the past through rational analysis of the evidence. On this basis, an advocate would mislead the court if s/he managed despite the trial judge's supervision to introduce irrelevant evidence in a way which reduced the chances of an accurate verdict. However it is not clear in the case of the jury that the rationalist assumption is always correct. Indeed one of the justifications for the jury is its capacity to return a verdict against the evidence, for example in a case where the decision to prosecute could be described as politically motivated[16]. As Lord Devlin has put it, 'Each jury is a little parliament'.[17]

Questions

1. Your client Norman, and his co-accused Steve, are charged with receiving stolen goods. The police found Norman and Steve in an alley transferring a stereo and TV from an abandoned car into the back seat of another car which they were about to drive away. The case hinges on whether the clients knew that the property was stolen. Norman says that when he borrowed his cousin's Volvo, he was given only the ignition key, not the boot key. But the prosecution seem unaware of this.

Is it misconduct to say in your closing address to the jury that *obviously* Steve and Norman had no idea that the property was stolen, else why would they have been loading it into the back seat, instead of concealing it in the boot?[18]

---

16   See the account of the trial of Clive Ponting in M Findlay and P Duff *The Jury Under Attack* (London, Butterworths, 1988) p 141.

17   P Devlin *Trial by Jury* (London, Methuen & Co Ltd, 1966) p 164.

18   William H Simon 'The Ethics of Criminal Defence' (1993) 91 Michigan Law Review 1703 at 1704.

2. The defendant is accused of violent attack upon a tourist late at night in a wealthy London suburb and is charged with assault occasioning actual bodily harm contrary to s 47 of the Offences Against the Person Act. One of the principal pieces of evidence against the accused is that of a police officer who says that he saw the accused running away from the scene of the crime (the accused has a long criminal record and was therefore well known to the police). The accused has elected for trial by jury and adamantly maintains his innocence. He says that though he was at the scene of the crime and witnessed the assault he was not involved. However, he also tells you that the jury at this trial centre has a reputation for being prosecution minded. Consequently, he is worried that he will not be believed, and you share his doubts. He has therefore arranged an alibi for himself.

i)   Is it *misconduct* to either a) suggest during the prosecution evidence that the witness was mistaken in his identification of your client? or b) allow the defendant and his friends to give the alibi evidence.

ii)   Is it *unethical* to do either of these things? What is the difference? How would a lawyer practising 'ethical discretion' resolve this case? Would the concept of 'broad framing' be relevant?

3. *Shorty's Case:* your client Harry (known as 'Shorty' to friends) is accused, along with a number of others of kidnapping and sexual assault. Along with many of the others, the client denies any involvement. The victim has stated that one of her assailants was known as 'Shorty'. The prosecution have identified another man, Peter, who is also know as Shorty and who has made a statement to the police admitting his (Peter's) presence at the scene of the crime but denying any involvement. Peter's statement implicates your client. The prosecution have decided not to call Peter on the grounds that he is an unreliable witness with a history of mental disturbance. You realise that if you call Peter and establish that he is known as 'Shorty' he will then refuse to answer any questions in order to avoid incriminating himself. You could then suggest to the jury that there is real doubt about the identity of 'Shorty'- even though none of the accused have implicated Peter[19]. Will this involve misleading the court?

4. Do you agree with Professor Freedman's suggestion that the duty not to mislead the court should give way to the duty of confidentiality?

5. What precisely should the defence lawyer do upon hearing an admission that the accused is guilty and intends to lead perjured evidence? In *Sankar* v *State of Trinidad and Tobago*[20], the defence lawyer facing this dilemma simply refused to allow accused to give evidence and sought merely to put the prosecution to proof. The defendants appeal against conviction was allowed by the Privy Council on the grounds that the lawyer ought to have informed the client that he could not be involved in such an attempt to mislead the court and that unless the client's instructions were changed he

19   This case is based on the Australian case of *R v Jamieson & Brugmans* (1993) 16 ALR 193.
20   [1995] 1 WLR 194 PC . It is clear that the Privy Council considered the principles applied in the case to be identical with those of English domestic law.

would have to withdraw. Is this a satisfactory position? Does it help in resolving the perjury trilemma? On the appropriate course where the client or a witness has already mislead the court see *Vernon v Bosley*[1] the material parts of which are set out in chapter 5.

Witnesses

Two questions fail to be considered here, namely harm caused to witnesses through the process of cross-examination and the question of the extent to which witnesses may be coached. As to the former, codes of conduct commonly restrict questions which are intended simply to vilify or annoy witnesses. Thus paragraph 21.08 of the LSGPC provides that:

> A solicitor must not make or instruct an advocate to make an allegation which is intended only to insult, degrade or annoy the other side, the witness or any other person.

and a barrister conducting a case at court:

> must not make statements or ask questions which are merely scandalous or intended or calculated only to insult or annoy either a witness or some other person;[2]

However, once again there is a thin line between misconduct and wholly appropriate professional zeal, for one of the most effective ways of minimising the effect of a witness' evidence is to impugn either their competence or their integrity. The latter tactic may involve questioning witnesses about aspects of their character which might make them appear to the jury to be an untrustworthy witness ('cross-examining as to credit'). How far back may the lawyer go when cross-examining as to credit in order to unearth ammunition which can be used to undermine a witness? Judges have an overriding discretion to control cross examination as to credit and in *Hobbs* v *Tinling*[3] Sankey LJ held that:

> (1) Such questions are proper if they are of such a nature that the truth of the imputation conveyed by them would seriously effect the opinion of the court as to the credibility of the witness on the matter to which he testifies.

> (2) Such questions are improper if the imputation which they convey relates to matters so remote in time, or of such a character, that the truth of the imputation would not effect, or would affect in a slight degree, the opinion of the court as to the credibility of the witness on the matter to which he testifies.

> (3) Such questions are improper if there is great disproportion between the importance of the imputation made against the witness's character and the importance of his evidence.[4]

1   [1997] 1 All ER 614.
2   Written Standards for the Conduct of Professional Work (CCB Annex H) para 5.10(e).
3   [1929] 2 KB 1 See further *Mechanical & General Inventions Co Ltd v Austin* [1935] AC 346 at 360 per Lord Sankey LC.
4   Ibid at p 29.

Nevertheless, it is clear that different judges will interpret these guidelines in differing ways. Moreover as a matter of principle respect for the presumption of innocence is likely to lead to doubts being resolved in favour of the accused. From a pragmatic point of view, judges' knowledge that restricting the conduct of the defence may lead to an appeal also suggests that defence lawyers have considerable scope for manoeuvre.

The distress which may be felt by a witness under cross-examination will undoubtedly be reduced if the lawyer calling the witness has explained what is involved in giving evidence and it would probably be regarded as a breach of duty to the client to fail to do so. A disorientated witness is unlikely to be credible. However, there is clearly a potential conflict here with the duty not to mislead the court since a witness might clearly be prepared by being told what answers are expected. An extreme example of this occurred in *Vernon v Bosely,* where lawyers acting in a custody dispute instructed experts to prepare a report on the basis that:

> We need to show that his mental health has improved dramatically since .... May 1993 and moreover that it has improved again since the conclusion of his big personal injury case.[5]

Consequently, most codes of conduct prevent 'witness coaching'. For example, paragraph 6.5 of the Law Society's Advocacy code provides that

> Advocates must not when interviewing a witness out of court:
> (a) place witnesses who are being interviewed under any pressure to provide other than a truthful account of their evidence;
> (b) rehearse, practice or coach witnesses in relation to their evidence or the way in which they should give it.

The CCB contains a very similar provision[6] which is reinforced by further provisions which allow barristers limited opportunities for discussing a case with a witness.[7]

These provisions are however made problematic by the law's insistence that the attitude, bearing, poise, presence and general behaviour of witnesses (usually termed their 'demeanour') are important clues as to their veracity. This is what lies at the heart of the Court of Appeal's reluctance to interfere with the findings of the judge or other fact finder (such as the jury) who saw the witnesses. The problem is of course that witnesses may be stuttering, (apparently) shifty, unwilling to look the advocate directly in the eye etc because they are lying – or, more prosaically, because of inherent personality traits or because the occasion is unfamiliar and unsettling. The dilemma, then, is whether to advise the witness about aspects of the witness' demeanour which might lead the jury to draw false inferences about his/her credibility. The temptation to cross the boundary of legitimate conduct is made all the stronger by the other sides

5   Supra note 1 at 620F-G.
6   CCB 705.1.
7   The CCB assumes that proofs of evidence will normally be taken by solicitors (paras 706-707) though a barrister who attends at Court may if necessary undertake this task if he/she has considered it appropriate in the interests both of the lay client and of justice to dispense with the attendance of the solicitor. Paragraph 705(c) provides that save with the consent of the representative of the other side (or of the court) no barrister may communicate with any witness about the case once the witness has begun to give evidence.

difficulties in exposing misconduct. If a client is asked what advice has been given by the lawyer about the process of testifying, s/he may claim that such conversations are privileged. Other witnesses must respond but the 'finality rule' provides that answers to questions which go only to credit must be accepted and that evidence cannot normally be led in rebuttal.

Questions

1. You are a criminal defence lawyer representing a defendant accused of attempting to bribe a public official. You know the case against the client is a strong one but that the chief prosecution witness has herself a previous criminal conviction which might be proved in court as weakening her credibility. You know that proving the conviction is unlikely to be terribly effective: the witness was convicted of child abuse many years ago and, logically, this conviction has little relevance to her propensity to tell the truth. Nevertheless, you also know that the judge assigned to the case is very reluctant to restrict counsel's freedom to present the defence case and will almost certainly allow you to proceed. However, disclosure of this conviction would be so damaging to the witness' reputation in the local community that she would in all probability refuse to testify if disclosure were a realistic possibility. If the defence indicates an intention to disclose the conviction, then the prosecutor may well feel bound to convey this to the witness with the result that the charge will probably be dropped.

Should you mention this to the client when advising her as to her plea?

2. In the film, *A Few Good Men*, Tom Cruise plays a US army defence lawyer whose client, a junior soldier, is charged with the murder of a fellow soldier. The defence seeks to prove that the assault was carried out on the orders of senior officers as part of an informal (and illegal) system of military discipline (a 'code red'). At the trial, Cruise cross-examines a senior general about military discipline and the general denies that the practice exists. Cruise then cross-examines the general as to his views on the role of the military as a bulwark against anarchy, casting ever greater slurs on the general's character. He protests that he is not on trial. The questions become less and less relevant and the atmosphere ever more emotionally charged. Cruise is warned repeatedly by the judge that he is about to be held in contempt. Finally, Cruise screams out the question 'Did you order the Code Red' and the general exploding with righteous anger, admits that he did and is proud of the fact. The judge orders his immediate arrest and the client's case takes on a different light.

Such cross-examination would almost certainly be regarded as misconduct in a UK court. But is it unethical? If not, why not?

3. Your client is the dean of a university law school and is charged with fraud in connection with expenses claims. Though once an academic, the dean many years ago

ceased serious academic study and became immersed in academic administration, exchanging, both literally and metaphorically, the academic's tweed jacket for the administrator's suit. At about the same time, the dean began to wear contact lenses instead of glasses. The defence is inadvertence. Should you advise your client to wear his tweed jacket instead of his suit and glasses instead of contact lenses on the grounds that this will make his evidence more credible?

4. You client is a teacher accused of raping one of his 18-year-old sixth form pupils. There is little evidence of physical struggle. The client's story is that the complainant had pursued him for many months and that he had at last succumbed to temptation late one evening at school after a drama rehearsal. He admits that she did not actively express consent but says that she did not resist and that he believed she was consenting in the light of her previous behaviour. The complainant admits that she had flirted quite regularly with the client but denies agreeing to have sex. She says that when they were alone together at school after the drama rehearsal, he forced himself upon her. She was too scared to resist.

i)   Is it misconduct to suggest that the defendant encourage his wife and 16-year-old daughter to attend the hearing?

ii)   Does it make any difference if you know that the wife intends to start divorce proceedings against the client after the conclusion of the criminal proceedings?

iii)   Does it make any difference that your client has a previous conviction for having under age sex with a pupil? Evidence of an accused's previous convictions is not generally admissible in evidence except inter alia where the defence leads evidence to the effect that the accused is of good character? (in which case the convictions can be admitted by way of rebuttal)?

iv)   Do the demands of ethics and professional conduct differ in relation to any of questions i-iii?

Justifying zealous advocacy

CONTAINING THE POWER OF THE STATE

Many of the arguments advanced in support of the 'Standard Conception' as an approach to criminal defence work are rooted in the liberal fear that state officials have an inherent tendency to abuse their powers. The police for example are on this view situated in an occupational culture in which crime control is so dominant a goal that the innocent are frequently in danger of being falsely accused. Bureaucrats may resist dissemination of information exposing them to public scrutiny and will abuse those provisions of the criminal law designed to protect official secrets in order to do so. Zealous advocacy defends civil liberties against such abuse. In the following passage, William Simon considers and criticises these concerns:

> Libertarians claim that aggressive advocacy is distinctively appropriate to the criminal sphere because it serves to check oppression by the 'state.' Such arguments invoke the

image of the 'isolated,' 'lone,' 'friendless,' or 'naked' individual faced with the 'enormous power and resources of the state.' Aggressive defense is supposed to level the playing field and turn the trial into a 'contest of equals,' or at least express the system's commitment to treat all citizens with respect.

Aggressive defense is also supposed to protect against the abuse of state power. The danger of abuse is most commonly attributed to the inherently corrupting nature of state power and the consequent aggression and rapacity of state officials. The aggressive defense lawyer inhibits such abuse by increasing the difficulty of conviction. In David Luban's rhetoric:

> We want to handicap the state in its power even legitimately to punish us, for we believe as a matter of political theory and historical experience that if the state is not handicapped or restrained *ex ante,* our political and civil liberties are jeopardized. Power-holders are inevitably tempted to abuse the criminal justice system to persecute political opponents, and overzealous police will trample civil liberties in the name of crime prevention and order.

This type of rhetoric has been exempt from critical reflection for so long that even a small amount should raise doubts. In the first place, the image of the lonely individual facing Leviathan is misleading. Let us grant the lonely part even though some defendants have lots of friends. But, what about the state? Libertarian rhetoric tends to suggest that the individual defendant takes on the entire state. But, of course, the state has other concerns besides this defendant. From the state's point of view, the defendant may be part of an enormous class of criminal defendants and suspects with which it can hardly begin to cope.

It is more plausible to portray the typical defendant as facing a small number of harassed, overworked bureaucrats. Of course, state agencies can focus their resources on particular defendants and, when they do so, their power can be formidable. But the state cannot possibly focus its power this way on all defendants or even most of them.

Yet, aggressive defense treats all defendants as if they faced the full concentrated power of the state.

Second, victims do not appear in the libertarian picture. Criminal actions are styled as claims by the state for punitive remedies. But in fact prosecutors often initiate such actions on behalf of particular individuals whose rights the defendant has violated and who have a strong personal stake in the outcome – not necessarily a claim for tangible compensation (although some criminal proceedings do involve restitutionary remedies), but a desire for vindication, retribution, or protection that the defendant's punishment might afford them.

The 'victims' rights' movement has worked for the past two decades to replace in the popular consciousness the defense lawyer's image of the criminal trial as a state-versus-defendant contest with that of a victim-versus-defendant contest. The movement is often naive, even blind, about the efficacy of criminal punishment in deterring future wrongs or aiding victims, but its imagery seems as plausible as that of the defense lawyer.

Now consider the suggestion that it is desirable to equalize the abilities of prosecution and defense, to level the playing field. If we really wanted to do this, we could 'handicap" state officials, to use Luban's word, the way we handicap horses in thoroughbred races by requiring the stronger ones to carry weights. It would certainly slow down prosecutors and police if they had to carry around belts with, say, forty pounds of lead weights. If we wanted to pursue equality, we would have to increase the weights in proportion to the probability of conviction. The prosecutor of a defendant caught red handed before a crowd of witnesses might have to drag around a ball and chain of several hundred pounds.

The reason why this sounds silly is that the premise that there is any interest in *categorically* remedying imbalances of power between prosecution and defense is silly. We want the prosecution to be strong in its ability to convict the guilty but weak in its ability to convict the innocent. Where these goals are in conflict, we make tradeoffs, more often than not in favor of the latter. But an indiscriminate weakening of state power, unfocused on any of the goals of the process, serves no purpose at all. The problem with aggressive defense is that it impedes the states' ability to convict the guilty without affording any significant protection to the innocent.

The state-focused arguments for aggressive defense are driven by what might be called the libertarian dogma. The right-wing version of the libertarian dogma is that the only important threat to liberty is the state. The left-wing version is that the only important threats are the state and powerful private organizations like business corporations. In the latter view, as Luban puts it, the central rule of the advocate is 'the protection of individuals against institutions.' The idea that informal, diffuse violence or oppression might threaten liberty is foreign to both versions of the dogma.

The libertarian dogma usually refers to totalitarian regimes like Nazi Germany and Soviet Russia and the absence of criminal defense rights in such regimes. These examples are supposed to illustrate the danger to liberty of the overpowerful state and the value of criminal defense in checking that danger. The point has merit, but it is incomplete. It ignores the dangers to liberty of the weak state. Both Nazi Germany and Soviet Russia emerged from weak states (the Weimar Republic and the Provisional Government), in part as a consequence of the illegal private terrorism and paramilitary aggression these states were unable to check. Since the end of colonialism, Latin America has seen many examples of weak states powerless to check the oppression of the paramilitary forces of landowners or narcotics traffickers.

Moreover, as an argument for defendants' rights in the criminal process, the libertarian dogma ignores that criminal law enforcement represents not only a danger that state power will be abused, but also an important *safeguard* against such abuse. The inability of certain weak Latin American states to prosecute effectively the crimes of their military officers tragically illustrates this.

. . . Luban's argument that aggressive defense desirably 'overprotects' liberty against its abuse by the state raises the question of why overprotection against state abuse is worth the resulting under protection against private abuse. To the extent one can discern an answer, it is the customary libertarian claim – typically unaccompanied by political or historical analysis – that the dangers of totalitarianism are greater than the dangers of anarchy.

If we put aside the problem, noted above, that these dangers are not entirely distinct, there is a further objection to this argument. The argument assumes that we must choose categorically between a criminal justice system that protects against one danger or a system that protects against another. But, in fact, the relevant choices are at the margin. We can all agree on a system that provides strong opportunities to establish innocence and to assert some intrinsic procedural rights. The question then becomes whether any net benefits are achieved by the addition of a categorically adversarial defense that includes, for example, active deception.[8]

Notes

1. Simon agrees that all criminal defendants have rights, eg to have the case against them proved beyond all reasonable doubt. Nor does he deny that zealous advocacy may be necessary in cases where abuse of State power has occurred. His point of disagreement is with those like David Luban who advocate its adoption for *all* criminal defence work. In accordance with his general approach, Simon urges the lawyer to seek justice meaning the correct resolution of the dispute according to the fundamental values of the legal system. In many cases, this will mean ceding judgment to some other institution (ie the jury) better placed for functional or constitutional reasons to make the decision. For Simon, the most problematic defence lawyering would be that which would prevent the dispute ever coming before the jury or which prevented relevant admissible evidence coming before the jury.

2. The debate about the relative resources of defences and prosecution has a parallel in England. The Criminal Bar has been arguing for some time that counsel for the prosecution are paid significantly less than their defence counterparts resulting in the prosecution being carried forward by inexperienced counsel.[9] Indeed, it is generally accepted that the Crown Prosecution Service has been under-resourced and badly managed for much of its history. However the prosecution do have the assistance of the police. By virtue of their control over interviews at the police station and (in many cases) their presence at the scene of the crime, the police are in a far stronger position than the defence to formulate a case and provide evidence to support it. What follows is a further response made by Luban in response to Simon's argument.

Political Legitimacy: More generally the state has enormous initial credibility because citizens believe it is democratic and legitimate. There is a nice paradox here. Liberal rhetoric promotes the policy of aggressive defence as a safeguard against totalitarianism. An independent bar, like an independent judiciary, has typically been among the first targets of totalitarian regimes, and history is replete with cases in which heroic and independent criminal defence lawyers have protected victims against the dangers of an

---

8   Simon supra note 18 at pp 1707-1708 and 1709-1710.
9   See *The Lawyer,* 30 September 1997 recording the submission of evidence to this effect to the DPP by the Chambers of James Hunt QC. The Review of the Crown Prosecution Service chaired by Sir Ian Glidewell (London, HMSO, 1998) ('The Glidewell Report') found evidence of a clear and unacceptable disparity between the fees offered to prosecuting counsel by the CPS and the fees paid to defence counsel by the Legal Aid Fund. It recommended that the government resolve the matter as a matter of urgency: see para 27 of its Summary of Conclusions and Recommendations.

oppressive and illegitimate state. Whether or not these arguments are right, critics such as Simon may argue that they are irrelevant in a non-totalitarian regime. But the paradox is that, just as zealous defence may be needed to counterbalance illegitimate government precisely because of its illegitimacy, a zealous advocate may also be needed to counter-balance a legitimate one, *precisely because of its legitimacy*.[10]

Questions

1. Do you wish to reconsider in the light of Simon's views your response to the case of the corrupt official? (p 198).

2. Your client is accused of assault with intent to cause grievous bodily harm following a fight with the leader of a rival gang. The client maintains his innocence (alleging that he was at home in bed alone at the time) but the prosecution intend to rely on identification evidence from two independent witnesses each of whom has identified the client as the assailant. You do not believe the client's story. You have read the Crown's witness statements which appear impressive. The client has a long list of previous convictions for violence many of them involving gang fights. You advise the client that though he may believe in his innocence, the jury is in your experience extremely unlikely to do so. If he pleads guilty, he will receive a sentence one third to one half less than that which he would receive if he insisted on going to trial. The client agrees to plead guilty, but on the morning of the trial the prosecution approach you and say that neither witness has arrived and that they intend to ask for an adjournment. They ask you to consent to their application.

What do you say? Should you ask for dismissal of the charges on the grounds that this latest delay (there have been several adjournments all of which have been due to the organisational incompetence of the police) is unfair to your client? What would William Simon say?

3. Would it make any difference in question 2 if you believed the witnesses had been intimidated by your client?

DEFENDANTS RIGHTS

A complimentary argument is that zealous advocacy is merely the instrument for the assertion of certain fundamental human rights. An example would be the right to be presumed innocent until proved guilty beyond reasonable doubt in a fair trial. Such rights have been recognised by the European Court of Human Rights, and its jurisprudence is now incorporated into English domestic law by the Human Rights

---

10   David Luban 'Are Criminal Defenders Different?'(1991) 91 Michigan Law Review 1729 at 1743.

Act. This is particularly important when the zealous advocate believes that the client is in fact guilty; it is the client's right to have guilt proved in a court of law and, in asserting that right, the lawyer may seek to discredit prosecution witnesses. In this way, the client may take advantage of the right to have guilt proved beyond all reasonable doubt. In the following extract, Nobles and Schiff develop these arguments as a part of a critique of the Royal Commission on Criminal Justice, chaired by Lord Runciman[11]. The Runciman Commission was set up to enquire into the workings of the criminal justice system following public concerns about a whole series of cases in which defendants had been wrongfully convicted. For many however, the report was immensely disappointing in its' failure to recommend strong measures to protect the suspect. In the following extract, Nobles and Schiff criticise what they see as the theoretical assumptions which undermined the Commission's work.

.....The Royal Commission was set up in response to cases in which large (or at least important) sections of the public had come to the conclusion that, in a number of cases, the wrong persons had been convicted of serious offences. Thus, whatever its specific terms of reference, its role was to respond to public awareness that the English system of criminal justice had produced miscarriages of justice. But beneath a consensus that miscarriages of justice had occurred, there are radically different notions of what constitute miscarriages of justice, and how one should respond to them.

Miscarriage of justice, as interpreted by the Royal Commission, is essentially about getting the verdict wrong – it is a rational conception linked to the outcome of trials. The Royal Commission's terms of reference required them to consider the effectiveness of the criminal justice system in securing the conviction of the guilty, as well as the acquittal of the innocent. These terms of reference immediately moved the focus away from another view of miscarriage of justice, one which could equally well be said to have concerned the public at the time the Commission was set up: the view that convictions had been secured in flagrant breach of the rules of criminal procedure – through, for example, non-disclosure (Stefan Kiszko, Darvell brothers, Judith Ward) and police malpractice (Guildford 4, Birmingham 6).

In the Commission's terms of reference, effectiveness is also a rational concept linked to the outcome of trials, associated in some way with probability. It is unacceptable to fail to convict too many of the guilty, or to convict too many innocents. 'Too many' is not quantified, but it is accepted that there will inevitably be some mistakes. As a Report in the rationalist tradition, it is perhaps not surprising to find that it is ahistorical. Although the Commissioners must be presumed to be aware of the long history of debate over the appropriate processes for separating the innocent from the guilty, their Report repeatedly reads as if the issue can be solved by a process of balancing, applied now, taking account of new evidence, or the effects of recent reforms. There is no sense of fundamental conflicts over ways of interpreting the criminal justice system. Perhaps this is deliberate. A brief statement of the history of the reform of criminal justice might have forced them to confront the fact that balances and trade offs are not matters of common sense or logic, but politics. In the absence of a consensus as to the appropriate aims and procedures for criminal justice there can be no simple balance. This may be the major reason why criminal justice has spawned so many commissions of enquiry, with such regularity.

The Commission's commitment to the Enlightenment project (the rational pursuit of truth) is well captured in the final paragraph of their introductory chapter:

> It may be argued that however practical our recommendations, and however cogent the reasoning behind them, there is a potential conflict between the interests of justice on the one hand and the requirement of fair and reasonable treatment for everyone involved, suspects and defendants included, on the other. We do not seek to maintain that the two are, or will ever be reconcilable throughout the system in the eyes of all the parties involved in it. But we do believe that the fairer the treatment which all the parties receive at the hands of the system the more likely it is that the jury's verdict, or where appropriate the subsequent decision of the Court of Appeal, will be correct. As will become apparent from our recommendations, there are issues on which a balance has to be struck. But we are satisfied that when taken as a whole our recommendations serve the interests of justice without diminishing the individual's right to fair and reasonable treatment, and that if they are implemented they will do much to restore that public confidence in the system on which its successful operation so much depends. (para 27)

The Commissioners' most important concern is the pursuit of truth in terms of the justice of 'correct' decisions. Fairness is welcomed to the extent that it contributes to the pursuit of truth, but must occasionally be balanced where the two conflict. The pivot for that balance is concern with public confidence. Without this, measures which might at first glance seem to increase the efficiency of criminal justice (eg increased police investigatory powers, the admissibility of all available evidence) can actually reduce efficiency (through a decline in the public's willingness to report crimes, be witnesses at trials, and, as jurors, to convict defendants).

But while the Royal Commission pursues truth at the point of trial court decisions, it fails to explore the 'truth' of public confidence in the system. Although it commissioned twenty-two separate pieces of research, none of them examined the basis of public confidence in, or public disquiet with, criminal justice. The Commissioners proceeded from the somewhat naive assumption that public confidence in criminal justice is based solely upon the statistical likelihood of mistakes. Therefore, measures which increase the accuracy of outcomes would also restore public confidence. The consequences of failing to consider other possible bases for public confidence (whether or not they can be measured empirically) is best illustrated by the fate of their recommendation for the abolition of the right to opt for jury trial (immediately questioned by the Home Secretary[11]). Despite stating in their introductory chapter that the jury is 'widely and firmly believed to be one of the cornerstones of our system of justice' (para 8), they recommended taking away the defendant's right to choose trial by jury. In making that recommendation, they only discussed the reasons why defendants might wish to take advantage of such a right and, believing that most defendants chose jury trial in order to

---

11   However a subsequent Home Secretary was to adopt the proposal: See the Criminal Justice (Mode of Trial) (No 2) Bill 2000 which provided that the mode of trial for offences triable 'either way' should be a matter for the magistrates. The Bill was rejected by the House of Lords and has not yet been reintroduced in the House of Commons.

maximize their chance of an acquittal, felt this was an illegitimate basis for the right. But the appropriate question is not simply why, or who, takes advantage of the right to jury trial (or many other rights) but why the availability of such a right creates public confidence in the legitimacy of the system. By making the crude assumption that legitimacy is mainly a function of accuracy, the Commission was led to make the crass mistake of recommending the abolition of such an important legitimating right...[12]

The problem however with the argument that zealous advocacy is merely the assertion of the procedural rights accorded to the defendant by the system is that those legal rights may conflict with others' moral rights. An advocate may damage the credit of a truthful witness by proving previous convictions or by an aggressive line of cross-examination which makes the witness look confused and unreliable. Doubt therefore arises in the jury's mind sufficient to secure an acquittal. The defendant's procedural rights may be vindicated but does this justify the harm inflicted upon a truthful witness? The position of witnesses is considered further below in relation to victims of sexual offences. At this point however, we focus on another problem with the defendant's rights argument, namely that unjustified harm is done to the victims of crime when the accused is acquitted because of the defence lawyer's skilful use of procedural rights. In the following extract, David Luban, a supporter of zealous advocacy in the criminal context, considers and concedes the force of the argument. In particular, Luban is responding to William Simon's critique (supra) of the arguments for zealous advocacy:

> Simon thinks not only that liberals have exaggerated the danger of the state, but that they have in addition neglected the danger posed by criminals. The liberal concern for protecting the accused typically assumes that little is lost if a guilty criminal escapes his just deserts. My own writing contains a clear example of this:
>
> > No tangible harm is inflicted on anyone when a criminal evades punishment. This is not to deny that people may be legitimately outraged, or that a 'moral harm' is inflicted on the community, or that there is a risk of further crime when the guilty go free. But no one's life is made materially worse off by acquittal as such.
>
> Plainly, the burden of this passage is carried by the wiggle-words *tangible* in the first sentence and *materially* in the third, and plainly the passage discounts the importance of legitimate outrage and moral harm. Simon is absolutely right to interpret this passage as a sign that 'victims [of crime] do not appear in the libertarian picture.' He insists that 'informal, diffuse violence or oppression might threaten liberty,' that 'formal institutions are not the only important threats to liberty, [and] that a wide and unspecifiable variety of social processes that are experienced as diffuse violence can do so as well.' Though Simon rejects many positions of the victims' rights movement, he insists that the movement's 'victim-versus-defendant' picture is 'as plausible' as the liberal's 'state-versus-defendant' picture.
>
> I am now inclined to agree with this criticism of my own earlier argument but it is worth exploring the grounds of agreement. What, exactly, is the victim's interest in a

---

12   R Nobles and D Schiff 'Optimism Writ Large: A Critique of the Runciman Commission on Criminal Justice' chapter 4 of *Criminal Justice In Crisis* (Lee Bridges and Michael McConville eds) (Aldershot, Edward Elgar, 1984) at pp 42-48.

perpetrator's criminal conviction? The answer turns in part on the justification of punishment. The victim has no greater stake in general deterrence than anyone else, and in any case our current practices of criminal punishment bear no demonstrable relationship to general deterrence. Furthermore, in many cases the victim will have no stake in specific deterrence or incapacitation, because it is unlikely that the same criminal will endanger that victim. Obviously, there are many exceptions to this observation – the victim of a stalker may well fear that if he is released he will stalk her again. But such cases are the exception. The victim may desire the emotional release of vengeance, but I see no reason to cater to that desire; civilization consists in large measure of the taming of vengeance.

Of the standard justifications for criminal punishment, that leaves what Simon calls 'vindication/retribution.' Simon's victims' rights argument makes sense, I think, only on a retributive theory of criminal punishment: victims have a legitimate interest – a right, perhaps – to see their victimizers punished.

Retribution may sound like vengeance, but I believe it is not. Vengeance is fundamentally an emotional response, whereas retribution, rightly understood, is at bottom cognitive. I am persuaded of this proposition largely by Jean Hampton's splendid essay, The Retributive Idea. Hampton argues that, when someone wrongs me, their act implicitly asserts that they are the sort of 'high' person who gets to do things like that to others; or that I am the sort of 'low' person that has to accept such indignities from others; or both. The wrongdoer's action has cognitive significance: it states a falsehood about the world of value and asserts an undeserved right of mastery that the wrongdoer possesses over the victim. The purpose of retributive punishment, on this analysis, is to enable the community to reassert the truth about value by inflicting a publicly visible 'expressive defeat' on the wrongdoer. Retribution, like wrongdoing itself, has cognitive significance and differs in this respect from vengeance. Hampton argues in addition that the motivation for deterrence derives at bottom from the same (fundamentally deontological) moral source as retribution: the community endorses the egalitarian truth about human value not only by inflicting ex post expressive defeats upon wrongdoers, but also by offering ex ante protection to potential victims. Importantly, Hampton also argues that precisely the same moral reason for engaging in retributive punishment in the first place constrains our practices of punishment: any punishment that degrades or denies the dignity of human beings undermines the cognitive and expressive purpose of retribution.

I am not as confident as Simon that retribution expresses the victim's standpoint rather than the community's. The victim no doubt has a passionate personal interest in a collective reaffirmation of her worth, but this is plainly an interest first and foremost of the community. When a derelict with no friends or family is murdered, no individual remains with a personal interest in reaffirming the victim's dignity, but that fact in no way diminishes the community's interest in finding and punishing the murderer. Quite the contrary: the fact that such murders are seldom noticed, investigated, or decried represents a moral failure on the part of the community. Retribution, unlike revenge, is the community's way of speaking the moral truth.

I have no idea whether Simon agrees with this version of retributivism. I do, however, and that is why I now regard my earlier pooh-poohing of legitimate outrage and moral harm as unjustifiably glib. Thus, I think it is only fair to acknowledge that the liberal argument for aggressive defense carries a significant moral price tag.[13]

Notes

1. Despite the concessions contained in this extract, Luban still maintains that zealous advocacy can be justified. For him, the American criminal justice system is so stained by pervasive racism and excessive sentencing practices that it can no longer claim legitimacy as a system which affirms individual moral worth by punishing the guilty. This is the 'social workers argument' considered in detail below.

2. In *Doorson v Netherlands*[14], the European Court of Human Rights has said that the right of a defendant to a fair trial under Art 6 (1) of the ECHR and in particular the right to examine witnesses under Art 6(3)d must be balanced against the interests of witnesses in personal security and privacy.

Questions

1. Do you think that victims have rights relevant to the moral evaluation of the conduct of the advocate who secures the acquittal of a guilty client?

2. *Doorsen v Netherlands* recognises the rights of witnesses in the criminal process. What is the significance to this for professional codes of conduct and for the ethics of criminal defence lawyers?

3. Your client is accused of stealing £10.00 from the till in a local shop and the evidence against him is very strong. Theft is an offence 'triable either way' which means that if the accused so chooses the offence must be tried in the Crown Court rather than in the magistrates court. You know that if your client opts for Crown Court trial, the prosecution will probably discontinue the prosecution. Your experience suggests to you that, though the practice is contrary to the Code of Practice for Crown Prosecutors[15], the prosecution is likely in a case such as this to regard the offence as too trivial to justify the expense of Crown Court trial.

i)   Should you tell your client this when advising on whether to plead guilty?

ii) Does it make any difference whether this practice is public knowledge or whether you have learned it in (breach of) confidence from a Crown Prosecutor?

---

13   Luban supra note 10 at 752-755.
14   (1996) 23 EHRR 330 especially at para 70. See further *Van Mechelen v Netherlands* (1998) 25 EHRR.
15   See paragraph 7.3 of the Code which is set out in the appendix to this chapter.

THE SOCIAL WORKER'S ARGUMENT

Very different from the preceding arguments for zealous advocacy is what some have called 'the social worker's argument'. This argument focuses upon the harshness of current penal practices and their disproportionate influence upon the poor and upon racial minorities. It follows on this view that the criminal justice system lacks the legitimacy necessary to ground an obligation to obey the law. This argument for zealous advocacy is very different from the previous two in that, in its extreme form, it implies that zealous advocacy should not even be constrained by professional codes of ethics. A lawyer adopting this position would be neither the disinterested advocate of the client's cause nor a faithful servant of the legal system. S/he would be a 'cause lawyer' that is a lawyer personally committed to a cause of which the client is merely the occasion for action.[16]

Once again the work of the Royal Commission of Criminal Justice provides a context in which the arguments can be considered. As noted, the RCCJ was established as a result of misconduct by the police and related State agencies such as the Crown Prosecution Service and the Forensic Science Service. Particularly alarming for many was the fact that several of these cases occurred after the introduction of the Police and Criminal Evidence Act. This brought into question the police claim that while historically there had undoubtedly been abuses of power, the safeguards introduced by PACE (such as the requirement that interviews with suspects at the police station be taped) had now dealt with the problems.

Given its origins, the Commission was roundly criticised for failing to recommend strong measures to protect the accused. For example, the Commission rejected the suggestion that it should not be possible for a defendant to be convicted solely on the basis of an uncorroborated confession. It therefore accepted that a defendant might be convicted solely on the basis of an officer's assertion that he had confessed even where this was denied by the defendant and where there was no further evidence. Particularly disturbing was the shallowness of the RCCJ's arguments. It was said for instance that an accused might refuse to confirm on tape a confession made on the way to the police station – which would not be surprising unless one was presuming guilt. It was said that any requirement of corroboration or that the confession be made in the presence of a solicitor might be subverted by fabrication or the exertion of pressure prior to the arrival of a solicitor – an argument which seems almost perverse. Most disturbing of all perhaps was the RCCJ's recommendations on plea-bargaining. It recommended formal recognition of the practice in the face of some strong counter arguments (considered further below). Given the context in which the Royal Commission was set up, this was a surprising outcome.

The following extract provides a useful perspective on the work of the RCCJ and on the fundamental questions of criminal justice raised by its' work. It also provides a flavour of 'the social worker's argument'.

16   See generally *Cause Lawyering* (Sarat and Scheinberg eds) (New York, Oxford, 1998) .

Following the Court [of Appeal]'s tardy recognition of miscarriages of justice in the Guildford, Maguire and Birmingham cases, there was a widespread sense of relief that the injustices done in these cases had finally been acknowledged. But the relief was accompanied, for many people (though apparently not for the Courts themselves), by a sense of collective shame about and responsibility for the failings of a system in which we were involved – as practitioners, as academic commentators, as politicians, as citizens. The setting up of the Royal Commission seemed to represent the only appropriately general institutional response to the underlying problems which had led to the miscarriages of justice. In this context, even relatively skeptical commentators (this one included) were perhaps somewhat slow to read the writing on the wall which, with hindsight, the Commission's terms of reference represent. The Commission was asked to, examine the *effectiveness* of the criminal justice system in England and Wales in *securing the conviction of those guilty of criminal offences* and the acquittal of those who are innocent, *having regard to the efficient use of resources ...*' [emphasis added]. The centre of gravity of these terms was, therefore, clearly distanced from that which would have been indicated by the circumstances which led to the Commission's appointment. Whether a more vociferous public debate about the assumptions underlying these terms of reference would have had any effect in encouraging the Commission to take a more critical approach to them is questionable. What is not in doubt is that the terms themselves reflect a clear view of the priorities of the criminal process, and one which is at odds with values which have long been taken, in establishment as much as oppositional ideology, to be at its heart.

On the face of it, the terms of reference construct the acquittal of the innocent, the conviction of the guilty and the efficient use of resources as joint and *equally important* instrumental concerns of the criminal process. In effect, they express a crude version of utilitarianism, with no recognition that special weighting should be given to individual justice, an idea which has long informed liberal critique of utilitarian theories of criminal justice. This implicit 'theory' calls into question the tenet that all are presumed to be innocent until proven guilty beyond reasonable doubt – perhaps the central institutional realization of the critical liberal concern. As we are all aware, this 'golden thread' of criminal justice is all too often broken in practice – in the conduct of interviews in police stations , in the practice of plea-bargaining, in the construction of certain doctrinal features of criminal law, in the style of judicial summing up to the jury and general conduct of trials, to mention just a few examples. Nonetheless, one would have expected a Royal Commission to concern itself with strengthening the institutionalization of this principle rather than the reverse...

THE COMMISSIONS MODE OF ANALYSIS:

...One of the most striking features of the Report is the level of detail at which it operates. Much of its' analysis, and most of its' 352 recommendations, engage with particular practices at specific stages of the criminal process. This focus on specifics was evident right from the start of the Commission's proceedings: for example, it was reflected in the consultation paper circulated to interested groups, which set out and solicited views on dozens of questions about detailed institutional reforms. Whilst its' grasp of detail is certainly impressive, and was inevitably an important part of the Commission's enterprise, questions can be raised about whether its' near-exclusive focus on practicalities debarred it from picking up on the underlying *causes* of the problems it sought to address, as opposed to the *symptoms* represented by the problems themselves.

For example, many of the Commission's initial consultative questions, like many of its' recommendations, focused on questions such as how far video-recording, tape-recording and other procedural reforms relating to the interviewing of suspects inside and outside police stations were feasible and might be expected to reduce the chances of inaccuracy and abuse in the construction of suspects' statements. Whilst these are undoubtedly important questions, there are equally important, broader questions which fall into the cracks between the detailed questions. These questions have to do with why abuses occur in the first place, and they can only be addressed through reflection on issues such as the way in which policing is socially constructed within a society preoccupied by 'law and order' as a major social problem; how adequate and humane policing is defined and rewarded and the institutional culture of the police and police work.

The nearest we get to a recognition of these broader questions in Chapter I is in the recognition that 'police malpractice, where it occurs, may often be motivated by an overzealous determination to secure the conviction of suspects believed to be guilty in the face of rules and procedures which seem to those charged with the investigation to be weighted in favour of the defense' (p 7, para 24). There is no analysis of the context in which this 'over-zealousness' occurs, nor any hint of recognition that it might be related to a system in which 'clear-up rates' have been a prime measure of police efficiency. We do get a glimpse of the Commission's awareness of the relevance of such issues later on, when it expresses its' approval of the fact that Home Office Circular 104/1991 provides for the assessment of police officers 'performance on the basis of their skills, abilities and attitudes rather than chiefly on numbers of arrests, searches and stops in the street' (p 2 1, para 62, see also Recommendation 31). But this insight is not developed in terms of any substantive discussion of what the relevant indicators of good performance should be....

...The predominant focus of the Commission's analysis on the level of practical detail therefore obscures some of the most important general issues which one might have expected it to address. The stance brings with it what might be called a technocratic approach to reform. The mode of analysis is to identify a specific 'problem' – abuses of power in police interviewing, wastage of resources as a result of 'cracked' trials, incompetence on the part of defense and prosecution lawyers – and to suggest a specific, practical solution. The assumption underlying this way of proceeding is a deeply instrumentalist and yet practically dubious one in which all functional problems are presumed to have regulatory solutions. Furthermore, a very significant proportion of the solutions proposed either take the form of *coercive* regulations backed by detailed sanctions or consist in rather general prescriptions for procedural reform which evade central substantive questions which would be likely to be politically controversial.

For example, the proposed solution to lawyers' incompetence and inefficiency is to set out detailed procedural rules backed up by disciplinary sanctions such as loss of fees; the solution to police malpractice is in terms of an extraordinarily comprehensive system of human and electronic surveillance (see Recommendation 50) and adjustments to the disciplinary structure. Failures within a system of coercive regulation are therefore dealt with by means of the elaboration of more and more coercive regulations – a mode of reform familiar to all acquainted with the criminal process and exemplified by the Police and Criminal Evidence Act 1984. It is all too obvious that such over-regulation is likely to be counter-productive. This is because perceptions among relevant practitioners that their activities have become regulated and bureaucratized to an unrealistic degree will breed precisely the kind of instrumentalist rule-avoidance which the Commission itself recognizes is already a feature of the system; because those charged with the sanctioning process may see the regulations as neither feasible nor fair; and because, most of all, the regulations respond to the problems but fail to address their causes. In this last respect, one particularly relevant factor is the extensiveness of the criminal justice system, whose growth over the last ten years has been very marked. This, arguably, is a direct result of an over-ready governmental resort to criminalisation as a quick 'fix' for a variety of perceived social problems. And this resort has been necessitated in part by the effects of the Government's own economic and social policies in damaging the networks and institutional infrastructure which supported more informal, consensual and local means of resolving conflict, and hence in reducing the array of repertoires available for the reproduction of social order.

Arguably, then, the resort to coercive regulation is one of the few tools available in a system which has become impoverished in terms of fora for substantive debate about the values underlying criminal justice practice and in which such values are deeply contested. The same is true of the other main kind of reform proposal – the instantiation of at first sight more proactive solutions such as better and more extensive training. For systems of police, judicial and legal practitioner training to have any hope of improving standards of criminal justice, there will have to be some consensus about what the values which inform the system are. Yet the nearest we get to any such substantive discussion lies in the ethically unsatisfactory consideration of the presumption of innocence and the undeveloped expression of approval for broader performance indicators for the police mentioned above. Beyond this, the Commission provides us with little above the level of platitudes, apart from the Report's thoroughgoing commitment to 'value for money' and the efficient use of resources. The key question of how effective resource management can be made compatible with the operationalisation of the presumption of innocence in a society with an over-extensive, under-resourced, criminal justice system and a commitment to divisive 'law and order' politics is outside the scope of the Commission's analysis.

REFORMING THE CRIMINAL PROCESS IN A 'LAW AND ORDER' SOCIETY

Finally, I want to consider whether it would have been realistic to expect the Royal Commission to produce anything other than a Report characterised by the features I have mentioned...

The Royal Commission was created by a Government which, in its' successive manifestations since 1979, had made its' status as the upholder of 'law and order' a central plank of both its' ideology and its' political programme. By the time the miscarriage of justice cases were acknowledged, this 'law and order' approach had begun to constitute something of a self-created noose around the Government's neck. For, as it poured resources into the police and the prison system and resorted liberally to criminalisation as a response to a wide range of 'social problems', the most apparent result of its' policies was an increase in the level of crime. This presented a major political problem, for once 'law and order' is set up as an index of governmental competence, it is hard to dismantle. The Government had consistently held up the image of the 'law-abiding' citizen as distinct from the 'criminal' – the ultimately undeserving and threatening 'other', excluded from political society by reason of his or her own individual wickedness. In doing so it had shifted political attention away from the social causes of crime and in particular, the relevance of its' own libertarian social policies to the increasing poverty, relative deprivation and urban infrastructural decay which are associated with many forms of crime in most 'developed' countries. But it had also constructed a Frankenstein's monster whose exigencies in terms of political capital and economic resources were huge – a monster which, by this time, was being fed by an Opposition which was keen to demonstrate its' macho credentials in an area in which it was generally regarded as electorally vulnerable.

In this context, the miscarriage of justice cases presented the Government with a very tricky problem. As a result of its' own policies, the (in itself proper) social concern with the threat of and harms done by crime to its' actual and potential victims had become extraordinarily intense. So much so, in fact, that almost any substantial political concern with injustice to actual or suspected offenders at a *systematic* level (rather than in the context of particular sensational cases) was in danger of being seen as the Government 'going soft' on crime and undermining its' own 'law and order' credentials. Its' solution, expressed clearly in the Royal Commission's terms of reference, was to reconstruct those cases as instances of a more general problem of the *efficient management* of the criminal process, and in particular of the process's failure in securing the conviction of the guilty. At a stroke, a spectacular instance of individual injustice and the abuse of power was converted into an instance of systemic inefficiency and wastage of resources......

Given the political and institutional context in which it operated, it was therefore always highly unlikely that the Royal Commission would engage in the kind of thoroughgoing critical analysis which many citizens and many commentators on and practitioners within the criminal justice system would have welcomed. For the really basic questions – questions about the social and economic conditions which foster crime; about the patterns of social division which mark out the social groups against whom criminal justice is enforced and, equally importantly, those against whom it is *not* enforced; about the long-term implications of a socially divisive 'law and order' politics, supported, in effect, by both major political parties, about the proper functions of the criminal justice system in a society such as ours; about the nature and role of policing and police culture; about the values underlying the presumption of innocence – are simply not on the political agenda in this country.[17]

Equally disturbing to many was the political reaction to the report, particularly in relation to the right to silence. The RCCJ in fact recommended that the law should not be altered so as to allow the prosecution to suggest that the jury draw adverse inferences from an accused's refusal to answer questions in the police station. Whilst the police contended in evidence that in a small number of cases professional criminals were able

17   Nicola Lacey 'Missing the Wood ... Pragmatism versus Theory ...' chapter 3 of *Criminal Justice in Crisis*.

to use their right to silence to fabricate defences, the RCCJ argued that abolition of the right to silence would have little impact. Professional criminals would probably have access to good legal advice. Consequently, they might refuse to answer questions in a way which would make it difficult for juries to make adverse inferences. Unsophisticated vulnerable suspects by contrast might seriously prejudice their position. Nevertheless, the government of the day were quick to abolish the right to silence[18]. As feared by commentators like Professor Lacey, the election of the Blair administration in 1997 failed to bring about a fundamental change in policy: one of the most controversial recommendations of the RCCJ was to remove the defendant's right to opt for trial in the case of certain 'non-serious' offences because, it was alleged, certain defendants were exercising it simply in order to improve their chances of acquittal. This proposal was not taken up at the time but was latter adopted by Jack Straw as Minister for the Home Office, though his Mode of Trial Bill was defeated in Parliament.

Amongst American liberals writing about legal ethics, the 'social workers' argument' is widely accepted. Though the American criminal justice system presents a context very different from our own, it is worth noting that commentators like David Luban and William Simon can agree upon the illegitimacy of the American criminal justice system but draw very different conclusions for the ethics of criminal defence. For Luban, the social workers argument justifies zealous advocacy in all cases. Simon's position is very different as is illustrated by the following extract:

> ...even if one concedes the view of contemporary criminal prosecution on which this argument is premised, it is inadequate as a justification for the current practice of aggressive defence. The problem is that the argument is under inclusive as long as one concedes that there is any substantial class of defendants for whom punishment would be just and otherwise appropriate. Aggressive defence is a practice of categorical or wholesale nullification; it does not focus on subverting only the prosecutorial and police practices that could plausibly be opposed as excessive and unjust.
>
> Thus, for the 'social worker's' or nullification argument to work, the practice of aggressive defence would have to be reformulated toward one of ad hoc or retail nullification. Aggressive defence should be limited to cases that present a threat of excessive or arbitrary punishment and only employed to the extent it is likely to counter that threat. The practice of aggressive defence ought to be part of a larger strategy designed to focus resources and effort on cases that present the greatest threats of injustice.[19]

Simon contends that the argument fails to justify aggressive defence in any case in which the defendant lawyer knows that the client committed a crime and deserves to be punished. In such cases, what does it matter if the criminal process is weighted against the accused if, in truth, justice demands punishment? Aggressive defence would be better focused on cases in which there is evidence of police malpractice or prosecutorial abuse, partly because it is damaging to lawyers' professional morale to be continually operating under an ethic which requires them to ignore the merits of

18　Section 34 of the Criminal Justice and Public Order Act 1994.
19　Supra p 194 note 18 at 1723 and 1725.

their clients' cases.[1] In addition, a blanket denial of concern by criminal defence lawyers with the substantive results of the criminal process is only likely to lead to a backlash from the law and order lobby. Those concerned with police and prosecutorial abuse are far more likely to gain public support if they focus their efforts on cases exhibiting those features. To this extent, the issue may be a political one.

Questions

1. What view if any does Professor Lacey advance as to the causes of crime? What difference does it make with respect to the 'social worker's argument' if you believe that certain crimes such as murder are clearly moral wrongs?

2. Do you think the 'social worker's argument' is a valid one in relation to the UK criminal justice system?

3. If the 'social worker's argument' is valid, do you find Simon or Luban more persuasive as to its implications?

3   Extending the criminal defence paradigm: problems and possibilities

At the heart of the argument for zealous advocacy is a concern to protect the individual against the power of the state. It can be argued however that the argument can and should be extended so as to provide individuals with protection against other forms of institutional power[2] such as that possessed by large corporations. One possible example might be the work of personal injury lawyers. There the battle is not between the individual and the powerful state but between an individual and a powerful insurance company. Nevertheless, it may be that the disparity in power will normally be such that zealous advocacy is justified. The lawyer is merely seeking to level a playing field otherwise strongly favouring the corporate defendant. Indeed, *Hard Bargaining*[3], Hazel Genn's empirical study of the UK personal injury process revealed that the problem facing most plaintiffs was precisely that their lawyers were insufficiently adversarial; those rare plaintiffs whose lawyers were prepared to push aggressively on towards trial were more likely to receive adequate settlements. Aggressive behaviour by lawyers representing the state in its attempt to regulate the behaviour of corporate

1   See Randy Bellows 'Notes of a Public Defender' in the *Social Responsibilities of Lawyers* 69 (Philip B Heymann and Lance Liebman eds 1988).

2   See generally David Luban *Lawyers and Justice: An Ethical study* (Princeton UP, New Jersey, 1988) chapter 4, at 58-67.

3   Hazel Genn, *Hard Bargaining: Out of Court Settlements in Personal Injury Cases* (Oxford, Clarendon, 1987) eg at 166-167. For a different view of the implications of *Hard Bargaining* see Dingwall et al 'Firm handling: the litigation strategies of defence lawyers in personal injury cases' (2000) 20 Legal Studies 1.

entities on behalf of otherwise vulnerable individuals might be seen as a further instance of the paradigm.

How far can this model be extended? A good context in which to answer that question is the cross-examining of rape victims about their prior sexual history. At common law, such evidence was considered relevant to the complainant's credibility – promiscuous women were considered untrustworthy – and in some circumstances, such as where the complainant was a prostitute, it was considered evidence from which a jury might infer consent. Victims however find the process to be intrusive and harrowing. When the issue was considered by the Heilbron Committee,[4] it concluded that evidence of previous sexual relations other than with the accused was irrelevant to credit. It was relevant to consent only in circumstances where the intercourse complained of took place in circumstances strikingly similar to proven incidences of sexual relations with other men. However, the legislation which followed was much less radical than that proposed by the Heilbron Committee. In effect, s 2 of the Sexual Offences (Amendment Act) 1976 simply left the issue to the discretion of the trial judge.[5] Unfortunately, there seems little doubt that this discretion was exercised in such a way that sexual history evidence tended to be admitted provided only that it had more than minimal relevance to the issue of consent. In the case of *R v SMS*[6] for example, the alleged rape took place in particularly sordid circumstance and the victim was a 14-year-old girl. The Court of Appeal held that the trial judge ought to have admitted evidence that she was not a virgin, since the jury might otherwise have inferred that she was a virgin and been inclined to infer that as such she was most unlikely to consent to sex in such circumstances. Cases like this were subject to strident criticism[7] and with good reason. Whether or not sexual history evidence can be said to be of any relevance – on which commentators disagree – a good argument can still be made for its exclusion in almost all cases. If the evidence is likely to influence the jury, then it will do so only by appealing to unjustified assumptions about women's propensity to make false accusations of rape. If the jury is sensible enough to dismiss the evidence as of little relevance, it ought not to be admitted because of the distress it is likely to cause to the claimant. Sustained criticism led to the passing of the Youth Justice and Criminal Evidence Act 1999.[8] This act severely restricts the circumstances in which judges may admit sexual history evidence in

4   *Report of the Advisory Group on the Law of Rape* Cmnd 6352 (1975).
5   Section 2 provided that,
    (1) If at a trial any person is for the time being charged with a rape offence to which he pleads not guilty then, except with the leave of the judge, no evidence and no question in cross-examination shall be adduced or asked at the trial, by or on behalf of any defendant at the trial, about any sexual experience of a complainant with a person other than the defendant.
    (2) The judge shall not give such leave in pursuance of the preceding subsection for any evidence or question except on an application made to him ....; and on such application the judge shall give leave if and only if he is satisfied that it would be unfair to that defendant to refuse to allow the evidence to be adduced or the question to be asked.
6   [1992] Crim LR 310.
7   See eg Jennifer Temkin, 'Sexual History Evidence-the Rape of Section 2' [1993] Crim LR 3.
8   See generally N Kibble 'The Sexual History Provisions: Charting a course between legislative rules and wholly untrammelled judicial discretion' [2000] Criminal Law Review 274.

relation to the issue of consent.[9] However, the act contains a loophole in that it may still be admitted if the defence alleges that it relates to the defendant's genuine but mistaken belief in the complainant's consent. If that is the defendant's case the judge can allow the evidence if 'a refusal of leave might have the result of rendering unsafe a conclusion of the jury.'[10]

It follows that unless future judges show greater sensitivity to the dangers of sexual history evidence than their predecessors, a defence lawyer may well be able to have admitted evidence which is of little relevance but which may lead to an unjustified acquittal. Even if the jury is unmoved, considerable distress will be caused to the complainant. The question is whether such tactics can be justified. In the following extract, David Luban argues that they cannot:

> The starting point of my analysis is the proposition that one-sided adversary advocacy in criminal defence is justified in order to protect individuals against a powerful institution, the state. ... however, there is nothing unique about the state: the real value underlying the advocate's role is the protection of individuals against institutions that pose chronic threats to their well-being. The state is the most conspicuous of these, but in point of fact no institution has ever posed a more chronic and pervasive threat to the well-being of individual women than that of patriarchy, the network of cultural expectations and practices that engenders and encourages male sexual violence.
>
> To appeal to the value underlying the advocate's role – the protection of individuals against institutions that pose chronic threats to their being – but to restrict that appeal to protection against the state is simply incoherent. Thus, the moral limits to the advocate's role in rape cases must be designed to maximise the protection of jeopardised individuals against *both* of these threatening institutions. Placing the brutal cross-examination of the truthful victim off limits serves precisely that function.
>
> One vital function of a vigilant defence bar is to deter the prosecution and police (the state) from abusing their power. But all observers agree that the prospect of a humiliating cross-examination also deters women from reporting rapes, particularly date-rapes, acquaintance rapes and marital rapes 'real rapes,' to use Susan Estrich's term, that form the vast majority of sexual attacks. The traditional advocate's role thereby serves to entrench 'notions of male power and entitlement and female contributory fault.' This is a powerful reason for tailoring the role so that the all-out assault on the victim at cross-examination is off limits....
>
> Matters would be different if rape was rare and false accusations of rape occurred regularly. Then the advocate's role would properly focus on the vulnerability of men, not of women. Suffice to say that the world is not this way. Estrich speculates that the law of rape has been shaped by '[t]he male rape fantasy ... a nightmare' in which the man is accused of rape after having sex with a woman who said no but did not resist. Certainly this improbable 'nightmare' lends urgency to the traditional advocate's role in rape cases; but unlike the male rape fantasy, the nightmare of the woman who has been

9   Broadly speaking, it may be admitted where the nature of the alleged behaviour either i) bears striking similarity to the complainant's behaviour during the incident complained of (s 41(3)(c)); or ii) occurred at or about the same time as the incident complained of.

10   Section 41(2)(b). The evidence must relate to specific instances of behaviour (s 41(6)) and must not be lead for the main purpose of impugning the witness' credibility (s 41(4)).

raped on a date and does not report it because she is afraid of what will happen to her reputation during the trial is real. In my view, then, the advocate's role should stop well short of an all-out assault on the prosecutrix[11].

Luban's views were the subject of much criticism, notably because the criminal paradigm seems to require the lawyer to be unconcerned if as a result a particular case succeeds contrary to the merits. As applied to the protection of women from patriarchy, it seems to imply that the defence lawyer need not be concerned if failure to cross-examine vigorously leads some defendants to be wrongly convicted. In the following extract, he defends a modified version of his thesis.

Consider two cases (in which) the client does not confess to the lawyer that he has raped the prosecutrix; on the contrary, he insists that she consented, and the lawyer is convinced that he is sincere. But what does 'consented' mean? Everything turns on the facts, so let me give two variants of the story.

3.[12] *Passive 'Consent'.* – When the lawyer asks the defendant what actually happened, he reports that they met for the first time on the night of the incident at a bar and had some drinks. She wore a sexy tank top and a short skirt. She flirted with him, brushing his hand with hers and trading dirty jokes with him. He drove her home, but she did not invite him in. He invited himself in. At first she said no, but he insisted and eventually she said all right, he could come in for a little while. The moment they were inside he began fondling and undressing her. She did not help or respond, but she also did not stop him, and never said a word. After his orgasm she said quietly 'Are you going to let me alone now?'- and he left. The next thing he knew, he was arrested. Her version of the story was substantially the same, except that she claimed that from the moment he insisted on entering her apartment she was scared witless: he was big and looked mean, he used a menacing tone of voice, and he began pulling her clothes off very roughly the moment the door was shut. She did not say anything because she thought that if she protested he would hurt her.

4. *Active Assent.* – The situation is the same as in variant 3, except that she invited him in on her own initiative, kissed him back with great passion, and said 'Let's make love.' They had sex and he left. Later the police came for him; he still does not know why she called them, and wonders if perhaps she is crazy.

In both variants of the story, the lawyer must decide whether to cross-examine her brutally . . . – that is, with the complete destruction of her credibility as the advocate's sole goal, and with her public humiliation as an unavoidable side-effect and perhaps even an instrumentally useful way of rattling her. The weakened version of the 'no brutal cross-examination even if she consented' thesis that I shall defend is that the lawyer clearly *should* go after the prosecutrix in case 4, but not in case 3. My reason is simple: *case 3* .... is really a rape. Case 4 was not..... the lawyer [in case 3] can ask the victim if she consented, and can then argue reasonable doubt. But that is all: the advocate cannot try to convince the jury that as a factual matter the prosecutrix's behaviour was

11   David Luban 'Partisanship Betrayal and Autonomy in the Lawyer-Client Relationship: A Reply to Stephen', (1990) 90 Columbia Law Review 1004 at 1026-1035.

12   In an earlier part of the article, Luban had considered two hypotheticals dealing directly with sexual history evidence.

tantamount to consent. It was not. You can drink and flirt and tell dirty jokes without agreeing to have sex. You can dress any way you wish without agreeing to have sex. You can accept a ride with a man and have him into your home without agreeing to have sex. And you can decide not to resist a sexual attack by a man who scares you without agreeing to have sex. These obvious truths are surprisingly easy to forget.

I think it is nevertheless plain that a great many people would hesitate to label case 3 a rape. But I have no hesitation on this score, for we have two overwhelming reasons for being confident that the victim had not assented to sex. First, she called the police afterward. Second, on her attacker's own admission she could not have assented to sex, since in fact she said nothing at all until the rape was over. Her silence logically implies lack of verbal assent, since it follows that she said nothing to indicate her willingness. Nor did she express willingness non-verbally by participating or responding.

One might object that the bare fact that she accused him of rape does not mean that he raped her: we do not simply take an accuser's word about such things. But in the present case, both parties are in substantial agreement about what happened; they have in effect stipulated to the facts. If she is simply lying, as in case 4, or if the advocate does not know whether she is lying or not, she may of course be cross-examined harshly to bring out the inconsistencies and implausibilities in her story. But here the disagreement is only about whether 'in her head' she assented to sex, and the fact that she called the police makes it overwhelmingly likely that she did not, the 'male rape fantasy' of false accusation to the contrary.

Perhaps, however, the disagreement was not over the contents of her head. Perhaps the defendant was entitled to presume the victim's consent from her previous behaviour and her lack of protest. That would almost certainly be the judgment of most courts, which have generally inferred consent in cases where the man behaved even more menacingly and the victim put up more resistance. The same point might be raised in response to the observation that her silence logically entails lack of consent: according to this response, the defendant was entitled to presume consent from her lack of protest.

Inferring consent from lack of protest collapses the distinction between *wanting sex* and merely putting *up with* sex. Many of us grew up thinking this way, but it not only misses the crucial distinction, it also amounts to a profoundly sexist way of viewing matters. Collapsing this distinction devalues a woman's subjective experience completely, since her wants are now insignificant; at the same time, entitling men to take sex from any woman who puts up with it kow-tows to the urgency of men's subjective wants. Men's desires are awarded high value, women's are awarded none. From a moral point of view, this is unacceptable, and it suggests that the question never should have been 'Did she consent to sex?' The question should have been 'Did she want it?' To preserve some parallelism in language, we may say that *assent*, not *consent*, is the real issue.

To construe the victim's behaviour in case 3 as assenting to sex is tantamount to adopting the viewpoint of a 19 year-old male out on a steamy Saturday night. At bottom he is completely uninterested whether the woman he meets *wants* to have sex with him; he is interested only in whether she *will* have sex with him. 'You're nice' means yes; silence means yes; perhaps even 'no' means yes. Her sexy clothes, her flirting earlier in the evening, her dirty jokes, her accepting a ride home, her reluctant acquiescence when he insists on coming in, all mean yes. Like a hawk-eyed auctioneer, he spots the slightest signal that might mean yes. Nothing short of a major show of protest on her part means no. He's got to have it.

And why doesn't she protest? She says she was scared, so shouldn't we believe her? It may be objected that a man's liberty should not be jeopardised simply because a woman was afraid, unless her fear was reasonable. But this objection is wrong in every, possible way. First, it is *always* reasonable to fear a man who is bigger and stronger than you, who has been drinking, who is insistent, who uses a menacing tone of voice, and who wants your body. Second, fear that is unreasonable for a man may be reasonable for a woman. As Estrich puts the point, the male 'version of a reasonable person is one who does not scare easily, one who does not feel vulnerable, one who fights back, not cries'. The reasonable woman, it seems, is not a schoolboy 'sissy'; she is a real man.

Third, and most important: *the man's liberty is not jeopardised because she is afraid, reasonably or otherwise. His liberty is jeopardised because he had sex with her without making sure that she wanted it.* He took a guess: if he had been right that she wanted sex, she would not have called the police. But his guess was wrong. Perhaps his lawyer could make it seem that the victim wanted sex with him; but she did not, and the lawyer should not.[13]

Notes

1. After a series of highly publicised rape trials in which defendants have represented themselves in person and subjected the complainant to a long and excruciating process of cross-examination (including, in one case, wearing exactly the same clothes worn on the occasion of the attack), s 34 of the Youth Justice and Criminal Evidence Act prohibits defendants in rape trials from cross-examining the victim in person. Section 38(4) allows the court to appoint a lawyer to represent the accused if he does not appoint one himself. Section 38(5) provides that 'A person so appointed shall not be responsible to the accused'.

2. It is *not* a breach of the lawyer's duty to his client to refuse to cross-examine witnesses in the manner which the client wishes. Hence in *Anderson* v *HM Advocate*[14], the Court of Session refused to overturn a conviction on the ground that the advocate had refused to impugn the character of witnesses for the prosecution in accordance with the client's instructions. In a wide-ranging survey of common law authorities the court held that the client could not give binding instructions to the advocate which overrode the lawyer's duty as an officer of the court.

3. Recent English legal history includes a number of examples of complainants in rape trials being successfully prosecuted for perjury on the basis that their complaint was a fabrication.[15] Luban seems therefore to be misleading when he speaks of a 'male rape fantasy'.

13   Supra p 218 note 11 at pp 1033–1035.
14   [1996] Scottish Law Times 155.
15   See I H Dennis *Rethinking Evidence* (London, Longmans, 1999) at p 470 n 46.

Questions

1. Craig's Case: You represent Craig who is accused of raping a fellow college student after a summer ball. The defendant, a 16-stone rugby player, admits he never asked her if she wanted to make love and that the intercourse was quite rough. He says he believed she was consenting because he had been told by two former boyfriends that she had slept with them on their first date and that she 'liked it rough'. The prosecution case at one time included convincing evidence that the defendant had committed two previous date rapes but you have been told that the relevant witnesses are now unwilling to testify. Most judges would in your experience refuse to admit the boyfriends' evidence but you also know that the judge listed to hear the case has a reputation for taking a generous view of the circumstances in which a defendant will be permitted to cross-examine a complainant as to her previous sexual history.

Are you ethically justified in applying to admit the evidence of the former boyfriends? Does it make any difference if the prosecutor tells you privately that if 'you're going to put her through that' the complainant will withdraw her complaint?

2. Do you agree with David Luban's revised position? For a critique of the assumptions on which it rests see Helen Reece 'When a woman says "No" she means "No" ' [1997] New Law Journal 1616.

3. What difference if any would it make to your answer in question 1 if you had been appointed to represent the accused under s 38(4) of the Youth Justice and Criminal Evidence Act?

4. What difference does it make to the ethical obligations of those defending alleged rapists that the 'male rape fantasy' is (*sometimes*) real?

4   Criminal defence and coloured collars

We have seen that the defendant in criminal proceedings is rarely defended with zeal. There are however exceptions, the most important being white collar defendants. This category includes all those charged with offences such as tax fraud or insider trading and which have some or all of the following characteristics: that the client has some degree of control over the evidence needed by the prosecution; that the evidence is widely dispersed amongst a number of potential witnesses; that the evidence is difficult to find and that the suspect has the resources and the sophistication to consult able lawyers at an early stage in the investigation. Kenneth Mann's study of the practices of the New York white collar defence bar, *Defending White Collar Crime*[16], shows that these lawyers are indeed zealous in the defence of their clients, an approach which

16   (New Haven, Yale University Press, 1985).

they justify by reference to the need to protect the individual against the state. The lawyers surveyed by Mann concentrated their efforts not on the trial process but on the investigatory phase prior to the laying of an indictment. Their aim was to prevent the government gaining sufficient information even to lay an indictment. Some of the tactics employed may serve only to illustrate what can be achieved by relying on the principle that the prosecution can be put to proof of its case. Other common tactics seem more dubious:

(1) *Avoiding knowledge of facts which would make it difficult to assert the client's ignorance:* the lawyers surveyed by Mann employed a variety of techniques to avoid being informed of incriminating information, such as exerting strict control over the dialogue as in the following exchange:

Client:	I want to tell you what my parents and I decided to do after we understood an investigation was to take place.
Lawyer:	Mr Sweet, before we begin, I want to set out the ground rules, because we want to be very efficient about how we use our time – we need to keep your expenses down. I'm going to ask you the questions, and when I think we are wasting time, I'll move you onto another subject.[17]

(2) *Explaining the law:* white collar suspects are frequently faced with official requests to disclose documents which may be crucial to the prosecution case. A common response observed by Mann was to explain to clients the significance and evidential weight of the documents sought and then to ask the client to search for them. Thereafter clients were asked not 'did you find any documents' but 'do you have any documents to declare in response to this subpoena?'.

(3) *Exploiting client control over witnesses:* in the name of information control, clients were encouraged to exploit any influence they might have over potential witnesses, particularly in the corporate context. In one case, the lawyer learned that the target of a bribery investigation was in a salary dispute with some employees who had overheard 'ambiguous' conversations. The lawyer's advice was forceful:

Let me put it to you as bluntly as I can. You need all these men on your side. Now is not the time to be concerned about cost efficiency and work productivity. If I were you, I would see to it that the salary issue is resolved and that you are on very good terms with all these people.[18]

(4) *Stonewalling:* The successful prosecution of white collar crime depends on access to information and one of the best sources of information is a participant who might be prepared to provide information in order to mitigate any possible criminal sanction. At the New York defence bar, one common tactic was to ensure that all the suspects were represented by the same lawyer. In this way, the defence could be conducted on the

17   Ibid at p 108.
18   Ibid at p 159.

basis of perfect knowledge about what information had been provided to the prosecution by the other participants each of whom could therefore say nothing in the knowledge that they were not thereby prejudicing their position.

Note

Doreen McBarnett's empirical study of the work of UK tax lawyers has shown that they too engage in preventive lawyering designed so as to ensure that the prosecuting authorities never have enough evidence to prosecute their clients for non payment of tax: See 'Whiter than White Collar Crime: Tax Fraud Insurance and the management of Stigma' (1991) 42 British Journal of Sociology 323 and 'Its not what you do, but the way that you do it' in David Downes (ed) *Unravelling Criminal Justice.*[19]

Questions

1. Paragraph 17.01 of the LSGPC provides that 'Solicitors must not act, whether in their professional capacity or otherwise, towards anyone in a way which is fraudulent, deceitful or otherwise contrary to their position as solicitors'. Is this principle breached by either of the first two of these four tactics? The first of them has been described by one commentator as 'innocent ignorance':

> The defence lawyer's avoidance of knowledge that incriminates his client provides an escape from the contradiction between the cognitive and normative reality of personal knowledge, and the cognitive and normative tableaux that the law uses for adjudication. Whatever moral sins the criminal lawyer may commit in living this contradiction, they are committed for the sake of due process and therefore for the sake of all of us. [20]

2. It is a well-accepted principle that lawyers should not attempt to interfere with the evidence to be given by a witness.[1] Is this principle breached by the third of these tactics?

3. What is the impact upon the final tactic of paragraph 15.01 of the LSGPC which provides that 'A solicitor or firm of solicitors should not accept instructions to act for two or more clients where there is a conflict or a significant risk of a conflict between the interests of clients.' Note 2 provides that a solicitor should not act in such a situation even where the client consents to the conflict. Can note 2 be justified as a way of preventing stonewalling?

4. What is the impact of this and other evidence of zealous white colour defence work on the debate between Luban and Simon about the validity of zealous advocacy by criminal defence lawyers?

19   London, Macmillan, 1992.
20   G Hazard Jnr 'Quis Custodiet ipsos custodies?' (1985) 95 Yale Law Journal 1523, 1530.
1   Supra text to pp 196-197 notes 2-7.

5   The case for the prosecution: prosecutorial ethics

In this section, we consider the question of prosecutorial ethics. Our discussion of the ethics of criminal defence lawyers would otherwise be incomplete. Moreover, the subject is important in itself, for the prosecutor has long been celebrated as the paradigm case of the 'lawyer as Minister of Justice', free and indeed required to put the interests of justice before victory. We must examine then whether the prosecutor's task is as free from moral ambiguity as the 'minister of justice' rhetoric would suggest. We consider three different facets of the prosecutor's work namely, the decision to prosecute, negotiated justice and contested trials.

The decision to prosecute

Our focus will be upon the work of the Crown Prosecution Service (the 'CPS'), which was set up following the report of the 1981 Royal Commission on Criminal Procedure. Previously, the decision whether to prosecute suspected offenders had been made by the police. Concern had arisen that police involvement in the process of investigating an offence might prevent its' officers giving sufficiently dispassionate consideration to the question of whether a prosecution should be brought.

The work of the CPS must be placed in context. To begin with, it should be noted that the police and the CPS are far from being the only investigatory/prosecutorial agency of the state. Their work is often described as being 'street crime', because they are usually concerned with high visibility crimes committed in public places, often by people of little or no public standing. Other crimes, particularly white collar crimes, are usually dealt with by other agencies such as the Serious Fraud Office. Some of the evidence indicates that the police are far more ready than these agencies to prosecute for past misconduct rather than achieve negotiated compliance for the future, even though the offences concerned are no less severe. This suggests that the prosecutorial system as a whole is discriminating unfairly against offenders with lower social status.[2]

A further contextual issue is that the work of the CPS is intimately related to that of the police in that its' primary function is to review decisions taken by the police that an alleged offender should be prosecuted. It is therefore vital to note that it is charged with the reviewing the work of a body which is almost universally recognised as being dominated by a very strong occupational culture ('Cop Culture'). One officer when asked by researchers about the impact of the Police and Criminal Evidence Act said 'I would say that we manipulate it in a way that it doesn't effect [the job] so much. It's about the same. You've got restraints but you've got the good bits, bad bits; its about

2   A Ashworth *The Criminal Process: An Evaluative Study* (2nd ed, Oxford, Clarendon, 1998) p 167.

the same I would say . But most police officers adapt it in such a way that it stays the same as it was for us.'[3]

In such a world, the police are a thin blue line against a tidal wave of crime and are being constantly hindered in their work by the introduction of rules designed to protect the suspect. Such rules must therefore be 'bent' if at all possible. Thus even the generally conservative Royal Commission on Criminal Justice accepted that as a response to the requirement that all interviews with suspects be taped, some police officers were ensuring that inculpatory conversations with suspects occurred on the way to the police station. The significance of this is that regardless of the ethical orientation of prosecutors, they may have very limited ability to review a police decision to prosecute because their review can only be conducted on the basis of evidence supplied in the police file. McConville et al found that this file can be and often is 'constructed' in such a way as to predetermine the consequences of the CPS review. One case was observed in which following an altercation between two school boys, the father of one of them became involved and allegedly assaulted the other, a ten-year-old boy. The officer dealing with the case decided that prosecution was appropriate and described the case as an 'Unprovoked attack by a 37-year-old man on a ten-year-old boy'. What was not mentioned was that inquiries had revealed that the victim was a known trouble maker with a reputation for picking on other boys at school. This was clearly relevant to the decision to prosecute and its omission is consistent with other research which found one Scottish prosecutor saying:

> the police can withhold information. They usually don't do it deliberately but they can do because they decide that the [prosecutor] doesn't want to know that or doesn't need to know that. [4]

Indeed, it is precisely because of the occupational pressures upon the CPS that many have argued unsuccessfully for the CPS rights of audience in the Crown Court to remain severely restricted. Heather Hallet QC the Chair of the Bar Council argued that:

> Whatever the pressures upon self-employed practitioners hungry for their next brief, there can be no comparison with the pressure which can be exerted upon lawyers by their employers or by the circumstances of their employment.[5]

It is against this background that we move to a consideration of the Code For Crown Prosecutors[6] (together with the Explanatory Memorandum[7] issued by way of further

---

3   M McConville, A Sanders and R Leng *The Case for the Prosecution* (London, Routledge, 1971) p 189.

4   S Moody and J Tombs *Prosecution in the Public Interest* (Edinburgh: Scottish Academic Press, 1982) pp 47-48.

5   Heather Hallet QC speech to the Annual Conference of the Bar, reported in *The Lawyer* (13 October 1998) at p 7.

6   Section 10 of the Prosecution of Offences Act 1985 requires the Director of Public Prosecutions to issue a code for Crown Prosecutors giving guidance on the general principles to be applied in prosecutorial decision making. The fourth edition of the Code was issued in October 2000.

7   Crown Prosecution Service, *An Explanatory Memorandum for use in Connection with the Code for Crown Prosecutors* (June 1994). At the time of publication, no explanatory memorandum had been issued for the 4th edition of the Code.

guidance) which sets out the CPS approach to its work. In deciding whether to proceed with charges laid by the police, the CPS considers two main questions, namely the evidential standard and the question of the public interest.

The evidential standard

The concern here is that the CPS should weed out weak cases prior to their coming to trial on the basis that even if the accused is acquitted substantial injustice may have been done. Even if the accused has not been remanded in custody prior to trial, the process of being tried for a criminal offence is nevertheless a stressful and damaging one. In the words of a well-known book on the subject, 'the Process is the Punishment'.[8]

There are questions however about just what standard is required by the Code. The momentum for the establishing of the CPS arose from concern that in practice cases were proceeding wherever there was a prima facie case ie wherever the evidence was such that a conviction would withstand an appeal based on the argument that there was insufficient evidence to lead a reasonable court to convict. This was felt to be too undemanding a standard. At first sight paragraphs 5.1 and 5.2 do indeed seem more demanding. There must be a 'reasonable prospect of conviction' meaning that a properly instructed court would be 'more likely than not to convict'. Since juries and magistrates must be satisfied beyond reasonable doubt this seems a demanding standard. However the waters were muddied by the Explanatory Memorandum which states that:

> Crown Prosecutors should not be looking for the same high standard of proof that a jury or bench of magistrates needs to find before it can convict. That is too high a standard for the Crown Prosecution Service to require and it would tend to usurp the role of the court. A test based on 'more likely than not' means just that. It requires Crown Prosecutors weigh the adequacy of the evidence in order to decide whether a conviction is more likely than an acquittal. *Only where it is clear that there is no realistic prospect of a conviction should Crown Prosecutors decide not to prosecute*[9]. [Emphasis added.]

The Explanatory Memorandum was new to the third edition of the Code and some critics saw its amplification of the evidential test as being in reality a relaxation and as part of a series of changes designed to encourage more prosecutions. Moreover the wording of paragraph 5.2 of the fourth edition of the Code seems to confirm that this was indeed what was intended. The new paragraph 5.2 specifically emphasises that the CPS applies a separate and less demanding test than that applied by the criminal courts.[10]

---

8   M Feeley *The Process is the Punishment* (New York, Russell Sage, 1979).

9   Explanatory Memorandum, supra note 7 at para 4.2. See A Sherr 'The Ethics of Prosecution' unpublished paper on file with the author at p 11.

10 The words 'This is a separate test from the one that the criminal courts themselves must apply. A jury or magistrates court should only convict if satisfied so that it is sure of the defendants guilt.' were not contained in the third edition.

The precise meaning of the code may not be crucial. In one study commissioned by the CPS itself, most prosecutors said they seldom used the Code because it was too basic[11]. Most relied on the CPS' own internal manuals rather than the Code which they regarded as a 'Noddy's Guide'. Moreover the empirical evidence suggests that in practice some CPS prosecutors apply a relatively undemanding evidential test. The most important evidence consists of the very high rate of judge ordered (where the prosecution offers no evidence) or judge directed (where the judge rules that the prosecution has failed to make out a case to be answered) acquittals in Crown Court trials. In 1998, 32% of Crown Court trials ended in this way.[12] By itself such statistics can be misleading since acquittals may be the result of an unexpected failure by a witness to give convincing evidence in accordance with a pre-trial statement. Nevertheless qualitative review by researchers suggests there is genuine cause for concern; analysis of 100 CPS files relating to cases in which acquittals were either ordered or directed revealed that in 75% of the ordered acquittals the result was foreseeable.[13] Interviews with Crown Prosecutors produced some forthright admissions of a relaxed approach to the evidential standard.

> Sometimes it is very difficult to decide which side is telling the truth, but I think that sort of case should go to a jury . I don't think that I should be the one to decide that we are not going ahead with it unless there is a very good reason for not going ahead with it.
>
> I have to say – and being absolutely frank – that the more serious the case and the more finely balanced it is, the more you stretch the point. It's got to be the case. I think it is a natural part of reviewing that you apply the realistic prospect of conviction test more rigorously in relation to minor matters. One always tries to stand back and make sure you are not being emotive about it, but there has to be a point where, if it is so finely balanced that you can't really make that decision, you have got to run it. I think there is a tendency in serious cases to let them run... I think that child abuse cases and domestic violence cases are two where you proceed if you possibly can. Often in that sort of case, we do stretch the realistic prospect of conviction test because so often it could be more serious next time. Certainly my tendency is to stretch the guidelines which may well lead to acquittals. By 'stretch', I mean you may bring your standard on what you consider to be a realistic prospect of conviction down in more serious cases.[14]

Related to questions about the sufficiency of the evidence is the question of its admissibility. Indeed such questions are logically prior since courts may only convict

---

11 Hoyano et al 'A study of the Impact of the Revised Code of Crown Prosecutors' [1997] Crim LR 556 at 558.

12 Criminal Statistics for England and Wales 1998 (HMSO) at para 6.25. The Glidewell Report (supra p 202 note 9) also expressed concern about this phenomenon but was unable to come to any firm conclusion as to its causes (see para 16 of its' Summary of Conclusions and Recommendation).

13 B Block, C Corbett and J Peay 'Ordered and Directed Acquittals In The Crown Court' (London, HMSO, 1993) p 100; John Baldwin 'Understanding Judge Ordered and Directed Acquittals' [1997] Criminal Law Review 537.

14 Baldwin supra at p 551.

on the basis of the evidence admitted. In relation to evidence whose admissibility is in doubt, paragraph 5.3 of the Code provides that prosecutors should ask whether

> it [is] likely that the evidence will be excluded by the court? There are certain legal rules which might mean that evidence which seems relevant cannot be given at a trial. For example, is it likely that the evidence will be excluded because of the way in which it was gathered or because of the rule against using hearsay as evidence? (paragraph 5.3)...Crown Prosecutors should not ignore evidence because they are not sure that it can be used or is reliable. But they should look closely at it when deciding if there is a realistic prospect of conviction. (paragraph 5.4)

The Explanatory Memorandum suggested that where judicial precedents make an item of evidence clearly inadmissible it should be ignored but that if in doubt the case could be continued and the disputed evidence left for the decision of the Court. Some commentators feel that this does not go far enough. Andrew Ashworth has commented in relation to the prosecutor's role as a minister of justice that:

> If the CPS discover that evidence has been obtained in breach of the PACE Codes or other rules, should they 'let the court decide' on admissibility or discontinue the case themselves? The answer to the question can be fudged in part by stating that there will be some cases where no breach is apparent on the file, and others where the breach or its significance leave room for doubt which is properly settled in court. But even the most casual reading of appellate decisions in the last seven years shows that many prosecutions have been brought in cases of manifest departure from central provisions of the Codes of Practice. This suggests that there is no ethical insistence on respect for fair procedures. A first step, therefore, would be to introduce an ethical statement that is not only general in its import but also accompanied by specific examples of the kinds of situation that might demand a principled approach. The second step is to convince Crown Prosecutors that the ethical statement is well founded and ought to be followed, and to dispel the rival notions of 'crime control' and 'prosecuting with one hand tied behind one's back.'[15]

Whether or not this is so, there seem to be clear examples in the case law where clearly inadmissible evidence has been relied upon in deciding to prosecute.[16]

Note

1. The Code of Practice for Crown Prosecutors to which reference should be made when responding to the problem questions posed in the rest of this chapter is set out in the appendix.

2. Paragraph 4.10 of the Explanatory Memorandum requires the CPS when applying the evidential standard to proceed in accordance with the intrinsic merits. That means the prosecutors should consider whether there is a realistic prospect of conviction by

---

15 *The Criminal Process: An evaluative study* supra note 2 first edition at p 191. The second edition contains the same argument in slightly different terms at p 205.
16 See *Miller* [1994] Crim LR 231 and *Wood* [1994] Crim LR 222.

a properly instructed court faithfully applying the law. What is known in fact about the peculiarities of the court/jury should be ignored.

Questions

1. Consider whether it would/should be a breach of the Code to bring a prosecution in the following cases:

i)   **Zachary's Case**: the defendant Zachary is a new age traveller, charged with assaulting a gamekeeper on a local landowner's estate. The landowner was at the relevant time attempting to clear a campsite full of new age travellers. The case turns on identification evidence (there were a lot of people there at the time) and you regard that evidence as thin. However you know the local magistrates have recently taken a dim view of the activities of new age travellers.

ii) **Horace's Case**: Horace, a police officer, is accused of assault occasioning actual bodily harm during the arrest of a suspect. The prosecutor regards the evidence as strong but knows that local juries are extremely reluctant to believe the word of suspect against that of a police officer.

2. What is the test for evidential sufficiency laid down by the Code and the Memorandum?

3. What principles should the evidential test seek to uphold?

4. Would it be preferable if the evidential test were to be that

> No prosecution shall proceed unless the prosecutor believes beyond reasonable doubt that the accused is guilty.

Is it relevant when considering this alternative that the Court of Appeal has power to quash a conviction if it has a 'lurking doubt' as to its validity? [17]

5. Why, if at all, are the approaches of the Crown Prosecutors interviewed by Baldwin unethical?

6. Do you agree with Andrew Ashworth that a prosecutor who seeks to be a minister of justice should not rely on evidence which may be admissible but which in the prosecutors view has been obtained in breach of the provisions of PACE. Under the Code, the prosecutor may proceed it if it remains arguable that the evidence should be admitted. Is it relevant to consider here the thought that anything is arguable if well-trained lawyers are paid well enough to make them think long enough about the question? If Ashworth is right, what might be achieved by inserting a provision in the Code to give effect to his views?

17   *R v Cooper* [1969] 1 QB 267.

The public interest

The notion that prosecution may not be in the public interest even if a crime has been committed is one of the distinctive features of the English criminal justice system, compared for example with that prevailing in most continental European countries. In Germany, for example, the principle[18] is that all offences are to be prosecuted. The English position reflects a belief that formal prosecution is not necessarily the appropriate response to criminal conduct and that formal warnings, cautions or even moral sanction may be a more appropriate response. Sanders et al's research[19] suggests that the CPS were reluctant in the early days to discontinue prosecutions on public interest grounds in order not to disrupt relationships with the police. However, research conducted for the RCCJ suggested that there had been some improvement in the position.[20] On the other hand, it was argued by critics that the third edition of the Code represented a move in the opposite direction[1]. Paragraph 21 of the second edition stated that juveniles should not be prosecuted unless 'exceptional circumstances dictate otherwise' whereas the equivalent provision of the third edition (paragraph 6.8) was much more prosecution orientated; references to the merits of cautioning instead of prosecuting were toned down. The fourth edition of the Code seems further to reinforce the trend towards prosecution. The relevant paragraph[2] omits a sentence[3] emphasising how damaging prosecution may be for a youth and there is a new paragraph[4] emphasising that the police will not normally refer a case to the CPS unless non-prosecutorial options have been tried and failed.

That the third edition of the Code was issued in June 1994, less than five months after the then Home Secretary Michael Howard issued to the police non-statutory guidelines restricting the use of cautions, raises the question of the legitimacy of changes which appear to have been prompted by governmental concerns about law and order. A final point of concern is that the Code is an incomplete guide to how the CPS address the prosecutorial function in general and the public interest in particular. Much of the guidance on which prosecutors rely is contained within CPS manuals which are not open to the public. Thus for example policy on which offences are not as a general rule to be prosecuted is contained within the manuals. This would seem to make democratic accountability impossible.

---

18 On the significance of the exceptions allowed in practice, see H Jung 'Criminal Justice in European Perspective' [1993] Crim LR 237.

19 Supra note 3.

20 See generally D Crisp and D Moxon *Case Screening by the Crown Prosecution Service: how and why cases are terminated* (London, HMSO, 1994).

1 See generally A Sherr 'The Ethics of Prosecution' supra note 9 and A Ashworth and Julia Fonda 'The New Code for Crown Prosecutors: (1) Prosecution, Accountability and the Public Interest' [1994] Crim LR 895.

2 Paragraph 6.9 which was found in paragraph 6.8 of the third edition.

3 Paragraph 6.8 of the third edition had a second sentence (omitted from the 4th edition) which read, 'The stigma of a conviction can cause very serious harm to the prospects of a youth offender or a young adult.'

4 Paragraph 6.10.

Questions

1. In each of the following two cases, you are a senior Crown Prosecutor and have been asked by your superior to set out the considerations relevant to the decision whether or not to proceed with prosecution. What advice would you give?

i)   **Graham's Case**: Graham, a former solicitor and currently a Crown Court judge, is charged with sexually assaulting a 10-year-old boy at his home. The evidence against Graham is strong, but you have now received a letter from the defence asking that the prosecution be dropped on the ground that the judge is suffering from clinical depression and that further proceedings would endanger his life. The letter contains a report in these terms from an eminent private specialist. News of this development has been leaked to the media where there is outrage that a member of the establishment might be 'let off' in this way.

ii)   **Quentin's Case**: Quentin is a doctor charged with murder. Quentin had been treating Tracy, a 25-year-old paraplegic who had suffered her injuries in a diving accident. Quentin is alleged to have given Tracy a lethal injection in response to repeated requests from Tracy and her family for assistance in ending her life. There is little dispute as to the facts and there is evidence (from an independent psychiatrist) that Tracy wanted to die and was not suffering from any form of mental illness. You think that the evidence is strong and that a rational jury should convict. However, there is considerable public sympathy for Quentin.

2. **Jim and Kevin's' Case**: You are reviewing the case of Jim and Kevin, two new age travellers who have been charged with being drunk and disorderly. The circumstances of the offence which are not in dispute are that Jim and Kevin were found to be singing loudly and tunelessly as they staggered down the high street of a small market town towards their camp site on the edge of town. You know the town well and such behaviour is a fairly common occurrence. In your considerable experience such behaviour has never previously led to prosecution. The file contains a police note to the effect that arrest was considered necessary to appease growing local resentment towards the travellers.

Should you proceed with the prosecution?

3. **Sarah's Case**: You are reviewing the case of Sarah, a woman of 36 who is charged with criminal damage to a small window at a probation office. She explained to the PC who interviewed her that she had broken the window in frustration when the staff at the office had refused to help her find accommodation. She further explained that she needs accommodation because she had left her previous flat after her landlord had tried to rape her. She gave fairly full details of this incident.[5]

What should you do?

5   Adapted from a case observed by Sanders et al supra p 225 note 3 at p 143.

4. Suppose the CPS were to decide that as a general principle they would not bring proceedings in respect of a particular offence, for example shoplifting where the value of the items stolen was less than £10.00. Is there anything unethical about keeping this decision secret?

5. Do you agree with criticism levelled at the CPS based on the assumption that the third edition of the Code reflected an increased concern to prosecute based on the government's concerns about law and order?

Negotiated justice

Once the prosecutor has decided to proceed, it is far from inevitable that the case will end in a contested trial. Such trials are in fact rare. 90 % of defendants in the magistrates courts and 65% in the Crown Court plead guilty[6]. Consequently, the prosecutorial function is more likely to be that of managing the production and processing of guilty pleas than that of an advocate. Central to this role are what are popularly called plea bargains but which are better distinguished as charge bargains, plea bargains proper and fact bargains.

The first of these occurs when the alleged facts are capable of supporting more than one charge. The accused might for example be alleged to have participated with others in the beating of the victim which left him with severe bruising following a scuffle outside a nightclub. On this basis, the prosecutor may find the accused charged with causing grievous bodily harm.[7] However, there may be doubts about the ability of the prosecution witnesses to identify the accused as a participant in the beating as opposed to the preceding scuffle. Consequently, the prosecutor adds a charge of assault knowing that, if the more serious charge fails, the accused is likely to be convicted of the lesser offence. The accused ultimately offers to plead guilty to the assault if the more serious charge is dropped and the offer is accepted. This is not surprising: the case will now proceed in the magistrates court and be dealt with more quickly under more limited sentencing powers. Proceeding with a lesser offence will usually offer advantages of this kind to both prosecution and defence. Deliberate overcharging is contrary to the Code of Practice for Crown Prosecutors[8] but empirical research suggests that bargains of this kind are made with great regularity in magistrates and Crown Courts up and down the country.[9]

Charge bargains rely on defendants pleading guilty to a lesser charge because it offers the prospect of a lower sentence. A true plea bargain occurs when even in the face of a single charge the accused pleads guilty at least partly because s/he knows that in the UK courts, a guilty plea will lead to a sentence between a third and one quarter lower than that which would have been passed following a contested trial. In

6   Ashworth *The Criminal Process* supra p 224 note 2 at p 269.
7   Section 20 of the Offences Against the Person Act 1861.
8   Paragraph 7.2.
9   See the research summarised in Ashworth supra p 224 note 2 at p 272 and p 196 notes 1-5.

most US states, plea bargaining is a much more explicit process. Counsel may meet with the judge in chambers and review the evidence. The judge will then indicate what sentence reduction he is willing to accept in return for a guilty plea. The judge's views are then conveyed to the accused. In the UK, American style plea bargaining is officially prohibited. In the case of *R v Turner*[10], the Court of Appeal held that it would be quite improper for a judge to give an indication of the likely sentence upon a guilty plea. Nevertheless, it *was* recognised in *Turner* that it was perfectly proper for a judge to give a discount on sentence of between one third and one quarter of the sentence which would have been passed after a contested conviction. In addition, counsel were permitted to advise their clients 'in strong terms' of the wisdom of pleading guilty. Consequently, it could be said that this constituted only a formal prohibition.

This was recognised by the RCCJ. Far from strengthening the prohibition, it was concerned to ensure that the court's time should be used efficiently. In particular, it wanted to reduce the high incidence of 'cracked trials' ie trials of defendants who had indicated an intention to plead not guilty but which were aborted by a late change of plea. In response, the RCCJ proposed a graduated sentencing discount whereby the reduction of sentence was proportionately reduced the later the entry of the guilty plea. More significantly for our purposes, it proposed that plea bargains should be formally permitted: *Turner* was to be overturned and the judge was to be permitted in the presence of both counsel to give an indication of the maximum sentence which would be handed down on a guilty plea at that point in the proceedings.

The RCCJ's proposals have not been fully taken up. Section 48 of the Crime and Disorder Act 1994 requires both the magistrates court and the Crown Court to take account of a guilty plea and the stage in the process when it was made when passing sentence. The court must state whether any discount was given. As yet, however, the proposal that the judge should indicate in advance the maximum sentence on a guilty plea has not been accepted. Even so the giving of sentence discounts for guilty pleas remains extremely problematic. Depending on the state of the evidence, it makes sense for innocent defendants to plead guilty. Moreover, in a study of Crown Court cases conducted by Zander and Henderson, 11% of guilty pleaders did claim innocence[11]. This is a disturbing statistic. While it is impossible to test the reliability of these claims, it is striking that when the question was asked, the defendants had no obvious motive for lying. Moreover, the significance of the statistic is magnified when we remember how many criminal trials end in guilty pleas. Clearly, plea bargains have the potential to produce false convictions. From the prosecutor's point of view, though, it should be noted whilst the sentencing discount may be a useful tool to be used in negotiations with defence counsel, it may equally operate quite effectively without the need for any active steps on the part of the prosecution. This follows from defence counsel's professional responsibility as set out in *Turner* to advise the defendant of the advantages of pleading guilty.

---

10   [1970] 2 QB 231.
11   M Zander and P Henderson RCCJ Research Study 19 (1993) 138-142.

Whether or not prosecutors actively exploit the leverage which the sentencing discount gives them, it arguably infringes the Human Rights Act 1998. Article 6(2) of the ECHR guarantees a presumption of innocence and from this it would seem to follow that the defendant has a right to put the prosecution to proof of its case. Yet the sentence discount imposes a penalty on defendants who do so[12]. Similarly if confessions are to be excluded when given under circumstances sufficient to render them unreliable, it might be argued that the same should apply to confessions taking the form of a guilty plea entered in the face of a sentencing discount. Finally, it should be noted that the discount seems discriminatory in that there is evidence that defendants of Afro-Caribbean and Asian backgrounds are more likely to plead not guilty and therefore to be penalised if found guilty than white defendants.[13] The sentence discount seems therefore to discriminate against such defendants on grounds of race contrary to the right of non discrimination conferred by Art 14 of the ECHR.

Fact bargains raise somewhat different considerations. These occur when, in exchange for a guilty plea, the prosecution agrees that it will not object if defence counsel in making a plea in mitigation presents the offence in a way which makes it appear less serious, leading to a reduced sentence. Suppose the defendant is charged with a serious assault and is prepared to plead guilty but only on the understanding that the victim provoked him by making racially abusive comments. The victim's story however is that the attack was completely unprovoked. There are obvious advantages to both defence and prosecution in the making of such a bargain, but the victim may feel outraged.

Questions

1. Reconsider Craig's Case[14] in which you are now the prosecutor. You estimate that there is a 60-70% chance of conviction, the main problem from the prosecution's point of view being that the defence has indicated that it intends to argue that the accused honestly believed that the complainant was consenting because of her reputation for 'liking it rough'. Like the defence lawyer you think that the defence is likely to succeed with an application to introduce evidence of the victim's sexual history and you think that this may prejudice the jury in favour of the defendant. Your research indicates that the sentence on a guilty plea is likely to be about nine years. The defendant has throughout protested his innocence. However, you are about to meet the defendant's lawyer outside the court . The case is due to begin in an hour.

What if anything should you say to the defence lawyer about the possibility of pleading guilty? Does it make any difference if the defence lawyer is clearly a very inexperienced barrister who has received the brief at the last moment?

12   See Ashworth supra p 224 note 2 at 289.
13   See Hood *Race and Sentencing* (Oxford, OUP, 1992) p 125.
14   Supra p 221.

2. Suppose that the defence lawyer acting in Craig's Case says that her client is prepared to plead guilty but only on the basis that it is put to the court in mitigation that the complainant initially agreed to intercourse but changed her mind at the very last minute. The complainant's story is that she never agreed but after an initial struggle was too frightened to resist. Should you agree to this?

3. Should prosecutors feel any sense of moral responsibility about the possibility of innocent defendants pleading guilty in order to attract a lower sentence? A conscientious prosecutor may wish to rely on Professor Fried's distinction between institutional and personal moral wrongs. Moral harm of the former kind (such as the distress caused by cross-examination) may be seen a consequence of the workings of a generally just system and the lawyers involved in that system are not personally morally accountable. Moral harm of the latter kind for which the lawyer is accountable occurs when the lawyer causes harm by stepping outside that system.[15] Consider whether the need to maximise the use of court time justifies the practice of giving discounts for guilty pleas. Is it relevant here that there is no sentence discount in Scotland nor Philadelphia, the fourth largest city in the US, where, however, far more cases are heard without a jury?[16]

The prosecutor at trial

The role of the prosecutor before and during the trial can usefully be separated for the purpose of exposition but the distinction should not be overemphasised. In particular the shape of the trial is or should be substantially affected by the prosecution's duty to disclose to the defence witnesses and other evidence which might assist the defence. The differing disclosure obligations of defence and prosecution are one of the features of the criminal process which correspond most closely with the idea that the prosecutor is a minister of justice and the defence lawyer a zealous advocate. At common law, the defence has no general duty to disclose information (be it the identity of crucial witnesses or the existence of incriminating documents). By contrast, English law has for many years required broad-ranging disclosure from the prosecution. However, a number of notorious miscarriages of justice in the 1980s involved non-disclosure by the prosecution of evidence vital to the defence. Consequently the Court of Appeal gave judicial force to and strengthened disclosure obligations previously contained within guidance issued by the Attorney-General. In the case of *Keane,* material was said to be disclosable if it could

> be seen on a sensible appraisal by the prosecution: (1) to be relevant or possibly relevant to an issue in the case; (2) to raise or possibly raise a new issue whose existence is not apparent from the evidence the prosecution proposes to use; (3) to

15   C Fried 'The Lawyer as Friend: The Moral Foundations of the Lawyer-Client Relation' 85 Yale Law Journal (1976) pp 1080-1085.
16   See Alschuler 'Implementing the Criminal Defendant's Right to Trial' (1983) 50 U Chi LR 931.

hold out a real (as opposed to a fanciful) prospect of providing a real lead on evidence which goes to (1) or (2).[17]

However two related concerns have led to changes which have reduced the contrast. The first was that the disclosure provisions had simply gone too far requiring the prosecution to spend time and money disclosing vast amounts of useless material. The second was that since the defence was not required to disclose even those areas in which it took issue with the prosecution case there arose the possibility for 'ambush' defences, ie defences disclosed for the first time at the trial thus making it impossible for the prosecution adequately to test the defence case. These concerns were articulated by the RCCJ and led to the passing of the Criminal Procedure and Investigations Act 1996.[18] The main feature of the new scheme is that the prosecution must

disclose to the accused any prosecution material which might undermine the case for the prosecution.[19]

Once this 'primary disclosure' has taken place, the defence comes under a duty to make a statement setting out

in general terms the nature of the accused's defence...indicating the matters on which it takes issue with the prosecution, and setting out, in the case of such matters the reason, why he takes issue with the prosecution.[20]

Failure to do this or to do so adequately is subject to sanctions[1] laid down in s 11(3) including adverse comment by the judge and, with his permission, by the prosecution. The further sanction is that the prosecution is required to make further disclosure ('secondary disclosure') only of material

which might be reasonably expected to assist the accused's defence as disclosed by the prosecution statement.[2]

A number of commentators have expressed concern about these provisions[3]. The defence may not realise that a particular defence is arguable until it has seen all the material in the hands of the prosecution. Yet on one reading of the provisions it is only when a defence has been advanced that the prosecution comes under a duty to disclose evidence which supports it. More generally, it can be said that unless trial judges take a very restrictive approach to the making of adverse comments the operation of these provisions may infringe the privilege against self-incrimination affirmed by the ECHR in *Saunders v UK*[4]. For example, an defendant accused of assault will have to admit that he struck the blow in his s 5(6) statement should he wish to plead self-

17   *R v Keane* [1994] 1 WLR 746 per Lord Taylor LCJ at 752C.
18   See, generally, Jack Sprack 'The Criminal Proceedings and Investigations Act 1996: (1) The Duty of Disclosure' [1997] Crim LR 308.
19   Section 3(1)(a).
20   Section 5(6).
1   Section 11(3).
2   Section 7(2)(a).
3   M Zander at pp 221-223 ('Note of Dissent') of the Report of the Runciman Commission. (supra p 204).
4   (1997) 23 EHRR 313.

defence. If the prosecution witnesses have difficulty identifying him as the assailant, the s 5(6) statement will, unless comment is prohibited, restrict his ability to change the course of his defence.

Whilst the gap between the disclosure obligations of defence and prosecution may have narrowed, it remains considerable. It therefore supports the argument that while the defence lawyer is a zealous advocate, the prosecutor is a minister of justice. A number of general rules relating to the trial process support this notion. For example, the prosecutor is expected to call any witnesses able to give reliable evidence whether it favours the prosecution or the defence even if the defence knows of the witness and is thus able to call the witness itself. The rule ensures that the defence rather than the prosecution will have the tactical advantage of being able to cross-examine. More generally, the prosecutor is expected to put the prosecution's case before the court with a view to seeking not victory but justice, ie the correct application of the law to the facts by the fact finder in accordance with the applicable rules of procedure. The LSGPC puts it this way:

> Whilst a solicitor prosecuting a criminal case must ensure that every point is made which supports the prosecution, the evidence must be presented dispassionately and with scrupulous fairness.[5]

Some have called this the 'cricket approach': like cricketers, prosecutors must refrain form doing certain things which are technically within the rules.

It should not be thought however that this approach is unchallengeable. It could be argued for example that a distinction should be made between the pre-trial and trial phases of prosecution. Whilst the cricket approach should prevail pre-trial (particularly in relation to disclosure), the prosecutor should behave at trial as a zealous advocate. If the defence *is* represented by a zealous advocate, failure to reciprocate means the legitimate interest of the state in conviction will be under-represented. Furthermore, it can be argued that the prosecutor must be immersed and committed to the prosecution case in order to present the case adequately let alone zealously. Finally, sympathy for victims provides a psychological impulse in the same direction. The point has been well put by an American Prosecutor[6]:

> When we decide to prosecute, it is because we decide that this is how justice will be done. The decision is reached only after we have satisfied ourselves of the defendant's actual guilt. When our belief in the defendant's guilt is fortified by the Grand Jury's decision that he be held for trial, we become fledgling advocates and our judicial function is relinquished to the judges who will sit on the various stages of the case. Then as the trial progresses and we see justice fighting a losing battle as the evidence is whittled away, we become more and more aggressive in our protection of the case that we believe to be right. Finally at trial when false issues are injected, unfair attacks are made on the witnesses, or perjured testimony is given by a defendant trying to lie his way out

5 Principle 21.19.
6 W Seymour 'Why Prosecutors Act Like Prosecutors' 11 Rec AB City NY 302 at 312-313 cited by K Crispin in 'Prosecutorial Ethics', chapter 5 (at p 187) of *Legal Ethics and Legal Practice – Contemporary Issues* (Charles Sampford and Stephen Parker (eds)), (Oxford, OUP 1995).

of a just conviction, the prosecutor becomes the most zealous champion of justice you can imagine. He is then a fully fledged advocate; and he should be. He must act with candour and fairness, but he must also fight for his cause. To do otherwise would be to violate his duty in the most real sense. His job is now to fight fairly and firmly with all his might to see that truth and justice prevail.

Questions

1. Reconsider *Shorty's* case (problem 3 at p 195 above). Suppose that as prosecutor you realise that the defence is likely to call Peter and also realise the likely effect of his refusing to give evidence. If you offer Peter immunity from prosecution he is likely to give evidence implicating Harry and ensuring his conviction. Is it ethical to do this without telling the defence of your intentions?

2. Comment critically upon the approach to prosecutorial trial advocacy suggested by Seymour.

Conclusion

Presenting a critique of particular prosecutorial decisions is not difficult. Evaluating the performance of prosecuting agencies more generally is fraught with difficulties. It is not clear for example what is the appropriate performance monitor. At the heart of the difficulty is the fact that the CPS is but one agent in a complicated process and its performance depends on that of the other elements in the process. Thus if the CPS appears to be discontinuing large numbers of cases the problem may lay in the police failure to supply complete information at the time when the decision to prosecute was made. Particularly problematic were the terms of reference of the Glidewell review of the work of the CPS which included consideration of 'whether the CPS has contributed to the falling number of convictions for reported crime.'[7] If individual prosecutors are evaluated internally by reference to the number of successful persecutions, the effect may be disastrous from an ethical point of view (can you see why?). Qualitative review of the kind carried out by Baldwin and Block et al[8] seems more promising but is expensive. Consequently, it is difficult to see how it could be applied broadly to individual prosecutors. Thus while the role of 'minister of justice' may appear attractive, it is not without its problems.

---

7   Glidewell Report supra note 29 at Conclusions para 14. The Report was unable to come to a conclusion on the question.
8   Supra text to p 218 notes 11-12.

APPENDIX

THE CODE OF PRACTICE FOR CROWN PROSECUTORS[9]

1. Introduction

1.1 The decision to prosecute an individual is a serious step. Fair and effective prosecution is essential to the maintenance of law and order. Even in a small case a prosecution has serious implications for all involved – victims, witnesses and defendants. The Crown Prosecution Service applies the Code for Crown Prosecutors so that it can make fair and consistent decision about prosecutions.

1.2 The code helps the Crown Prosecution Service to play its part in making sure that justice is done. It contains information that is important to police officers and others who work in the criminal justice system and to the general public. Police officers should take account of the Code when they are deciding whether to charge a person with an offence.

1.3 The Code is also designed to make sure that everyone knows the principles that the Crown Prosecution Service applies when carrying out its work. By applying the same principles, everyone involved in the system is helping to treat victims fairly and to prosecute fairly but effectively.

2. General principles

2.1 Each case is unique and must be considered on its own facts and merits. However, there are general principles that apply to the way in which Crown Prosecutors must approach every case.

2.2 Crown Prosecutors must be fair, independent and objective. They must not let any personal views about ethnic or national origin, sex, religious beliefs, political views or the sexual orientation of the suspect, victim or witness influence their decisions. They must not be affected by improper or undue pressure from any source.

2.3 It is the duty of Crown Prosecutors to make sure that the right person is prosecuted for the right offence. In doing so, Crown Prosecutors must always act in the interests of justice and not solely for the purpose of obtaining a conviction.

2.4 It is the duty of Crown Prosecutors to review, advise on and prosecute cases, ensuring that the law is properly applied, that all relevant evidence is put before the court and that obligations of disclosure are complied with, in accordance with the principles set out in this Code.

2.5 The CPS is a public authority for the purposes of the Human Rights Act 1998. Crown Prosecutors must apply the principles of the European Convention on Human Rights in accordance with the Act.

3. Review

3.1 Proceedings are usually started by the police. Sometimes they may consult the Crown Prosecution Service before starting a prosecution. Each case that the Crown Prosecution Service receives from the police is reviewed to make sure it meets the evidential and public interest tests set out in this Code. Crown

9   The Code For Crown Prosecutors (4th ed) (London, CPS, 2000).

Prosecutors may decide to continue with the original charges, to change the charges, or sometimes to stop the case.

3.2   Review is a continuing process and Crown Prosecutors must take account of any change in circumstances. Wherever possible, they talk to the police first if they are thinking about changing the charges or stopping the case. This gives the police the chance to provide more information that may affect the decision. The Crown Prosecution Service and the police work closely together to reach the right decision, but the final responsibility for the decision rests with the Crown Prosecution Service.

4.   The code tests

4.1   There are two stages in the decision to prosecute. The first stage is the evidential test. If the case does not pass the evidential test, it must not go ahead, no matter how important or serious it may be. If the case does meet the evidential test, Crown Prosecutors must decide if a prosecution is needed in the public interest.

4.2   This second stage is the public interest test. The Crown Prosecution Service will only start or continue with a prosecution when the case has passed both tests. The evidential test is explained in section 5 and the public interest test is explained in section 6.

5.   The evidential test

5.1   Crown Prosecutors must be satisfied that there is enough evidence to provide a 'realistic prospect of conviction' against each defendant on each charge. They must consider what the defence case may be, and how that is likely to affect the prosecution case.

5.2   A realistic prospect of conviction is an objective test. It means that a jury or bench of magistrates, properly directed in accordance with the law, is more likely than not to convict the defendant of the charge alleged. This is a separate test from the one that the criminal courts themselves must apply. A jury or magistrates' court should only convict if satisfied so that it is sure of a defendant's guilt.

5.3   When deciding whether there is enough evidence to prosecute, Crown Prosecutors must consider whether the evidence can be used and is reliable. There will be many cases in which the evidence does not give any cause for concern. But there will also be cases in which the evidence may not be as strong as it first appears. Crown Prosecutors must ask themselves the following questions:

Can the evidence be used in court?

a   Is it likely that the evidence will be excluded by the court? There are certain legal rules which might mean that evidence which seems relevant cannot be given at a trial. For example, is it likely that the evidence will be excluded because of the way in which it was gathered or because of the rule against using hearsay as evidence? If so, is there enough other evidence for a realistic prospect of conviction?

Is the evidence reliable?

b   Is there evidence which might support or detract from the reliability of a confession? Is the reliability affected by factors such as the defendant's age, intelligence or level of understanding?

c   What explanation has the defendant given? Is a court likely to find it credible in the light of the evidence as a whole? Does it support an innocent explanation?

d   If the identity of the defendant is likely to be questioned, is the evidence about this strong enough?

e   Is the witness's background likely to weaken the prosecution case? For example, does the witness have any motive that may affect his or her attitude to the case, or a relevant previous conviction?

f   Are there concerns over the accuracy or credibility of a witness? Are these concerns based on evidence or simply information with nothing to support it? Is there further evidence which the police should be asked to seek out which may support or detract from the account of the witness?

5.4   Crown Prosecutors should not ignore evidence because they are not sure that it can be used or is reliable. But they should look closely at it when deciding if there is a realistic prospect of conviction.

6.   The public interest test

6.1   In 1951, Lord Shawcross, who was Attorney General, made the classic statement on public interest, which has been supported by Attorneys General ever since: 'It has never been the rule in this country – I hope it never will be – that suspected criminal offences must automatically be the subject of prosecution'. (House of Commons Debates, volume 483, column 681, 29 January 1951.)

6.2   The public interest must be considered in each case where there is enough evidence to provide a realistic prospect of conviction. A prosecution will usually take place unless there are public interest factors tending against prosecution which clearly outweigh those tending in favour. Although there may be public interest factors against prosecution in a particular case, often the prosecution should go ahead and those factors should be put to the court for consideration when sentence is being passed.

6.3   Crown Prosecutors must balance factors for and against prosecution carefully and fairly. Public interest factors that can affect the decision to prosecute usually depend on the seriousness of the offence or the circumstances of the suspect. Some factors may increase the need to prosecute but others may suggest that another course of action would be better.

The following lists of some common public interest factors, both for and against prosecution, are not exhaustive. The factors that apply will depend on the facts in each case.

Some common public interest factors in favour of prosecution.

6.4   The more serious the offence, the more likely it is that a prosecution will be needed in the public interest. A prosecution is likely to be needed if:

a   a conviction is likely to result in a significant sentence;

b   a weapon was used or violence was threatened during the commission of the offence;

c   the offence was committed against a person serving the public (for example, a police or prison officer, or a nurse);

d   the defendant was in a position of authority or trust;

e   the evidence shows that the defendant was a ringleader or an organiser of the offence;

f   there is evidence that the offence was premeditated;

g   there is evidence that the offence was carried out by a group;

h   the victim of the offence was vulnerable, has been put in considerable fear, or suffered personal attack, damage or disturbance;

i   the offence was motivated by any form of discrimination against the victim's ethnic or national origin, sex, religious beliefs, political views or sexual orientation, or the suspect demonstrated hostility towards the victim based on any of those characteristics;

j   there is a marked difference between the actual or mental ages of the defendant and the victim, or if there is any element of corruption;

k   the defendant's previous convictions or cautions are relevant to the present offence;

l   the defendant is alleged to have committed the offence whilst under an order of the court;

m   there are grounds for believing that the offence is likely to be continued or repeated, for example, by a history of recurring conduct; or

n   the offence, although not serious in itself, is widespread in the area where it was committed.

Some common public interest factors against prosecution

6.5 A prosecution is less likely to be needed if:

a   the court is likely to impose a nominal penalty;

b   the defendant has already been made the subject of a sentence and any further conviction would be unlikely to result in the imposition of an additional sentence or order, unless the nature of the particular offence requires a prosecution;

c   the offence was committed as a result of a genuine mistake or misunderstanding (these factors must be balanced against the seriousness of the offence);

d   the loss or harm can be described as minor and was the result of a single incident, particularly if it was caused by a misjudgement;

e   there has been a long delay between the offence taking place and the date of the trial, unless;

    •   the offence is serious;
    •   the delay has been caused in part by the defendant;
    •   the offence has only recently come to light; or
    •   the complexity of the offence has meant that there has been a long investigation;

f   a prosecution is likely to have a bad effect on the victim's physical or mental health, always bearing in mind the seriousness of the offence;

g   the defendant is elderly or is, or was at the time of the offence, suffering from significant mental or physical ill health, unless the offence is serious or there is a real possibility that it may be repeated. The Crown Prosecution Service, where necessary, applies Home Office guidelines about how to deal with mentally disordered offenders. Crown Prosecutors must balance the desirability of diverting a defendant who is suffering from significant mental or physical ill health with the need to safeguard the general public;

h   the defendant has put right the loss or harm that was caused (but defendants must not avoid prosecution solely because they pay compensation); or

i   details may be made public that could harm sources of information, international relations or national security.

6.6   Deciding on the public interest is not simply a matter of adding up the number of factors on each side. Crown Prosecutors must decide how important each factor is in the circumstances of each case and go on to make an overall assessment.

The relationship between the victim and the public interest.

6.7   The Crown Prosecution Service prosecutes cases on behalf of the public at large and not just in the interests of any particular individual. However, when considering the public interest test Crown Prosecutors should always take into account the consequences for the victim of the decision whether or not to prosecute, and any views expressed by the victim or the victim's family.

6.8   It is important that a victim is told about a decision which makes a significant difference to the case in which he or she is involved. Crown Prosecutors should ensure that they follow any agreed procedures.

Youths

6.9   Crown Prosecutors must consider the interests of a youth when deciding whether it is in the public interest to prosecute. However Crown Prosecutors should not avoid prosecuting simply because of the defendant's age. The seriousness of the offence or the youth's past behaviour is very important.

6.10   Cases involving youths are usually only referred to the Crown Prosecution Service for prosecution if the youth has already received a reprimand and final warning, unless the offence is so serious that neither of these were appropriate. Reprimands and final warnings are intended to prevent re-offending and the fact that a further offence has occurred indicates that attempts to divert the youth from the court system have not been effective. So the public interest will usually require a prosecution in such cases, unless there are clear public interest factors against prosecution.

Police Cautions

6.11   These are only for adults. The police make the decision to caution an offender in accordance with Home Office guidelines.

6.12   When deciding whether a case should be prosecuted in the courts, Crown Prosecutors should consider the alternatives to prosecution. This will include a police caution. Again, the Home Office guidelines should be applied. Where it is felt that a caution is appropriate, Crown Prosecutors must inform the police so that they can caution the suspect. If the caution is not administered because the suspect refuses to accept it or the police do not wish to offer it, then the Crown Prosecutor may review the case again.

7.   Charges

7.1   Crown Prosecutors should select charges which:

a   reflect the seriousness of the offending;

b   give the court adequate sentencing powers; and

c   enable the case to be presented in a clear and simple way.

This means that Crown Prosecutors may not always continue with the most serious charge where there is a choice. Further, Crown Prosecutors should not continue with more charges than are necessary.

7.2 Crown Prosecutors should never go ahead with more charges than are necessary just to encourage a defendant to plead guilty to a few. In the same way, they should never go ahead with a more serious charge just to encourage a defendant to plead guilty to a less serious one.

7.3 Crown Prosecutors should not change the charge simply because of the decision made by the court or the defendant about where the case will be heard.

8.   Mode of trial

8.1 The Crown Prosecution Service applies the current guidelines for magistrates who have to decide whether cases should be tried in the Crown Court when the offence gives the option and the defendant does not indicate a guilty plea. (See the 'National Mode of Trial Guidelines' issued by the Lord Chief Justice.) Crown Prosecutors should recommend Crown Court trial when they are satisfied that the guidelines require them to do so.

8.2 Speed must never be the only reason for asking for a case to stay in the magistrates' courts. But Crown Prosecutors should consider the effect of any likely delay if they send a case to the Crown Court, and any possible stress on victims and witnesses if the case is delayed.

9.   Accepting guilty pleas

9.1 Defendants may want to plead guilty to some, but not all, of the charges. alternatively, they may want to plead guilty to a different, possibly less serious, charge because they are admitting only part of the crime. Crown Prosecutors should only accept the defendant's plea if they think the court is able to pass a sentence that matches the seriousness of the offending, particularly where there are aggravating features. Crown Prosecutors must never accept a guilty plea just because it is convenient.

9.2 Particular care must be taken when considering pleas which would enable the defendant to avoid the imposition of a mandatory minimum sentence. When please are offered, Crown Prosecutors must bear in mind the fact that ancillary orders can be made with some offences but not with others.

9.3 In cases where a defendant pleads guilty to the charges but on the basis of facts that are different from the prosecution case, and where this may significantly affect sentence, the court should be invited to hear evidence to determine what happened, and then sentence on that basis.

10. Re-starting a prosecution

10.1 People should be able to rely on decisions taken by the Crown Prosecution Service. Normally, if the Crown Prosecution Service tells a suspect or defendant that there will not be a prosecution, or that the prosecution has been stopped, that is the end of the matter and the case will not start again. But occasionally there are special reasons why the Crown Prosecution Service will re-start the prosecution, particularly if the case is serious.

10.2 These reasons include:

a   rare cases where a new look at the original decision shows that it was clearly wrong and should not be allowed to stand;

b   cases which are stopped so that more evidence which is likely to become available in the fairly near future can be collected and prepared. In these cases, the Crown Prosecutor will tell the defendant that the prosecution may well start again; and

c   cases which are stopped because of a lack of evidence but where more significant evidence is discovered later.

CHAPTER SEVEN

Lawyer-client confidentiality

...a fundamental condition on which the administration of justice as a whole rests.[1]

In 1996, Leigh Day & Co, a UK firm specialising in personal injury litigation, announced that it was bringing proceedings on behalf of a number of former smokers against two of the UK's leading tobacco companies, Imperial Tobacco and Gallahers. Right from the start this seemed a very bold move on Leigh Day & Co's part because the litigation was funded on a conditional fee basis. Consequently, the plaintiffs' lawyers were bound to be seriously out of pocket should the case be lost[2] as was always a serious possibility; even in the US which many see as being so favourable to tort plaintiffs, the tobacco industry has historically been extremely successful in defeating damages claims by smokers.

However, the decision to litigate in the UK may well have been prompted by a turning of the tide in favour of American tobacco plaintiffs, leading to a number of expensive settlements.[3] One of the most significant blows to the tobacco industry world wide occurred in May 1994 when the University of California in San Francisco received more than 4,000 copies of confidential documents belonging to the American tobacco company Brown & Williamson. These documents were said to reveal that contrary to what it had always claimed the tobacco industry had known for many years that nicotine was addictive. Such knowledge would seriously undermine arguments that smokers had knowingly and freely taken the risk of damage to their health and were therefore barred from claiming.

1   Lord Taylor of Gosforth LCJ in *R v Derby Magistrates Court, ex p B* [1995] 1 All ER 526 at 541A.
2   The case was lost. Leigh Day and Co and Irwin Mitchell (the other firm leading law firm in the case) are thought to have lost £2.5 million in fees. See 'Tobacco Firms Avoid Cancer Court Battle' *Times* 27 February 1999.
3   This account draws upon that appearing in *The Lawyer* on 24 June 1997 entitled 'Staring Down the Barrel of a Smoking Gun.'

These documents were 'leaked' by Merrell Williams, a law clerk working for a firm representing Brown & Williamson. Yet, under the LSGPC, such disclosure, albeit arguably in the public interest, would be a breach of the lawyer's duty of confidentiality under Principle 16.01.[4] Lawyers are thus indistinguishable from many other occupational groups in two very important respects. Firstly, they may in the course of their employment come across information disclosure of which would further the interests of identifiable third parties or broader social concerns. Secondly, lawyers have a duty of confidentiality to their clients.

As we shall see, lawyer-client confidentiality is protected by a number of different bodies of law and its precise scope is difficult to discern. Nevertheless, the scope and limits of lawyer-client confidentiality are of enormous significance for legal ethics. Confidentiality will generally be in the client's interests and if it is not the client can authorise disclosure. However, disclosure may sometimes serve other important interests. It follows that the scope of the confidentiality obligation is an important test of the legal professions' commitment to the public interest.

This has led to a vigorous debate on the scope of lawyer-client confidentiality in the US and this chapter briefly considers that debate before attempting to clarify the interrelationship of the various systems of rules which cumulatively define lawyers' obligations of confidentiality in England. Next we focus on the scope and bases for the duty of confidentiality. This is followed by an examination of the major exceptions to the duty of confidentiality recognised by the professional bodies. In the remaining sections the impact of the general equitable duty of confidentiality is described and set in the context of the occupational pressures working against the urge to 'blow the whistle'.

Note

Some moral philosophers have argued that the purpose of ethics is to act as a guide to conduct. Therefore any purported ethical duty must be one which is capable of fulfilment by the majority of those to whom it is addressed. They use the term 'supererogatory' to describe conduct worthy of praise but beyond the bounds of duty because it is 'asking too much' of most people.

Questions

1. Do you agree with the view of ethics set out in the preceding note? If not, why not and what alternative view do you prefer?

---

4   If the reports were prepared for the purposes of pending litigation they would be covered by litigation privilege and consequently confidential. If not so prepared, they would be discoverable and the solicitors would have a duty to ensure that their client disclosed them (*Myers v Ellman* [1940] AC 282). However if the client refused to do so, it would seem that withdrawal rather than disclosure would be the proper course.

2. Was Williams conduct supererogatory in this sense? Why, if at all could it be said that Williams would have been (morally) wrong to refrain from disclosure? Does it make any difference that Williams was a lawyer?

1 The American experience

The provisions of the American Bar Association's Model Rules of Professional Conduct relating to confidentiality[5] proved to be highly contentious. Particularly controversial was MR1.6(b)(2) which allows disclosure in the interests of preventing crime only if the crime is likely to result in imminent death or substantial bodily harm. The Kutak Commission had proposed that it should be sufficient if the crime would cause serious financial loss, but the ABA House of Delegates inserted the narrower provision contained in the current MR1.6(b)(2). Thus a lawyer who discovered that his services had been used in furtherance of a financial fraud, whilst required to withdraw (MR1.2(d)), would nevertheless be required to refrain from revealing the fraud either to victim or to regulator. Almost as controversial was MR4.1(b) which prevents a lawyer disclosing information in order to correct fraudulent statements by the client even if the information is necessary to correct a misrepresentation by the client during negotiations. By contrast, Rule 3.3 requires disclosure even of confidential information if this is necessary to prevent the client deceiving a court, for instance by giving perjured testimony.

Critics have seen in these provisions a highly self-interested hierarchy of interests. Bottom of the pile comes harm to third parties or the legal system which must almost always give way to the interests of the clients who pay lawyers' fees. However, clients' interests must give way when they conflict with the lawyers' interests. Hence MR1.6(2) allows client confidences to be revealed if this would serve the lawyer's interests in a dispute whether with the client or a third party (contrast the position of English lawyers with respect to wasted costs orders; See *Ridelhalgh v Horsfield* page 102 supra). In addition, comments 14 and 15 to MR 1.6 allow a lawyer who fears that his/her innocent assistance of a client now seen to be engaged in a fraud might later be seen as knowing complicity to give notice to third parties that he/she no longer stands by documents or opinions previously produced for the former client – even if such notice would in effect breach confidentiality. Even the exception in the case of fraud on a tribunal can be seen as self-interested regulation: many of the ruling voices in the ABA are transaction lawyers not litigators. They are therefore more interested in negotiation (covered by the restrictive MR4.1) than litigation.

In the following extract, the American writer Fred Zacharias considers the arguments in favour of strict confidentiality rules. Many of these arguments have been advanced in support of the English rules on lawyer-client confidentiality and all of them could be relied on for this purpose.

---

5   See Appendix: 'Anglo-American Confidentiality Provisions' infra p 280.

A. THE JUSTIFICATIONS FOR CONFIDENTIALITY

The primary argument in favour of attorney-client confidentiality in civil cases rests on a three-step syllogism. First, for the adversary system to operate, citizens must use lawyers to resolve disputes and the lawyers must be able to represent clients effectively. Second, attorneys can be effective only if they have all the relevant facts at their disposal. Third, clients will not employ lawyers, or at least will not provide them with adequate information, unless all aspects of the attorney-client relationship remain secret. Thus, the systemic argument goes, attorney-client confidentiality is the foundation of orderly and effective adversarial justice.

The bar, however, has relied on other justifications for confidentiality. By encouraging clients to communicate information they would otherwise withhold from their lawyers, confidentiality enhances the quality of legal representation and thus helps produce accurate legal verdicts. Proponents also claim that confidentiality improves the attorney-client relationship. It can foster aspects of lawyer and client 'dignity.' And, in theory, confidentiality helps lawyers discover improprieties that the client plans, advise against them, and ultimately stop the misconduct.

Undoubtedly, each of these justifications has played some role in convincing code drafters to favour rules preserving secrecy. But in many ways, strict confidentiality also serves personal interests of segments of the bar. For example, the rules relieve some lawyers from the psychological costs of having to make difficult ethical decisions. Consider this hypothetical case:

> An attorney obtains information from a client that would prove that another person, falsely accused of a crime, is innocent. The attorney could reveal the information without implicating the client in the crime. The client refuses to disclose the information voluntarily.

Strict confidentiality absolves the lawyer from deciding between betraying her client's (perhaps capricious) wishes and letting an innocent victim suffer. Confidentiality rules also may benefit an attorney financially. For example:

> A tax lawyer learns, from working with the books of a client, that the client has received large sums from the Russian government. The client will only say that the money is income for services rendered. The lawyer knows that the client has access to classified government documents.

A lawyer forbidden to disclose need not fear repercussions if her affiliation with the client's actions later becomes public. When questioned about the propriety of assisting the client, the attorney can hide behind the nondisclosure rules. A smile or 'no comment,' suggesting that the questioner would act like the lawyer 'if he only knew,' enables the attorney to avoid the cost of bad publicity and community disapproval of her conduct. In contrast, when silence subjects lawyers to accusations of wrongdoing, most codes authorise lawyers to speak.

The extent to which the profession's personal or economic interests have influenced the scope of confidentiality rules can never be known. Yet their mere existence leads one to wonder whether the attorney-drafters of the strict codes -- perhaps even unintentionally -- have overemphasised the systemic justifications for confidentiality or undervalued the social benefits of less restrictive rules. A code that explicitly acknowledges lawyers' right to follow their own moral instincts despite a financial risk might produce a more ethical bar that can serve society better. The following sections thus evaluate the strength of the traditional justifications for strict confidentiality and the societal costs of avoiding exceptions.

B. ARE THE TRADITIONAL JUSTIFICATIONS SOUND IN THEORY?

At the heart of attorney-client confidentiality rules is the notion that lawyers are clients' agents, and often their fiduciaries. Agency law requires preservation of principals' confidences and forbids agents to profit personally from information the principal has disclosed in secret. Attorney-client rules, however, expand the responsibility of lawyers to maintain client secrets beyond agency law standards. Ordinary agents may not sell or attempt to benefit personally from disclosing confidences. But they are 'privileged to reveal information confidentially acquired by [them] in the course of [their] agency in the protection of a superior interest of [themselves] or of a third person.'[6]

This disclosure privilege is reflected in the everyday practice of non-legal professionals, such as physicians, who normally keep confidentiality. In contrast, the strict versions of attorney-client confidentiality limit an attorney's right to disclose situations involving dangerous future crimes. Not even the most liberal of lawyer codes includes a catch-all 'superior interest' provision.

As a result, strict confidentiality rules forbid attorneys to disclose in a variety of situations in which other agents might have free rein to follow their consciences. In the absence of a client's declared intent to commit or participate in a crime, strict rules might well forbid an attorney to disclose a confidence to protect third parties from criminal harm…Standard disclosure exceptions also do not cover situations in which the client plans to commit potentially tortious, but non-criminal, activity. For example:

> The general counsel to a firm that produces a metal alloy used in the manufacture of airplanes learns of a company study that suggests that in some high-altitude flight patterns the alloy might weaken and cause a plane to explode. The alloy does, however, meet the minimum safety standards set by the government. The lawyer urges the Board of Directors to recall the alloy or at a minimum to inform users of its potential danger. The Board decides that the study is too inconclusive to warrant action, in light of the dire financial consequences of disclosure to the company.

…lawyers usually must keep evidence of past criminal activity secret, as in this scenario:

> A client fortuitously receives an undeserved payment from the government (eg, a duplicate welfare check or tax refund) and deposits it in a savings account. The client then contacts his attorney, who advises the client to return the money. The client refuses.

And rarely, if ever, do strict rules allow lawyers to disclose politically or morally disturbing (but noncriminal) information about their clients, such as the fact that a client organisation is secretly a Nazi front…

---

6   By virtue of the broad public interest exception to the equitable duty of confidentiality, the position is similar in the UK: see p 171 infra.

1. Confidentiality's Systemic Justification

To accept the modern systemic arguments in favour of confidentiality, one must reach one of two conclusions: first, that clients would use lawyers significantly less if more exceptions existed; second, that clients who employ lawyers would reveal substantially less information. Both conclusions are questionable.

The proponents of confidentiality posit that in this complex, litigious society, our need for 'trained [legal] technicians to advise men how to order their conduct' militates in favour of artificial rules that encourage the use of lawyers. Yet in theory, this very need suggests that potential clients will use lawyers even if confidentiality is circumscribed. As matters become complex, laypersons have no choice but to consult the experts. The threat of being sued or the need to sue for redress of grievances necessarily drives clients to lawyers. When litigation is not involved, the inability to understand or deal with a legal matter is usually the catalyst.

The notion that clients may, absent the promise of full confidentiality, withhold important information from their attorneys is intuitively more palatable. A client who expects the lawyer to reveal embarrassing or damaging facts may not be willing to tell all. Again, however, for the strictness of confidentiality rules to be significant in assuaging client fears, several premises about the actual practice of law must hold true. Attorneys must regularly inform clients of the rules, or clients must learn of them from independent sources. Clients must understand the explanation of confidentiality's scope. The rules must be sufficiently clear that clients can know which of their statements will remain secret. For if these premises do not hold true, hesitant clients will withhold information despite the existence of firm confidentiality guarantees.

Supporting the premises may be difficult. Even if a lawyer makes a good faith effort to explain the rules to clients, the clients are likely to remain confused at least as to details. Many aspects of confidentiality are ambiguous. A few universal exceptions to confidentiality exist, some of which are subject to hot debate. Often the distinction between disclosable communications and secrets rests on 'vague and open-textured criteria.' To the extent clients learn of confidentiality from sources other than their lawyers -- such as television, literature, or friends -- the explanations they receive are likely to ignore details or distinctions among the various jurisdictions' codes.

As a practical matter, clients thus probably end up with only a general understanding that attorney-client conversations usually remain confidential but occasionally may be revealed. If that is the case, creating limited additional disclosure exceptions is unlikely to affect a client's decision to confide. Absent supporting empirical evidence, it is problematic to assume that clients would avoid lawyers to any significant degree merely because they cannot speak in absolute secrecy.

2. Enhancing the Quality of Legal Representation and Maintaining Adversarial 'Truth-seeking'

Stated broadly, the claim that lawyers can be effective only when informed of all relevant facts is simply untrue. Attorneys do without information in a broad variety of contexts. To make sense, the argument in support of confidentiality must thus be redefined as follows: Lawyers whose clients hide information are likely to perform less ably. By encouraging client disclosure through secrecy guarantees, the state protects clients who otherwise would jeopardise their case by withholding information.

Professor Morgan long ago questioned the need to protect uncooperative or deceitful clients. The client who receives bad advice because he fails to inform the lawyer has only himself to blame. Alternatively, if the client lies to the lawyer and later finds himself confronted by the truth, the government has little reason to aid the client. The law should probably not be written for the benefit of liars or perjurers.

Morgan's position, however, does not do full justice to one type of client: the genuinely confused client who needs advice and representation, but unthinkingly hesitates to confide for fear his secrets will become public. Yet by definition, this category of client feels sufficiently troubled to seek legal advice. He is unlikely to undermine that advice by withholding information, particularly when told by the lawyer that full disclosure is important. If the client does withhold particularly embarrassing items, it is not clear that the representation will be significantly affected. In some settings, lawyers actually would prefer not to be told everything the client knows. Even a lawyer who ideally would like to know all relevant facts often can provide good legal advice based on partial information. Studies suggest that criminal defendants rarely are frank with their lawyers. Yet the criminal justice system relies on the presumption that these clients are nevertheless fairly and well represented.

I do not suggest that confidentiality rules have no effect on client forthrightness or the quality of representation. But in the abstract, it is difficult to determine the extent of any effect. If the number of clients needing and deserving the protection of absolute rules are indeed few, the interest in 'assuring effective representation' may be outweighed by society's alternative interests in allowing limited disclosures.

3. Client Dignity and the Trust Relationship

Absolute confidentiality can enhance lawyer client relations. It often makes the client feel as if the lawyer is a true fiduciary, with loyalty to no one other than the client. It also avoids the unseemly situation in which a lawyer induces the client to be open and then informs on the client.

But these considerations alone do not justify the strictest of rules. In an ideal world, the government would promote the relationship between clients and all agents. But that does not mean it is essential to preserve confidentiality to an extreme degree. Even if we accept client 'autonomy' as an important value, there are limits to how comfortable we want clients to be in the belief that their lawyers will never take a stand against them. Arguably, client distrust will increase if the lawyer insists that she will always act in accord with the client's wishes. So long as the attorney informs the client at the outset of the relationship that she may feel compelled to disclose particular types of information, subsequent disclosures are not unseemly. The client may more readily accept her as an ally within the defined boundaries, both because the lawyer has exhibited integrity and because the limitations on the alliance make the total package more believable.

The argument that confidentiality gives 'appropriate regard' to client dignity is equally vulnerable. For one, the same argument applies to all professions. More importantly, too much secrecy can be counter-productive. As the Supreme Court implicitly recognised in approving a lawyer's threat to disclose a client's proposed perjury, the lawyer who contributes to the notion that the client can get away with anything demeans the client as a moral individual.

4. Preventing Client Misconduct

The most appealing secondary justification for attorney-client confidentiality is that helping lawyers obtain information enables them to advise clients against committing improper acts or filing frivolous claims. Yet the same empirical questions that plague the systemic justification for strict confidentiality are present here. Confidentiality probably does allow some lawyers to prevent some misconduct before it occurs. But adding limited exceptions might not substantially affect lawyers' ability to dissuade improper acts.

Moreover, it is unclear that strict confidentiality is what provokes client candour about potential improprieties. In most cases, lawyers impress upon clients the importance of full disclosure to the lawyer's ability to evaluate the case. This warning alone may procure the type of information lawyers need to prevent misconduct. As a factual matter, the additional disclosures strict confidentiality fosters may only marginally improve the lawyer's ability to enforce the law.

Enabling clients to discuss planned misconduct with impunity sometimes might even promote misconduct. In consulting with clients, lawyers often serve the function of psychiatrist, social worker, or priest-confessor. They provide some clients with a psychological outlet that helps the clients persist in misconduct. Empirical research might show that lawyers play this role only rarely, that the risk of promoting misconduct deserves little weight. Yet proponents of the dissuading misconduct rationale have not relied on such evidence; they do not even consider strict confidentiality's possible costs.[7]

Questions

1. In what way may the arguments for strict confidentiality rights be tested?

2. Upon whom should the burden of proof concerning the consequences of limiting lawyer–client confidentiality lie, for example in relation to Zacharias example of the unsafe airplane?

3. Do lawyers need to be fully informed in order to represent their clients effectively? Consider the implications for lawyer-client confidentiality of the practices of lawyers defending those suspected of white collar crimes. See chapter 6 at pp 221-223 supra.

2   Clarifying confidentiality

In the US, the proper scope of lawyer-client confidentiality is controversial, but its actual scope is relatively easy to determine. The Model Rules purport to be a self-contained Code binding on lawyers to such an extent that lawyers are urged to presume that State and Federal Statutes requiring disclosure of confidential information do not

---

7   Fred C Zacharias 'Rethinking Confidentiality' [1989] 74 Iowa L Rev 351 at 358-370.

apply to lawyers[8]. Moreover this presumption must be maintained by appealing any contrary judicial decision.

In England, the CCB is so perfunctory as to be of little assistance in determining what standards are observed by or expected of the Bar.[9] The LSGPC is not only controversial. It is also far less user-friendly than the Model Rules because it can only be understood in the light of the doctrine of legal professional privilege. The Guide purports to set out a duty of confidentiality which is distinct from the doctrine of legal professional privilege: see principle 16.01 comment 1[10]. With respect to the type of communication covered by the principle this is true: the doctrine of privilege protects only communications made for the purpose of obtaining legal advice. The duty of confidentiality by contrast covers all matters disclosed by the client to the lawyer however unrelated to the obtaining of legal advice.

The claim is however misleading in relation to the exceptions to the duty of confidentiality. The most significant general exception[11] to the duty is coextensive with the major exception to privilege known as the 'crime-fraud exception.' Thus comment 1 to principle 16.01 provides that

> The duty of confidentiality does not apply to information acquired by a solicitor where he or she is being used by the client to facilitate the commission of a crime or fraud because that is not within the scope of the professional retainer.

The adoption by reference of the doctrine of privilege which, as we shall see, gives lawyer-client confidentiality an exalted legal status is open to criticism. It is true that in some cases the autonomy of a self-regulating profession may be circumscribed by the general law. If the profession accepts the state's claim to obedience, its code of professional ethics may not permit conduct which is prohibited by the general law. Hence comment 6 to Principle 16.02 of the LSGPC provides that:

> A solicitor should reveal matters which are otherwise subject to the duty to preserve confidentiality where a court orders that such matters are to be disclosed or where a warrant permits a police officer or other authority to seize confidential documents. If a solicitor is of the opinion that the documents are subject to legal privilege or that for some other reason the order or warrant ought not to have been made or issued, he or she without unlawfully obstructing its execution should normally discuss with the client the possibility of making an application to have the order or warrant set aside.

However, the privilege doctrine does not require the exceptions to confidentiality to be coextensive with exceptions to the law on privilege. That doctrine formally states that a lawyer is not *obliged* to give evidence in court against a current or former client

---

8   MR 1.6 comments 19 and 20.
9   CCB para 603 provides, '…a practising barrister must preserve the confidentiality of his lay client's affairs and must not without the prior consent of his lay client or as permitted by law lend or reveal the contents of his papers…' .
10   Infra p 280.
11   It is often said that the crime-fraud doctrine sets out not an exception but a set of circumstances in which privilege never attaches in the first place. This however seems to be a matter of semantics.

of communications between lawyer and client[12]. It does not therefore purport to state when a lawyer may *voluntarily* disclose client communications, for example to third parties.[13] Indeed, the courts have decided that the fact that a document is privileged, so that its production cannot be compelled by legal process, is not per se sufficient grounds for the issuing of an injunction to restrain unauthorised use by third parties. That issue is regulated by the equitable law of confidential information.[14]

Of course, a self-regulating profession may prohibit what is permitted by the general law. Indeed it is at the heart of the case for self-regulation that the profession is well-placed to decide cheaply and accurately what limits should be imposed upon its members professional activities beyond those imposed by the general law. Thus the courts have recognised the appropriateness of the LSGPC imposing stricter rules for the prohibition of conflicts of interest than those imposed and enforced by the courts as part of its inherent jurisdiction over solicitors.[15] For this reason, there is nothing inconsistent with the nature of self-regulation in the adoption by the Guide of the privilege doctrine. But unlike the requirement that judicial orders for disclosure of confidential information be obeyed which can be justified by reference to rule of law arguments, the adoption of the privilege doctrine requires independent substantive justification. Why, it might be asked, should not the profession like the courts prohibit only those disclosures which are prohibited by the equitable duty of confidence. As we shall see, much turns on whether the privilege doctrine can itself be justified.

However, it may be a mistake when trying to ascertain the scope of lawyer-client confidentiality to concentrate too closely on professional codes. We have seen that there are doubts about the efficiency of the Law Society as an enforcement agency (see chapter 4 supra). Consequently it may be argued that lawyers' real obligations are determined by the extent to which the courts will actually grant remedies to those whose confidences they disclose. This provides another reason to look at the general equitable duty of confidentiality, and, in addition to look at the protections available to lawyers who do 'blow the whistle'.

Note

As well as the exception contained in comment 1 and the further exception contained in comment 3 (discussed in section 4 below) there are a number of specific statutory exceptions, of which the most important are perhaps those imposed by the Drug Trafficking Act 1994 and the Criminal Justice Act 1988. These two statutes impose upon lawyers who suspect their clients may have been involved in laundering the

12 Two kinds of communication are privilege by this doctrine. Communications made for the purpose of obtaining legal advice ('legal advice privilege') and communications between lawyer and third party (such as an expert witness) for the purpose of obtaining information relevant to advising the client about forthcoming litigation.

13 See the case of 'Waxo Ltd', question 2 p 289 infra.

14 Infra text to pp 272-273 notes 6-8. For a different view of the relationship between privilege and confidentiality, see p 273 note 8 infra.

15 See Browne-Wilkinson V-C in *David Lee & Co (Lincoln) Ltd v Coward Chance* [1991] Ch 259 at p 266B-H.

proceeds of drug trafficking or other criminal activity an obligation to report the matter to the authorities.[16] Moreover, note 4 to principle 16.02 countenances disclosure of otherwise confidential information by solicitors in cases involving harm to children.

Question

Is the diligence of the Law Society in its' enforcement of the confidentiality provisions of the Guide relevant to a consideration of lawyers' 'real' obligations of confidentiality (See chapter 4 above esp pp 124-127)?

3   The UK position

It has been argued that the lawyer's duty of confidentiality is conceptually distinct from the doctrine of privilege. Nevertheless, it is undeniable that the privilege doctrine exerts significant influence upon the duty of confidentiality. In addition, privilege is the context in which the rationale for confidentiality has been considered by the judiciary. For these reasons we consider in this section the basis of the privilege doctrine.

It is a well-established rule of the English law of evidence that communications between lawyer and client for the purpose of obtaining legal advice are privileged regardless of whether legal proceedings of any kind are contemplated.[17] The strength of English laws commitment to privilege was however severely tested in the case of *R v Derby Magistrates, ex p B* [18] where the principle was in conflict with the interests of a defendant in a criminal trial.

B was charged with the murder of a 16-year-old girl. At first, B admitted the charge, but at his trial, B blamed his stepfather and alleged that he had been involved only under duress exerted upon him by his stepfather. Following B's acquittal, his stepfather was himself tried for murder and B gave evidence for the prosecution. The stepfather sought to compel B and his solicitors to testify about B's instructions to his solicitor during the period when he was admitting guilt. In this way, the stepfather hoped to undermine B's credibility but also to uncover evidence that B was in fact responsible. B claimed these conversations were privileged, an issue on which the House of Lords was ultimately asked to rule.

Lord Taylor of Gosforth:

> The stipendiary magistrate considered that it was his duty to weigh the public interest which protects confidential communications between a solicitor and his client against the public interest in securing that all relevant and admissible evidence is made available

16   See especially, ss 51 and 52 of the Drug Trafficking Act 1994 and s 93B of the Criminal Justice Act 1988.
17   *Greenough* v *Gaskell* (1883) 1 My &K 98.
18   [1995] 4 All ER 526.

to the defence. In his view the balance came down firmly in favour of production. The appellant could no longer be regarded as having any recognisable interest in asserting privilege. The overriding consideration was the need to secure a fair trial for the stepfather. In holding that he was obliged to weigh competing public interests against each other, the stipendiary magistrate was following the decision of the Court of Appeal, Criminal Division in *R v Ataou* [1988] 2 All ER 321, [1988] QB 798. If *R v Ataou* was correctly decided, then the stipendiary magistrate was plainly entitled to take the view he did. Indeed, McCowan LJ in the Divisional Court described the balancing exercise which he had carried out as flawless. I would not disagree. For there could be no question of the appellant being tried again for murder, and it is most improbable that he would be prosecuted for perjury.

The important question remains, however, whether *R v Ataou* was correctly decided, and in particular whether, when there is a claim for privilege in respect of confidential communications between solicitor and client, there is a balancing exercise to be performed at all...

[Having considered the history of the privilege doctrine, Lord Taylor continued]

I may end with two more recent affirmations of the general principle. In *Hobbs v Hobbs and Cousens* [1959] 3 All ER 827 at 829, [1960] P 112 at 116–117 Stevenson J said:

'... privilege has a sound basis in common sense. It exists for the purpose of ensuring that there shall be complete and unqualified confidence in the mind of a client when he goes to his solicitor or when he goes to his counsel that that which he there divulges will never be disclosed to anybody else. It is only if the client feels safe in making a clean breast of his troubles to his advisers that litigation and the business of the law can be carried on satisfactorily ... There is ... an abundance of authority in support of the proposition that once legal professional privilege attaches to a document ... that privilege attaches for all time and in all circumstances.'

In *Balabel v Air-India* [1988] 2 All ER 246, [1988] Ch 317 the basic principle justifying legal professional privilege was again said to be that a client should be able to obtain legal advice in confidence.

The principle which runs through all these cases, and the many other cases which were cited, is that a man must be able to consult his lawyer in confidence, since otherwise he might hold back half the truth. The client must be sure that what he tells his lawyer in confidence will never be revealed without his consent. Legal professional privilege is thus much more than an ordinary rule of evidence, limited in its application to the facts of a particular case. It is a fundamental condition on which the administration of justice as a whole rests...

Mr Richards, as amicus curiae, acknowledged the importance of maintaining legal professional privilege as the general rule. But he submitted that the rule should not be absolute. There might be occasions, if only by way of rare exception, in which the rule should yield to some other consideration of even greater importance. He referred by analogy to the balancing exercise which is called for where documents are withheld on the ground of public interest immunity and cited the speeches of Lord Simon of Glaisdale in *D v National Society for the Prevention of Cruelty to Children* [1977] 1 All ER 589 at 607,

[1978] AC 171 at 233 and in *Waugh v British Railways Board* [1979] 2 All ER 1169 at 1175–1176, [1980] AC 521 at 535. But the drawback to that approach is that once any exception to the general rule is allowed, the client's confidence is necessarily lost. The solicitor, instead of being able to tell his client that anything which the client might say would never in any circumstances be revealed without his consent, would have to qualify his assurance. He would have to tell the client that his confidence might be broken if in some future case the court were to hold that he no longer had 'any recognisable interest' in asserting his privilege. One can see at once that the purpose of the privilege would thereby be undermined.

As for the analogy with public interest immunity, I accept that the various classes of case in which relevant evidence is excluded may, as Lord Simon of Glaisdale suggested, be regarded as forming part of a continuous spectrum. But it by no means follows that because a balancing exercise is called for in one class of case, it may also be allowed in another. Legal professional privilege and public interest immunity are as different in their origin as they are in their scope. Putting it another way, if a balancing exercise was ever required in the case of legal professional privilege, it was performed once and for all in the sixteenth century, and since then has applied across the board in every case, irrespective of the client's individual merits.

In the course of his judgment in the Divisional Court, McCowan LJ indicated that he not only felt bound by *R v Ataou*, but he also agreed with it. He continued:

> 'These further points were made by Mr Francis. He says that if a man charged with a criminal offence cannot go to a solicitor in the certainty that such matters as he places before him will be kept private for all time, he may be reluctant to be candid with his solicitors. Surely, however, it ought to be an incentive to him to tell the truth to his solicitors, which surely cannot be a bad thing. Mr Francis went on to suggest that his client's reputation would be damaged if the disclosures were to go to suggest that he was the murderer. For my part, I would be able to bear with equanimity that damage to his reputation. In the interests of justice and of the respondent, it would be a good thing that that reputation should be so damaged.'

One can have much sympathy with McCowan LJ's approach, especially in relation to the unusual facts of this case. But it is not for the sake of the appellant alone that the privilege must be upheld. It is in the wider interests of all those hereafter who might otherwise be deterred from telling the whole truth to their solicitors. For this reason I am of the opinion that no exception should be allowed to the absolute nature of legal professional privilege, once established. It follows that *R v Barton* [1972] 2 All ER 1192, [1973] 1 WLR 115 and *R v Ataou* [1988] 2 All ER 321, [1988] QB 798 were wrongly decided, and ought to be overruled.[19]

Lord Nicholls of Birkenhead commented:

> Legal professional privilege is concerned with the interaction between two aspects of the public interest in the administration of justice. The public interest in the efficient working of the legal system requires that people should be able to obtain professional legal advice on their rights and liabilities and obligations. This is desirable for the orderly

19   Supra at 535H-536B; 540F-542E.

conduct of everyday affairs. Similarly, people should be able to seek legal advice and assistance in connection with the proper conduct of court proceedings. To this end communications between clients and lawyers must be uninhibited. But, in practice, candour cannot be expected if disclosure of the contents of communications between client and lawyer may be compelled, to a client's prejudice and contrary to his wishes. That is one aspect of the public interest. It takes the form of according to the client a right, or privilege as it is unhelpfully called, to withhold disclosure of the contents of client-lawyer communications. In the ordinary course the client has an interest in asserting this right, in so far as disclosure would or might prejudice him.

The other aspect of the public interest is that all relevant material should be available to courts when deciding cases. Courts should not have to reach decisions in ignorance of the contents of documents or other material which, if disclosed, might well affect the outcome.

...Mr Goldberg QC and Mr Richards submitted that the balance between competing aspects of the public interest should not be struck once and for all on a generalised basis. The law should no longer adopt such a crude 'all or nothing' approach. Instead, in each individual case the court should weigh the considerations for and against disclosure of the privileged material. The court should attach importance to any prejudice the client might suffer from disclosure. The court should also attach importance to the prejudice an accused person might suffer from non-disclosure. The court should then carry out a balancing exercise. The interest of the client in non-disclosure should be balanced against the public interest in seeing that justice is done. If disclosure were confined to truly exceptional cases, the public interest underlying legal professional privilege would not be at risk of serious damage.

This is a seductive submission, but in my view it should be resisted. The end result is not acceptable. Inherent in the suggested balancing exercise is the notion of weighing one interest against another. On this argument, a client may have a legitimate, continuing interest in non-disclosure but this is liable to be outweighed by another interest. In its discretion the court may override the privilege against non-disclosure. In *R v Ataou* [1988] 2 All ER 321 at 326, [1988] QB 798 at 807 the Court of Appeal expressed the matter thus:

'The judge must ... decide whether the legitimate interest of the defendant in seeking to breach the privilege outweighs that of the client in seeking to maintain it.'

There are real difficulties here. In exercising this discretion the court would be faced with an essentially impossible task. One man's meat is another man's poison. How does one equate exposure to a comparatively minor civil claim or criminal charge against prejudicing a defence to a serious criminal charge? How does one balance a client's risk of loss of reputation, or exposure to public opprobrium, against prejudicing another person's possible defence to a murder charge? But the difficulties go much further. Could disclosure also be sought by the prosecution, on the ground that there is a public interest in the guilty being convicted? If not, why not? If so, what about disclosure in support of serious claims in civil proceedings, say, where a defendant is alleged to have defrauded hundreds of people of their pensions or life savings? Or in aid of family proceedings, where the shape of the whole of a child's future may be under consideration? There is no evident stopping place short of the balancing exercise being potentially available in support of all parties in all forms of court proceedings. This highlights the impossibility of the exercise. What is the measure by which judges are to ascribe an appropriate weight, on each side of the scale, to the diverse multitude of different claims, civil and criminal, and other interests of the client on the one hand and the person seeking disclosure on the other hand?

In the absence of principled answers to these and similar questions, and I can see none, there is no escaping the conclusion that the prospect of a judicial balancing exercise in this field is illusory, a veritable will-o'-the wisp. That in itself is a sufficient reason for not departing from the established law. Any development in the law needs a sounder base than this. This is of particular importance with legal professional privilege. Confidence in non-disclosure is essential if the privilege is to achieve its raison d'être. If the boundary of the new incursion into the hitherto privileged area is not principled and clear, that confidence cannot exist.[20]

Notes

1. *Ex p B* has been distinguished on a number of occasions. In *Re L*[1] the House of Lords had to decide whether an experts report, obtained during proceedings under the Children Act 1989, on a mother alleged to have subjected her child to involuntary substance abuse, was privileged. Their Lordships held that it was not. Privilege was impliedly excluded by the non-adversarial nature of proceedings under the Children Act which were concerned primarily with the welfare of the child. Consequently (though the point was not decided) legal advisers might have a duty to disclose adverse expert reports to the court even if they were not ordered to do so.

2. In *Saunders v Punch*[2], Lindsay J held that decided that the assertion in *Ex p B* that legal professional privilege was absolute did not require the court automatically to order a journalist to disclose the source of information leaked in breach of legal professional privilege. On the contrary, s 10 of the Contempt of Court Act 1981 required the court to refuse to make such an order unless the applicant established one of the grounds set out in the statute.

3. The question of how confidentiality arguments could be tested was asked earlier in this chapter. One obvious answer is to undertake empirical investigation of clients' attitudes to lawyer-client confidentiality. However, very few such surveys have been done. Zacharias himself undertook such a survey and found some evidence that wider exceptions to the duty of confidentiality would produce some increase in clients' reluctance to disclose to lawyers. He also found however that most clients thought

---

20   Supra at 543G–545G.
1   [1996] 2 WLR 395 HL.
2   [1998] 1 All ER 281. See infra text to p 273 notes 8-9.

lawyers would disclose in order to prevent a variety of harms in circumstances where, in fact, the professional rules currently prohibit disclosure.[3]

Questions

1. **Damien's Case**: Harriet has been asked to represent Damien who has been accused of an horrific ritual killing. Damien confesses to Harriet that he killed an earlier victim in a similar way. He describes the previous killing in such a way that he is almost certainly telling the truth. Harriet knows that George, a friend of Damien's, was convicted of the earlier killing despite his protestations of innocence. However, Damien refuses to confess to the earlier killing.

What should Harriet do?

2. What are the implications for the court's judgment in *Ex p B* of the arguments put forward by Zacharias?

Rights based justification for confidentiality

Despite the occasional use of the language of rights, most of the arguments for strict confidentiality rules considered thus far have been consequentialist in character, which is to say that they depend on the alleged negative effects on the legal system of allowing exceptions. Many years ago, Jeremy Bentham raised a famous objection to the consequentialist argument that lawyer-client communications must remain privileged if legal representation is to be effective. The innocent, Bentham argued, would have nothing to fear from frank disclosure whilst the concerns of the guilty are of little merit.

However, innocent but anxious and/or unsophisticated clients may mistakenly think they have something to fear from disclosure and, hence, absent confidentiality guarantees, may conceal information which vindicates them. This is likely to be a particular problem in relation to criminal defence work. Suppose the client has killed her husband in order to avoid an imminent beating. In the absence of confidential advice, she may not know that she can plead self-defence and be tempted to deny, however implausibly, that she was in any way involved.

Yet if our sole concern is the efficiency of the legal system, ie with maximising the number of correct verdicts, cases like that of the battered wife do not provide much of an argument for strict confidentiality rules. Such cases are likely to be few and would be outweighed by the increase in the number of accurate outcomes which would follow if lawyers were required to testify as to their conversations with their clients.

---

3   Supra p 254 note 7 and see further Note: 'Functional Overlap Between Lawyers and Other Professionals: its implications for the privileged communications doctrine' [1962] 72 Yale LJ 1226.

As a result, lawyer-client confidentiality is likely to be more successfully defended by reference to the client's rights and following the passing of the Human Rights Act 1998 we can expect greater reliance on rights-based arguments in this area. The case of *General Mediterranean Holdings SA v Patel*[4] may therefore represent a significant development. In that case the claimant had brought an action against the defendant alleging fraud. Shortly before trial the defendant abandoned a defence which it had maintained for many months and which the claimant had investigated at huge cost. The claim was eventually settled but the claimant applied for a wasted costs order alleging against the defendant's solicitors alleging that the solicitors had been aware all along that the defence was false. The solicitors applied under CPR r 48(3) for an order permitting them to disclose to the court privileged documents which they claimed would show that the claimant's case against them was misconceived. The application was opposed by the defendant who alleged that the rule was ultra vires the Civil Procedure Act 1997. The Act provides that 'Civil Procedure Rules may modify rules of evidence as they apply to proceedings in any court within the scope of these rules[5].' Having considered the English, Canadian and Australian authorities on legal professional privilege, the judge concluded that,

> the common law recognises (1) the right to legal confidentiality which arises between a person and his legal adviser (save where the client is trying to use the relationship for an unlawful purpose) as a matter of substantive law, and (2) regards it as a right of constitutional importance, because it is seen as a necessary bulwark of the citizen's right of access to justice whether as a claimant or a defendant. Legal professional privilege is an attribute or manifestation of that right. It is also as Lord Taylor CJ said in *R v Derby Magistrates Court, ex p B* ... much more than an ordinary rule of evidence being considered a fundamental condition on which the administration of justice rests.[6]

It followed that r 48.7(3) was ultra vires because of the principle that fundamental common law rights cannot be abrogated by delegated legislation[7] or in the absence of clear words[8]. The judge added that he would in any case have refused to make an order in the light of the protection accorded to privacy by Art 8 of the ECHR. No exception was required to the defendant's right to privacy in its communications with its' lawyers by the right of the lawyers to have their civil obligations determined in a fair and public hearing[9]. The lawyers could be protected by the courts making favourable assumptions about the contents of the privileged communications. Whether *Patel's* case undermines earlier decisions[10] supporting the interrelationship described in the text between privilege and confidentiality is not yet clear.

In fact, however, the rights-based argument may be at its' strongest in the context of criminal defence work. For criminal defendants are special in that under the European

---

4   [1999] 3 All ER 673, QBD, Toulson J.
5   Civil Procedure Act 1997, s 1(2) and para 4 to Sch 1.
6   [1999] 3 All ER 673 at 688D-F.
7   *R v Secretary of State for Home Department , ex p Leech* [1993] 4 All ER 539.
8   *R v Secretary of State for Home Department, ex p Simms* [1999] 3 All ER 400.
9   Article 6, ECHR.
10   Eg *Webster v James Chapman & Co* infra text to note 48; supra text to note 14.

Convention on Human Rights and therefore under the Human Rights Act 1998, they have both the right to the assistance of a lawyer in preparing a defence and the right not to incriminate themselves.[11] It can be argued that lawyer-client privilege is necessary if these rights are to be respected. If there is no guarantee of confidentiality, the accused must forego either his right to legal representation or his privilege against self-incrimination. For if he chooses a lawyer unrestrained by lawyer-client privilege, the client risks giving self-incriminating testimony via his lawyer. The strength of the privilege against self-incrimination was affirmed by the European Court of Human Rights in the case of *Saunders v UK*[12]. The Secretary of State for Trade and Industry had appointed inspectors pursuant to ss 432-436 of the Companies Act 1985 to investigate the affairs of Guinness. The inspectors were a barrister and a solicitor and they interviewed Saunders in the presence of his expert lawyers having given him notice of the nature of their concerns. After the interview, Saunders was sent a copy of the transcript and given an opportunity to comment upon it. It was accepted by all concerned that the proceedings were investigatory (ie undertaken with a view to establishing the facts so as to enable others to make decisions) not judicial. Saunders was required to answer the inspectors' questions. Failure to do so was by statute a contempt of court. Subsequently he was charged with various offences in relation to the Guinness share support operation. At his trial, the Crown relied on several of his answers to the inspectors in order to undermine his credibility and to impugn his honesty. Saunders was convicted and subsequently brought proceedings in the ECHR.

It held that a right to silence and a right not to incriminate oneself were implicit within Art 6(1). This Article was therefore violated when the Crown used Saunders compelled testimony in subsequent judicial proceedings. It is a mark of the strength of the right not to incriminate oneself that it was violated by an obligation to testify after receiving privileged advice from expert lawyers. It follows a fortiori that Art 6(1) would be violated by the disclosure of privileged communications at a criminal trial. Thus it can be argued that a right to lawyer-client confidentiality is implied by the rights to a fair trial and to legal representation.

Note

Article 6 of the ECHR provides:

(1) In the determination of his civil rights and obligations or of any charge against him, everyone is entitled to a fair and public hearing within a reasonable time by an independent and impartial tribunal established by law.

Article 8 provides:

(1) Every one has the right to respect for his private and family life, his home and his correspondence.

11   See ECHR, Arts 6(1) and (3).
12   (1997) 23 EHRR 313.

(2) There shall be no interference by a public authority with the exercise of this right, except such as is in accordance with the law and is necessary in a democratic society in the interests of national security, public safety or the economic well-being of the country for the prevention of disorder or crime, for the protection of health or morals, or for the protection of the rights and freedoms of others.

Questions

1. Consider whether rights-based arguments for confidentiality in the criminal context justify the decision in the *Derby Magistrates* case.

2. Consider in relation to Damien's case (supra), the suggestion that while Harriet should not be required to testify about Damien's instructions (ie the privilege rule should remain), the relevant professional code should be amended so as to permit a criminal defence lawyer to disclose confidential communications if such disclosure was necessary to prevent serious physical injury to or the wrongful conviction of a third party. Such communication could only be made to the prosecutor and only on the basis that it would not be used against the client.

3. What are the implication of *Patel's* case for the status of exceptions to lawyer-client confidentiality permitted by the professional codes, for example the permission given solicitors by comment 3 to principle 16.02 to disclose confidential information in order to prevent the client committing a criminal act which the solicitor believes on reasonable grounds is likely to result in serious bodily harm?

4. What is the purpose of the jurisdiction to make wasted costs orders (see chapter 4 supra)? How will these purposes be effected by the decision in *Patel*?

5. Is there a rights-based justification for the jurisdiction to make wasted costs orders? Consider for example Art 6 of the ECHR (supra). Does the decision in *Patel* adequately take account of *all* relevant rights?

4   Exceptions to confidentiality

As we have seen, the LSGPC contains a number of important explicit exceptions many of which are statutory.[13] However we concentrate here on the general exceptions. The first is the exception to the privilege doctrine known as the crime-fraud exception and the second is exception provided by Comment 3 to principle 16.02. The issues arising where disclosure of confidential information might be necessary to prevent a client (or a witness testifying on the client's behalf) deceiving the court have been dealt with in chapter 6.

13   See the note on pp 256-257 supra.

Crime/fraud

Based on the 19th century case of *R v Cox and Railton*,[14] the crime-fraud exception establishes that where a solicitor is consulted by a client who seeks advice for the purpose of carrying out a settled intention to commit a fraud, privilege does not apply regardless of whether the solicitor knew of the client's intention. This exception was considered and to some degree extended in *Finers v Miro*[15]. The plaintiff was a firm of solicitors which from 1982 onwards had arranged for the hiding of certain assets belonging to its client, believing quite innocently (as the court held) that the defendant wished to protect these assets from political appropriation. The solicitor held the assets on trust for the defendant through a maze of offshore trusts/companies.

The plaintiff became aware that it was being alleged in the US that the defendant was systematically defrauding an insurance company which he ran in Louisiana. In May 1991, the firm's senior partner was required to give evidence on deposition in civil proceedings begun by the liquidator of the Louisiana company and the firm realised that the assets might well be the proceeds of fraud.

It therefore ceased to act for the client, froze the assets and applied to the court asking whether it should give notice to the liquidator.

Dillon LJ held:

> The difficulty about that is of course that in the present case any communication to the liquidator or his solicitors which gives enough information to be of any practical use must breach the secrecy which was the whole object of the defendant's instructions to Mr Stein, and must breach the legal professional privilege to which the defendant is consequently entitled as against the plaintiffs.

> It is well established, however, that that privilege is lost by the criminal or fraudulent intent of the client, whether or not the solicitor was aware of that intent: see *Gamlen Chemical Co (UK) Ltd v Rochem Ltd* [1979] CA Transcript 777 per Templeman LJ. He elaborated this where he said:

>> 'In the present case the plaintiffs seek discovery and disclosure of communications between the defendants and their solicitors. In the light of the existing evidence and without knowing if, at the trial, that evidence will be disproved, we must ... determine whether it seems probable that the defendants may have consulted their legal advisers before the commission of fraud and for the purpose of being guided and helped wittingly or unwittingly in committing the fraud. A fortiori if the defendants embarked on a fraudulent activity, communications between the defendants and the solicitors, made in the course of that activity, cannot be entitled to privilege and must be disclosed so that ... 'the whole transaction should be ripped up and disclosed in all its nakedness to the light of the Court' [see *Williams v Quebrada Railway Land and Copper Co* [1895] 2 Ch 751 at 755 per Kekewich J].'

> That is in line with the passages in the speech of Lord Wrenbury in *O'Rourke v Darbishire* [1920] AC 581 at 632–633, [1920] All ER Rep 1 at 19 where he referred to assertions

14   (1884) 14 QBD 153.
15   [1991] 1 All ER 182.

of fraud which 'are such as to be regarded seriously as constituting prima facie a case of fraud resting on solid grounds', and went on to explain how this can be shown.

It was urged for the defendant that the advice obtained by the defendant from Mr Stein was not advice on how to commit a fraud but advice after the fraud, if there was one, had been committed. I note however that in *O'Rourke v Darbishire* [1920] AC 581 at 613, [1920] All ER Rep 1 at 10 Lord Sumner refers to a party consulting a solicitor 'in order to learn how to plan, execute, or stifle a fraud'. The privilege cannot, in my judgment, apply if the solicitor is consulted, even though he does not realise this and is himself acting innocently, to cover up or stifle a fraud.

On the material before us I conclude that it does seem probable that the defendant may have consulted Mr Stein for the purpose of being guided and helped, albeit unwittingly on the part of Mr Stein, in covering up or stifling a fraud on Insurance of which there is a prima facie case resting on solid grounds.

Does it matter that it is the solicitor himself who is seeking in the present case to tear aside the client's privilege, and not a third party with a hostile claim? In my judgment it does not; the privilege does not require the court to compel the solicitor to continue, at his own personal risk, to aid and abet the apparently fraudulent ends of the defendant in covering up the original fraud of which there is such a prima facie case.[16]

Comment 3

From the perspective of privilege, the crime-fraud situation should be distinguished from that in which the client asks the solicitor for advice about a proposed course of action and upon being informed that such action would be criminal nevertheless proceeds. This much was made clear by *Butler v The Board of Trade*[17] . There the plaintiff was charged with offences under the Companies Act 1948 in relation to companies under liquidation. The plaintiff's solicitors had inadvertently given to the Board of Trade (the prosecutor) a letter prior to the alleged offence written by the plaintiff's previous solicitor warning the plaintiff that his proposed conduct might be criminal. One question in these proceedings was whether the letter was privileged. Goff J held:

It is submitted on behalf of the defendants, however, that as the plaintiff is charged with criminal offences, and the letter is relevant thereto, which it undoubtedly is, the privilege does not apply. Now, it is clear that a sufficient charge of crime or fraud will in certain circumstances destroy the privilege, but there is a dispute between the parties about what it is necessary to show for that purpose. The defendants say that relevance is alone sufficient, and the position is in effect so stated in the *Supreme Court Practice 1970*. The plaintiff submits, however, that it is necessary to go further and to show that the professional advice was in furtherance of the crime or fraud...

As questions of this nature have to be determined on a prima facie basis, often without seeing the documents or knowing what was orally communicated, the two tests will,

16   Supra 186F–187D.
17   [1970] 3 All ER 593.

I think, in many and probably most cases be found in practice to produce the same result because in most cases of relevance the proper prima facie inference will be that the communication was made in preparation for or in furtherance or as part of the criminal or fraudulent purpose. However, the two tests are not the same and in the present case cannot, I think, possibly produce the same result. On the information before me, the letter was nothing but a warning volunteered, no doubt wisely, but still volunteered by the solicitor that if her client did not take care he might incur serious consequences, which she described. I cannot regard that on any showing as being in preparation for, or in furtherance or as part of, any criminal designs on the part of the plaintiff. I must, therefore, decide which test is correct, and I prefer the narrow view.

First, that appears to me to be the true effect of *R v Cox and Railton*. Counsel for the defendants argued to the contrary and he relies on the passage where Stephen J said ((1884) 14 QBD at 165, [1881–85] All ER Rep at 70):

> 'We must take it, after the verdict of the jury, that so far as the two defendants, Railton and Cox, were concerned, their communication with Mr Goodman was a step preparatory to the commission of a criminal offence, namely, a conspiracy to defraud.'

That passage, he argues, cannot mean that the criminal trial disclosed that they went to see Mr Goodman with an already-formed criminal intention, for that the verdict did not show, and, therefore, the true explanation must be, that the evidence was held rightly admitted because it was relevant to the criminal offence subsequently proved to have been committed. I do not so read it. The court by then knew that a criminal offence had been committed and the evidence which had been admitted showed that criminal purpose existed in the minds of Cox and Railton when they saw Mr Goodman, since ((1884) 14 QBD at 156): 'It was expressly arranged that the partnership should be kept secret'. As I see it, the court having to decide ex post facto whether the evidence had been rightly admitted, inferred that the advice was preparatory to the crime proved, and it will be observed that immediately after the passage in question Stephen J went on to say ((1884) 14 QBD at 165, [1881–85] All ER Rep at 70):

> 'The question, therefore is, whether, if a client applies to a legal adviser for advice intended to facilitate or to guide the client in the commission of a crime or fraud, the legal adviser being ignorant of the purpose for which his advice is wanted, the communication between the two is privileged? We expressed our opinion at the end of the argument that no such privilege existed.'

If relevance alone is the test, it follows that privilege could never be claimed in cases of crime or fraud, except as to communications in connection with the defence. That, in my judgment, is too narrow, and inconsistent with the whole tenor of *R v Cox and Railton*. Stephen J said ((1884) 14 QBD at 166, [1881–85] All ER Rep at 71) that they would first state the principle on which the present case must be decided, then set out in the forefront the nature of the privilege itself and then draw the exception to it in these terms ((1884) 14 QBD at 167, [1881–85] All ER Rep at 76):

> 'The reason on which the rule is said to rest cannot include the case of communications, criminal in themselves, or intended to further any criminal purpose, for the protection of such communications cannot possibly be otherwise than injurious to the interests of justice, and to those of the administration of

justice. Nor do such communications fall within the terms of the rule. A communication in furtherance of a criminal purpose does not 'come into the ordinary scope of professional employment'.'

Further, the relevance test is in my judgment negatived by the conclusions of the court, ((1884) 14 QBD at 175, 176, [1881–85] All ER Rep at 76) and in particular the words:

'We are far from saying that the question whether the advice was taken before or after the offence will always be decisive as to the admissibility of such evidence.'

Secondly, in my judgment all the members of the House of Lords in *O'Rourke v Darbishire* with the possible exception of Lord Wrenbury, clearly adopted the narrower test, and that is binding on me.[18]

However, while a solicitor cannot be compelled to disclose such communications, there may be an option to do so under Comment 3 which provides

A solicitor may reveal confidential information to the extent that he or she believes necessary to prevent the client or a third party committing a criminal act that the solicitor believes on reasonable grounds is likely to result in serious bodily harm.

Note

Having assisted albeit innocently in the laundering of the proceeds of fraud, Finers had an interest in disclosing what they knew in order to minimise the risk that the liquidator and perhaps subsequently a court would conclude (albeit erroneously) that they had known all along about the client's activities. In that case they would have been liable to compensate the victims of the fraud for dishonest assistance in their client's breach of fiduciary duty. Given that fraudsters will often be impecunious and/ or fugitives, their victims may well seek redress against the fraudsters' professional advisers. (CF 'noisy withdrawal' under MR1.6 comment 14 and 15[19]). Such liability attached to accountants running companies as channels for the flow of client funds in *Agip (Africa) v Jackson* [1990] Ch 265; [1991] Ch 547.

Questions

1. You are partner in a large London law firm which specialises inter alia in charities law. You are consulted by Marcus, the chief executive and majority shareholder of Mint Ltd, a wealthy private company. Several years ago Mint set up the Marcus Educational Charitable Trust which makes an educational grant to children from disadvantaged backgrounds so as to enable them to pay their university fees. The trust now has substantial capital assets in the form of share holdings but is heavily dependent on annual contributions from Mint Ltd.

18   Supra at pp 596D-597H.
19   Supra p 268.

Marcus tells you that Mint Ltd is in serious financial trouble and he wants to know if he can borrow money on the security of the Trust's shares to tide Mint over the next few months. Marcus says he has received legal advice from the Trust's regular solicitors that such a transfer would not be a breach of trust because the health of the Trust is dependent on that of the company. Marcus and the other independent trustees are inclined to accept this advice but your research convinces you that a) the transfer would be a breach of trust and b) that criminal prosecution might well follow should the deal go wrong, though the first opinion is likely to make it difficult for the prosecution to establish mens rea. You advise Marcus of this but he tells you that he intends to proceed. What do you do?

2. Your firm specialises in environmental law. Your firm has just been retained by Waxo Ltd, a chemical manufacturer. Waxo asks your firm to do an audit of its main site, to ascertain whether its current mode of operation exposes them to a risk of legal liability. When you conduct the audit you come across internal company documents which reveal that for many years the company has been disposing of waste material by dumping it in a disused mine shaft beneath the site. Your report points out that the dumping of chemicals in this way is clearly contrary to environmental regulations.

You are surprised to receive a letter some weeks later thanking you for your work on the audit and expressing relief at the 'clean bill of health'. When you take this up with Waxo, you are informed 'off the record' that the company has known for years about its breach of regulations but that the cost of making alternative arrangements would be prohibitive. You are concerned because dumping the chemicals in this way will almost certainly damage a nature reserve which borders the plant. You know too that you could easily inform the environmental agency of what is going on at the plant.

Would it be misconduct to inform the regulator? Would it be unethical?

3. Should clients be able to claim privilege for legal consultations following which the client decides to pursue a course of conduct which the lawyer has indicated is criminal or fraudulent?

4. Should lawyers be under a *duty* to warn potential victims of a client's intended crime or fraud enforceable in the event of breach by an action in tort. In *Tarasoff v Regents of the University of California*[20], a psychiatrist was held to owe a duty of care to a person who had been threatened by one of the psychiatrist's patients. It is clear that such a duty would be highly unlikely to arise under current UK tort law. Consider however the material in chapter 4 on regulatory institutions. Is it likely that such a duty could play a useful role in the regulation of lawyers' conduct?

5. The auditors to a number of regulated financial institutions such as insurance companies, banks, building societies and friendly societies owe a duty to report

20   17 Cal 3d 425 (1976) 133.

irregularities in the running of these institutions to the industry regulator.[1] Does the existence of such duties count as an argument for or against the imposition of similar duties on lawyers?

6. Stuart is an in-house lawyer advising a large car manufacturing company. He is consulted by the product development director about whether the company would be negligent in putting on the market its new Mark 7 Sports Car even though the design department are concerned that it is highly likely to explode after any significant impact. Stuart advises that this would be negligent but his advice is rejected by the product development director. What should Stuart do? What is/should be the significance of whether in these circumstances the state would be able to gather enough evidence to mount a criminal prosecution for manslaughter should a death occur?

7. Does it make any difference to Stuart's position if he is convinced that the directors judgment is clearly contrary to the interests of the company (the potential liability costs are enormous) and that the director's judgment has been skewed by the pressure s/he feels personally to produce a new product?

8. What is the problem peculiar to the corporate setting which is being addressed by MR 1.13 [2] (which has no equivalent under the LSGPC) ? Would this rule have been better dealt with by an earlier draft of MR 1.13 which read

> 1.13(c) When the organisation's highest authority insists upon action, or refusal to take action, that is clearly a violation of a legal obligation to the organisation, or a violation of law which might be imputed to the organisation, and is likely to result in substantial injury to the organisation, the lawyer may take further remedial action that the lawyer reasonably believes to be in the best interests of the organisation. Such action may include revealing information otherwise protected by Rule 1.6 only if the lawyer reasonably believes that:
> (1) the highest authority in the organisation has acted to the personal or financial interests of members of that authority which are in conflict with the interest of the organisation: and
> (2) revealing the information is necessary in the best interests of the organisation.

5   The equitable duty of confidence

It is important to consider the scope of the protection afforded to confidential information by the general law. To the extent that the general law takes greater account of the need to prevent harm to others or to the legal system, it raises questions about whether the position taken by the professional codes is justifiable. Moreover, the general law will determine the extent to which a lawyer may be liable in damages for disclosing

---

1   See the statutory instruments cited in Y Cripps *The Legal Implications of Disclosure in the Public Interest* (London, Sweet & Maxwell, 2nd ed, 1994) p 94.
2   Set out in the appendix to this chapter.

confidential information. In addition, doubts about the enforceability of professional codes make it arguable that the general equitable duty of confidentiality is in reality a much more significant restraint on the disclosure by lawyers of client confidences.

Save where the plaintiff is a public body (in which case the plaintiff must show that confidentiality would be in the public interest), the courts will usually restrain unauthorised disclosures of confidential information by awarding an injunction. However, there is an exception to this general rule where disclosure is in the public interest. Most reported instances of the Courts refusing to restrain disclosure have involved the disclosure of criminal or other forms of misconduct. Nevertheless, it is clear that the exception is broader than this. In *Fraser v Evans* for example, Lord Denning stated that

> No person is permitted to divulge to the world information which he has received in confidence, *unless he has just cause or excuse for doing so*.[3] [Emphasis added]

In *Lion Laboratories v Evans*[4], the plaintiff was a company seeking to prevent the disclosure by two former employees of evidence that its scientists had doubts about the accuracy of a device it was currently supplying to the police for measuring the levels of alcohol in motorists' blood. The Court of Appeal refused to grant an injunction. Even though the plaintiff was not committing any legally recognised wrong, the prospect that, in the absence of disclosure, innocent motorists would be convicted meant that there was a 'just cause or excuse' for disclosure.

Whilst the exact limits of the public interest defence are not clear, it seems that information which is privileged may nevertheless be discloseable on this basis. Indeed, prior to the case of *Butler v Department of Trade and Industry* it was thought that the Court of Appeal had decided in *Calcraft v Guest*[5] that once privileged documents came into the hands of third parties secondary evidence of them could always be given in court proceedings. It was not argued in *Calcraft v Guest* that the equitable duty of confidence could be invoked to protect the client. In *Butler*, Goff J, having held that the information was privileged[6], continued:

> There remains, however, the final question whether the law or equity as to breach of confidence operates in the terms of para 14 of the special case to give the plaintiff—
>
>> 'any equity to prevent the Defendants from tendering a copy of the letter in evidence in any of the said criminal proceedings'
>
> where, if tendered it would, as I see it, clearly be admissible: see *Calcraft v Guest* ([1898] 1 QB 759 at 764, [1895–99] All ER Rep 346 at 349), subject of course to the overriding discretion of the trial court to reject it if it thought its use unfair. The plaintiff relies on the decision of the Court of Appeal in *Lord Ashburton v Pape*, where, a party to certain bankruptcy proceedings having by a trick obtained a copy of a privileged letter, Neville J granted an injunction restraining him and his solicitors from publishing or making use of it, save for the purposes of those proceedings, and the Court of Appeal varied the order by striking out the exception, so that the injunction was unqualified. . .

3   [1969] 1 QB 349 at 361B-C.
4   [1984] 3 WLR 539, CA.
5   [1898] 1 QB 759.
6   Supra text to note 18.

In the present case there was no impropriety on the part of the defendants in the way in which they received the copy, but that, in my judgment, is irrelevant because an innocent recipient of information conveyed in breach of confidence is liable to be restrained. I wish to make it clear that there is no suggestion of any kind of moral obliquity on the part of the solicitors, but the disclosure was in law a breach of confidence. Nevertheless, that case does differ from the present in an important particular, namely that the defendants are a department of the Crown and intend to use the copy letter in a public prosecution brought by them. As far as I am aware, there is no case directly in point on the question whether that is merely an immaterial difference of fact or a valid distinction, but in my judgment it is the latter because in such a case there are two conflicting principles, the private right of the individual and the interest of the State to apprehend and prosecute criminals: see per Lord Denning MR in *Chic Fashions (West Wales) Ltd v Jones* ([1968] 1 All ER 229 at 236, [1968] 2 QB 299 at 313) and in *Ghani v Jones* ([1969] 3 All ER 1700 at 1704, 1705, [1970] 1 QB 693 at 708).

In my judgment it would not be a right or permissible exercise of the equitable jurisdiction in confidence to make a declaration at the suit of the accused in a public prosecution in effect restraining the Crown from adducing admissible evidence relevant to the crime with which he is charged. It is not necessary for me to decide whether the same result would obtain in the case of a private prosecution, and I expressly leave that point open.[7]

Thus Goff J held that in principle the equitable duty of confidence could be relied upon to restrain the unauthorised use of privileged documents but held that even in the case of privileged documents the court would refuse to exercise the equitable jurisdiction where the documents had come into the hands of a prosecutor. The position seems to be that:

Protection [is] given as an exercise of the Court's discretion. Whether the unauthorised use of confidential information or of confidential documents will be restrained is essentially discretionary and must, in my opinion, be dependent on the particular circumstances of the particular case. The privileged nature of the document is bound to be a highly material factor but would not in my view, exclude from the scales other material factors.[8]

Notes

1. Lawyers contemplating disclosure should note that the courts have tended to look with less favour upon disclosure to the press than to regulatory bodies[9]. In *Initial Services* v *Puterill,* Lord Denning commented that:

---

7   Ibid at pp 599C–600A.
8   *Webster v James Chapman &Co A Firm* [1989] 3 All ER 939 at 945H-J per Scott J. For a contrary view see *Derby v Weldon (No 8)* [1991] 1 WLR 73 where Vinelott J held that absent a waiver of privilege the court would always grant an injunction to prevent the threatened use of a privileged document in legal proceedings. See also the judgment of Nourse LJ in *Goddard v Nationwide Building Society* [1987] QB 670.
9   See also *Re a Company Application* [1989] 3 WLR 265 per Scott J with respect to the disclosure of corporate malpractice to FIMBRA and the IRC.

> The disclosure must, I think be to one who has a proper interest to receive the information. Thus it would be proper to disclose a crime to the police; or a breach of the Restrictive Trade Practices Act to the Registrar. There may be cases where the misdeed is of such a character that the public interest may demand, or at least excuse, publication on a broader field, even to the press.[10]

Similarly, the courts tend to look with less favour on paid rather than gratuitous disclosure on the basis that disclosure which is truly in the public interest should be gratuitous.

2. Analogous issues arise in relation to documents disclosed during the discovery process. Such documents are not (ex hypothesi) privileged but they are protected by an obligation which though described as an 'implied undertaking' is in reality imposed by the court. In effect, a party receiving documents through the discovery process is obliged not to use the documents for any purpose ulterior to the litigation (until the documents have been read out in open court). Breach of this undertaking is a contempt of court and may be punishable by a fine or imprisonment. The purpose of the undertaking is to protect the disclosing party's confidentiality and hence it has been accepted that in principle the public interest exception might make the undertaking inapplicable. Nevertheless, the courts have been reluctant in practice to accept that documents disclosed pursuant to discovery may legitimately be used for some other purpose. This was illustrated by the case of *Distillers v Times Newspapers*[11]. Distillers had been sued by a group of Thalidomide victims for negligence, the actions being subsequently settled with all allegations of negligence being withdrawn. Other writs were then issued. Distillers had disclosed documents to the victims in the settled actions which their solicitors had passed to an expert for the purposes of preparing an experts report. Following the settlement of the action, the expert sold the documents to a journalist working for Times Newspapers who proposed to write a newspaper article about the Thalidomide tragedy based on these documents. Talbot J issued an injunction restraining the journalist from making use of the documents on the grounds that any public interest in an informed discussion of the Thalidomide tragedy was outweighed by Distiller's interest in the confidentiality of it's documents and the public interest in maintaining the integrity of the discovery process. This decision reflects a judicial preference for the trial of disputes by courts not by the media. The decision would have been different if the documents had been read out or referred to in open court because they would then no longer be confidential.

Questions

1. **Sarah's Case**: Herbert is consulted by Sarah about whether a particular transaction will legitimately avoid liability to tax. Herbert advises, correctly, that the transaction

---

10   [1968] 1 QB 396 at 405.
11   [1974] 3 WLR 728.

will involve tax liability whereupon Sarah states that she intends nevertheless to proceed because 'the revenue are unlikely to find out and I'm certainly not about to tell them' Herbert is troubled and asks you for advice. Does it make any difference to your advice whether Herbert is a lawyer or an accountant? Should it? What are the implications of any difference for the market for professional services?

2. One of the undisputable features of the legal landscape in the last two decades of the 20th century was the tendency of law firms to grow in size, with the consequence that many more solicitors than previously were likely to be employees rather than partners.[12] What sort of influence are these developments likely to have upon lawyers' willingness to disclose?[13]

6   Lawyers and whistleblowing

Information is sometimes discovered in the workplace such that disclosure is at least arguably in the public interest.[14] Yet the desire to avoid retaliatory action by an employer is a powerful disincentive to 'blowing the whistle'. This emphasises the importance of the legal issues relating to whistleblowing. Widespread recognition of the public importance of the issues involved in disclosing misconduct in the workplace led to the passing of the Public Interest Disclosure Act 1998. Broadly speaking, the Act protects employees who disclose in an appropriate manner information which tends to show one or more of the following:

(a)   that a criminal offence has been committed, is being committed or is likely to be committed,

(b)   that a person has failed, is failing or is likely to fail to comply with any legal obligation to which he is subject,

(c)   that a miscarriage of justice has occurred, is occurring or is likely to occur,

(d)   that the health of any individual has been, is being or is likely to be endangered,

(e)   that the environment has been, is being or is likely to be damaged,

(f)   that information tending to show any matter falling within any one of the preceding paragraphs has been, is being, or is likely to be deliberately concealed.[15]

Any employee who is victimised by his employer for making such a disclosure may complain to an industrial tribunal which has power to award compensation. Dismissal which is motivated wholly or principally by the fact that the employee has made such

---

12   According to Professor Richard Abel, there were no firms in the 1960s having more than 20 principals. By 1977, there were 25 such firms and by 1985 there were 66 (*Legal Profession in England and Wales* (Oxford, Blackwell, 1989) at p 202).

13   See further Richard Painter 'Towards a market for Lawyer Disclosure Services: In Search of Optimal Whistleblowing Rules' (1995) 63 George Washington Law Review 221.

14   See generally, Yvonne Cripps *The Legal Implications of Disclosure in a the Public Interest* (London, Sweet & Maxwell, 2nd ed, 1994) pp 7-16.

15   Section 43A of the Employment Rights Act 1996 as inserted by the Public Interest Disclosure Act 1998.

a disclosure will automatically count as an unfair dismissal[16], for which unlimited compensation is available.[17] Generally speaking, disclosure will only be regarded as made appropriately if it is made in accordance with an employer's internal procedures or to an industry regulator authorised by statutory instrument to receive such disclosures. Other disclosures are given more limited protection, the basic requirements being either that internal/regulatory disclosure has been ineffective; or that the employee reasonably fears victimisation if disclosure is made to the regulator; or that wider disclosure is necessary to prevent a cover-up.

There is clearly much to be said for these provisions in general terms. With regard to lawyers, however, matters are very different: disclosure of a communication subject to legal professional privilege is excluded from the protection of the Act.[18] Accordingly those who regard legal professional privilege as paying insufficient regard to third party interests will find the act disappointing.

Given the limitations of the Public Interest Disclosure Act, anonymous disclosure is likely to remain attractive to potential whistleblowers. This raises different questions for lawyers according to their role in the drama. Firstly, lawyers may be asked to advise clients considering blowing the whistle upon their employer. Indeed widespread concern about the position of whistleblowers has led to the founding of a charity Public Concern at Work, staffed partly by lawyers to provide advice and support to potential whistleblowers. Concerns about retaliatory action may lead the client to ask the lawyer to disclose anonymously on the client's behalf. Unfortunately, no English court has held that the client's identity is privileged.[19] Hence, a lawyer is principally subject to the courts' jurisdiction[20] to order disclosure of the identity of a wrongdoer. The victim of any wrong including breach of confidence can bring an action against a third party who knows the identity of the wrongdoer in order to compel disclosure. The starting point is that disclosure will never be ordered if the third party shows that the information disclosed was within the public interest exception to the duty of confidentiality[1]. Even if this is not so, however, the court has a discretion whether or not to grant relief which recognises a public interest in protecting the identity of a person who provided information on an anonymous basis, perhaps in the mistaken belief that the public interest exception to the duty of confidence applied. This has to be weighed against considerations such as any damage to national security, the prevention of crime or, more generally, the interests of justice which would follow from not ordering disclosure of the whistleblower's identity. Indeed the passing of the Public Interest Disclosure Act may make it more likely that disclosure will be ordered since a court may take the

---

16   Ibid, s 103(A).

17   The Public Interest Disclosure (Compensation) Regulations 1999 SI 1999/1548, remove the limit on compensation previously contained in s 4 of the Public Interest Disclosure Act.

18   Section 43B(4) of the Employment Rights Act 1996.

19   The contrary is normally thought to be established by a number of authorities eg *Bursill v Tanner* (1865) 16QBD 1. See *Cross and Tapper on Evidence* (8th ed, 1995) 473. However it has been convincingly argued (see Morrick (1980) 124 Sol Jo 303) that these cases have no application when the client asks for anonymity in order to facilitate a public interest disclosure. The argument has been accepted in New Zealand: see *Police v Mills* [1993] 2 NZLR 592.

20   *Norwich Pharmacal v Customs & Excise* [1974] AC 133.

1   *Secretary of State for Defence v Guardian Newspapers* [1984] 3 WLR 986 at 991.

view that since Parliament has defined when disclosure is in the public interest and provided protection in such cases a deserving whistleblower has nothing to fear from disclosure, whereas an undeserving whistleblower should be exposed. For this reason, the client might well be advised to make disclosure to a journalist on the basis that s 10 of the Contempt of Court Act 1981 provides special protection for the anonymity of journalists' sources, the extent of which is considered below.

Given the exclusion of privileged communications from the protection of the Public Interest Disclosure Act, anonymous disclosure may be particularly attractive for lawyers who are themselves considering blowing the whistle. Like their clients, lawyers are more likely to remain anonymous if they disclose to journalists. Section 10 of the Contempt of Court Act 1981 which was intended to create a presumption against disclosure of a journalist's sources provides:

> No court may require a person to disclose, nor is any person guilty of contempt of Court for refusing to disclose, the source of information contained in a publication for which he is responsible, unless it be established to the satisfaction of the Court that disclosure is necessary in the interests of justice or national security or for the prevention of disorder or crime.

It is perhaps not surprising that disclosure can be ordered when it is really necessary to prevent damage to national security or to prevent crime. The breadth of the protection provided by s 10 depends crucially on when disclosure is likely to be held to be in the interests of justice. Disclosure has on several occasions been ordered on this ground if it is the only way the person seeking it can establish a defence to a criminal charge. This would need to be borne in mind by a lawyer contemplating a disclosure which might lead to prosecution but, again, it is not surprising that the interests of justice includes the accused's interest in access to witnesses. More surprising however was the decision of the House of Lords in *X Ltd v Morgan Grampian (Publishers Ltd)*[2]. The plaintiffs (X) were small private companies who were planning to refinance their operations. Details of these plans were contained in a number of binders, one of which was stolen from an unlocked office. Goodwin was a trainee journalist working for a publication called *The Engineer*. A day or two after the theft, he received a call from a source disclosing certain information which it was accepted must have come from the stolen files. Goodwin proposed to write a story about the companies' plans and rang X to check some of the information. In response, X sought and obtained an interlocutory injunction restraining publication of its confidential information.

X then sought disclosure of the source. The managing director testified that it feared further disclosures, the effect of which would be to jeopardise its restructuring plans and consequently the future of the companies. In the House of Lords, their Lordships inferred, perhaps questionably, that the only motive for the disclosures could have been malice or a desire to further Goodwin's career, and denied that there might be any public interest in disclosure. Might not the source have genuinely believed

---

2   [1990] 2 WLR 1000 HL, cf *Secretary of State for Defence v Guardian Newspapers* [1984] 3 WLR 986 though since that case involved national security the legitimation of the plaintiff's desire to dismiss the mole is perhaps less surprising.

that there was a public interest in knowing that an apparently thriving company had financial problems?

The question before the House of Lords was whether the trial judge had been correct in ordering disclosure. The House of Lords unanimously affirmed the decision to order disclosure. It was held that contrary to the dicta of Lord Diplock in *Secretary of State v Guardian Newspaper*[3] 'the interests of justice' in s 10 did not refer to the administration of justice in the course of legal proceedings. The interests of justice was a broader concept which included the consideration:

> ...that persons should be enabled to exercise important legal rights and to protect themselves from serious legal wrongs whether or not resort to legal proceedings will be necessary to obtain these objectives. Thus *to take a very obvious example, if an employer of a large staff is suffering grave damage from the activities of an unidentified disloyal servant, it is undoubtedly in the interests of justice that he should be able to identify him in order to terminate his contract of employment, notwithstanding that no legal proceedings may be necessary in order to achieve that end.*[4]

Once the plaintiff established that disclosure was necessary for the protection of such an interest, disclosure did not automatically follow. The interests of justice required that disclosure had to be balanced against the public interest in the protection of journalists' sources. A number of factors could be added to either side of the balance. Any public interest in the information given to the journalist and the fact, if such it was, that the information was obtained from the plaintiff in an honourable manner pointed in favour of anonymity[5]. The seriousness of any damage which might follow to the plaintiff from continued anonymity and any reprehensible features of the mole's conduct pointed in the opposite direction[6]. In this case, the mole's identity should be disclosed because of the severity of the potential damage which might arise from further leaks, viz destruction of an economic concern and the lack of any public interest in disclosure of the information. In addition, the source had behaved reprehensibly.

However, on Goodwin's application to the European Court of Human Rights[7], it was held that the decision of the UK court violated Goodwin's right to freedom of expression under Art 10 of the European Convention on Human Rights. It was noted that whilst freedom of expression could be limited in order to protect the rights of others, the confidentiality of journalists sources was of such importance to freedom of expression that any restrictions should be as limited as possible. In this case, the fact that the injunction was effective to prevent further publication through the press made the chances of further breach of confidence so small as to make disclosure of the source unjustified. The implications of this decision are that if the mole discloses to a journalist who informs the employer, giving the employer a chance to seek an injunction, then one of two results will usually follow. Either the court will find that the information

3   Supra note 2.
4   Lord Bridge AC pp 43F-H.
5   Ibid, 44F-G.
6   Ibid, 44D.
7   *Goodwin v UK* [1996] 22 EHRR 123.

is disclosable under the public interest exception to the law of confidence. Or it will hold the contrary, and hence issue an injunction. If so, however, the reasoning of the ECHR in Goodwin suggests that the issuing of the injunction will undermine the argument for disclosure of the source.

In *Saunders v Punch*[8], where the mole may well have been a lawyer, the protection which this line of argument offers to whistleblowers was amply demonstrated. Punch published an article which suggested that Saunders was deliberately delaying publication of an official inquiry into the Guinness affair in order to pre-empt criticisms of him which might damage his prospects of employment as a consultant. The article claimed to be based on documents which recorded conversations between Saunders and his solicitors which were privileged. Punch did not resist Saunders' application for an interlocutory injunction restraining publication of his conversations with his solicitor. Indeed, Punch submitted to an injunction even though the judge thought that it was arguably in the public interest for it to be known that Saunders' objections to the publication of the report were in fact motivated by his desire to protect his earning power.[9] Saunders then sought but failed to obtain an order for disclosure of Punch's sources. In a judgment imbued with the spirit of the ECHR decision in *Goodwin*, Lindsay J held that Saunders' interests were effectively protected by the grant of an injunction.

Questions

1. The exclusion of privileged communications from the Public Interest Disclosure Act may be explained by the desire to encourage potential whistleblowers to seek legal advice. Such an interpretation is supported by the fact that communications with a lawyer for the purpose of obtaining legal advice are given protection equivalent to that afforded to disclosures in accordance with employers' internal procedures[10]. Does this concern justify the exclusion of privileged communications from the protection otherwise given by the Act?

2. Does the fact many other classes of employee are given protection and therefore enabled to blow the whistle reduce the need for lawyers to be given equivalent protection?

3. Do you wish to add anything to your advice to Stuart, the in-house lawyer to the sports car manufacturer (question 6 page 290 supra)?

---

8   [1998] 1 All ER 281.
9   The explanation may be that Punch took the view that satisfying the burden of proof as to the application of the public interest exception would itself involve disclosure of the source.
i0 Section 43D of the Employment Rights Act 1996.

Appendix : Anglo-American Confidentiality Provisions

THE LAW SOCIETY'S GUIDE TO THE PROFESSIONAL CONDUCT OF
SOLICITORS[11]

16.01 General duty of confidentiality

A solicitor is under a duty to keep confidential to his or her firm the affairs of clients
and to ensure that the staff do the same.

1. It is important to bear in mind the distinction between the duty to keep client
    affairs confidential and the concept of law known as legal professional privilege.
    The duty in conduct extends to all matters communicated to a solicitor by the
    client or on behalf of the client, save as mentioned in 16.02, 16.03 and 16.07[12].
    Legal professional privilege protects communications between a client and solicitor
    from being disclosed, even in a court of law. Certain communications, however,
    are not protected by legal professional privilege and reference should be made to
    an appropriate authority on the law of evidence. Non-privileged communications
    remain subject to the solicitor's duty to keep the client's affairs confidential.

2. Disclosure of a client's confidences which is unauthorised by the client or by the
    law could lead to disciplinary proceedings against a solicitor and could also render
    a solicitor liable, in certain circumstances, to a civil action by the client arising out
    of the misuse of confidential information.

3. The duty of confidentiality applies to information about a client's affairs irrespective
    of the source of the information...

4. A solicitor who acquires information on behalf of a prospective client may be
    bound by the duty of confidentiality even if there is no subsequent retainer at law.

5. Information given to the solicitor in the context of a joint retainer must be available
    between the clients; they must however all consent to a waiver of the duty of
    confidentiality before that information may be disclosed to a third party. However,
    information communicated to the solicitor in the capacity of solicitor for only
    one of the clients in relation to a separate matter must not be disclosed to the
    other clients without the consent of that client.

6. Where firms amalgamate, information which each firm has obtained when acting
    for its clients will pass to the new firm as a result of any express or implied retainer
    of the new firm, and conflicts of interest could arise from the competing duties of
    confidentiality and disclosure.

16.02 Circumstances which override confidentiality

The duty to keep a client's confidences can be overridden in certain exceptional
circumstances.

1. The duty of confidentiality does not apply to information acquired by a solicitor
    where he or she is being used by the client to facilitate the commission of a crime
    or fraud, because that is not within the scope of a professional retainer. If the

---

11   8th ed London, Law Society, 1999 at 324-327; 331-333. For the very brief provision of the
     CCB on this topic see note 9 supra.
12   This provision which deals with money laundering is not set out here. It is summarised supra
     text to p 257 note 16.

solicitor becomes suspicious about a client's activities the solicitor should normally assess the situation in the light of the client's explanations and the solicitor's professional judgement.

2. Express consent by a client to disclosure of information relating to his or her affairs overrides any duty of confidentiality, as does consent by the personal representatives of a deceased client.

3. A solicitor may reveal confidential information to the extent that he or she believes necessary to prevent the client or a third party committing a criminal act that the solicitor believes on reasonable grounds is likely to result in serious bodily harm.

4. There may be exceptional circumstances involving children where a solicitor should consider revealing confidential information to an appropriate authority. This may be where the child is the client and the child reveals information which indicates continuing sexual or other physical abuse but refuses to allow disclosure of such information. Similarly, there may be situations where an adult discloses abuse either by himself or herself or by another adult against a child but refuses to allow any disclosure. The solicitor must consider whether the threat to the child's life or health, both mental and physical, is sufficiently serious to justify a breach of the duty of confidentiality.

5. In proceedings under the Children Act 1989 solicitors are under a duty to reveal experts reports commissioned for the purposes of proceedings, as these reports are not privileged. The position in relation to other documents or solicitor/client communications is uncertain. Clearly advocates are under a duty not to mislead the court (see 21.01). Therefore, if an advocate has certain knowledge which he or she realises is adverse to the client's case, the solicitor may be extremely limited in what can be stated in the client's favour. In this situation, the solicitor should seek the client's agreement for full voluntary disclosure for three reasons:
    (i)   the matters the client wants to hide will probably emerge anyway;
    (ii) the solicitor will be able to do a better job for the client if all the information is presented to the Court.
    (iii) if the information is not voluntarily disclosed, the solicitor may be severely criticised by the Courts.
    If the client refuses to give the solicitors authority to disclose the relevant information, the solicitor is entitled to refuse to continue to act for the client if to do so will place the solicitor in breach of his or her professional obligations to the court.

6. A solicitor should reveal matters which are otherwise subject to the duty to preserve confidentiality where a court orders that such matters are to be disclosed or where a warrant permits a police officer or other authority to seize confidential documents. If a solicitor is of the opinion that the documents are subject to legal privilege or that for some other reason the order or warrant ought not to have been made or issued, he or she without unlawfully obstructing its execution should normally discuss with the client the possibility of making an application to have the order or warrant set aside. Advice may be obtained from the Professional Adviser.[13]

8. Occasionally a solicitor is asked by the police or a third party to give information or to show them documents which the solicitor has obtained when acting for a

---

13 The Law Society runs a 'hotline' which practising solicitors can use to obtain confidential advice in relation to problems of conduct and ethics.

client. Unless the client is prepared to waive confidentiality, or where the solicitor has strong *prima facie* evidence that he or she has been used by the client to perpetrate a fraud or other crime and the duty of confidence does not arise, the solicitor should insist upon receiving a witness summons or subpoena so that, where appropriate, privilege may be claimed and the court asked to decide the issue. If the request is made by the police under the Police and Criminal Evidence Act 1984 the solicitor should, where appropriate, leave the question of privilege to the court to decide on the particular circumstances.

...

11. In the case of a legally aided client, a solicitor may be under a duty to report to the Legal Aid Board information concerning the client which is confidential and privileged. See regulations 67 and 70 of the Civil Legal Aid (General) Regulations 1989, regulation 56 of the Legal Aid in Criminal and Care Proceedings (General) Regulations 1989...

12. A solicitor may reveal confidential information concerning a client to the extent that it is reasonably necessary to establish a defence to a criminal charge or civil claim by the client against the solicitor or where the solicitor's conduct is under investigation by the Office for the Supervision of Solicitors or under consideration by the Solicitors' Disciplinary Tribunal.

16.05 Duty not to profit

A solicitor must not make any profit by the use of confidential information for his or her own purposes.

1. In such circumstances a solicitor may be liable to civil action by the client in an action for account and could also be liable to disciplinary proceedings or, in some cases, criminal proceedings...

16.06 Duty to disclose all relevant information to client

A solicitor is usually under a duty to pass on to the client and use all information which is material to the client's business regardless of the source of that information. There are, however, exceptional circumstances where this duty does not apply.

1. A breach of this duty may be actionable in law and might involve the solicitor in disciplinary action.

2. Some provisions in the money laundering legislation effectively prohibit solicitors from passing on information to clients in certain circumstances. ...

3. In general terms, since the solicitor is the agent of the client, all information coming into his or her possession relating to the client's affairs must be disclosed to the client. Consequently, it is undesirable that a solicitor should seek to pass on to the solicitor on the other side information which is not to be disclosed to the other side's client. Equally, the recipient should decline to accept or receive confidential information on the basis that it will not be disclosed. If a confidential letter is written to the solicitor on the other side, the writer cannot insist on the letter not being shown to the client. When offered information from another solicitor, or any other source, which the solicitor is asked to treat as confidential and not to disclose to the client, the solicitor should consider carefully before accepting such confidential information.

4. There might, however, be certain circumstances where the imparting to the client

of information received by the solicitor could be harmful to the client because it will affect the client's mental or physical condition. Consequently, it will be necessary for a solicitor to decide whether to disclose such information to the client, eg a medical report disclosing a terminal illness.

5.   Generally, a solicitor should not seek, or encourage a client to obtain access to, or information from private confidential correspondence or documents belonging to or intended for the other side. This includes not opening or reading letters addressed to someone other than himself or herself or the firm. If, however, the contents of such documents otherwise come to the solicitor's knowledge (and other than in circumstances described in note 6… below), the solicitor is entitled, and may have a duty, to use the information for the benefit of the client. The intention to do so should, however, be disclosed to the other side.

6.   Where it is obvious that privileged documents have been mistakenly disclosed to a solicitor on discovery or otherwise, the solicitor should immediately cease to read the documents, inform the other side and return the documents. The solicitor may tell the client what has happened. As to the use of privileged documentation and possible repercussions as to costs should injunctions be necessary, see any text on the law of evidence. See also *English and American Insurance Company Ltd v Herbert Smith* [1988] FSR 232 and *Ablitt v Mills and Reeve, The Times,* 25th October 1995 for cases where counsel's papers have accidentally been sent to the wrong side.

8.   Where a solicitor acts for two or more clients on related matters, a conflict may arise between the duty of disclosure owed to a client under one retainer and the duty of confidentiality owed to a client under another retainer. For example, a solicitor acting for borrower and lender in the same transaction has two separate retainers and if the borrower does not consent to relevant but confidential facts being brought to the attention of the lender, the solicitor must honour the duty of confidentiality to the borrower. Should that situation arise, however, the solicitor will be faced with a conflict of interests and must cease to act for the lender and probably also the borrower .

THE ABA MODEL RULES OF PROFESSIONAL CONDUCT [14]

Rule 1.6 Confidentiality of Information

(a)   A lawyer shall not reveal information relating to representation of a client unless the client consents after consultation, except for disclosures that are impliedly authorised in order to carry out the representation, and except as stated in paragraph (b).

(b)   A lawyer may reveal such information to the extent the lawyer reasonably believes necessary:

(1)   to prevent the client from committing a criminal act that the lawyer believes is likely to result in imminent death or substantial bodily harm; or

(2)   to establish a claim or defence on behalf of the lawyer in a controversy between the lawyer and the client, to establish a defence to a criminal charge or civil claim

---

14   2000, Selected Standards on Professional Responsibility, Thomas D Morgan and Ronald D Rotunda eds (Foundation Press, New York, 2000) at 18-22; 40-41; 62 and 76.

against the lawyer based upon conduct in which the client was involved, or to respond to allegations in any proceeding concerning the lawyer's representation of the client.

Comment:

[1] The lawyer is part of a judicial system charged with upholding the law. One of the lawyer's functions is to advise clients so that they avoid any violation of the law in the proper exercise of their rights.

[2] The observance of the ethical obligation of a lawyer to hold inviolate confidential information of the client not only facilitates the full development of facts essential to proper representation of the client but also encourages people to seek early legal assistance.

[3] Almost without exception, clients come to lawyers in order to determine what their rights are and what is, in the maze of laws and regulations, deemed to be legal and correct. The common law recognises that the client's confidences must be protected from disclosure. Based upon experience, lawyers know that almost all clients follow the advice given, and the law is upheld.

[4] A fundamental principle in the client-lawyer relationship is that the lawyer maintain confidentiality of information relating to the representation. The client is thereby encouraged to communicate fully and frankly with the lawyer even as to embarrassing or legally damaging subject matter.

[5] The principle of confidentiality is given effect in two related bodies of law, the attorney-client privilege (which includes the work product doctrine) in the law of evidence and the rule of confidentiality established in professional ethics. The attorney-client privilege applies in judicial and other proceedings in which a lawyer may be called as a witness or otherwise required to produce evidence concerning a client. The rule of client-lawyer confidentiality applies in situations other than those where evidence is sought from the lawyer through compulsion of law. The confidentiality rule applies not merely to matters communicated in confidence by the client but also to all information relating to the representation, whatever its source. A lawyer may not disclose such information except as authorised or required by the Rules of Professional Conduct or other law.

[6] The requirement of maintaining confidentiality of information relating to representation applies to government lawyers who may disagree with the policy goals that their representation is designed to advance.

Authorised Disclosure

[7] A lawyer is impliedly authorised to make disclosures about a client when appropriate in carrying out the representation, except to the extent that the client's instructions or special circumstances limit that authority. In litigation, for example, a lawyer may disclose information by admitting a fact that cannot properly be disputed, or in negotiation by making a disclosure that facilitates a satisfactory conclusion.

[8] Lawyers in a firm may, in the course of the firm's practice, disclose to each other information relating to a client of the firm, unless the client has instructed that particular information be confined to specified lawyers.

DISCLOSURE ADVERSE TO CLIENT

[9] The confidentiality rule is subject to limited exceptions. In becoming privy to information about a client, a lawyer may foresee that the client intends serious harm to another person. However, to the extent a lawyer is required or permitted to disclose a client's purposes, the client will be inhibited from revealing facts which would enable the lawyer to counsel against a wrongful course of action. The public is better protected if full and open communication by the client is encouraged than if it is inhibited.

[10] Several situations must be distinguished.

[11] First, the lawyer may not counsel or assist a client in conduct that is criminal or fraudulent. See Rule 1.2(d). Similarly, a lawyer has a duty under Rule 3.3(a)(4) not to use false evidence. This duty is essentially a special instance of the duty prescribed in Rule 1.2(d) to avoid assisting a client in criminal or fraudulent conduct.

[12] Second, the lawyer may have been innocently involved in past conduct by the client that was criminal or fraudulent. In such a situation the lawyer has not violated Rule 1.2(d), because to 'counsel or assist' criminal or fraudulent conduct requires knowing that the conduct is of that character.

[13] Third, the lawyer may learn that a client intends prospective conduct that is criminal and likely to result in imminent death or substantial bodily harm. As stated in paragraph (b)(1), the lawyer has professional discretion to reveal information in order to prevent such consequences. The lawyer may make a disclosure in order to prevent homicide or serious bodily injury which the lawyer reasonably believes is intended by a client. It is very difficult for a lawyer to 'know' when such a heinous purpose will actually be carried out, for the client may have a change of mind.

[14] The lawyer's exercise of discretion requires consideration of such factors as the nature of the lawyer's relationship with the client and with those who might be injured by the client, the lawyer's own involvement in the transaction and factors that may extenuate the conduct in question. Where practical, the lawyer should seek to persuade the client to take suitable action. In any case, a disclosure adverse to the client's interest should be no greater than the lawyer reasonably believes necessary to the purpose. A lawyer's decision not to take preventive action permitted by paragraph (b)(1) does not violate this Rule.

WITHDRAWAL

[15] If the lawyer's services will be used by the client in materially furthering a course of criminal or fraudulent conduct, the lawyer must withdraw, as stated in Rule 1.16(a)(1).

[16] After withdrawal the lawyer is required to refrain from making disclosure of the clients' confidences, except as otherwise provided in Rule 1.6. Neither this Rule nor Rule 1.8(b) nor Rule 1.16(d) prevents the lawyer from giving notice of the fact of withdrawal, and the lawyer may also withdraw or disaffirm any opinion, document, affirmation, or the like.

[17] Where the client is an organisation, the lawyer may be in doubt whether contemplated conduct will actually be carried out by the organisation. Where necessary to guide conduct in connection with this Rule, the lawyer may make inquiry within the organisation...

Dispute Concerning Lawyer's Conduct

[18] Where a legal claim or disciplinary charge alleges complicity of the lawyer in a client's conduct or other misconduct of the lawyer involving representation of the client, the lawyer may respond to the extent the lawyer reasonably believes necessary to establish a defence. The same is true with respect to a claim involving the conduct or representation of a former client. The lawyer's right to respond arises when an assertion of such complicity has been made. Paragraph (b)(2) does not require the lawyer to await the commencement of an action or proceeding that charges such complicity, so that the defence may be established by responding directly to a third party who has made such an assertion. The right to defend, of course, applies where a proceeding has been commenced. Where practicable and not prejudicial to the lawyer's ability to establish the defence, the lawyer should advise the client of the third party's assertion and request that the client respond appropriately. In any event, disclosure should be no greater than the lawyer reasonably believes is necessary to vindicate innocence, the disclosure should be made in a manner which limits access to the information to the tribunal or other persons having a need to know it, and appropriate protective orders, or other arrangements should be sought by the lawyer to the fullest extent practicable.

[19] If the lawyer is charged with wrongdoing in which the client's conduct is implicated, the rule of confidentiality should not prevent the lawyer from defending against the charge. Such a charge can arise in a civil, criminal or professional disciplinary proceeding, and can be based on a wrong allegedly committed by the lawyer against the client, or on a wrong alleged by a third person; for example a person claiming to have been defrauded by the lawyer and client acting together. A lawyer entitled to a fee is permitted by paragraph (b)(2) to prove the services rendered in an action to collect it. This aspect of the rule expresses the principle that the beneficiary of a fiduciary relationship may not exploit it to the detriment of the fiduciary. As stated above, the lawyer must make every effort practicable to avoid unnecessary disclosure of information relating to a representation, to limit disclosure to those having the need to know it, and to obtain protective orders or make other arrangements minimising the risk of disclosure.

Disclosures Otherwise Required or Authorised

[20] The attorney-client privilege is differently defined in various jurisdictions. If a lawyer is called as a witness to give testimony concerning a client, absent waiver by the client, Rule 1.6(a) requires the lawyer to invoke the privilege when it is applicable. The lawyer must comply with the final orders of a court or other tribunal of competent jurisdiction requiring the lawyer to give information about the client.

[21] The Rules of Professional Conduct in various circumstances permit or require a lawyer to disclose information relating to the representation... In addition to these provisions, a lawyer may be obligated or permitted by other provisions of law to give information about a client. Whether another provision of law supersedes Rule 1.6 is a matter of interpretation beyond the scope of these Rules, but a presumption should exist against such a supersession.

Former Client

[22] The duty of confidentiality continues after the client-lawyer relationship has terminated.

Rule 1.13 Organisation as Client

(A) A lawyer employed or retained by an organisation represents the organisation acting through its duly authorised constituents.

(B) If a lawyer for an organisation knows that an officer , employee or other person associated with the organisation, is engaged in action, intends to act, or to refuse to act in a matter related to the representation that is a violation of a legal obligation owed to the organisation, or a violation of law which might reasonably be imputed to the organisation and is likely to result in substantial injury to the organisation the lawyer shall proceed as in reasonably necessary in the best interests of the organisation. In determining how to proceed, the lawyer shall give due consideration to the seriousness of the violation and its consequences, the scope and nature of the lawyer's representation, the responsibility in the organisation and the apparent motivation of the person involved, the policies of the organisation concerning such matters and any other relevant consideration. Any measures taken shall be designed to minimise disruption of the organisation and the risk of revealing information relating to the representation to persons outside the organisation. Such measures may include among others:

(1) asking reconsideration of the matter:
(2) advising that a separate legal opinion on the matter be sought for presentation to appropriate authority in the organisation: and
(3) referring the matter to higher authority in the organisation, including if warranted by the seriousness of the matter, referral to the highest authority that can act in behalf of the organisation as determined by applicable law.

(C) If, despite the lawyer's effort in accordance with paragraph (b), the highest authority that can act on behalf of the organisation insists upon action, or a refusal to act that is clearly a violation of law which might reasonably be imputed to the organisation and is likely to result in substantial injury to the organisation the lawyer may resign...

Rule 3.3 Candour Toward the Tribunal

(a) A lawyer shall not knowingly:
(1) make a false statement of material fact or law to a tribunal
(2) fail to disclose a material fact to a tribunal when disclosure is necessary to avoid assisting a criminal or fraudulent act by the client;
(3) fail to disclose to the tribunal legal authority in the controlling jurisdiction known to the lawyer to be directly adverse to the position of the client and not disclosed by opposing counsel; or
(4) offer evidence that the lawyer knows to be false. If a lawyer has offered material evidence and comes to know of its falsity, the lawyer shall take reasonable remedial measures.

(b) The duties stated in paragraph (a) continue to the conclusion of the proceeding, and apply even if compliance requires disclosure of information otherwise protected by rule 1.6.

Rule 4.1 Truthfulness in Statements to Others

In the course of representing a client a lawyer shall not knowingly:

(a) make a false statement of material fact or law to a third person; or

(b) fail to disclose a material fact to a third person when disclosure is necessary to avoid assisting a criminal or fraudulent act by a client, unless the disclosure is prohibited by Rule 1.6.

CHAPTER EIGHT

Negotiation

at the heart of negotiation there will always be opportunistic interaction – less than fully open motives and methods, self-interested manoeuvres.[1]

1 Introduction

Legal education often and perhaps unwittingly portrays litigation as the lawyers central task and advocacy as the pre-eminent skill. Contract law for example is studied through the law reports, in which judges adjudicate upon the contentions of advocates for parties whose contractual relationship has broken down. Yet negotiation is at least as significant to our understanding of contract law as advocacy and adjudication. Prior to the formation of a binding contract, the parties may well engage in intense pre-contractual negotiations. Thereafter the contract may well be modified on one or more occasions and, in the absence of full performance, the parties may well have to engage in settlement negotiations if litigation is to be avoided. While many lawyers do not become litigators, there are very few whose professional role will not require them to negotiate. They may negotiate with their partners over profit shares, with clients over fees and will probably negotiate with third parties on their clients' behalf. Even a simple residential conveyancing transaction will usually involve negotiations between solicitors representing buyer and seller. Moreover, as noted above, even litigators will often end up settling their cases for the simple reason that it is usually in both sides' interests to do so in order to save costs.

---

1 *Learning Lawyer's Skills by Phillip A Jones* (London, Blackstone Press, 3rd ed 1995 Philip A Jones ed) p 177 at para 24.4. The current (8th, 2000) edition of the book does not contain this quotation, nor is Professor Jones one of the authors.

Yet negotiation raises some very difficult ethical issues. To begin with it should be noted that the 'Standard Conception of Lawyers Ethics' (see chapter 5) is most often and perhaps most easily defended by reference to the operation of the adversary system. However, it is crucial to the operation of the 'adversary system excuse' that the contest between the two adversarial lawyers be refereed by a neutral umpire – the judge/jury[2]. In negotiation, there is no such figure.

In addition, negotiation provides opportunities for the use of tactics which are at least arguably unethical. Let us begin with the question of lying, defined for these purposes as the inducing by any act or omission of a belief in the mind of another which is at variance with one's own.[3] On this definition, statements like 'my client will never accept less than £50,000 in settlement of this claim' when the client has given authority to settle of £35,000 or 'this claim is worth at least £50,000' when the advice was to settle for £35,000 seem morally problematic. On this broad definition, omissions may also amount to lies. Imagine that you are negotiating as a lawyer on behalf of a local authority with a power of compulsory purchase over land needed for a motorway. Prior to exercising the power, the authority enters into negotiations with one of the property owners. Assume that the opposing lawyer, a person of marginal competence, concludes incorrectly from a statement that you have made that you have been purchasing similar houses for £20,000 when in fact you have been paying £60,000. When he says, 'Now I understand that you have been buying similar houses for £20,000', can you remain silent?[4]

Case law provides evidence that lawyers sometimes grasp with both hands the opportunities for sharp practice afforded by negotiation. In *Commission for the New Towns v Cooper (Great Britain) Ltd,*[5] the plaintiff was the landlord of leasehold premises which the defendant had acquired by assignment when taking over a business. When the business proved unsuccessful, the defendant sought a way out of its obligations under the lease. The previous tenant had enjoyed options both to extend its' leasehold rights and obligations should the business prosper and an option to surrender the lease should it fail. Unfortunately, these rights had lapsed. The defendant's lawyers sought to further their client's interests and to exploit the principles of the common law to the uttermost in a manner which the Court of Appeal was latter to label 'dishonest' and 'disgraceful'.[6] The lawyers called a meeting with two of the plaintiff's senior officials for the purpose of settling a long-running dispute concerning liability for works carried out on the premises. The lawyers offered a sum in settlement of the outstanding issues provided its client was allowed *all* (emphasis added by the writer but not surprisingly omitted by the defendant) the rights enjoyed by the previous tenant. They managed to give the impression that the client's concern was with the

2   See generally Murray L Schwartz 'The Professionalism and Accountability of Lawyers' (1978) 66 California LR 669.
3   See G Wetlaufer 'The Ethics of Lying in Negotiations' (1990) 75 Iowa LR 1223.
4   This example is based on that given by Professor James White in 'Machiavelli and the Bar: Ethical Limits on Lying in Negotiation' [1980]ABF Res J 926 at p 939.
5   [1995] Ch 259 CA.
6   Evans LJ at 292E.

right to extend. The plaintiff agreed in principle and subsequently received a proposal that the defendant should pay £45,000 in return for the plaintiff's agreement that:

> [the defendant] will continue to have all such rights previously granted to [the previous tenant].

The plaintiff agreed without checking just what rights had been granted to the previous tenants. Shortly afterwards the defendant sought to terminate the lease. Subsequently, the Court of Appeal held that it was not entitled to do so on a number of grounds[7]. So justice was done, but only after the plaintiff had incurred the costs of litigation in the Court of Appeal and the defendant's lawyers' negotiation ethics remain problematic. So negotiation provides ample opportunities for deception. This is not to deny that deception may sometimes be justified, a point to which we will return. Nevertheless it is important to recognise that some justification is required.

Threats are another tactic which can appear problematic. Suppose you act for the wife of a Church of England minister in negotiations for a financial settlement following the breakdown of the marriage. The husband has proved difficult. May the wife's lawyers warn that unless a suitable offer is forthcoming, the press will undoubtedly get to hear of the wife's allegations of cruelty and adultery? Similarly, tactical use of the rules of procedure may allow lawyers engaged in litigation to put pressure on the other side to agree to a generous settlement. For example, those who successfully resist claims by legally-aided plaintiffs are normally unable to claim their costs either from the loser, or from the Legal Services Commission. Lawyers funded by legal aid can use exploit the pressures generated by these cost provisions, and there is evidence that they have not been slow to take advantage. In her ground-breaking empirical study of UK personal injury litigation, Professor Hazel Genn interviewed one barrister who commented that:

> There's always the nuisance value to a claim. Now as a plaintiff one can play on that, and particularly so, I think, and it's probably naughty to do it, but if one is legally aided, as of course so many plaintiffs are, then even if the defendant wins, there is a nuisance value to the extent of their costs, and so in a small claim it shouldn't be too difficult to get something out of the defendant.[8]

But are these tactics in fact forbidden by the law on lawyering? The lawyer for the minister could not make the threatened disclosure once proceedings had been issued because this would then constitute contempt of court. Otherwise, however, the general law imposes very few restrictions. In particular, the law of contract excludes from the category of actionable misrepresentation anything which might be described as a

7   That i) the agreement on its true construction did not confer a right to surrender (277B, 291G) ii) even if the Court was wrong in relation to i) the plaintiff was entitled to rectification of the contract because even if the defendant did not actually know of the plaintiff's mistake it had behaved unconscionably (280D); iii) the plaintiff's representatives had no authority to agree to grant a right to surrender (282H); iv) the plaintiff's were victims of a misrepresentation and v) the correspondence did not satisfy the formalities of s 2 of the Law of Property (Miscellaneous Provisions) Act 1989.

8   Hazel Genn *Hard bargaining, Out of Court Settlements in Personal Injury Actions.* (Oxford Socio-Legal Studies Series, Oxford, Clarendon Press, 1987) p 115.

'mere puff' or 'mere sales talk', so untrue statements about a client's negotiating position may not amount to misrepresentations. There is no general obligation to disclose material facts. As to the LSGPC, a number of provisions seem to be relevant.

17.01 FAIRNESS

Solicitors must not act, whether in their professional capacity or otherwise, towards anyone in a way which is fraudulent, deceitful or otherwise contrary to their position as solicitors. Nor must solicitors use their position as solicitors to take unfair advantage either for themselves or another person.

1. A solicitor must not deceive anyone: however any information disclosed must be consistent with the duty of confidentiality.

19.01 DUTY OF GOOD FAITH

A solicitor must act towards other solicitors with frankness and good faith consistent with his or her overriding duty to the client.[9]

These provisions are open to criticism both on formal and substantive grounds. As a matter for form, they seem hopelessly vague, for example in the reference in 17.01 to action contrary to the position of a solicitor. Substantively, principle 19.01 suggests that if lack of candour and bad faith are required by the client's interests, then there is no objection from the perspective of professional conduct. Finally note 1 to principle 17.01 seems to place solicitors in an unenviable position if they discover that statements made on their client's behalf in negotiations were in fact false. Note 1 would seem to prevent correction by the solicitor of a representation now known to be false.

2   The ethics of negotiation

Whatever the precise scope of the LSGPC, we have seen that it is not necessarily conclusive of the wider ethical question.[10] As to this, recall our discussion of Stephen Pepper's powerful argument that whatever the demands of common morality or the lawyer's own conscience, the lawyer's role morality renders permissible and even mandatory any conduct taken in the client's interests provided only that it is technically legal. Here however, we focus on arguments more specific to the negotiation context, the most striking of which is that such an approach is made inevitable and even desirable by the nature of negotiation. Thus, Professor James White has argued that:

Like the poker player, a negotiator hopes that his opponent will overestimate the value of his hand. Like the poker player, in a variety of ways he must facilitate his opponent's inaccurate assessment. The critical difference between those who are successful negotiators and those who are not lies in this capacity both to mislead and not to be misled. Some experienced negotiators will deny the accuracy of this assertion,

9   *The Guide to the Professional Conduct of Solicitors* (8th ed) (London, Law Society, 1999) pp 346, 359.
10 See for example chapter 1 supra.

but they will be wrong. I submit that a careful examination of the behaviour of even the most forthright, honest and trustworthy negotiators will show them actively engaged in misleading their opponents about their true position...To conceal one's true position, to mislead any opponent about one's true settling point, is the essence of negotiation.[11]

This view of negotiation is known as the competitive approach and draws heavily on the recent economic analyses of contract law. It treats contractual exchange as the natural outcome of a situation in which one economic agent (the seller) possesses an asset which s/he values less than the buyer. As applied to the settlement of legal claims, this means settlement of a legal claim will occur when the lowest figure for which the plaintiff will settle ('sell') the claim is lower than the highest figure for which the defendant is prepared to settle ('buy'). The difference between the plaintiff's and defendant's 'reservation prices' represents a zone of settlement such that settlement at any point between those prices makes both parties better off than the alternative of going to court. The situation can be represented by the following diagram:

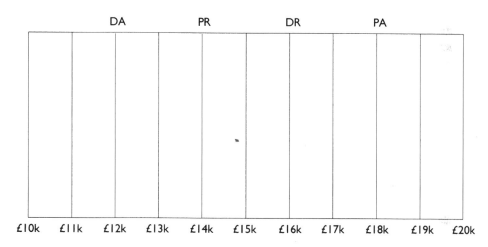

Here PA represents what the plaintiff would like to receive from settlement and PR the plaintiffs reservation price. DA represents the sum which the defendant would ideally like to pay and DR the reservation price. The shaded area PR-DR represents the zone of settlement. As both parties are made better off by settlement at any point within this zone, the sum PR-DR can also be seen as a pie, the consensual division of which is the goal but also the intractable problem of negotiations. For if both parties are seeking to capture as large a share as possible of the pie, settlement will only occur if one side can deceive the other as to its true reservation price either by making false statements about its reservation price or by exaggerating the strength of its evidential or legal position. Thus in our diagram settlement will occur at PR if the defendant can convince the plaintiff that PR=DR (leaving D with the whole of the pie) and at DR if the plaintiff can convince the defendant that DR=PR. It should now be clear why our diagram

1 1   White supra note 4 at 928.

looks like an American football pitch. The process of negotiation is a war of attrition in which each side seeks to capture territory by brute force.

This conception of negotiation has recently been criticised by a number of theorists led by Professors Fisher and Ury. In their ground-breaking book, *Getting to Yes*[12], Fisher and Ury make a claim everyone would like to be able to accept. They urge us to remember:

> that the first thing you are trying to win is a better way to negotiate – a way that avoids your having to choose between the satisfaction of getting what you deserve and of being decent. You can have both.[13]

At the heart of what has become known as the 'problem-solving approach' to negotiation are three ideas. The first is that it is often a mistake to view negotiations as a zero-sum game in which one side is attempting to enlarge its own share of a fixed resource (money) at the expense of the other. Instead parties should seek to expand the pie. Structured settlements in personal injury litigation are an example of this process. If an insurer's reservation price is £100,000 and the plaintiff's is £110,000 it looks as if agreement is impossible. However, the government offers tax incentives to plaintiffs willing to accept an annuity purchased by the defendant instead of a lump sum settlement. Consequently, the defendant may be able to purchase for £100,000 an annuity having a capital value (because of the tax concession) of £120,000, thus making settlement possible. A second and closely related aspect of the problem-solving approach is the need to concentrate on the parties' real needs rather than on their negotiating positions. In this way, the parties may find to their surprise that their needs are complementary rather than opposed. One classic example involves the negotiations between Israel and Egypt over the future of the Sinai Peninsula. These negotiations seemed deadlocked by Egypt's insistence on nothing less than full sovereignty, which was completely unacceptable to Israel. Deadlock was broken by focusing on the needs underlying the parties' positions. Israel was concerned about its security, Egypt about vindicating its historic rights. Consequently, the parties were able to agree that Egypt should regain sovereignty over a demilitarised Sinai. One crucial difference between this approach and the competitive approach is that problem solvers have an incentive to disclose information rather than to conceal it – only in this way can complementary needs be identified.

Finally, once the pie has been expanded as far as it will go, problem solvers should resolve any remaining disagreements by reference to objective standards rather than by a trial of strength in which the actors behave 'as if the negotiators were living on a desert island with no history, no customs, and no moral standards'.[14] Objective standards may be of two types: substantive (market value; precedent; morality; professional standards; efficiency; tradition; reciprocity (do unto me as you would have done unto yourself)) or procedural. A powerful example of a procedural standard

---

12 Roger Fisher and William Ury *Getting to Yes Negotiating Agreement Without Giving In* (Boston, MA Houghton Mifflin Company, 1981)
13 Supra at p 182.
14 Supra at p 85.

can be found in the behaviour of a divorcing couple who resolve their disagreement over visitation rights for the non-custodial partner by agreeing that they will negotiate over visiting rights before they negotiate or ask the court to adjudicate upon custody.

The claim that a problem-solving approach allows negotiators to be both successful and decent has led to a fierce debate between Professors White and Fisher. Professor White opened the debate:

> Getting to Yes is a puzzling book. On the one hand it offers a forceful and persuasive criticism of much traditional negotiating behaviour. It suggests a variety of negotiating techniques that are both clever and likely to facilitate effective negotiation. On the other hand, the authors seem to deny the existence of a significant part of the negotiation process, and to oversimplify or explain away many of the most troublesome problems inherent in the art and practice of negotiation. The book is frequently naive, occasionally self-righteous, but often helpful.
>
> Initially, one should understand what the book is and what it is not. It is not a scholarly work on negotiation; . . . The book is not rigorous and analytical, rather it is anecdotal and informative. It does not add fundamentally to our understanding of the negotiation process. Rather it points to a need for change in our general conception of negotiation, and points out errors of emphasis that exist in much of the thinking about negotiation.
>
> The book's thesis is well summarised by the following passage:
>
>> Behind opposed positions lie shared and compatible interests, as well as conflicting ones. We tend to assume that because the other side's positions are opposed to ours, their interests must also be opposed. If we have an interest in defending ourselves, then they must want to attack us. If we have an interest in minimising the rent, then their interest must be to maximise it. In many negotiations, however, a close examination of the underlying interests will reveal the existence of even more interests that are shared or compatible than ones that are opposed.
>
> This point is useful for all who teach or think about negotiation. The tendency of those deeply involved in negotiation or its teaching is probably to exaggerate the importance of negotiation on issues where the parties are diametrically opposed and to ignore situations where the parties' interests are compatible. By emphasising that fact, and by making a clear articulation of the importance of co-operation, imagination, and the search for alternative solutions, the authors teach helpful lessons. The book therefore provides worthwhile reading for every professional negotiator and will make sound instruction for every tyro.
>
> Unfortunately the book's emphasis upon mutually profitable adjustment, on the 'problem solving' aspect of bargaining, is also the book's weakness. It is a weakness because emphasis of this aspect of bargaining is done to almost total exclusion of the other aspect of bargaining, 'distributional bargaining,' where one for me is minus one for you. Schelling, Karrass and other students of negotiation have long distinguished between that aspect of bargaining in which modification of the parties' positions can produce benefits for one without significant cost to the other, and on the other hand, cases where benefits to one come only at significant cost to the other. They have variously described the former as 'exploring for mutual profitable adjustments,' 'the efficiency

aspect of bargaining,' or 'problem solving.' The other has been characterised as 'distributional bargaining' or 'share bargaining.' Thus some would describe a typical negotiation as one in which the parties initially begin by co-operative or efficiency bargaining, in which each gains something with each new adjustment without the other losing any significant benefit. Eventually, however, one comes to bargaining in which added benefits to one impose corresponding significant costs on the other. For example, in a labour contract one might engage in co-operative bargaining by the modification of a medical plan so that the employer could engage a less expensive medical insurance provider, yet one that offered improved services. Each side gains by that change from the old contract. Ultimately parties in a labour negotiation will come to a raw economic exchange in which additional wage dollars for the employees will be dollars subtracted from the corporate profits, dollars that cannot be paid in dividends to the shareholders.

One can concede the authors' thesis (that too many negotiators are incapable of engaging in problem solving or in finding adequate options for mutual gain), yet still maintain that the most demanding aspect of nearly every negotiation is the distributional one in which one seeks more at the expense of the other. My principal criticism of the book is that it seems to overlook the ultimate hard bargaining. Had the authors stated that they were dividing the negotiation process in two and were dealing with only part of it, that omission would be excusable. That is not what they have done. Rather they seem to assume that a clever negotiator can make any negotiation into problem solving and thus completely avoid the difficult distribution of which Karrass and Schelling speak. To my mind this is naive. By so distorting reality, they detract from their powerful and central thesis.

Chapter 5, entitled 'Insist on Objective Criteria,' is a particularly naive misperception or rejection of the guts of distributive negotiation. Here, as elsewhere, the authors draw a stark distinction between a negotiator who simply takes a position without explanation and sticks to it as a matter of will, and the negotiator who is reasonable and insists upon 'objective criteria.' Of course the world is hardly as simple as the authors suggest. Every party who takes a position will have some rationale for that position; every able negotiator rationalises every position that he takes. Rarely will an effective negotiator simply assert 'X' as his price and insist that the other party meet it. The suggestion that one can find objective criteria (as opposed to persuasive rationalisations) seems quite inaccurate. As Eisenberg suggests, the distributive aspect of the negotiation often turns on the relative power of the parties. One who could sell his automobile to a particular person for $6,000 could not necessarily sell it for more than $5,000 to another person, not because of principle, but because of the need of the seller to sell and the differential need of the two buyers to buy. To say that there are objective criteria that call for a $5,000 or $6,000 price, or in the case of a personal injury suit for a million dollars or an $800,000 judgment, is to ignore the true dynamics of the situation and to exaggerate the power of objective criteria. Any lawyer who has been involved in a personal injury suit will marvel at the capacity of an effective plaintiff's lawyer to appear to do what the authors seem to think possible, namely to give the superficial appearance of certainty and objectivity to questions that are inherently imponderable... Every lawyer who has ever been involved in a lawsuit in which experts have been hired by each side will have a deep scepticism about the authors' appeal to scientific merit as a guide in determining a fair outcome in the negotiation of any hotly disputed problem.

In short, the authors' suggestion in Chapter 5 that one can avoid 'contests of will' and thereby, eliminate the exercise of raw power is at best naive and at worst misleading. Their suggestion that the parties look to objective criteria to strengthen their cases is a useful technique used by every able negotiator. Occasionally, it may do what they suggest: give an obvious answer on which all can agree. Most of the time it will do no more than give the superficial appearance of reasonableness and honesty to one party's position.

The authors' consideration of 'dirty tricks' in negotiation suffers from more of the same faults found in their treatment of objective criteria. At a superficial level I find their treatment of dirty tricks to be distasteful because it is so thoroughly self-righteous. The chapter is written as though there were one and only one definition of appropriate negotiating behaviour handed down by the authors.

Apart from the rather trivial concern about their self-righteousness, their discussion is troublesome because it discloses an ignorance of, or a disregard for, the subtleties involved in distinguishing between appropriate and inappropriate conduct in negotiation. There is no concession to the idea that certain forms of behaviour may be acceptable within certain regional or ethnic groups; that Jews may negotiate differently than Quakers, or city people differently than those in the country. There is no recognition that the setting, participants, or substance may impose a set of rules. Rather a whole host of things labelled 'dirty tricks.... deliberate deception, psychological warfare, and positional pressure' are out of bounds. Consider their treatment of threats:

> Good negotiators rarely resort to threats. They do not need to; there are other ways to communicate the same information if it seems appropriate to outline the consequences of the other side's action, for example, suggest those that will occur independently of your will rather than those you could choose to bring about. Warnings are much more legitimate than threats and are not vulnerable to counter threats: 'Should we fail to reach agreement, it seems highly probable to me that the news media would insist on publishing the whole sordid story. In a matter of this much public interest, I don't see how we could legitimately suppress information. Do you?'

The statement which they approve (and label as a 'warning' and not a 'threat') would likely be construed as a threat. One who wishes to threaten his opponent in a negotiation is not likely to say, 'if we do not reach agreement I will see to it that the information concerning your client becomes public.' Rather he is likely to say what the authors suggest, 'In a matter of this much public interest, I don't see how we could legitimately suppress information, do you?' In fact, the authors have suggested merely a more subtle and more Machiavellian form of threat.

The question of deception is dealt with in the same facile way:

> Less than full disclosure is not the same as deception. Deliberate deception as to facts or one's intentions is quite different from not fully disclosing one's present thinking. Good faith negotiation does not require total disclosure. Perhaps the best answer to questions such as 'What is the most you would be willing to pay if you had to?' would be along the following lines: 'Let's not put ourselves under such a strong temptation to mislead. If you think no agreement is possible, and that we may be wasting our time, perhaps we could disclose our thinking to

some trustworthy third party, who can tell us whether there is a zone of potential agreement,' In this way it is possible to behave with full candour about information that is not being disclosed.

The authors seem not to perceive that between 'full disclosure' and 'deliberate deception' lies a continuum, not a yawning chasm. They seem to ignore the fact that in one sense the negotiator's role is at least passively to mislead his opponent about his settling point while at the same time appearing to engage in ethical behaviour.

Most who have engaged in significant negotiation will concede the tension between those two responsibilities. How does one answer a question about his authority? Can one ethically allow a bumbling opponent who has drawn the incorrect inference about one's statement to continue in ignorance? ...Each [lawyer] has a different point on the continuum where he will stop. Notwithstanding superficial agreement on generalisations among lawyers, if one stimulates open discussion about lying and dissembling in negotiation, he will find large differences of position among lawyers on specific cases. To suggest that drawing the line between appropriate disclosure and inappropriate deception is easy is to mislead the reader.[15]

Professor Fisher was given the opportunity to respond:

To some extent, I believe, White is more concerned with the way the world is, and I am more concerned with what intelligent people ought to do. One task is to teach the truth – to tell students the unpleasant facts of life, including how people typically negotiate. But I want a student to negotiate better than his or her father. I see my task as to give the best possible prescriptive advice, taking into account the way other human beings are likely to behave as well as one's own emotions and psychological state.

Suppose a husband and wife come to an expert in negotiation asking advice on how best to negotiate the terms of a separation agreement that will involve children and jointly-held property. What is the best advice that such an expert could give to both about the process – about the manner of negotiating that would be most likely to produce a wise and fair outcome while maximising their ability to deal with future problems, and minimising their costs in terms of time, resources, and emotional stress? If one of them alone asked for such advice, in what ways would wise recommendations differ? These are the questions I am interested in.

The world is a rough place. It is also a place where, taken collectively, we are incompetent at resolving our differences in ways that efficiently and amicably serve our mutual interests. It is important that students learn about bluffing and hard bargaining, because they will certainly encounter it. It is also important that our students become more skilful and wise than most people in dealing with differences. Thus, to some extent, White and I are emphasising different aspects of what needs to be taught.

Are distributional issues amenable to joint problem solving? The most fundamental difference between White's way of thinking and mine seems to concern the negotiation of distributional issues 'where one for me is minus one for you.' We agree on the importance of co-operation, imagination, and the search for creative options where the task is to reconcile substantive interests that are compatible. White, however,

15   'The Pros and Cons of "Getting to Yes"' (1984) 34 Journal of Legal Education 115 at 119.

sees the joint problem-solving approach as limited to that area. In his view, the most demanding aspect of nearly every negotiation is the distributional one in which one seeks more at the expense of the other. Distributional matters, in his view, must be settled by the ultimate hard bargaining. He regards it as a distortion of reality to suggest that problem solving is relevant to distributional negotiation.

Here we differ. By focusing on the substantive issues (where the parties' interest may be directly opposed) White overlooks the shared interest that the parties continue to have in the process for resolving that substantive difference. How to resolve the substantive difference is a shared problem. Both parties have an interest in identifying quickly and amicably a result acceptable to each, if one is possible. How to do so is a problem. A good solution to that process-problem requires joint action.

The guts of the negotiation problem, in my view, is not who gets the last dollar, but what is the best process for resolving that issue. It is certainly a mistake to assume that the only process available for resolving distributional questions is hard bargaining over positions. In my judgment, it is also a mistake to assume that such hard bargaining is the best process for resolving differences efficiently and in the long-term interest of either side.

Two men in a lifeboat quarrelling over limited rations have a distributional problem. One approach to resolving that problem is to engage in hard bargaining. A can insist that he will sink the boat unless he gets 60 per cent of the rations. But A's and B's shared problem is not just how to divide the rations; rather it is how to divide the rations without tipping over the boat and while getting the boat to safer waters. In my view, to treat the distributional issue as a shared problem is a better approach than to treat it as a contest of will in which a more deceptive, more stubborn and less rational negotiator will tend to fare better. Treating the distributional issue as a problem to be solved ('How about dividing the rations in proportion to our respective weights' or 'How about a fixed portion of the rations for each hour that one of us rows?') is likely to be better for both than a contest over who is more willing to sink the boat.

Objective criteria. It is precisely in deciding such problems that objective criteria can play their most useful role. Here is a second area of significant disagreement. White finds it useful to deny the existence of objective standards: 'The suggestion that one can find objective criteria (as opposed to persuasive rationalisations) seems quite inaccurate.' To his way of thinking, the only approach is for a negotiator first to adopt a position and later to develop rationalisations for it: '....every able negotiator rationalises every position that he takes.'

No one has suggested that in most negotiations there is a single objective criterion that both parties will quickly accept as determinative. The question is rather what should be treated as the essence of the negotiation, and what attitude should be taken toward arguments advanced in the discussion. White thinks it better to treat positions of the parties as the essence of the negotiation, and objective standards advanced by either party as mere rationalisations. That is one approach. A different approach is possible and, I believe, preferable.

Two judges, in trying to reach agreement, will be looking for standards that should decide the case. They may have their predispositions and even strongly-held views, but they will jointly look for an agreed basis for decision. Each will typically advance law, precedent, and evidence not simply as rationalisations for positions adopted for other reasons, but honestly, as providing a fair basis for decision. White's example of litigation is the very one I would advance to demonstrate that however great the disagreement, the wise approach is to insist upon using objective criteria as the basis of decision. It is better for the parties in court to be advancing objective standards which they suggest ought to be determinative than to be telling the court that they won't take less (or pay more) than so many dollars. The same, I believe, is true for negotiators.

Two negotiators can be compared with two judges, trying to decide a case. There won't be a decision unless they agree. It is perfectly possible for fellow negotiators, despite their self-interest, to behave like fellow judges, in that they advance reasoned arguments seriously, and are open to persuasion by better arguments. They need not advance standards simply as rationalisations for positions, but as providing a genuine basis for joint decision.

What we are suggesting is that in general a negotiator should seek to persuade by coming up with better arguments on the merits rather than by simply trying to convince the other side that he is the more stubborn. A good guideline is for a negotiator to advance arguments as though presenting them to an impartial arbitrator, to press favourable bases for decision, but none so extreme as to damage credibility. (On the receiving side, a good guideline is for a negotiator to listen to arguments as though he were an impartial arbitrator, remaining open to persuasion despite self-interest and preconceptions.) My experience suggests that this method is often more efficient and amicable than hard positional bargaining and more often leads to satisfactory results for both parties.

White seems to find the concept of 'raw power' useful for a negotiator. I do not. For a negotiator, the critical questions of power are (1) how to enhance one's ability to influence favourably a negotiator on the other side and (2) how to use such ability as one has. My ability to exert influence upon the other side depends upon the cumulative impact of several factors: skill and knowledge, interests, the state of our relationship, the legitimacy of our respective interests, the elegance of a proposed solution, my willingness and ability to commit myself, and the relative attractiveness to each side of its best alternative.

During a negotiation I can orchestrate my use of these factors so that they reinforce and augment each other or I can use some elements in ways that undermine others. Unless I am careful, a threat to use 'raw power' will weaken rather than enhance my total ability to influence the other side, since it is likely to deprive me of knowledge , damage a relationship, and undercut my legitimacy.

Incidentally, I consider warnings (of what it will be in my interest to do, or of what will happen independent of my action) to be not simply a more Machiavellian form of threat. Being more legitimate than a threat (of harm I could cause you), a warning tends to exert more influence.

Deception. White correctly calls attention to the difficult issue of ethical behaviour, where disclosure of what a negotiator would be willing to do if he or she had to in order to reach agreement would be damaging to self-interest. The problem is particularly acute if the substance of the negotiation is haggling over positions over statements of what one is willing or unwilling to do. With such positional bargaining in mind White sees the negotiator's role as being 'to mislead his opponent about his settling point while at the same time to engage in ethical behaviour.'

I believe White falls to appreciate the extent to which the ethical problem is reduced if instead of negotiating by making a series of offers and counteroffers (each often intended to deceive the other as to what one is really willing to do), one treats negotiation as a joint search for an appropriate objective basis for decision, taking into account legitimate interest. If one tries to persuade the other side on the merits, as one would try to persuade an arbitrator, the rewards for – and need for – misleading are far less.

Changed thinking. Getting to Yes says 'Don't Bargain Over Positions.' Students have now taught me that there are categories of negotiations where positional bargaining is the best way to proceed. On single-issue negotiations among strangers where the transaction costs of exploring interest would be high and where each side is protected by competitive opportunities, haggling over positions may work better than joint problem solving. A typical case would be negotiating a sale on the New York Stock Exchange.[16]

Questions

1. Why do Fisher and White disagree? Who do you think is correct and why?

2. You represent an insurance company defending a personal injury claim against an insured driver. During settlement negotiations, the plaintiff's lawyer offers to settle for £100,000 and adds 'You do have authority to settle for £100,000 don't you?' Your client has given you authority to settle for £110,000 but you think the claim is worth £80,000 at most. What do you say?

3. Is it helpful, when considering the ethical status of a negotiating tactic, to distinguish between threats and warnings?

4. You are negotiating an international construction contract on behalf of a firm based in the UK. The developer is the State Development Corporation of an African republic. During the course of negotiations which occur in the foreign capital, the agent acting for the development corporation asks you to pay his 'fees'. On further inquiry from local lawyers you learn that such 'fees' will not be disclosed to the principal but that they are a universal practice in this country. Without it your client will never be awarded the contract. You refer the matter to the client who says that the contract is important and that you should pay the fees which will later be reimbursed to your firm. What do you do? Are there any and if so what further matters which you would wish to investigate? See *Mahesan v Malaysian Government Officers Co-operative Housing Society* [1979] AC 374 and *Logicrosse v Southend Football Club* [1988] 1 WLR 1256.

16   Ibid at pp 120-123.

In addition to these arguments about the nature of negotiations other defences may be offered for the tactics described earlier. One of the most common is the argument that such tactics are 'part of the rules of the game', an argument that is attractive because it enables distinctions to be made between different practice contexts (what is ethical in commercial litigation is different from what is ethical in family litigation) and different cultural settings. In the following extract, Gerald Wetlaufer considers these arguments in relation to lying.

It is often asserted that lying in negotiations is within 'the rules of the game' and therefore ethically permissible. For a number of reasons, however, the application of this justification to the ethics of lying in negotiations is highly problematic. In assessing this claim, it is essential that we be clear about the nature of the rules in question and about the reliability of the information that people claim to have concerning the specific provisions of those rules.

First, some rules speak directly to the question of what is ethically permissible. While the golden rule and the ten commandments may be rules of this kind, what we refer to as the rules of the game with regard to lying in negotiations are not. That is not necessarily to say that these rules are not relevant to ethical discourse or that they may not, for some reason that has not yet been specified, distinguish between what is ethically permissible and what is not. In the first instance, though, they are something less than that. They are a description of how people conduct their affairs; of what people believe to be permissible, perhaps even ethically permissible; of how people may believe their adversaries are conducting their affairs; or of what people believe their adversaries believe to be ethically permissible.

Moreover, some rules can be found in a form that is consultable and authoritative. Once again, however, the rules of the game with regard to lying in negotiations are not of this kind. Finally, some rules are sufficiently clear and sufficiently well-understood that we can draw strong inferences concerning our adversaries' beliefs as to those rules. For two quite separate reasons, the rules of the game with regard to lying in negotiations are not of this kind. One reason, of course, is that they do not exist in a consultable and authoritative form and, perhaps as a result just of this, we do not all agree on what they are. Another reason is that the rules with regard to lying in negotiations are quite different from, say, the rules of checkers in that one player cannot tell simply through the course of the play whether she and her adversaries are playing by the same rules. One's conduct with respect to lying in negotiations is generally invisible.

What follows from all this is that the statement that lying is permitted by the rules of the game may be relevant to an inquiry into the ethics of lying in negotiations but only as a part of some larger argument. The ethical permissibility of lies is not established by the fact that 'the rules' may permit them. If, for instance, Ms Buyer wanted to claim that such lies are ethically permissible, she would have to argue more than simply the fact that they are permitted under the rules. In theory, there appear to be three such further arguments that are open to her.

Under one of these arguments, Ms Buyer might assert that the rules tell us what is ethically permissible not because that is the nature of these rules but rather because that is the nature of ethics. Let us assume, for instance, that what Ms Buyer means by 'the rules' is a description of how people who negotiate actually behave. She might then assert that custom is the measure of ethics and that, accordingly, those things that people actually do is the proper measure of what is ethically permissible. One problem with this argument is that her evidence as to what people actually do, as to the rules of the game, is likely to be a good deal weaker and less reliable than she might have us believe. The other problem is that, even if her description happens to be exactly right, her argument still relies entirely upon the claim that custom is the full measure of ethics, an understanding of ethics that is impoverished and unacceptably narrow.

The second argument available to Ms Buyer involves the assertion that the rules of the game are relevant not because they are directly normative but, instead, because of what they tell us about the expectations and the future conduct of the person with whom she is negotiating. Thus Ms Buyer might argue that lying is ethically permissible because it is permitted by the rules of the game, because we therefore know that Mr Seller believes such lies to be permissible and will tell them if he gets a chance, and because it is ethically permissible to lie to people about whom that is true. There are several reasons that might then be offered for the proposition that it is ethically permissible to lie to people who believe lying to be permissible and who will lie if they get a chance. Perhaps there will be no harm because Mr Seller will know better than to believe the lie, or no net harm because her lies will simply cancel out his. Perhaps her lies are justified as a matter of self-defence or retaliation, or perhaps he has somehow forfeited his right to honest treatment. Or perhaps lying is necessary or useful to the efficient conduct of negotiations. Or perhaps, finally, her lies are justified because he has consented to them or agreed to play by these particular rules of the game. Most of these arguments are taken up elsewhere and can readily be shown to be wholly unpersuasive. As to those forms of the argument which are uniquely within the province of the rules of the game, Ms Buyer again faces the problem of persuading us that she really knows the rules according to which people generally behave and, still less likely, that she can sustain the inference that Mr Seller understands the rules and has chosen to play by them. Her argument about 'consent' is, of course, wholly fictitious.

The third argument differs from the second because, instead of resting on an assertion about Mr Buyer's expectations and future conduct, it rests only on an assertion about his expectations. Here Ms Buyer asserts that the rules of the game permit lying, that Mr Seller knows the rules of the game permit lying, and that it is therefore permissible to lie to Mr Seller even though he may be one of those persons who, perhaps for reasons of ethics, will not lie to his adversary. Under these circumstances, Ms Buyer might argue that Mr Seller is on notice as to how others will play the game, that this notice provides him with the opportunity to protect himself from her lies, and that, while he is free to choose to play to a higher set of standards than are to be found in the rules of the game, he is not free unilaterally to change the rules of the game or to require Ms Buyer to play by the rules he might prefer.

There are, again, several difficulties with this argument. First, Ms Buyer's argument depends upon two assertions of fact, one concerning the rules of the game and the other concerning Mr Seller's knowledge of those rules, that will rarely be sustainable. Second, her arguments about the irrelevance of Mr Seller's probable conduct are unsound when, as is the case with this argument, lying is said to be justified not because the rules of the game actually distinguish what is ethically permissible from what is not but because of what the rules of the game may tell us about a particular adversary's expectations or probable conduct. Third, the substantive justifications for lying under these circumstances are both fewer and weaker than those that were available under the second argument.[17]

A common excuse for competitive negotiation focuses on the behaviour of the other side or the other side's lawyer. It can be argued for example that otherwise unethical behaviour might be justified as a way of establishing a credible deterrent to such behaviour on the part of the other side. This argument seems implausible in relation to lying, for the deterrence argument requires the aggressor to know that s/he is being punished whereas the whole point of lying is that the truth will remain undiscovered, at least in the short term. However, in relation to the tactical use of procedure, the argument assumes greater plausibility. In this way, a negotiator may reduce the possibility that a problem-solving approach might be exploited by the other side to the disadvantage of the problem solver's client. Indeed, in one of the few empirical studies of the strategies adopted by UK personal injury litigators, Andy Boon found that some solicitors were willing to adopt a co-operative approach to negotiation until they became convinced that the other side were adopting an aggressive approach in which case they would respond in kind.[18]

It is important also to consider the argument that apparently dubious practices are justified by the need to prevent some greater evil. It should be noted that in her study of personal injury litigation, Professor Hazel Genn concluded that such were the systematic advantages possessed by insurance companies in personal injury settlement negotiations that adequate representation of the client required aggressive lawyering. David Luban's criminal defence paradigm (see chapter 6 above) suggests a similar conclusion.

It is difficult to argue that lying is always wrong. Consider the position of the citizen of a country occupied by the Nazis during World War II. If the citizen is hiding Jewish refugees in the attic, it is surely not wrong to lie when a Gestapo officer calls asking if there are Jewish refugees in the house? It should be noted that even the Bible, which generally upholds the importance of telling the truth, seems to countenance lying in such extreme situations: Rahab lies in order to save the Israelite spies from the King of Jericho (Joshua 2) and is later described as a heroine of faith (Hebrews 11:31).

However, even if we agree that it is ethically permissible to lie to Nazi soldiers, it is not clear that we are thereby committed to a utilitarian view that lying is always permissible to prevent some greater evil. It may simply mean that lying is wrong save in certain narrowly defined exceptional circumstances. In any case, the position of a lawyer representing a client will normally be very different in that the 'evil' to be prevented (losing the client's case!) will normally be far less severe than the loss of human life. The 'greater good' argument may also be psychologically dangerous. Lawyers are unlikely to represent their clients effectively without at least some degree

---

17   Wetlaufer, supra note 3 at pp 1248-1250.
18   A Boon 'Ethics and Strategy in Personal Injury Litigation' (1985) 22 Journal of Law and Society 353.

of identification with the client. Unfortunately, there is always the danger that a lawyer will identify too closely with the client and hence be too ready to conclude that the other side's claim amounts to an evil to be prevented by all available means. In an attempt to test empirically the generality of the 'Standard Conception of Legal Ethics' Robert Nelson conducted a survey of Chicago litigators[19]. Most respondents did not say that they regarded themselves as freed by their professional role from moral responsibility for clients whose goals or methods they regarded as immoral. That is to say they did not rely upon on the 'Principle of Neutrality'.[20] Rather they said that they had never been asked to act for such a client. This suggests that lawyers do indeed identify very closely, perhaps too closely, with the client's cause.

Questions

1. Is it wrong to lie? Why? When is it not wrong to lie?

2. Do the superior resources possessed by institutional defendants in personal injury litigation justify any, and if so which, of the problematic tactics described above?

3 Reform of negotiating practices

Structural reform

If current negotiation practices give cause for concern, then a number of corrective strategies may be appropriate. The possible contribution of legal education has already been considered. Another possibility is structural reform, ie the changing of those features of the environment in which lawyers work which provide the opportunity for unethical behaviour. This is the general strategy underlying the fundamental reforms of civil procedure in the UK which were introduced following Lord Woolf 's inquiry into *Access to Justice*[1]. These reforms are considered in more detail in chapter 10. In the following extract[2], I consider the impact of cost-shifting rules on settlement negotiations.

> Settlement through private negotiation or, as it is sometimes called, bargaining in the shadow of the law[3] is an enormously important dispute resolution mechanism the continued legitimacy of which requires that it be perceived as fair. When it is not, the

---

19 R Nelson et al. 'Ideology Practice and Professional Autonomy: Social Values and Client relationships in the Large Law Firm' (1985) 37 Stanford Law Review 503.
20 See chapter 5 text to p 134 note 4.
1 Access to Justice – Final Report by the Right Hon Lord Woolf (London, HMSO, 1996).
2 This extract is taken from DRF O'Dair 'Lawyers' Ethics, Settlement Negotiations, and the Maintainers Liability for Costs: Cases in Search of a Principle' [1997] LMCLQ 156 but has been modified slightly to take account of recent developments.
3 See Robert H Mnookin and Lewis Kornhauser 'Bargaining in the Shadow of the Law: The Case of Divorce' (1979) 88 Yale LJ 950.

blame, will often be laid at the door of the parties' legal advisers.[4] Whilst the professional ethics of the lawyers involved are vital to ensuring fairness the problem also has structural features, making pertinent the warning issued by a leading US ethics expert against the common human tendency to explain ethical misconduct in terms of individual deviance rather than institutional constraints[5].

The point is illustrated by reference to the impact upon the settlement process of the rules and principles governing liability for costs. On several occasions recently, the Courts have had to consider whether those who fund litigation brought by others should be made liable for the costs of the opposing party should the assisted party be unsuccessful.[6] Following the decision of the House of Lords in *Aiden Shipping Co Ltd v Interbulk Ltd[7]*, jurisdiction to make such an order for the payment of costs undoubtedly exists pursuant to s 51(1) and (3) of the Supreme Court Act 1981. There has been debate however as to the exercise of that discretion. Whilst the question of who should pay costs is largely within the discretion of the trial judge[8], it is clearly desirable that cases be decided consistently on the basis of defensible principles. In my opinion, the Courts should adopt the following principle: that where the assisted[9] party is a private rather than a corporate party and a plaintiff rather than a defendant an order that the funder pay the successful unassisted party's costs ought normally to be made even in the absence of bad faith. Otherwise, there will be unfair prejudice to the unassisted party because the resulting distribution of liability for costs amounts to a form of one way cost shifting similar to that effected by the current legal aid scheme. This places the unassisted party at an unfair disadvantage in settlement negotiations....

The need for s 51 orders in cases where the assisted party is a private[10] plaintiff is graphically illustrated by *Murphy v Young & Co's Brewery plc.[11]* The plaintiff brought a claim for wrongful dismissal against his employer claiming £60,000 and the defendant counterclaimed for £16,000. The plaintiff's claim failed and the counter-claim succeeded and consequently the plaintiff was ordered to pay £42,000 in costs. The plaintiff had the benefit of legal expenses insurance under which he was entitled to indemnity against both his own and his opponent's costs but subject to a limit of £25,000 which had been

---

4   This suggestion clearly underlies the government's concern in its recent White Paper Striking The Balance – The Future of Legal Aid in England and Wales (Cmn 3305 Lord Chancellors Department, HMSO, June 1986) with the difficulties faced by unassisted parties in settlement negotiations with assisted parties: 'Legally aided parties have little incentive to keep costs down and may drive up their costs unnecessarily. Faced with this, unassisted parties are often under pressure to settle cases in their opponents favour.' Ibid at para 1.9.

5   Deborah L Rhode 'Institutionalising Ethics' (1994) 44 Case WL Rev 665, 686.

6   See generally, I R Scott 'Towards Understanding the Maintainers Liability for Costs' (1995) 14 CJQ 271.

7   [1986] AC 965.

8   'There is only one immutable rule in relation to costs, and that is that there are no immutable rules.': *Taylor v Pace Developments Ltd* [1996] BCC 406, at p 408 per Lloyd LJ.

9   In this note the terms 'assisted' and 'unassisted' refer to parties being assisted otherwise than by the state unless the context indicates otherwise. The term 'legally aided plaintiff' is generally used when funding is provided by the state though the defendant is still referred to as the unassisted party.

10   Where the plaintiff is a corporate party, the defendant may seek protection by asking for an order for security for costs, ie an order that the plaintiff satisfy the court of its ability to pay costs should it lose. Failure to do so will result in the action being dismissed.

11 [1996] 1 IRLR 60.

exhausted by the plaintiff's own solicitors costs. The defendant applied for an order under s 51 that the plaintiff's legal expenses insurers be ordered to pay its' costs.

Simon Brown J refused to grant the order.[12] The key question was whether the insurer had been guilty of 'wanton meddling' in the litigation, which on the facts it had not. Nor as a separate point was it contrary to public policy for litigation to be funded under a contract of insurance which limited liability for the other side's costs. His Lordship noted that as legal aid declined in its' scope it was vital that arrangements such as these be encouraged, whereas the insurers' evidence had shown to the judge's satisfaction that the imposition of unlimited liability for the other side's costs would lead to cover becoming less widely available. As to the question of unfairness to the defendant, his Lordship noted that the insurer like the Legal Aid Board had a strong financial incentive not to finance hopeless claims. Indeed the contract contained provisions governing the evaluation of the insured's prospects of success strikingly similar to those found in the legal aid regulations. Thus the chances of the unassisted party succeeding and then finding itself liable for its' own costs were kept within acceptable bounds.

A number of comments are appropriate. The first is that his Lordship is quite correct in his identification of the relevance of the analogy with legal aid but draws the wrong conclusion. One of the problematic features of the judicare legal aid scheme has been that save in exceptional cases, neither the state assisted party nor more importantly the Legal Aid Fund will pay the successful parties costs if the state assisted party loses. However, if the legally aided party succeeds costs will be payable by the loser. Therefore in most cases costs are shifted only one way. Consequently victory in litigation may for the unassisted party may be somewhat pyrrhic since the 'victor' loses the costs for which it is liable to its' own legal advisers. Knowledge that this is likely to be the case gives the state assisted party an unfair advantage in settlement negotiations. Suppose, to adapt the facts of Murphy's case, a legally aided party brings a claim for wrongful dismissal against an employer for £16,000 which the employer reasonably believes to be unfounded. If the employer knows that his own irrecoverable costs are likely to be in the region of £42,000 it is worth settling the claim provided only that the costs incurred prior to settlement plus the sum paid by way of settlement do not exceed £42,000. Moreover the legally aided party's ability to recover costs in the event of success prevents it being subject to a corresponding[13] pressure to settle, thus strengthening its' position in settlement negotiations. It is noteworthy that these pressures to settle exist regardless of whether the legally aided party's lawyer conducts the litigation in a particularly adversarial and hence perhaps unethical way. The point here though is that apparent unfairness arises without the need for any overtly adversarial behaviour. It is simply a natural consequence of the settlement dynamics created by the rules governing liability for costs. For this reason, the Courts repeated suggestion that they will be

12 The decision and reasoning of Simon Brown J were subsequently affirmed by the Court of Appeal. See [1997] 1 WLR 1591.
13 To the extent that the taxed costs payable by the unassisted party fail to cover the assisted parties costs, these will be recouped by the Legal Aid Board from the damages payable via the operation of the statutory charge. Since, in this sense, the assisted party does bear its own costs, there is clearly some incentive to settle. However it is most unlikely that the incentive will counter-balance that faced by the unassisted party which bears all its own costs in any event. In addition, it should be noted that solicitors must report to the Legal Aid Board any assisted client who declines an unreasonable settlement offer. However this seems unlikely to insulate the other side from the need to take account of the realities of the costs situation.

more ready to make an order for costs against third parties in cases of litigation brought in bad faith does little to resolve the problem.

Unless the successful party has a realistic chance of recovering costs from the assisted litigant personally, a similar settlement dynamic to that arising from legal aid is created by the decision in *Murphy*. It is doubtful whether the legal aid model is one which should be adopted in respect of private legal expenses arrangements. For one thing, it is disappointing that note was not taken of the governments contemporaneous expressions of concern about the one way cost shifting resulting from the legal aid scheme. In the consultation paper 'Legal Aid Targeting Need'[14], which was issued at the same time as *Murphy*, it was noted that

> Hardship can be caused to a person not on legal aid who, even if successful will very rarely be able to recover any of his or her costs. Such a person will often withdraw from or settle proceedings on unfavourable terms because of the advantage which legal aid gives the opposing party on the question of costs. Legally aided status can give rise to an unfair bargaining advantage[15]. (emphasis added).

This concern led the Major administration to propose in its' White Paper *Striking the Balance* that the unassisted successful party should have an effective means of recovering its' costs.[16] It was proposed that the costs be paid by the loser in instalments or by means of a charge on the equity in the assisted person's home. The reform of legal aid enacted by the Access to Justice Act 1999 was on this point rather less radical: it was proposed that as previously costs should not in general be recoverable from assisted parties. However, in assessing whether or not, it is, exceptionally, reasonable for costs to be paid, the Court will for the first time be able to take account of any equity in the assisted person's house.[17] They will also have regard not just to the resources of the assisted party, as previously but also to the resources of the victor.[18] Despite this partial retreat, the concerns about unfairness in negotiation which they express make it very difficult to support opposition to the principle here proposed by analogy with the legal aid scheme.

It has to be recognised that plaintiffs are also shielded from liability for their own lawyer's costs by conditional fees and in cases where the lawyer acts pro-bono. In the *Tolstoy-Miloslasky v Lord Aldington*[19] the Court of Appeal made it clear that only under exceptional circumstances would a court impose upon solicitors acting pro-bono liability for the costs of the other side in the event of the litigation proving unsuccessful. Such an approach was necessary in order to encourage pro-bono work and hence access to justice.[20] Conditional fees have been endorsed by the legislature[1], also as means of improving access to justice. Moreover, in *Hodgson v Imperial Tobacco*[2], the Court of

14   Legal Aid – Targeting Need (Cmnd 2854) May 1995.

15   Ibid at para 12.26.

16   Supra note 4 at para 12.24-28.

17   See Access to Justice Act 1999, s 11 (1)(a) and (4)(c) and Annex A to the LCD's explanatory notes.

18   See s 11(1)(a) Access to Justice Act 1999.

19   [1996] 1 WLR 736 CA.

20   Ibid at p 746 per Rose LJ.

1   See s 58 of the Courts and Legal Services Act 1990.

2   [1998] 1 WLR 1056, CA.

Appeal indicated that it was not in itself misconduct (justifying the making of an order for costs against a lawyer personally) to bring a case on a conditional fee basis on behalf of clients who had been unable to obtain insurance and would not therefore be able to meet any order that they pay their opponents costs. However, these developments can be reconciled with the suggested principle even though these fee arrangements also involve a distorting effect on the settlement process. The distinguishing feature in the case of pro-bono and conditional fee work is that the plaintiffs freedom from liability for its' own lawyer's costs is counterbalanced by the fact that the lawyer will not get paid in the event of failure. This provides a degree of security against the bringing of unmerited claims which many now feel to be lacking in the judicare legal aid scheme.[3]

Whatever the merits of the suggested reform, it is now clear that it has not been embraced by the courts. It is recognised that as a general principle the courts should seek to ensure that the loser is in a position to pay the winners costs, this being of 'fundamental importance in deterring plaintiffs from bringing and defendants from defending actions which they are likely to lose.' [4] However, this principle must give way before the competing right of access to the courts. Steps will not be taken to protect the winner's position on costs which will deter the exercise of this right. [5] This as was clearly illustrated by the decision of the Court of Appeal in *Metalloy Supplies Ltd v MA (UK) Ltd*.[6] The liquidator of the plaintiff company brought an action against the defendants for the price of goods sold by the plaintiff to the defendant. It was clear however from the start that the liquidator lacked the funds to bring the case to trial if, as proved to be the case, the defendant had a substantial defence. Indeed once the defendant obtained an order for security for costs, the claim was dismissed. The defendant then sought an order that the liquidator pay personally the costs incurred to date. The Court of Appeal refused to make such an order for the reasons set out in the following extract.

Waller LJ

Mr Irvin (counsel for the defendants) argued that once the liquidator realised that he had not sufficient funds to pay the plaintiffs own costs of taking the matter to trial, it was unreasonable or irresponsible of the liquidator to continue with the action. That is not in fact in my view an allegation of impropriety at all in the sense required to lay the foundation for an application against a liquidator to pay costs personally as a non party; but in any event I do not, for my part, think that it was unreasonable because the liquidator must have hoped in the context of this action[7] ... that if he could keep the action going some recovery might be made. Mr Irvin suggested that this would be encouraging some sort of blackmail, but it seems to me that that starts from the assumption that the defendants are really bound to win on the merits and should not

---

3   Supra p 305 note 2 at pp 156-157, 161-163.
4   *Roache v News Group Newspapers Ltd* (1992) Times, 23 November per Sir Thomas Bingham MR.
5   See *Abraham v Potter* [1997] 4 All ER 362 CA.
6   [1997] 1 WLR 1613.
7   Doubts had been expressed at an early stage by the trial judge about the merits of the defence, though it was ultimately deemed arguable.

be forced to settle because of the impecuniosity of the plaintiff company. In fact, the pressure or blackmail is two-sided in a case of this kind. The defendants , it may be said by the plaintiff company, are able by counterclaiming and fighting interlocutory battles to exhaust the resources of the liquidator so that ultimately the plaintiff company must discontinue. No one court can tell where the merits of these respective arguments lie prior to a trial, and to brand one or other as unreasonable or as acting improperly could only be justified if the action or defence was not being conducted bona fide in the sense of being reasonably arguable....

[Millet LJ] It is not an abuse of the process of court or in any way improper or unreasonable for an impecunious plaintiff to bring proceedings which are otherwise proper and bona fide while lacking the means to pay the defendant's costs if they should fail. Litigants do it every day with or without legal aid. If the plaintiff is an individual, the defendant's only recourse is to threaten the plaintiff with bankruptcy. If the plaintiff is a limited company, the defendant may apply for security for costs and have the proceedings dismissed if the plaintiff fails to provide whatever security is ordered.[8]

Note

One of the strongest affirmations of the principle that costs should follow the event occurred in *TGA Chapman Ltd v Christopher*[9]. There, the plaintiffs were the owners of a large warehouse which had been burned down after the defendant threw a match into a tin of bees wax. The plaintiffs premises insurers ('PI') indemnified them and sought to exercise rights of subrogation against the defendant, who was penniless but covered for the first £1 million of liability under his mother's insurance policy. The defendant's insurers ('DI') eventually paid out £1 million in damages. The Court of Appeal held that it was right to order DI to pay PI's costs under s 51(3) since DI had defended the case in its own interests. However this case has now been effectively overruled: see *Cormack v Washbourne* ((2000) Times, 30 March).

Questions

1. Does the approach of the Court of Appeal in the *Metalloy* case hold an appropriate balance between the need to ensure that costs follow the event and the need to avoid fettering access to the courts?

2. Reconsider the frameworks for lawyers' ethics advocated by William Simon and Stephen Pepper[10]. Which if any of these approaches represent an appropriate response to the impact upon settlement negotiation of liability for and ability to pay costs?

8   Ibid at pp 1619 B – 1620B.
9   [1998] 1 WLR 12, CA.
10   Supra chapter 5.

Reforming the code of ethics

We have seen that the professional conduct of negotiators is not directly addressed by the UK codes. How might the current position be improved? In the following extract, Murray Schwartz notes that whatever the merits of the adversary system, it provides no moral excuse for the lawyer acting as negotiator and goes on to consider the merits of a rule of professional conduct, providing that:

> when acting in a non advocate capacity on behalf of a client, a lawyer must, within the established constraints upon professional behaviour, attempt to achieve the client's objectives, unless to do so would require that the lawyer use unfair unconscionable, or unjust, though not unlawful, ends, in which event the lawyer must not accept or continue the representation.

[Professor Schwartz contends that] the arguments against the kind of prohibition contained in the second rule fall into three categories: the first has to do with unfairness to lawyers, the second with the impact of such a prohibition on the integrity of the lawyer-client relationship, and the third with unfairness to the client.

A. UNFAIRNESS TO LAWYERS

One immediate objection is that terms like 'unfair', unconscionable,' or 'unjust' are too vague to be used in a rule of professional responsibility. One lawyer's concept of unconscionability may be another's consummation devoutly to be wished. It would be unconscionable, the argument might run, to discipline a lawyer for behaviour that others – but not the individual lawyer – might regard as unconscionable in retrospect.

[A] possible response to the argument of vagueness would be to define 'unconscionability' not in terms of a lawyer's subjective assessment, but rather by reference to an objective body of law, that is, by measuring a lawyer's conduct against a standard of how others in similar circumstances would regard the proposed transaction. Courts are not unfamiliar with an 'unconscionability' standard, and lawyers may refer to an existing body of law for an explanation of the term. If the standard explicitly posed the question 'Would a court of equity regard this course of action as 'unconscionable'?,' the vagueness objection, though not eliminated, would have less force.

Closely related to the objection of vagueness is the objection that such a standard would be arbitrarily enforced or even be unenforceable. That objection has several facets.

First, the contribution of a lawyer acting in a non-advocate capacity is much less visible than that of the advocate. In most cases, the lawyer's conduct will not surface at all. To impose discipline in the few cases where it does surface would be to create an arbitrary system of enforcement.

Second, use of such a standard may result in abusive discrimination against lawyers who represent unpopular causes or oppressed persons, or who themselves are for personal, political, or other reasons *personae non gratae* at the bar. Whatever safeguard against this kind of abuse is obtained by limiting the scope of the professional rule to criminal or fraudulent conduct is lost *pro tanto* by expanding its scope to reach other kinds of conduct. The argument is not without force. Its persuasiveness depends upon the extent to which the disciplinary process is seen as concentrating unfairly on these types of lawyers. Expanding the grounds for discipline necessarily increases opportunities for using enforcement as a harassment device.

On the other hand, it may well be that concepts like unfairness, injustice, and unconscionability are just as likely to run in favour of poor or oppressed clients as against them, for the concepts as substantive law have for the most part aided these groups. Confining the reach of the terms to established legal understandings could further reduce the possibility of discriminatory enforcement.

A third facet is the question of whether professional disciplinary and enforcement systems can handle such types of conduct. Imposition of discipline upon lawyers for criminal and fraudulent conduct, both of which are now professional violations, is rare. How much will be gained or lost by the addition of an 'unconscionable' category?

In answering this question it is necessary to consider the functions of a professional code apart from actual enforcement. One such function is analogous to the use of the criminal law for deterrence. Although the incidence of actual professional discipline is, like the use of criminal sanctions, remarkably low, the existence of sanctions itself has a deterrent effect. Moreover, the professional code serves an important reinforcement function. It enables lawyers who do not want to assist clients in questionable transactions to decline on the grounds that the Code does not permit them to go forward, and thus to avoid the unpleasantness of refusing to assist on a basis that is seen by the client as a personal condemnation. A professional code is also an informational document. It tells lawyers how to behave. More than one lawyer has wanted to know the answer to the question, 'What should I do?,' in circumstances which would be covered by the prohibitory rule being considered here.

B: INTEGRITY OF THE LAWYER-CLIENT RELATIONSHIP

A different set of objections to a rule prohibiting a lawyer from using unconscionable means or pursuing unconscionable ends has to do with the integrity of the lawyer-client relationship.

First, there is the negative impact upon the trust and confidence necessary to that relationship if the lawyer is cast as the 'conscience' of the client. Clients come to lawyers for help and assistance, not moral lectures, it may be said. Yet the aspiration of the bar now is for the lawyer 'to point out those factors which may lead to a decision that is morally just as well as legally permissible. He may emphasise the possibility of harsh consequences that might result from assertion of legally permissible positions.'[11]

From the point of view of the client, there may be little difference between a mandatory rule and a mere permissive caution; a mandatory rule might, therefore, be expected to have only minimal impact upon the lawyer-client relationship.

At least as important is the objection that clients will not tell lawyers all that is relevant to the proposed course of action out of fear that the lawyer will conclude that the proposal is unconscionable and refuse to assist. This argument is similar to, and often confused with, the doctrine justifying a testimonial privilege for lawyer-client

11   ABA Model Code of Professional Responsibility and Ethical Consideration 7-8.

communications. Whether such client concerns are actually reflected in the extent to which clients make full and frank disclosure to their lawyers is unclear. There is evidence that professional and legal rules have little effect on the willingness or unwillingness of clients to talk to their lawyers. For example, Professor Uviller asserts that the testimonial privilege is rarely the factor that determines the client's decision to talk freely to the criminal defence lawyer. Lawyers may have more trouble convincing clients not to talk to other people than establishing open communications within the lawyer-client relationship. It is reported that defendants who have been given the *Miranda* warnings and admonished by their own lawyers not to talk with the police nevertheless do so to their own detriment. The Code of Professional Responsibility now permits a lawyer to breach the confidence wall by disclosing the client's intention to commit a crime and the information necessary to prevent it. Yet how many clients are aware of this exception and because of it do not talk to lawyers about their criminal intentions? With respect to a different client group, in today's world of increased liability of corporate officers, directors, accountants, and lawyers, it is doubtful that lawyers will be satisfied with incomplete answers or clients will be willing to risk liability due to insufficient disclosure because of their concern that lawyers will refuse to aid in their proposed courses of action.

Suppose, however, that some clients will be less than fully candid out of fear of their lawyers' reluctance to proceed. How undesirable would that be? Presumably, there is a danger that the client who mistakenly believes that the lawyer will regard the proposed course of action as 'unjust' will make incomplete disclosures and consequently will receive inadequate counsel. Yet the alternative of allowing lawyers to co-operate in bringing about unjust results may be too high a price to pay to relieve the minds of clients who have those concerns. Finally, whatever the justification for the application of an evidentiary privilege to lawyer-client communications outside the context of litigation, a privilege that excuses lawyers from revealing what a client has told them need not oblige lawyers to behave as if they never heard the client's story. The testimonial privilege of the advocate stands upon a different footing from the non-advocate lawyer's general obligation not to disclose the client's confidences; there is no necessary reason for the two to be treated as coextensive for these purposes. Thus, while it may be wrong to urge lawyers to reveal to the investing public confidences obtained from the client which might disclose the inaccuracy of a financial statement, it is a different question whether the securities lawyer should continue to assist the client as if the information were accurate.

C. UNFAIRNESS TO THE CLIENT

This third set of challenges to the proposed prohibitory rule derives from the claim ...[that]... a rule that prohibited lawyers under any circumstances from assisting clients could result in depriving those clients of rights to which they are presumably entitled under the law.

There are two ways in which such a result would arguably be unfair to clients. One is that to deny a client assistance even though the transaction involved is neither criminal nor fraudulent would be to prohibit the client from reaching concededly legal objectives. The other is that to require that lawyers refrain from assisting clients when they view the proposed course of action as 'unconscionable' is to run the danger of imposing the standards of an elite upon segments of the population that are not fairly represented at the bar, since lawyers are hardly a cross-section of the community in socio—economic, racial, ethnic, or political terms.

The first of these objections can be at least partly answered by acknowledging that not all outcomes which are neither criminal nor fraudulent are 'legal.' There is a range of agreements, for example, which, though they are neither criminal nor fraudulent, the law regards as either unenforceable or subject to rescission or reformation. It would not be a great extension to generalise that body of law into a professional rule which limits the lawyer's ability to assist the client where the ends are unconscionable. Moreover, if what is regarded as 'unconscionable' is limited to existing judicial interpretation of the term, the limitation upon those who would represent minority or indigent clients seems less severe. Indeed, as previously suggested, the standard could be more often a shield for protecting such clients from oppressive action than a sword to wield against them.

As the preceding discussion reveals, there are a number of legitimate objections to be made to a professional rule which would prohibit a non-advocate lawyer from engaging in 'unconscionable' conduct. But that discussion also points to an appropriate way to take the force out of those objections – to define the professional limitation in terms of a body of substantive law. This is the approach recommended here.

The proposed Professional Rule for the Non-advocate reads:

> A) When acting in a professional capacity other than that of advocate, a lawyer shall not render assistance to a client when the lawyer knows or if it is obvious that such assistance is intended or will be used:
> (1)   to facilitate the client in entering into an agreement with another person if the other person is unaware
>   (a)   of facts known to the lawyer such that under the law the agreement would be unenforceable or could be avoided by the other person, or
>   (b)   that the agreement is unenforceable or could be avoided under the policy of the law governing such agreements; or
> (2)   to aid the client in committing a tort upon another person, provided that this rule applies in business or commercial transactions only to torts as to which it is probable that the other person will in the circumstances be unable to obtain the remedy provided by the law; or
> (3)   to allow the client to obtain an unconscionable advantage over another person.
> (4)   For the purpose of this rule, 'assistance' does not include advice to a client that a particular course of action is not unlawful.

The general purpose of this rule is to prohibit a lawyer from assisting a client to achieve an advantage over a third party which the law would regard as illegitimate in that it would render an agreement unenforceable. The rule's provisions are phrased in terms of existing substantive law.

An important feature of the proposed rule, which significantly limits its reach, is its *mens rea* requirement. It could be argued that the appropriate *mens rea* element would be the 'belief' of the lawyer; such a requirement is, in fact, used in some of the Disciplinary Rules of the ABA Code of Professional Responsibility. But the phrase 'knows or it is obvious that' also is used in the Code, notably in the rules under canon 7 mandating that a lawyer represent the client 'Within the Bounds of the Law'. The difference is not metaphysical. A lawyer may believe that a proposed course of conduct is tortious, for example, but recognise that there are reasonable arguments to the contrary. Such a situation is posited by Disciplinary Rule 7-I0I(B)(2), which provides that a lawyer may – and impliedly may not – 'refuse to aid or participate in conduct that he believes to be unlawful, even though there is some support for an argument that the conduct is legal.' As long as the professional code permits lawyers to assist clients when they believe (but do not know) that the client's proposed course of conduct is unlawful, it would be inconsistent to prohibit assistance in 'lawful' but unenforceable transactions where the lawyer merely believes but does not know that the transactions would be unenforceable. The limitation of the *mens rea* requirement in the proposed rule thus accords with existing provisions of the ABA Code and also with the rule's reference to the substantive law.

Subsection (a)(I)(a) comprehends transactions in which the lawyer is aware of a mistake made by the other party which, if it subsequently became known to the other party and the matter were litigated, would render the agreement unenforceable or avoidable. The position taken in the rule is that the client has no 'legal right' to a non-criminal or non-fraudulent result which would nonetheless be unenforceable or which could be avoided were a court to review the transaction, and that, therefore, the client has no right to receive professional assistance for this purpose. A lawyer has a professional responsibility to decline to accomplish on behalf of a client that which the formal processes of the law themselves would not tolerate.

To the extent that such a restriction precludes fraud and deceit, its substance is already incorporated in Disciplinary Rule 7-102(a)(7) of the current Code of Professional Responsibility: 'a lawyer shall not counsel or assist a client in conduct that the lawyer knows to be illegal or fraudulent. The proposed rule goes further. By focusing on the other party's unawareness of facts which would render the transaction unenforceable, subsection (a) both avoids controversies over the definition of 'fraud' and also reaches transactions which are unenforceable on grounds other than fraud. For example, the proposed rule would apply where a unilateral mistake of one party known to the other results in a contract that does not reflect the 'true intent' of the contracting parties.

Subsection (a)(I)(b) is addressed to those circumstances where all the parties are aware of the facts, but a court would nonetheless declare the agreement unenforceable or voidable because of an overriding social policy such as that underlying the Statute of Frauds. Where the other party, although aware of the facts, is unaware of the unenforceability or avoidability of the transaction, the rule would prohibit the lawyer from assisting the client to take advantage of that unawareness. Where the other party is aware of the unenforceability of the agreement but nevertheless desires to proceed – as, for example, in an industry practice of closing a deal with a handshake rather than a formal writing the lawyer may assist the client. Of course, in today's world of professional liability, a lawyer who assists a client in entering into an unenforceable or voidable transaction without being aware or advising the client of that potential outcome would be risking a substantial lawsuit from the client.

The first clause of subsection (a)(2) ('to commit a tort upon another person') casts the professional responsibility of the lawyer in terms of substantive tort law. That law already imposes civil liability upon a lawyer who knowingly assists a client to commit a tort for which the client is liable to a third person. No immediate reason appears why such a provision should not be incorporated in a professional code, except perhaps in the circumstances addressed in the proviso. Certain types of conduct in the business and commercial world are classified as either torts or breaches of contract, depending upon the purposes of the classification (eg, measure of damages, statute of limitations). Inasmuch as a substantial, if not dominant, body of opinion would hold that there is nothing improper about an intentional breach of contract since the law provides ample remedies, it would be unfortunate to let the lash of professional rules fall upon the shoulders of a lawyer because a particular breach of contract happens to carry tortious implications. On the other hand, lawyers should not be immunised from professional liability for assisting in tortious conduct merely because for some purposes the tort could also be regarded as a breach of contract. The proviso in the rule therefore imposes restrictions on a lawyer's ability to assist a client to commit a tort even in the business and commercial world, but limits those restrictions to circumstances in which the tort remedy is not practicable.

Subsection (a)(3) of the proposed rule would bar a lawyer from assisting a client to gain 'an unconscionable advantage over another person.' At first glance, this subsection would seem to raise the objections to an unconscionability standard reviewed above. But its context takes much of the force from those objections – in a rule that refers to areas of substantive law, the term 'unconscionable' is to be understood first of all as referring to means and ends which have been specifically condemned under that term in statutes and judicial opinions. It's applicability, then, depends not upon whether a lawyer personally regards the transaction as unconscionable, but rather upon an objective determination of whether the means and ends would be regarded as unconscionable under existing law. This interpretation of 'unconscionable' is further mandated by the *mens rea* requirement of the rule: discipline is to be imposed only when the lawyer 'knows or it is obvious that' the proposed conduct is unconscionable.

Yet at the same time as the *mens rea* requirement lends precision to the term 'unconscionable,' it is flexible enough to adjust to future developments in substantive law. Judicial or legislative definitions of unconscionability would be included as they become clearly established. There is room, too, for developments of the concept in less traditional ways, for example, through the reflections of committees on professional ethics. Ethics committees might serve the non-coercive functions of a professional code – the reinforcing and informing functions – by responding to lawyers' inquiries about whether proposed behaviour would result in an 'unconscionable advantage' over another person.

Of course, it is open to question whether ethics committees composed of legal practitioners should have the authority to opine on issues of unconscionability where legislatures and courts have not yet spoken. But the suggestion may be less objectionable if it is seen as a device for evaluating lawyer tactics rather than as a means of determining the unconscionability of client objectives, for lawyers may possess special competence to assess the 'procedural' conscionability of their own techniques of negotiating and counselling.

Assignment to ethics committees of the task of explicating 'substantive' unconscionability is more difficult to justify. Is it fair to assume that a group of lawyers serving in an advisory capacity, drawing on well-accepted sources of law and their own familiarity with the customs of the community, will reach reasonable conclusions as to whether a proposed course of conduct is 'unconscionable'? Would it be easier to endorse this approach if such committees were to include non-lawyers? At the least, it would be illuminating to lawyers to have designated bodies to advise them on matters of this kind. Promulgation of subsection (a)(3) with the understanding that the term 'unconscionable' is somewhat open ended would provide an opportunity to gain experience with this type of advisory committee.

Subsection (B) of the proposed rule is intended to distinguish between advising clients that their proposed course of action is not unlawful, which the rule would permit, and assisting clients in that course of action through active participation, which the rule would prohibit.

The subsection may be unnecessary, for a lawyer would not face the problems contemplated by the rule until after determining that the proposed transaction was not unlawful.

Whatever the client's own moral standards, the client is entitled to expect an honest response from the lawyer. Thus, the proper response under the proposed rule to a client's unenforceable or avoidable, but otherwise lawful, proposal is for the lawyer to tell the client that although the proposal is not unlawful, professional standards prohibit the lawyer from assisting the client in pursuing that course of action.[12]

Note

Professor Schwartz's proposed rule would, under certain circumstances, prohibit lawyers from taking advantage on their client's behalf of the ignorance/ vulnerability of the other side. Its impact however would be wider so that it would prohibit a lawyer drafting a standard form contract including a term known or believed to be unenforceable but which might never be challenged by consumers.

Questions

1. Should the rule proposed by Professor Schwartz be incorporated into the LSGPC and the CCB?

2. How would Professor Schwartz's rule differ from the current Principle 12.01 of the LSGPC (Principle 12.01 is set out at p 348, n 20).

3. **Harry's Case**: You are a solicitor acting for Harry who is seeking to sell his newsagency business to George. In the preliminary negotiations, Harry tells George that the business is earning at least £25,000/annum net profit. Having seen the accounts

12   Schwartz supra p 290 note 2 at pp 681- 690.

you know that this is true. Just before the second round of negotiations, however, Harry receives a new set of accounts (which he passes on to you) which indicate that in the latest financial year the business made a net profit of only £3,000. To your astonishment, Harry says nothing about these figures during the second round of negotiations, as a result of which George agrees to buy the business for £500,000. Harry asks you to draw up the necessary contract.

What should you do? What difference would it make if Professor Schwartz's proposed rule had been incorporated within the LSGPC? See *With v O'Flanagan* [1936] Ch 375.

4. **Horatio's Case**: You are a solicitor acting for Horatio, a small business man. Horatio has discovered that Laura, aged 23 and one of his employees' has for some time been stealing money from the business. She has stolen a total of £10,000. Horatio plans to tell Laura's parents that unless they enter into an agreement to repay the money backed by a legal charge over their (large) home, Horatio will tell the police. Horatio is confident that Laura's parents will sign. Her father hopes to become a magistrate and the bad publicity would be fatal to his chances. Horatio wants you to draw up the documentation.

What should you do? What difference would it make if Professor Schwartz's proposed rule had been incorporated within the LSGPC? See *Williams v Bayley* (1866) LR 1 HL 200 and *Mutual Finance v John Wetton & Sons* Ltd [1937] 2 KB 389.

4   Lawyers' ethics and negotiations – a case study

Recall Fisher and Ury's claim that it is unnecessary to choose between the satisfaction of getting what you want and of being decent. The truth of this claim is the issue underlying this chapter. An appropriate way to come to a conclusion on this and related issues is to end with a case study: *Ernst and Young v Butte Mining plc*[13] concerned BM's dispute with EY (the Gramcol action) over EY's role as reporting accountants to BM upon the latter's flotation on the stock market in mid-1987. BM wished to claim damages amounting to about £100 million on the grounds of fraud, breach of contract and constructive trust.

In May 1992, BM began the Gramcol action in Montana because this would enable the claim to be prosecuted with the benefit of the contingency fee system and would also allow the assertion of certain causes of action peculiar to the US, thus inflating the damages to £2 billion. At almost the same time, EY began an action in England to recover unpaid fees of about £315,000 in respect of later transactions on which EY had also advised BM.

There matters rested while EY sought to persuade the English courts to issue an injunction prohibiting BM from proceeding with its claim in the US on the grounds

13   [1996] 1 WLR 1605.

that those proceedings were oppressive given that the dispute had little to do with the US. By July 1995, EY had been successful. Meanwhile in March 1995, EY had obtained judgment by default against BM because BM (inadvertently, as they later said) had omitted to serve a defence and BM almost immediately applied to have this judgment set aside.

EY's success in halting the US proceedings presented both sides with a problem. For BM the problem was that the claims they now wished to assert against EY in the UK were time-barred. However, if they could be asserted as a counterclaim to EY's fees action, then s 35 of the Limitation Act 1982 would allow them to proceed. Procedurally, they could not make a counterclaim in an action which they had already lost, but it is relatively easy to set aside a default judgment provided the costs of the other side are paid.

But both sides were equally aware that on the setting aside of the default judgment EY would have an unfettered right to discontinue their claim for fees and that once that had occurred it would be too late to make the counterclaim. However, each side hoped the other side did not know this and had no intention of informing them. On 15 January 1996, EY decided after consulting counsel that they should agree to the setting aside of the default judgment and then discontinue as quickly as possible.

So everything depended upon which would happen first following the setting aside of the judgment: EY's notice of discontinuance or BM's counterclaim. There followed on 23 January and 25 January two conversations in which the parties' solicitors discussed the question of whether EY would agree to set aside the default judgment and the procedure which would govern BM's counterclaim. They eventually agreed to seek the following consent order:

> It is by consent ordered (1) that the default judgment dated 7 March 1995 be set aside (2) that the defendant be at liberty unconditionally on or before [date] to serve on the plaintiff its defence and counterclaim.[14]

Ms B (a partner in the firm of FCB acting for BM) thought that this meant that Ms C (a partner in the firm BLG acting for EY) had agreed not to discontinue their claim and therefore agreed to allow EY to carry out the formalities necessary to get the order approved by the court. EY obtained the order at midday on 1 February. At 1.20 the same day, they faxed a notice of discontinuance to BM. At 1.50pm they faxed to BM a copy of the order. In these proceedings, BM sought to establish that EY's claim had not been effectively discontinued. Robert Walker J held that he had jurisdiction to set the discontinuance aside as an abuse of the process of court. He continued as follows:

> I must return to the facts and the important telephone conversation which took place on 25 January 1996. [Ms B] made the call. The exhibits include her contemporaneous manuscript note and a typed attendance note which [Ms B] actually dictated on 2 February; and [Ms C]'s contemporaneous manuscript note and a typed attendance note prepared within a day or two.

---

14 Ibid at p 1619C.

It is common ground that the conversation took between five and ten minutes and that much of it was taken up with [Ms B] reading out a draft consent order which she had prepared. The first three paragraphs of the draft were as follows:

1.   The default judgment dated 7 March 1995 be set aside.
2.   The defendant do have unconditional leave to defend and counterclaim.
3.   The defendant do serve a defence and counterclaim within seven days of the date of this order.

These paragraphs were followed by further directions as to pleadings and costs, with liberty to apply.

[Ms B] evidence was that after reading the draft she returned to paragraph 2 and reiterated or emphasised it (I have already referred to some of her evidence on this point). [Ms C] had no recollection one way or the other as to whether [Ms B] returned to the point, but she firmly denied that [Ms B] said that she wanted to be sure that Butte could defend and counterclaim. None of the attendance notes cast any clear light on this except that [Ms B]'s manuscript note says 'Agree to c/c;' this appears in the typed note as 'Confirmed agreement to counterclaim and defence.'

In the course of the conversation there was also discussion of costs, the Gramcol action and the preparation of the consent order. [Ms C] had still not got an estimate of costs, but that does not seem to have been an obstacle. The solicitors discussed the possibility of consolidating the fees action and the Gramcol action, but [Ms C] did not indicate any definite agreement to that course. She did indicate her agreement to the directions to be given in the Gramcol action mirroring those embodied in the draft consent order. [Ms C] proposed that her assistant Miss Jenny Brown should prepare the draft order (on which she was, [Ms C] said, already engaged) and that BLG should have carriage of the order. [Ms B] said that she agreed to this (although the summons to set aside was Butte's application) because she no longer saw discontinuance as a threat....

His Lordship then held that on these facts there was no enforceable agreement not to seek a discontinuance and turned to the law on abuse of process.

....it is necessary to have regard to the overall position of the parties, and what the plaintiff is trying to achieve by discontinuance. Looking at the overall position cannot in my view exclude looking at any allegation that one side has misled the other and has thereby put itself in a position to serve a notice of discontinuance which it might not otherwise have been able to serve.

Mr Boyle did not shrink from submitting, in unequivocal terms, that BLG deliberately (and at several stages) misled FCB as to [EY's] intentions. The deception which Mr Boyle asserts was practised (if it was practised by anyone) by [Ms C]; and [Ms C] herself did not in her oral evidence seek to disclaim responsibility, though she did refer to the plan (which I take to mean plan A, or if it failed plan B) being discussed at the consultation on 15 January. In the course of his submissions Mr Hirst candidly said that if the plan was improper, he apologised because he had advised on it. I have no idea how far the detail of the plan was discussed in consultation, and in any case I am not prepared to say that the plan, as a plan, was improper. But it was to my mind imprudent because of the predictable difficulty, which in the event occurred, of carrying out plan A without prevarication, and in particular of deciding when proper professional conduct required plan A to be aborted, whatever its attractions in the client's interests.

The first matter that calls for consideration is the telephone conversation on 23 January. [Ms C] readily agreed in her oral evidence that she did not mention [EY's] intention to discontinue, because she did not want to alert [Ms B] to the idea. That by itself is plainly unexceptionable; [Ms B] did just the same. But [Ms C] agreed that the discussion of directions would give the impression that the action was to continue. The transcript of cross-examination provided to me by Mr Boyle (from which Mr Hirst did not dissent, and which largely coincides with my note) records these exchanges.

Q. At [Ms C]'s manuscript note of the 23 January call] there is a reference to a timetable for directions and the conduct of the action. You must have known it would have created the impression for [Ms B] that you would continue with the action?

A. I suppose it would.

Q. [Ms B] was misled?

A. In so far as she would not realise that we were planning to discontinue.

Q. You were prepared to mislead her?

A. I did not look at it like that. I did not know we were going to discontinue until the final decision. We might have changed our minds if we were not able to pursue plan A.

Q. You would only have changed your mind if you could not achieve plan A?

A. Yes.

So [Ms C] went some way to accepting that the discussion of directions on 23 January gave [Ms B] a misleading impression.

There was further discussion of directions, both for the fees action and for the Gramcol action, during the second telephone conversation on 25 January. This was the subject of cross-examination.

Q. You agreed in your first conversation that reference would be made to directions for further conduct so you expected [Ms B] would telephone you to discuss the terms of an agreement?

A. The debate on terms was only whether [BM] would pay costs.

Q. Not terms?

A. I did not look upon future directions as 'terms.' Obviously we were going to agree directions. I was aware of my intention to stop the action in its tracks as soon as the order was made.

Q. You were prepared in the conversation on 25 January to agree further conduct of the action although you knew your client would stop the action the moment the order was made?

A. Yes.

Q. You knew the discussion would mislead [Ms B]?

A. No, because the important thing was not to confirm we were not going to discontinue.

Q. What would be the point of discussing directions if they were not going to be carried out?

A. One would normally agree directions.

Q. The real reason was you wanted [Ms B] to believe that your clients would continue with the action?

A.   I did not care what she believed as long as I gave no confirmation that we were not going to discontinue.'

In relation to the Gramcol action [Ms C] was referred to her typed attendance note of this conversation which recorded her as commenting 'that she could see no obvious difficulty with it-and would consider it as a possibility.' She was asked whether this was a fair statement:

A   I cannot remember saying it but I take my attendance note as accurate. It was dictated after the conversation for my assistants.

Q.   So a discussion about consolidation would not be misleading but agreeing to it would be?

A   Yes, I treated it the same way as directions.

Q.   If you had agreed, it would have been misleading?

A   Yes, because it would imply an intention to continue and one can only consolidate a live action.

Q.   Exactly.

A   We were solicitors talking in hypotheticals about the concept of consolidation.

Q.   You draw a distinction between agreement and discussion?

A   Yes.

Q.   Should solicitors be able to trust what other solicitors say?

A   It depends on the circumstances, the conversation they are having.

A third matter which calls for special mention is [Ms C]'s success in seeing that BLG obtained the carriage of the consent order.

This was an important part of plan A, as [Ms C] acknowledged:

Q.   You wanted to have carriage of it?

A   Yes, because then we would know when it was sealed.

Q.   Did you have that in mind during your conversation on 25 January?

A   It was my preference.

Q.   You expressed that preference to [Ms B] in your conversation?

A   Yes, it was not debated, she just agreed.

Q.   Having regard to your strategy plan A, you realised that it was crucial that she agreed?

A   It helped.

Q.   It was crucial?

A   It was what I wanted. I had not considered what would happen if there was not agreement.

Q.   You wanted the discontinuance before they got their counterclaim in?

A   Yes, I intended to serve the notice of discontinuance and the order at the same time.

The practice as to which solicitor has carriage of an order is a procedural nicety on which I was not referred to any authority (it is touched on, but not fully explained, in the Chancery Division practice directions in *The Supreme Court Practice 1995*, vol 2, p 165, para 810, sub-para (d)). But Mr Hirst did not dispute Mr Boyle's submission that in having carriage of an order a solicitor would be acting as an officer of the court, and should not use that responsibility in order to secure some partisan advantage. But that is, as I must conclude, what [Ms C] tried to achieve in this case. The fact that [Ms B] readily agreed to [Ms C] having carriage of the consent order is to my mind the clearest indication that she had come to believe that EY were not going to discontinue in the near future. I must also regretfully conclude that misleading conduct on the part of [Ms C] was the major cause of [Ms B]'s mistaken belief. It is to [Ms C]'s credit that she was so candid on these matters in her oral evidence.

In deciding whether the service of the notice of discontinuance in these circumstances amounted to an abuse of process, and if so what should be done about it, I have well in mind Mr Hirst's submission (put colloquially, but then developed) that EY did not owe BM any favours. I have well in mind that BM's initiation and conduct of the Montana action has been characterised by Rix J and Miss Dohmann QC as oppressive, and that is why EY were successful in the anti-suit action. But it is a commonplace that two wrongs do not make a right.

Heavy, hostile commercial litigation is a serious business. It is not a form of indoor sport and litigation solicitors do not owe each other duties to be friendly (so far as that goes beyond politeness) or to be chivalrous or sportsmanlike (so far as that goes beyond being fair). Nevertheless, even in the most hostile litigation (indeed, especially in the most hostile litigation) solicitors must be scrupulously fair and not take unfair advantage of obvious mistakes: see the decision of the Court of Appeal in *Derby & Co Ltd v Weldon (No 8)* [1991] 1 WLR 73 (this was not cited by counsel but the general principle is, I think, uncontroversial). The duty not to take unfair advantage of an obvious mistake is intensified if the solicitor in question has been a major contributing cause of the mistake.

For these reasons I conclude that the service of the notice of discontinuance was, in all the circumstances, an abuse of process.

Questions

1. How if at all do Principles 17.01[15] and 19.01[16] of the LSGPC effect this situation?

2. Would you expect Ms B and/or Robert Walker J to report Ms C's conduct to the Law Society? Would the *Guide to Professional Conduct* be improved by a rule requiring the reporting of misconduct?

3. Was Ms C's conduct in this case justified by Ms B's? Or by the fact that this was commercial litigation?

4. Ms C's manoeuvre ultimately failed and her client had to pay the costs of this hearing. Does the existence of the court's discretion justify her behaviour? Consider in this regard the conclusion of the Woolf Committee that civil litigation had become unacceptably slow and expensive and the frequent claim that there is currently a shortage of judicial manpower. Would the ethics of the situation be altered by plans to

15   Supra text to p 292 note 9.
16   Ibid.

make parties bear an ever greater share of the costs of litigation through increased court fees, thus in effect privatising judicial time?

5. Would this be a case where problems might have been avoided by the setting up by the firms involved of an internal review procedure designed to ensure litigators consult with colleagues not involved in the case before making tactical use of rules of procedure? What seems to have been the role of counsel in this case?

6. Is it significant that both the leading solicitors in this case were women? (See chapter 3 supra.)

CHAPTER NINE

Lawyers, clients and power

(Counsel) has nothing to do with his client except to protect him in court... in court he has the whole conduct of the case, ... and he has the power to act without asking his client what he can do. He has no master, but he is regulator and conductor of the whole thing[1] .

This chapter considers the distribution of power in the relationship between lawyer and client and more generally the values which ought to guide lawyers as they interview and advise their clients. By way of introduction we consider some models for the lawyer-client relationship suggested by Professor Thomas Shaffer (section 1). We then move to consider the extent to which the UK's 'law on lawyering' promotes client autonomy (section 2). This is followed by a consideration of the meaning and ethical status of autonomy (section 3); the relationship between autonomy and the rights of third parties (section 4); the justifications if any for lawyer paternalism (section 5); and finally the question of whether lawyers are ever justified in infringing their client's autonomy to failing to educate their clients about the limits of the law's coercive power. Many of these issues are most likely to arise in practice where the client is a private individual with little familiarity with or knowledge of the legal system. Lawyers working for large companies or powerful, wealthy private clients are likely to have little opportunity to be paternalistic and the problems facing these lawyers have already been discussed in chapter 5.

1 Models for the lawyer–client relationship

Thomas Shaffer has suggested that it is useful to consider four possible goals for the lawyer-client relationship namely, client victory, client autonomy, client rectitude and

1   *R v Registrar of Greenwood County Court* [1885] 15 QBD 54 at 58 per Lord Brett MR CA.

client goodness. He describes the lawyer adopting these aims as the 'Godfather', the 'Hired Gun', the 'Guru' and the 'Friend'.[2]

The godfather and client victory

The Godfather assumes that the client wants victory (meaning, in most cases, maximum financial returns) and that the lawyer's role is that of a technician ready to pull any of the levers of the legal machine which are likely to achieve success. The Godfather proceeds in this way even if the non-legal cost to the client in terms of damaged relationships, bitterness and animosity is enormous. Characteristic of this lawyer is the further assumption that the client's problems can only be addressed through the strictly legal techniques in which the lawyer has been trained.

The hired gun and client autonomy

The Hired Gun may have read that lawyers are often excessively paternalistic and is concerned to maximise the client's autonomy, ie to ensure that the client is fully apprised of all the options available and makes an informed rational choice in accordance with his or her own values. The Hired Gun therefore practises client-centred counselling. The decision must be that of the client and the client alone. For this reason, s/he attempts to ensure that the client makes the decision free from the influence of others. Those others include the lawyer and so the lawyer should refrain from non-legal advice, at least until the client has made his or her own decision. At that point, the lawyer may tender his or her own opinion and, according to some commentators, withdraw if that opinion is rejected. Another view is that the lawyer should nevertheless continue to act in order to facilitate the client's autonomy.

The lawyer as guru and client rectitude

The Guru is concerned that the client will do the right thing regardless of the client's opinion on the matter. Characteristic of the Guru is a willingness to override the client's decisions either in the interests of third parties (in which case s/he acts as a moral police(wo)man) or in the client's own interests (in which case s/he acts as a paternalist). For either of these two reasons , the Guru is prepared to manipulate the client in order to achieve the right result. This will be what the lawyer does if s/he makes a credible threat to withdraw should the client refuse to follow the lawyer's advice. Sometimes such manipulation may be unavoidable. Indeed it may be required by a code of conduct. For example, if the client in a criminal trial admits guilt but continues to insist upon advancing a defence, then in England the lawyer will be required to withdraw unless

---

2   Thomas L Shaffer and Robert F Cochran Jnr *Lawyers, Clients and Moral Responsibility* (St Paul, Minn, West Publishing) pp 42-47.

the client changes his instructions. If the client is persuaded by the threat of withdrawal, the lawyer has acted as Guru. Whilst this may be perfectly justifiable in this case because of the constraints of the Code, there are others where it may be more problematic, for example where the lawyer refuses to engage in a line of cross-examination which is legal but which the lawyer regards as unnecessarily oppressive to witnesses and therefore morally wrong.

The lawyer as friend and client goodness

The lawyer who wishes to be a friend to the client ('LAF'), has a deeper concept of friendship than that presupposed by Professor Fried's famous article of the same name.[3] LAF is concerned about the impact of the lawyer-client relationship on the client's personality and relationships. Unlike the Godfather, LAF takes time and trouble to discover what the client's real values are and explores their implications for the problem at hand. S/he does not assume that the client is concerned simply to manipulate the law to his own ends. Unlike the Hired Gun, LAF does not view the client as an isolated individual free to choose amongst values and relationships. Rather the client is understood as a product of a series of communities and relationships (family, neighbourhood, faith) by which the client's goals will be and should be moulded. Unlike the Guru, LAF is not content that the client do the right thing. LAF sees conduct as being determined by character not by rules (moral or legal). LAF wants the client to embrace a course of action which will not only impact beneficially upon others but also represent a positive episode in the client's personal development. The crucial question for LAF is whether the lawyer-client relation has been such as to influence helpfully other aspects of the client's life as well resolving the problem which led the client to the lawyer.

Client autonomy is widely viewed as the pre-eminent value which lawyers should seek when interviewing and advising their clients. Professional power in general and paternalism in particular are viewed with an extreme suspicion perhaps as a relic of earlier times in which not only wealth but also moral judgment were regarded as appropriately confined to a narrow elite[4]. In more egalitarian times, this is regarded as unacceptable both in morals and in economics. This suspicion may be unwarranted. Indeed Thomas Shaffer has argued that this suspicion is based on a corrupt understanding of fatherhood:

3   Charles Fried 'The Lawyer as Friend: The Moral Foundations of the Lawyer-Client Relationship' (1976) 85 Yale LJ 1060.
4   See D Kennedy 'Distributive and Paternalist Motives In Contract and Tort With Special Reference to Compulsory Terms and Unequal Bargaining Power' (1982) 41 Maryland LR 563 at p 588.

There are trends in both popular and scholarly views of families. The popular trends are evident... and changes in fashion are evident among ethics scholars too -- prominently with regard to what has been said about paternalism.

Paternalism, in most writing on the professions, is a bad word. But pater (father) is not a bad word. The Hebraic religious tradition chose and retains the word, if only as metaphor, to describe God, despite the difficulty of a theology of patriarchy. The description approximates with a family metaphor the understanding of the Hebrew prophets that the God of Israel is a God with feelings -- the 'divine pathos,' as Abraham Joshua Heschel called it. God's pathos means that He feels as a father feels; the prophetic response to God is thus sympathy. Father, consequently, is not a bad word; it cannot be. Writers on professionalism erred in thinking otherwise.

It is not a moral condemnation of standards of professional conduct, then, to call them 'fatherly' (paternalistic); nor would it be a moral condemnation to call them 'motherly' (maternalistic) or even parent-like (parentalistic). If we take our theological metaphors seriously, to analogise behaviour to the parental is to fit it to our traditions. The retreat from parental metaphors in modern writing on professionalism is subject to two criticisms. First, the analysis has not proceeded deeply enough; writing on professionalism has been duped into announcing a moral principle when it should have been concerned with description -- truthfulness -- in the comparison of a professional person and a parent, and of the virtues of good parents and the failures of bad parents. Writing on professionalism should describe the moral reasons that we use family metaphors, in theology and in professional life and it then should turn those reasons into doctrine. Second, the condemnation of paternalism (parentalism) in modern writing on ethics in the professions is the product of the lonely-individual doctrine in philosophical ethics, and of the philosophical distinction between fact and value, particularly in its disposition to turn the parental metaphor into a moral principle.[5]

Nevertheless this mistrust of paternalism is undeniable. This chapter proceeds by considering the extent to which lawyers are encouraged to respect their client's autonomy as a matter of law and professional conduct before moving on to consider the meaning and moral claims of the idea of autonomy. In particular, we consider three possible limits to the claims of autonomy namely, the moral claims of third parties, the best interests of the client (paternalism) and the lawyer's obligation not to advise or assist the client to break the law.

2   Autonomy in law and in conduct

Even if there is a strong case in moral terms for the view that lawyers should seek to promote their clients' autonomy, the substantive law and the codes of conduct provide little incentive to do so. Lawyers are agents for their clients and in the absence of express agreement to the contrary, they will have the implied authority granted to them as a matter of law by virtue of their status. When conducting litigation, lawyers have

5   Thomas L Shaffer 'The Legal Ethics of Radical Individualism' (1987) 65 Texas Law Review 963 at pp 986-987.

very broad implied powers to take all decisions necessary to the conduct of a case in court. Consequently unless the client has expressly restricted their authority, the client will be bound by the lawyer's decisions in the sense that they cannot be said to be a breach of duty. Nor does the protection of the lawyer's autonomy stop at the door of the court. In *Waugh* v *HB Clifford*[6] , the Court of Appeal held that a lawyer had implied authority to compromise litigation without reference to the client save where it would be unreasonable to do so, for example because of the size of the settlement. If, as in the case of doctors seeking consent to medical treatment, the need to seek consent is circumscribed only by what professionals regard as reasonable[7] the qualification does little for client autonomy. The position is only marginally better as a matter of conduct. Solicitors are advised that 'As a matter of good practice it would not be appropriate for a solicitor to rely upon implied authority for non-routine matters other than in exceptional circumstances eg where it was impossible to obtain express instructions'.[8] However, solicitor and client might have very different perceptions of what amounted to a routine matter or exceptional circumstances. The one area where the LSGPC does attempt to promote autonomy is with respect to costs. The 1999 edition of the *Guide* contains stringent provisions[9] requiring solicitors to give their clients full and accurate information about likely costs. In this way, it could be argued, the *Guide* addresses one of the preconditions of an autonomous decision by the client to begin or continue the lawyer-client relation, namely full information. The CCB has very little to say about the matter and what it does say seems to do little to promote client autonomy. Thus para 603 provides that a barrister must not accept instructions which would cause him or her to be professionally embarrassed and adds that there will be such embarrassment

> if the instructions seek to limit the ordinary authority or discretion of a barrister in the conduct of proceedings in Court.[10]

The undervaluing of client autonomy is perhaps most prominent with respect to criminal defence work. Thus in *R v Ensor*[11] , the defendant had been tried simultaneously on two counts of rape and found guilty of both. Each offence was alleged to have occurred in similar circumstances in the course of his job as a security guard at a night club. The defendant expressed a strong wish to apply for severance, ie to apply to be tried separately for the two offences. He not unreasonably thought that the jury would give undue weight in assessing each case to the fact of complaint in the other. The Court of Appeal later agreed that the application would probably have succeeded, but his counsel decided that it was not in his interest tactically speaking to do so. Having been convicted of both offences, the defendant appealed on the basis that failure to

---

6   [1982] 1 All ER 1089, CA.
7   See *Sidaway v Board of Governors of the Bethlehem Royal Hospital and the Maudsley Hospital* [1985] AC 871.
8   Principle 12.08 note 2.
9   See Practice Rule 15 (paragraph 13.01 of the LSGPC) and the Solicitor's Costs Information and Client Care Code.
10   CCB para 603 (c).
11   [1989] 1 WLR 499, CA.

apply for severance made the conviction unsafe and unsatisfactory. The appeal was dismissed by the Court of Appeal on the ground that 'generally speaking this court will always proceed on the assumption that what counsel does is done with the authority of the client who instructed counsel to take the case'[12]. A court would only intervene if it had a lurking doubt 'that the appellant might have suffered some injustice as a result of *flagrantly incompetent* advocacy' [emphasis added]. That counsel's view was plausible seems beside the point if the client's autonomy is a significant value.

The issue of autonomy also arose in the case of *R v Turner*[13]: The defendant in that case was accused of stealing his own car from a garage at a time when the garage had a repairer's lien over the vehicle. The proprietor gave evidence which indicated that he thought he was giving evidence in civil proceedings for the recovery of the debt. At that point, the defendant's position was clearly a strong one. However, the defendant wished to allege that the whole case was a result of a conspiracy between the police and the garage owner. Counsel was concerned that this would lead to the defendant's numerous previous convictions being put before the jury leading to his conviction and that conviction following a defence along these lines would might lead to an increased sentence, perhaps even to a custodial sentence. Counsel sought to persuade the defendant of the merits of a guilty plea in an interview lasting from 1.50pm to 3.30pm throughout which the defendant maintained his intention to plead not guilty. However, in a further discussion in the cells just before the court resumed, the defendant finally agreed to plead guilty. One of the grounds of his subsequent appeal was that the guilty[14] plea was induced by undue pressure on the part of counsel. Dismissing this ground of appeal, Lord Parker commented

> [the defendants argument on appeal] is a very extravagant proposition, and one which would only be acceded to in a very extreme case. The Court would like to say with emphasis that they can find no evidence here that counsel then representing the appellant exceeded his duty in the way he presented his advice to the appellant. He did it in strong terms. It is perfectly right that counsel should be able to do it in strong terms, provided always that it is made clear that the ultimate choice and a free choice is in the accused person. The one thing that is clear from all the evidence is that, at every stage of these proceedings, certainly up to the interview in the cell, it was impressed on the appellant by counsel, by the solicitor acting for the appellant by [the defendants girlfriend] that the choice was open to him, and, insofar as the appeal rests on undue influence by counsel, the court is satisfied it wholly fails.

Question

Do you agree with Lord Parker's statement of the duties of defence counsel? Did the appellant in *Turner* have a free choice? What are the implications for the lawyer's moral responsibility in such situations of the practice of discounting the sentences of those who plead guilty? (Supra pp 232-234.)

12   Ibid at 502B.
13   [1970] 2 All ER 281.
14   Ibid 283A-B.

3   Autonomy and morality[15]

Like any concept with popular appeal and persuasive value, the notion of individual autonomy is used in a variety of different and inconsistent senses. Nevertheless, Gerald Dworkin has plausibly defined autonomy as:

> the second order capacity of persons to reflect critically upon their first order preferences desires, wishes and so forth and the capacity to accept or attempt to change these in the light of higher first order preferences and values. By exercising such a capacity, persons define their nature, give meaning and coherence to their lives and take responsibility for the kind of person they are[16].

Individuals may be said to be act autonomously when they view living their lives as like writing a novel. The novel has immense possibilities and until the final chapter is written no fixed destination. Autonomous individuals reflect on the sort of person they want to be and then act to give their lives that particular shape. As Dworkin implies, this may involve discarding the values and concerns of the moment for others more consistent with the plot devised by the author. To give up your job because, though enjoyable, you felt it was making you a different and less attractive person would be to act autonomously in this sense. Something of the attractiveness of autonomy to modern eyes emerges when it is contrasted with older notions of how the story is written. In the Old Testament, the prophet Jeremiah writes that

> I went down to the potter's house, and I saw him working at the wheel. But the pot he was shaping from the clay was marred in his hands; so the potter formed it into another pot, shaping it as seemed best to him. Then the word of the Lord came to me:' O house of Israel , can I not do with you as this potter does' declares the Lord.'Like the clay in the hand of the potter so are you in my hand , O house of Israel.'[17]

To modern eyes the notion of the individual (let alone that of a whole nation) being shaped by another is distinctly unattractive. As stated, however, the notion of autonomy contains a crucial ambiguity. The question is whether one can claim to be acting autonomously and yet say that ' I have [autonomously?] decided to do whatever my husband, priest, communal traditions tell me...'. The alternative view is that a person is morally autonomous if and only if he refuses to accept others as moral authorities; that is, he does not accept without independent consideration the judgment of others as to what is morally correct. The former is a weak view of autonomy because it does not regard as inconsistent with autonomy any particular decision, even a decision to cede judgments to others; the latter is a strong view of autonomy precisely because it rules out for the autonomous agent a decision to cede judgment to another.

The relative merits of strong versus weak conceptions of autonomy have assumed practical importance for contract lawyers in the working out of the doctrine of undue influence (which is summarised in chapter 1 above). The strong concept of autonomy

---

15   In this section, I draw heavily upon Gerald Dworkin *The Theory and Practice of Autonomy* (Cambridge, CUP, 1988).
16   Ibid at p 20.
17   Jeremiah 18: 3-7 (NIV).

is illustrated by the judgment of Lord Justice Millet in the case of *Crédit Lyonnais Nederland NV v Burch*[18]. The case concerned a girl (Burch) in her mid-twenties who had been a junior employee in a company run by a wealthy Italian businessman (Pelosi). Burch was very committed to the business and enjoyed a close personal relationship with Pelosi and his family. When the business need further credit facilities, Burch agreed to Pelosi's request that she give an unlimited guarantee and charge as a condition of the bank's continued assistance. She rejected the advice of the bank's solicitors that she consult an independent solicitor. The bank's solicitor informed her that the charge and guarantee were unlimited in time and extent, but she was never told that the company had already borrowed £163,000 against a limit of £250,000. Nor was she told that the proposed extension was only to £270,000. The court set aside the transaction against the bank. Whilst the relationship of employer and employee was not one such as automatically attracted a presumption of undue influence, it was common knowledge that employer-employee relationships do sometimes lead to employees placing excessive trust in their employer. This together with the manifestly disadvantageous terms of the transaction did combine to create a presumption that the guarantee was being offered as a result of Pelosi's undue influence. The bank had not itself exerted undue influence, but it knew of the facts giving rise to the presumption. It therefore had to take reasonable steps to ensure that its guarantee had not in fact been procured by undue influence[19]. Merely to advise Burch to seek independent advice was not enough. She needed actually to have independent advice since an independent advisor would have ascertained the undisclosed facts and advised her not to proceed.

Millett LJ went on however to consider what would have been the position if Burch had had independent legal advice He said:

> ...no competent solicitors could possibly have advised her to enter into [the transaction]. He would be bound to warn her against it in the strongest possible terms, and to have refrained from acting for her further if she had persisted in it against his advice (see *Powell v Powell* [1990]1 Ch 243 at 247).

> ...it would [not] necessarily have made any difference even if Miss Burch had entered into the transaction after taking independent legal advice. Such advice is neither always necessary nor always sufficient. It is not a panacea. The result does not depend mechanically on the presence or absence of legal advice. I think that there has been some misunderstanding of the role which the obtaining of independent legal advice plays in these cases.

> It is first necessary to consider the position as between the complainant and the alleged wrongdoer. The alleged wrongdoer may seek to rebut the presumption that the transaction was obtained by undue influence by showing that the complainant had the benefit of independent legal advice before entering into it. It is well established that in such a case the court will examine the advice which was actually given. It is not sufficient that the solicitor has satisfied himself that the complainant understands the legal effect of the transaction and intends to enter into it. That may be a protection against mistake

18 [1997] 1 All ER 144 CA.
19 *Barclays Bank v O'Brien* [1994] 1 AC 180, HL.

or misrepresentation; it is no protection against undue influence. As Lord Eldon LC said in *Huguenin v Baseley* (1807) 14 Ves 273 at 300, [1803–13] All ER Rep 1 at 13: 'The question is, not, whether she knew what she was doing, had done, or proposed to do, but how the intention was produced ...' Accordingly, the presumption cannot be rebutted by evidence that the complainant understood what she was doing and intended to do it. The alleged wrongdoer can rebut the presumption only by showing that the complainant was either free from any undue influence on his part or had been placed, by the receipt of independent advice, in an equivalent position. That involves showing that she was advised as to the propriety of the transaction by an adviser fully informed of all the material facts (see *Powell v Powell, Brusewitz v Brown, Permanent Trustee Co of New South Wales Ltd v Bridgewater* [1936] 3 All ER 501 at 507 and *Bester v Perpetual Trustee Co Ltd* [1970] 3 NSWLR 30 at 35–36).

Some of those cases were concerned with the equity to set aside a harsh and unconscionable bargain rather than one obtained by the exercise of undue influence, but the role of the independent adviser, while not identical, is not dissimilar. The solicitor may not be concerned to protect the complainant against herself, but he is concerned to protect her from the influence of the wrongdoer. The cases show that it is not sufficient that she should have received independent advice unless she has acted on that advice. If this were not so, the same influence that produced her desire to enter into the transaction would cause her to disregard any advice not to do so. They also show that the solicitor must not be content to satisfy himself that his client understands the transaction and wishes to carry it out. His duty is to satisfy himself that the transaction is one which his client could sensibly enter into if free from improper influence; and if he is not so satisfied to advise her not to enter into it, and to refuse to act further for her if she persists. He must advise his client that she is under no obligation to enter into the transaction at all and, if she still wishes to do so, that she is not necessarily bound to accept the terms of any document which has been put before her but (where this is appropriate) that he should ascertain on her behalf whether less onerous terms might be obtained.[1]

This represents a clear preference for a strong concept of autonomy. Burch should not be allowed even with the benefit of full information to cede judgment to Pelosi.

A common and widely accepted argument for the strong concept of autonomy is the view that moral statements are, in Arthur Leff's terms, evaluative statements[2]. As such, they are *necessarily* matters of opinion personal to the maker on which no external authority can be accepted. On this view, moral judgments may be contrasted with statements of fact such as those generated by the natural sciences (eg the world is round) about which individuals are not free to differ. This argument seems however to misrepresent what is going on when we make moral statements. Is the statement that widow burning (a practice long accepted in India) really just a statement about what the speaker prefers? At the very least a moral claim seems to be not just statement of personal preference but also an application of a principle accepted by a social

---

1   Ibid at p 155. This dictum was affirmed by Stuart Smith LJ giving the judgment of the Court of Appeal in *Bank of Scotland v Etridge (No 2)* [1998] 4 All ER 705.
2   See chapter 2 supra p 36.

group. Moreover, the argument understates the extent to which scientific statements depend upon *opinions* strongly and widely held within the scientific community about what makes a scientific proposition acceptable. Thus the theory of evolution is sometimes described as a fact. In one sense, however, this is to misstate the position. The theory of evolution is a theory about the inferences to be draw from certain pieces of primary evidence as to the origins of the universe. It is clearly not a fact in the sense of being something that someone has directly observed. It is a fact only in that it is regarded as the best explanation of the origins of the universe *according to the criteria currently regarded as decisive within the scientific community.* This can be seen when critics like Philip Johnson[3] challenge the theory of evolution by challenging the evaluative criteria on which it is based. Such challenges though made by very able men (Johnson is a law professor at the University California at Berkeley) provoke not merely disagreement but outrage.

This suggests then that the supposed contrast between morals (allegedly subjective) and science (allegedly objective) is overstated and that each involves some degree of deference to the opinions of others. If so, the objection to the weaker concept of autonomy that it allows deference to the moral judgments of other individuals or of a community seems insubstantial. Moreover, the weaker notion of autonomy, allows room for values other than autonomy such as loyalty, fidelity, commitment to one's community or relationships which are otherwise in danger of being squeezed out of our moral perspective by a strong concept of autonomy. The outcome of the debate about the respective merits of strong versus weak concepts of autonomy will also have important implications for the lawyer when advising about the choice between the possible courses of action permitted by the law. The weaker notion of autonomy will require, or at least permit, the lawyer to remind the client about his or her prior relationships and commitments including obligations to family. This was the view taken in America by the drafters of the Model Code:

> In assisting his client to reach a proper decision, it is often desirable for a lawyer to point out those factors which may lead to a decision which is morally just as well as legally permissible. He may emphasise the possibility of harsh consequences from assertion of legally permissible positions.[4]

By contrast, a strong concept of autonomy will be more suspicious of such advice. Thus the leading US textbook[5] on advising the client seems to suggest that respect for the client's autonomy requires the lawyer to refrain from discussing the moral implications of a proposed course of action.

Questions

1. **Mrs Smith's Case**: You are defending Mrs Smith, an elderly black lady charged with assault, who is due to appear in the local magistrates court. Her story is that as she was

---

3   See generally Philip E Johnson *Darwin on Trial* (IVP, Downers Grove, Illinois , 2nd ed, 1993).
4   MCPR EC 7-8.
5   See generally DA Binder and SC Price *Legal Interviewing and Counselling: a client-centred approach* (St Paul, Minn, West Publishing, 1977).

wandering around the local supermarket with her 14-year-old son, they were stopped by a security guard who asked them to accompany him to the manager's office. When she protested that she had done nothing, the officer seized her by the arm. When she went to push him away, he attempted to wrestle her to the floor, slipped and fell. The police were called and arrested her. In Mrs Smith's opinion, this was a case of racial harassment. The detectives' account says Mrs Smith was the aggressor throughout. You tell Mrs Smith that if she pleads guilty she will probably receive a conditional discharge, in view of her previous unblemished record and fine reputation within the local community. On the other hand, if she alleges racial harassment and pleads not guilty, a more serious sentence will follow if she is convicted. Mrs Smith is outraged and says she is innocent but says she just does not know what do. She asks for your opinion as to what she should do, saying repeatedly 'You're the lawyer, you know the system, tell me what I should do. That's what you're paid for, isn't it?'

What do you do?

2. You are one of five partners in a provincial practice which undertakes a broad range of work. Mary James, one of your oldest clients, was a highly successful local businesswoman until her retirement five years ago. In the course of assisting her on a broad range of legal matters, you have built up a good working relationship with her. You know she trusts your judgment. Two years ago, you drew up a new will for her in which she disinherited Harold, one of her three sons, because he had married outside the faith (Mary is Jewish). Mary now has cancer and has less than a year to live. On several occasions recently she has discussed with you Harold's position and said that she is not sure if she has done the right thing. She has asked you several times if she should reinstate Harold. You think she would probably reinstate Harold if you suggest that she should. What do you do?

3. Consider again the case of *Crédit Lyonnais Nederland NV v Burch*. Do you agree with Millet LJ's analysis of the duties of an independent legal adviser to people like Ms Burch?

4. Is the analogy of an author writing a novel helpful as a way of understanding and justifying individual autonomy?

4   Autonomy and third parties

A lawyer may attempt to justify an apparent infringement of client autonomy on one of a number of grounds. One is that what was done was in the interests of the client even if it was contrary to his or her wishes. This seems to be paternalism and as such a difficult claim to make. A more promising line is to argue that what the client was proposing to do whilst undoubtedly legal would have resulted in a serious moral wrong to a third party. This argument might be made by a lawyer in defence of a refusal to carry out a client's wish for an application for the introduction of irrelevant sexual history evidence in a rape trial. This argument has already been considered in detail in chapter 5 but can nevertheless usefully be reconsidered at this point. It might be objected that such an infringement of the client's autonomy though not tarred with the paternalistic brush is nevertheless unjustified because it is for the client to decide what morality requires. This argument seems though to involve the confusion identified earlier about the nature of moral reasoning.[6] It also seems to involve a confusion between two different spheres of operation for the idea of autonomy. One is the political sphere, where autonomy operates as an argument that the state should not impose upon its citizens any particular vision of the good life. The other is the social sphere in which the argument is that other citizens should not question each other's exercise of their legal freedom on moral grounds even if the moral case includes...iew that morally wrongful harm to a third party is about to occur. The problem is that one may accept the political argument without accepting the social argument. Indeed one may argue that the state may only be kept within bounds if citizens *do* obstruct each others exercise of freedoms allowed by the law if such exercise is likely to cause unjustified harm. Consequently, the defence for the lawyer as hired gun which depends on arguing that client autonomy requires the lawyer to assist the client to exercise each and every freedom allowed by the law seems unpersuasive. The choice would seem to be between the lawyer as Guru and the Lawyer as Friend. The Lawyer as Friend is attractive because s/he displays moral humility. In discussing the moral implications of a proposed course of action, the lawyer may find his or her moral views changing in the light of what the client says. But if they do not, the LAF has a difficult dilemma.

Question

Spaulding v Zimmerman[7] : you represent an insurance company which is defending an action against a motorist who is alleged to have negligently run down the plaintiff. You receive a medical report from your own doctor which says that unless the plaintiff receives immediate treatment his injuries may become much more serious, indeed fatal. The plaintiff's doctor does not appear aware of this. What do you do? Can you both respect the client's autonomy and protect the plaintiff? If so, how?

5   Autonomy and paternalism

Soft paternalism

Interviewing and advising the client so as to promote the client's autonomy and avoid paternalism may be an exceedingly difficult thing to do. Lawyers may find themselves

---

6   Supra text to notes 2-3.
7   116 NW 2d 704 (1962).

manipulating their clients in very subtle perhaps even unintended ways. For example in an effort to ensure client autonomy, lawyers taught the art of interviewing will often be urged to proceed with open questions which allow the client to speak without interruption. They will be urged to listen empathetically, ie in a manner which conveys understanding and acceptance rather than a judgmental disapproval. Yet if the lawyer in fact disapproves of the client's behaviour (few lawyers will approve of the client who says 'I want to leave my wife and five children because I'm bored with being tied down') effective empathetic listening will be deceptive. It will therefore infringe the client's autonomy because it induces a full account of the facts under the influence of a lie, namely that the lawyer approves. When it comes to advising, it is sobering to realise that many studies show that respondents will often answer two questions involving logically identical choices in a contradictory manner depending on just how the question is put.[8] Similarly, lawyers who attempt to present all the options in a way which avoids influencing the clients may find that the order in which the options are presented, the tone of voice with which they are conveyed and a host of other factors nevertheless have a powerful impact on the client.[9] Whilst such problems may be mitigated by appropriate training and practice of the art of client-centred lawyering, there are deeper problems at the level of principle. The difficulty arises because the capacity to exercise autonomy is distinct from the capacity to express preferences between possible courses of action. Those suffering from senile dementia lack the former but may well have the latter even if acting upon those preferences would clearly be disastrous. Most would agree that a commitment to autonomy does not require respecting the choices of those suffering from impaired rationality. Indeed it may require overruling of their apparent preferences in order to restore full autonomy in the long term. This is what doctors do when they commit patients to mental hospitals for treatment against their will.

Once we move beyond cases such as these where the capacity for rational choices and therefore for the exercise of autonomy is so clearly impaired, it becomes difficult to know which choices cannot be regarded as fully rational. In approaching this issue, David Luban argues that it is helpful to distinguish between wants, values and interests. An individuals' wants are subjective preferences (such as a taste for pickled cabbage) which are rarely the subject of discussion and criticism.

> [by contrast] values are reasons, and thus intersubjective and open to criticism and public assessment . . . values are definitive of the person who holds them. Both aspects are crucial. Because of the former aspect, we feel entitled to judge a person as having *wrong* values, *inadequate* values, *irrational* values, and so on. Because of the latter aspect, we nevertheless sense that attempting to change a person's values by main force, or to override them, directly assaults the integrity of his or her personality. I suggest that the former aspect is the deep reason for our temptation to act paternalistically toward someone whose values are weirdly different from our own; the latter aspect explains why we find paternalism offensive. The account I am offering helps to explain our conflicting intuitions toward paternalism.

8   David Luban 'Paternalism and the Legal Profession' [1981] Wisc LR 454 at note 77.
9   See William H Simon 'Mrs Jones Case' (1991) 50 Maryland Law Review 213.

Different from both a person's values and wants are his *interests*. I will use this term in a somewhat special way – a lawyerly way, if I may say so – to refer to freedom, money, health and control over other people's actions: what I have earlier called 'generalised means to any ultimate ends.' (These are the interests that our laws protect and regulate, and that lawyers are trained to obtain for clients.) The concept of interests that I am employing is meant to be an objective concept. A person's interests can be understood as those goods that enable the person to undertake the normal range of socially available actions. On this characterisation, interests can differ from society to society. Money is not among a person's interests in a barter economy, because it does not enable a person to do anything. Freedom in the sense of a wide range of career options is not among a person's interests in a strict caste society, because choosing among such options is not part of the normal range of socially available activities.

But, while interests may differ from society to society, they will not differ from individual to individual within a society, because to talk of the normal range of socially available actions is already to talk to the entire community. This objective sense of 'interests' is meant to capture the meaning of the concept in sentences such as 'Like it or not, I'm going to look out for your best interests.' Whether or not a person wants money or values freedom, in our society it is in the person's interest to have money and freedom. And just as the concept of liberty is ambiguous, in that it can mean either liberty to act on your values or liberty to do what you want, so the concept of a *person's own good* is ambiguous: it can refer either to what is good according to a person's own values, or to what is in the person's best interest. Sometimes these coincide, but often they do not.[10]

On this basis, paternalism is justified only when the individual's decision represents either

a)   a preference for his or her own *wants* over his or her own *values*; or
b)   a preference for his or her own *wants* over his or her own *interests*.

The problem is diagnosing when a particular preference falls into one of these two categories, the problem being that outside the academy many people form their values by a process which is far less deliberate and analytical than academic discourse.

The argument may be expanded in this way: if a person has odd – imprudent – preferences, the preferences may nevertheless be the result of calm deliberation, and therefore unexceptionable. Or the preferences may be formed by a mental process different from that of the 'fully rational individual.' But one can be a competent human being and still make decisions in a way that the 'fully rational individual' would not: one can prefer improvisatory decisions to deliberate ones (most people do, at least some of the time.) So before we are entitled to judge an individual impaired on the basis of his exceedingly odd preferences, we owe an independent causal account of how he came to be impaired.

This requirement, however, may be too strong a condition, because causal accounts of human behaviour in the fine are extremely hard to come by. Surely there comes a time when the irrationality of a person's wants is so manifest that it is itself evidence of a causal account lurking in the background, undiscovered by us and perhaps undiscoverable

10   D Luban supra note 8 at pp 460-464.

given our current ignorance of what makes people tick. How are we to discover, in such a case, whether the individual is genuinely addled? The obvious way is to ask him why he wishes to follow an obviously disadvantageous path. If he can give us an account of his reasons, then we should dismiss the hypothesis of incompetence and abandon our paternalistic designs.

Thus consider once again motorcycle helmet laws. We may wish to consider a motorcycle rider who objects to helmets as an example of 'a person irrationally attaching weights to competing values.' Let us ask a Hell's Angel why he prefers to risk his life by leaving the helmet at home. He tells us – at least this is the gist of what he says in admittedly livelier terms – that if he wore a helmet he would lose status in his club, that he might even be 'stomped,' that his opportunities for sexual intercourse would vanish, and that he would miss the thrill that comes from high-speed motorcycling without a helmet. These are perfectly coherent reasons, and it would be absurd to consider him incompetent.

But what if instead he told us, with perfect sincerity, that he doesn't need a helmet because his head is made of unbreakable plastic? (at each stage of our argument the question of rationality seems to reappear.) Doesn't the fact that the belief is obviously absurd rule out the claim that he has reasons for his preference? The answer seems to be yes, but there is a problem here. People frequently base their choices on matters of superstition, articles of faith, religious convictions, or coherent systems of unacceptable beliefs. Michael Herr tells us that superstitious methods to avoid death were universal in the American Army in Vietnam. Does that mean that all of the soldiers were incompetent? Somewhere there is a boundary to be drawn, separating unacceptable from acceptable bad reasons for a preference.

These bad reasons should be demarcated, I think, in two ways. The first way derives from the intersubjective character of reasons, that is their tacit claim to group acceptance. This suggests taking as a hallmark of an acceptable reason its acceptance by a recognised group. Obviously, this involves a logical fallacy: the fact that a group accepts a certain reason does not make it valid. But recall that all we are looking for is a line of demarcation between acceptable and unacceptable *bad* reasons; and here my suggestion is that a reason is acceptable if it is accepted by a group and therefore more than the product of an individual's idiosyncrasy.

The point here is one of pluralist political theory: if an individual adopts a group's values, this should be viewed as a political act (joining a voluntary association) and not a mere psychological quirk. Perhaps in some cases political reasons will exist for assaulting those values (think, for example, of the values that lead one to join the Ku Klux Klan); but it will not do simply to declare them incompetent by administrative ukase. In this context, anti-paternalism should be viewed as an essential policy safeguarding the rights of participatory politics.

Sometimes, however, we are confronted by bad reasons for a preference that are peculiar to the individual. The individual, let us say, is a self-harming eccentric with bad reasons for his preferences. Here, too, the problem is separating the acceptable bad reasons from the unacceptable.

My suggestion is that we apply a test given in *Matter of Will of White*, an 1890 New York testament case: 'But if there are facts, however insufficient they may in reality be, from which a prejudiced or a narrow or bigoted mind might derive a particular idea or belief, it cannot be said that the mind is diseased in that respect.' The idea here is that if any process is going on in the person's head that can be called 'inference from real facts,' the person is competent. It is too much to require that the inference be valid, or objective, or correct, for that is more than competent people can manage. Relative to a trained, intelligent mind, many of us are bad infers; relative to extra-terrestrials, our greatest scientists may seem cretinous. All we can reasonably require is that the person be connecting beliefs to real facts by *some* recognisable inferential process – then the mind is not 'diseased in that respect.'.[11] ...

As Luban recognises these tests are far from being value neutral:

> The outcome of our argument is very tolerant: the *White* test will countenance some strange folk as capably rational. It is important to notice, however, that this argument does not clear the way to a liberal theory of paternalism, for recall that rationality in the sense we have discussed it is committed to a theory of the good: it is biased toward the protection of interests and rationalist values. Let us call this the Ideal of Prudence. Our argument now concludes that when we are faced with an incompetent, imprudent individual, it is perfectly all right – justified paternalism – to foist on him the Ideal of Prudence. While the justification of paternalism I have offered contains the liberal toleration of alternative values, its bias toward the Ideal of Prudence is revealed in the case of incompetence: when a person's wants do not express coherent values, as shown by his inability to pass the *White* test, it is the Ideal of Prudence that the paternalist imposes, rather than any other theory of the good.

> The lawyer is caught in the same dilemma as the liberal paternalist. On the one hand, he is committed to advancing his client's stated ends, however peculiar they might seem to him, in order to advance the client's autonomy. On the other hand, '[t]he responsibilities of a lawyer may vary according to the intelligence, experience, mental condition or age of a client,' and

>> [a]ny mental or physical condition of a client that renders him incapable of making a considered judgment on his own behalf casts additional responsibilities upon his lawyer ... If the disability of a client ... compel[s] the lawyer to make decisions for his client, the lawyer should ... act with care to safeguard and advance the interests of his client.

> Since the lawyer may make a seat-of-the-pants judgment that the client is 'incapable of making a considered judgment on his own behalf,' ... and the lawyer's assessments of the client's affairs are angled in favour of maximising ends, the lawyer will sometimes act paternalistically to override the client's stated preference and substitute the Ideal of Prudence or, as I called it in less charitable language, Philistine values.

> On balance, this does not seem to me to be an objectionable state of affairs. There is nothing wrong with a profession which is the embodiment of Philistine values. Plato thought that the state is a macrocosm of the soul: employing this conceit, we could say that the function of lawyers in the division of labour in our society is to assert the Reality Principle against the more extravagant claims of the id and superego. If the client

11   Supra at pp 478-480.

expresses ends which, due to imprudence or excessive moralism, seem self-destructive, it is the lawyer's job to voice the conservative and restrained point of view.[12]

Luban thus urges lawyers to be 'soft paternalists', ie to ignore some of client's preferences in order to ensure that the clients' decisions are made in a calm, reflective, rational manner. The aim is to ensure that the client makes decisions autonomously where autonomy is identified with a particular mode of decision-making which may seem natural to the lawyer but which as Luban concedes may come less naturally to some clients. Soft paternalism allows those committed to autonomy to justify apparently inconsistent behaviour if in all the circumstances it is necessary to overcome impediments to the client's exercise of autonomy. Thus if empathetic listening is manipulative, it appears at first sight to be inconsistent with a commitment to autonomy. However, the soft paternalist may argue that inconsistency is only apparent. If the client is nervous or in the grip of strong emotions, there is the danger that all the information necessary to the client's decision may not be disclosed. Even if this problem is resolved there is the further danger that the final decision may be unduly swayed by strong emotions and thus not reflect the client's values in Luban's sense. Consequently, it may be argued that any manipulation involved in empathetic listening is justified by the need to promote trust and confidence between lawyer and client and generally to 'take the heat out of the situation'. If successful, this manipulative behaviour will prove to have been a valuable tool in the promotion of autonomy. Such arguments may be deployed to defend the freedom from client control granted to lawyers by English law in relation to trial tactics. Clients could not possibly hope to make informed decisions about trial tactics unless the lawyer were to invest considerable time in educating the client about trial advocacy. In the real world, however, this is impractical and so the lawyer must make the tactical decisions, but this is not an infringement of the clients autonomy. Rather it is an attempt to reach a decision which an informed autonomous client would make.

Questions

1. A commitment to soft paternalism may be indistinguishable from a commitment to autonomy. William Simon comments that

... the defining and problematic feature of paternalism is (said to be) is its commitment to particular conceptions of the good life. But the most notable theory of the good to have come out of the law schools in recent years defines the good in terms of the choices people make when not under domination. This sound very much like a theory of autonomous choice.

A genuine conflict between autonomy and paternalism would require both a thick theory of the good that did not depend on individual choice and a notion of individual choice capable of violating the good as autonomous. It is not hard to find examples of

12 Supra at pp 483-484 and 491.

such views – for example most versions of Christianity and other scriptural religions- but they seem to have had little direct influence on the legal profession.[13]

What does Simon mean? Do you agree?

2. The client is involved in a bitter custody dispute with his ex-wife. The client was a successful advertising agent with little time for family life until one day, to his complete surprise, his wife left him. Having recovered from the shock, the client has become a devoted and fulfilled father. His world is shattered (again) when, three years after leaving him, his wife reappears and asks for custody. During a brutal cross-examination, you suggest to the wife that by leaving she showed herself to be failure in the only roles she had ever assumed, those of wife and mother, to the evident distress of the witness *and* your client. On sitting down, your client says 'Did you have to be so rough on her?' What is your response? Have you acted ethically?

3. Do you think the court's decision in *R v Ensor*[14] can be justified as an example of soft paternalism?

4. Reconsider *Mrs Smith's Case*[15] and suppose that Mrs Smith finally accepts that the decision should be hers. If Mrs Smith pleads not guilty and is convicted there is a small (you estimate the probabilities to be less than 5%) chance that she will go to jail for a month. Should you tell Mrs Smith this? Does it make any difference if Mrs Smith is clearly so terrified of jail that disclosure of this risk would induce her to plead guilty however strong her case?

5. You are a provincial solicitor in general practice and have just been asked to handle the conveyancing needed for the purchase of a house by David Jones, the 21-year-old son of one of your oldest clients. David is shortly to marry Rebecca Batten. You know that both David and Rebecca come from deeply religious families in which marriage is seen as being for life. Should you suggest to David that he consider with Rebecca drawing up an ante-nuptial contract to govern the consequences of any subsequent divorce. (Such contracts have recently been made binding under matrimonial law.) Should you insist that David discuss this with Rebecca? Should you insist that Rebecca obtain independent legal advice?

Hard paternalism[16]

Arguments that defend apparent infringements of client autonomy by reference to the need for soft paternalism are very similar to efficiency arguments. The latter are often

---

13   William H Simon 'Lawyer Advice and Client Autonomy: Mrs Jones Case' supra p 337 note 9
       at p 225.
14   Supra p 330 note 13.
15   Supra p 334.
16   In this section, I draw heavily upon Duncan Kennedy supra p 327 note 4.

employed to justify state interference in the workings of the free market whereas the former are usually employed in the context of professional relationships. This difference however is only one of context. In each case an interference with individual's apparent choices is said not to be a disregard of their values but rather an attempt to realise their values by bringing about situations which would in fact be chosen but for the existence of 'transaction costs' for example the costliness of the information necessary to make an informed choice.

As Duncan Kennedy points out such arguments are enduringly popular even though they depend upon empirical assertions which are never really substantiated (how long *would* it really take to educate the client about the criminal procedure to which s/he is subject: might not the hardened criminal know as much as the inexperienced advocate?). For Kennedy, this raises some provocative questions.

> Why is it that the patent manipulability of efficiency arguments does not undermine their effectiveness, while distributive and paternalist arguments, which are actually easier to grasp and to apply seem excessively fuzzy?
>
> At least part of the answer I think is that the move to efficiency transposes a conflict between groups in civil society from the level of a dispute about justice and truth to a dispute about facts – about probably unknowable social science data that no one will ever try to collect but which provides ample room for fanciful hypotheses.[17]

In Kennedy's opinion soft paternalism may be a way of disguising what is in fact the overruling of value judgments ('hard paternalism'). Kennedy does not feel such a disguise is necessary. Just as we would praise an adult who overruled a child's choice because it was likely to be disastrous for the child's personal development, so we should recognise that sometimes adults should act so as to prevent other adults behaving in a similar way. Consider for example the case of an academic lawyer whose colleague, though very able, has an obsessive fear of criticism and hence refuses to publish the clearly valuable work she is doing. It might under these circumstances be right to suggest to the dean that she be heavily bullied into giving and the publishing a series of highly public lectures. This would be a stressful experience for her, but it might be transformative and as such the gateway to a highly successful academic career. In the following passage, Kennedy describes the motivation of and the judgments to be made by a hard paternalist.

> [paternalism arises] from two circumstances in a relationship between the actor and the beneficiary. The actor feels he has intuitive access to the other's feelings and perceptions about the world, and that he participates directly in the suffering and the happiness of the other. In other words, the basis of strong paternalism is lived intersubjectivity. The actor is not in the position of supposing or hypothesising that the other feels in a particular way – it's much more immediate than that. It feels like unity.
>
> In this condition of unity, the actor comes to believe that the other is suffering from some form of false consciousness that will cause him to do something that will hurt him, physically or financially or morally or in some other way. The actor's sense that

the other's consciousness is false is an intuition of error – that the clue to what the other is about to do is having it wrong. The basis of this kind of intuition is one's own experience of being mistaken, and of having other people sense one's mistake.

It is almost never possible to verify the intuition in a positivist sense, and this has great significance. But it is also important that intuitive certainties are real knowledge. To my mind they are more real and more reliable than knowledge of the other built up by formulating and testing hypotheses and models (though that is a form of knowledge, too).

The actor will certainly try hard to persuade the other out of his false consciousness, and sometimes persuasion works. Or it may turn out that it is the other who persuades the actor that the actor was wrong, thereby removing any motive for paternalist action. But sometimes it doesn't happen that way: at the end of the discussion, the actor still feels that the other is mistaken, and is about to do something not in his best interests. Or perhaps there is a limited time or no time at all for persuasion, and the actor has either to act paternalistically right away or not at all.

The actor has to decide whether to act to prevent the injury he sees coming. In the strong kind of paternalism, he doesn't see this issue in terms of, say, a reduction in total utility through the other's threatened behaviour, but in terms of anticipated pain for the actor himself. The impulse to save the other is the impulse that caused parents, putting on the brakes before the era of safety belts and armoured kiddie car seats, to reach across to keep their inattentive children from hurtling into the windshield. If they hurt themselves, you are hurt – that's the basic experience. Nonetheless, there are strong reasons for not acting.

The first is that your intuition that they suffer from false consciousness may be wrong. You may be mistaken in just the way you thought they were – it's all backwards, so to speak. This is the relatively cognitive version of mistake. The pea was really under the left-hand rather than the right-hand cup, so if you'd let them bet the way they wanted to, we'd all be millionaires now.

Another possibility is that their conduct was based not on the mistake you'd wrongly intuited, but on a larger plan you hadn't understood. They knew all along what you thought they didn't know, but because they had intentions you didn't grasp, their knowledge was perfectly compatible with what they were doing. You thought the developer tricked the condominium buyer into accepting a sweetheart contract with a management company. In fact, this contract, which eliminated just about all legal power of the condo owners to meddle in one another's lives, was one of the greatest attractions of this particular development. If you're wrong in one or both of these ways, your intervention will probably make things worse rather than better. If it will make things *much* worse if you're wrong, and only a little better if you're right, maybe intervention is too risky.

There is also the possibility that it would be best for the other to make the mistake and suffer the consequences. It may be a developmentally desirable mistake, with consequences limited enough so the other will survive to do better the next time. It may be more than that – it may be a mistake the other has to make if the other is to survive without the actor's constant paternalistic intervention to bail him out. In every case, the actor has to be aware of the possibility that intervention is breeding more intervention – perpetuating dependence and incompetence just as the apostles of self-reliance are always saying it does. Sometimes the actor must take the chance that the other will destroy himself, in the hopes that if he doesn't he will emerge at a new level of autonomy.

If the actor decides to act, the experience will be complex and contradictory. On the one hand, the action affirms intersubjective unity with the other. One acts out of the sense that one knows the other's mind, motivated by the fact that one suffers the other's pain. Sometimes these forms of knowledge are immediate and so intense that one feels no choice in the matter, any more than one does when acting out of the instinct of *self-preservation*. But even if it's a matter of reflection, paternalist action, when it works, has a strong positive connotation. Care is something we need; the ability to give care coercively but beneficially is one of the qualities we admire most intensely, whether in parents dealing with young children, in children dealing with aged parents, or in political leaders dealing with the base impulses and misguided beliefs of their constituents. When you feel you have done it right, you will feel fulfilment.

But there is a bad side to it as well, even when it works. The paternalist intervention is aggressive: it involves frustrating the other's project by force (or by fraud, in the case of withholding information in order to control the other's behaviour or spare the other pain). Along with frustration, the other is likely to feel rage against unjust treatment. From her point of view, the actor has come along not only with force, but with the self-righteous claim that the force is altruistic so she has no basis for objecting. Paternalist action is inherently risky because it will make someone you are intersubjectively one with furious at you, and they may be right.

If they are right, you will suffer twice: you will suffer with them the pain of the frustration of a valid project, and you will suffer on your own behalf the hurt of their anger at you, along with guilt that you have done them not just an injury, but an injustice. Even if it turns out that they were indeed suffering from false consciousness and that your intervention spared them a serious evil, they may not forgive you for taking things into your own hands. When you intervene in someone else's life, they may turn against you though you were in the right to do as you did. While we admire and honour some people in some roles for their successful paternalism, we quite rightly scorn and condemn other people for playing God, for not minding their own business, for degrading and infantilising those they are trying to help, and for acting out of selfish motives behind a facade of concern for others.[18]

The dilemma for the hard paternalist as conceived by Kennedy is that there is no principal or rule such as that proposed by advocates of soft paternalism to assist in determining when paternalism is appropriate. It is largely a matter of intuitive judgment.

Questions

1. You are a middle-aged, middle class female lawyer educated in London who now works in a community law centre in a mining community in Yorkshire. You have been

18   Kennedy, supra p 327 note 4 at pp 638-640.

consulted several times by Mrs Stewart, the middle-aged wife of an ex-miner who is now unemployed. On each occasion, Mrs Stewart complains of physical abuse by her husband, but rejects your suggestions that she take proceedings to remove Mr Stewart from the family home. She says angrily that you don't understand ('How could you?'). In her community, men regularly hit their wives and it is accepted that they do. It is indeed part of the deal. It seems that Mrs Stewart just wants to talk.

Last time you saw Mrs Stewart she had clearly been badly beaten but reacted much as before. In frustration, you consult a colleague. Your colleague suggests that you should threaten to refuse to see Mrs Stewart in future unless she agrees to your seeking an injunction banning Mr Stewart from the house. Your colleague's view is that once Mrs Stewart is freed from the physical presence of her husband, her self-esteem may rise and her view of the situation change. She may even be persuaded to bring criminal charges against her husband which would further the process of releasing her from a disempowering relationship.

Would the suggested action be paternalism? Would it be justified and if so why?

2. To what extent is it an objection to hard paternalism by lawyers that they lack personal knowledge of their clients such as that which exists between parent and child and husband and wife?

3. Consider again the duty which Millet LJ considered would be owed to a client in the position of Helen Burch. Would this be a paternalistic duty? If so what kind of paternalism would be involved? Would such paternalism be justified?

4. In John Grisham's novel *A Time to Kill*, Jake Briggance defends Carl Lee. Lee, who is black, has shot two white men who had raped his 10-year-old daughter. Just before his first court appearance, Carl Lee asks Jake, who has decided that insanity is the only possible defence, what he should say at the hearing...

CL: What can I say tomorrow?

JB: What do you wanna say?

CL: I wanna tell the judge why I shot them boys. They raped my daughter. They needed shootin'.

JB: And you want to explain that to the judge tomorrow?

CL: Yeah.

JB: And you think he'll turn you loose once you explain it all?

Carl Lee said nothing.

JB: Look, Carl Lee, you hired me to be your lawyer. And you hired me because you had confidence in me, right? And if I want you to say something tomorrow, I'll tell you. If I don't, you stay quiet. When you go to trial in July, you'll have the chance to tell your side. But in the meantime, I'll do the talking.

CL: You got that right[19].

Is Jake's behaviour paternalistic and, if so, in what way? Is it justified?

5. You are a solicitor acting for Simon Harris. Simon comes from humble origins and has little formal education. However, he has made a great deal of money in business, most recently as the director of a large plc. Now however Simon faces criminal charges in relation to the alleged misappropriation of shares owned by the company pension scheme. The main issue at the trial is likely to be dishonesty. Simon is an arrogant bullying entrepreneur confident in his ability to convince the jury. After all, he has never failed in his life. You are doubtful of the wisdom of this strategy and want Simon to plead guilty to a series of lesser charges, since this would lead to a far lower sentence, but he appears highly resistant. Consequently, you have asked Simon to attend a meeting with counsel to obtain a second opinion. You know that Simon is likely to be highly deferential to the social and professional status of the barrister concerned (a man from a highly upper class Oxbridge background) particularly as the meeting is due to take place in counsel's chambers. You also know that the barrister concerned is heavily dependent on your firm for work so that if you disclose your opinions on the matter the barrister is likely to give strong advice about the merits of a guilty plea.

Should you disclose your views to counsel? If you do will you have acted paternalistically? If so, is your behaviour justified?

6   Client autonomy and advising on the limits of the law

Question

The Polluting Client: Regulations have been issued to protect inland rivers from industrial pollution and widely publicised to relevant industries. The regulations prohibit discharge of ammonia at amounts greater than .050 grams per litre of effluent. Your client owns a rural plant that discharges ammonia in its effluent, the removal of which would be very expensive. The lawyer knows from informal sources that: (1) violations of .075 grams per litre or less are ignored because of a limited enforcement budget; and (2) inspection in rural areas is rare, and in such areas enforcement officials usually issue a warning prior to applying sanctions unless the violation is extreme (more than 1.5 grams per litre).

Should you educate the client concerning these enforcement-related facts even though it may motivate the client to violate the .050 gram limit?

19   John Grisham *A Time to Kill* (London, Arrow, 1992) p 153.

It is not only the interests of third parties or of the client which may induce the lawyer to infringe the client's autonomy. Such an infringement may be provoked, even required, by the injunction common to most codes of conduct that a lawyer shall not assist the client in breaking the law.[20] Recall Stephen Pepper's first class citizenship model of legal representation. That model was based on the premises that:

1) law is a public good intended to be available for the assistance of individuals in planning their lives; and
2) the primary function of lawyers is to assist their clients by informing their clients about the law and refraining from moral judgment of their client's intentions; and
3) lawyers should not assist clients in illegal conduct.

This model was designed to further the client's autonomy. However premises two and three create a problem, for in some situations providing information about the law may simultaneously both further the client's autonomy and simultaneously increase the probability that the client will engage in illegal conduct. Suppose you act for a father in a bitter custody dispute. On losing custody of the children, the father asks you to tell him which countries do not have treaties providing for the return to the UK of children illegally abducted by a non-custodial parent. Telling your client which countries are in effect safe havens will clearly increase the chances of an illegal abduction and therefore seems intuitively wrong. On the other hand, many would argue that telling a client that the applicable judicial remedy for breach of contract is nominal damages is the lawyer's professional responsibility, even if such advice makes it inevitable that the client will breach the contract. In between these two positions, are a host of difficult examples of which the 'Polluting Client' is just one. In the following extract, Stephen Pepper considers a number of possible principles which might be used to identify those rare occasions when informing the client about the law would be wrongful assistance in illegal conduct. As Pepper himself notes, most of these principles raise one of two fundamental questions. The first is whether what the law requires is morally required. The second is what we mean by 'law' when we speak of informing the client about the law. The fundamental insight of American legal realism was after all that it may be very difficult to state what the law is without reference to the actual behaviour of officials. If so, advising a client about the law must be understood very broadly (see *The Lawyer's Amoral Defense Role: A Defense, a Problem and Some Possibilities* supra chapter 5).

B. THE DISTINCTION BETWEEN LAW AS 'COST' AND LAW AS 'PROHIBITION' (THE CRIMINAL/CIVIL LINE)

Legal provisions can convey at least three rather different messages. First, the law can tell you that if you want to accomplish x, you will have to do a, b, and c in certain prescribed ways. If you want to create a contract, you will have to have an offer, an acceptance, and consideration. If you want to create a corporation, the necessary actions are prescribed by statute. Second, the law can indicate that some specific conduct will

---

20   Thus Principle 12.01 note 1 of the LSGPC provides that 'A solicitor must not accept instructions which would involve the solicitor in a breach of the law or the rules or principles of professional conduct.'

have certain prescribed negative consequences; that some specific conduct creates liability for certain costs or penalties. Failure to comply with a valid contractual obligation renders one liable for some of the damages caused to the promisee and to a limited class of third parties. A corporation that fails to conduct its business as required by the state of incorporation, by not holding required annual meetings, for example, may forfeit some of the benefits of being a corporation, such as limited liability. Third, the law can indicate that certain conduct is prohibited and will not be tolerated by society. A person who murders or steals will be punished by being forcibly removed from society for some period of time, in part to demonstrate how serious society is about the prohibition and in part to prevent repetition of the violation. Legal provisions in the first two categories indicate that some conduct is favoured and some disfavoured, and legal consequences will reflect the differences, but the third category involves a different and stronger message.

The ethical line for legal advice could be based on this distinction. Under such a rule or guide, a lawyer could not give legal advice in a context in which that advice is likely to lead to conduct prohibited by law, but such advice could be given in a context in which it is likely to lead to conduct to which the law only attaches a cost or penalty. The distinction between criminal and civil law is traditionally understood as distinguishing the prohibited from the tolerated, the prohibited from the 'merely' wrongful.

1. The Ends of the Spectrum

The principal advantage of this distinction lies in its apparent congruence with accepted legal culture and practice at both ends of the range of examples. Holmes' 'bad man' understanding of contract law has become so descriptively accurate that few would contest the notion of a 'right' to breach a contract, and where a citizen has a right, it is difficult to envision a rule of lawyers' ethics that would prohibit a lawyer from informing the client of that right or a malpractice rule that would allow a lawyer to choose to leave the client in ignorance of a right she might profit from exercising. At the other end of the spectrum, it is hard to countenance the notion that a citizen (client) has a 'right' to murder or steal, as long as she is willing to accept the law's penalty if she is caught. The dominant legal rules and culture are certainly in accord with this perception. Legal advice that facilitates such criminal conduct may be prohibited by the current versions of lawyers' ethics, and the lawyer is more likely to face tort liability for providing such legal advice than for withholding it.

Even at the ends of the range the distinction is not without problems, however. Breach of contract can cause serious harm, and our society (and perhaps our law) perceive some level of normative obligation not to breach contracts. It is not pleasant to contemplate a legal regime in which the primary message of the law as transmitted through lawyers is that breaching contracts is perfectly acceptable if it is to one's economic advantage to do so after having calculated potential compensatory damages as a cost, discounted by the probability and expense of enforcement by the promisee. This is perhaps just another example of the two-edged nature of law with which we began: all law, not just breach of contract, can be used to harm or to wrong. Here, however, the law has specifically recognised the harm and the wrong and has placed a cost or penalty on it. (Is it inaccurate to refer to the sanction as a 'penalty' because compensatory damages only include the cost of the damages one's 'wrong' has caused, and there is no additional sum whose only purpose is to discourage the conduct? Note that torts are normally considered 'wrongs,' but are ordinarily 'punished' only with 'compensatory' damages.)

At the other end of the spectrum, the euthanasia example also gives pause. Here we have contemplated murder, surely one of the core examples that makes the criminal/ civil distinction intuitively plausible, yet the notion that the client has a 'right' to know the law under which her behaviour will be judged and the procedures through which that law will be applied does not seem so far-fetched. To prohibit the lawyer from giving the advice means that the prosecutor has lawful discretion to apply the law to the facts in a fully contextualised, nuanced fashion and to choose not to prosecute; the jury has power to choose not to apply the law at all if it finds that the facts and justice lead that way; but the lawyer must keep the client in ignorance of these aspects of the legal system regardless of the specific facts of the situation.

2. The Middle Range of the Spectrum

The intuitive appeal of the criminal/civil distinction as applied to limiting lawyer advice about the law is substantially weaker when the examples come from the middle range. In that category, I would include non-obvious or non-traditional crimes, much regulatory law, and torts.

Indiscriminate usage of the criminal sanction creates a problem for drawing our line between civil and criminal wrongs. To the extent that conduct is criminalised when it is not intuitively obvious that the conduct involves a serious moral wrong, the justification for the criminal/civil distinction becomes obscure. The criminal sanction is supposed to announce that we are particularly serious about a legal rule, that we really mean a particular act is prohibited. But when applied to conduct that in no obvious way involves serious moral wrongdoing, the question irresistibly pushes up: why are we so serious about this? If no persuasive reason is available, we are reduced to the circular, positivist, formal justification: because it's criminal.

A few years after the national speed limit of fifty-five miles per hour was imposed, the reason for the rule -- conserving gasoline -- no longer seemed to be a strong national priority. Imagine the small trucker in a spacious, flat western state who wants to reimburse his drivers for fines imposed for driving between fifty-five and seventy miles per hour. He has asked his lawyer if it is permissible to do so and if he could deduct such reimbursement as an expense of the business. Or imagine a retailer just within the border of a state with a Sunday closing law, in competition with stores just across the state line, who asks his lawyer about the penalties for remaining open. The lawyer finds out that the penalty is a criminal fine of only twenty-five dollars per Sunday. In such situations, is the message sent by the law that the conduct is prohibited, that it is disfavoured and comes with a cost, or some mixture that is difficult to interpret?

This problem is particularly pervasive in major areas of regulatory law administered by agencies. Here much conduct is 'prohibited' by law, but the sanction can either be civil or criminal, at the discretion of the administrative agency, and civil enforcement is the norm, with criminal enforcement unusual. ...this [might] mean that the lawyer does not even know which side of the criminal/civil line she is on until the agency has chosen to act and draw that line in relation to the client's conduct.

A final problem with the criminal/civil line is contemplated tortious conduct. Nineteenth-century tort opinions speak of negligent conduct not only as wrongful in a strong normative sense, but also often as if it were forbidden. The thrust of the shift in tort thinking over the last eighty years or so has been to drain tort law of much of its normative content, to move away from a focus on the 'wrongfulness' of the conduct of defendant and plaintiff and toward allocation of the costs of accidental injury on the bases of compensation, loss spreading, and efficiency. Where the language of the courts once seemed to assimilate tortious conduct to criminal conduct, the language of much torts scholarship and at least some judicial opinions now seems to assimilate tortious conduct to breach of contract. One is free to be negligent so long as one is willing to pay compensatory damages to persons injured by that negligence. Tort law is civil law. Tortious conduct is not prohibited, but it may, after litigation, result in the imposition of an obligation to pay damages. And thus it would seem that the client is free to commit torts, has a right to commit torts (unless stopped by injunction), and the lawyer has an obligation to educate him about all this if the circumstances make it relevant.

Imagine: The owner of a small chain of run-down motels has discovered that his twenty-year-old water heaters, all identical in make and model, are starting to malfunction and release scalding hot water with no warning. There is no way to know which one will go next. The owner does not have funds to replace all the units, and he already carries so much debt that financing to remedy the problem is unavailable. He has consulted his lawyer for legal advice concerning his obligations. The severity and foreseeability of potential injuries to guests using the showers probably make further use of the water heaters negligent, but the probability of suit is unclear because neither the injured party nor his or her lawyer will have reason to know of the pattern of malfunction absent suit and discovery. Also, the client's liability insurance is sufficient to cover likely compensatory damages. The lawyer knows that the client is very attached to his business, and that he may have no realistic option to avoid injuries except to close down -- at least temporarily -- and this is likely to be fatal to the enterprise. The client is free to commit the tort -- has a right to commit the tort -- and, under the criminal/civil dichotomy, the lawyer is free (and possibly obligated) to give the advice likely to lead to that result.

Pepper goes on to argue that even if the lawyer is free to advise the client about the possibility of regarding a legal sanction as no more than a cost to be taken account of in choosing between courses of action, s/he should discuss with the client the moral dimension including the possibility of causing unjustified harm to others and/or to the fabric of society. In short, lawyer and client should enter into moral dialogue. He then continues:

C. THE LAW/ENFORCEMENT DISTINCTION

Is a distinction between law and enforcement of law the solution to the problem of legal advice that may facilitate unlawful conduct? The lawyer's obligation to provide access to the law could be considered to be fulfilled by informing the client concerning substantive law. The line would then be drawn at information about the various contingencies involved in the future application of that substantive law to the client's facts: advice about the enforcement rules or practices that might reveal to the authorities a violation of the substantive law and the legal procedures through which any enforcement or penalties would be applied would be out of bounds. The constraints that channel application of the substance of the law to the client would be information the lawyer could not convey to the client. To the extent the problem is the perception of law as cost -- the conflation of law with enforcement -- this seems the most direct answer for the lawyer giving advice.

Imagine that lawyers have access to a bulletin board behind the counter at the police station with a weekly list of the frequency of patrol of city neighbourhoods by day and time. The client, previously represented by a lawyer on burglary charges, wants to know the frequency for [a notoriously violent inner city ghetto] Sunday, 2-4 a.m. Intuitively we know the lawyer ought not to supply this information. The law/ enforcement dichotomy provides an explanation. The two-percent audit rate information in our tax return hypothetical appears to be directly analogous under the law/ enforcement dichotomy, which would disallow this more generally accepted legal advice.

…

The law/enforcement distinction is not consistent with the two possibilities previously discussed. Desuetude[1] is a matter of enforcement under this dichotomy, and thus not something the lawyer could communicate to the client. Likewise, the sanction for law violation, whether it be conceived as 'cost' or as 'prohibition,' falls on the 'enforcement' side of the dichotomy and would therefore be out of bounds for lawyer advice. Distinguishing between 'law' and 'enforcement,' while intuitively attractive, thus presents significant difficulties, several of which are canvassed below.

1. The Problem of Disentangling Civil Law from Enforcement

Imagine being asked to advise a client with a contract or tort problem, but being unable to discuss the nature of the sanctions or the mechanisms of enforcement for breach of contract or for tortious conduct. Could one communicate to the client the nature of contract or tort without telling her how they are enforced; without describing the nature of a civil lawsuit and civil damages? What would the lawyer say? Could you tell the client that breach of contract is 'prohibited' by the law, or is 'unlawful'? Could you characterise tortious conduct as 'prohibited' or 'unlawful'? Or are those characterisations sufficiently inaccurate that you would be misleading the client in giving such advice? The distinction between civil and criminal law is fundamental, and to a large extent it is a difference in the nature and mechanisms of enforcement. If discussion of future consequences is out of bounds, it becomes truly difficult to imagine the lawyer's discussion with the client in the area of civil law.

Return to the situation of the client who owns the run-down motels with water heaters likely at some point in the future to seriously injure a customer. If it is not criminal under these circumstances to proceed with business at the motels, it would be misleading to tell the owner that the law 'prohibits' further use of the water heaters, or that further use is 'illegal' or 'unlawful.' And informing the client only that the conduct is 'negligent' doesn't tell him much if he hasn't been to law school. To communicate adequately to the client the nature of liability for negligence will require the attorney

---

1   The first part of Professor Pepper's article, which is not set out here, considers the doctrine of desuetude whereby a rule of law may be regarded as non-binding due to its not having been enforced for a specified period. This doctrine does not form part of English law.

to provide some account of a civil lawsuit and civil damages. But once one is conveying the nature of a civil lawsuit and civil damages, one has entered the area of enforcement, and that is not acceptable under the guideline we are considering.

The situation becomes even clearer if we imagine giving advice about the obligations of contract to one who is either contemplating entering a contract or contemplating breach of an existing contract. To convey that breach of contract is 'prohibited' by the law (is 'illegal' or 'unlawful') is to suggest to the client that society does not tolerate breach of contract. This would be very misleading, however, because the regime of contract law clearly does tolerate breach. (Some would argue that on occasion it encourages breach.) The message of contract law is nuanced, one might even say, conflicted.

Perhaps the example of bankruptcy makes the point most forcefully. What is bankruptcy law other than an elaborate set of procedures dealing with both the enforcement and the extinguishment of debt? If discussion and explanation of these procedures and their consequences is out of bounds for the lawyer, bankruptcy law could not function as intended.

It seems, then, that disentangling civil law from enforcement simply is not possible. That may be, of course, an underlying part of the fundamental problem we are examining. But it also suggests the law/enforcement distinction is not as useful for lawyers as it first appears. There are, however, three other possible understandings of the distinction that might be useful.

2. Advice About Legal Procedures in Relation to Contemplated Conduct as Opposed to Pending Litigation

Ethical Consideration 7-3 of the Code of Professional Responsibility distinguishes between the advocate role and the adviser role of the lawyer in relation to 'doubts as to the bounds of the law.' Because the advocate 'for the most part deals with past conduct and must take the facts as he finds them,' he should resolve doubts about the law in favour of his client. As an adviser, however, the lawyer 'primarily assists his client in determining the course of future conduct,' and therefore must assess 'the bounds of the law' in a more neutral fashion. This Article is concerned with the lawyer as adviser, and with how advice about the law influences client behaviour. Once the client has acted, however, that concern is no longer relevant. Thus if the law/enforcement distinction is to function at all there is at least one necessary adjunct. The prohibition on advice about enforcement, at least as it is related to civil and criminal procedure, would apply only in regard to advice about contemplated conduct by the client that might entail a legal sanction, and not to pending litigation that involves actions already performed. Litigation is enforcement, and once the client is involved in litigation, legal advice is impossible if it does not deal with enforcement mechanisms and rules. If this additional distinction were not applied, the role of the lawyer in litigation would become totally paternalistic: the lawyer would make all decisions because participation by the client would require educating the client about the process, which would be prohibited. Such a nightmarish, Kafkaesque vision of the client in litigation clarifies that during litigation, at least, advice about legal procedures (enforcement) is not only entirely appropriate, but is a core function of lawyering. The client is allowed to have a lawyer (in the criminal context, there is a constitutional right to a lawyer) and the lawyer's primary loyalty is to the client. This is the case precisely so that the party involved in litigation will not be solely an object of the legal process, but will also have some control over (and necessarily, therefore, some knowledge about) the process.

This distinction, in combination with the impossibility of disentangling civil law from enforcement, yields an additional possibility. Our spectrum of examples begins with the effect on the client of learning about the limited sanction for breach of contract, and then moves to the additional effect of learning about the burdens of civil litigation entailed in enforcing that limited sanction for breach of contract. As a refinement of the law/enforcement dichotomy, one could educate the client about the nature of contract law but refuse to disclose information about the process of enforcing civil damages. Advice about civil procedure (and its attendant burdens and consequent discounts) would be out of bounds until litigation was pending or contemplated. Such a line might also function in the tort example of the motel owner. The nature and function of tort damages might be explained, but not the burdens imposed on potential plaintiffs by the discovery and litigation process.

Two other, previously explored examples help to illustrate this possibility. First, in the euthanasia situation, the substance of the law of murder (including the grades and defences) can be communicated without elaborating on criminal procedure. The law/enforcement line as here modified would allow meaningful legal advice about the contemplated conduct and the punishment for law violation, but would rule out the whole area of advice dealing with how that law would be enforced (including prosecutorial discretion and jury nullification).

Second, application of this discrimination to bankruptcy is more difficult, but still conceivable. Consider the person entering into substantial debt, or a course of business involving constant, refinanced debt. Before the debt is undertaken, the client can certainly be advised of the civil nature of the various mechanisms for debt collection, and the various forms of security. But can the client contemplating debt be instructed on the possibilities of bankruptcy? That would seem to be advice about enforcement procedures (really, avoidance procedures) in regard to contemplated conduct, and thus would fall on the wrong side of this version of the law/enforcement line. The client already legally obligated and in a position to consider bankruptcy (or the client who is a creditor of such a person) could be told of the bankruptcy alternative -- which debts could and could not be discharged -- but could not be told of the elaborate procedures through which this would occur...

3. 'Enforcement' of Law: Discovery of Underlying Conduct or the Procedures of Prosecution and Adjudication?

There is a clear distinction between two senses of 'law enforcement.' On the one hand this phrase can refer to the process and procedures that will be applied to determine the legal consequences of a particular set of facts. Thus the prosecutor's evaluation of a situation and consequent exercise of discretion as to whether or not to prosecute is an act of law enforcement, as is the police officer's decision as to whether or not to ticket a vehicle going four miles per hour over the speed limit. Similarly, the standard of proof that will be required to show future medical expenses or lost future income in a tort case is an aspect of the enforcement of law between two private parties, as are rules governing the number of persons who will serve on the jury and the rule as to whether lawyers' fees are included in compensatory damages. All of criminal and civil procedure are a part of law enforcement in this sense. On the other hand, 'law enforcement' can refer to the discovery of a particular set of facts, which may then be subject to legal evaluation and process. The facts must be known -- discovered, gathered, and reported -- before the prosecutor can evaluate; the vehicle must be observed and its speed known before the police officer can decide whether or not to ticket. The person who has been injured by the tortious conduct of another must discover at least (1) the identity of the person whose conduct caused the injury, and (2) that the conduct was tortious.

Advice from lawyer to client about 'law enforcement' in the first sense is intuitively far more palatable than is advice about law enforcement in the second sense to any lawyer educated in the post-legal realist era. How one's acts will be judged -- the procedure of the law -- does appear inextricably bound up with the substance of the law. On the other hand, the likelihood that one's conduct will become subject to legal evaluation appears much less a part of the law, although it is certainly part of the administration of the law. Advice about procedure (in the broad sense) may well be relevant to the client who intends to obey the law; advice about discovery is more likely of concern to the client who believes the conduct will be perceived as unlawful.

A possibly attractive alternative for giving content to a distinction between law and enforcement of law for use in limiting advice from lawyer to client is, therefore, to think of enforcement as discovery by government (or a potential civil plaintiff) of the client's conduct, and to prohibit advice concerning it. Under this alternative all other enforcement-related advice would be allowed. This has the obvious attraction of the notion that lawyers will not be in the business of assisting clients in hiding illegal conduct. For example, this form of the prohibition clearly covers the information on the police bulletin board about frequency of neighbourhood patrol.

Unlike the previous two possibilities, one can imagine lawyers making useful distinctions under the guidance of this alternative, and it thus offers some promise. It would require, however, changes in currently accepted practices. For example, it would appear to prohibit advice about audit frequency in the tax context, advice that many tax practitioners give their clients. And in the motel example, one of the factors mentioned was that the probability of suit is unclear because neither the injured party nor his or her lawyer will have reason to know of the pattern of malfunction. This is the sort of fact that most lawyers would assume is appropriate to convey to a client. It relates, however, to discovery of a relevant aspect of the client's conduct by the plaintiff, the analogue to police and prosecutor in the civil context. Thus the criterion we are considering would prohibit the discussion of this factor with the client... In the water pollution hypothetical, the distinction cuts an interesting line. It rules out informing the client that inspection in rural areas is rare, but allows advising that violations of .075 grams per litre or less are ignored. In sum, as applied to the police bulletin board and tax audit situations, the alternative appears to yield sensible results; as applied to the motel and water pollution situations, the sense of the distinction is less apparent.

4. Intended and Unintended Lax Enforcement

The water pollution hypothetical raises another problem with distinguishing between enforcement and law. It is possible that a disparity between a written rule and the way it is enforced is intended government policy, and thus amounts to a de facto amendment of the law by a governmental actor with the power to make such a change. On the other hand, it is also possible that the lax enforcement is not a matter of policy, but rather results from unintended circumstances such as budget limits, incompetence, or happenstance.

Imagine two possible reasons why enforcement inspections might be rare in rural areas. First, it might be that rural water tends to be significantly cleaner than urban water (at least in regard to ammonia) and that pollution, if it is occurring, is far less likely to be harmful in the rural environment than in the urban environment. Multiple sites discharging the same pollutant are also far less likely. These facts may have been known when discharge limits for the particular effluent were promulgated, but more detailed regulation defining 'urban' as opposed to 'rural' and articulating differential limits for the two types of area, or otherwise more accurately calibrating the limit to the environmental context, may not have been feasible. The agency thus may have framed the limit with the most typical area and the most serious harms in mind, with the intention of exercising regulatory discretion to fine tune the regulation to different areas and conditions. The regulation was promulgated with knowledge that it was intended more for urban areas than rural, and the enforcement disparity known to the lawyer might well be part of the regulator's policy. Alternatively, the .05 gram ammonia limit may be the regulator's best judgment as to the amount sufficiently likely to cause significant harm regardless of the presence of other effluents or multiple sites. The less frequent testing in rural areas may be attributed solely to insufficient funds for enforcement, and the fact that it is less expensive to test in the urban areas.

In the first situation, it is meaningful to say that the .05 limit is not 'really' the legal limit in rural areas. The source of law -- the regulatory agency -- has intentionally made the law-as-enforced different from the law-as-written for reasons related to its legal mission. (The situation is akin to the desuetude example where prosecutors refuse to enforce an anachronistic statute.) Since the harm the agency is to prevent is unlikely to occur in the rural area, even over the .05 limit, the agency has tailored the law through enforcement decisions. Such intentional use of enforcement policy for substantive reasons appears to break down the 'law/enforcement' distinction; enforcement is part of the 'real' law here. When, however, lax enforcement is based simply upon cost, incompetence, or inadvertence, rather than substantive reasons, the 'law/enforcement' distinction retains meaningful content.

If the lawyer knows the reasons for a significant differential between the law-as-written and the law-as-enforced, then the 'law/enforcement' distinction might be used in deciding what information to convey to the client. Frequently, however, the lawyer does not know. Absent information, ought the lawyer to assume that such a differential is not substantively based? Or, is it more likely the case that in most such decisions substantive and cost factors are mixed in a complicated way? Is it likely that enforcement policy is usually partly law -- that is, partly assessment of what is more and less important, more and less wrongful, and so on -- and partly 'just' enforcement? If the latter is true, the utility of the 'law/enforcement' distinction is substantially diluted.

In sum, the distinction between law and enforcement has significant intuitive attraction. A citizen's access to the law ought not mean access to the means to evade the law; and distinguishing law from enforcement of the law appears to speak to that difference. Our exploration of the possible ways of framing and applying the distinction, however, reveals substantial difficulties. The distinction will assist a lawyer's understanding of the situation, but these difficulties render a thorough analysis complex and problematic.

D. THE DISTINCTION BETWEEN PUBLIC INFORMATION AND PRIVATE INFORMATION

Imagine, once again, that you are the lawyer anticipating counselling your client concerning the ammonia effluent limits for her rural plant in the situation where: (1) .05 grams per litre of effluent is the written limit, (2) .075 grams per litre is the enforced limit, (3) inspection is infrequent in rural areas, and (4) in such areas violators are issued a warning (given a second chance) prior to any penalty. In deciding what information to convey to your client, ought it to be relevant whether or not a given piece of information is generally known to either lawyers giving advice regarding these matters or to the industry in general? If, for example, items (2) and (3) are generally known among lawyers for the industry, but you are the only non-government lawyer who knows item (4), ought you to convey all the information except item (4)? If so, we have yet another possible guide for what legal information to give and what to withhold from the client who may use the information to facilitate unlawful conduct.

Even though knowledge of items (2) and (3) may facilitate (or lead to) unlawful conduct by the owner of the rural plant, withholding such information might well put your client at a competitive disadvantage if the rest of the industry has the information. And if the industry knows, then the government must know that the industry knows, and continuation of the .075 gram limit and infrequent rural inspections then takes on the characteristics of a conscious 'legal' decision by the agency, a policy it knows the regulated use as a guide. In other words, if the lawmaker knows its conduct is known by and guiding the regulated, that conduct looks and sounds like 'law' to a contemporary lawyer. It doesn't seem fair to put your client at a disadvantage in regard to information available to her competitors, and part of why it doesn't seem fair is that what the competitors have access to and are being guided by looks a lot like 'law.'

On the other hand, if the industry does not know of the practice of giving a warning, there appears to be less reason for your client to know; it doesn't seem unfair for her not to know. Indeed, if the 'second chance' practice is a government decision, it would appear to be unfair for only your client, and not the rest of the industry, to know. If it is a limit coming from the government -- that is, if it is law -- it is wrong for information about the penalty not to be publicly available. Thus, one distinction we could apply in limiting information about the law that lawyers ought to give to clients is whether or not the information is public. And this line dovetails with what we consider law to be: rules and related conduct by the government intended to limit and channel behaviour . . .

Although not likely to be precise, the public information/private information distinction provides helpful guidance for lawyers. It connects with both our notions of fairness concerning the government treating its citizen equally and our understanding of law as public. It appears legitimate for much information about the enforcement of law not to be available to the public. If such information has been successfully kept from the public, the lawyer would not have an obvious obligation to provide it to a client. The wide legal realist understanding of law, however, would certainly define such information as 'law.' Under that view, we have here a narrow category of justifiably secret law.

E. DIFFERENTIATING MALUM IN SE FROM MALUM PROHIBITUM

Intuitively we know that it is wrong to give the client information available to the lawyer from the police bulletin board about the frequency of police patrols in a particular neighbourhood. That intuition explains, in part, the attractiveness of distinguishing between law enforcement as discovery of the client's possibly unlawful conduct and law enforcement as the procedures following such discovery. The fact that this distinction would also prohibit providing information about the frequency of tax audits in particular categories of returns or information about the frequency of testing of rural water effluent seems, however, to undermine significantly that intuition. What accounts for the difference? The answer is that there is a clear and strong consensus that burglary is wrong. On the other hand, whether or not it is wrong to discharge .060 grams of ammonia per litre of water effluent in a rural area is a question to which most of us would not have an immediate answer. For all we know, such a discharge could be quite harmless; or, if kept up for a period of five years, it may be likely to cause several additional cancer deaths in the next forty years. Knowing that the discharge is unlawful adds relevant information, and makes the conduct 'wrongful' in at least one sense, but not on a parallel with burglary.

The discharge may be a technical legal violation, but it may not be wrongful in any other significant sense. (It is quite possible, as noted above, that the lack of enforcement resources devoted to discovery of violations in rural areas is based upon the regulators' conclusion that the conduct is not harmful to a significant degree.) The difference between burglary and this instance of regulatory violation seems to be that the former is clearly wrong in its very nature in addition to being unlawful, and the latter is unlawful, but may or may not be otherwise wrongful.

That difference corresponds to the old distinction between crimes mala in se, wrong in their very nature, and crimes mala prohibita, crimes wrong only because prohibited by positive law. This distinction also helps in understanding our intuitions concerning the criminal/civil dichotomy. The latter seemed to fit in some circumstances, particularly at the ends of the spectrum. But it did not do so well with regulatory criminal law, as in the water pollution example. A prohibition on giving the client legal information that might assist in the commission of a crime rings the right chord when the conduct is something we perceive as 'really criminal,' but strikes quite another note with vast areas of regulatory law. The malum in se/malum prohibitum distinction appears, in older garb, to formulate the difference between law as true prohibition (that is, the identification of conduct not to be tolerated) and law as cost (that is, the identification of conduct to be penalised in some legal fashion, but which the citizen is still free to choose to do).

We have a strong sense that somehow lawyers' ethics must differentiate these two. For example, William Simon notes that lawyers 'insist that a person has a 'right' to breach a contract,' but 'never argue that a person has a right to commit murder so long as he does not leave behind proof beyond a reasonable doubt of his act.' While the distinctions between criminal and civil law and between law and enforcement of law do not provide the ordinary practising lawyer with an answer to Professor Simon, something like the malum in se/malum prohibitum distinction does.

Lawyers' ethical rules have already used what appears to be this distinction in one core provision. The ABA Code of Professional Responsibility allows a lawyer to reveal '[t]he intention of his client to commit a crime.' In the current ABA Model Rules of Professional Conduct, this has been narrowed to allow disclosure 'to prevent the client from committing a criminal act that the lawyer believes is likely to result in imminent death or substantial bodily harm.' Although the organised bar may not have articulated its reasons this way, I suspect that the large and amorphous category of criminal conduct appeared to be too wide an exception to the obligation to keep information learned from the client confidential, and I surmise that no legal classification seemed to do the job better. So the drafters appear to have been forced back upon an old distinction: if what the client is going to do is really wrong, you can reveal it. But that way of putting it is too vague -- and too subject to individual interpretations of 'really wrong' -- to work well as a rule, so an operational definition was used: it is 'really wrong' if it is going to kill someone, or hurt someone in a significant, physical way.

An attempt along these lines to translate the malum in se/malum prohibitum distinction into guidance for practising lawyers in giving legal advice in situations where the client might use it for unlawful conduct could take a narrower or broader form. A narrow rule could be framed to simply track the one on confidentiality quoted above: when it appears likely that the client will use knowledge of the law to facilitate unlawful conduct likely to cause death or substantial bodily harm, the lawyer shall not provide that knowledge.

Alternatively, a rule could be formulated to track the underlying perception of the 'wrong in itself' concept, and apply that concept to a larger area of potential client conduct. Such a rule might state: when it appears more probable than not that the client will use legal information or advice to facilitate conduct that (1) is clearly prohibited by law and (2) involves what is by clear societal consensus a serious and substantial moral wrong, the lawyer shall not provide the client with the legal advice or information.

Such rules effectively accord with our intuitions in ruling out advice in the most troubling situations. For example, the situation in which the childless, middle-aged client is interested in whether legal authorities consider children under ten years old competent to testify in sexual abuse cases easily fits within the prohibition if there appears to be no legitimate basis for the client to be interested in this information. The more general form of the rule also assists us in understanding our hesitance to rule out advice about possible prosecutorial discretion and jury nullification in the euthanasia hypothetical. Although the contemplated euthanasia is clearly criminal, the client's particular circumstances may make it unlikely that the conduct would be a 'serious and substantial wrong by clear societal consensus.'

Thus, a rule constructed along these lines to reflect the difference between malum in se and malum prohibitum could function to rule out advice from lawyer to client in the most egregious situations. A rule of this kind would be of value to practising lawyers, reinforcing the intuition that certain advice ought to be out of bounds, and announcing at least one category of circumstances in which the client's right of access to the law is trumped by considerations that justify a refusal to allow the lawyer's knowledge to become instrumental to a violation of the law.

Note here that the suggested rules focus upon the results of the particular client conduct at issue, not on the classification of the legal violation or crime. 'Murder' is certainly a category of crime we would normally consider malum in se. It is murder under the particular circumstances of the euthanasia example that perhaps is not wrong in itself. And the ABA exception regarding confidentiality refers not to the category of 'crimes of violence,' but to any criminal act (including, conceivably, a violation of the water pollution prohibition) 'likely to result in imminent death or substantial bodily harm.' Such approaches move away from the old malum in se/malum prohibitum distinction by moving away from legal categories, and looking more at the particular conduct at issue. The larger categories seem too large to function well for the basic right/wrong distinction we are considering.

Even having made this move, however, these possible rules are relatively narrow. They function to give support and justification where the lawyer is likely to know already, on one level or another, that under the circumstances the advice is improper. They would not function, however, to give guidance in the vast areas of legal advice that remain: contracts, much of torts, most criminal violations that are 'only' mala prohibita, regulatory law (substantial parts of which include criminal penalties, but most of which would be classified mala prohibita), civil procedure, and so on. Relatively little advice in these areas of law would fall on the prohibited side of either of the two rules articulated above.

It is possible that the basic perception underlying the distinction could be extended to these less precise, more problematic areas. A flexible 'standard' might be constructed according to which each lawyer must judge under the particular circumstances whether the client's prospective unlawful conduct is 'really wrongful' in some fundamental or serious way, or is 'merely penalised' in some legal fashion. Thus a client's intentional breach of contract that was likely to bankrupt the business of an innocent, unsophisticated individual might be treated quite differently from an intentional breach that would cost a Fortune 500 company $ 100,000. The lawyer's decision to give all the relevant legal information in the motel example would depend upon that lawyer's categorisation of the tortious conduct as 'really wrongful' or as 'merely penalised' with the cost of damages. The absence of the clear societal consensus that underlies the concepts of malum in se and malum prohibitum would mean that the guidance would be more subjective and contextually determined, but it would still provide the lawyer with a framework for considering the situation and making a decision. Because such a standard would move away both from clear societal consensus and from somewhat more objective lines, it might be that the direction given the lawyer would not be to withhold the legal information. The lawyer might instead be required to provide the information only in tandem with the lawyer's assessment that the conduct not only would be 'unlawful' in some sense or other (breach of contract, tortious), but also that it would be 'really wrongful,' and ought not to occur.

F. WHO INITIATED DISCUSSION OF THE POSSIBLY ILLEGAL CONDUCT: LAWYER OR CLIENT?

Many lawyers suggest that the ethical propriety of providing legal information that may lead to conduct contrary to law depends, at least in part, on whether or not the client has asked. Under this line of thought, if the client has requested information about 'the law' or legal consequences, the lawyer's primary function is to provide that information. If, however, the client has not asked, providing the information may well amount to the lawyer's suggesting unlawful conduct, and thus would be improper.

Assume, for an initial example, that the client has suffered recent financial difficulties, and current contractual obligations entail further serious financial harm. The client has not, to the lawyer's knowledge, considered breaching these contracts, although the lawyer believes the consequences of breach will be significantly less deleterious to the client than will continuing to fulfil the obligations. Is it wrong for the lawyer to inform the client of the legal consequences likely to follow from breach, and of the lawyer's opinion that these would leave the client in a better position? Is it wrong to fail to give such advice? Is it malpractice?

Second, imagine that the client in our motel example assumes that because the malfunctioning water heaters may do serious harm to a customer he has a legal obligation to remove them, even though this is likely to lead to closure and loss of the business, a possibility he finds very difficult to face. Ought the lawyer to educate the client concerning (1) the difference between the nature of the obligations of criminal law and tort law, (2) the difficulties and contingencies that an injured person would face in pursuing a claim (including whether he happens to consult a lawyer and the difficulties of discovery and trial), and (3) the significance of the client's liability insurance, including the insurer's obligation to defend? (Ought the more creative lawyer raise in addition the possibility of purchasing and installing the water heaters on credit, almost certainly defaulting on the obligations, and then working toward an extended payout with the creditors, knowing they would probably prefer such a workout to taking either the heaters or the motel, which are security for the debt? Is this advice merely anticipating the advice about breach of contract in the previous paragraph, or has it crossed the line to suggesting a future fraud? Note that even if it is fraud, it appears to be a solution that prevents the substantial possibility of serious physical injury to an innocent customer.)

Finally, consider the affluent client who owns four investment condominiums, each with a federally insured mortgage, for whom it has become uneconomical (but possible) to continue payments. The lawyer knows that the client can walk away from the properties without paying anything further as long as he defaults on only one of the mortgages in any two-month period. Is it wrong for the lawyer to provide information to the client about the government's enforcement policy, which is highly likely to lead to the client's breaching the contract and to substantial loss for the government? Is it malpractice to fail to give the advice? (Is it a form of fraud to 'misuse' the operational definition distinguishing 'investors' from 'ordinary owners' that the government is attempting to draw with its enforcement policy?)

Does it make a determinative difference, in each of these situations, that the client has not asked? Two quite different basic perceptions about the role of the lawyer point in different directions. First, for the lawyer to be the originator of conduct contrary to law certainly doesn't sound right. Law, to a large extent, is society's formal vehicle for channelling people into conduct the polity has judged beneficial in some significant way, and away from conduct it considers harmful or deleterious. For lawyers actively to counsel clients in opposition to that channelling would appear to be plainly antisocial conduct, the kind of conduct that earns lawyers the negative half of their image.

The strength of this perception, however, is dependent on all the factors discussed earlier in this article: Is the legal provision really 'law,' or has it been eroded by desuetude or enforcement policy into something society appears not to be very concerned about? Is the conduct really prohibited, or just freighted with a legal cost or penalty? Is the conduct really wrongful, or just legally prohibited?

The second, quite different perception concerns the apparent unfairness of advantaging the more legally sophisticated client over the less knowledgeable client, or of advantaging the less scrupulous client over the more scrupulous one. (I assume here that the less sophisticated or more scrupulous client is less likely to initiate the problematic discussion with the lawyer.) The prime function of lawyers -- providing access to the law -- suggests that it may not be fair. Law is intended to be a public good; the prospect of differentially available law is troubling. Lawyers function to make law available and thus to equalise citizen access to one major public resource: use of the law. The distinction considered here appears to subvert that positive role of lawyering. The person wise enough to ask gains access to the law; the less knowledgeable or curious or sophisticated client does not. Lawyers generally pride themselves on understanding that the client may not be knowledgeable enough about the law to know what he wants or needs. Frequently a lawyer must engage in skilful interviewing in order to discover enough about her client to educate him about where his situation and the law intersect. Lawyers often need to counsel the client to understand what options the law presents. In this way the sophisticated and unsophisticated are significantly equalised through the assistance of lawyers.

Just as with the first perception, however, the problem of what counts as 'law' to which there should be equal access remains. We are cycled back to the questions considered earlier. If we knew which kinds of law a client has a 'right' to violate and take the consequences, or under what circumstances clients have such an option as part of the law, then we might know when the lawyer could initiate discussion of such an option, and when it would, to the contrary, not be a legal option for the client, and hence not appropriate for the lawyer to raise. But such a taxonomy is not available to practising lawyers.[2]

Questions

1. Which of these distinctions seem most useful to you? Why?

2. Consider as an alternative the principle that
i)   Subject to principle ii) below, the lawyer shall not give the client information about the law where the lawyer believes that the giving of such advice will in all probability lead the client to disregard his legal obligations, as set out in the decision of the Courts and other relevant rules of law.
ii)   The lawyer shall give the clients information about the law even though the lawyer believes that the giving of such advice will in all probability lead the client to disregard his legal obligations, but only if the lawyer believes that client has a moral right to disregard his legal obligations.

3. How, if at all, would your view of Pepper's argument be effect by the existence of an obligation to obey the law?

2   Stephen Pepper 'Counselling at the Limits of the Law: An Exercise in the Jurisprudence and Ethics of Lawyering' (1995) 104 Yale Law Journal 1547 at 1554-1556, 1559-1582.

4. What advice would you give i) in the case of the polluting client and ii) to the owner of the hotel with the dangerous water heaters?

5. Your client is a university lecturer who is preparing her tax return for the year which has just finished. In that year she earned £9,000 from consultancy work which must be declared. She used £4,000 of that money to purchase a new computer and would like to put this down as expenses. You know that the IRC would contend that this was a capital expense and allow only £1,000/annum capital allowance for four years. If the matter were litigated, you think the Revenue would have a 2/3 chance of success. However, for earnings under £10,000, the IRC requires only a declaration of the taxable sum – the calculations do not have to be disclosed. Moreover under self-assessment, calculations are in any case left to the taxpayer and there is only a 5% chance of an audit of such a small taxpayer.

What is your advice? Does it make any difference if official figures have just been published showing that undeclared earnings are costing the country £11 million per annum in lost revenues?

6. You are a lawyer in general practice in a provincial town. You are consulted by Dr Snow, the President of the local Association of Rural General Practitioners. Dr Snow says that one of their members has been treating a 35-year-old man who about a year ago was left completely paralysed by a diving accident. The patient who is not suffering from depression has begged his doctor several times to give him an overdose sufficient to end his life. Dr Snow wants to know what the legal position will be if the doctor agrees to the patient's request. In your view giving the overdose would in the circumstances amount to murder. But you also know from a friend of yours working at CPS headquarters in London that the CPS has just taken (though this has not been made public) a decision not to prosecute in such cases. What is your advice ?

7   Concluding comments on the lawyer-client relationship

Our consideration of the scope and limits of the notion of autonomy provides a backdrop against which to consider Shaffer's four models for lawyer-client relationships. For example, Stephen Pepper has suggested that none of the principles of decision he discusses provides a decisive test in hard cases of how to resolve the tension between the principle that the client is entitled to know the law and the principle that the lawyer should not assist the client in illegal conduct. The lawyer's only recourse is to enter into moral conversation with the client, that is to attempt to discuss with the client as sympathetically as possible exactly what the client hopes to achieve in the hope that the client as s/he is then revealed to be less like Oliver Wendell Holmes bad man than the lawyer may have assumed.[3] Pepper then seems to regard the Lawyer as Friend as

3   Supra at pp 1599-1607.

the model best able to resolve the tension between the conflicting goals of fully informed client decision-making and fidelity to the law.

Questions

1. Which of the four models for lawyer-client relationships do you prefer?

2. You represent a small company which makes baby walkers. Recent scientific evidence produced by the company shows that they pose a significant risk to health if not used under proper supervision. Some of this research is in the public domain and has caused an outcry. Your client for whom you have acted for many years and with whose managing director you have a close relationship fears the introduction of government regulations banning their sale. You know however that extensive lobbying could delay these regulations for several month and think that any negligence actions resulting from injuries sustained in the meantime could be vigorously defended. After discussion, the client says he does not consider it appropriate to withdraw the product. After all, it is not illegal to sell and such a precipitate withdrawal would mean ruin, for the company, the MD and his family, and the small workforce. What would you do?

3. Consider the objection to the moral dialogue suggested by Professors Shaffer and Pepper that 'I couldn't bill my clients for that sort of advice'.

4. Has your legal education made you more likely to adopt any and if so which of these counselling models?

CHAPTER TEN

Lawyers, ethics and access to justice

A legal aid lawyer died and went to heaven. At the Pearly Gates, he met St Peter who confirmed that he was expected within. 'Wonderful' said the lawyer 'but, without wishing to seem ungrateful, I'd like to know why He summoned me now. I am, after all, only 52.' St Peter checked his notes and replied, 'That's odd. According to the hours you've billed you're 132.'[1]

'The Rule of Law' is often given as a reason why citizens have a moral obligation to obey the state's laws. At its simplest, the argument is that the law should be obeyed because everyone is equally subject to its benefits and burdens. One of the many difficulties with this argument is that citizens may find that the substantive benefits formally guaranteed by the law are illusory unless they have access to the specialised knowledge and assistance required for the realization of their legal rights. In many situations, this will mean access to the services of professional lawyers. Hence, lawyers, access to justice and the Rule of Law are intimately linked.

This explains the depth of the concern which has recently emerged in the UK that the cost of purchasing lawyers' services is so great as to be unaffordable for all accept the wealthy and those sufficiently poor to qualify for legal aid. This is seen as an unacceptable barrier to access to justice[2]. This chapter considers this problem from the perspective of legal ethics and asks whether the problem can be traced in any sense to the ethical failings of lawyers. In addition, it considers the implications for legal ethics of the various institutions which might be, or currently are, employed to address the problem. The chapter therefore considers in turn judicare legal aid, legal aid contracting, conditional fees, procedural reform, pro bono lawyering and legal

---

1   Anon.
2   Lord Woolf *Access to Justice: Final Report* (London, HMSO, 1996) at p 2 para 2 and p 72 para 1 and, generally, *Access to Justice, Interim Report* (Lord Chancellors Department, June 1995).

expenses insurance. None of these institutions is in principle exclusive of the others. Nevertheless, they must be seen in their historical context. With the establishment of the welfare state following the Second World War, judicare legal aid was the principal method through which the problems of access to justice were addressed. The other institutions to be discussed owe their importance, and in some cases their existence, to the decline of the judicare system.

Question

Why should society provide the less well off with gratuitous or subsidised legal services rather than simply allowing its income to be redistributed via the taxation system? In 1994-1995, the legal aid scheme spent £130 for every household eligible for help.[3] If those helped by the legal aid scheme were given the money, it might make an appreciable difference to their tight budgets. The recipients *might* then choose to spend this additional income on legal expenses insurance.[4]

1 Judicare legal aid

After the Second World War, there was an increasing awareness that the distribution of legal services could not be left to the operation of market forces . Consequently, the advent of the welfare state led in most western European states to some form of state subsidised access to legal assistance. In Great Britain, the stimulus for the introduction of what was to become the legal aid scheme was a liberalisation of the divorce laws in the 1940s. This, combined perhaps with wartime conditions, led to a steep rise in the divorce rate, particularly amongst service personnel. This in turn stimulated demand for legal services by consumers lacking the means to purchase such services themselves. During the war, a number of temporary expedients were devised, notably a salaried solicitor service run by the Law Society. After the war, when optimism about the state's ability to provide for the needs of its' citizens 'from the cradle to the grave' was at its height, came the birth of the welfare state. It became accepted that the state had an obligation to ensure access to justice. The obligation extended not only to those who would generally be classed as poor but also to persons of 'moderate means' and this principle underlay the Legal Aid Act 1949. This Act laid the foundations for a scheme which was to dominate subsidised legal service provision for 45 years.

Behind the bare bones of this account, there lies real controversy over how to analyse and evaluate the origins of the legal aid scheme, the central puzzle being why those with power and wealth should seek to redistribute wealth (in the form of legal services) and thus power to those who would otherwise lack it. For market control

---

3   Alan Paterson and Tamara Goriely at p 10 of the Introduction to A *Reader on Resourcing Civil Justice* (Paterson and Goriely eds, Oxford, OUP, 1996).

4   Legal expenses insurance is dealt with in section 6 infra.

theorists, it is natural to see legal aid as a form of demand creation by the legal profession. This is consistent with the fact that the legal aid scheme has historically made a very significant contribution to its income. In 1992, 11.8% of solicitors' income came from legal aid and for the Bar the figures are even more striking: in 1989, 27% came from legal aid with a further 11% coming from the Crown Prosecution Service.[5] However, market control theory has great difficulty explaining the origins of legal aid in the UK: for the initiative came from the government and was initially opposed by the Law Society which feared that solicitors would become employees of the state. Its support for the scheme was by way of making the best of something (state funding of legal services) rendered inevitable by events beyond its control.[6] It may be that market control theory fails here because it assumes that social developments must be explained by actions taken in the interests of economic advancement. Consider the alternative explanation suggested by the following description of post-war Britain.

> First, it was a time of hope. As *Picture Post* kept reminding its readers, it was time to plan for a brave new Britain. The popular acclaim following the publication of Beveridge's report in November 1942 had forced Churchill to accept that government had to do something about the old giants of want, disease, ignorance, squalor, and idleness. Over the next three years, a multitude of official committees started to design a better country after the peace. The Rushcliffe report was a very small and unobtrusive part of the plans for a New Jerusalem.

> Secondly, it was a time of social solidarity. Disaster was no longer individual but something whole communities had shared. As the Home Intelligence reports of the time noted, there was a strong desire for equality, even if it was an equality of misery. In 1942 most people had positively welcomed increased rationing as a way of reducing the 'big bugs' who took more than their fair share of petrol and food. They now wanted equal shares in forthcoming prosperity. The basis of the welfare state was not to be minimum benefits for the few but equal benefits for all. The middle classes were prepared to give the welfare state their support provided it also gave them tangible benefits.[7]

The judicare model

Perhaps the most striking feature of the UK scheme is that it has traditionally been a judicare scheme. The significance of this term and the contrasting salaried model through which legal aid is largely provided in the USA are explored by Professor Alan Paterson in the following extract. Writing in 1991, Professor Paterson describes the

5   Solicitors' income is based on the Law Society's *Annual Statistical Report* (1993). The figures for barristers income are based on estimates compiled by the General Council of the Bar (General Council for the Bar *Strategies for the Future* (1990) chapter 4). See generally Bevan, Partington and Holland 'Organizing Cost Effective Access to Justice' chapter 14 of *'A Reader on Resourcing Civil Justice'* (supra note 3).
6   A Paterson and D Nelken 'The Evolution of Legal Services in Britain: Pragmatic Welfarism or Demand Creation?' chapter 10 of *A Reader on Resourcing Civil Justice* supra note 3.
7   Tamara Goriely at p 215 of *Resourcing Civil Justice* supra note 3.

legal aid scheme and its problems prior to the process of reform which is considered in the rest of this chapter. Having considered pro bono work ('the first model') as a solution to the problem of unmet legal need he continues:

> The second model of legal aid is usually referred to under its American title, namely the 'Judicare Model' in order to distinguish it from other legal aid models. Under this approach the state funds the private profession to provide legal services to individuals. This model exists in most of the leading industrial countries in the Western world. In some (for example, the United Kingdom, the Netherlands, Germany, Norway, Sweden, most Canadian provinces, Australia, New Zealand and Hong Kong), it is the dominant mode of providing legal services. In most western countries it took over from the first model in the second half of the twentieth century but in a few, for example, France, Italy, Spain and Ireland, the first model still prevails *de facto* if not also *de jure*.

I. THE UNITED KINGDOM

The primary characteristics of the judicare model owe much to the version of it which has developed in the United Kingdom since it was here that the model was first introduced on a large scale (in 1950). As is well known, the principal features of legal aid here are that it is:

(1)   State Funded: providing access to justice is seen more as a State obligation rather than a charitable duty of the profession;

(2)   Independent: responsibility for the administration and award of legal aid is placed in the hands of an independent body, board or court;

(3)   Demand-led: expenditure is open-ended although it is subject to constraints and monitoring before, during and after the provision of the service;

(4)   Broad in scope: much wider than under the charitable model. Nevertheless some restrictions on coverage exist in that certain types of action are excluded, eg defamation, simplified divorces and small claims; it is not available in tribunals and it is designed to support individual rather than collective actions;

(5)   Subject to multiple eligibility criteria including means and merits testing and an expectation that funding from other sources, eg a trade union are not available to the applicants

(6)   Contributory: with the exception of criminal legal aid in Scotland, assisted persons may be required to contribute towards the cost of their cases, depending on their means. In practice only between 10 per cent and 20 per cent of assisted parties have an initial contribution. One of the significant features of the United Kingdom model is that the Legal Aid Fund is expected to bear the bulk of the risk of loss if assisted parties are unsuccessful in their actions. However, for successful assisted parties legal aid is a loan, not a grant and should they be unable to recover the cost of their lawyer from the other side it will be deducted from their winnings through the mechanism of the statutory charge;

(7)   Provided by private practitioners: the overwhelming majority of legal aid and advice and assistance is provided by private practitioners. In Scotland there are only two law centres which operate legal aid and nearly a thousand private firms that do so. Nor is advice and assistance used by advice agencies. In England there are no figures available as to the amount of legal aid cases undertaken by law centres but in 1989/90 less than a quarter of 1 per cent of payments to solicitors went to law centres.

Recent research suggests that advice agencies and law centres account for less than 2 per cent of advice and assistance[8] work.

(8) Open panel: hitherto assisted parties have had a very wide choice of lawyer to act for them in legal aid cases. This is a major advantage over the charitable model, in that assisted parties can be represented by some of the best and most experienced court lawyers in the country.

Commentators have tended to see most of the features outlined above as strengths, stressing particularly the importance of state funding; independence; breadth of coverage, risk protection and choice. Nonetheless, viewed from the standpoint of the profession, consumers and the government there are also a number of weaknesses in the model.

1. The profession's perspective

Leaving aside the inevitable teething problems connected with the restructuring of legal aid on both sides of the border, the principal complaints of the profession are that:

(1) the coverage of the scheme is deficient, for example, in not extending to tribunals and that it is being reduced in small ways by recent and ongoing reforms;

(2) bureaucratic hurdles are increasing, necessitating delays, abandonment or the option of doing work for nothing;

(3) there is no payment mechanism which supplies the necessary working capital to support firms through cash-flow problems;

(4) the level of remuneration for legal aid work is inadequate. Legal aid rates (particularly in Scotland) are now significantly below the private rates set by the profession and the court. This, however, does not prove the rates are inadequate. The policy question is what profit margin should be built into legal aid rates. Here much depends on whether legal aid is seen as a pro bono activity for the majority of the profession or a specialism to be pursued by a minority of firms.

These drawbacks are said to be causing an increasing number of specialist or sizeable firms to give up doing legal aid, although there are no reliable figures on the issue. Equally disturbing for the public is the argument that the workload of these firms is increasingly going to junior and less experienced fee-earners in smaller practices thus recreating one of the major weaknesses of the charitable model.

2. The consumer's perspective

A reduction in the quality of service or the availability of legal aid lawyers would be obvious drawbacks from the consumers' perspective. In fact it has already been established that access problems exist. Thus it is clear that there are considerable shortages of practitioners who are experts in the fields of housing, welfare, consumer, immigration, employment and child law. Moreover the figures suggest individuals with problems in these areas are much more likely to consult law centres than private practitioners offering legal aid in the shape of Advice and Assistance. Repeated Annual Reports of both law societies have confirmed that contrary to original hopes Advice

---

8   Ie basic advice on the client's legal position which might include assistance with the writing of a letter but would stop well short of the issuing of proceedings.

and Assistance continues to be used primarily in the traditional areas of family and criminal work (about 60 per cent of Scots cases and 75 per cent of English cases). (The same is true for legal aid.) It is partly because of this that provision for tendering for advice, assistance and representation was suggested in the Scrutiny Review.

Apart from the eligibility criteria, the level of contributions and the statutory clawback-points which I shall return to the other principal concerns of consumers in relation to legal aid relate to its scope. The recommendations of both the Benson and the Hughes Commissions that legal aid should be extended to tribunal representation have been strongly reinforced by the Genn report which graphically demonstrates the advantage secured by those who are represented at tribunals. A further deficiency that has been highlighted recently is the individualised nature of legal aid. As the Opren affair demonstrated legal aid does not lend itself to collective actions, for example, disaster cases where many victims are suing the same defender in respect of the same alleged wrong...

3. The Government's perspective

Inevitably western governments are concerned at the increasing cost of providing legal aid through the private profession, particularly since the rise in cost seems often to be running ahead both of inflation and productivity in terms of numbers of cases handled. As we shall see some countries have begun to respond to the problem by placing a greater proportion of the funds available into salaried lawyers for cost-efficiency reasons. The Lord Chancellor's Department and the Legal Aid Board on the other hand seem to be focussing more on improving efficiency and quality controls, eg through the Franchising experiment. (One of the major aims of the Franchising project is to try to measure the quality of service provided by legal aid practitioners-a task that is not without difficulties). However a consensus has yet to be reached between the profession, the public and the authorities as to the standard of service to which legally aided clients are entitled.

Despite being open-panel in character, legal aid in England and Wales (there is no comparable Scottish data) is not evenly distributed throughout the profession but highly concentrated with 7 per cent of all offices receiving 42 per cent of the payments and 32 per cent of offices receiving less than £5,000 per annum in legal aid fees. This not only complicates the problem of fixing on an appropriate level for legal aid remuneration (legal aid work done in small amounts is never likely to be cost-effective) but also raises the question whether it is desirable that there should be more specialist legal aid practitioners. Many legal aid solicitors are already specialising and specialist panels of legal aid lawyers already exist in England in the fields of mental health and child care law...

A final area of concern to the government is the inefficiency in administrative terms of the differing rates of remuneration for various forms of legal aid work and indeed of a piecework based payment scheme. Discussions over the introduction of more block or standard fees are continuing with the profession but we are a long way from the Dutch and German situation where most payments are in the form of lump sums.

The author goes on to discuss the judicare model in other European jurisdictions noting that 'In surprisingly few are there significant or interesting variations on the UK model except that few share its scope' and continues:

III. ELIGIBILITY CRITERIA

The lack of up to date information in English makes it difficult to produce an informed comparison between the financial eligibility tests of western industrialised countries. Some countries, eg the United Kingdom, France, Germany and Sweden use detailed financial limits. Others, eg Austria, Spain, Italy, Finland and Southern Australia use flexible criteria whereby those who cannot afford to go to law without causing 'hardship to the applicant or his family' are eligible for legal aid. Often there is little to choose between the two approaches. Nevertheless, it would be wrong to say that in practical terms about the same proportion of the population is eligible for judicare in most western countries. Even from the limited information available, it is clear that some countries (notably, the Netherlands, Sweden and the United Kingdom) have intended their programmes to include not just the poor but also part of the middle classes while others in part because of the extensive penetration of legal expenses insurance in Europe focus primarily on the poor. However, rising costs have led the former countries to reexamine coverage and there are signs that some are opting for a transfer of resources to salaried lawyers (on cost-effectiveness grounds) while others, such as the United Kingdom, appear to be failing to up-rate eligibility limits with inflation. In addition, applicants are increasingly being expected to make direct or indirect (eg the statutory charge) contributions towards the cost of the legal services they receive.

As in the United Kingdom, it is normal for there to be a merits test in the judicare scheme in other jurisdictions. In some, as in the United Kingdom, the probable cause requirement is separated from the reasonableness requirement, in others the two requirements are integrated. German judges apply the dual test requiring that 'applicants must not be careless risk takers. 'In France the case must not be 'manifestly inadmissible or devoid of foundation,' while Swedish applicants are deemed ineligible if they have no justifiable reason for pursuing a matter. In most Australian states, however, the merits test is simply whether it is reasonable in the circumstances that the applicant should be granted legal aid, although this criterion is usually amplified with legislative guidelines, one of which is often the English 'reasonableness' yardstick of the 'hypothetical paying client' test

C The Salaried Model

There are relatively few jurisdictions in the western world (the United States of America and Quebec being the most prominent) in which the third or 'salaried' model of legal aid provision predominates. Nevertheless, the model is to be found in a number of other western countries (including the United Kingdom, the Netherlands, Canada, Australia, New Zealand, Sweden and Finland). For the purposes of exposition, it will be argued that this model comes in two polar forms: strategic and service orientation. In reality, the work style of most salaried legal services lawyers lies on a continuum between these poles. However, all forms of the salaried model share certain characteristics in that they are:
(1) Publicly funded: the overwhelming majority of salaried programmes are supported from public funds (whether central, local or, as in England, a mixture of both),
(2) Independent: the management of salaried programmes is intended to be independent of the profession and of funders of the service although these bodies will frequently be represented on the management committee/board of the programme. (In the United States of America and Australia independence is further

secured by the fact that the central funding is channeled through independent Corporations or Commissions similar to the Legal Aid Boards). Many salaried programmes are committed to the notion of management by representatives of the community served by the programme (community control), but this is a difficult management style to achieve in practice;

(3) Limited in scope: partly in response to the initial hostility of the profession to salaried programmes when they were first established, it is common for the salaried programmes to restrict the scope of the assistance which they provide to their client communities. In the Netherlands, the *Buros* generally restrict themselves to initial advice before referring clients to private practitioners. In Australia and the United Kingdom the limits are enshrined in formal agreements, elsewhere the programmes' own priorities ensure that rarely (except in Sweden) are they in competition with the private profession. In the United States of America the Legal Services Corporation salaried programmes are also banned from taking cases to do with school desegregation, abortion, or engaging in political activities such as picketing, striking, lobbying or working for political campaigns;

(4) Limited in eligibility terms: salaried programmes generally operate much more rough and ready means tests than judicare programmes;

(5) Free: most salaried programmes, especially community law centres, provide their services free of charge, particularly where only advice is being offered. In the United Kingdom and Australia this is regarded as a very significant factor in improving access by helping to overcome the public's fear of the expense of going to law;

(6) Salaried: by definition the services in these programmes are provided by salaried lawyers as opposed to private practitioners. However, in most jurisdictions the division of labour between the salaried programmes and judicare is such that a symbiotic relationship grows up between the public and the private sector. Far from competing with each other, each sector generates work for the other. Moreover it is not uncommon for private practitioners to act as volunteers at law centres by providing evening advice sessions. Secondly, the salaried programmes, like private practice, are demonstrating an increasing reliance on paralegal or unqualified staff;

(7) Closed panel in form: salaried programmes inevitably offer restricted choice of lawyer as compared with judicare programmes.

I The Strategic version

In addition to these features the strategic form of the salaried model has four other characteristics. It is:

(1) Proactive: rather than adopting the reactive stance of most practitioners and judicare programmes, the salaried programmes which are committed to the strategic model frequently pursue a proactive strategy of targeting the local problems which they wish to focus on, collecting data and making submissions to relevant bodies and attempting to reach potential clients by advertising, circulars and public meetings.

(2) Controlled: unlike demand-led judicare programmes or service model salaried programmes, strategic programmes frequently control demand for their services by adopting a 'closed door' policy, only accepting cases which are referred by third party agencies who have weeded out irrelevant cases or only taking clients off the street on certain days in the week.

(3) Community orientated: strategic programmes devote a considerable proportion of their time to community projects including educating the community about legal rights and remedies, the production of leaflets, booklets and videos and tackling the problems of the community or a group as opposed to an individual basis, for example, by the pursuit of collective or class actions. Although community organisation is an important goal for strategic programmes, lawyers have not found this an easy path to follow. One particular form of community orientation is the salaried programme which is set up to handle the legal problems of a particular constituency group.

(4) Reformist: strategic programmes, particularly in the United States of America, quickly learned the importance of pursuing law reform through test-cases or lobbying. While this was objected to as political activity, it was in fact no more than Washington lawyers were doing routinely for their corporate clients.

Despite its advantages in terms of focus, flexibility and cost-effectiveness (see below) the strategic model has always attracted more attention and criticism (since its version of preventive lawyering is often seen as being too akin to political activity) than its limited presence in reality would seem to merit. Before lobbying was banned for salaried lawyers in the United States of America, less than 5 per cent of their time was devoted to such pursuits. Practically none of the 60 or so law centres in the United Kingdom have adopted a wholeheartedly strategic approach. The position is somewhat similar in the clinics in Quebec, Ontario and the Australian states. In the Netherlands it is only in the very recent past that any strategic element has emerged in the practice of the law centres. In Finland and Sweden the salaried programmes contain few strategic elements.

II The Service version

This is the predominant form which the salaried model takes. In some senses it is the antithesis of the strategic model. Thus in addition to the characteristics shared by most salaried programmes the service model is essentially-

(1) reactive in that the programmes wait to see which clients come through the doors;
(2) demand-led in the sense that the programme encourages take-up by its location, publicity and work-style and places no limits on meeting the resulting demand except the capacities of the staff;
(3) individual oriented in the sense that the problems of individuals rather than those of groups or of the community are the primary focus; and
(4) routinised in the sense that staff time is spent mainly on highly routine, non-researched legal work with little impact in the law or the legal system.

The reality of the service model in practice is that it is not entirely reactive, that ways are found to reduce demand, for example, by limiting the type of client or the areas of work which will be handled, that some group work will be done even if it is only community education and most programmes are willing to take test cases in appropriate circumstances.

III The Salaried and Judicare Models compared

Any discussion of the strengths and weaknesses of the salaried model invites a comparison between it and the judicare model. At first blush salaried programmes would appear to be the solution to a number of the problems with the judicare model as it operates in the United Kingdom. They can and do cover areas excluded from judicare, such as tribunal representation. Moreover, law centres in the United Kingdom devote most of their resources to the areas of law which have traditionally been neglected by legal aid lawyers here. This also holds true for Australian community legal centres and Legal Services Corporation lawyers in the United States of America who have developed expertise in welfare rights, child law, mental health, prisoners' rights, housing, consumer law and anti-discrimination. In short, in most jurisdictions where the two models co-exist a *de facto* (and sometimes a *de jure*) division of labour exists between them particularly in civil law areas.

Secondly, to the extent that salaried programmes adopt a proactive, community oriented style, they provide not only a more accountable service, but a more flexible, planned, prioritised and targeted service which in its focus on group work and collective problems represents a more cost effective use of scarce resources than any judicare plan. Surprisingly, there have been no studies designed to test whether community satisfaction is greater with a service which is tailored to its perceived needs, than a reactive judicare programme. (In part this may be attributable to the division of labour between salaried and judicare plans.) However, a limited pilot study in England and an extensive evaluation project ('The Delivery Systems Study') conducted by the Legal Services Corporation were unable to detect any significant difference in the satisfaction rate of individual clients using salaried and judicare programmes.[9]

The most controversial question relating to salaried schemes is their relative cost and effectiveness in comparison with judicare schemes.[10] Critics of salaried schemes usually point to the US experience of salaried defenders which have generally yielded very low standards of representation. However, the absence of quality controls within the US system plus the peculiar problems generated by its urban crime rate mean make the Canadian experience more informative. In Canada, legal aid delivery services are organised provincially. Consequently, there are 12 different schemes between which comparisons can be made. Moreover since the Federal Government contributes 40% of the cost it has incentive to monitor for cost and does so. The evidence in relation to criminal representation is that salaried systems have lower costs per case because their lawyers spend less time on the case than judicare lawyers. However, there is also evidence that quality does not really suffer. Most studies find that criminal defendants using salaried lawyers are more likely to plead guilty, but that if they do contest the case they are no more likely to be convicted than defendants using judicare lawyers. In addition, those using salaried lawyers tend to do better at the sentencing stage. Even the conservative Canadian Bar association has commented that:

[i]n the criminal field, where some hard data on quality is available, albeit crude, it appears that the staff model is capable of delivering the same outcomes for lower costs that the judicare model, or slightly better outcomes for the same costs.[11]

---

9   'Legal Aid at the Crossroads' [1991]10 CJQ 124 at pp 126-129, 131-135.
10   On this see Tamara Goriely 'Legal Aid Delivery Systems in Mass Casework: Which offers the best value for money?'. LCD Research Study 10/97.
11   Ibid at p 17.

This is not to deny however that there are not problems with salaried offices. In particular, there is the problem of staff overload because managers can increase caseload at no extra cost to the institution.

Notes

1. On the 'franchising experiment' referred to by Paterson, see the discussion of contracting in section 2 infra.

2. Paterson concludes by arguing that a mixture of judicare and service models would be the optimum but notes that nowhere has the interaction of judicare and service models been planned. Note in this respect that one of the primary functions of the Legal Services Commission (created by the Access to Justice Act 1999 to replace the Legal Aid Board) was to systematically plan and co-ordinate the work of the various different legal service providers.[12]

3. The Access to Justice Act created a Criminal Defence Service to take over the running of criminal legal aid[13]. Despite strong opposition the Act allowed the CDS to provide legal representation through employed lawyers.[14] Criminal defence services have been piloted in Scotland.

4. The merits test for civil litigation referred to was then contained in s 15 (2) of the Legal Aid Act 1988 which provided that legal aid could not be granted 'unless [the applicant] satisfies the Legal Aid Board that he has reasonable grounds for taking, bringing or being a party to the proceedings' This related to the prospects of success. Even if the prospects were reasonable assistance might be refused if in the circumstances it appeared 'unreasonable that he should be granted representation' (s 15(3)). The principal purpose of the funding code introduced by the Access to Justice Act and discussed below was to provide more detailed and focused tests for different categories of legal assistance according to their importance.

Legal Aid in crisis

By the early 1990s, the UK was spending more on legal aid per capita than almost any other European country[15]. Yet as Professor Paterson implies many of the relevant participants were highly dissatisfied with the working of the scheme. Consumer groups were alarmed at the poor quality of service provided by some of the solicitors and barristers doing legally aided work (see in particular chapter 6 on criminal legal aid).

12   Access to Justice Act 1998, s 5(5).
13   Section 13.
14   Section 14.
15   See Goriely and Paterson supra note 3 at p 13.

The same constituency also complained that the legal aid scheme was taking a very narrow view of legal services, defining them largely in terms of the litigation skills and traditional practice areas of solicitors and barristers. Hence most legal aid work was being done in matrimonial, personal injury, and criminal law. Yet the legal problems of the poor are equally if not more likely to arise in relation to housing, welfare benefits, debt and employment law – areas left largely untouched by most legal aid practitioners.

Legal aid practitioners were themselves dissatisfied claiming that falling rates of pay required them to deal ever more quickly with ever higher numbers of clients in order to make ends meet, leading to diminished occupational satisfaction. One criminal law practitioner commented that:

> I'm only going to continue this work as long as I have to and then I'd like do something else. Still in the law, because that's the only thing I'm competent to do, but not private practice. Maybe lecturing, CPS or something. I'm tired of being called out at night. I have two kids, I'm 42 – in six-seven years I won't have to pay for their schooling. When I was younger, my work was everything to me, but I'm less keen now.[16]

The loudest voice raised in protest however was that of government which was understandably alarmed by the escalating costs of the scheme. Between 1992-1993 and 1997-1998, spending on all forms of civil and family legal aid rose by 35% (as compared with general inflation of 13%) from £586 million to £793 million. Over the same period the number of full civil legal aid cases started fell by 31%, implying an increased unit cost.[17]

As the following extract shows, the Major administration sought to explain the increase by means of two well-known economic models. The first (the principal-agent problem) deals with the difficulties facing relatively inexpert principals (ie the state) employing relatively expert agents (ie lawyers) to complete a task. The second (the 'problem of moral hazard') assumes a tendency on the part of those consuming services free at point of delivery to use the service unnecessarily.

THE INCENTIVE PROBLEM

3.29 Under the existing scheme, lawyers are encouraged and are bound to define problems as needing legal solutions. This includes seeking redress in the courts, when alternative remedies might be as effective, cheaper and more popular with clients. The current system gives little or no encouragement to lawyers to pursue or adopt these alternative solutions, either by using non-solicitor agencies or by seeking out ways of resolving problems which do not involve the courts. The main reason for this is that there is an incentive within the system of fees to pursue court based solutions to problems.

3.30 Within the existing scheme the client, the Legal Aid Board and the lawyer or supplier all have different aims. The client wishes to have his or her problem resolved. The solicitor wishes to help the client but is also running a business and wishes to

16 Solicitor talking to researchers cited in R Baldwin et al *Standing Accused: A Study of Criminal Defence lawyers in Britain* (Clarendon, Oxford, 1994) p 23.

17 *Modernising Justice: The Government's plans for reforming legal services and the Courts* (Cmn 4155, 1999) para 3.8.

make a profit. The Board (the payer representing the taxpayer) wishes to ensure that publicly funded legal services are available to those who most need them in the most cost-effective way.

3.31 The information which the solicitor has about the case is superior to that of the Board and of the client. This gives the solicitor great power to make decisions about the way the case is run. The way that the solicitor chooses to run the case may not be the way that either the Board or the client would wish the case to be run, if they had the same information. As a result, it is very difficult for the Board to assess when it is receiving value for money from suppliers. Nor can it easily assess the strength of continuing need for legal aid at any stage in the case.

3.32 There is little consequence for the solicitor in failing to pursue the aims of the Board. The Board has few sanctions against inefficiency under the present system and anyway may not always be aware of a failure to pursue its objectives because of the inferior information which it has compared with the solicitor. As for the client, he or she may often have no financial interest in the costs of the case, because unlike a private client they may not be paying. In such cases, the client has no incentive to ensure that costs are kept to a minimum. This can be contrasted with the position of the privately paying client, who is only too well aware of the fees that have to be paid.[18]

These economic models gained a remarkable hold on policy makers and were still being used to explain legal aid cost inflation five years later when the Labour government published its White Paper *Modernising Justice*.[19] Some independent researchers doubted whether the explanation could really be that simple.[20] Some of the increased cost may have been due to improved quality or increased procedural complexity, for example when increased procedural safeguards were introduced into child care proceedings by the Children Act 1989. Moreover, it is striking that the first category of cases to be removed from the legal aid scheme was personal injury work since most of these cases were in fact won thus ensuring a relatively low net cost to the legal aid fund[1]. Be that as it may, these economic models remained highly influential and helped to precipitate the fundamental reforms discussed in the next two sections.

Questions

1. What does the principal-agent analysis suggest about the ethics of lawyers?

18 *Legal Aid – Targeting Need* Cmnd 2854 (London, HMSO, May 1994) pp 18-19.
19 'The scheme provides *few effective means or incentives for improving value for money.* Because any lawyer can take a legal aid case, there is little control over quality and no scope for competition to keep prices down. Lawyers' fees are calculated after the event, based on the amount of work done, so there is *little incentive to work more efficiently*' 'Modernising Justice' (London, HMSO,1998) at para 3.8 emphasis added.
20 See T Goriely 'The Governments Legal Aid Reforms' chapter 10 of *The Reform of Civil Procedure* (Zuckerman and Cranston eds) (Clarendon Press, Oxford, 1995) p 350.
1   See Alan Tunkel 'Legal Aid, Politics and Statistics' (1997) New Law Journal, 11 July and in reply, Geoffrey Hoon MP (Parliamentary Secretary at the Lord Chancellors Department) (1999) New Law Journal, 25 July.

2. Review the analysis of professionalism put forward by market control theorists (chapter 3 supra). To what extent does governmental determination to reform the legal aid system represent a collapse of professional power?

2 Reform of the legal aid scheme – contracting

Whatever the true nature and cause of the problems with the judicare scheme, the principal-agent/moral hazard diagnosis precipitated fundamental reforms, the precise consequences of which will only emerge over the next decade. The process was initiated by the Major administration's green paper *Legal Aid – Targeting Need*[2] and the subsequent White paper *Striking the Balance – the Future of Legal Aid in England and Wales*[3] and continued by the subsequent Labour administration. At the forefront of the new approach were the encouragement of conditional fee litigation (considered below) and contracting.

As originally conceived, contracting involved a radical change in the way in which the state's commitment to the subsidizing of legal services was to be determined. The judicare scheme had been demand led: any case of sufficient merit presented by a client of insufficient means to a qualified solicitor would be given assistance. Under the new scheme the legal aid budget would be capped: a fixed budget would be allocated each year to each of the major categories of legal aid (ie criminal, matrimonial etc) implying a need for rationing decisions. More radically still, there was to be an attempt to stimulate and capture the benefits of a competitive market amongst legal service providers. Only those firms of solicitors who had been awarded a contract to do a particular category of work could be retained by the assisted person. Contracts would be awarded on the basis of value for money after a competitive tendering process and each contract would specify the number of acts of assistance to be provided and the unit price. Payments would be staged over the life of the contract rather than being in lieu of work done in order to answer solicitors' complaints about the previous system – the LAB's slowness in making payment.

This was an attempt to deal with the defects in the present system as diagnosed by principal-agent and moral hazard models. Informational asymmetries were to be addressed by giving a more active supervisory role over a smaller number of solicitors to a more proactive LAB. Thus an expert principal (the state) would replace an inexpert lay client as the dominant figure in evaluating the lawyer's services. It was envisaged that the competitive tendering process and the fixing of unit prices in the contract would give lawyers an incentive to minimise costs. Moreover, the new system would ensure that value for money did not simply mean low price and low quality by putting in place quality control measures. Contracts would be awarded to and renewed with solicitors who provided value for money having regard to quality of output as well as to price.

---

2   Supra note 18.
3   Cmnd 3305 (London. HMSO, 1996).

As originally conceived, these proposals raised some difficult ethical problems for lawyers such as the question of rationing: it was envisaged that each contractor would have a fixed budget to provide a fixed number of acts of assistance. How was the lawyer to decide which among the applicants whose cases had the necessary minimum merit would be given assistance if, in a given period, there were more applicants than available funds?

However, the contracting regime as it currently exists within the framework provided by the Access to Justice Act 1999 is significantly less radical. The overall budget for what is now called the Community Legal Service is to be capped by central government in accordance with its overall spending plans. The Lord Chancellor will determine limits on expenditure for the component parts of the budget (such as family legal services; clinical negligence litigation; basic advice and assistance etc) and the money will then be spent by the Legal Services Commission as successor to the Legal Aid Board. However, the budget for the Criminal Defence Service is not to be capped. To deny legal representation for criminal defendants solely for financial reasons would have put the government in breach of Art 6(1) of the ECHR.

The emerging contracting system is much less clearly market orientated and might indeed be more accurately termed 'exclusive licensing'. Most categories of state subsidised legal work will be restricted to those to whom a contract has been awarded by the Legal Services Commission, thus reducing the number of solicitors doing legal aid work from over 10,000 to about 3,000. However, the emphasis will be on ensuring the appropriate quality of service rather than competition amongst potential contractors with respect to price. Thus contracting represents no more than a development of the preexisting practice of awarding legal aid franchises (and consequently improved terms of payment) to firms able to comply with quality assurance procedures. This may reflect a learning of the lessons to be drawn from the United States experience of competitive contracting for criminal defence services which has led to cost containment at the expense of quality.[4]

Moreover, remuneration for work done under the contract is not to be fixed in advance by the contract. Instead it will be fixed by regulations made by the Lord Chancellor and administered by the LSC. These will provide either for payment on an hourly basis (but with strict limits on the amount of work that can be done) or for the payment of a fixed fee, for example for a contested trial in the magistrates court. Nor, in most cases, will the question of whether a client's case has sufficient merit be one for the lawyer.[5] Instead, the Legal Services Commission has published a funding code setting out detailed criteria for deciding whether a particular applicant will receive assistance with a particular category of case. Most importantly, it is envisaged that assistance will only ever be refused because of the need to ration resources in the case of very expensive cases (defined as those involving costs in excess of £75,000).[6] With such cases, it is anticipated that the LSC might deem an applicant's case to be of

4   See generally Roger Smith, *Legal Aid Contracting – Lessons from North America* (London, Legal Action Group).
5   See The Funding Code (Legal Services Commission, 2000) Part II. A para A.2.
6   Ibid Part I para 6.5; Part III 'Decision Making Guidance para 15.1.4(b).

sufficient merit but refuse immediate funding in case even more meritorious cases should emerge during the financial year. Expensive cases will be put out to competitive tender and awarded on a fixed price basis.

Note

1. A further aim of the contracting system is to permit the channelling of public money away from professional lawyers and the services (such as litigation) they have historically provided. Thus in *Modernising Justice,* Lord Irvine commented that:

> As part of the Community Legal Service, legal aid spending will be refocused on the people and cases where it is most needed and can do most good. More money will reach the not-for-profit sector (which has particular expertise at dealing with the types of problems faced by poor people) and better ways of resolving disputes.[7]

2. Under s 15(2)(a) of the Access to Justice Bill, there is a provision for those accused of crimes to be restricted in their choice of legal representative to contracted criminal defence firms.[8]

Questions

1. Is the restriction of state-funded legal services to contracted providers an unacceptable restraint on freedom to choose one's own lawyer?[9] What is the likely impact of these constraints on client's autonomy? It has been argued that 'the restriction of personal choice returns the [client] to a position of dependency, as the generally voluntary, formally equal relationship between practitioner and client is replaced by one which is more coercive as clients go to solicitors because they have nowhere else to go.'[10]

2. The Legal Service Commission has no power to fund legal services such as the law reform campaigning of the type carried out by some of the strategic salaried law offices described by Professor Paterson.[11] Should it have such a power?

---

7   Supra note 17.
8   But they may not be restricted to lawyers employed by the Criminal Defence Service: s 15(4).
9   Note that Legal Services Commission is likely to be even less receptive than its predecessor the Legal Aid Board to client's requests for a change of solicitor given the wasted costs involved. See 'The Funding Code – a new approach to funding civil cases' (London, Legal Aid Board, 1999) para 13.21.
10 H Sommerlad 'Ethical and Philosophical Concerns Arising Out of Conditional Fee Arrangements and Contracting' (1999, unpublished paper on file with the author) p 19.
11 See s 5(2) of the Access to Justice Act.

Particular ethical problems: rationing and quality control

While the devolution of rationing decisions from government to solicitors has for the moment been largely avoided, this is not entirely the case. Contracts for the provision of 'Legal Help' and 'Help at Court'[12] restrict the number of 'new starts' each provider may make and leave it to the provider to decide which clients should be assisted. Moreover, the restrictions on the work which the LSC is prepared to allow providers to carry out mean that if the case requires work going beyond what the LSC is prepared to pay for, the provider must choose whether to provide such work 'pro bono'. The obvious limits on the amount of such work any firm can do require, in effect, rationing decisions. Finally, lawyers will be permitted to make representations to the LSC about whether their client's case should receive funding[13]. Such arguments will be effective only to the extent they advocate a coherent approach to rationing.

Questions

1. William Simon has argued that lawyers should welcome the opportunity to be involved in rationing decisions. It is inevitable, he argues, in a world of limited resources, that choices have to be made among would-be clients. For lawyers to be involved in these choices is for them an opportunity to exercise ethical discretion and thus to seek justice.[14] Hilary Somerlad by contrast argues that this process is destructive of lawyers' sense of vocation because it makes it much more difficult to argue that they are servants of justice. Instead their primary loyalty is owed to the Treasury and thus to the taxpayer.[15] Which view do you prefer?

2. What are the advantages and disadvantages from a public interest perspective of having rationing decisions made by, on the one hand, lawyers (or other legal service providers) and, on the other, the Legal Services Commission and its employees. Note that the Legal Services Commission consists of up to 12 members appointed by the Lord Chancellor subject only to certain very broad constraints.[16] Moreover, the Lord Chancellor has numerous powers to require the LSC to carry out its various functions as he directs. [17]

12 Ie legal advice and assistance in relation to a legal problem which may in the case of 'Help at Court' include assistance with litigation falling short of formal representation. Funding Code (supra note 25) Part II Part A.
13 Ibid at 13.22.
14 William H Simon 'Ethical Discretion in Lawyering' (1988) 101 HLR at pp 1092-1096.
15 H Somerlad supra note 10 at pp 12-16.
16 Section 1(5) of the Access to Justice Act provides that in appointing members of the LSC the Lord Chancellor shall 'have regard to the desirability of securing that the Commission includes members who (between them) have experience in or knowledge of – a) the provision of services which the Commission can fund as part of the Community Legal Fund or Criminal defence service b) the work of the Courts c) consumer affairs d) social conditions and e) management.'
17 See for example s 4(10) (the LSC's planning functions) and s 5(6) (the priorities for the expending of the Community Legal Service Fund).

3. You work for a law firm in inner city London which has a contract for the provision of advice and assistance. You are consulted by Ned who lives on a local council estate from which the local authority is seeking to evict him. While Ned seems (on the basis of the brief account of events he has given you) to have ground for complaint, you are aware that he is known in the area as a racist troublemaker and you suspect that the this may be why the council are seeking to evict him. You are also aware that your firm is approaching the limit in terms of new clients permitted by its contract for the current year. Your knowledge of local authority housing policy convinces you that there will be many other evictions needing to be contested before the end of the current year. Should you assist Ned? Is it relevant to consider whether or not other contracted firms in your area have 'spare capacity'? [18]

4. The LSC funding code attempts wherever possible to quantify the value of a case using a cost benefit criterion. Generally speaking, eligibility for legal representation with respect to claims for damages will be granted on the following basis[19]:

(i)   if prospects of success are very good (80% or more), likely damages must exceed costs;

(ii)   if prospects of success are good (60%-80%), likely damages must exceed costs by a ratio of 2:1;

(iii) if prospects of success are moderate (50%-60%), likely damages must exceed likely costs by a ratio of 4:1.

However it was accepted by the LSC that not all claims can be evaluated in this way, particularly where questions of wider public interest are involved. What arguments could be made to the LSC in support of an application for 'litigation support funding'[20] in the following cases?

a) Your client Mary claims to have been raped two years ago by her doctor whilst she was under sedation in his surgery. The case was referred to the Crown Prosecution Service which refused to proceed because it felt there was no realistic prospect of conviction. The prosecutor concerned laid particular stress on Mary's failure to complain immediately and the absence of evidence of physical injury. Mary now wishes to bring a claim for assault in the civil courts. Damages are unlikely to be more than £65,000 and your own costs are likely to be in the region of £50,000. Given the lower standard of proof in a civil trial, you rate the prospects of success at between 60% and 70%.

---

18   The LSC's guidelines for funding decisions state that 'the conduct [of the putative client] can only be taken into account insofar as it relates to any application for funding. The general character and conduct of the client and whether they have a criminal record or high public profile are not relevant to funding decisions' but adds delphically that 'There may be some cases where the conduct of the client in relation to the case is so dishonest, abusive or violent that it would not be reasonable for further services to be provided' (Funding code supra note 25, Part III at paras 9.10.2 -9.10.3.).

19   Supra note 5. Part I para 5.7.3.

20   See p 390 note 11 (infra) and accompanying text.

b) Your client Adjit is the personal representative of his 17-year-old son Sachin. Sachin was killed after the police failed to respond to his emergency call. Sachin had called for assistance from a mobile phone when he found himself being pursued through a multi storey car park by a racist mob. The police were given the correct location but went to the wrong multi-storey car park and, as a result, Sachin was brutally murdered. Adjit wants to bring a negligence claim against the police under the Fatal Accidents Act. Damages are likely to be small (under £27,000) and the costs are likely to be high (about £100,000). In any case, Adjit has said that he will give any damages away to charity. There are legal difficulties with the case: English authority[1] suggests the police have immunity from suit but there is case law in the European Court of Human Rights[2] suggesting that these decisions are contrary to Art 6(1) of the ECHR. The prospects of success are rated as being 60%.

Quality control

As contracting develops, quality control is likely to be crucial. The Major administration's White Paper *Striking the Balance* envisaged two principal ways in which this might be done. The first was through transaction criteria: the funding body's audit of files would require the solicitor to be able to demonstrate that the steps deemed to be typical of that class of case had been taken. In personal injury cases involving loss of earnings, for example the auditor would expect the solicitor to have sought proof of earnings. The second method was via outcome criterion. These evolved from the government's fear that solicitors were litigating too many unwinnable cases because payment would be made independent of success or failure. Accordingly contractors would be expected to show that most of their cases reached a successful outcome. In the following extract, Tamara Goriely considers some of the problems with the concept of quality.

THE DIFFERENT DIMENSIONS OF QUALITY

… concepts such as quality and competence are multi-faceted. Not only do people measure quality in different ways, they also measure different things. Most British experimental studies have focused on one or two of the following dimensions of quality:

1. Was the service *client-orientated?* For example, did clients think that the solicitor was approachable and sympathetic? Were they able to explain their problem? Did they understand the advice given? Were solicitors easy to contact? Did they keep in touch and explain any delays? In the past, surveys concentrated on simple satisfaction scores, but recent studies have been considerably more sophisticated. Thus a study by Hisock & Cole used depth interviews to compare the service of law centres and solicitors, while the National Audit Office has conducted a major survey of the views of legally aided clients.

---

1   See *Alexandrou v Oxford* [1993] 4 All ER 328; *Osman v Ferguson* [1993] 4 All ER 344.
2   See *Osman v UK* [1999] 1 FLR 193.

2. Was the advice *accurate*? For example, did the solicitor accumulate all the necessary information, come to a legally correct conclusion and give advice about all the available options?
3. Was the service *efficient*? For example, was the work carried out quickly and cheaply? Although it is dangerous to measure speed and cost in isolation, efficiency may be measured alongside other aspects of quality. Thus Domberger & Sherr's small scale study of industrial tribunal advisers found that the law centre adviser dealt with cases more efficiently, without appreciable differences in outcome or client satisfaction.
4. Was the service *effective*? Did it achieve tangible benefits for the client? Here the focus is on the outcome of the case. Did the client win and, if so, how much money did they gain? Studies which measure outcomes suffer from the difficulty of comparing like with like, but meaningful results are possible. Thus Genn & Genn's research into tribunal representation provides useful information about the comparative success rates of different types of representatives.

Most people would agree that all four dimensions of quality have a part to play in assessing the service solicitors provide. But when it comes to the stress that should be put on each, the consensus breaks apart. Commentators usually feel that one aspect is more important: when confronted with other people, who stress different aspects, the result can be blank incomprehension. It is possible to identify a number of different views, each underpinned by an implicit model of 'good lawyering'.

THE TRADITIONAL VIEW

The most traditional, professional view lays stress on legal accuracy. This is, after all, the basis of most legal teaching. Before lawyers are allowed to practice, they are examined through the 'problem question'. Here students are given hypothetical scenarios from which they must identify the salient facts and to which they must apply the correct law. It matters little if the result is written in jargon, or incomprehensible to the lay client that they are notionally advising.

The same view of quality was stressed in the 1980 ALI-ABA discussion draft analysed by Bryant Garth. This states that the good lawyer must first gather all the appropriate facts and formulate the material issues. The attorney is then 'responsible for an accurate determination of the applicable law' and 'for identifying alternative legal responses'. After devising a strategy to deal with the case, the lawyer is responsible for following it through. A very similar approach has been adopted by the transaction criteria, within the constraints of the budget and methodology. The transaction criteria attempt to check whether the lawyer has identified the salient facts, applied the correct law and carried through the agreed strategy. They follow the approach identified by Carlson in 1976 as the most promising way forward: that process measurements should be applied to individual 'episodes of service'.

Lying behind this approach is a model of good lawyering which is based on knowledge of the law. It is assumed that there is a correct answer to any given problem, which can be applied as a unitary standard to the whole profession; as Garth points out, under the ALI-ABA code *all* lawyers are required to identify *all* salient facts, and apply *all* relevant law. The Benson Commission asserted a unitary standard as a matter of principle:

'All those who receive legal services are entitled to expect the same standard of legal service irrespective of their personal circumstances.'

The transaction criteria also assume that there is a right answer to any given legal problem. It is quite possible for a case to score 100%, with no omissions. This would be considered as 'excellence', to which all practitioners should aspire, and which many practitioners will reach, at least some of the time. The Board has, however, tempered the Benson Commission's sanguinity with commercial reality. It accepts that not all legal aid practitioners will be perfect all the time, and it will permit a certain level of omissions. The exact cut-off for omissions has not yet been set, but is expected to be around a third. Practitioners will be expected to be better than barely competent – but not excellent. In the terminology of the researchers, the level is said to be somewhere between 'competence' and 'competence-plus'. The tacit assumption is that legal aid solicitors have a lower 'quality' than large city solicitors acting for corporate clients. On the other hand, they should be as good, if not better, than many high street firms acting for private, individual clients.

THE SPECIALIST VIEW

For some experienced or specialist lawyers, this legal knowledge approach is too redolent of their student days. Hence the often repeated comment that the criteria are fine for training new recruits, but are not suitable for experienced practitioners. Smith quotes two typical reactions along these lines:

'Housing specialist Duncan Forbes considers the housing criteria, 'useful particularly if you have not got experience' . . . Criminal expert Ed Cape makes a similar point: 'They would be quite good in terms of training and supervision. The problems arise if they are being relied upon to perform a weightier function.'

To the specialist, legal work is not simply a matter of identifying the facts and applying the law. It is about developing new strategies to further the interests of the client. Rather than following the law teacher or the textbook, it leads them. Instead of applying the notionally 'correct' answer, it goes one step better. Such practitioners justify their work on the grounds that it gets results. Hence their preference for outcome measures, whatever the practical problems such measures pose...

What model of legal services underpins such views? The trade union and law centre specialists who express such views are often politically committed to their client's cause. They see the role of lawyers as using the law to further the interests of their clients in an essentially disputatious society. Their quality therefore depends on how far their clients' interests are furthered. In this model, there are no absolute answers: excellence is an infinitely receding goal.

THE FUNDERS' VIEW

The view of quality adopted by the Lord Chancellor's Department and the Legal Aid Board is very different. Here the overriding emphasis is on efficiency: carrying out tasks more quickly with less waste. Thus John Pitts, Chairman of the Legal Aid Board, commented that improving quality in legal services had much in common with improving quality in manufacturing industry:

'Managing quality is important, therefore, not only to satisfy the legitimate demands of the client, but also to reduce the wastage resulting from faulty work. Wide experience of quality objectives shows that their use leads to lower costs rather than higher costs.

In addition to reducing the cost of wasted effort, the greater attention that has to be paid to management usually leads to improvements in efficiency in other areas. I believe the same effects will be observed if this approach is applied to legal services.'

If one assumes that improving quality is about working more efficiently and reducing waste, then it follows that improving quality will reduce costs: a view which flatly contradicts the traditional professional view that the higher the quality, the higher the cost. Lying behind the Legal Aid Board's approach is a model of mass legal aid work which provides good value for the limited amount of money that can be spent on it. It sees legal aid as an essentially high-volume, low-cost operation, in which efficiency gains can be achieved through improved 'routinisation'. The belief is that better management systems will allow the work to be undertaken with less waste and to a more consistent standard. The absolute level of the standard, however, must be dependent on the money available.

In Ian Harden's terminology, this approach concentrates on the 'supply side' aspects of quality, that is on how services are delivered once priorities have been set and the level of resources prescribed. It carries the danger that key 'demand' decisions over priorities and resources will be neglected. Proponents of the supply side view often make analogies with goods produced for the private market, in which consumers with only limited budgets prefer to buy Minis rather than Rolls Royces. Both Minis and Rolls Royces may, in their own terms, be 'quality' cars – it depends on how well they meet consumers' requirements within the budget available. The analogy, however, does not cover a situation in which the state rather than the consumer sets the standard, and where the state may be tempted to set a standard which the consumer finds unacceptable. It may be worth recalling that the only motorised vehicles the British welfare state has provided to private individuals were the much condemned invalid tricycles, withdrawn in the late 1970s because they were found to be dangerous. John Pitts' views raise the spectre that the Legal Aid Board may be about to provide the invalid tricycle of legal services.

Despite the protests of the traditionalists, routinisation is hardly new to legal aid work. It was first identified by Bridges et al in 1975, who found a limited number of firms undertaking a high volume of legal aid work on a 'strictly routinised basis'. These firms positively chose to do legal aid work and found it profitable, but were reluctant to take on relatively rare kinds of work which did not 'fit into their organisational patterns'. One solicitor in the study contemptuously dismissed such firms as 'sausage machines'. At the time, 'sausage machines' undertook around half of all legally-aided work. The other half was carried out by a much larger number of general practitioners, who did small numbers of legally aided cases alongside other work. Returning the insult, these general firms could be designated 'fruit machines', in which the quality of service provided was a gamble. Some legally aided clients undoubtedly struck lucky and were given excellent service, similar to that provided to well-to-do paying clients. Others may have found themselves with conveyancers who were out of their depth with complex litigation, and who buried their files in the back of the drawer. The Legal Aid Board

Annual Reports suggest that from the mid 70s to the late 80s the ratio of 'sausage machines' to 'fruit machines' remained fairly constant: in both 1978-79 and 1989-90, 10% of offices within the legal aid scheme received 49% of payments.

Over the last few years, however, both ideological and economic pressures have been towards increased routinisation...

THE CONSUMER VIEW

For many years, advice centres and consumer bodies have stressed the need for solicitors to improve the client-oriented aspects of their work. They have castigated lawyers for their poor communication skills, their inability to deal with clients' emotional concerns, their failure to keep clients informed and their inadequate information about costs.

The traditional professional view was that such issues were relatively unimportant. Thus, in 1989 the Solicitors Complaints Bureau described poor communication and misunderstandings as ranking 'low on the scale of seriousness'. This view would no longer be expressed so boldly. Most quality checklists now make some mention of communicating with clients. The Law Society requires that solicitors comply with 'client care' rules and these have been incorporated within the Legal Aid Board's management criteria. Meanwhile the transaction criteria attempt to measure communication with clients by looking at the letters on the files.

To the consumer bodies, this misses the point. Not only must the appropriate letters be given, but they must be read and understood. Furthermore, the tone must address clients' emotional concerns. The only way of finding out whether this is done is to ask clients. Even more important is the demand that clients should have some say in the standards to be applied. Thus the National Consumer Council argues that:

'Consumers' concerns should be established before service standards are set, so that performance can be evaluated to improve the quality of the service ...'

'The Board and its suppliers should be required to find out more directly from consumers about the services they are receiving and to pay particular attention to improving those aspects of service that are important to consumers. There needs to be further work which collects both qualitative and quantitative information from consumers.'

The debate about whether clients can judge the quality of their lawyers is often portrayed as a methodological question – how can one measure agreed characteristics? In fact, it goes much deeper than this. It is about how quality is defined, and the implicit model of what makes a 'good lawyer'.

The difference between the traditional and the client-centred model of legal practice was first identified by Douglas Rosenthal in 1974. He argued that while a traditional view considers that professional problems are 'routine and technical' with a 'best solution inaccessible to lay understanding', a more participatory model considers that such problems involve 'open, unpredictable individualised choices, understandable to a layman, for which there is no single best answer'. Clients should not simply sit back and trust their lawyers, but make 'an active, sceptical effort to be informed and to share responsibility, making mutually agreeable choices'. Rosenthal's own research of New York personal injury practice found that clients who actively participated did significantly better than those who passively delegated decision-making responsibility, as often the best strategy depended on the 'unique circumstances and subjective feelings of each client'.

A client- or consumer-centred model of lawyering starts with what the client wants. This does not mean that it ignores accuracy, efficiency or outcomes. Indeed, it assumes that no consumer would be happy to think that they had been given inaccurate advice. Furthermore, many consumers want cases dealt with quickly. When clients are paying (and in legally aided cases they often are, either through contributions or the statutory charge), they want cases done cheaply. They also care deeply about the outcome. All these issues are important – yet, as most consumers would only too readily admit, they are not in the best position to judge them. In an ideal world, they would like others to judge them, and to tell them the result. But there are other specifically consumer-oriented measures of quality which other models of lawyering either downgrade or ignore. A consumer-centred model assumes that finding out what clients want, and giving personal, understandable advice is central to what a lawyer does. It is not an optional extra, to be added to other, more 'professional', views of quality. As David concludes:

> 'A degree of sensitivity to the client's emotional state . . . is essential if [the solicitor] is to discharge his more technical, or purely 'legal' responsibilities. A solicitor who lacks this understanding is likely to be ineffective in all aspects, including that of conveying sound legal advice'.

One client in the Hisock & Cole study complained that her solicitors were 'giving answers to the problems and not to the person who had them'. A consumer-centred model requires solicitors to give answers to people. And the only way to judge if they have done this, is to ask the client.

Goriely concludes by describing the adversarial model of good lawyering. This is the model which theorists such as Luban have advocated as being appropriate for criminal defence practice in the interests of safeguarding the rights of the criminal defendant. She notes however empirical work suggesting such a model is rarely encountered in practice – see chapter 6 above.[3]

Note

The initial work on transaction criteria was conducted by academic legal researchers and based on the actual practices of (then) current franchisees. The criteria derived from observed practice were then adjusted in the light of normative standards gleaned from theoretical literature and further developed through a process of consultation with leading practitioners and consumer groups.[4]

---

3   T Goriely 'Debating the Quality of Legal Services: Differing Models of the Good Lawyer' (1994) 1 International Journal of the Legal Profession pp 160-166.
4   See A Sherr, Richard Moorhead and Alan Paterson 'Assessing the quality of legal work: measuring process' [1994] 1 International Journal of the Legal Profession 135.

Questions

1. What effect would you expect the need to comply with the transaction criteria would have on the lawyer–client relationship? Are any of the qualities needed by a good client interviewer difficult to demonstrate on paper? If so, how could the LSC monitor this aspect of the process?

2. How could one measure whether a settlement amounted to a successful outcome?[5]

3. Are contractual quality controls a threat to or protective of lawyers?

4. To what extent is it appropriate for government to take into account the views of clients (solicited for example by questionnaires) when assessing the quality of subsidised legal work? One critic[6] has noted that 'in spite of the status of the client as the rhetorical pivot of the reforms, the client voice is likely to be regarded as marginal to quality assessment because they would probably demand a level of service higher than 'competence plus.'[7]

5. Consider again the material in chapter 6 on zealous criminal defence lawyering and see p 374 and following notes above. Are there any features of that work which make contracting/quality control particularly problematic? Are these problems likely to be magnified or reduced if criminal defence work is done by salaried lawyers employed by the Criminal Defence Service?

6. Are the issues raised by quality control technical, political, or ethical?

7. Exclusive contracting and block contracting present alternative models to the Judicare and Salaried Models described by Paterson (supra). Which model seems to you most attractive and why?

8. How do the ethical challenges posed by each of the various models referred to in the previous question differ?

3   Reforming legal aid – conditional fees

Another main response to dissatisfaction with the judicare scheme has been the legitimation and encouragement by government of what are commonly (though, as we shall see, misleadingly), called 'no win, no fee' arrangements which provide for the

---

5   In controlled experiments in the US, several pairs of practising personal injury lawyers were asked to negotiate a settlement on the basis of the same set of facts. The resulting settlement figures varied enormously. See T Goriely supra note 3 at p 361 note 66.

6   Sommerlad supra p 380 note 10 at p 22.

7   Ie a level of service deemed acceptable but below that which would be obtained by a privately paying client. Supra note 4 at p 142.

lawyer to be paid only if s/he wins the case. For many years, such contracts were thought to be rendered illegal by the common law doctrines of maintenance (which restricts the funding of litigation by third parties) and champerty (which prohibits contracts for the division of the spoils of litigation). These common law doctrines were reinforced by further prohibitions contained in the Solicitors Practice Rules made pursuant to the Solicitors Act 1974 and incorporated within the LSGPC. Such was the opposition to these agreements that the doctrines of champerty and maintenance were thought to strike down not only arrangements ('conditional fees') providing for the lawyer to be paid extra in the event of success (and nothing in the event of failure) but also contracts ('speculative fees') under which the normal fee was to be paid if but only if the case was won; *British Waterways Board v Norman* [1993] 26 HLR 695.

However, we have seen that since the election of the first Thatcher administration in 1979, successive governments have been anxious to control public expenditure. In such a climate, no win no fee arrangements have many attractions, offering the possibility that the legal profession might be persuaded to replace the state as underwriters of the cost of ensuring access to justice. Consequently, the 1989 Green paper 'The Work and Organization of the Legal Profession'[8] was accompanied by another Green Paper 'Contingency Fees'[9] calling for reconsideration of the idea. Subsequently, s 58 of the Courts and Legal Services Act gave the government power to validate conditional fee arrangements ie contracts under which a successful lawyer would be paid as a reward for success the lawyers ordinary costs plus a percentage (known as an 'uplift') of those costs.[10] The initial delegated legislation covered only personal injury litigation, human rights cases and insolvency work. As governmental attention has turned towards concrete proposals for the reform of legal aid, support for conditional fee litigation has grown. Indeed the election of the Blair administration in 1997 was followed by a quickening of the pace. For example, Lord Mackay's White Paper 'Targeting Need' focused on block contracting by the state as a means of ensuring access to justice. Conditional fee agreements were seen as a complementary but not as an alternative strategy. By contrast, the incoming Lord Chancellor, Lord Irvine, was to place greater emphasis on conditional fees. The Access to Justice Act 1999 validated conditional fees for all non-matrimonial civil litigation and removed personal injury claims except for those involving clinical negligence from the legal aid scheme.[11] In future, the Legal Services Commission will in principle refuse legal aid if

8   Cmnd 570 (London HMSO, 1989).

9   Cmnd 571 (London. HMSO, 1989).

10   Conditional fee uplifts have always been subject to a statutory maximum of 100%. The relevant provision is currently reg 4 of the Conditional Fee Agreements Order 2000, SI 2000/823.

11   Section 6(6) and Sch 2 para 1(a). Note however that the Lord Chancellor has power under s 6(8) to disapply Sch 2 and has used this power so as to permit the LSC to fund the costs of investigating whether a personal injury claim is strong enough to justify a solicitor entering a conditional fee arrangement. In addition, some limited financial contribution ('litigation support') can be granted in cases otherwise being litigated on a conditional fee basis if the total costs of the case are likely to exceed £20,000: Funding Code (supra note 00) Part III para 3.3 (7-8). Cases involving a 'significant wider public interest' are also removed from the general prohibition; ibid para 3.3 (4(a)).

a case can be litigated under a conditional fee arrangement. In parallel with these legislative developments, speculative fees were reconsidered judicially. In *Thai Trading Co (a firm) v Taylor*[12] the Court of Appeal reconsidered the legality of contracts under which the solicitors' hourly rate would be payable only in the event of success and overruled *British Waterways Board v Norman*. This decision was confirmed by s 27 of the Access to Justice Act.

Conditional fees: for and against

Conditional fees remain controversial in principle. Critics remain concerned that lawyers with a financial interest in the outcome of litigation will be tempted to breach their duty to the court and/or their duty to the client. In the following extract, these arguments are considered with particular reference to personal injury litigation. In such cases, individual plaintiffs experience what they hope will be their one and only encounter with civil litigation ('one-shot players') and confront insurance company defendants ('repeat players')[13] who litigate on a regular basis.

THE ADVANTAGES OF CONDITIONAL FEES

Risk Distribution and Bargaining Endowments:

Simply put, conditional fee agreements remove from plaintiffs the risk of having to pay their lawyers if they lose and this significantly improves their chances of obtaining a settlement somewhere near that which their case deserves. This argument can only be understood in the context of three fundamental and well established features of personal injury litigation. The first of these is that most cases settle. The Pearson Commission report stated that only 8.2% of High Court cases come to trial, the remainder settling out of court[14], and most studies put the figure at between 8 and 20%.[15] Therefore for most plaintiffs, the trial is important only as the backdrop against which they negotiate a settlement. The second is that most cases settle for sums well below what one would expect given the levels of damages awarded by judges after contested hearings. Thus when in 1984, Harris et al published their survey of accident victims experiences with the tort system (subsequently know as 'the Oxford Study'), they found the mean compensation agreed in settlements to be only £1,135 and the median only £500, their explanation being that

---

12   [1998] 1 WLR 893 CA. Ironically, after conditional and speculative fees had been validated for most non criminal and matrimonial cases by legislation, the Court of Appeal was to change its mind on the position at common law: see *Awwad v Geraghty & Co* [2000] 1 All ER 608.

13   On this terminology and the thinking which lies behind it, see M Galanter 'Why the "Haves" Come Out Ahead: Speculations on the Limits of Legal Change' [1974] 9 Law and Society Review 95.

14   *The Royal Commission on Civil Liability and Compensation for Personal Injury* Cmnd 7054 (1978), vol 2, para 516.

15   *Compensation and Support for Personal Illness and Injury* (Harris Maclean, Genn, Lloyd-Bostock , Fenn and Brittan) 1984 hereafter referred to as the Oxford Study put the figure at 7.5%; *The Taxed Cases Study* (reported by Swanson in 'The Importance of Contingency Agreements' (1991) 11 OJLS 193) put the figure at 20%.

Many pressures on claimants led them to accept amounts which heavily discounted the full award which a court would make.[16]

A later study found that plaintiffs who actually went to trial ie refused the insurance companies final offer were awarded sums which were on average over 400% higher than the final offers received by themselves and also by plaintiffs who did accept the final offer[17]. Consistently with this, Professor Hazel Genn's recent study of the experiences of personal injury plaintiffs in the years following settlement revealed large numbers of plaintiffs who had found their damages insufficient for needs which were within the scope of the damages rules and which were included within their claim[18]. Thirdly, and perhaps most controversially, the phenomenon just noted is due to a very significant extent to institutional defendants indulging in hard bargaining in order to induce a low settlement. The latter point is controversial for a number of reasons. To begin with, there is the question of proof. Forthright and statistically significant confessions by institutional lawyers are a priori unlikely, though Professor Genn's London County Court Mediation study produced a frank admission by one insurance company lawyer that

> I'm acting for an insurance company. I have to use any tactic I can, to pay as little attention as possible to the plaintiff, in order to pay as little as possible.[19]

Moreover, many either in government or having the ear of government seem sceptical about the hard bargaining thesis. Thus Sir Peter Middleton who was asked by Lord Irvine as incoming Lord Chancellor to review the previous administration's proposals for the reform of civil justice clearly indicated that hard bargaining was not a problem.

> insurance companies are in a very competitive market. I do not believe that in the great majority of such cases, they seek to drive up cost in the way suggested. This might happen in a few cases that are likely to set a precedent. But such cases ... should be dealt with by the greater powers that judges will have to control 'oppressive' conduct in litigation.[20]

The subsequent White Paper *Modernising Justice*[1] was full of similar sentiments. Plaintiffs, we were told on several occasions, must think very carefully about whether their claims are significant enough to merit the attention of the Court system. In order to focus their minds on the issue they must pay Court fees at each and every successive stage of the process. On only one occasion is there any recognition that it takes two to tango ie that defendants by their attitude to the claim made upon them also have an important influence on whether legal process is necessary.[2]

---

16 *The Oxford Study* ibid at p 318.

17 *The Taxed Cases Study* cited in Swanson ibid at p 210.

18 H Genn *How Much Is Enough? A Study of the Compensation Experiences of Victims of Personal Injury* (Law Commission Working Paper No 225 (1994)) chapter 11.

19 H Genn *The Central London County Court Pilot Mediation Scheme: Evaluation Report*, LCD Research Series 5/98 at p 10. See generally H Genn *Hard Bargaining: Out of Court Settlements in Personal Injury Actions* (Oxford Socio-Legal Studies Series, Oxford, Clarendon Press, 1987).

20 Sir Peter Middleton *Review of Civil Justice and Legal Aid* (London, LCD, 1997) para 2.24.

1 *Modernising Justice – The Governments Plans for Reforming Legal Services and the Courts* (Cm 4155) (London, HMSO, 1998).

2 Supra note 20 at para 2.38, where Sir Peter Middleton's confidence in the restraining powers of judicial case management is echoed.

In fact however, such scepticism is quite unmerited. Even if industry wide confessions are unlikely to be obtained, the hard bargaining hypothesis is the best explanation for some very striking data. Consider, for instance, the fact that settlement often occurs within a month of trial 'at the door of the Court' ie when most of the expense of preparing for trial has already occurred. Given that it ought to be in the interests of both sides to save money (ie lawyers fees) by settling out of court, this is surprising. Again, consider the fact that when personal injury plaintiffs go to trial they very often win. Most recent research indicates that 75-90% of personal injury plaintiffs prevail at trial.[3] The Civil Justice Review[4], the Taxed Cases Study and the Oxford Study all showed that plaintiffs were prevailing in 66%-75% of the cases going to trial[5]. Why is it that well paid highly expert lawyers are taking to trial so many cases which they ultimately lose?; economic theory predicts that when litigation occurs in order to clarify uncertainties in the law, plaintiffs and defendants ought to prevail equally often.[6] Finally, amidst what Lord Woolf assures us is a consensus that the current system of civil litigation is too costly and too slow, a survey of insurance companies showed that 77% of surveyed respondents were satisfied with the pre-Woolf system of civil litigation[7]. The obvious interpretation of this evidence and more generally of the evidence previously cited concerning settlement figures is that defendants are investing in a reputation for hard bargaining which, while costly in the cases which settle only at the door of the court or when it leads to defeat at trial, pays off in the long run because it induces low settlements in other cases.

Conditional fees can do something to redress this problem. Ordinarily, one factor pushing plaintiffs towards settling for low sums is that if forced to go to trial, they face the prospect if they lose of being left not only with uncompensated injuries but also with the need to pay their lawyers' large legal bills. With a conditional fee arrangement in place, this risk is removed: the conditional fee contract acts like an insurance policy under which the lawyer assumes the risk of irrecoverable fees in return for a premium consisting of a fee uplift payable only after and on the event of success.

This gives lawyers a considerable ethical opportunity in the sense that it offers them an opportunity to contribute to a process leading to more just outcomes than would occur if the plaintiff were personally liable for costs. Professor Hazel Genn's analysis on behalf of the Law Commission of the experiences of personal injury plaintiffs showed that a sizeable minority were dissatisfied with the settlement they accepted but nevertheless accepted their lawyer's advice to compromise the claim[8]. It seems very likely that at least some of those lawyers regarded the settlement as less than what the plaintiff deserved but the best that could be achieved given the unacceptable risks of trial. For lawyers sharing this perception, there is potentially at least an opportunity for increased occupational satisfaction. It may even be the case that this opportunity

3   See the research summary by Stella Yarrow in *The Price of Success* (London, Policy Studies Institute, 1997) 41.
4   *Report of the Review Body on Civil Justice* (The 'Civil Justice Review') Cmnd 394 (1988).
5   Swanson supra note 15 at p 214.
6   See G Priest and B Klein, 'The Selection of Disputes for Litigation' (1984) 13 Journal of Legal Studies 1.
7   'Litigation Reform: the Client's Perspective' (Herbert Smith, January 1995) cited in Hazel Genn 'Access to Just Settlements: The Case of Medical Negligence' in *The Reform of Civil Procedure* supra p 377 note 20.
8   *How Much is Enough* supra note 18, at chapter 4, esp 76ff.

extends to lawyers acting for institutional defendants. Consider for example the comments of a US insurance company lawyer interviewed by Douglas Rosenthal;

> Frankly we are in business to wear out plaintiffs... We're not a charity out to protect plaintiffs welfare. Take the case I was trying today. The other lawyer... doesn't know what he's doing. His client's got a good claim for a fractured skull. *I want this bastard to win* ... and I know he'll blow it. Today I laid the foundation for contributory negligence, which is very doubtful, and the other lawyer made no attempt to knock it down. The plaintiff is a sweet gentle guy-a Puerto Rican. I met him in the john at recess and I told him that there was nothing personal in my working against him, that I was just doing my job...It's not my fault, I want him to win. Its his lawyer's fault and his own fault for not getting a better lawyer like me.[9]

This lawyer was experiencing a tension between the demands of his occupational role and his personal ethics. The phenomenon of cognitive dissonance whereby the tension between personal ethics and occupational role is resolved by altering ones personal ethics will ensure that this is a less than universal phenomenon. Nevertheless, conditional fees can alter the dynamics of the settlement process so as to produce more just outcomes for plaintiffs not only in the eyes of their lawyers but also from the perspective of their opponents.

Aligning of Incentives

It is often thought to be a weakness of 'no win no fee' arrangements that they weaken the lawyer's loyalty to the client by giving him/her a financial interest in the case. But in fact this may very often be a good thing because it concentrates the lawyer's mind on the question of whether to proceed. Thus if a lawyer is hesitating to proceed because fees are at risk then it is probably not in the client's interests to proceed either. After all, the client has more to lose than the lawyer. S/he is a one shot player who will (hopefully) never have another PI case. The lawyer will have other cases. Similarly, if the lawyer is happy to go ahead and risk not being paid, this is one indication that the case, however speculative it may seem, is worthy of a hearing. Thus far from creating a conflict between the interests of the lawyer and the interests of the client, conditional fees may reduce the conflict otherwise inherent in contractual arrangements which allow the lawyer to be paid regardless of outcomes. One of the criticisms made by government of the judicare legal aid scheme was that because it paid lawyers an hourly rate regardless of the outcome of the case, it created an incentive for lawyers to begin and continue cases which ought never to have been brought or which ought to have been settled earlier. Conditional fees have been seen by government as an alternative to legal aid precisely because they eradicate this incentive. This is not to suggest that there will never be conflicts of interest between lawyer and client in relation to conditional fee arrangements (see below). It is however to suggest that these conflicts are not as universal and therefore as damaging as is sometimes thought.

This argument does not assume that all lawyers are motivated by self-interest so that only a system under which their fees were at risk would induce them to make correct decisions about which cases to litigate or settle. Many lawyers probably can be trusted

---

9   Douglas E Rosenthal *Lawyer and Client: Who's in Charge?* (New York, Sage, 1974) 82-83.

to make wholly appropriate decisions about when to begin and continue cases on their clients' behalf irrespective of whether their fees are at stake. But equally some cannot: it seems impossible for example to deny that at least part of the reason for the spiraling upwards of legal aid costs in this country over the last 20 years is the potential for abuse within the historic system of judicare legal aid whereby lawyers are paid by the hour and regardless of the outcome. One of the advantages of replacing legal aid with conditional fees is that it provides a sanction against misconduct of this kind. Moreover, the imposition of this sanction should be welcomed by the ethical majority because it protects them against the damage to their collective reputation which might otherwise be done by those who would act unprofessionally. It is abundantly clear at present that the legal profession has an image problem. In this climate, the embracing of conditional fee agreements whereby lawyers stake their fees upon their judgment can act as a means of regaining public trust. It is just as logical for lawyers to agree to forgo their fees should a case be lost regardless of their best efforts as it is for the manufacturer of a product lacking an established reputation in the market to offer a strict product warranty. Undertaking to bear part of the cost should things go wrong is a way of signaling to consumers what you know to be true, namely that you offer a high quality service.[10]

Moreover, conditional fees can in fact be seen to have had precisely the impact which this argument predicts. As we have seen, conditional fee plaintiffs usually take out insurance against liability to pay the defendant's costs in the event of defeat. A number of insurers delegate to the solicitors the decision whether or not to proceed with and grant insurance to a particular claim. This is in marked contrast to the bureaucratic approach of the current Legal Aid Board and of the quality controls to be imposed with respect to work done under legal aid contracts. The explanation is that the insurers are willing to trust the lawyers to exercise their professional skills because the lawyers are willing to accept at least partial financial responsibility for the consequences of their choices. In this way, conditional fees facilitate to some degree the occupational independence which has always been a central goal of professional aspirations.

Finally, to criticize incentive arguments as presupposing that all lawyers are always self-interested may be to assume that each of us is either wholly saint or wholly sinner. In fact, almost everyone lawyers included is a mixture of both. As a consequence, our propensity for ethical conduct is likely to be increased if we work in a supportive institutional environment and vice-versa.[11] Put in older language, most of us find it helpful when attempting to stick to the straight and narrow not to have endless contrary temptations put in our path. Lawyers paid by the hour regardless of results may not consciously, deliberately and systematically make decisions which maximize their earnings at the expense of the client (or the State) but may nevertheless find their decisions being subtly influenced by the pull of self-interest. If so, to remove the incentive (which is to some extent what conditional fees do) may simply be a means of supporting preexisting dispositions to behave ethically.

---

10   See generally G Priest 'A Theory of the Consumer Product Warrenty' (1987) 90 Yale LJ 1297.

11   See Charles Sampford and Christine Parker 'Ethical Standard Setting, and Institutional Design' chapter 1 of *Legal Ethics and Legal Practice: Contemporary Issues* (Charles Sampford and Stephen Parker eds) (Clarendon, Oxford, 1996).

DISADVANTAGES OF CONDITIONAL FEES

Conflict of Interest

Whilst I have already suggested that conditional fees may reduce or eliminate some conflicts of interest between lawyer and client, it is also true that they create conflicts of interest. The potential conflicts are in general terms of two kinds. On the one hand, there is the question of conflict between the lawyer's own interests and the duties which are owed to the court, such as the duty to ensure that the client complies with the rules of discovery. On the other hand, there is the possibility of conflict between the lawyer's own interests and the duty of loyalty which, as a fiduciary agent, s/he owes to the client. I want to deal with the first of these conflicts here as part of my argument about the ethical opportunity offered by conditional fees.

... it is true that if the lawyer is not going to be paid unless the client prevails, this creates an incentive not to comply with any given duty to the Court if, on the facts, compliance will reduce the probability of the case succeeding. Nevertheless, it should not be forgotten that conditional fee lawyers are not alone in confronting this tension. The same problem exists whenever the lawyer is strongly motivated to ensure that the client will prevail and such motivation may arise for many other reasons than the presence of a conditional fee arrangement. It is for precisely this reason that the conferral upon employed lawyers of rights of audience in the Access to Justice Act is accompanied by a statutory restatement of the priority of the lawyer's duty to the Court.[12] The fear is that the pressure of representing the interests of one's employer will otherwise be a temptation to ignore duties owed to the court. Yet employed lawyers are obviously not employed under conditional fee contracts. Most pertinently for our purposes, the need to retain the custom of a sophisticated long term institutional client which pays at generous rates creates exactly similar pressures. Indeed such a conflict is inherent within the adversary system relying as it does upon lawyers retained and for the most part paid by litigants to present arguments in an adversarial fashion within the narrow constraints of the duties owed by the lawyer to the Court. All that can be done is to ensure that the institutions within which lawyers work are not such as to make the tension unbearable.

Furthermore it is useful at this point recall that in general terms the problems of legal ethics can said to be of two types. On the one hand, there is the problem of over-representation, which occurs when lawyers subvert the purposes of the legal system (or deprive third parties of their substantive rights) in the interests of their client. But there is also the problem of under representation which occurs when lawyers fail to assert their clients interests with sufficient zeal, a problem which McConville et al in their book *Standing Accused*[13] have shown to be endemic within the arrangements made

12   Section 42 of the Access to Justice Act inserts into s 27 of the Courts and Legal Services Act 1990 a new s 27(2A). This provides that every person exercising rights of audience has
'(a) a duty to the court to act with independence in the interests of justice; and
(b) a duty to comply with rules of conduct of the body relating to the right ...
and those duties, shall override any obligation which the person may have (otherwise than under the criminal law) if it is inconsistent with them.'

13   Michael McConville, Jacqueline Hodgson, Lee Bridges and Anita Pavolvic *Standing Accused – The Work and Organisation of Criminal Defence Lawyers in Britain* (Clarendon, Oxford, 1994).

for the representation of suspects in police custody. Prior to the introduction of conditional fee arrangements, personal injury plaintiffs were vulnerable to under representation and often experienced it.[14] Consequently, the new arrangements may address a problem of legal ethics equally as real in this sphere of practice as over representation in other spheres. There is of course the danger that conditional fees will overcorrect the balance but the detection and deterrence of such abuses is precisely why the Court has an inherent jurisdiction to discipline officers of the Court.[15] Finally, it is precisely because all lawyers live with a tension between the interests of the client and their duties to the Court that the norms of professional ethics, both the formal norms contained in rules of conduct and the informal norms of the professional culture are so important.[16]

The extract refers to but does not address the issue of conflicts between the lawyer's own interest and the fiduciary duty of loyalty owed to the client. One aspect of this problem is the possibility that the lawyers will enter into extortionate conditional fee contracts requiring the payment of large uplifts in cases involving negligible risk. The leading UK expert on the legal profession, Professor Michael Zander, has described conditional fees as nothing but 'a bonanza for lawyers'[17] and predicted that lawyers would uniformly charge their clients the statutory maximum uplift[18]. At the heart of the concern is the widespread acknowledgment that well over 90% of personal injury cases are successful in the sense that some damages are received, usually after settlement. On this view, conditional fee litigation will usually be a very low risk exercise. If so, it is difficult to justify any substantial uplift, for conditional fees without risk are, as one critic has put it, like Hamlet without the Prince of Denmark[19]. Michael Napier and Fiona Bowden, co-authors of one of the leading professional books on the topic, recommend that the uplift should be calculated using a formula $(F/P \times 100) + U$[20] where F is the chances of failure, P is the chances of success and U is a small additional percentage to reflect the fact that fees and, if applicable, disbursements will not be paid until the end of the case. They are thus in a sense covered by a loan to the client for what may well be a very long case. Using this formula, a case having a 90% chance might justify an uplift of $(10/90 \times 100) + 5 = 16\%$. Yet in an early study of conditional fee contracts[1], it was found that the average uplift was 43%. Whilst the author of the

---

14 *Hard Bargaining* supra p 392 note 19 esp 166ff.

15 In the case of barristers this jurisdiction has been delegated by the courts to the Bar Council: see Sydney Kentridge QC 'A Quiet Revolution' *Counsel* December 1998 at p 24.

16 This extract, slightly modified and updated, is taken from D R F O'Dair 'Legal Ethics and Legal Aid – the Great Divorce' (1999) 53 CLP 418 at pp 419-434.

17 'Well Anyway, Conditional Fees Should Be a Bonanza for Lawyers' (1995) NLJ 920, 933. The early research on the use of conditional fees has left Professor Zander only marginally less sceptical: see 'Two Cheers for Conditional Fees' (1997) NLJ 1438.

18 Supra p 390 note 10.

19 Lester Brickman 'Contingent Fees Without Contingencies: Hamlet Without the Prince of Denmark' (1998) 37 UCLA Law Review 29.

20 Michael Napier and Fiona Bowden, *Conditional Fees – A Survival Guide* (London, Law Society, 1995) 90-94.

1 Stella Yarrow *The Price of Success* (London, Policy Studies Institute, 1997) pp 56-61.

study viewed inexperience in risk assessment as a possible cause the high uplifts, the government was concerned and responded by making success fees recoverable from the other side[2]. The loser was given a corresponding right to challenge the reasonableness of these fees in taxation proceedings.

Questions

1. Are hourly fees and fixed fee scales more or less likely to create a conflict of interests between lawyer and client than conditional fee arrangements?

2. Do you agree with the writer's dismissal of the ethical difficulties created by conditional fee litigation?

3. How could you test empirically whether the uplifts observed in current conditional fee arrangements are a result of extortion or of some other (and if so what) cause?

4. Is the concern about excessive uplifts resolved by the provisions in the Access to Justice Act for uplifts to be recoverable from defendants?

5. Professor Shaffer has argued that the lawyer-client relationship should be seen as analogous to friendship.[3] Do you agree? On this basis, it can be argued that at least one element in friendship is commitment, ie a willingness to stand by the other when it is costly to do so. It has been argued that, if so, there emerges

> ...another way in which conditional fees provide ethical opportunity, for by entering into such arrangements lawyers are committing themselves to their clients causes in a very concrete way. Conditional fee contracts therefore add credibility to the service orientation which has always been at the heart of the professional ideal.[4]

Do you agree?

Conditional fees in the UK

Leaving aside the broad issues of principle, the implementation of the decision to permit conditional fee litigation has given 'no win, no fee' litigation in the UK its own distinctive features and raised further questions.

---

2   Section 58A(6) of the Courts and Legal Services Act 1990 (inserted by s 29(1) of the Access to Justice Act 1999). In addition, regulations provide that solicitors may not recover from their clients any part of the uplift which is not recovered from the other side unless the Court makes an order permitting them to do so. See reg 3(2)(b) and (c) of the Conditional Fees Regulations 2000, SI 2000/692.

3   Supra chapter 9.

4   Supra note 16 at pp 427.

Conditional and contingency fees: conditional fee litigation in the UK involves the lawyer agreeing that if s/he is unsuccessful no fee will be paid (though as we shall see disbursements[5] may remain payable). In the event of success, the ordinary fee will be payable plus an extra percentage of that fee, as a success fee. In the US, by contrast, the equivalent arrangement is known as a contingency fee and the lawyer is paid in the event of success, a percentage (typically 33%) of the client's damages. In the UK, opposition to contingency fees has remained strong and they are still largely prohibited. However, for a number of reasons, the contingent fee model remains important. To begin with, concern over the possibility that clients' damages would be swallowed up by payment of the uplift led the Law Society to recommend that solicitors limit their success fee to 25% of the client's damages and early evidence points towards the almost universal adoption of this cap. Since many low value personal injury claims have a very high costs to value ratio, this means that the effective success fee will in many cases be 25% of the client's damages.[6]

In addition, contingency fees have only ever been prohibited in 'contentious business' as defined by the Solicitors Act 1974. Consequently, contingency fees may be used in industrial tribunal proceedings and were made substantially more attractive when the limits on the compensation awarded by such tribunals was raised from £12,000 to £50,000. Moreover any form of dispute settlement which does not involve the prospect of litigation can be conducted on contingency fee basis. Hence, it was on this basis that Leigh Day and Co represented Allied POWs used as slave labour during World War II in attempts to get compensation from the German government.

Cost shifting and insurance: in further contrast to the US, where each side normally bears its own costs, the normal rule in England is that 'costs follow the event' meaning that the loser pays the winners costs. This rule applies to litigation conducted under conditional fee agreements and is one reason why the popular term 'no win, no fee litigation' is misleading: a litigant losing a case conducted under a conditional fee contract will *not* have to pay the losing lawyer but *will* be liable to pay the opponent's costs. However, the insurance market will sometimes provide a solution to this problem. For example, members of the Law Society's Accident Line (a panel of accredited specialist personal injury lawyers) were from the outset[7] able to take advantage of Accident Line Protect. In return for a premium, the insurer will cover any costs payable to the other side and any disbursements payable to the client's solicitors in the event of the claim failing. Initially, premiums were modest, a premium of £90 buying £100,000 worth of cover for a routine road accident case. However, premiums soon began to rise quite steeply: by November 2000, Accident Line Protect was charging £300-£2,900

---

5   A charges made by a solicitor consist inter alia of disbursements, which are the costs paid by the lawyer on the clients behalf eg to obtain an expert's report and the costs of the solicitor's own time. It is important to distinguish these two elements because they are or can be treated very differently under conditional fee contracts.

6   Yarrow supra note 1 at xi and pp 63-64. Yarrow's research preceded s 27 of the Access to Justice Act which makes success fees recoverable from the other side. It remains to be seen whether they will continue to be as widely used under the new regime.

7   A number of other insurers have since entered the market.

depending on the level of cover.[8] For complex and risky litigation, such as medical negligence cases, premiums may be much higher in some cases, as much as 40% of cover.[9] One factor determining the impact of conditional fees upon access to justice will be the ability of clients to bear such premiums. Another is the ability of the market to offer a premium at all: the attempt in the late 1990s by tobacco smokers to sue the tobacco companies proved uninsurable. Indeed, there is evidence that insurers are adopting a very conservative attitude to risk. In 1999, insurers were requiring firms seeking cover to maintain a 95% success rate. This is a much stricter attitude even than that proposed by the Legal Services Commission for contracted legal aid[10] and suggests that conditional fees will have to be supplemented by considerable state funding if access to justice is to be maintained.

The Law Society's Model Conditional Fee Agreement: given widespread reservations about conditional fee contracts, it is not surprising that such agreements are heavily regulated. The Conditional Fee Agreements Regulations 2000[11] provided for example that the agreement must state whether or not there is a cap on the proportion of damages that may be paid by way of success fee. In addition, the client must be given advice about other methods of financing the claim.[12] Furthermore, solicitors contemplating conditional fee work will almost certainly use one of the model agreements available to them, such as the Law Society's model conditional fee contract for use in personal injury work[13]. These model contracts have been drawn up on the advice of counsel and are attractive because the consequences of failing to satisfy the regulations are drastic: the agreement becomes unenforceable and the client cannot claim costs from the other side. If the client loses, the lawyer may be liable for the other sides costs under s 51 of the Supreme Court Act. For this reason, the pressure to use the model which was formulated on the advice of leading counsel is likely to be overwhelming. This agreement contains a number of complex provisions and the LSGPC[14] requires solicitors to undertake the formidable task of explaining the agreement in detail to clients. The agreement contains some very striking provisions such as a condition that if the client refuses to accept the solicitor's advice to settle, the lawyer can end the agreement forthwith leaving the client liable to pay the lawyer's costs and disbursements incurred up to that point. Moreover, cover against liability for the opponent's costs will also terminate at that point. The clients only recourse in cases of disagreement is to seek a second opinion for which the client must pay.[15]

---

8   See Litigation Funding (November 2000) p 10.
9   See Litigation Funding (July 1999) p 7 citing a case involving a premium of £4,868 for £50,000 worth of cover. More generally, see The Society of Advanced Legal Studies *Report of the Working Party On the Ethics of Conditional Fee Arrangements* (London, SALS, 2000) chapter 2 'Conditional Fees in England and Wales: Law, Policy and Context'.
10   The LSC will fund a case with only 50% chance of success if prospective damages are 4 times as great as the costs; supra text to p 382 note 19.
11   SI, 2000/692, reg 2(1)(d).
12   Ibid reg 4(2).
13   This agreement is set out in the annex to this chapter. Other model agreements have been drawn up, for example by the Association of Personal Injury Lawyers.
14   See LSGPC principles 13.01-13.03.
15   Condition 7.

Notes

1. The general approach adopted in the Access to Justice Act is to make the costs of using conditional fee agreements recoverable from the other side. Section 27(6)-(7) and s 30 will make conditional fee uplifts and insurance premiums respectively recoverable as costs in the event of success. One effect of these changes is to make it possible to defend claims on a conditional fee basis.

2. As noted, insurance is not currently available for all the classes of claim which may be litigated on a conditional fee basis. In *Hodgson v Imperial Tobacco*[16], plaintiffs brought claims based on alleged negligence in allowing them to continue to smoke cigarettes with high levels of tar even when the consequent health risks were known. The claims were brought under conditional fee arrangements even though the plaintiffs were unable to obtain insurance against costs payable to their opponents in the event of failure. The ethical issues arising from proceeding on this basis were considered in chapter 8.

3. Many insurers allow their panel of approved solicitors to operate delegated authority schemes. This means that cases may be granted cover by the solicitors without reference to the insurer who then monitors the solicitors' performance over time to ensure that the authority is being exercised carefully. However, it is invariably a condition of the scheme that the firm agrees to do all its conditional fee cases with the benefit of that insurance.[17]

4. It is possible to obtain after the event insurance ('full after the event insurance') which covers both the other sides costs *and* the client's own costs, thereby making a conditional fee arrangement unnecessary. The premium for such policies will inevitably be higher than that payable for insurance covering only the other side's costs.[18]

Questions

1. Is the introduction of conditional fees instead of legal aid a good thing or a bad thing for defendants who might otherwise be sued by plaintiffs on legal aid? See chapter 8 supra.

2. Consider in the light of the above extract the likely impact upon settlement levels of the incentives offered to a) lawyers and b) insurers by conditional fees? Are contingency fees any different in this respect?

---

16   [1998] 1 WLR 1056, CA.
17   Bowden supra note 20 at p 109.
18   See 3 Litigation Funding (July 1999) p 4.

3. Is there a conflict of interest between solicitor and (prospective?) client in the process by which the conditional fee contract is formulated. If so, and if the lawyer-client relationship can be regarded as fully constituted even before the contract is formed, then the client may require independent advice in order for the contract to be valid.[19]

4. What are the implications for the conditional fee agreement if the solicitor discovers a witness whose testimony substantially increases the client's chances of success? As a fiduciary agent the solicitor owes a general duty to pass on to the client all information which is material to the clients affairs.[20]

5. Read the Law Society's model conditional fee agreement for use in personal injury cases (Appendix infra). In what ways is it misleading to speak of no win no fee litigation? To what extent is it realistic to expect lawyers to explain fully to clients the implications of the agreement? How might modern methods of communication be used to make the task easier?

4   Lord Woolf and procedural reform

The problem diagnosed

In 1994, Lord Woolf was appointed by the (then) Lord Chancellor, Lord Mackay of Clashfern, to conduct a wide-ranging inquiry into civil justice. In his Interim and Final Reports[1], Lord Woolf reported widespread dissatisfaction with the costs and delays of the civil justice system. These impressionistic findings were confirmed by empirical evidence in the form of a survey of taxed solicitors' bills conducted by Professor Hazel Genn. The survey reported striking disproportion, particularly in relation to low value claims, between the value of claims and the costs incurred in disposing of them. Among claims with a value between £12,500 and £25,000, costs as a percentage of claim value ranged from 41% in relation to personal injury disputes to 96% in relation to Official Referees (ie construction law) disputes. Moreover, these represented only the costs of the party prevailing so that the cumulative costs of both parties were in most cases likely to exceed the value of the claim.

Whilst a number of factors contributed to these problems, Lord Woolf's diagnosis was that much of the responsibility lay with the excessively adversarial approach of litigators:

> Litigants and their lawyers need to have imposed upon them an obligation to prosecute and defend their proceedings with efficiency and dispatch[2] ... the litigation process is too often seen as a battlefield where no rules apply. In this environment, questions of

---

19   Cf Bowden supra note 20 at p 46 where the difficulty is acknowledged but not resolved.
20   Cf Principle 16.06 of the LSGPC. See also *Specter v Ageda* [1973] Ch 30.
1   Supra p 365 note 2.
2   Interim Report para 7(b), p 5.

expense, delay compromise and fairness may have only low priority[3] ...the conduct, pace and control of litigation are left almost completely to the parties. There is no effective control of their worst excesses. Indeed, the complexity of the present rules facilitates the use of adversarial tactics and is considered by many to require it[4] ... The powers of the Courts have fallen behind the more sophisticated and aggressive tactics of some litigators... the main procedural tools for conducting litigation efficiently have become subverted from their proper purposes.[5]

These excesses were exacerbated by the passivity of the judiciary who had been excessively reluctant to intervene, preferring instead to leave the content form and pace of the litigation to be shaped by the parties. (Can you see the connection here with the views of Fuller and Randall which are set out in chapter 5?)

In the following extract, Adrian Zuckerman, a cautious supporter of Lord Woolf's proposals expands upon this analysis:

THE DIMENSION OF SELF-INTEREST

Although Lord Woolf has not systematically investigated the reasons for which parties tend to complicate and protract litigation, he draws attention to some of the principal causes. He points out that parties tend to exploit the rules of practice to their own advantage. It is not uncommon for the financially stronger or more experienced party to 'spin out proceedings and escalate costs, by litigating on technical points or peripheral issues instead of focusing on the real substance of the case. All too often, such tactics are used to intimidate the weaker party and produce a resolution of the case which is either unfair or is achieved at a grossly disproportionate cost or after unreasonable delay.' (Report, 27.) There is considerable evidence, he says, that individual plaintiffs in personal injury cases are often forced to settle for inadequate compensation because of delaying tactics employed by insurance companies and their own financial inferiority.

Lord Woolf's observations – that, first, litigants will tend to exploit the procedure to their own advantage and, second, that there is at present a very considerable scope for doing so – are undoubtedly correct. But it is essential not to lose sight of the distinction between these two very different factors. The pursuit of self-interest is a fundamental human trait in any socio-economic context which it is neither possible nor desirable to change. It is therefore an immutable factor. By contrast, the scope for the pursuit of self interest in the conduct of litigation is largely a function of the system of rules governing the civil process.

It is natural that litigants should seek to exploit procedure to their advantage. Litigants do not resort to legal proceedings for altruistic disinterested motives. They go to law in order to advance their own interests. In so doing they will take whatever advantage the rules of court afford. Litigants want to win, and they can be hardly condemned for having such a desire or, indeed, for following the course which is most conducive to their objective.

A party to a dispute would wish to secure a favourable result at minimum cost and in the shortest time. It follows that the commencement of proceedings, the pre-trial

3   Ibid para 4, p 7.
4   Ibid para 6, p 7.
5   Ibid para 7, p 8.

process, trial and final judgment are all means to an end, rather than ends in themselves. The end is to secure interests: the remedy sought (such as a money payment) by the plaintiff, or the freedom of not having to make good the plaintiff's demand, in the defendant's case. Parties would much rather achieve their goals without having to take proceedings; having taken proceedings, without the need to go to trial, and so on. In other words, they desire to secure their interest with the minimum of effort and cost.

It is, therefore, normal for litigants to seek advantage from whatever superiority they possess, be it greater economic resources or wider experience or strong nerves. The degree to which one is able to sustain litigation and bear the consequence of an eventual loss has a direct bearing on one's prospects of recovering one's entitlement in a settlement. Defendants who know that their plaintiffs cannot afford even the initial cost of commencing proceedings, need hardly respond to claims made against them. Defendants who cannot make a show of being able to defend their case, must expect to pay in full the plaintiffs' demands. Quite plainly, the less one is able to commit resources to litigation and bear the risk of failure, the less one can expect in settlement; and vice versa: the more a litigant can sustain litigation, the greater the prospect of biting into the opponent's entitlement. Where the plaintiff has only a limited ability to sustain litigation, the defendant is in a position to insist on a settlement that is tailored not to the plaintiff's prospects of winning but to his ability to finance litigation.

While no one can, or should, change the tendency of people to pursue their self-interest within the bounds allowed by the rules, it is legitimate to try and limit these bounds. Lord Woolf is therefore right to deal with the second of the factors mentioned above: the scope for procedural manipulation. He is justified in seeking to restrict the extent to which litigants are free to use the process of the law regardless of the complexity of their cause or its importance. Indeed, it is imperative in the interests of justice to circumscribe the degree to which the litigants with deep pockets are able to use their financial advantage to undermine the entitlements of their poorer opponents. For where a decision to settle a claim or a defence is driven not by the strength of a party's case on its merits but by his poverty, the outcome cannot be considered just.

The parties are not the only participants in the litigation process with an interest. Although lawyers are on the whole interested in the pursuit of justice, their professional activities are not wholly altruistic. They too have an interest at stake: professional remuneration. Just as it is natural that litigants should be keen to further their objectives so it is normal for lawyers to be concerned about their own financial interests. This is not to say that the legal profession is dominated by greed. On the contrary, the prevalent ethical standards in England are rather high. But it would be wholly unrealistic to suppose that the legal profession is unique amongst all professions in being indifferent to financial rewards.

We must therefore accept that, as in any other context, economic considerations do play a part in the development of professional practices. Accordingly, we need to consider the economic factors that may influence lawyers. Solicitors are commonly paid for their services on an hourly basis. Barristers have traditionally charged according, to the complexity of the case and on the basis of days spent in court, though there seems to be an increasing trend for them too to seek an hourly return. Whether charging is by the hour or in proportion to complexity, it seems obvious that lawyers have no direct incentive to economize in the provision of services. On the contrary, the more complex and protracted litigation becomes the more they earn.

Not only do lawyers have an interest in making litigation more complex and lengthy, but their clients' ability to resist costs is neutralized by the clients' lack of information about the legal process. Lay clients do not have independent means for making decisions about the cost efficiency of particular procedural moves. They must rely on their lawyers to judge whether this or that procedural step is necessary or cost efficient. Moreover, it is largely in the hands of lawyers to determine, by the custom of professional practice, the parameters of acceptable procedural deployment. It is in the nature of things that forensic practices should, without any self-conscious decision on the part of individuals, follow the most rewarding path.

Self-interest finds expression not only in seeking maximal remuneration, but also in acquiring immunity from claims in negligence. In order to minimise liability for negligence lawyers would naturally tend to follow all procedural avenues open to their client. Since reasonable standards of litigation practice are determined by what practitioners normally do, it follows that here too we have a mechanism which continually expands the intensity of litigation.

Lord Woolf's views about the influence of the lawyers' financial interest on the cost of litigation are unclear. On the one hand, he says: 'there is a misconceived view that the entire problem is due to the scale of lawyers' charges. This is not so.' (Report, 199) On the other hand, however, he makes two points. First, that 'market forces, which in other contexts have acted as a restraint on prices, operate rather weakly in relation to the supply of professional services' (id). Secondly, he points out that hourly pay rates have 'an inflationary effect on costs' (Report, 200). Sadly, he does not consider any further the correlation between the hourly payment system and the intensity of use of procedural devices. Yet, given the scope for procedural maneuvering and low client resistance, it would be a miracle if there were no substantial connection between lawyers' financial interests and litigation practices.

In fact it is not difficult to find signs of this correlation, and witness statements provide a good illustration. Lord Woolf condemns the practice of drafting lengthy witness statements at exorbitant expense (Report 175-7). But he believes that the reason for this is to be found in the rule that witness statements stand in place of examination in chief. The fear that witnesses would not be allowed to supplement their statements has lead, Lord Woolf suggests, to a practice whereby lawyers try to cover every possible angle of the dispute in their witness statements.

This explanation is, however, unconvincing. There is no substantial body of case law to encourage or justify such a fear. There are no reported decisions suggesting that litigants have suffered a reversal because something was missing from a witness statement which they were not allowed to supplement during the trial. There is no hint in the *Chancery Guide, 1995*, which has been produced to help expedite litigation, that the problem with witness statements is due to the fact that they stand in place of evidence in chief. Although the *Chancery Guide* acknowledges that witness statements have tended to be too elaborate and lengthy, the Chancery Division does not believe that it is necessary to alter the rule that witness statements will normally stand in place of evidence in chief. Under the Chancery Guide, a party is allowed to supplement his witness statement, if he can persuade the judge of the need to do so. Since this is already the position at present it seems clear that the source of trouble with witness statements must be found elsewhere.

The witness statement process, like most other procedural aspects, is strongly influenced by the prevalent professional culture. In this culture, lawyers possess no incentive to exert an effort to produce concise witness statements which only reproduce the witness's words and which are narrowly confined to the issues on which the witness is called to testify. On the contrary, lawyers have an incentive to elaborate these statements, for the greater the elaboration the greater the lawyer's reward. It is not suggested that individual lawyers make conscious decisions to spin out the witness statement process for gain. But the supposed advantage that may be gained from embellishing and expanding witness statements has provided the excuse for the development of a practice which coincides with the financial interests of practitioners.

As this last point suggests, the professional incentive to complicate and protract the process does not operate in isolation. Its influence is most powerful when it combines with the litigant's self-interest. Where lawyers can show that by investing a little extra in procedure the client would thereby obtain some advantage, they can justify to themselves recommending that the client undertake the extra expenditure. Indeed, at times the pursuit of the extra advantage can lock both opponents in a competition of investment in procedure; each trying to undo the other by raising the procedural stakes.

The indemnity rule, whereby the loser in litigation has to pay the winner's costs, also makes a contribution here. Given that success brings with it not only the sum claimed but also the expenses laid out in securing judgment, a litigant who believes that an increase in the amount spent on litigation will increase his chances of success has a very good reason for progressively raising his stakes. Once one party has increased the stakes, the opponent would feel compelled to follow suit for fear that by using inferior procedural devices, be it a less celebrated lawyer or a less qualified expert, he would compromise his chances of success and run a greater risk of having to pay the other party's costs as well on losing the subject matter in dispute. Indeed, a point may come where the parties would have reason to persist with investment in litigation not so much for the sake of a favourable judgment on the merits, as for the purpose of recovering the money already expended in the dispute, which may well outstrip the value of the subject matter in issue. On their part, the parties' lawyers have of course no interest in breaking such a spiral of costs and persuading their clients to desist.

It is a serious omission in the Report that it does not address the mechanisms which help ratchet up the cost of litigation; that it does not draw attention to the economic aspects which explain why the legal profession has tended to resist any drive for economy and efficiency in procedure. This inattention to the incentives possessed by lawyers weakens Lord Woolf's proposals concerning court control of litigation.[6]

Lord Woolf's analysis of the causes of delay was not without its ambiguities. Whilst his formal reports seem to lay much of the blame at the door of the legal profession, he

---

6   A Zuckerman 'Reform in the Shadow of Lawyer's Interests' chapter 3 of *The Reform of Civil Procedure* infra note 20 at pp 61, 62-67.

has elsewhere praised the legal profession's support for the reform process and commented that:

> all the blame for the problems which I believe exist is not to be laid at the door of the legal profession. However too often in individual cases, lawyers are at least partly to blame. More important as a cause of the problems is the disproportionate way the present adversarial system operates which encourages excessive delay, expense and unnecessary complexity. *It is the system, not the lawyers, that explains, for example, the hostility and bitterness which distorts medical negligence litigation.*[7] [emphasis added]

Lord Woolf also acknowledged the whilst adversarial approaches to litigation may sometimes be a result of clients' inability to control their lawyers' zeal, adversarialism may on other occasions be exactly what the client requires.[8]

Others offered radically different diagnoses. Professor Michael Zander has argued that the causes of delay may be much more diverse than Lord Woolf assumed, noting that a number of previous reports on civil justice had identified inefficient working practices rather than tactical manoeuvring as the most prominent cause of delay. A study by KPMG for the LCD in 1995 came to a similar conclusion.[9] Professor Genn raises a still more radical question:

> ... how cheap would legal costs have to become before they were cheap enough to satisfy consumers of legal services? Losers in litigation currently face large bills for legal costs, and a disproportionate amount when the sums in issue are small. Current concern about the courts is driven largely by the costs issue. The argument is that if costs could be reduced, more people would be able to engage in litigation (presumably a social good) and people would complain less about legal aid withering away, because more people could afford to pay for themselves. The extent of legal costs is related to the requirements of the substantive law and the procedures for proof. So the argument runs that if we cut down on procedures, costs will fall and potential litigants, currently denied access to the system, will flock to the courts.
>
> However, something that has never been investigated, but worth considering, is the attitude of ordinary people to the cost of legal services. What is the perception of the value of legal knowledge and skills? Why are people shocked at having to pay £40 for a solicitor's letter or £550 to read a lease when they will pay £2.50 for a glass of fizzy water, £40 for a workman to inspect a faulty appliance, or £5000 to an estate agent, with relatively little complaint? Is it the sheer scale of legal costs? Is it the uncertainty about the extent of risk as a result of the costs indemnity rule and the fact that costs liability is open-ended? Or is it also something to do with a lack of value in the good that is being purchased? That what people seek from legal assistance is what they believe they are entitled to?[10]

---

7   Lord Woolf 'Medics, Lawyers and the Courts' (1997) 16 CJQ 305.
8   Charles Plant *Blackstone's Guide to the Civil Procedure Rules* (London, Blackstone Press, 1999) p 31 citing Lord Woolf in House of Lords on 14 December 1998.
9   See M Zander 'The Woolf Report: Forwards or Backwards for the New Lord Chancellor' [1997] 16 CLQ 208 at p 240 and 'Woolf on Zander' (1997) 147 New Law Journal 768.
10   H Genn 'Understanding Civil Justice' chapter 6 of *Law and Opinion at the End of the 20th Century* (Michael Freeman (ed), Oxford, OUP,1997) pp 180-181.

Questions

1. Is the view that, on the one hand, lawyers have hitherto subverted the rules of civil procedure but are, on the other hand, enthusiastic supporters of reform credible? Does the Standard Conception of Legal Ethics help here? What modifications to our understanding of the Standard Conception are suggested by this enthusiasm for reform?

2. That many practising lawyers have contributed much to the reform process is a fact which Lord Woolf interprets as an indication of support for his proposals. Are there any other interpretations which should be considered?

3. Noting the satisfaction expressed by 77% of insurance companies defending personal injury claims with the unreformed system of civil litigation[11], Professor Genn has criticised Lord Woolf for failing to consider the fundamental problems of lawyers ethics[12]. Can you see why?

4. What assumptions, if any, does Zuckerman make about the ethics of lawyers and their clients? What are the implications of these assumptions, according to Zuckermann for the reform of civil litigation?

The solution prescribed

Whatever the doubts about Lord Woolf's analysis, it was accepted by government, leading to a set of revolutionary changes in civil procedure, most of which were implemented when on 26 April 1999 the new Civil Procedure Rules came into effect. At the heart of the new regime, is the view that since the discretion allowed to litigators by the old regime had led to excessive adversarialism, litigation must in future be governed by tightly drawn procedural rules and, in complex cases, proactive judicial case management. Thus the control of litigation is to be transferred from the lawyers to the courts. Thus it is significant that the new Civil Procedural Rules speak first to the courts, providing as follows:

THE OVERRIDING OBJECTIVE

1.1 (1) These Rules are a new procedural code with the overriding objective of enabling the Court to deal with cases justly.

(2) Dealing with a case justly includes so far as practicable -

(a) ensuring the parties are on an equal footing

---

11   *Litigation Reform: the Client's Perspective* (Herbert Smith, January 1995) cited at p 399 of Hazel Genn 'Access to Just Settlements: the Case of Medical Negligence' chapter 20 of *The Reform of Civil Procedure* (supra p 377 note 20).

12   Ibid at p 398.

(b) saving expense
(c) dealing with the case in ways which are proportionate -
   i.   to the amount of money involved
   ii.   to the importance of the case
   iii. to the complexity of the issues; and
   iv.   to the financial position of each party;
(d) ensuring that it is dealt with expeditiously and fairly; and
(e) allotting to it an appropriate share of the court's resources, while taking into account the need to allot resources to other cases.

APPLICATION BY THE COURT OF THE OVERRIDING OBJECTIVE

1.2 The court must seek to give effect to the overriding objective when it -
(a) exercises any power given to it by the Rules: or
(b) interprets any Rule.

Particularly crucial is the principle of proportionality, which dictates that the disputes should be resolved by means of procedures proportionate in their complexity and cost to what is at stake. This principle is to be given effect by means of a series of procedural 'tracks' to which cases will be allocated by procedural judges depending largely on the value of the claim. Most claims worth less than £5,000 will be allocated to the small claims procedure. Disputes are dealt with informally by a district judge and the presence of lawyers is discouraged because no costs are awarded to the winner. At the other end of the scale, cases worth more than £15,000 will be dealt with on the multi-track where the court will impose a procedural regime appropriate to the complexity of the case and ensure that the parties and their lawyers comply. Non-compliance will be visited with sanctions, whether consisting of a disadvantage in the subsequent litigation (such as the inability to rely on an expert's report served out of time) or costs penalties payable by either the lawyer or the client. In the more complex cases, this may involve one or more case management conferences, in which the procedural judge will meet with the parties and actively ensure steps are being taken to progress or, if possible, settle the case.

At the heart of the new regime however is the 'fast track' designed to deal with cases having a value of between £5,000 and £15,000. Once a case is allocated to the fast track, the court will impose a timetable designed to bring the case to trial within 30 weeks. Dates will be set for all the intermediate steps (such as disclosure of witness statements) with automatic sanctions specified for failure to comply. The trial itself will usually last no more than one day and be firmly controlled by the judge. Expert evidence will usually be in writing (though the parties may put questions to the expert witness in advance) and if possible consist of the evidence of an agreed expert or, alternatively, an expert appointed by the court. Judges will not be required to give detailed reasons for their decisions and costs will normally be assessed summarily on the basis of questionnaires filled in by the parties in advance of the hearing.

Perhaps the most radical feature of Lord Woolf's original vision for the fast track was its approach to costs. In England the loser pays the winner's costs, in contrast to the position in the United States where each side pays its own costs. Both economic theory and empirical evidence suggest that under the English regime each side spends more on a given case than under the American rule.[13] For this reason and to allow litigants to know in advance their maximum liability to pay the other sides costs, Lord Woolf proposed that the costs to be awarded to the prevailing party should be fixed. In the following extract Lord Woolf describes some of the details of a possible fixed cost regime.

SOLICITOR AND OWN CLIENT COSTS

7. The fast track costs regime will provide a standard system of fixed inter partes costs. It will result in the individual litigant knowing at the outset of the proceedings the maximum extent of his liability for his opponent's costs if he loses, and the amount that he will recover from his opponent if he wins.

8. However, the litigant also needs information on what he will pay his own solicitor. To provide this certainty, it is imperative that solicitors explain their basis of charging to their clients. They must go beyond quoting an hourly rate to enable clients to appreciate their real maximum exposure. The fact that the fast track provides a greater degree of certainty as to the procedure involved should enable them to do this. It is also my hope that the fixed costs regime will enable clients to negotiate their own solicitors' costs on a more informed basis, and to make a better assessment of whether they wish to pay more than the fixed costs and, if so, what they will receive for the extra expense. I therefore recommend that, unless there is a written agreement between the client and his own solicitor which sets out clearly the agreed terms of business, the costs payable by a client to his own solicitor should be limited to the level of the fixed costs plus disbursements. The agreement will need to set out the likely level of fixed recoverable costs, the basis of charging specifying the hourly rate actually charged, and the likely level of disbursements and expert fees. It should include the best possible information, including all the relevant figures, on the amount which the client will be liable to pay. This information should be updated in the event of a change of circumstances.

13. The working group has not undertaken detailed work on the costings for the new regime. Its effort has been directed at establishing the initial structure. Further detailed work will be required to establish the final figures. In paragraph 6 above, I have recommended that this might be assisted by a series of detailed case studies in different areas of the country. This will provide further information on the realistic cost of progressing cases on the fast track. In the light of information available to me at present, from the initial work on activity profiles, examination of current county court bills by District Judge Greenslade and Professor Hazel Genn, and information on the current cost of legally aided cases, I consider that it should be possible to litigate even the upper band of fast track cases at a total legal cost of up to £2,500, excluding VAT and disbursements. This is based on a preliminary assessment, undertaken chiefly to inform the structure rather than the actual level of costs. Those responsible for implementation

---

13 N Rickman 'The Economics of Cost-Shifting Rules' chapter 17 of *The Reform of Civil Procedure* (supra p 377 note 20).

will establish the specific figures. It will then be for solicitors together to work within this figure.

PROPORTIONALITY

14. There are a number of possible options for achieving a proportionate costs regime. The issues paper on the fast track canvassed views on whether the best approach would be to devise a single level of costs for all cases up to £10,000[14], several bands within the £10,000 limit or a sliding scale of percentages related to case value. While the responses indicated some support for a sliding scale of percentages, since this would provide absolute proportionality in every case, this approach would make it impossible for solicitors to put a figure on the likely costs until the end of the case. There was particular concern that it would be very difficult to achieve both proportionality and a realistic figure at the lower end of the scale - that is, personal injury cases under £3,000 - since there is a basic minimum amount of work which has to be done in all cases. The weight of responses favoured broad bands related to case value.

15. I propose that there should be two value bands: up to £5,000 and up to £10,000. The lower band will include claims up to £5,000 not dealt with within the present[15] small claims limit of £3,000. As now, costs will depend on the award for successful claimants and the amount of the claim for successful defendants. This approach will encourage claimants to make a realistic assessment of their claim. It will also allow solicitors greater certainty at the start of the case because they will be able to assess at the outset the fixed costs for which clients will be liable if they lose (based on the value of the claim) and either the likely amount they will recover or, in cases likely to be near the boundaries of a band, a lower and upper figure.

18. While it would be attractive, in terms of certainty, to assess whether a case required more or less work according to the type of case, particular case types may vary in the amount of work required. I therefore recommend that individual cases should be considered against specified criteria. This approach should enable litigants and their solicitors to assess with a reasonable degree of certainty into which fee band their case will fall. The district judge will determine the costs band into which the case will fall at the paper review stage once the defence is filed by assessing whether the individual case meets these criteria.

19. A number of criteria which might be good indicators of whether a case will require additional work have been suggested. Some criteria, such as disclosure exceeding that laid down as standard or a multiplicity of experts, are more relevant to the decision on whether the case should be in the fast track or the multi-track. Others, such as a split trial or a limitation issue, would be better taken account of by an additional fee since they relate to procedural activities which occur in only a minority of cases. In the case of children, the vast majority of such cases will be personal injury cases and will meet the first of the identified criteria.

20. I have therefore identified the following criteria as being valid indicators of additional work required on a case:
(a)   the need for expert evidence;

14   The upper limit for the fast track was subsequently set at £15,000.
15   The small claims limit was subsequently raised to £5,000.

(b)   parties who are patients (as defined by the Mental Health Act 1983) and therefore require a next friend;

(c)   parties who are unable to give adequate instructions in English; and

(d)   multiple defendants with different interests where the case is otherwise suitable for the fast track.

21.   The Law Society has recommended that the same level of costs should be payable for cases valued up to £5,000 requiring additional work and straightforward cases valued between £5,000 and £10,000. I consider that this approach adds to the simplicity of the costs regime, and I therefore accept this recommendation. Thus there will be three bands of costs:

Band A   £5,000 ceiling and straightforward

Band B   £5,000 ceiling and additional work factors £10,000 ceiling and straightforward

Band C   £10,000 ceiling and additional work factors.

STAGES

24.   Cases finish or settle at different stages. To ensure that remuneration broadly corresponds to the activity required at different stages within the new fast track procedure, the fixed costs will be divided into tranches relating to the stage the case has reached, although the costs will only become payable at the conclusion of the case. This approach will allow clients to assess their exposure to costs at each stage of the case and give effect in part to my general recommendation that clients should know how much their case is costing as it progresses. It will ensure that the costs regime provides certainty as to costs for litigants whose cases settle as well as for those who go to trial. It will be important for clients with solicitor and own clients costs agreements to be kept informed about the costs of their cases.

Adrian Zuckerman, a supporter in principle of fixed costs, was critical of the details of Lord Woolf's proposals, arguing that they gave lawyers too many opportunities to increase their own remuneration and hence the costs of the case.[16] For example, Lord Woolf's original proposal excluded disbursements from the fixed sum, leading Zuckermann to predict a steep rise in the costs of preparing bundles of documents for trial. He argued instead for a system closer to that adopted in Germany where recoverable costs (including disbursements) are rigidly limited by a statutory scale depending on the value of the claim. Moreover, the statutory costs are recoverable only to the extent the judgment awarded matches the sum claimed thus preventing parties exaggerating the value of their claim so as to earn the higher fees which are assigned to higher value claims. Lower value claims (for which the fees are very low) do not in fact seem to receive a poor quality service. Zuckermann's research indicated that lawyers in Germany (where firms are generally much smaller) handle a mixture of cases so that the more generous fees which apply to higher value claims (regardless of complexity) can set off the miserable fees which apply to low value claims even when the case is complex.[17] German lawyers seem to thrive financially by processing much larger volumes of small

16   See A Zuckerman 'Lord Woolf's Access to Justice: Plus Ca Change' (1996) 59 Modern Law Review 773.

17   Ibid at p 794.

claims than their English equivalents.[18] Moreover, the predictability of costs has led to a thriving market in legal expenses insurance.[19]

However, partly because of the difficulty of fixing an appropriate level of fixed costs, the idea was implemented in a very limited way when the new system was adopted. Part 46 of the Civil Procedure Rules (CPR) fixes advocates' trial fees according to the value of the claim. For a successful case, the value of the claim is the amount of the judgment excluding interest, costs and any reduction for contributing negligence. For a successful defendant, the amount of the claim is the sum specified on the claim form.[20] Pre-trial costs are still within the judge's discretion. Nevertheless, it is very likely that special restrictive rules on pre-trial costs will be made for fast track cases in the relatively near future. Following the publication of Lord Woolf's report, a number of different ways have been proposed for dealing with these cases. One[1] is that for cases having a value of up to £5,000, solicitors' profit costs and counsel's fees would be capped at £2,500. In cases worth between £5,000 and £15,000, the cap would be at 50% of the value of the claim. However, in these cases, lawyers would still have to justify their costs under the summary or other procedure for costs assessment. This will be so as to avoid windfalls for solicitors on some cases by which they might subsidise other cases.

Note

Allocation to one of the three tracks will normally be based on information provided by the parties in an allocation questionnaire[2] which the parties are required to file shortly after the filing of defences. The court may hold an allocation hearing if it thinks this is necessary but this is likely to be the exception rather than the rule. Normally therefore allocation decisions will be made on the basis of the questionnaire. Consequently, parties are permitted to file additional information with their allocation questionnaires to assist the court in making its decisions. Such information should only be filed if it is agreed between the parties or, if it is not agreed, on the basis that it has already been served on the other party.[3]

The first factor on which allocation will depend[4] is the financial value of the claim. However, the court has power to take into account a number of discretionary factors including the likely complexity of the facts, law or evidence and the amount of oral evidence which may be required.

---

18   Ibid at p 794 note 1.
19   Ibid at p 791.
20   CPR r 46.2.
1   See the LCD consultation paper *Justice at the Right Price* (June 1998).
2   CPR r 26
3   Practice Direction 26 para 22.2.
4   CPR r 26.6.

Questions

1. Reconsider the various possible regimes for the regulation of lawyers ethics considered by Wilkins in chapter 4. Which of those regimes does the new system of civil litigation most closely resemble? What does that suggest about the likely effectiveness of the new regime?

2. Does this approach leave any room for ethical discretion on the part of lawyers? And what about judges? One question about the Woolf Report's emphasis is whether by placing upon the judiciary the responsibility actively to move cases to settlement, there will in effect be a shifting of ethical difficulties from the lawyer to the judge, with consequent damage to the traditional judicial role of neutral impartial arbiter. See further Resnick 'Failing Faith: Adjudicatory Procedure in Decline' (1986) 53 Univ Chicago L Rev.

3. CPR r 3 imposes upon clients an obligation to comply with 'the overriding objective'. What is the likely impact of this obligation upon the approach adopted by lawyers when conducting litigation on their client's behalf?

Prognosis

Professor Zander has argued that a large-scale study by the Rand Corporation shows that in the United States judicial case management, whilst apt to cut delay, may in fact increase the cost. This is because much of the work for trial is done earlier even in the many cases which ultimately settle.[5] At this stage, however, the impact of the Woolf reforms upon costs and delays in civil litigation is very difficult to predict. What is clear though is that the new system raises three questions of particular relevance to lawyers ethics. The first is whether an excessively adversarial culture can be changed from above by a combination of procedural reform plus sanctions of various kinds. In the following extract, Adrian Zuckerman considers this issue.

> [Lord Woolf is] right in thinking that in order to affect a substantial change in the practice of litigation it is not enough to change the rules of procedure; rather, it is necessary to bring about a change in attitudes to the conduct of litigation. What is less clear is that court control on its own could produce the desired cultural change.
>
> We have seen that it is in the nature of things that litigants should desire to win and that they would tend to use all legitimate means to that end. We have also seen that this natural attitude combines with the financial incentives that lawyers have to encourage ever increasing investment in procedure. If this powerful cost driving combination is left untouched, judicial control of litigation would be going against the grain of the interests of the participants in the civil process, lawyers and their clients.

5   See generally Michael Zander 'The Woolf Report: Forwards or Backwards for the New Lord Chancellor' (1997) 16 CJQ 209 and 'How does judicial case management work?' (1997) 14 NLJ 539. Lord Woolf's reply is contained in 'Medics, Lawyers and the Courts' p 407 note 7.

A system in which the courts continually have to pitch themselves against the professional instincts of lawyers is bound to be inefficient. It can hardly be denied that the judicial task of controlling litigation is bound to be easier when its objective is shared by practitioners, and much harder when the court's aim runs counter to that of practitioners. Moreover, not only is the court's task likely to be more difficult to achieve in these circumstances, it risks being defeated altogether. This is because professional culture is as likely to influence judicial practices as the latter are likely to shape forensic practice. One should not overlook the fact that there is a two way traffic of influence between the courts and practitioners. It is plainly not the case that the courts can lay down standards of their own choosing which practitioners will observe as the courts envisage. The courts are as likely to be influenced by the professional standards as the profession is likely to observe standards laid down by the courts. This is especially true in a system such as ours, where judges are drawn from the ranks of the profession.[6]

The second question relates to the goal of fixing recoverable costs on the fast track. Critics have argued that far from protecting the less well-resourced litigant, such a change would give wealthy litigants a tactical advantage. Money spent on litigation which is not recoverable under a fixed cost regime may nevertheless increase the chances of success. Wealthier litigants will however be much better placed to withstand such losses. Hence fixed costs may in fact create an additional downwards pressure on settlements. This is a view shared by at least some defendants. One insurance company claims negotiator commented that:

Unfortunately a lot of the time, because of legal aid and legal expense insurance the cost pressure is more on us than on the actual plaintiff…We are really up against the wall. I've never seen a claim where legal expenses insurance has withdrawn funding. Unfortunately not. I think that's where you get a lot of these actions taking up court time. They run the distance. I think fixed costs will really concentrate the mind on that – then these cases will go a lot faster.[7]

Lord Woolf has considered this objection:

Many of those responding to the fast track issues paper were concerned that it might reduce equality between the litigants. That is the opposite of what should be the position. Equality is furthered by setting out the requirements in terms of activity and timetable for both parties at the very start of the case. There will be very limited scope for any party to undertake extra work and no reward for doing so. The timetable will be sufficient for parties to undertake the work that is needed but not so generous as to encourage elaboration. While the fixed costs will be set at a level sufficient to reward the winning party for this work, the resultant procedure will mean that there is little potential for a powerful opponent to drive up costs in a way which is intimidating to the weaker litigant, as can happen in the current system. Sanctions will be more effective, whether they are cost related or inhibit a party's ability to present material in the case.

6   Zuckerman supra p 406 note 6 at 67-68.
7   H Genn 'Understanding Civil Justice' chapter 6 of *Law and Opinion at the End of the 20th Century* (Michael Freeman ed, Oxford, OUP, 1997) at 179.

> It is particularly important on the fast track for the court to provide protection, on both a preventative and a curative basis, against oppressive or unreasonable behaviour.[8]

This response however only serves to raise the third question that of the extent to which the civil litigation can be designed in such a way as to eliminate tactical manoeuvring on the part of well-resourced litigants.

Questions

1. What are the implications for the likely impact of the reforms of the different diagnoses of the problem set out above?

2. What opportunities, if any, remain for well-resourced litigants wishing to pursue litigation aggressively in the provisions of the CPR relating to
i)   expert witnesses[9]
ii)   allocation decisions[10]:
Consider in relation to point ii) the relationship between the existence of a difficult question of law or fact and the skills and resources of the lawyers considering the matter.

3. What are the implications for a sanctions-based approach to civil justice reform of the law on wasted costs orders (chapter 4 supra)?

4. 'Lord Woolf and those who have built upon his work have attempted to build a system so perfect that ethically responsible behaviour on the part of individual lawyers is redundant. Alas this particular Brave New World is likely to be as illusory as that described by Aldous Huxley.' Do you agree?

5   Pro bono – the lawyer as altruist?

The absence of adequate State support for the provision of legal services to lower income groups inevitably leads to pressure on the professions to provide pro bono services. Yet Galanter and Palay's[11] survey of large London solicitors firms in the early 1990s did not demonstrate any widespread conviction that the problem of ensuring access to justice was a question of professional responsibility. This finding represented a stark contrast to the position in the United States where the 1980s had seen an explosion in pro bono work particularly amongst large law firms. In the following

---

8   Woolf Report (supra note 2) chapter 2 para 30.
9   See 'The Solution Prescribed' supra p 409.
10   See text to p 413 notes 2-4 supra.
11   M Galanter and T Palay 'Large Law Firms and Professional Responsibility' in R Cranston (eds) *Legal Ethics and Professional Responsibility* (Oxford, OUP, 1995) p 201.

extract, Galanter and Paley discuss this phenomenon and, in particular, its connection with large law firms.

> ...there is pressure from within the [American legal] profession to address the problems of access and disparity by embracing the notion of mandatory *pro bono* service. In February 1993 the American Bar Association's House of Delegates modified its model ethical rule commending *pro bono*, to provide that every lawyer 'should aspire' to devote fifty hours a year to *pro bono publico* service, of which a 'substantial majority' should go to the poor and to organisations that help the poor. Since the enforceable ethical rules are enacted by the courts and bar in each state, this provision is not enforceable as such, but it provides a powerful push for bar groups to consider how to implement *pro bono* requirements. Four state bars had enacted such 'hours' obligations before the ABA pronouncement and a fifth enacted one by mid-1994. Like the ABA rule, all provided 'should' rather than 'shall': they were ethical obligations but not enforceable through the disciplinary process. A few local bars, in which membership is voluntary, have imposed *pro bono* requirements as a condition of membership.
>
> The idea of mandatory *pro bono*, which has been around for the last twenty years or so, appeals to those who share the public justice critique of the profession. Joining these supporters are many who are alarmed by external attacks on the legal profession. Mandatory *pro bono* commends itself for its equalising thrust and its display of professional *noblesse*.
>
> The supporters of mandatory *pro bono publico* service seem to be reading public opinion accurately. Almost three-quarters of the respondents to the aforementioned 1993 National Law Journal poll thought lawyers should be required to spend some of their time on community service – a sharp increase since the 1986 poll. Other survey data suggests that this is a passive low intensity preference: when asked to volunteer a change that would improve the legal system only five per cent proposed equalising access to justice or expanding *pro bono* services. Still, hearing about lawyers providing free legal service to the needy ranked highest among items improving respondents' opinion of the profession.
>
> Of course this notion of an obligation to devote a portion of one's time to public service applies to all lawyers, not just to lawyers in large firms. But there is a substantial connection between large firms and support for *pro bono*. Large firms have had the most visible *pro bono* programmes – and large firm lawyers have been the most enthusiastic and outspoken supporters of the concept. The amount of *pro bono* activity by law firms is uneven among firms of all sizes, but media accounts suggest that generally there is more *pro bono* among the largest firms and the amount is increasing.
>
> To test this impression, we matched the *American Lawyer's* annual surveys of *pro bono* activity (available since 1990) with the *American Lawyer* reports on firm size, revenues, and estimated profits and with our own data set on firm growth rates. In general we found that *pro bono* activity was positively related to the size and economic performance of the firm. We used four measures of *pro bono* activity (total hours of *pro bono* activity for the firm, the number of lawyers providing twenty or more hours of *pro bono* service during the year, hours per lawyer engaged in *pro bono* work, and the percentage of lawyers at the firm who reported twenty or more hours of *pro bono* activity). *Pro bono* activity, as measured by each of these four measures, increased between 1990 and 1993.

In the fifty-nine firms for which complete data were available for both 1990 and 1993, total hours of *pro bono* work increased forty-five per cent. This resulted from more lawyers contributing more hours each: the number of attorneys reporting twenty or more hours of *pro bono* activity increased by over sixty per cent while the average hours per attorney increased by almost one-third. The percentage of attorneys at these firms who contributed twenty or more hours increased by thirty-four per cent (but still totalled less than forty per cent of lawyers at these firms). Overall, *pro bono* activity grew faster than the size, revenue, or profits of these firms. In general the level of *pro bono* activity was positively related to firm performance.

Thus the data suggests that the larger the firm and the greater its gross revenues, the more willing it is to encourage or permit *pro bono* activity. Why should this be? Some would argue that large firms, or at least some of them, have been the site of a long tradition of public service, even though that tradition is presently in some disarray. Conceding that 'public service' is a category far broader than '*pro bono*' as currently understood, it is evident that *pro bono* work by large firms has been neither typical nor continuous.

The present *pro bono* surge is not the large firms' first encounter with expectations of organised *pro bono* work. In the late 1960s there was a great contraction in the supply of talented associates. The Vietnam War draft diverted law graduates to other occupations in which they could obtain deferments. Simultaneously, when 1960s activism induced disdain for corporate practice among students seeking work in poverty law and public interest law, the percentage of elite law graduates entering private practice fell precipitously. Confronted by criticism that their work was unfulfilling and inimical to the public interest, many firms acceded to demands that recruits be able to spend time on '*pro bono publico*' activities. In 1970 the *Wall Street Journal* reported that 'now it's common for [the big corporate law firms] to permit their attorneys to spend substantial portions of their time in non-commercial work'. But just a few years later, this commitment had largely dissipated, only to be rekindled in the 1980s, when 'voluntary *pro bono* programs enjoyed an unparalleled level of support, funding and growth'.

We submit that there are structural reasons why large firms find regular organised *pro bono* service more congenial than do their smaller counterparts. On the whole, large firms with hundreds of lawyers can adapt readily to the *pro bono* obligation by appointing partners (or retaining outside specialists) to manage it, and assigning staff to deal with the logistical problems of finding and screening suitable cases. A large volume of *pro bono* work projects a favourable image of public service at the same time that it provides both an asset for recruitment of young lawyers and regular opportunities for development of professional skills such as trial advocacy. Smaller firms, unable to enjoy similar economies of scale in organising their *pro bono* work, find it considerably more disruptive and burdensome.

The large firm setting is home to the most intense efforts to institutionalise *pro bono* obligations. In May 1993 the American Bar Association launched its 'Law Firm *Pro Bono* Challenge' calling on the five hundred largest law firms in the country – that is, roughly all firms with more than seventy lawyers – to contribute an amount of time equal to three to five per cent of the firm's total billable hours each year. This effort was resoundingly endorsed by Attorney General Janet Reno. By late May some 155 law firms had signed on. Some of the largest firms declined to participate on the ground that the programme's definition of *pro bono* work was too restrictive and objected to the requirement that a law firm commit a percentage of its total hours rather than a fixed number. Unlike the American Bar Association Model Rules, which declares the obligation of individual attorneys, the Challenge includes an undertaking to modify firm arrangements by eliminating barriers to *pro bono* work and nurturing 'a firm culture in which *pro bono* service is a routine and valued part of each individual's professional life'. A year after the Challenge was issued, the total number of signatory firms was 164, only slightly higher than the initial sign up. Subsequently, news about the programme has been sparse.

If *pro bono* were to become mandatory for all lawyers, it would very likely include arrangements for making *pro bono* obligations transferable. That is, there would be a market in which lawyers could arrange to pay others to discharge their obligation, or be paid to do *pro bono* work for others. Existing legal services offices would be strengthened and a whole new category of *pro bono* providers might appear. But it seems likely that most large firms would operate their own *pro bono* programmes, with long term effects that no one can predict.

So, to summarise, we have a curious situation in which lawyers are under attack by elites, but are seen as flawed yet useful champions by the poor and less advantaged. Major regulatory initiatives promise to make large firms hold themselves more independent of their major business clients – at the very time that these clients are trying to reduce their dependence on outside law firms and gain more control over costs. And, finally, the large law firms, embracing *pro bono* representation of the poor, are the leading edge of the profession's initiative in redefining itself as a vehicle of public justice.

We do not argue that such service is a necessary and inevitable feature of the large business law firm – a claim which its history surely falsifies. But neither is it incompatible – at least from the point of view of the lawyers in those firms. It remains to be seen how their clients will react and how they will respond to client pressures.

As the American style large firm spreads around the globe, it is an open question whether the *pro bono* gene will manifest itself elsewhere. Our interviews of lawyers in large London solicitors firms from 1990 until 1994 elicited little sense of distress about the increasingly commercial character of law practice. Interviewees unselfconsciously spoke of 'the law business'. For the most part they were quite sanguine about recent changes and free of expressions of nostalgia about lost professional virtue. There was no sense that the profession was under attack. And there was hardly a glimmer of interest in expansive *pro bono* activity, although inquiry revealed that several of the firms we visited had substantial *pro bono* programmes. Such interest, where it exists, remains low key, valued more as a recruiting device than a bulwark protecting professional identity from attack. Perhaps we failed to ask the right questions, but we detected no counterpart in the London large firm world to the American sense that large firms might have a special obligation to remedy serious deficiencies in access to justice. In May 1994, a Law Society working party firmly rejected any mandatory contribution of legal services or compulsory financial support.

Perhaps this should not surprise us, for legal aid for the poor was firmly institutionalised in Britain as a state responsibility prior to the emergence of large firms. And lawyers there have not been subjected to withering attack by elite groups and broader public opinion. But these contrasts, in turn, are located in a world in which many forces are driving the legal systems of the industrialised nations in a common direction. The development in England of the large law firm is in itself a striking instance of such convergence. So before we take the present divergence on *pro bono* as permanent, it is useful to recall that in their 'Golden Age' in the 1950s and early 1960s no one would have predicted that the thrust for strong *pro bono* commitment in the United States would come from the large firms.[12]

It is clear however that the late 1990s have seen a surge of interest in pro bono work amongst the UK legal profession. In 1996, the Bar founded a pro bono unit which within two years was able to report that it had 900 barristers including 155 QC s committed to giving at least three days of free legal assistance per year. At about the same time, a number of law firms founded the Solicitors Pro Bono Unit to publicise and co-ordinate the pro bono work of the solicitors profession and at about the same time many of the largest firms began to appoint full time pro bono coordinators. The Privy Council, as final court of appeal to many former British colonies in the Caribbean, has been inundated with death penalty appeals. Most of these have involved pro bono representation by large commercial law firms. So extensive was this pro bono contribution that Lord Browne-Wilkinson was led to express concern that it was taking up as much as 25% of the time of the senior judiciary.[13] Clients too are conscious that the image of their lawyers may impact upon that of their clients. Early in 1999, British Aerospace Engineering announced that, in future, it would ask for evidence of substantial pro bono commitment from firms wishing to be on their panel of commercial law firms.[14]

At this point it should be noted that the Model Rules of Professional Responsibility contain the following provision in relation to pro bono work.

A lawyer should aspire to render at least (50) hours of pro bono publico legal services per year. In fulfilling this responsibility, the lawyer should:
(a) provide a substantial majority of the (50) hours of legal services without fee or expectation of fee to:
   (1) persons of limited means or
   (2) charitable, religious, civic, community, governmental and educational organisations in matters which are designed primarily to address the needs of persons of limited means; and
(b) provide any additional services through:
   (1) delivery of legal services at no fee or substantially reduced fee to individuals, groups or organisations seeking to secure or protect civil rights, civil liberties or public rights, or charitably religious, civic, community, governmental and educational organisations in matters in furtherance of their organisational

12   Ibid at pp 197-201.
13   (1999) The Lawyer, 11 May, p 17.
14   (1999) The Lawyer, 8 March.

purposes, where the payment of standard legal fees would significantly deplete the organisation's economic resources or would be otherwise inappropriate;

(2)   delivery of legal services at a substantially reduced fee to persons of limited means; or

(3)   participation in activities for improving the law, the legal system or the legal profession.

In addition a lawyer should voluntarily contribute financial support to organisations that provide legal services to persons of limited means.

Whilst failure to comply is not a disciplinary matter, the question arises of whether the UK codes ought to be changed so as to incorporate a similar or stronger provision. David Luban has argued[15] that the state grants lawyers a monopoly over the provision of certain services and erects barriers to entry to those seeking to enter the profession. In addition some of the complexity of the legal system which creates the need for legal services can be directly traced to the activities of lawyers. Consequently, the state is entitled to demand pro bono services in return. Professor Fried in one of the earliest defences of the 'Standard Conception of Legal Ethics'[16] argued that critics of the standard conception were mistaken. Their error was to require lawyers to regard the interests of society as equally important as those of clients. This argued Professor Fried was the same philosophical error lying at the heart of utilitarianism in that it regarded the lawyer as a resource to be deployed for the maximum good of society. This in turn involved an inadequate concept of the self (ie of the lawyer). It is in fact one of our basic intuitions that each individual is entitled to treat himself with special concern and respect ('Love your neighbour as yourself'). Similarly we feel entitled to treat with special concern those with whom we enter into special personal relationships. Professor Fried used this insight to argue that lawyers were entitled to prefer their clients' interests to those of third parties. For similar reasons lawyers were entitled to choose as client-friends whomsoever they wished. Consequently, if society was not prepared to meet the financial costs involved in fulfilling the moral right to legal services it was mere humbug to expect the legal profession to do so.

One argument against mandatory pro bono is that many lawyers simply lack the knowledge to deal with the legal problems of the relevant clientele. One possible response would be to allow lawyers to fulfill their pro bono obligation in the initial years by undergoing relevant training. Another would be to allow those lawyers pleading incompetence to pay into a fund at the equivalent of their hourly rate in respect of any unfulfilled commitment. This fund could then be used to pay for legal representation for clients otherwise unrepresented whose cases are too long and complex to be handled pro bono.[17]

---

15   *Lawyers and Justice: An Ethical Study* (Princeton UP, 1988) chapter 11.

16   Charles Fried 'The Lawyer As Friend: The Moral Foundations of the Lawyer-Client Relationship' (1976) 85 Yale Law Journal 1060.

17   See Luban supra note 15.

Notes

1. In one survey of pro bono work by UK law firms, the most common motivation for pro bono activity was said to be staff development ie the development in pro bono practice of important skills which many of their staff were unable, due to lack of seniority, to develop through contact with paying commercial clients.[18]

2. In *Count Tolstoy v Lord Aldington*[19], the Court of Appeal ordered lawyers acting for a plaintiff whose case was deemed to be hopeless to pay personally the costs incurred by the defendant. The court stressed that such an order would be made only rarely, but that those acting pro bono should take particular care to ensure that the case was bona fide.

Questions

1. Is it fair to regard the complexity of the legal system and hence the need for legal services as an artificial creation of the state/lawyers?

2. Should the state require monopoly suppliers of electricity to provide free services to those on very low incomes?

3. How strong is the 'incompetence argument'? What does the argument presuppose about what is involved in being a good lawyer? To what extent should legal education be capable of dealing with the problem?

4. Consider Thomas Shaffer's comment on lawyers and vocation in chapter 1.[20] What does the concept of pro bono service imply about the moral worth of paid professional work?

5. Reconsider in the light of the material on pro bono work, the question of whether professionalism can survive in modern practice conditions.

6. What other motives might there be for lawyers and law firms to engage in pro bono activity other than altruism and, as noted, staff development?

7. Some have expressed considerable cynicism about the genuineness of firms' commitment to pro bono work. Reconsider the impact of computers upon modern practice described at the end of chapter 3. Does this suggest a way in which the commitment of law firms to pro bono work might itself be measured?

18   See (1999), The Lawyer, 15 March at p 12.
19   [1996] 1 WLR 736, CA.
20   Supra pp 1-2.

8. What are the competing policy considerations facing a court when considering whether to make lawyers acting pro bono personally liable for costs?

9. You are a partner in a firm which permits all assistant solicitors to spend up to 40 hours per year on pro bono activity, but it is a requirement that all proposed activity be approved by a partner as being 'in the public interest.' This condition was inserted to prevent some historic abuses (ie acting for friends) and is generously interpreted. You receive a proposal from a young male assistant who wishes to spend his time doing research for an organization campaigning against the extension of gay rights on religious grounds. Should you approve the proposal?

Legal expenses insurance

Legal expenses insurance is a policy of insurance under which the insured is indemnified in return for a premium against the costs of bringing and defending litigation usually up to a specified limit in relation to specified categories of claim. In the UK usually such insurance is provided as an additional benefit under another policy such as householders public liability insurance. LEI is very small at the moment but this may change as the legal aid schemes decline.

In Germany, the state spends very little on legal aid[1] but LEI is very widespread. The German position may in part be due to the fact that costs in German courts are paid on a fixed scale which makes insurers' exposure predictable. (Can you see the link here with Lord Woolf's proposed procedural reforms?) Similarly in the United States, where LEI is also very widespread, it has operated through legal clinics. Such clinics are similar to HMOs found in the health care sectors. Information asymmetries are restricted by using in-house lawyers and the clients pays for legal services on an instalment basis. Costs are kept down by using economies of scale with clients being attracted by mass advertising campaigns. There were 1,000 such clinics in the US in 1990, with two of the largest constituting the 2nd and 42nd largest law firms.

Even if legal aid's decline does represent one factor suggesting a growth of LEI, there remain formidable problems. Consumers seem to underestimate the importance of LEI leading to an insufficient volume of business to enable its provision at acceptable cost. Moreover insurers face similar information asymmetries and third party payer problems (moral hazard) to those faced by the state. Insurance companies often seek to solve this problem by restricting the insured to a choice between private practitioners on an approved panel.[2]

---

1   As a proportion of GDP, Germany's expenditure on legal aid is less than half that of the UK. See A Gray and N Rickman 'The Role of Legal Expenses Insurance in Securing Access to Justice' chapter 16 of *The Reform of Civil Procedure* (supra note 20) p 31.
2   Solicitors are not generally permitted to be party to restrictions on a clients choice of solicitor but this is permitted (subject to exceptions) in the case of legal expenses insurance by the Insurance Companies (Legal Expenses Insurance) Regulations 1990.

Note

Note 1 to Principal 6.01 of the LSGPC provides that

> The solicitors principal duty is to the insured, not to the legal expenses insurer but the insured has a duty to mitigate loss and keep the insurer informed of progress.

Questions

1. To what extent is Legal Expenses Insurance a threat to professional independence?

2. Does the tripartite relationship between client, solicitor and insurer create any significant conflict of interest?

3. If LEI involves problems similar to those facing the legal aid system, in what ways do they differ as a means of providing access to justice? See *Murphy v Young & Co's Brewery.*[3]

4. Should LEI be made compulsory?

3   Supra chapter 8 text to pp 295-304 notes 10-18.

Appendix

CONDITIONAL FEE AGREEMENT

FOR USE IN PERSONAL INJURY CASES, BUT NOT CLINICAL NEGLIGENCE

This agreement is a binding legal contract between you and your solicitor/s.

Before you sign, please read everything carefully.

Words like 'our disbursements', 'basic charges', 'win' and 'lose' are explained in condition 3 of the Law Society Conditions which you should also read carefully.

. . . . .Agreement date

. . . . I/We, the solicitor/s

. . . . You, the client

What is covered by this agreement?
* Your claim against [   ]
  for damages for personal injury suffered on [   ]
* Any appeal by your opponent.
* Any appeal you make against an interim order during the proceedings.
* Any proceedings you take to enforce a judgment, order or agreement.

What is not covered by this agreement?
* Any counterclaim against you.
* Any appeal you make against the final judgment order.

Paying us

If you win your claim, you pay our basic charges, our disbursements and a success fee. The amount of these is not based on or limited by the damages. You are entitled to seek recovery from your opponent of part or all of our basic charges, our disbursements, a success fee and insurance premium. Please also see conditions 4 and 6.

It may be that your opponent makes a Part 36 offer or payment which you reject and, on our advice, your claim for damages goes ahead to trial where you recover damages that are less than that offer or payment. We will not add our success fee to the basic charges for the work done after we received notice of the offer or payment.

If you receive interim damages, we may require you to pay our disbursements at that point and a reasonable amount for our future disbursements.

If you receive provisional damages, we are entitled to payment of our basic charges our disbursements and success fee at that point.

If you win but on the way lose an interim hearing, you may be required to pay your opponent's charges of that hearing. Please see conditions 3(h) and 5. If on the way to winning or losing you win an interim hearing, then we are entitled to payment of our basic charges and disbursements related to that hearing together with a success fee on those charges if you win overall.

If you lose, you pay your opponent's charges and disbursements. You may be able to take out an insurance policy against this risk. Please also see conditions 3(j) and 5. If you lose, you do not pay our charges but we may require you to pay our disbursements.

If you end this agreement before you win or lose, you pay our basic charges. If you go on to win, you pay a success fee. Please also see condition 7(a).

We may end this agreement before you win or lose. Please also see condition 7(b) for details.

Basic charges

These are for work done from now until this agreement ends.

How we calculate our basic charges

These are calculated for each hour engaged on your matter [from now until the review date on   ]. Routine letters and telephone calls will be charged as units of one tenth of an hour. Other letters and telephone calls will be charged on a time basis. The hourly rates are:

*   Solicitors with over four years' experience after qualification
£

*   Other solicitors and legal executives and other staff of equivalent experience
£

*   Trainee solicitors and other staff of equivalent experience
£

[We will review the hourly rate on the review date and on each anniversary of the review date. We will not increase the rate by more than the rise in the Retail Prices Index and will notify you of the increased rate in writing.]

Success fee

This is [   ] % of our basic charges.

The reasons for calculating the success fee at this level are set out in Schedule 1 to this agreement.

You cannot recover from your opponent the part of the success fee that relates to the cost to us of postponing receipt of our charges and disbursements (as set out at paragraphs (a) and (b) at Schedule 1). This part of the success fee remains payable by you.

Value added tax (VAT)

We add VAT, at the rate (now [   ] %) that applies when the work is done, to the total of the basic charges and success fee.

Law Society Conditions

The Law Society Conditions are attached because they are part of this agreement. Any amendments or additions to them will apply to you. You should read the conditions carefully and ask us about anything you find unclear.

Other points

Immediately before you signed this agreement, we verbally explained to you the effect of this agreement and in particular the following:

(a)   the circumstances in which you may be liable to pay our disbursements and charges;

(b)   the circumstances in which you may seek assessment of our charges and disbursements and the procedure for doing so;

(c)   whether we consider that your risk of becoming liable for any costs in these proceedings is insured under an existing contract of insurance;

(d)   other methods of financing those costs, including private funding, Community Legal Service funding, legal expenses insurance, trade union funding;

(e)   (i)   in all the circumstances, on the information currently available to us, we believe that a contract of insurance with [   ] is appropriate. Detailed reasons for this are set out in Schedule 2.

(ii)   In any event, we believe it is desirable for you to insure your opponent's charges and disbursements in case you lose.

(iii)   We confirm that we do not have an interest in recommending this particular insurance agreement.

Signatures

Signed for the solicitor/s

. . . .

Signed by the client

. . . .

I confirm that my solicitor has verbally explained to me the matters in paragraphs (a) to (e) under 'Other points' above.

Signed

. . . . (Client)

I specifically confirm that I verbally explained to the client the matters in paragraphs (a) to (e) under 'Other points' and confirm the matters at (e) in writing in Schedule 2.

Signed

. . . . (Solicitors)

This agreement complies with the Conditional Fee Agreements Regulations 2000 (SI 2000 No 692)

SCHEDULE 1   The success fee

The success fee is set at [   ]% of basic charges and cannot be more than 100% of the basic charges.

The percentage reflects the following:
(a) the fact that if you win we will not be paid our basic charges until the end of the claim;
(b) our arrangements with you about paying disbursements;
(c) the fact that if you lose, we will not earn anything;
(d) our assessment of the risks of your case. These include the following:

. . . .
. . . .

(e) any other appropriate matters.

The matters set out at paragraphs (a) and (b) above together make up [   ]% of the increase on basic charges. The matters at paragraphs (c), (d) [and (e)] make up [   ]% of the increase on basic charges. So the total success fee is [   ]% as stated above.

SCHEDULE 2   The insurance policy

In all the circumstances and on the information currently available to us, we believe that a contract of insurance with [   ] is appropriate to cover your opponent's charges and disbursements in case you lose.

This is because:

. . . .
. . . .
. . . .

We are not, however, insurance brokers and cannot give advice on all products which may be available.

LAW SOCIETY CONDITIONS

1.   Our responsibilities

We must:
- always act in your best interests, subject to our duty to the court;
- explain to you the risks and benefits of taking legal action;
- give you our best advice about whether to accept any offer of settlement;
- give you the best information possible about the likely costs of your claim for damages.

2.   Your responsibilities

You must:
- give us instructions that allow us to do our work properly;
- not ask us to work in an improper or unreasonable way;
- not deliberately mislead us;
- co-operate with us;
- go to any medical or expert examination or court hearing.

3.   Explanation of words used

(a) Advocacy

Appearing for you at court hearings.

(b) Basic charges

Our charges for the legal work we do on your claim for damages.

(c) Claim

Your demand for damages for personal injury whether or not court proceedings are issued.

(d) Counterclaim

A claim that your opponent makes against you in response to your claim.

(e) Damages

Money that you win whether by a court decision or settlement.

(f)   Our disbursements

Payment we make on your behalf such as:
- court fees;
- experts' fees;
- accident report fees;
- travelling expenses.

(g) Interim damages

Money that a court says your opponent must pay or your opponent agrees to pay while waiting for a settlement of the court's final decision.

(h) Interim hearing

A court hearing that is not final.

(i) Lien

Our right to keep all papers, documents, money or other property held on your behalf until all money due to us is paid. A lien may be applied after this agreement ends.

(j) Lose

The court has dismissed your claim or you have stopped it on our advice.

(k) Part 36 offers or payments

An offer to settle your claim made in accordance with Part 36 of the Civil Procedure Rules.

(l) Provisional damages

Money that a court says your opponent must pay or your opponent agrees to pay, on the basis that you will be able to go back to court at a future date for further damages if:
- you develop a serious disease; or
- your condition deteriorates in a way that has been proved or admitted to be linked to your personal injury claim.

(m) Success fee

The percentage of basic charges that we add to your bill if you win your claim for damages and that we will seek to recover from your opponent.

(n) Win

Your claim for damages is finally decided in your favour, whether by a court decision or an agreement to pay you damages. 'Finally' means that your opponent:
- is not allowed to appeal against the court decision; or
- has not appealed in time; or
- has lost any appeal.

4. *What happens if you win?*

If you win:
- You are then liable to pay all our basic charges, our disbursements and success fee – please see condition 3(n).
- Normally, you will be entitled to recover part or all of our basic charges, our disbursements and success fee from your opponent.
- If you and your opponent cannot agree the amount, the court will decide how much you can recover. If the amount agreed or allowed by the court does not cover all our basic charges and our disbursements, then you pay the difference.
- You will not be entitled to recover from your opponent the part of the success fee that relates to the cost to us of postponing receipt of our charges and our disbursements. This remains payable by you.
- You agree that after winning, the reasons for setting the success fee at the amount stated may be disclosed:

(i)   to the court and any other person required by the court;

(ii) to your opponent in order to gain his or her agreement to pay the success fee.

- If the court carries out an assessment and disallows any of the success fee percentage because it is unreasonable in view of what we knew or should have known when it was agreed, then that amount ceases to be payable unless the court is satisfied that it should continue to be payable.

- If we agree with your opponent that the success fee is to be paid at a lower percentage than is set out in this agreement, then the success fee percentage will be reduced accordingly unless the court is satisfied that the full amount is payable.

- It may happen that your opponent makes an offer that includes payment of our basic charges and a success fee. If so, unless we consent, you agree not to tell us to accept the offer if it includes payment of the success fee at a lower rate than is set out in this agreement.

- If your opponent is receiving Community Legal Service funding, we are unlikely to get any money from him or her. So if this happens, you have to pay us our basic charges, disbursements and success fee.

You remain ultimately responsible for paying our success fee.

You agree to pay into a designated account any cheque received by you or by us from your opponent and made payable to you. Out of the money, you agree to let us take the balance of the basic charges; success fee; insurance premium; our remaining disbursements; and VAT. You take the rest.

We are allowed to keep any interest your opponent pays on the charges.

Payment for advocacy is explained in condition 6.

If your opponent fails to pay

If your opponent does not pay any damages or charges owed to you, we have the right to take recovery action in your name to enforce a judgment, order or agreement. The charges of this action become part of the basic charges.

5.   *What happens if you lose?*

If you lose, you do not have to pay any of our basic charges or success fee. You do have to pay:

- us for our disbursements;

- your opponent's legal charges and disbursements

If you are insured against payment of these amounts by your insurance policy, we will have a claim on your behalf and receive any resulting payment in your name. We will give you a statement of account for all money received and paid out.

If your opponent pays the charges of any hearing, they belong to us.

Payment for advocacy is dealt with in condition 6.

6.   *Payment for advocacy*

The cost of advocacy and any other work by us, or by any solicitor agent on our behalf, forms part of our basic charges.

We shall discuss with you the identity of any barrister instructed, and the arrangements made for payment.

Barristers who have a conditional fee agreement with us

If you win, you are normally entitled to recover their fee and success fee from your opponent. The barrister's success fee is shown in the separate conditional fee agreement we make with the barrister. We will discuss the barrister's success fee with you before we instruct him or her. If you lose, you pay the barrister nothing.

Barristers who do not have a conditional fee agreement with us

If you win, then you will normally be entitled to recover all or part of their fee from your opponent. If you lose, then you must pay their fee.

7. *What happens when this agreement ends before your claim for damages ends?*

(a) Paying us if you end this agreement

You can end the agreement any time. We then have the right to decide whether you must:
- pay our basic charges and our disbursements including barristers' fees when we ask for them; or
- pay our basic charges, and our disbursements including barristers' fees and success fees if you go on to win your claim for damages.

(b) Paying us if we end this agreement
(i) We can end this agreement if you do not keep to your responsibilities in condition 2. We then have the right to decide whether you must:
   - pay our basic charges and our disbursements including barristers' fees when we ask for them; or
   - pay our basic charges and our disbursements including barristers' fees and success fees if you go on to win your claim for damages.
(ii) We can end this agreement if we believe you are unlikely to win. If this happens, you will only have to pay our disbursements. These will include barristers' fees if the barrister does not have a conditional fee agreement with us.
(iii) We can end this agreement if you reject our opinion about making a settlement with your opponent. You must then:
   - pay the basic charges and our disbursements, including barristers' fees;
   - pay the success fee if you go on to win your claim for damages.
   If you ask us to get a second opinion from a specialist solicitor outside our firm, we will do so. You pay the cost of a second opinion.
(iv) We can end this agreement if you do not pay your insurance premium when asked to do so.

(c) Death

This agreement automatically ends if you die before your claim for damages is concluded. We will be entitled to recover our basic charges up to the date of your death from your estate.

If your personal representatives wish to continue your claim for damages, we may offer them a new conditional fee agreement, as long as they agree to pay the success fee on our basic charges from the beginning of the agreement with you.

8. What happens after this agreement ends?

After this agreement ends, we will apply to have our name removed from the record of any court proceedings in which we are acting unless you have another form of funding and ask us to work for you.

We have the right to preserve our lien unless another solicitor working for you undertakes to pay us what we are owed including a success fee if you win.

CHAPTER ELEVEN

Conflicts of interest

... a faithful man, who can find?[1]

Introduction

Lawyers' codes of ethics usually lay down detailed rules designed to prevent conflicts of interest. In common law countries breach of these rules will often constitute both misconduct and, simultaneously, a breach of the fiduciary duties imposed upon lawyers by the substantive law, with serious remedial consequences. This injunction to avoid conflicts of interest is common, familiar and rarely questioned. On reflection, however, it can be seen that conflict of interest doctrine is intimately linked with a particular model of good lawyering and thus has an ideological aspect. 'Good lawyers' are on this view completely detached in their professional lives, zealously asserting the interest of their clients without regard to their own moral or financial interests and without regard to the interests of others.

This chapter examines selected aspects of conflict of interest doctrine and raises the question of whether their model of good lawyering is workable. Is it realistic to expect lawyers to avoid any conflict between their own interests and their clients' interests? Indeed, conflict of interest doctrine may be historically contingent. Ethical rules on conflict of interest are derived from the fiduciary duties governing principal-agent relationships. This body of law was developed by the courts in the 19th century, an era in which agency relationships normally involved individual agents acting for individual principals on an ad hoc basis. The modern context for principal-agent relationships is often very different, particularly in commercial transactions. Both

1   Proverbs 20:6 (NIV).

principal and agent may be large institutions making it difficult and costly to comply with a strict injunction to avoid conflicts of interest.[2] Even if the model is workable the question is whether it is desirable. As we shall see, the avoidance of conflict of interests may impose unacceptable costs, both financial and moral, for the lawyer and for society.

The chapter follows a basic taxonomy of the various forms in which conflicts may arise. There are three basic forms. There may be a conflict between the lawyer's own interests and those of the client. In such situations paragraph 15.04 of the LSGPC[3] provides that:

> A solicitor must not act where his or her own interests conflict with those of a client or a potential client.

Thus in one case considered by the Legal Services Ombudsman, a firm of solicitors was negotiating on the client's behalf for the purchase of a domestic property. These negotiations eventually broke down. In the meantime, one of the solicitors in the firm (who was not personally acting for the buyer) learnt of the property and indeed subsequently purchased it. The Legal Services Ombudsman was critical of the firm for continuing to act under circumstances involving an apparent conflict of interest between the client's interest and that of one of its employees.[4]

Secondly, the conflict may between the interests of two or more current clients. In this situation paragraphs 15.01 and 15.03 of the LSGPC provide as follows:

> 15.01: A solicitor or firm of solicitors should not accept instructions to act for two or more clients where there is a conflict or a significant risk of conflict of interest.[5]

> 15.03: A solicitor or firm of solicitors must not continue to act for two or more clients where a conflict of interests arises between those clients.

The CCB provides that a barrister must not accept instructions:

> if there is or appears to be a conflict or risk of conflict of interest ...between the interests of any one or more clients (unless all relevant persons consent to the barrister accepting instructions);[6]

and must cease to act

> if having accepted instructions on behalf of more than one client there is or appears to be
> (i)   a conflict or risk of conflict between the interests of any one or more of such clients; or

---

2   See P Finn ' Fiduciary Law and the Modern World' in *Commercial Aspects of Trusts and Fiduciary Obligations* (Clarendon Press, Oxford, 1992, Ewan Mckendrick ed) pp 19-23.

3   The CCB does not seem directly to address these conflicts, providing only that a barrister will be professionally embarrassed and must therefore refuse to act 'if there is or appears to be a conflict between the interests of the Barrister and some other person... (unless all relevant persons consent to the Barrister accepting the instructions' (CCB para 603(e).)

4   5th Annual Report of the Legal Services Ombudsman, p 9, para 3.17.

5   Note 2 states that the solicitor may not act even if the client consents.

6   CCB para 603 (e).

(ii) the risk of breach of confidence;

and the clients do not all consent to him continuing to act. [7]

The CCB is thus very similar to the LSGPC but with the important difference that a barrister may continue to act with the consent of the clients. Such conflicts are known as simultaneous conflicts of interest. Finally, there are successive conflict of interests which arise where a lawyer is asked to represent a client whose interests conflict with those of a previous client. One problem in this situation is that the lawyer may, whilst representing the first client, have acquired confidential information which would be useful to the second client. Hence Paragraph 15.02 of the LSGPC provides:

> If a solicitor or firm of solicitors has acquired relevant confidential information concerning a former client during the course of acting for that client, the solicitor or firm must not accept instructions to act against the client.[8]

As we shall see the standards imposed by substantive law in relation to these three areas of conflict are closer to those of the Bar because they generally allow a lawyer to act in the face of a conflict of interest provided the client consents. The rest of the chapter deals in turn with each of these three types of conflict of interest .

1   Conflict of interest between lawyer and client

The principle that solicitors must not act where their own interests conflict with those of the client is a reflection of the fact that solicitors are viewed by the law as fiduciary agents. As such, they owe a duty of loyalty to the client which requires them to subordinate their own interests to those of the client and to avoid acting in situations where self-interest might tempt them to compromise their duty of loyalty. Hence a lawyer will not be allowed to retain any substantial gift , for example under a will, unless the client has independent advice. Similarly, contracts entered into between lawyer and client are prima facie suspect. English law presupposes that contractual negotiations are inevitably adversarial[9] and this is inconsistent with the fulfilment of fiduciary duties. Hence, a solicitor who purchased a house from a client might well find that the transaction would be set aside in the absence of independent advice. Whilst transactions such as the purchase of the client's house are unlikely to occur often in practice, these principles would also apply to arrangements made between lawyer and client for the giving of security by the client for sums expended by the lawyer on the client's behalf.

This latter example raises the troubling question of whether conflict of interest may be inherent in lawyer-client fee negotiations. Established principles do not go so far

---

7   CCB paras 608(b)(i) and (ii).
8   Paragraph 603 (f) of the CCB provides that a barrister must not accept instructions 'if there is a risk that information confidential to another client or former client might be communicated to or used for the benefit of anyone other than that client or former client without their consent' Once again however the difference is that the barrister may act with the consent of the client.
9   *Walford v Miles* [1992] 2 AC 128 per Lord Acker at p 138E.

perhaps because in formal terms these negotiations precede the formation of the lawyer-client relationship which gives rise to fiduciary duties[10]. On the other hand, it could be argued that recognition of such conflict is implicit in the right accorded clients to have their solicitor's bills assessed by the court, in the case of litigation or by the Law Society in other cases. This process may lead to a reduction of the bill if it is found to be excessive. Even so it may be said that such provisions fail to address the fundamental conflict between lawyers' professional interest in maximising fee income and clients' interests in value for money. Indeed on one view these conflicts are irresolvable. If the lawyer is employed at an hourly rate then there is every incentive to leave no stone unturned. If the lawyer is employed for a fixed fee, then there will be the temptation to cut corners. Only a very sophisticated client will be able to ensure the lawyer is providing value for money. (See further Chapter 10 above.)

Notes

1. Principle 12.09 of the LSGPC provides that:

> A solicitor must not abuse the solicitor/client relationship by taking advantage of the client.

> I.   A solicitor must not abuse his or her position to exploit a client by taking advantage of a client's age, inexperience, ill health, want of education or business experience or emotional or other vulnerability. For example: ...

>> (B)   Whilst it would not necessarily be so, it may be an abuse of the solicitor/client relationship for a solicitor to enter into a sexual relationship with a client.

2. Paragraph 15.06 of the LSGPC provides:

> A solicitor must decline to act where either the solicitor or a partner, employee or relative of the solicitor holds some office or appointment as a result of which:

> (a)   a conflict of interests or a significant risk conflict of arises;

> (b)   the public might reasonably conclude that the firm had been able to make use of the office or appointment for the advantage of the client: or

> (c)   the solicitor's ability to advise the client properly and impartially is inhibited.

Questions

1. Does the idea that fiduciaries should subjugate their own interests to those of the client justify the 'Standard Conception of Legal Ethics'? (See Stephen Pepper, chapter 5 at p 137ff supra.)

---

10   See M Napier and F Bawden *Conditional Fees – A Survival Guide* (London, Law Society, 1995) pp 46 and 87 suggesting that some clients might require independent advice before entering some conditional fee contracts.

2. Should all lawyer-client transactions be invalid in the absence of independent advice? What view of the distribution of power within the lawyer client relationship does the current rule presuppose? For what modern practice settings is this appropriate?

3. Your firm specialises in information technology law and has been asked to act for a newly formed company with few assets save for a potentially very profitable computer program. The company is likely either to make a lot of money in the medium term or to become insolvent very quickly. It has no money to pay your fees but its directors have proposed that you accept 50% of the equity in lieu of fees. Can you proceed on this basis?

4. Consider the view that fee related conflicts of interest between the role of lawyer and client are inevitable. What does this assume about the aims of lawyers? Are these assumptions consistent with the any, and if so which, of the theories of professionalism considered earlier? Do you know of any relevant empirical evidence?

5. **Percy's Case**: You represent Percy, a personal injury claimant, who is funding his own case. Quantum is not in dispute and has been agreed at £120,000 but there is a dispute about liability, though you consider the case to be very strong. Two days before the scheduled hearing, the lawyers acting for the defendant insurers offer to settle for £70,000 plus payment of all costs you have incurred so far (which you estimate to be £30,000), such costs to be paid without assessment.
i)   In what sense, if any, does this represent a conflict of interest for you as Percy's lawyer?
ii)   Would it be desirable to introduce a practice rule to the effect that in settlement negotiations discussion of the substance should be separate from and prior to discussion of costs?
iii)   How, if at all, does the analysis alter if the arrangement is funded through a conditional fee arrangement with a 25% uplift and the defendant offers £70,000 in damages plus your costs of £30,000 plus an uplift of £7,500.

6. **Humphrey's Case**: Humphrey has been advising Julia, who is in the process of divorcing her wealthy husband for several months. Humphrey travels with Julia to a number of meetings with her husband and his advisers both within the UK and abroad. After one trip abroad, Humphrey announces that he is to leave his wife and set up home with Julia. Should Humphrey continue to act for Julia? Has Humphrey breached his fiduciary duty to the client?

7. In what practice settings are sexual relationships between lawyer and client likely to be problematic? Should these issues be the subject of provisions in a professional code? Does principle 12.09 correctly capture the implications for lawyer-client relations of the fact that the relationship is a fiduciary relationship? Note the Canadian case of *Norberg v Weinrib* (1992) DLR 4th 449 in which the Supreme Court of Canada had to consider a claim for damages by a former drug addict whose doctor had prescribed

further drugs in return for sexual favours. The majority held the doctor liable in the tort of battery, the patient's consent having been vitiated by the inequality of bargaining power between them. The minority however held the doctor liable for breach of fiduciary duty.

8. Principle 15.04 of the LSGPC provides in note 2 that 'A solicitor should not enter into any arrangement or understanding with a client or prospective client prior to the conclusion of the matter giving rise to the retainer by which the solicitor acquires an interest in the publication rights with respect to that matter.'

Why should a client on trial for murder not remunerate the lawyer by granting the lawyer the right to publish the client's story?

9. Mary is an assistant solicitor in a firm which regularly acts for defendant insurers in personal injury litigation concerning accidents at work. John is an assistant at another firm in the same town which regularly acts for trade union funded claimants. Mary and John act against each other in a number of cases as a result of which they become friendly and, eventually, begin to live together.

What are the implications of this situation for Mary, John and the senior partners of their respective firms? Consider also s 6 of the Sex Discrimination Act 1975 and *Skyrail Oceanic v Coleman* [1981] ICR 864, CA.

2 Simultaneous conflict of interests

Consider the following questions in the light of principles 15.01 and 15.03 of the LSGPC and where relevant paras 603(e) and 608(b) (i) and (ii) of the CCB.[11]

1. **Clive's Case**: You have been engaged by an insurance company which covers dentists against professional negligence claims. The master policy provides cover up to a limit of £1 million and allows the insurance company to engage lawyers to undertake the defence of any claims made. In the event of a dispute about settlement, the dispute is to be referred to arbitration by leading counsel. Clive, the insured, is alleged to have cut a nerve whilst operating upon Glenda, causing her to suffer partial facial paralysis. Glenda is now suing Clive for negligence. You interview Clive who, after giving his account, indicates his indignation at what he considers to be an unwarranted claim and stresses the importance of settling the claim lest his professional reputation be damaged. After all the expert and medical evidence is disclosed, damages are agreed with the claimant's solicitors at £100,000. In your view, Glenda has only a 30% chance

---

11   Supra text to notes 5-7.

of succeeding on liability. The other side have indicated that they would be prepared to settle for £25,000 but the insurance company claims assessor instructing you has refused to pay this much and now proposes to take the case to trial. What, if any, are your professional obligations to Clive? (See further *Groom v Crocker* [1939] 1 KB 194.)

2. **Bill and Ben's Case**: You have been asked to represent Bill and Ben, aged 15 and 18 respectively, who are charged with obtaining goods by deception contrary to s 15 of the Theft Act 1968. The prosecution alleges that whilst they were in Azdo, a local sportswear shop, one of the boys switched the label on a pair of sports shoes so that the shoes bore a price tag lower than that at which Azdo intended to offer them for sale. The chief prosecution witness (the store detective) alleges that he saw the one of the boys switch the labels but admits to being unsure which one was the culprit (the boys are of similar height, hair colour and build). Though Ben admits to having been involved in shoplifting on a number of occasions he denies any wrongdoing on this occasion. Both boys deny switching the labels and allege a mistake on the part of the store.

May you represent both boys? Supposing that you do decide to represent both boys, does it make any difference if, on the day of the trial, the older boy admits that he switched the labels and says that he intends to plead guilty?

3. **Mr and Mrs James' Case**: You are a small-town provincial solicitor who has for many years acted in a number of matters for Mr and Mrs James. Indeed you consider them to be personal friends. One day Mrs James rings and tells you that she and her husband have separated and have resolved all matters between themselves. Mrs James tells you that she knows from previous experience that you are a good, sensible solicitor and she and her husband wish to consult you jointly. They would like you to prepare all the documents necessary to wrap the matter up. She adds that they do not want the matter to be blown out of all proportion and would like to resolve things in an amicable manner. How do you respond?

4. **Peter Morris' Case**: David Morris and Sarah Mason are partners in a law firm which has for many years represented David Morris' father Peter. Peter, who recently died, ran a profitable photographic business helped (part-time) by David. Peter's will left all his assets on trust for equal division between his four children (Irene, David, Mary and Sophie), all assets to be sold if division could not be agreed. Whilst the business was very profitable during Peter's lifetime it has little sale value. Sarah has been asked to act as solicitor to the executors (Mary and Sophie). She thinks that the best way forward is for David to continue to run the business. The best way to facilitate this would be for David to form a new company that would then lease the business premises and equipment from the estate in return for a monthly rent. However she is concerned that the situation may raise some difficult issues of professional ethics. Advise her.

The substantive law relating to simultaneous representation of clients with conflicting interests was thoroughly, if controversially, reviewed by the Privy Council in *Clark Boyce v Mouat*.[12] Mr Mouat wished to borrow money to pay for household repairs and persuaded his mother to borrow the money on the security of her house, with himself as guarantor. The intention was however that he should pay the mortgage. Mr Davis, Mr Mouat's normal solicitor and a family friend, refused to act so Mr Mouat took his mother to see Mr Boyce who agreed to act for both Mr and Mrs Mouat. When Mrs Mouat came to his office with her son for the signature of the documents, Boyce explained the nature of the transaction, pointing out to her that her home might be at risk and the conflict of interest between her and her son. Boyce urged Mrs Mouat to seek independent advice and offered to make the necessary arrangements. However, Mrs Mouat refused, indicating that she had made up her mind to support her son and did not require advice as to the wisdom of the transaction. At Boyce's request, she signed a letter acknowledging that she had been urged to seek independent advice but did not wish to do so. Mr Mouat later went bankrupt and Mrs Mouat was called upon to repay the loan. In these proceedings, she sued her solicitors for breach of contract and breach of fiduciary duty. She alleged that the solicitors should have refused to act for her in the absence of independent advice and, in relation to their fiduciary duty, that they had failed to make the full disclosure necessary to validate her consent to the joint representation. In particular, it was alleged that she ought to have been informed that i) Mr Mouat's normal solicitor had refused to act and ii) that Clarke Boyce & Co had no knowledge of her son's ability to service the mortgage. The Privy Council held that the solicitors were not liable, the judgment being given by Lord Jauncey.

> There is no general rule of law to the effect that a solicitor should never act for both parties in a transaction where their interests may conflict. Rather is the position that he may act provided that he has obtained the informed consent of both to his acting. Informed consent means consent given in the knowledge that there is a conflict between the parties and that as a result the solicitor may be disabled from disclosing to each party the full knowledge which he possesses as to the transaction or may be disabled from giving advice to one party which conflicts with the interests of the other. If the parties are content to proceed upon this basis the solicitor may properly act. In *Boulting v Association of Cinematograph Television and Allied Technicians* [1963] 1 All ER 716 at 729, [1963] 2 QB 606 at 636 Upjohn LJ said:
>
> > '...the client is entitled to the services of his solicitor who may not charge more than he is legally entitled to and must not put himself into a position where he may owe conflicting duties to different clients (see, eg, *Re Haslam and Hier-Evans* ([1902] 1 Ch 765)). But the person entitled to the benefit of the rule may relax it, provided he is of full age and sui juris and fully understands not only what he is doing but also what his legal rights are and that he is in part surrendering them.'
>
> *Farrington v Row McBride & Partners* [1985] 1 NZLR 83 concerned a solicitor who advised a client to invest money in a company which was also a client of his without disclosing that fact to the potential investor. Richardson J said (at 90):

12   [1993] 3 All ER 268 on appeal from the New Zealand Court of Appeal.

'A solicitor's loyalty to his client must be undivided. He cannot properly discharge his duties to one whose interests are in opposition to those of another client. If there is a conflict in his responsibilities to one or both he must ensure that he fully discloses the material facts to both clients and obtains their informed consent to his so acting: "No agent who has accepted an employment from one principal can in law accept an engagement inconsistent with his duty to the first principal from a second principal, unless he makes the fullest disclosure to each principal of his interest, and obtains the consent of each principal to the double employment" (*Fullwood v Hurley* ([1928] 1 KB 498 at 502,[1927] All ER Rep 610 at 611) per Scrutton LJ). And there will be some circumstances in which it is impossible, notwithstanding such disclosure, for any solicitor to act fairly and adequately for both.'

In the last sentence of that dictum Richardson J no doubt had in mind a situation where one client sought advice on a matter which would involve disclosure of facts detrimental to the interests of the other client.

In determining whether a solicitor has obtained informed consent to acting for parties with conflicting interests it is essential to determine precisely what services are required of him by the parties. In this case Holland J was satisfied that Mrs Mouat was not concerned about the wisdom of the transaction and was 'merely seek[ing] the services of the solicitor to ensure that the transaction [was] given proper and full effect by way of ascertaining questions of title and ensuring that by appropriate documentation the parties achieve[d] what they [had] contracted for'. Gault J considered that this finding was amply supported by the evidence. As has already been observed, Sir Gordon Bisson drew a different conclusion from the evidence, as did McGechan J. In their Lordships' opinion Holland and Gault JJ drew the correct conclusion. As Viscount Haldane LC observed in *Nocton v Lord Ashburton* [1914] AC 932 at 957, [1914–15] All ER Rep 45 at 54: 'it is only in exceptional circumstances that judges of appeal, who have not seen the witness in the box, ought to differ from the finding of fact of the judge who tried the case as to the state of mind of the witness.' Holland J had the advantage of seeing and hearing all the witnesses and of forming an impression therefrom as to their states of mind and what had occurred during the meeting in Mr Boyce's office. There are no exceptional circumstances which would justify differing from his conclusions on these matters.

Their Lordships are accordingly satisfied that Mrs Mouat required of Mr Boyce no more than that he should carry out the necessary conveyancing on her behalf and explain to her the legal implications of the transaction. Since Mrs Mouat was already aware of the consequences if her son defaulted Mr Boyce did all that was reasonably required of him before accepting her instructions when he advised her to obtain and offered to arrange independent advice. As Mrs Mouat was fully aware of what she was doing and had rejected independent advice, there was no duty on Mr Boyce to refuse to act for her. Having accepted instructions he carried these out properly and was neither negligent nor in breach of contract in acting and continuing to act after Mrs Mouat had rejected his suggestion that she obtain independent advice. Indeed not only did Mr Boyce in carrying out these instructions repeat on two further occasions his advice that Mrs Mouat should obtain independent advice but he told her in no uncertain terms that she would lose her house if Mr Mouat defaulted. One might well ask what more he could reasonably have done .

When a client in full command of his faculties and apparently aware of what he is doing seeks the assistance of a solicitor in the carrying out of a particular transaction, that solicitor is under no duty whether before or after accepting instructions to go beyond those instructions by proffering unsought advice on the wisdom of the transaction. To hold otherwise could impose intolerable burdens on solicitors.

It remains to consider the conclusion of the Court of Appeal that Mr Boyce was in breach of fiduciary duties. Sir Gordon Bisson's observations on this matter have already been set out. McGechan J agreed with these observations, albeit at somewhat greater length. That a solicitor owes a fiduciary duty to a client is not in doubt. The classic case where the duty arises is where a solicitor acts for a client in a matter in which he has a personal interest. In such a case there is an obligation on the solicitor to disclose his interest and, if he fails so to do, the transaction, however favourable it may be to the client, may be set aside at his instance (*Lewis v Hillman* (1852) 3 HL Cas 607, 10 ER 239). Another case of breach is where a solicitor acts for both parties to a transaction without disclosing this to one of them or where having disclosed it he fails, unbeknown to one party, to disclose to that party material facts relative to the other party of which he is aware. A fiduciary duty concerns disclosure of material facts in a situation where the fiduciary has either a personal interest in the matter to which the facts are material or acts for another party who has such an interest. It cannot be prayed in aid to enlarge the scope of contractual duties. Thus, there being no contractual duty on Mr Boyce to advise Mrs Mouat on the wisdom of entering into the transaction, she cannot claim that he nevertheless owed her a fiduciary duty to give that advice. Furthermore, any duty of disclosure can only extend to the solicitor's knowledge of facts and not to his lack of knowledge thereof.

Both Holland and Gault JJ considered that Mr Boyce's failure to disclose that Meares Williams had declined to act for Mr Mouat was not a failure to disclose information material to the transaction. Given the information which was then available to Mr Boyce and the fact that he saw nothing sinister in Meares Williams's refusal to act, their Lordships are satisfied that that information was not material information which should have been disclosed. It therefore follows that Mr Boyce was not in breach of any fiduciary obligation owed to Mrs Mouat.[13]

Notes

1. The New Zealand Court of Appeal has since suggested that there might be exceptional circumstances where a lawyer *is* required to give unsolicited advice as to the wisdom of a transaction: see *Haira v Burbery Mortgage Finance and Savings Ltd* [1995] 1 NZLR 396.

2. *Clarke Boyce* was decided at a time when the Law Society was considering requiring buyers and lenders involved in a domestic conveyance to have separate representation (the proposal was eventually dropped). Opponents and supporters of the scheme each claimed support from the Privy Council's judgment. Supporters alleged that

---

13   Ibid at pp 273-275H.

separate representation was warranted because buyers were not given sufficient information about the solicitors duty to the lender so as to enable them to consent to dual representation. Accepting that this was so, opponents argued that the judgment was based on the absence of an obligation to give unsolicited advice on the merits if merely technical legal services had been sought. See Richard Sayer and Robert Hegarty SJ (1994) 138(46) Sol Jo. Which view represents a correct interpretation of the judgment?

Questions

1. Did Mrs Mouat have sufficient information to enable her to give informed consent to the joint representation?

2. Dr Paul Finn, a leading expert on fiduciary law, has suggested in relation to informed consent to dual representation that:

> in some instances the point can surely be reached where no matter how full the disclosure, the consent of the [client] cannot and should not be regarded as binding. The subject matter in which the fiduciary's services are retained may be so complex and specialised, the beneficiary so untutored in that matter, that even with full disclosure he could not on his own make an intelligent judgment as to how his interests are to be best served. And that after all is the reason why ordinary members of the public engage professional advisers.[14]

Do you agree?

3. Lord Jauncey says lawyers are not required to give unsolicited advice about the wisdom of a transaction to adults of full age and capacity. What moral values does this view seek to promote?

4. What difference might the law of undue influence (which was not considered in the case) make to the situation in *Clarke Boyce?* See chapter 1 pp 22-23 supra.

5. Does the substantive law differ with respect to the issues considered in *Clarke Boyce* from the LSGPC? Should the Privy Council have considered the equivalent provision of the professional code in NZ (which were similar to those found in the LSGPC) when defining the solicitors' contractual duties?

The decision in *Clark Boyce v Mouat* has been the subject of considerable criticism on the grounds that a stricter approach was called for.[15] To these critics, Mrs Mouat's

---

14   P D Finn 'Conflicts of Interest, The Businessman and the Professional' (Papers from the Legal Research Foundation Seminar, University of Auckland, May 1987) p 28 citing American authorities collected in [1981] 94 Harv LR 1244 at 1311ff.

15   See for example R C Nolan (1994) 53 Cambridge Law Journal 34 and R Tobin [1994] Conveyancer 404.

unhappy experience shows the risks involved in relaxing the rules about conflict of interest. For others, however, a strict approach to conflicts of interest involves a narrow vision of legal work. The problem is that when faced with conflicting interests, the lawyer's role, according to the narrow view, is not to broker a solution to the conflict but rather to act as partisan advocate for one of the conflicting individuals, leaving the other(s) to be represented, if at all, by other lawyers. In some situations, such an approach may be wholly appropriate. In others, however, it seems either morally inappropriate or impractical or both. In this section, we consider two possible contexts for an alternative approach, namely family representation and multi-party litigation.

Family representation – the lawyer for the situation?

Since legal aid became available after the Second World War, matrimonial disputes have typically been resolved through a process in which each side is represented by and negotiates through a lawyer acting in faithful obedience to the values embodied in conflict of interest doctrine. Recently however, this process has been subjected to severe criticism. Not only is it viewed as overly expensive, but the involvement of lawyers is felt to lead to unnecessary adversarialism and hostility. Consequently, the Family Law Act 1996 paved the way for the withdrawal of legal aid from matrimonial disputes and its replacement by state funding of mediation. Similarly the Access to Justice Act 1999 imposes upon the Legal Services Commission's funding strategy a presumption that mediation is more appropriate than court proceedings[16]. Whatever the merits of this in general terms, what is striking for present purposes is the Law Society's acquiescence in the assumption that mediating solutions to conflict is not typical of lawyers' work. The LSGPC does in principle permit a solicitor to act as a mediator or conciliator in a domestic or commercial dispute[17]. However this permission is restricted in two important ways. The lawyer may not mediate if s/he has previously acted for and acquired confidential information about one of the parties to the dispute. This restricts the lawyer's ability to act in situations where their is a pre-existing relationship with the married couple, whereas it might be thought that it is in precisely those situations that mediation by a lawyer is most likely to succeed. Secondly, if a lawyer is engaged to act as an advocate then the lawyer may not subsequently act as a mediator or vice versa.[18] Richard Tur has argued has argued that these restrictions should be relaxed and lawyers encouraged to act as mediators. In the following extract, he considers some objections to his proposals and the further question of whether lawyers are in any way particularly well qualified to act as mediators.

16   Access to Justice Act 1999, s 8(3).
17   Principle 15.01 note 3.
18   Principle 22.03 of the LSGPC provides that: 'A solicitor must not provide an ADR service in connection with a dispute in which he or she has, or a member of his or her firm, has acted as a professional adviser to any party. nor, having provided an ADR service, may a solicitor or member of his firm act for any participant individually in relation to the dispute.'

One possible objection to my proposal is that lawyers are simply too combative and adversarial to function as mediators…

(however) some commentators suggest that critics of the legal system and lawyers have paid too much attention to adversarial aspects and the ethics of trial advocacy and not enough attention to the diversity of legal practice: the lawyer's role as an advocate, though a notorious one, is but one role that he plays in the legal system. It is no secret that many disputes settled by means of negotiation, mediation and arbitration, and the lawyer's role, in addition to one of advocate, is to be a counsellor, negotiator/conciliator, and adviser. But if this is so, then too much concern with the ethics of advocacy gives a false unity to the field of legal ethics.

In the resolution of divorce disputes in England, for all the current interest in mediation in divorce, there is no doubt that solicitors continue to dominate the scene. The solicitor is more than just a partisan and a degree of sensitivity to the client's emotional state … is essential … a solicitor who lacks this understanding is likely to be ineffective in all aspects, including the conveying of sound legal advice. Since family lawyers have a degree of sensitivity to clients' emotional states and also have training and experience in financial, property, and trust matters, family lawyers are well placed to assist parties reach the optimum outcome through a process of legally-informed but ethically-sensitive mediation.

Parties to a matrimonial breakdown may, of course, be prone to irrational acts and decisions. In some ways the present system of separate representation and communication only through their legal advisers creates a situation analogous to the 'Prisoner's Dilemma':

> Two prisoners are held by the police for a crime. The police separate the two prisoners, and inform each that if he will give evidence against the other, he can go free. The prisoners are aware that if only one gives evidence, the other will receive the maximum penalty, say 20 years; but if both give evidence, each will receive a moderate sentence, for example, 10 years. However, if neither gives evidence, each will be tried on a minor charge, with a penalty of a fine and less than a year in prison. Each would prefer to go free, but if both give evidence, both will go to jail for years. On the other hand, opting for the minor charge by refusing to give evidence may in fact result in the most severe penalty if the other gives evidence. Refusing to give evidence is defined as a co-operative response, since both must do so for the choice to yield mutually beneficial payoffs. Giving evidence may be seen as competitive – an effort to obtain the best outcome for oneself at the expense of the other, or as defensive, in an effort to thwart the competitive intention of the other. Experimental subjects who have played this game typically make competitive choices despite the collectively poor payoffs this strategy yields

The implications of the Prisoner's Dilemma for handling divorce disputes are significant. There is quite often an atmosphere of mutual mistrust, exacerbated by :a total breakdown in communications either by choice or imposed on the parties by their lawyers, and one spouse is readily deterred from making co-operative choices by the reasonable apprehension that the other will make competitive choices. In that state of belief, the rational thing to do is also to make a competitive, not a co-operative, choice.

But, as the Prisoner's Dilemma so clearly illustrates, both parties are worse off if both make competitive choices. Faced with this insight into human psychology it is difficult to see that the attitudes of lawyers towards combat or negotiation can have much impact other than at the margins. If psychological imperatives lead clients into mutually damaging competitive choices, then a psychological solution must be found. Happily there is one.

Psychologists interested in social interaction have carried out empirical studies of co-operation and competition. The classic study is Muzafer Sherif's 'Robbers' Cave' field experiment:

> Boys (perhaps female or mixed subjects would act differently) at a summer camp were divided into two groups which were then separated. In the first phase of the study, each group was put into situations designed to develop group solidarity and group identity. In the second phase, the two groups participated in a series of contests aimed at producing competitiveness and increased group solidarity. This led to considerable rivalry and even hostility between the two groups. The last phase of the study addressed the question of how two hostile groups can be brought into harmony. Simply bringing the groups together for social events only increased hostility. However when the experimenters created a series of 'urgent' problems which required the collaborative efforts of the two groups to overcome – such as a breakdown in the camp water supply – intergroup hostility gradually decreased, new friendships developed across group lines, and a spirit of co-operativeness ensued..

Psychologists have concluded from such experiments that co-operative activity is most likely where interacting parties share a common goal and a common means of achieving that goal. Applied to the choices facing divorcing parties, the Robbers' Cave experiment suggests that if the divorcing coupes could acknowledge the seriousness of their situation they would be more likely to adopt co-operative rather than competitive strategies.

The Prisoner's Dilemma can only occur in circumstances of ignorance. If the two prisoners could collude both would refuse to give evidence. It is essential, therefore, for the police to keep them apart. Mediation has the great advantage of seeking to open up to the parties themselves access to information necessary to make rational choices. In addition, a mediator is much less likely than either party's own lawyer to harbour or encourage false optimism. A lawyer acting for one client may well seek to re-assure that client that things will work out well in the end, and for all sorts of reasons divorce lawyers are anxious to soothe their own clients. This may encourage a belief on both sides that the situation is less serious than it is and that belief renders co-operative choices less likely. If the parties meet with one lawyer-mediator, information can be exchanged and a real sense of emergency generated. Attention can be directed towards solving the problem rather than in winning a victory which, given the costs of the battle, is very likely to be pyrrhic. It appears that the lawyer-mediator has (or can acquire) the necessary skills to act for both parties in an 'amicable' divorce. It also seems that the one-lawyer option offers enhanced prospects of settlement by promoting the psychological conditions for co-operative choices. Clearly, there are ethical and economic payoffs too. Parties are likely to be better off given this option and family lawyers could take moral credit for their achievements...

...one remaining question is – what is it about lawyers that fits them for this central role in family matters? The prevailing conception of the 'good lawyer' is instrumentalist.

An alternative conception might be developed in terms of virtue. Given some basic assumptions about the necessary indeterminacy of and conflicts among legal rules and principles there is more or less room, depending on circumstances, at the point of application for choice. That choice involves moral judgement. Since the legal system makes contact with peoples' lives at least sometimes, perhaps often, through the mediation of lawyers, the manner in which these lawyers understand, interpret and apply the law becomes very important and their choices at the point of law-application have privileged status.

If lawyers approach their tasks critically, sensitively and imaginatively, theirs is a creative, developmental role. Of course, there are no guarantees that these lawyers will apply their ingenuity to the production of 'good' outcomes. Given the contested and polarised context of law-application at least some lawyers, some of the time, will be seeking to produce outcomes that some members of society, perhaps a majority, would regard as morally problematic. In this, the lawyer is no different from the non-lawyer. Some non-lawyers, too, seek outcomes that some members of society, perhaps a majority, would regard as morally problematic.

Good lawyers are to be valued not for the results that they can achieve but because of their intrinsic characteristic virtues; analytical rigour, discriminating judgment, ethical sensitivity, creative imagination, and fidelity to a cluster of core values internal to law, and lawyering. The good lawyer is in the balancing business answering judgement calls about synthesising conflicting objectives and values such as justice and certainty, freedom and security, individualism and communitarianism, private objectives and public interest. This brings us to applied ethics and the interface between general moral principles and individual discretion. Reasonable individuals may reasonably differ, not only at the margins but also as to the basic commitments that constitute character, lifestyle, and objectives. Ethics is not about arriving at the one right answer. Nor can ethical problems be solved once and for all by legislative fiat. Judgement calls will always be made and there will always be a margin of individual appreciation in the application of rules and principles of law, procedure, and ethics to the concrete and particular facts of real life circumstances. These judgement calls are necessarily ethical, calling upon the lawyer conscientiously to address questions of right and wrong in a bewildering range of particular circumstances. A life in the law is, necessarily, an adventure in applied ethics.

Good lawyers understand and can express the parties' position as well, perhaps even better, than the parties themselves. In addition, they can see ways of reconciling parties' apparently conflicting objectives with each other and with the requirements of law. Since this is what lawyers do, lawyers could (in my view should be allowed to) do it for families and for divorcing couples where the reconciliation of the competing objectives is the point of the exercise. This is, as Shaffer suggests, an ethically worthwhile pursuit and presents the family lawyer as a professional family friend.[19]

Leaving aside pragmatic arguments about the costs which are undoubtedly incurred when those with interests which are perceived to be in conflict are urged by their lawyer to obtain independent advice, perceptive critics of conflict of interest doctrine

19   R H S Tur 'Family Lawyering and Legal Ethics' in C Parker and C Sampford (eds) *Legal Ethics and Legal Practice: Contemporary Issues* (Clarendon, Oxford, 1995) pp 162, 164-166 and 168-170. I have omitted the internal citations.

(such as Professor Thomas Shaffer whose work is considered in chapter 2[20]) have pointed out that underlying the doctrine is the contested notion that law and therefore lawyers exist to vindicate individual autonomy and rights. For these critics, the established approach begs the question of why there should be one individual client to whom undivided loyalty should be shown, for the individual cannot be understood or identified outside the web of relationships of which the individual is but a part. Why in Mr and Mrs James case (supra) should we not say that the client is the family just as we say that lawyers owe duties to companies rather than to its individual directors or members. Indeed current law recognises that the person funding legal services may not necessarily be the client and that the lawyer may therefore have problems identifying which of several individuals is the client. Critics go one step further however and refuse to try and find a single individual whom the lawyer may be said to represent. In the words of Louis Brandeis, later a Justice of the US Supreme Court, the lawyer is 'the lawyer for the situation.'

Note

Conflict of interest doctrine requires a prior determination of exactly who has become the lawyer's client for example in Clive's case (supra p 440). As a matter of law, undertakings to apply professional skills for the benefit of another may become legally binding even in the absence of contract.[1] It follows that a lawyer-client relationship may arise as between the lawyer and someone other than the person paying the lawyer's fee, for example where a contract of liability insurance gives the liability insurer the right to instruct (and pay the fees of) the defendant's lawyer.

Questions

1. What are the lessons of *Clark Boyce v Mouat* for the notion that a lawyer may represent the family as such rather than its individual members?

2. Do you agree that a strict application of the prohibition of conflict of interest doctrine is appropriate in some but not all of the problems set out above (pp 440-441) ? If so, what criteria distinguish those cases where it is and is not appropriate?

3. Identify the client(s) in Clive's case and Khan's case (chapter 1 pp 19-23 supra). How may a lawyer who already has a client avoid entering another lawyer-client relationship which leads to a conflict of interest, for example in Khan's case?

---

20   See chapter 2 at p 51 and also Thomas L Shaffer 'The Legal Ethics of Radical Individualism' (1987) 65 Texas Law Review 963.

1   *Hedley Byrne & Co Ltd v Heller & Partners* [1964] AC 465; *Midland Bank Trust Co Ltd v Hett Stubbs & Kemp* [1979] Ch 384; *Henderson v Merret Syndicates Ltd* [1995] 2 AC 145.

4. Do you agree that it is sometimes appropriate for lawyers to act as 'the lawyer for the situation' and represent clients with conflicting relationships in order to further ongoing relationships? Peter Morris' Case (supra p 441) above is modelled on a real-life incident in the practice of Louis Brandeis for which he was severely criticised during hearings to test his fitness for nomination to the US Supreme Court. See further J P Frank 'The Legal Ethics of Louis D Brandeis' (1964-1965) 17 Stanford Law Review 683.

5. Do you agree with Richard Tur that lawyers are by virtue of their professional and academic training peculiarly suited to be mediators?

Multi-party litigation

One area where a strict approach to conflicts of interest may be inappropriate is multi-party litigation. Multi-party litigation may arise in a number of different ways. It may arise, for example, when a large number of people are injured at the same time by one act of negligence, such as the police failure to control football supporters which led to many people being crushed to death in what became known as the Hillsborough Disaster. Alternatively, it may arise when a large number of people suffer personal injuries at different times due to a single act of negligence, such as the negligent design and testing of a pharmaceutical product. Finally, a large number of consumers may suffer identical economic losses when a commercial concern breaches an undertaking given to all its customers – for example a computer company breaks its promise to provide free support after sale. A distinctive feature of multi-partly litigation is that there are huge cost savings to be made from disposing of a large number of claims in one set of proceedings. Indeed, in some instances the low sums at stake for each individual plaintiff mean that it is the aggregation of their claims which makes litigation economically feasible.

In many jurisdictions[2], such claims are dealt with by a class action procedure. Typically, these proceedings can be brought only when the court is willing to certify that a number of potential claims involve common issues so that the common issues can be dealt with most efficiently by allowing a representative party to litigate these issues on behalf of other claimants. In some jurisdictions, claims may even be brought on behalf of plaintiffs who have as yet no accrued cause of action, for example plaintiffs who have been exposed to asbestos as a result of the defendant's tort but who have not as yet developed any asbestos-related illness. Claimants will normally be bound by the result unless they opt out of the action, which can be settled only with the approval of the judge. Approval may be given to aggregate awards, that is to a settlement which provides for payment of a lump sum by the defendant in satisfaction of all claims of that class. The award is then distributed via an administrative mechanism established by the settlement applying criteria significantly more flexible than the formal rules on the assessment of damages. As a result, the litigation may yield not a

---

2   The following account draws on the report of the Scottish Law Commission *Multi-Party Actions* (Edinburgh, HMSO, 1996).

lump sum for each plaintiff but an institution procedurally similar to the social security system, though funded by the defendant. Whilst such procedures have traditionally been regarded as valuable tools making cost effective claims which would otherwise be impractical, recent developments in the US have revealed a new perspective. Commentators[3] have noted that defendants may also have much to gain from class actions, namely early settlement at a defined cost of a potentially protracted series of legal disputes. The problem is that in a class action there may be only very weak client control over the performance of the lawyers. Consequently, a settlement containing very generous provisions for payment of fees may tempt the lawyers to agree to arrangements that provide only very inadequate compensation. Judges concerned to see the speedy disposal of cases may acquiesce in what is in effect a collusive settlement, a possibility recently recognised by the Supreme Court.[4]

In England, the special features of multi-party litigation were not formally recognised until special provisions were introduced into the new Civil Procedure Rules to allow the making of 'Group Litigation Orders'. Nevertheless multi-partly litigation grew enormously during the last 15 years of the 20th century, its growth being concealed perhaps by the fact that most of the cases were settled rather than being litigated to judgment. In the absence of a class action procedure, first instance judges were allowed by the Court of Appeal a wide discretion to fashion appropriate procedures on an ad hoc basis. Directions could be given for example that all plaintiffs having a particular claim against a defendant should be represented by a named solicitor and should adopt a master statement of claim to be served by that solicitor. One formal difference between these ad hoc procedures and a true class action procedure was that a plaintiff's claim could not be subsumed within the group action without their consent. Consequently, there was the possibility of individual plaintiffs refusing to litigate and therefore accept liability for costs but being able nonetheless to take the benefit of any judgment obtained by current litigants. In many cases, however, there were strong incentives to join the group: the Legal Aid Board might refuse to fund those who did not and the relatively short limitation periods applying to personal injury actions soon required those who knew they might have a claim to issue proceedings and thus submit themselves to the jurisdiction of the court.

The chief problem for litigants in this country was, and perhaps remains, the uncertain contours of the procedures being evolved by the courts. Some leading UK practitioners have complained that

> Participants in multi-party cases in the UK have on occasion found themselves in a position not unlike that of the members of a football team who have started a match only to find out just before half-time that the referee is operating a changed set of rules, by which time half the players have been sent off for breaching those rules, leaving behind too few players to continue the match[5] .

3   J Coffee Jnr 'Class Wars: the Dilemma of the Mass Tort Class Action' (1995) 13 Columbia Law Review 1343.
4   See *Georgine v Amchem Products Inc* 157 FRD 24b (ED Pa 1964).
5   M Day, Paul Balen, and Geraldine McCool *Multi-Party Litigation – A Practitioners Guide to Pursuing Group Claims* (London, Legal Action Group, 1995) p 13.

If this is an accurate diagnosis of the problem, then the new Civil Procedure Rules are unlikely to solve it since they are extremely brief and leave maximum discretion in the hands of procedural judges. It is unclear for instance whether the court may make an an order which binds claimants who have not chosen to join the group. Nor is it clear whether judicial approval is ever required for settlement.[6]

Group litigation is similar in important ways to what in the United States is called institutional reform litigation, in which claims are brought under a class-action procedure that a large institution typically an organ of the state is organised in such a way as to infringe the claimants' civil rights. For example, it might be alleged that the provision of racially segregated schooling infringes the rights of black schoolchildren to equality before the law. The aim of the litigation would be not simply a declaration of the illegitimacy of current arrangements but a decree specifying and requiring the setting up of alternative legitimate arrangements. In the following extract, Deborah Rhode considers the challenge posed by this sort of litigation for conflict of interests doctrine.

> A fundamental premise of American adjudicative structures is that clients, not their counsel, define litigation objectives. Thus, the American Bar Association's current and proposed ethical codes both emphasise that an attorney must defer to the client's wishes on matters affecting the merits of legal action. However, by presupposing an individual client with clearly identifiable views, these codes elide a frequent and fundamental difficulty in class action proceedings. In many such cases, the lawyer represents an aggregation of litigants with unstable, inchoate, or conflicting preferences. The more diffuse and divided the class, the greater the problems in defining its objectives.
>
> Much of the renovation required concerns our concept of class representation. In particular, we need a more coherent theory of class interests and of the role plaintiff preferences should play in defining class objectives. As a first cut at reconceptualisation, this article posits a theory of representation mandating full disclosure of, although not necessarily deference, to class sentiment. A central premise is that the class as an entity has interests that may not be coextensive with the preferences of its current membership. Often those able to register views will be insufficiently disinterested or informed to speak for the entire constituency of present and future class members who will be affected by the court's decree. Nonetheless, preferences matter, not because they are conclusive of class interests, but because their disclosure is critical to the efficacy and legitimacy of judicial intervention ...
>
> School desegregation cases provide the most well-documented instances of conflict. Both commentators and litigators have described in some detail the balkanisation within minority communities over fundamental questions of educational policy. Dispute has centred on the relative importance of integration, financial resources, minority control, and ethnic identification in enriching school environments. Constituencies that support integration in principle have disputed its value in particular settings where extended bus rides, racial tension, or white flight seem likely concomitants of judicial redistricting. Some minority administrators, teachers, and parental organisations have opposed

---

6   Rule 19.11 (3)(b) and r 19.12 (1)-(3) suggest that such orders may be made and that the binding effect on those outside the group may be dependent on a settlement being embodied in a court order, thus in effect making judicial approval necessary. However the position is unclear.

interdistrict remedies that would close minority schools or dilute minority control. Even class members who accept the necessity of some busing will often divide on the merits of particular desegregation plans, which involve disproportionate burdens on minority students or transportation of primary grade students...

As noted previously, the violations at issue in most structural reform cases do not admit of only one resolution; prevailing doctrine will be indifferent as to at least some remedial choices. Many technical aspects of school desegregation, prison reform, or employment discrimination remedies 'incorporate considerations that might not be rooted in any direct and obvious way in the constitutional value that occasions the intervention'. To be sure, in some instances, principles of comity and federalism will argue for deferring to defendants' remedial proposals so long as they fall within constitutionally acceptable boundaries. But the location of those boundaries will frequently be open to dispute. Indeed, as Owen Fiss has suggested, 'more often than not the dynamics that led to the initial violation prevent the defendant from using its own expertise effectively to control its own behaviour.' Institutional politics, inertia, and concerns for self-exoneration may unduly constrain opposing parties' choices of alternatives. For that reason, plaintiffs typically play an active role in designing indeterminate remedies. Moreover, accommodating class preferences on issues of profound personal, but little doctrinal, significance will often prove a desirable implementation strategy.

Of course, in many cases, to be amplified at length below, those preferences will not be controlling; current plaintiffs or their guardians will be insufficiently disinterested or informed to speak for the entire class that will be bound by the court's decrees. But even if their views are not dispositive, those litigants have a strong stake in seeing their position put forward on issues that could materially affect the quality of their lives. Insofar as prevailing legal norms afford scope for accommodating plaintiff concerns, the judge should have information regarding the full range of class sentiment.

Frequently that sentiment will not be self-revealing. Much institutional reform litigation presents opportunities for dispute that are less easily identified than in other class actions, or individual suits. Where a claim is for monetary damages alone, the interests of various plaintiff subgroups are readily apparent. An adequate working assumption is that for any fraction, more compensation is better than less. So too, in much private-law litigation with broad precedential impact, the court can predict the preferences of those not present. Tort victims will generally wish the broadest possible liability and damage rules; insurer's interests are to the contrary. But when remedial choices involve complex forms of injunctive relief, with many opportunities for trade offs among subgroups within a plaintiff class, prediction becomes far more difficult. Thus, reported decisions reflect a broad variety of circumstances in which courts and counsel failed to appreciate the nature and intensity of class concerns until after entry of a decree.

That sort of failure is troubling in several respects. Most obviously, it will increase the expense and delay of proceedings, if disaffected parties subsequently challenge the adequacy of their representation and attempt to reopen matters already resolved. Moreover, misperceptions about party preferences may unnecessarily diminish the efficacy of judicial intervention.

It is, of course, difficult to document in any concrete fashion the causal linkages between participation, legitimacy, and effective implementation of legal norms. In some contexts those linkages may have been overstated. Yet virtually all of our governance structures presuppose some relationship. As political theorists since Burke have argued, no decision making process dependent on representative relationships can have a 'long or sure existence' without some grounding in constituent support. In both concept and implementation, all systems of representation demand some measure of consent...

CLASS COUNSEL

A familiar refrain among courts and commentators is that lawyers assume special responsibilities in class litigation. According to one circuit court of appeals, the duty to ensure adequate representation rests 'primarily upon counsel for ... in addition to the normal obligations of an officer of the court, and ... counsel to parties of the litigation, class action counsel possess, in a very real sense, fiduciary obligations to those not before the court'. Principal among those duties is the responsibility to apprise the trial judge of conflicting interests that may warrant separate representation or other corrective measures.

Although unobjectionable in concept, that role definition has frequently proved unworkable in practice. To be sure, many attorneys make considerable efforts to appreciate and accommodate the broadest possible spectrum of class sentiment. Particularly if conflicts are likely to come to the court's attention through other sources, counsel may find it prudent to broad the issue first. A demonstrated sensitivity to dissension could persuade the court that other procedural safeguards are unnecessary. Of course, these are precisely the circumstances in which an activist role for class counsel is least needed. Indeed, absent pre-emptive action by the class attorney, other parties may be able to provide a fuller record on the merits of separate representation. Moreover, where the range and intensity of divergent preferences within the class are unlikely to surface without counsel's assistance, he often has strong prudential and ideological reasons not to provide it. One need not be a raving realist to suppose that such motivations play a more dominant role in shaping attorney's conduct than Rule 23's directives and the accompanying judicial gloss.

PRUDENTIAL INTERESTS

An attorney active in institutional reform class actions is subject to a variety of financial, tactical, and professional pressures that constrain his response to class conflicts. Of course, none of these constraints is unique to this form of litigation. And the intensity of such pressures varies considerably depending inter alia, on the sources of funding and organisation support for particular cases. Nonetheless, it is important to identify, in generic form, the range of prudential interests that can affect counsel's management of internecine disputes, and the inadequacy of conventional correctives.

The most patent of these interests arises from the financial underpinnings of institutional reform litigation. Support for such cases derives largely from limited public interest funding and from the award by Courts to prevailing parties of counsel's fees. Among the factors affecting the attorney's fee award are the relief obtained, the costs of attaining it, and the number of other counsel who have contributed to the result. Given the expense of institutional reform class actions, few litigators can remain impervious to fee-related considerations or organisational budget constraints. And flushing out dissension among class members can provide costly in several respects.

For example, opposing parties often seek to capitalise on class dissension by filing motions for decertification. If such efforts prove successful, class counsel may lose a substantial investment that he cannot, as a practical matter recoup from former class members. At a minimum, such motions result in expense, delay, and loss of bargaining leverage, and deflect resources from trial preparation. Certification disputes may also trigger involvement of additional lawyers, who would share the limelight, the control over litigation decisions and, under some circumstances, the resources available for attorneys' fees.

Exposing conflict can also impede settlement arrangements that are attractive to class counsel on a number of grounds. As in many other litigation contexts, attorneys often have a bias to settle not shared by their clients. Since institutional reform plaintiffs generally do not underwrite the costs of litigation, their primary interest is in the result attained; the time and effort necessary to attain it are of less concern. Yet from the attorney's perspective, a modest settlement may generate a result 'bearing a higher ratio to the cost of the work than a much larger recovery obtained only after extensive discovery, a long trial and an appeal'. For example, if the prospects for prevailing on the merits are uncertain, some plaintiffs will see little to lose and everything to gain from persistence. That viewpoint may be inadequately aired by class counsel, who has concerns for his reputation as well as completing claims on his time and his organisation's resources to consider.

The potential for attorney-client conflicts is compounded when a proposed settlement makes extremely generous, or totally inadequate, provision for class counsel. Of course a lawyer may attempt to avoid compromising influences by refusing to discuss fees until agreement on all other issues is final. However, that strategy is not necessarily in anyone's interest if it inhibits favourable settlement offers, and many defendants are reluctant to compromise without some understanding of their total liability. Moreover, in an escalating number of civil rights cases, defendants have sought to make settlement on the merits conditional on counsel's waiver or curtailment of claims to statutory compensation.

Although the difficulty arising from simultaneous negotiation over fees and substantive issues has not escaped professional notice, neither courts nor bar associations have adequately monitored the practice or its results. Apart from broad injunctions against conflicting interests, the ABA's current Code and proposed Model Rules take no position on the issue of simultaneous discussion, and only one bar ethics committee has taken steps to control it. The Supreme Court declined a recent opportunity to provide further guidance, and lower courts have proved similarly reticent.

Thus except in a small minority of jurisdictions that have unequivocally prohibited simultaneous negotiation over fees and substantive issues, class attorneys are left in a vulnerable position. By refusing to make package agreements or to waive adequate compensation, the lawyer risks pre-empting settlement. By accepting a liberal reward for his services, the attorney may in fact or appearance be recouping his own investment at his clients' expense. Thus, no matter what course he elects, counsel will have difficulty

---

7   The Model Rules of Professional Conduct were still under discussion when this article was written.

preventing fee related considerations from affecting his assessment of settlement opportunities and his willingness to expose contrary views.

A final set of problems emerges in test-case litigation. In some instances, counsel may be reluctant to espouse positions that are at odds with those he has taken or intends to take in other proceedings or that could establish an unwelcome precedent. Moreover, test case litigation often generates settlement biases directly converse to those discussed above. Once a lawyer has prepared a claim with potentially significant impact, he may be disinclined to settled. He almost certainly would not share some plaintiff's enthusiasm for pre-or post-trial agreements promising generous terms for the litigants but little recognition and no precedential value for similarly situated victims. Few professionals, class attorneys included, can make decisions wholly independent of concerns about their careers and reputations among peers, potential clients, and funding sources. Litigating well-publicised institutional reform cases can provide desirable trial experience, generate attractive new cases, legitimate organisational objective in the eyes of private donors, and enhance attorneys' personal standing in the legal community. Where such rewards are likely, counsel may tend to discount preferences for a low-visibility settlement, particularly if it falls short of achieving ideological objectives to which he is strongly committed.

COURTS

Both Rule 23 and the due process clause vest ultimate responsibility for ensuring adequate representation in the trial judge. To discharge that obligation, he has a broad range of procedural options, explored in some detail below. As a threshold matter, however, what bears emphasis is the court's frequent lack of information – or incentive to demand it – concerning the need to invoke these procedural devices.

Despite the judiciary's formal responsibilities, constraints of time and role militate against an active oversight posture. In this context, departures from the courts' traditional umpireal stance often seem a thankless enterprise. Effectively monitoring class counsel's representation could require more personal innuendo and factual investigation than many trial judges are disposed to supply. As one federal district court has noted, a judge who took seriously his mandate to police the fee aspects of settlement agreements would necessarily find himself 'in the posture of a bad guy'; where neither defence counsel nor any class members complained, why should the judge want to 'interject himself into the arrangement?' It is, as Shirley Hufstedler has observed, difficult enough to induce trial courts to assume the unaccustomed role of superintending complex institutions. To ask that they also become self-initiated proctors of counsel's performance requires an even less congenial departure from conventional judicial functions.

Moreover, many trial courts face staggering caseloads and seemingly interminable claims on their time. Where the pressures to clear dockets are substantial, the costs of smoking out conflict may seem prohibitive. For if finding one set of class representatives and their counsel inadequate does not terminate proceedings, it will likely prolong them. From a trial court's perspective, more is seldom merrier. Multiple representation multiplies problems, both administrative and substantive. More parties means more papers, more scheduling difficulties, and more potential for objection to any given ruling or settlement proposal. Increasing the visibility of class cleavages may also increase their intensity, thereby reducing the possibility for settlement or exposing the trial court to greater risks of reversal on appeal...

The potential benefits attending independent advocacy are readily apparent. Constituencies whose concerns are antithetical or peripheral to those of the class representatives receive a hearing. Such participation may assist courts in formulating remedies that best accommodate all interests affected by judicial decree. Since many civil rights litigators operate under severe resource constraints, the inclusion of additional advocates with separate funding sources could often improve factual deliberations. Particularly in contexts such as school desegregation, where the concept of a litigating amicus first took hold, the contribution of Justice Department attorneys and private practitioners, as well as civil rights organisations, has been enormous. And insofar as dissenters believe their values have been forcefully advocated, they may be more supportive of both the process and result of judicial deliberations.

How frequently separate representation will in fact improve or legitimate particular decisions, is however, open to question. In this as in other decision making contexts, problems of bias, timing, manageability, and expense all render the pluralist model less attractive in practice than in theory.

As long as a given constituency's views are still mediated through self-appointed representatives and their counsel, the potential for biased advocacy remains. Certainly the pluralist approach cannot fully redress difficulties arising from attorneys' prudential or ideological concerns. If, for example, counsel representing intervenors has substantive commitments to a particular remedial strategy, or strong professional stakes in certain settlement offers, he may consciously or unconsciously shade his communications with class members. As has been amply documented in other contexts, lawyers' techniques of 'impression management' can readily reshape client sentiment. Given the absence of any adequate mechanisms for assuring counsel's accountability to his clients, a proliferation of participants will at times simply exacerbate problems of bias.

Similarly, adding attorneys can be counterproductive if it generates a more distorted account of membership concerns than that emerging from a single advocate's presentation. Like other interest groups, each litigant faction is likely to overstate the extent and intensity of its support. Since would be intervenors or amici need not voice interests other than their own, their involvement may distort the trial court's perception of aggregate class preferences and skew settlement negotiations accordingly. As one experienced public interest litigator has observed, it does not help to have 'lawyers representing ten different interest groups objecting to ten different aspects of a proposed decree, if the court has no sense of how substantial a constituency each represents'. When self-appointed volunteers lack a significant following within the class, tailoring remedial responses to meet their preferences may ill serve plaintiffs' collective interests. This is not, of course, to suggest that separate representation is inadvisable wherever distortion might occur. Excluding some concerned participants solely because others have not stepped forward may enhance neither the quality nor the perceived legitimacy of decision making. The point, rather, is that where the court is interested in obtaining a fair cross-section of class concerns, separate representation is not in itself a sufficient response.

Related difficulties with the pluralist strategy involve issues of timing. To avoid unnecessary expense and complication, courts certifying diverse classes may resist subdivision at the outset but reserve it is an option should schisms later develop. Yet the extent of conflict frequently will not be apparent until the parties propose a settlement or the court enters a remedial order. At that point, defining subclasses whose separate counsel could upset the proposed disposition will be costly to all concerned. Precisely when conflicts are most concrete, the pressures on the parties and courts to overlook them are most intense...

THE MAJORITARIAN RESPONSE: DIRECT PARTICIPATION THROUGH PLEBISCITES AND PUBLIC HEARINGS

Under the federal rules governing injunctive suits, trial courts must afford class members notice and an opportunity to be heard before approving a pre-trial settlement, and may mandate notification in other circumstances as a matter of discretion. Soliciting opinions directly from class members can serve two purposes. Through questionnaires or invitations to convey comments, the trial judge may attempt to assess the extent of conflict and the appropriateness of separate representation. Alternatively, the expression of class sentiment can enable courts or counsel to gauge support for particular litigation objectives or remedial alternatives. The following discussion focuses on the utility of majoritarian strategies for the latter purpose, that of identifying aggregate class preferences. Insofar as membership sentiment serves only to signal a need for independent advocates, its ultimate usefulness is, of course, subject to the pluralist limitations analysed above.

As a means of conveying information to the court and a sense of participation to class members, majoritarian strategies seemingly offer several advantages over pluralist devices. The first is economic. Relatively speaking, talk is cheap, at least when it occurs among class members rather than through separate counsel. Even with large classes, trial judges can often minimise notice and processing costs through reliance on non-individualised methods of communication and information from court appointed experts. Moreover, soliciting class preferences directly, rather than through the mediating influence of attorneys' or named representatives, may reduce distortion and enhance individuals' sense of efficacy and confidence in the decision making process. In practice, however, this approach is vulnerable to three serious objections, largely overlooked by advocates of enhanced client control in class proceedings. Absent extraordinary expenditures, the views elicited from notice and hearings will frequently be unrepresentative, uninformed, and unresponsive to a range of concerns particularly significant in institutional reform litigation.

To provide meaningful evidence of class preferences, responses to written notices or attendance at open meetings must reflect a fair cross section of the class as a whole. The scant empirical data available raise significant doubts about how frequently this condition could be met. Even in cases affording strong incentives for written response, where class members are notified that they can recover damages merely by mailing a single proof of loss, only 10% to 15% have done so. Absent some efforts to ascertain the representativeness of respondents – efforts that are rarely if ever undertaken in injunctive class actions - the reliability of survey replies is questionable. Yet even judges who acknowledge that deficiency seem unperturbed. After conceding that class responses to proposed prison regulations 'may not be a statistically sufficient sample', one district court blandly asserted that the returns 'more than adequately' conveyed plaintiff sentiment.

Reliance on views expressed at public meetings or settlement hearings presents similar difficulties. Interviews with class action litigators confirm the difficulty of convincing a representative sample of the class to attend. Attorneys who have held open meetings in school desegregation and employment cases generally report poor attendance. Judicial decisions that disclose the percentage of class members present at settlement hearings reflect equally low turnouts, even when there is evidence of strong opposition to a proposed decree. That community organisers generally experienced comparable attendance rates at the height of the War on Poverty suggests that the problems of mobilisation are deep seated if not intractable.

Although class members' failure to register dissent has often been taken to denote satisfaction, such inferences are troubling on several grounds. Rarely will class members have sufficient understanding of the meaning of notice, the positions of counsel, or the remedial alternatives to make informed decisions about whether or how to respond...

Analogous problems arise when class sentiment is gauged by votes at public meetings. Particularly when class counsel orchestrates the plebiscite on a proposed settlement, the potential for biased presentations is unavoidable. As public choice models amply demonstrate, agenda can determine outcome. Even assuming concerted attempts at objectivity, lawyers may unwittingly shape results through the formulation of issues and the sequence of voting. Neither training nor experience equips most attorneys in the mechanics of 'democratic consultation'.

In some instances ....courts minimise the likelihood of distortion by appointing a special master or magistrate to superintend open meetings. But even assuming a wholly neutral oversight, public discussion is of limited use in eliciting informed preferences. The complexity and confidentiality of the bargaining process in many institutional reform cases precludes adequate description of remedial alternatives. Excessive 'posturing' by vocal participants may divert audience attention from difficult trade offs that negotiators cannot so readily avoid. So too, public votes or petition signatures may reflect peer pressure rather than independent judgment.

These considerations, coupled with problems of timing and expense, militate against soliciting class sentiment during the negotiating process. Yet if, as is often the case, class members are invited to register preferences only after agreement is reached, they will have too little appreciation of plausible alternatives to make independent and informed evaluations. Some individuals may miscalculate the likelihood of obtaining a more attractive remedial package after trial, appeal, or further bargaining. Others might too readily accept counsel's less than disinterested assessment of particular proposals. And of course, simple plebiscites cannot adjust for differentials in voter comprehension, acuity, or intensity of concerns. Thus, as political theorists remind us, the more technical the issue, the less the point in counting noses. ...

Even absent such conflicts, current plaintiffs will not always be reliable trustees for classes that include their successors. Thus, if trade-offs are necessary, incumbent employees have obvious reasons to prefer compensation for past discrimination rather than opportunities for prospective job applicants. And where current class members are not directly subsidising litigation, they may be insufficiently appreciative of broader interests in encouraging settlement.

Similarly, minority parents, whose children will bear the immediate consequences of disruptive school closures or white hostility, are poorly situated to project the preferences of future generations. The inequity of busing only blacks is immediately apparent; the principal benefits in pre-empting white flight and maintaining an adequate tax base are by comparison remote and conjectural. So too, a defendant school board's offer to increase dramatically the funds available for ghetto schools may seem attractive to existing class members. From the perspective of future generations, the 'gold-plated school house' without secure fiscal foundations has far less appeal. Ironically enough, the more volatile the issues and the greater the demand for participation, the less comfortable we may be in equating class interest with class preferences.

These considerations undoubtedly account for many judges' reluctance to demand systematic evidence of class sentiment, or to view it as controlling. Thus, settlement hearings tend to be pro forma gestures. Only overwhelming opposition is likely to convince trial or appellate courts to jettison a proposed agreement. Even then, they generally are at pains to emphasise that vigorous dissent by 'large numbers' of class members does not necessarily render a settlement unfair. No 'simple percentages' are determinate.

Although these opinions fail to explain why majority vote should not control in instances of conflict, their reasoning may rest on an unarticulated premise: The class as an entity has interests beyond those expressed by its current constituents. As in many other decision making contexts, we do not trust the individuals capable of registering preferences to make adequately informed or disinterested judgement. And if, in the final analysis, courts are unprepared to defer to majoritarian sentiment, there are compelling reasons not to solicit it. To persuade either the class or the public of the legitimacy of a particular outcome becomes far more difficult once eligible voters have recorded their opposition. From this perspective, relying on class counsel as a mediating presence has obvious advantages. Such reliance maintains a convenient legitimating myth of client sovereignty, without an inconvenient substantive reality. That we have more frequently employed pluralist than majoritarian responses to class conflicts is at least partly, albeit not openly, explained on these grounds. We often wish to provide some mechanism for conveying plaintiffs' views that does not expose the limits of our confidence in their judgments.[8]

Question

In what ways is private (usually tort) law multi-party litigation similar to institutional reform litigation? Which of the subclasses of multi-party litigation considered above[9] most closely resemble institutional reform litigation?

8   Deborah L Rhode 'Class Conflict in Class Actions' (1982) 34 Stanford LR 1183 at 1183;1185; 1189;1191-1193; 1198-1201; 1204-1210; 1218-1220; 1222-1224; 1232-1235; 1236-1238 and 1240-1242.
9   Supra text preceding note 2.

Case study: The Exan Valley Disaster

Tumnus Ltd owns a highly profitable chemical factory in Onescome, a small town at the head of the Exan Valley, where it has for many generations been one of the main employers. 8,000 people live in the valley, of whom 1,500 are employed in the factory and a further 1,500 people are economic dependants of these employees. 2,000 people are unemployed, many of them as a result of recent downsizing at the factory. Another 1,000 or so are employed in tourism and a further 500 in farming. The rest of the inhabitants of the valley are employed in other occupations or are dependants of such people.

In December 2000, an explosion occurs at the factory due, it is alleged, to the negligence of the company. 100 employees die in the explosion. Another 200 employees suffer burns of varying degrees of severity: 50 of them will never work again. Poisonous fumes are emitted from the plant in the aftermath of the explosion and are blown by the wind in a thick black cloud down the valley and then out to sea. As a consequence, many of the trees in the beautiful forests on the valley side are left coated with a thin black film.

A number of those suffering physical injury contact local solicitors and, with the help of a national charity specialising in assisting victims of mass disasters, a support group 'the Exan Valley Disaster Association' is founded. Just before the association meets to consider legal proceedings, an advert appears in the local newspaper:

EXAN VALLEY – TOXIC COMPENSATION

Evidence has been discovered in the US that those inhaling fumes such as those emitted by the recent explosion at the Tumnus factory have a significantly increased risk of contracting cancer of the throat within the next 10 years. There is also a risk that those exposed could become carriers transmitting the disease to future generations.

If you think you may have suffered significant exposure to toxic fumes as a result of the recent explosion, you may have a claim for compensation against Tumnus Ltd.

This firm is experienced in dealing with mass disasters and would be keen to meet with you to discuss without charge the possibility of your making a claim.

Our senior partner Mr Knight will be visiting the valley next week. If you would like to meet him, ring Knight and Co on 0207 655 0980.

Following the advert, 25 people who claimed to have been exposed to the fumes engage Knight and Co to act on their behalf. Most of these join the 'the Exan Valley Disaster Association'. At its next meeting, those present are addressed by local solicitors representing victims employed at the factory. Despite the protests of local solicitors, they are also addressed by Knight & Co which describes its own expertise in the field of mass disasters and suggests that the chances of obtaining compensation will be much increased if they are appointed to bring proceedings on behalf of all of those injured. Following much discussion the meeting agrees by a large majority to retain Knight & Co. Exan Valley is a tightly knit community and all members of the association feel themselves morally bound to retain Knight and Co.

Knight and Co issues proceedings on behalf of a number of those who suffered physical injury in the explosion and applies for legal aid. The Legal Services Commission, having considered bulky submissions by lawyers acting for Tumnus Ltd refuses the application on the grounds that insufficient evidence has been presented either that the claim is likely to succeed or that there are sufficient plaintiffs to justify the phenomenal costs involved. Consequently, the firm agrees to take the case on conditional fee basis. Meanwhile, an application is made to the court for a group litigation order. The class is described as ' all those who have suffered or may in future suffer damage as a result of the explosion at the Tumnus chemical factory on 28 December 2000.' The court gives directions such that anyone having a cause of action based on the explosion whether or not it has yet accrued will be bound by the proceedings.[10] The court possesses power to appoint the solicitors for the claimant class and taking express note of the vote of the EVDA appoints Knight and Co. Over the next two years extensive discovery of documents occurs but liability remains in dispute because the explosion appears to have been caused by the accidental mixing of large quantities of two solvents which were normally stored separately. Whether this could have been foreseen so as to require Tumnus to take stricter precautions to prevent the mixing is controversial within the scientific community. Settlement negotiations are attempted but prove largely unfruitful.

Two weeks before trial is due to take place, Knight and Co are approached by lawyers acting for Tumnus' liability insurer. Having stressed their oft repeated doubts about the strength of the claimants' case and emphasised that the defendant's liability cover extends only to £160 million (so that any award in excess of that would most likely lead to bankruptcy), they offer the claimants £135 million by way of full and final settlement of all the claims of those bound by the group action. The insurers propose a mechanism for the division of the damages to be administered by Knight and Co. However, it is proposed that the settlement be embodied in a judgment which means that the judge's approval must be sought. After a series of informal consultations with the judge assigned to the case, Knight and Co draw up a settlement scheme the material provisions of which are as follows.

1) that the defendant pay to the claimants' solicitors as Trustees of the Exan Valley Settlement Scheme, a total sum of £135 million, of which

a) £2 million is to be paid to Knight and Co to cover its' fees (including 40% conditional fee uplift) and expenses. (The defendants agree that these will be paid directly to Knight and Co without assessment).

b) £100 million is to be spent on compensation for earnings lost
   i)   by those killed or injured by the explosion; and
   ii) by those who in subsequent years contract cancer as a result of exposure to the fumes.
   With respect to cancer victims the settlement provides a set of criteria determining eligibility which are much less demanding than the legal principles on causation. As regards compensation, the settlement provides a formula for determining

10   Whether the court has power to do this is not clear from the relevant provisions of the CPR
     – supra note 6.

compensation levels similar to the principles governing damages in tort but much simpler to apply and rather less generous. Each claimants' entitlement will be determined by the trustees on the basis of a written application with supporting medical evidence.

c)   £13 million is to be used to provide compensation for non pecuniary losses to be distributed at the absolute discretion of the trustees.

d)   £10 million is to be spent on the funding of screening procedures designed to provide early warning of and thereby facilitate the treatment of lung cancer.

e)   £10 million is to be spent on the making good of the environmental damage caused by the explosion and on the building of community facilities catering especially for the needs of those disabled as a result of the accident.

Knight and Co arrange for details of the scheme to be sent to each home in the Exan Valley. Included in the package is a letter from the judge urging acceptance of the settlement and a form allowing the recipient to vote for or against the settlement within three weeks. Recipients are urged to attend a meeting to be held in Onescome at which Knight and Co explain the details. The meeting is attended by a total of 1,000 people most of whom seem satisfied with the settlement. When the votes are counted, it is estimated that 50% of the inhabitants of Onescome have replied, of whom 95% are in favour of the settlement. At a subsequent hearing the judge, citing the votes cast in favour, gives his approval.

Questions

1. Do you regard the settlement as satisfactory? How could it have been improved?

2. What conflicts of interest occur for Knight and Co in this account? What techniques do they adopt for dealing with these conflicts?

3. What other techniques could Knight and Co and/or the court have adopted?

4. Is it possible to evaluate Knight and Co's performance by reference to the model of lawyering presupposed by conflict of interest doctrine? If not, why not? What alternative model might be more appropriate?

5. When evaluating Knight and Co's conduct what is the significance of the judge's approval of the settlement?

6. What pressures, if any, impact upon the judge's exercise of the power of approval? (See chapter 10 section 4 supra.) Are these pressures accurately described as conflicts of interest? Should formal judicial approval of multi-party action settlements be required? When considering multi-party litigation, the Scottish Law Commission[11] recommended

11   Paragraph 4.89 supra note 2.

that the judge's approval of the settlement should *not* be required on the grounds that this would pose the following difficult questions:

> If a class member objected to the proposed amount of a settlement, how is the court to satisfy itself that it should grant approval?
>
> What kinds of settlement offer should the defender be entitled to make?
>
> Would there be a separate offer to each class member or would it be a lump sum offer on behalf of the class as a whole? If the latter, how would the sum be allocated among the class members?
>
> What happens if a minority of the class do not wish to accept the offer?
>
> What information relative to the proposed abandonment or settlement would be supplied to the judge?
>
> Would the judge have to assess both the prospects of success on the merits and the amount of any likely awards, if liability had been established?
>
> What happens if the judge refuses approval? Are the class members obliged, against their will, to continue the litigation?

Do you think answering these questions is a legitimate judicial function? See further Schuck 'The Role of the Judge in Settling Complex Cases: The Agent Orange Example' (1986) 53 U Ch L Rev 337.

7. Are there any other ethical difficulties facing Knight and Co in this account?

3 Successive conflicts of interest

Receipt of confidential information

There are a number of reasons why the prospect of a lawyer acting against a former client might be thought problematic. Most obviously, there is the prospect that the lawyer might misuse information communicated in confidence. And even if there is no reasonable prospect of misuse, the former client may view things differently. Consequently, public confidence in the legal system may be undermined.

In England the public interest in the integrity of the legal system is expressed in the fact that an aggrieved client has remedies beyond those available against other recipients of confidential information. The client may invoke the inherent jurisdiction of the court to restrain his former solicitor from acting against him and, as we shall see, the standard of proof which the courts apply is lower than that applied in other proceedings for an injunction to restrain a threatened breach of confidence. Nevertheless, the emphasis in this country has been more upon the essentially private interest in the protection of confidential information than upon the public interest in the reputation of the legal system . In America, greater emphasis on the public interest point has been influential in the formulation of a set of rules in relation to successive conflicts of interest which, as we shall see, are stricter in some respects than those pertaining in England.

When a former client seeks to restrain a lawyer from acting against him a threshold question is that of how the former client is to prove that the solicitor has received confidential information without disclosing the very information the client wishes to withhold. Rule 1.9 of the Model Rules resolves this dilemma by providing that:

> A lawyer who has formerly represented a client in a matter shall not thereafter represent another person in the same or a substantially related matter in which that person's interests are materially adverse to the interests of the former client unless the client consents after consultation.

The point of the 'substantial relation' test is that the client is required to prove only that the type of transaction in which s/he retained the lawyer was such that information might be disclosed which would be relevant to the current transaction. English Law has taken a different line, holding that:

> On the issue whether the solicitor is possessed of relevant confidential information... it is in general not sufficient for the client to make a general allegation that the solicitor is in possession of relevant confidential information if this is in issue: some particularity as to the confidential information is required; But the degree of particularity required must depend upon the facts of the particular case and in many cases identification of the nature of the matter on which the solicitor was instructed, the length of the period of original retainer, the date of the proposed fresh retainer and the nature of the subject matter for practical purposes will be sufficient to establish the possession by the solicitor of relevant confidential information.[12]

Questions

Consider the following problems in the light of Principle 15.02 of the LSGPC and para 608 (b)of the CCB.[13]

1. Anchor & Co, a firm having 10 partners and 6 assistant solicitors, practice in a medium-sized provincial town and undertake a broad range of work. Over the last five years, Mary (one of the partners) has been retained on a number of matters by Airmiles, a travel agency owned run by David Miles. Mary helped set the business up. Since then she has advised Airmiles on various matters relating to tax and acted when one of its employees sued Airmiles for unfair dismissal. Mary also drafted the standard terms and conditions upon which Airmiles contracts with its holiday makers.

Last year, Mary had an argument with David Miles and, as a consequence, David ceased to instruct the firm, using instead its biggest local rival Apt and Co. Later that year Hugo, one of Airmiles' customers, was seriously injured when he slipped on the

12 Re *A Firm of Solicitors* [1995] 3 All ER 483 at pp 489J-490A, per Lightman J.
13 Supra text to p 437 notes 7 and 8.

floor of a hotel in a Greek island. Hugo now wishes to claim compensation from Airmiles alleging that it was in breach of an implied term of the contract making Airmiles strictly liable for the negligence of the foreign holiday operators for whom they act as agents. The claim seems prima facie to be excluded by a clause in the contract.

Hugo has engaged Mary to act on his behalf. Can David prevent her doing so?

2. Clair qualified in 1997 upon completion of a training contract with a medium-sized firm of London solicitors which gave her experience of a wide variety of work including medical negligence litigation. She then joined the in-house legal department of the Blairdale NHS Trust, a newly-created NHS trust. Whilst working there she was involved in defending a number of medical negligence claims. In May 2000, having become dissatisfied with her career prospects, she joined Queue and Co, a firm of solicitors which acts almost exclusively for the victims of medical negligence. Six months later, Clair is consulted by Elizabeth who wishes to bring a medical negligence claim on behalf of her two-year-old child Joshua based on injuries which he received at birth. The birth took place at the Blairdale Trust Hospital.

i)   Can Clair act for Joshua? What further information would you want to know? What information would the trust have to provide to the court if it were to apply for an injunction to restrain Clair from acting?

ii)   Would the trust's position be improved if the 'substantial relation test' were to be applied in the UK?

Disclosure of confidential information and Chinese Walls

Another difficult issue is that of 'imputed' knowledge. Assume that a solicitor is undoubtedly in receipt of confidential information about the affairs of a former client such that principle 15.02 prevents that solicitor from acting for a prospective client against the former client. The question is whether other lawyers in the firm are similarly disqualified. Developments in the market for legal services and particularly the growth over the last 20 years in the size of law firms makes this issue very topical. For, as the number of lawyers in a firm grows, so too does the number of its current and former clients. Consequently, the possibility of conflict between present and former clients increases. In America, Model Rule 1.10 provides that

(a) While lawyers are associated in a firm, none of them shall knowingly represent a client when any one of them would be prohibited from doing so by Rule 1.9.

Thus all the lawyers in a firm are deemed to be in possession of confidential information actually disclosed to any of them. Such a rule operating in a large law firm context is likely to bar a significant number of large firms from representing a significant number of clients. If, on the other hand, knowledge is not to be imputed in this way, the question is under what circumstances other lawyers in the firm can nevertheless act for the prospective client. An important issue here has been whether the former client's confidential information can be kept from those acting for the prospective client by means of information barriers (popularly known as 'Chinese Walls').

For many years, the leading UK case on these issues was *Rakusen v Ellis Munday & Clarke*[14], aspects of which are considered below. The whole subject was however reconsidered by the Court of Appeal in *Re A Firm*. In that case, the applicants (AA) took over a number of companies involved in the management of Lloyd's insurance syndicates. However, it soon became concerned about possible misconduct by one of the companies (AHA) and in particular by a number of individuals who were later to become known as the gang of four. In order to protect the members of the syndicates, AA set up an independent company known as ASM to conduct the future management of the syndicates and to investigate the past. ASM was advised in its work by the firm between 1982 and 1985. AA co-operated with the investigation even though there was always the possibility of proceedings against AHA, to such an extent that the Court of Appeal considered that AA should be treated as the firm's client. Proceedings were duly brought against AHA and settled, after which time the firm ceased to act.

In 1994 SD, another of the subsidiaries, had begun an action against a number of names including one Denby who appointed the firm to represent him. Denby's defence to SD's action was based on the same misconduct by the same individuals which had been investigated by the firm on behalf of ASM. SD and AA applied for an injunction to restrain the firm from acting. The firm argued that its representation of Denby would be carried out by different personnel, situated in different buildings and that the documents from the first representation would forever remain locked away.

By a majority (Staughton LJ dissenting) the Court of Appeal granted an injunction restraining the firm from acting.

Parker LJ:

> The principal case on this subject is *Rakusen v Ellis Munday & Clarke* [1912] 1 Ch 831, [1911–13] All ER Rep 813, a decision of this court. The facts of that case were unusual. The defendant firm consisted in two partners only, Munday and Clarke. Their custom was to do business entirely separately, neither having any knowledge of each other's clients and each of them having the exclusive services of different clerks. In June 1911 the plaintiff, Mr Samuel Rakusen, consulted Mr Munday with regard to a possible claim against S & H Rakusen Ltd for wrongful dismissal. He had several interviews with Mr Munday and gave him much confidential information in regard to the matters in dispute between himself and the company. At that time Mr Clarke was away on holiday and knew nothing of the consultations. He had not seen any of the papers. In October 1911 the plaintiff changed his solicitors and issued a writ against the company claiming damages for wrongful dismissal. The matter was referred to arbitration. In the course of the arbitration the firm were appointed solicitors to the company. It dealt wholly with Mr Clarke.

> Not surprisingly Mr Rakusen objected. He applied for an injunction to restrain the firm from acting for the company. The application was heard by Warrington J, who granted

14   [1912] 1 Ch 831 .

the injunction despite undertakings offered by Munday not to act in any way in the arbitration proceedings or say anything about his consultations with Mr Rakusen and a further undertaking that Clarke's name alone should appear on the papers as solicitor to the company. The firm appealed to this court offering a further undertaking by the company not to consult Munday in any way. The appeal succeeded.

Having held that the judgments of the Court of Appeal were not easy to harmonise, Parker LJ continued:

> Some help is in my view to be gained from Buckley LJ's test 'whether there may reasonably be anticipated to exist a danger' of breach of the duty not to communicate confidential information. This appears to me to suggest that the proper approach is to consider whether a reasonable man informed of the facts might reasonably anticipate such a danger.
>
> To approach the matter in this way has the advantages, in my judgment, that an over-sensitivity on the part of the objector would be excluded and that public confidence in the process of litigation would not be undermined. If a reasonable man with knowledge of the facts would say 'If I were in the position of the objector I would be concerned that, however unwittingly or innocently, information gained while the solicitor was acting for me, might be used against me', the court in my judgment can and should intervene. Were it not to do so the court would be permitting to exist a situation of apparent unfairness and injustice. That this should be avoided is in my view every bit as much a matter of public interest as the public interest in not unnecessarily restricting parties from retaining the solicitor of their choice.
>
> At this point it is convenient to consider certain of the provisions of chs 11 and 12 of *The Law Society's Guide to the Professional Conduct of Solicitors* (1990).Chapter 11 is entitled 'Conflict of Interests'. Paragraph 11.02 sets out the following principle:
>
>> If a solicitor or firm of solicitors has acquired relevant knowledge concerning a former client during the course of acting for him, he or it must not accept instructions to act against him.
>
> Paragraph 1 of the commentary which follows is:
>
>> Any knowledge acquired by a solicitor whilst acting for the former client is confidential and cannot be disclosed without that client's consent. ... However, a solicitor is under a duty to his present client to inform him of all matters which are material to his retainer. ... Consequently, a solicitor in possession of knowledge concerning his former client which is, or might be relevant, is put in an impossible position and he cannot act against that client. Moreover, if a solicitor would feel embarrassed in acting against his former client, he should not act.
>
> Since the plaintiff companies were at no time clients of the firm this is not directly applicable. For my part, however, I consider that the principle is one which the court should enforce for the reasons set out in para 1 of the commentary. It is to be observed that the principle is absolute in the case of relevant knowledge and applies whether as in *Rakusen's* case the matter concerned is the same as or different from the matter in which the solicitor acted for the former client. This is clearly necessary. When acting

for a former client a solicitor may for example have acquired knowledge relevant to a totally different matter in which he seeks to act for another client against his former client.

Chapter 12 is headed 'Confidentiality'. Paragraph 12.07 sets out this principle:

> A solicitor is usually under a duty to pass on to his client and use all information which is material to his client's business regardless of the source of that information. There are, however, exceptional circumstances where such duty does not apply.

Bearing in mind the special circumstances prevailing when the firm's clients were strictly ASM but A & A and subsidiaries were providing information and, in my view, were informal or quasi clients, I regard principles 11.02 and 12.07 as equally applicable in the present case.

Apart from the question of the 'Chinese wall' to which I next turn I would regard it as clear that in the present case the court should intervene to prevent the firm from continuing to act for Mr Denby in the main action. As to the 'Chinese wall', although not then so-called, it was on the basis that, in the very particular circumstances of *Rakusen's* case the undertakings given coupled with the retainer being not of the firm but of Mr Clarke personally, afforded an impregnable barrier against leakage or misuse of information that the court allowed Mr Clarke to act. The situation here is very different. The firm is a very large one and it acted for three years in a matter which attracted great public interest and much discussion in the legal profession and in the insurance world. Those who were then immediately concerned for ASM will almost certainly have discussed it extensively with others not immediately concerned. All may genuinely believe that they have forgotten all about what then happened but anyone in the legal profession knows that a chance remark may bring details of an apparently forgotten case flooding back. In *Supasave Retail Ltd v Coward Chance (a firm)* [1991] All ER 668, [1991] Ch 259 Nicolas Browne-Wilkinson V-C had to consider whether the arrangements there proposed for preventing leakage, ie a 'Chinese wall', eliminated the risk which prima facie arose. He held that they did not. In the present case we have much more background evidence than was available to Sir Nicolas Browne-Wilkinson V-C. I do not doubt for one moment that the firm intend that such proposals will eliminate any risk and believe that they will do so. For my part, however, I am not satisfied that they would do so. Moreover, even if for a period they would, no one can tell whether in the course of the litigation something might occur which would put the firm in an embarrassing position. That would be disastrous.

In my judgment any reasonable man with knowledge of the facts, in the present case, including the proposals for a 'Chinese wall', would consider that some confidential information might permeate the wall and would indeed regard it as astonishing that the plaintiffs should be faced with solicitors on the other side to whom, over a considerable period, they had forwarded much confidential information concerning matters being investigated in the main action.

Sir David Croom-Johnson:

> Putting aside the facts for the moment, what is the correct question which the court should ask itself before exercising its jurisdiction? It must, in answering it, obviously

take into account what has come to be called the 'Chinese wall'. It would not be right to require that there should be no risk at all. Human affairs being what they are, it is impossible to say that there is never a risk of confidential information being revealed or leaked, or professional duty being breached. But in my view it is relaxing the necessary precautions required to be taken to protect confidential information too much to ask whether the test is one of probability as the applicant firm ask us to do. They submit that the requirement of probability before a quia timet injunction is granted is what is appropriate, but that is too broad a test in the exercise of this jurisdiction. Cozens-Hardy MR said in *Rakusen's case* [1912] 1 Ch 831 at 834–835, [1911–13] All ER Rep 813 at 814:

> We expect and indeed we exact from solicitors, who are our officers, a higher standard of conduct than we can enforce against those who are not our officers.

The appellant firm have in good faith, which nobody doubts, erected what reads like a formidable Chinese wall to prevent leakage of information within their organisation. For this injunction to continue there must be a possible, but real, risk of such a leakage, inadvertent or not. It is the inadvertent which matters here. I agree with the test set out by Parker LJ, based as it is on that put forward by Buckley LJ in *Rakusen's* case and echoed by Sir Nicolas Browne-Wilkinson V-C and Hoffman J. This is that the court will act if danger of a breach of duty may reasonably be anticipated.

Adopting that test, what is the position in this case? The firm have put all the documents relating to the earlier inquiries and actions in special store. There seems to be no risk of leakage of those. The staff and personnel who are handling the present litigation are not those who were concerned in the earlier cases. But in view of the complexity of the issues in all the cases, the reasonable man knowing of the overlap could not be confident that in the course of the present case some inadvertent revelation might not take place, caused perhaps by the awakening of a memory or by someone consciously or unconsciously availing himself of information which had in the past been obtained from A A and communicated to him in the course of his work or even in social meetings with other members of the firm. He might well not appreciate the origin of the information, but the risk is there. There is no analogy to be drawn from the two-man firm in *Rakusen's* case to a large firm of 107 partners and obviously a correspondingly large staff of executives and other employees. The reasonable man would recognise the existence of a risk of use of the earlier information no matter what steps the firm had taken to protect it.

The Law Society's Guide to the Professional Conduct of Solicitors (1990), ch 11 on 'Conflict of Interests', may be perhaps more strict than the general law (it could not be less so), but I find that the principle set out in para 11.02 is persuasive:

> If a solicitor or firm of solicitors has acquired relevant knowledge concerning a former client during the course of acting for him, he or it must not accept instructions to act against him.

Once one puts A A in the position of having been tantamount to a client, that principle applies.[15]

---

15   [1992] 1 All ER 353 at 357-358, 361-362 and 368-369.

Notes

1. Staughton LJ(dissenting) thought that on the facts before the court, there was only a remote possibility of unauthorised disclosure. *Rakusen*'s case was binding on the court and decided that the test to be applied was ' whether there is or is not a reasonable anticipation of mischief' and required such remote possibilities to be ignored. The court should not be swayed by the maxim that justice must not only be done but also be seen to be done for

> alongside the need for justice to be seen to be done there is a countervailing public interest, that the choice of solicitors open to the public should not be unduly and unnecessarily restricted. In *Rakusen's* case it was argued that such restriction, 'would work great hardship in small towns where there were few solicitors'...The same may occur in a large city where there are many solicitors, but only a few of them have experience in a recherché and specialised field. To deprive a litigant of his chosen solicitor may cause him inconvenience and dismay, which may be why (so we are told) it is not uncommon practice for his opponent to attempt to do so in the United States. It is a step which should only be taken on solid grounds.[16]

2. Parker LJ was much impressed with the argument that a solicitor owes a duty to pass on to his client all relevant information in his possession including information confidential to a former client. This duty, which was recognised by Megarry J in *Specter v Ageda*[17], and the avoidance of such a conflict of duties is one reason to avoid acting against a former client. The problem is that, if Megarry J's view is correct, a firm might find itself liable for negligence if the confidential information which it refuses to disclose because of its duty to the former client renders its advice to the current client misleading[18]. The possibility of such liability increases the likelihood of unauthorised disclosure. Staughton LJ in his dissenting judgment refused to accept that a large law firm had a duty to disclose to a current client all information known to any of its staff whether or not they were personally acting for the client.[19]

Questions

1. Is the approach to successive conflicts of interest in the LSGPC different in any way from that of the courts? What are the implications of any difference for solicitors and for the LSGPC?

2. Puddle & Co, a medium-sized 12-partner London law firm, is contemplating merging with Max and Co a Leeds based firm with 4 partners. They wish to merge because each of the firms has strengths in different areas of commercial law. However, the London

16 [1992] 1 All ER 353 at 366C-D.
17 *Specter v Ageda* [1973] Ch 30.
18 Finn, supra p 436 note 2 at pp 30-35.
19 [1992] 1 All ER 353 at 365G-H.

firm is concerned that each of the two firms has current clients with interests adverse to those of the other's former clients so that conflict of interest problems may arise. They therefore decide to enter into an agreement under which each firm undertakes to refer current and prospective clients to the other firm when the client requires legal services in which the other firm has expertise. Each firm will maintain its separate partnership and there will be no fee sharing. However, the firms will market themselves as 'Puddle/Max & Co, a member of Leeds/London Legal Services'.

To what extent should this agreement be regarded as solving their problem? Would you require any further information?

3. Would the Court of Appeal's decision have been any different if the lawyers who acted for ASM had all left by the time the firm was engaged by SD? Model Rule 1.10 provides that
(a) While lawyers are associated in a firm, none of them shall knowingly represent a client when any one of them practising alone would be prohibited from doing so.
(b) When a lawyer has terminated an association with a firm, the firm is not prohibited from thereafter representing a person with interests materially adverse to those of a client represented by the formerly associated lawyer and not currently represented by the firm unless:
(1) the matter is the same or substantially related to that in which the formerly associated lawyer represented the client; and
(2) any lawyer remaining in the firm has (confidential information) that is material to the matter.

4. In *Rakusen's* case, the court seems to have been assuming that it was exercising its inherent jurisdiction to regulate the conduct of solicitors, and Sir David Croom Johnson sees this as the justification for granting an injunction without proof that breach of confidence was likely, as would be required of a claimant seeking a quia timet injunction to restrain breach of confidence by a non-solicitor defendant. What would be the implications of this approach for competition between lawyers and other professionals eg accountants, seeking to provide services to business clients? See further however *Prince Jefri Bolkiah v KPMG* below.

5. Do you agree with Staughton LJ's criticisms of the majority's decision? One important issue is the likely impact of Chinese Walls. The following extract is from an article which reviews a line of US cases which have allowed the presumption of imputed knowledge to be rebutted by proof of a Chinese Wall sufficient to make disclosure improbable. The writer considers whether Chinese Walls can meet this test in the light of their use over many years in financial institutions.

A. CHINESE WALLS IN FINANCIAL INSTITUTIONS

Securities firms and banks, plagued by conflict of interest problems analogous to those of law firms, routinely build Chinese walls to protect their clients. Given the legal profession's lack of experience with walls, the effectiveness of walling procedures in financial institutions merits examination.

Conflicts of interest arise in a securities firm because of its multiple functions, as investment banker on the one hand and as securities broker, dealer, and investment adviser on the other. In its capacity as investment banker, a securities firm has a duty to guard the confidentiality of financial secrets it receives from its customers. At the same time, however, the firm's broker-dealer or investment advising department may be making recommendations concerning the securities of these very same customers, and the investment management arm of the securities firm may be buying or selling those securities for accounts it manages.

In the performance of these functions, the securities firm owes a conflicting [legal] duty ... to disclose inside information or to refrain from using it in trading or recommending the securities in question. Like their counterparts in securities firms, commercial-bank employees also receive confidential information as investment bankers, direct lenders, and board members. Because banks also buy and sell securities, both on their own accounts and as trustees and investment managers, they encounter conflicts of interest substantially identical to those faced by securities firms.

To prevent such conflicts from arising, financial institutions have developed structural, procedural, and educational methods for containing confidential information. Structurally, separate financial roles – investment banker, broker-dealer, trustee have been assigned to distinct groups of employees, and this division of labour is reflected in discrete departments in almost every financial institution of appreciable size. Recently, these internal structural arrangements have even acquired legal status through incorporation, a trend one observer thinks may serve to reduce the probability of information leaks by creating a heightened sense of corporate identity. Organisational separation may be supplemented by physical separation, a practice intended to reduce the possibility that a department, either accidentally or in deliberate violation of company policy, will gain access to prohibited information.

Physical separation, like incorporation, is also thought to increase the sense of departmental identity. Routine, internal procedures for the handling of confidential information constitute another screening method prevalent in financial institutions. At the heart of these procedures is restricted access to files. Thus, banks typically attempt to prohibit access by trust department personnel with investment responsibilities to files containing commercial credit information and securities firms utilise equivalent procedures.

A third ingredient in the construction of a Chinese wall is educational in nature. Although outside sanctions may apply to conduct that breaches a wall some employees may not adequately be acquainted with the relevant legal standards. And if the firm's policy remains unspoken, even those employees who are more knowledgeable may be led by their desires for self-advancement to bend or break the law. Thus, a strong policy statement from the management against passing information to other departments, accompanied by an educational program for employees, is considered essential if a Chinese wall is to be even minimally effective.

Despite these measures, Chinese walls in financial institutions have not been free from criticism. In part, problems have arisen from a failure to adopt, and when adopted to apply, adequate procedures. Some large banks, for example, were slow to establish policies against transfer of information from their commercial banking to their trust departments. Even when such policies were announced, commercial credit files sometimes remained open to trust department employees. In other cases, the procedures were adequate but were applied only to a small segment of the full range of confidential information in need of protection Occasionally, too, the wolves are left to guard the sheep: individuals who were themselves subject to the rules bore the duty of enforcement and performed the task of distinguishing protected from unprotected information.

Although such problems could be avoided by stricter observance of walling methods, walls in financial institutions have also suffered from defects that may be irremediable. If the bank or firm is small, so that the same employees performance diverse functions a wall may be impossible to build. Some mingling of functions may be unavoidable even in large institutions when integrated decision making procedures increase the likelihood that confidential information will be exchanged among higher-ups. Particular kinds of transactions, such as a firm's investing for its own account in securities concerning which it has acquired inside information, may present temptations too great to resist. And it may be that structural, procedural, and educational methods all combined are no match for the natural tendency of co-workers to talk shop at company-wide social gatherings and in chance encounters. At any rate, studies of Chinese walls in financial institutions have found frequent breaches. Despite these drawbacks, the bulk of considered commentary on the problem endorses the Chinese wall as a significant aid in solving the information conflicts of financial institutions.

B.   FINANCIAL WALLS COMPARED TO LAW-FIRM WALLS

The experience of financial institutions with Chinese walls indicates that walls are not impermeable barriers to information flow. Although in some respects law-firm walls are similar, important differences exist. On balance, a comparison of financial and law firm walls suggests that Chinese walls in law firms will successfully impede the flow of confidential information in successive representation cases.

Similarities between financial institutions and law firms make their walls comparable. Like employees of financial institutions' individual lawyers in small law firms may perform potentially conflicting functions. Large law firms typically have a departmental structure and branches in several locations. In large firms, however, as in large financial institutions, important decisions are often made by committees whose membership cuts across organisational lines. Interdepartmental and interbranch transfers of personnel are not uncommon in large firms, and some firms even require departmental rotation by young associates. Like financial institutions, law firms recruit new business from other departments and encourage firm unity at social gatherings attended by all the lawyers associated with the firm. To the extent that the effectiveness of law firm walls depends upon a strict observance of the separation of departments and branches, these similarities suggest that Chinese Wall in law firms will suffer the same defects as walls in financial institutions.

Some of the differences between financial institutions and law firms would appear to indicate that walls in law firms will be even less reliable than their financial cousins. The information problems in financial institutions arise because different departments offer different services, – whereas in law firms information problems may arise within a single department. Because these problems are inherent when a multiplicity of services is provided, as in financial institutions, financial walls are permanent. By contrast, law-firm walls are typically created after a conflict arises; so they attempt to screen a particular matter, rather than all matters handled by a particular employee or group of employees. The ad hoc and post hoc nature of law-firm walls means that no barrier to the flow of confidential information will be erected until the ethical problem is discovered.

Despite these gloomy indicators, persuasive evidence supports a sunnier forecast for the effectiveness of Chinese walls in successive representation cases. First, the softness of departmental lines in law firms would be relevant chiefly in concurrent representation cases, in which separate teams of lawyers contemporaneously pursue conflicting representations. But, in such cases the... studies that show the permeability of financial walls are of questionable relevance to legal walls in successive representation cases, because the conflicts in financial institutions are mostly concurrent, and there is good reason to believe that Chinese walls are more likely to be effective in cases of successive rather than concurrent representation.

Second, the ad hoc nature of law-firm walls operates in successive representation cases to create a greater, not a lesser, likelihood of prevention. Unlike financial walls, law-firms are not used to screen an entire department, but only the individual lawyer or lawyers tainted by reason of their former representations. As the number of people to be walled off grows smaller the prospects for a successful wall increase. Furthermore, because law firms erect walls with the expectation that their procedures will be subjected to judicial scrutiny upon a motion for disqualification, strict adherence to walling measures may be presumed. The attorneys whose activities are responsible for the screening procedures can also count on testifying under oath concerning their conduct and thus will have every reason scrupulously to observe the wall. In contrast, walls in financial institutions are standard operating procedure, and outside scrutiny is likely to be infrequent.[20]

The factors to be taken into account when deciding what restrictions are to be imposed on lawyers by virtue of their receipt of confidential information are not in doubt. On the one hand, clients must be assured that their lawyers will respect their confidences and the reputation of the legal system must be protected; on the other hand, as Staughton LJ points out, there is the need to allow clients a broad choice of lawyers. Nor, if possible, should lawyers be prevented from moving (and firms be prevented from merging) by over stringent rules. The problem is how to balance these conflicting considerations. It is perhaps not surprising therefore that the issue was ultimately considered by the House of Lords in the case of *Prince Jefri Bolkiah v KPMG*[1]. From 1983 onwards, KPMG had acted as auditors to the Brunei Investment Agency, whose function was the management of the assets of the Government of Brunei. Until 1998, the BIA was managed by Prince Jefri, the youngest of the Sultan's brothers. During

---

20 'The Chinese Wall Defence To Law Firm Disqualification' (1980) 128 U Penn LR 677, 705-711.

1 [1999] 1 All ER 517.

that period, the auditors were obliged to accept the certificate of the Board that certain 'special transfers' of its funds were legitimate.

From 1996-1998, the forensic accountancy department of KPMG provided litigation support services to Prince Jefri of a kind normally provided by solicitors in connection with litigation of his own against third parties. This work was known as 'Project Lucy' and came to an end in May 1998.

Meanwhile, Prince Jefri had fallen out with his brother, the Sultan of Brunei, and been dismissed from his post as Chairman of BIA. The BIA then alleged that Prince Jefri had misappropriated BIA funds and made plans to recover them ('Project Gemma'). The Audit group at KPMG was initially asked only to ascertain the amount of the special transfers which it did by looking at past audit papers.[2] BIA then sought to engage the forensic accounts department of KPMG to trace the money. KPMG realised the possibility of conflict but took measures to minimise it. These measures included

1) The selection of staff: no one who worked on Project Lucy was allowed to work on Project Gemma, save for 11 people who had done minor administrative work after KPMG had been satisfied they had no confidential information. All Project Gemma staff were interviewed by KPMG's solicitors about their knowledge of Prince Jefri's affairs and asked to confirm on affidavit that they had no relevant knowledge; and

2) Physical separation: most of the work on Project Gemma was done in Brunei. Any work undertaken in London was done in a separate room with restricted access. Special computer servers were provided for Project Gemma. Project Lucy information was deleted from KPMG's servers.

Having taken these steps, KPMG decided to act and proceeded to do so without informing Prince Jefri. After KPMG had been working for about three months, Prince Jefri sought and obtained an injunction. This injunction was discharged by the Court of Appeal and restored by the House of Lords where the leading judgment was given by Lord Millet.

THE BASIS OF THE JURISDICTION

In *Rakusen's* case the Court of Appeal founded the jurisdiction on the right of the former client to the protection of his confidential information. This was challenged by counsel for Prince Jefri, who contended for an absolute rule, such as that adopted in the United States, which precludes a solicitor or his firm altogether from acting for a client with an interest adverse to that of the former client in the same or a connected matter. In the course of argument, however, he modified his position, accepting that there was no ground on which the court could properly intervene unless two conditions were satisfied: (i) that the solicitor was in possession of information which was confidential to the former client and (ii) that such information was or might be relevant to the matter on which he was instructed by the second client. This makes the possession of

---

2   In the House of Lords, Lord Millet viewed this as no more than an extension of the audit function.

relevant confidential information the test of what is comprehended within the expression 'the same or a connected matter.' On this footing the Court's intervention is founded not on the avoidance of any perception of possible impropriety but on the protection of confidential information.

My Lords, I would affirm this as the basis of the court's jurisdiction to intervene on behalf of a former client. It is otherwise where the court's intervention is sought by an existing client, for a fiduciary cannot act at the same time both for and against the same client, and his firm is in no better position. A man cannot without the consent of both clients act for one client while his partner is acting for another in the opposite interest. His disqualification has nothing to do with the confidentiality of client information. It is based on the inescapable conflict of interest which is inherent in the situation...

Where the court's intervention is sought by a former client, however, the position is entirely different. The court's jurisdiction cannot be based on any conflict of interest, real or perceived, for there is none. The fiduciary relationship which subsists between solicitor and client comes to an end with the termination of the retainer. Thereafter the solicitor has no obligation to defend and advance the interests of his former client. The only duty to the former client which survives the termination of the client relationship is a continuing duty to preserve the confidentiality of information imparted during its subsistence.

Accordingly, it is incumbent on a plaintiff who seeks to restrain his former solicitor from acting in a matter for another client to establish (i) that the solicitor is in possession of information which is confidential to him and to the disclosure of which he has not consented and (ii) that the information is or may be relevant to the new matter in which the interest of the other client is or may be adverse to his own. Although the burden of proof is on the plaintiff, it is not a heavy one. The former may readily be inferred; the latter will often be obvious. I do not think that it is necessary to introduce any presumptions, rebuttable or otherwise, in relation to these two matters. But given the basis on which the jurisdiction is exercised, there is no cause to impute or attribute the knowledge of one partner to his fellow partners. Whether a particular individual is in possession of confidential information is a question of fact which must be proved or inferred from the circumstances of the case. In this respect also we ought not in my opinion to follow the jurisprudence of the United States.

THE EXTENT OF THE SOLICITOR'S DUTY

Whether founded on contract or equity, the duty to preserve confidentiality is unqualified. It is a duty to keep the information confidential, not merely to take all reasonable steps to do so. Moreover, it is not merely a duty not to communicate the information to a third party. It is a duty not to misuse it, that is to say, without the consent of the former client to make any use of it or to cause any use to be made of it by others otherwise than for his benefit. The former client cannot be protected completely from accidental or inadvertent disclosure. But he is entitled to prevent his former solicitor from exposing him to any avoidable risk; and this includes the increased risk of the use of the information to his prejudice arising from the acceptance of instructions to act for another client with an adverse interest in a matter to which the information is or may be relevant.

DEGREE OF RISK

It follows that in the case of a former client there is no basis for granting relief if there is no risk of the disclosure or misuse of confidential information. This was the ground on which the Court of Appeal discharged the injunction in *Rakusen's* case [1912] 1 Ch 831. The test for disqualification was expressed in different terms by each of the three members of the court, but the case has been taken to indicate that the Court will not intervene unless it is satisfied that there is a 'reasonable probability of real mischief.' This test has been the subject of criticism both in this country and overseas, particularly in relation to solicitors, and a more stringent test has frequently been advocated: (see for example Professor Finn Conflicts of Interest and Professionals published by the New Zealand Legal Research Foundation in the volume Professional Responsibility) cited with evident approval by Gummow J in *National Mutual Holdings Pty Ltd v The Sentry Corporation* (1989) 22 FCR 209. It has been abandoned in Canada: see *Macdonald Estates v Martin* (1990) 77 DLR (4th) 249 where it has been replaced by two rebuttable presumptions: (i) that confidential information will have been communicated by the former client in the course of the retainer and (ii) that lawyers who work together share confidences. The clear trend of the authorities is towards a stricter approach.

My Lords, I regard the criticisms which have been made of the test supposed to have been laid down in *Rakusen's* case as well founded. It imposes an unfair burden on the former client, exposes him to a potential and avoidable risk to which he has not consented, and fails to give him a sufficient assurance that his confidence will be respected. It also exposes the solicitor to a degree of uncertainty which could inhibit him in his dealings with the second client when he cannot be sure that he has correctly identified the source of his information.

It is in any case difficult to discern any justification in principle for a rule which exposes a former client without his consent to any avoidable risk, however slight, that information which he has imparted in confidence in the course of a fiduciary relationship may come into the possession of a third party and be used to his disadvantage. Where in addition the information in question is not only confidential but also privileged, the case for a strict approach is unanswerable. Anything less fails to give effect to the policy on which legal professional privilege is based. It is of overriding importance for the proper administration of justice that a client should be able to have complete confidence that what he tells his lawyer will remain secret. This is a matter of perception as well as substance. It is of the highest importance to the administration of justice that a solicitor or other person in possession of confidential and privileged information should not act in any way that might appear to put that information at risk of coming into the hands of someone with an adverse interest.

Many different tests have been proposed in the authorities. These include the avoidance of 'an appreciable risk' or 'an acceptable risk.' I regard such expressions as unhelpful: the former because it is ambiguous, the latter because it is uninformative. I prefer simply to say that the court should intervene unless it is satisfied that there is no risk of disclosure. It goes without saying that the risk must be a real one, and not merely fanciful or theoretical. But it need not be substantial. This is in effect the test formulated by Lightman J in *Re a Firm of Solicitors* [1997] Ch 1, at p 9 (possibly derived from the judgment of Drummond J in *Carindale Country Club Estate Pty Ltd v Astill* (1993) 115 ALR 112) and adopted by Pumfrey J in the present case.

THE ADEQUACY OF THE PROTECTIVE MEASURES TAKEN BY KPMG

Once the former client has established that the defendant firm is in possession of information which was imparted in confidence and that the firm is proposing to act for another party with an interest adverse to his in a matter to which the information is or may be relevant, the evidential burden shifts to the defendant firm to show that even so there is no risk that the information will come into the possession of those now acting for the other party. There is no rule of law that Chinese Walls or other arrangements of a similar kind are insufficient to eliminate the risk. But the starting point must be that, unless special measures are taken, information moves within a firm. In *MacDonald Estates v Martin* 77 DLR (4th) 249, Sopinka J said at p 269 that the court should restrain the firm from acting for the second client 'unless satisfied on the basis of clear and convincing evidence that all reasonable measures have been taken to ensure that no disclosure will occur.' With the substitution of the word 'effective' for the words 'all reasonable' I would respectfully adopt that formulation.

APPLICATION TO THE FACTS OF THE PRESENT CASE

Chinese Walls are widely used by financial institutions in the City of London and elsewhere. They are the favoured technique for managing the conflicts of interest which arise when financial business is carried on by a conglomerate. The Core Conduct of Business Rules published by the Financial Services Authority recognise the effectiveness of Chinese Walls as a means of restricting the movement of information between different departments of the same organisation. They contemplate the existence of established organisational arrangements which preclude the passing of information in the possession of one part of the business to other parts of the business. In their Consultation Paper on Fiduciary Duties and Regulatory Rules the Law Commission (1992) (Law Com No 124) describe Chinese Walls as normally involving some combination of the following organisational arrangements:

(i)   the physical separation of the various departments in order to insulate them from each other - this often extends to such matters of detail as dining arrangements;

(ii) an educational programme, normally recurring, to emphasis the importance of not improperly or inadvertently divulging confidential information;

(iii) strict and carefully defined procedures for dealing with a situation where it is felt that the wall should be crossed and the maintaining of proper records where this occurs;

(iv) monitoring by compliance officers of the effectiveness of the wall;

(v)   disciplinary sanctions where there has been a breach of the wall.

KPMG insist that, like other large firms of accountants, they are accustomed to maintaining client confidentiality not just within the firm but also within a particular team. They stress that it is common for a large firm of accountants to provide a comprehensive range of professional services including audit, corporate finance advice, corporate tax advice and management consultancy to clients with competing commercial interests. Such firms are very experienced in the erection and operation of information barriers to protect the confidential information of each client, and staff are constantly instructed in the importance of respecting client confidentiality. This is, KPMG assert, part of the professional culture in which staff work and becomes second nature to them. Forensic projects are treated as exceptionally confidential and are usually given code names. In the present case KPMG engaged different people, different servers, and ensured that the work was done in a secure office in a different building. KPMG maintain that these arrangements satisfy the most stringent test, and that there is no risk that information obtained by KPMG in the course of Project Lucy has or will become available to anyone engaged on Project Gemma.

I am not persuaded that this is so. Even in the financial services industry, good practice requires there to be established institutional arrangements designed to prevent the flow of information between separate departments. Where effective arrangements are in place, they produce a modern equivalent of the circumstances which prevailed in *Rakusen's case* [1912] 1 Ch 831. The Chinese Walls which feature in the present case, however, were established ad hoc and were erected within a single department. When the number of personnel involved is taken into account, together with the fact that the teams engaged on Project Lucy and Project Gemma each had a rotating membership, involving far more personnel than were working on the project at any one time, so that individuals may have joined from and returned to other projects, the difficulty of enforcing confidentiality or preventing the unwitting disclosure of information is very great. It is one thing, for example, to separate the insolvency, audit, taxation and forensic departments from one another and erect Chinese Walls between them. Such departments often work from different offices and there may be relatively little movement of personnel between them. But it is quite another to attempt to place an information barrier between members all of whom are drawn from the same department and have been accustomed to work with each other. I would expect this to be particularly difficult where the department concerned is engaged in the provision of litigation support services, and there is evidence to confirm this. Forensic accountancy is said to be an area in which new and unusual problems frequently arise and partners and managers are accustomed to share information and expertise. Furthermore, there is evidence that physical segregation is not necessarily adequate, especially where it is erected within a single department.

In my opinion an effective Chinese Wall needs to be an established part of the organisational structure of the firm, not created ad hoc and dependent on the acceptance of evidence sworn for the purpose by members of staff engaged on the relevant work.[3]

Notes

1. One of KPMG's arguments in this case was that only a limited number of firms possessed the skills and resources to undertake an investigation of the required scale. This was disputed by Prince Jefri and the court noted that Arthur Andersen had been able to do 'at least some' of the Project Gemma work following the grant of the injunction.[4]

---

3   [1999] 1 All ER 517 at 525H- 530H.
4   Ibid at 524G-J.

2. It was accepted by KPMG (and affirmed by the court) that its obligations were the same as those of solicitors because they were providing litigation support services and receiving privileged information.[5]

3. The Court of Appeal in this case had followed the different approach developed by the New Zealand Court of Appeal in *Russell McVeagh Mckenzie Bartlett v Tower Corp*[6]. The alternative approach required the court to ascertain the sensitivity of the information which the client sought to protect and the degree of risk of disclosure should the lawyer act for a subsequent client. The mere existence of a real risk was not however decisive. The risk had to be balanced against other factors such as the need to sustain competition between the providers of legal services, the right of lawyers to offer their services to the public and the need to encourage intra-firm mobility. The Court of Appeal accordingly discharged the injunction, in part because Prince Jefri had known, when engaging KPMG, that the firm had already acted as auditors to the Brunei Investment Agency. Lord Millet disapproved the alternative test. In his view, Prince Jefri's knowledge of KPMG's relationship with the BIA was relevant only in so far as it implied consent to any subsequent representation of BIA by KPMG. On the facts, Prince Jefri had consented only to further audit work.

4. Despite Lord Millet's apparent disapproval of ad hoc Chinese Walls, such walls were held sufficient in the subsequent case of *Young v Robson Rhodes*[7]. There the defendant accountants had been engaged to provide forensic accountancy services in support of the plaintiffs' action for breach of contract against another firm of accountants (PKF) with respect to the latter's involvement in the Lloyd's insurance syndicate, of which the plaintiffs were members. Some 12-18 months before the trial, Robson Rhodes told the plaintiffs that they intended to merge with PKF and could not therefore continue to act. The plaintiffs sought an injunction to restrain the merger on the basis that, applying the test laid down in *Bolkiah*, it created a real risk of unauthorised disclosure. The judge held that the merger could only proceed

i)   if PKF identified all involved in the incidents forming the subject of the litigation and all who had worked and were likely to work on the litigation; and

ii) if the Robson Rhodes personnel who worked for the plaintiffs were housed in separate premises for the duration of the litigation; and

iii) if the Robson Rhodes personnel undertook to have no professional contact with the relevant persons within PKF.

The case may however be exceptional because of the small number of people (three) requiring to be screened behind Chinese Walls.

---

5   Ibid at 526C-D.

6   [1998] 3 NZLR 361. For a critique See Duncan Webb 'Client's Secrets; Confidentiality and Disclosure in the Court of Appeal' (1999) 5 New Zealand Business Law Quarterly 91.

7   [1999] 3 All ER 524, Ch D.

Note

Empirical research has shown that many firms of solicitors continue to act even when the LSGPC would seem to prohibit them doing so. They attempt to manage the problems through the use of Chinese Walls and justify ignoring the LSGPC on the grounds that they have the (informed?) consent of clients: see Janine Griffith-Baker (1999) 49 New Law Journal 162 and *Conflict of Interest, Fiduciary Duties and Chinese Walls: the Problems of Modern Legal Practice* (forthcoming, Hart Publications).

Questions

1. What are the implications of *Bolkiah* for the future of Chinese Walls as a solution to conflicts of interest?

2. What are the implications of *Bolkiah* for competition between solicitors and accountants in relation to the provision of litigation support services?

3. If a strict rule on conflicts of interest causes problems for large firms offering specialised legal services does this make the rule inappropriate?

4. What are the implications for self-regulation of solicitors by the Law Society of the fact that large law firms regularly ignore its provisions on conflict of interest?

5. Which solution to the problem of successive conflicts of interest do you prefer; MR10.1[8]; the decision of the House of Lords in *Bolkiah v KPMG* or that offered by the New Zealand Court of Appeal in *Russell McVeagh*?

Conflict of interest and occupational mobility

One striking feature of working life at the end of the 20th and the beginning of the 21st centuries has been the frequency with which employees change jobs. At one time many trainee solicitors would expect to be offered a job by their training firm with the prospect in due course of a partnership which would last till retirement. By contrast lawyers, including partners, now regularly move from one firm to another. Such mobility may be motivated simply by the desire for economic improvement. In addition, there are a number of factors which suggest that in future a high proportion of training contracts are likely to be offered by a small number of firms. Increased Law Society regulation, increasing specialisation and the increasing complexity of the substantive law increase the costs to firms of training and limit the number of firms able to undertake it. Moreover, large firms have a significant volume of routine work which can be handled by trainees and can afford to pay the salary necessary to attract them. However,

8   Supra text to p 468 note 14.

many lawyers are unlikely to be either willing or able to remain in the firm which trained them.

This poses problems for conflict of interest doctrine. If a lawyer has acted for clients A, B and C whilst working at Firm 1 both the lawyer and (subject to the latitude remaining for Chinese Walls after the *Bolkiah* case) all other lawyers at Firm 1 will be bound by Principle 15.02. What is the position however if the lawyer moves to another firm? This issue recently came before the UK courts as a result of some highly complex patent litigation.[9] The partner was one of 10 partners in a leading intellectual property firm which was retained in 1992 to advise the client in its patent actions against the defendant in which it alleged that the defendant had infringed its patent for the production of kits used to test for the Hepatitis C virus. Issues had arisen as to whether the defendant's actions had depressed prices for the client's products and as to whether the client had acted in breach of EC competition law. Consequently, the firm received much highly sensitive information about the client's approach to and attempts to develop their market.

The partner was not involved in this litigation, but lawyers at the firm had general conversations with him about how the litigation was proceeding and no steps were taken to keep the confidential information from members of the department not directly involved. One assistant had had on the wall of her office a strategy setting out the plaintiff's plans for dealing with 'obviousness' attacks on the validity of the patents. In addition, the partner attended departmental meetings at which the general progress of the litigation was discussed. In October 1992, he left the firm and joined a rival firm as Head of Intellectual Property. Meanwhile the litigation continued. In March 1995, the new firm was retained to act for the defendant with the partner having a leading role. The client sought an injunction to restrain the partner's new firm from acting. Lightman J held that a lawyer who had not personally received confidential information about a client's affairs would be able to act against that client if she left that firm and moved elsewhere. His Lordship continued:

> the issue raised in this case is as to the approach to be adopted in determining whether a solicitor is possessed of relevant confidential information where his firm was retained and his partners (or employees) received relevant confidential information. The former partner in this case contends that the onus is upon the clients to prove on the balance of probability his possession of relevant confidential information and in particular that relevant confidential information was communicated to him. On the other hand, the clients argue that they have only to show that there is a real risk that such confidential information has been communicated. There are involved, as it seems to me, two separate questions. The first is that of the test to be applied; and the second is as to the burden of proof. In the ordinary case, where it is alleged that a defendant has received confidential information and should be restrained from using it, the burden must be on the plaintiff to identify the confidential information and prove on the balance of probabilities the communication of the same to the defendant: see eg *G D Searle & Co Ltd v Celltech Ltd* [1982] FSR 92 at 109. But the position of a partner in a firm of solicitors retained by a client is in no wise ordinary: it is extraordinary and special. The contract

9   *Re A Firm of Solicitors:* [1995] 3 All ER 483.

of retainer creates a close fiduciary relationship between the client and the firm and each partner, a relationship to which the law attributes unique incidents, eg legal professional privilege, reflecting its unique importance in the eyes of the law. Having regard to such fiduciary relationship, (in the absence of the informed consent of the client) the burden must surely be upon any person who was a partner in a firm which was retained whilst he was a partner in the firm and which in the course of such retainer became possessed of confidential information, to establish that there is no risk of his misusing confidential information before he can thereafter act against that client. The solicitor must show that there is no reasonable prospect of any conflict between his duty to his previous client and his personal interest in obtaining the new retainer and his duty to his new client, and accordingly not merely that he is not in possession of any relevant confidential information, but that there is no real risk that he has such information. All the members of the Court of Appeal in Re a firm of solicitors agreed that the members of a firm wishing to act against a former client are disqualified from so acting if there is any real risk of subsequent communication to them of relevant confidential information by members of the same firm possessed of such information; and the same strict test (ie the need to establish the absence of any real risk) is appropriate in determining whether the solicitor is already possessed of such information...

DECISION

The former partner was one of ten partners in the intellectual property department of a firm not large by modern standards. He was in no wise engaged in the clients' matters. There was in the firm no secrecy in respect of the clients' matters or perception of the need for secrecy between the partners and assistants so engaged and the former partner.

The evidence establishes that the former partner had informal conversations (I would infer in general terms) with the partner in charge and two assistant solicitors working on the clients' case as to how the litigation was proceeding. He may have attended departmental meetings when aspects of the litigation may have been discussed. The confidential files (including a wall chart) were available to him to see if he wished to do so. There is no evidence that anything confidential was ever communicated to the former partner and in his affidavits he firmly states that it was not and that he was at no time possessed of any confidential information. His honesty and integrity are in no wise challenged. He met Mr Blackburn on the stairs at the firm and exchanged pleasantries. It is not suggested that anything confidential was said on this occasion. I cannot avoid feeling that against this background of fact it is unfortunate, perhaps undesirable, that there should be the perception of impropriety or unfairness resulting from the former partner now acting for the defendant. A client in the position of the clients need not be unduly sensitive to be affronted and the goodwill of the firm may be seriously prejudiced. But that is not the applicable test. The test is the existence of a real risk that relevant confidential information is possessed by the former partner. On the facts of this case, I do not think that there is any such risk. The former partner has satisfied me that there is no real possibility that confidential information was ever communicated to him. The clients' evidence suggests the possibility (and no more than the possibility) of such communication. In the light of the former partner's evidence, even after applying the discount appropriate to the need to protect the clients in respect of information in the former partner's mind of which he is presently unaware, but recollection of which may subsequently be triggered, I do not think that there is any real possibility. On the facts of this case, if I were to find the existence of any real risk in this case, I would in reality be adopting the test adopted in the United States of America, which is not legitimate. I also find that the overwhelming probability is that if any confidential information was ever communicated to the former partner, with the lapse of time, the progress of the proceedings and the disclosures in evidence and on discovery in the proceedings and having regard to the highly technical issues, there can be no real risk that such information will any longer now be (1) confidential (2) relevant and (3) recallable.[10]

Questions

1. Does Lightman J give appropriate weight to the partner's statement about what he had and had not been told?

2. If (as his Lordship assumes and the *Bolkiah* case probably confirms) the obligation to protect the client's confidences would have prevented the partner from representing the defendants whilst still a partner at his original firm, *should* the position have been any different because the partner was now in a new firm?

3. If the court had held that the partner had received confidential information, could other partners at his new firm have acted for the defendant?

4. Should the desire not to restrict the occupational mobility of lawyers (not mentioned by Lightman J) be regarded as a consideration to be weighed against the need to protect client confidentiality? Is this a matter of the private interests of lawyers or a matter of public policy?

5. You are one of six partners in a firm specialising in insurance work having joined the firm as a partner two years ago. For much of your time as a partner in this firm you have been acting for a client (whom you inherited from the former senior partner who has now retired) who is a road haulier and is in dispute with his indemnity insurers. The client is claiming indemnity from the insurer with respect to goods stolen from his depot. The insurers deny liability, relying by way of defence on clauses in the contract excluding liability in the case of theft by employees and upon failure by the insured to take specified measures to protect the premises. You have just learned from one of your partners that Mary, the solicitor acting for the insurer, was for a period of two years (ending two years ago) a trainee solicitor in your firm. During that time she worked for the senior partner when he was advising the client with respect to a number of claims for indemnity against the insurer. The former senior partner tells you that the solicitor was mainly involved in legal research, though she may have been present when confidential issues relating to the client's business were discussed.

---

10   Ibid at 487-490.

You must now decide whether to ask the court to restrain Mary from acting for the insurer.

i) Do you think the court would restrain Mary in these circumstances?

ii) Suppose you conclude that it is possible though unlikely that a court would issue an injunction. Should you nevertheless issue the proceedings? Does it make any difference if, in your view, the client's case is a good one and the insurer's refusal to pay seems unreasonable? What ethical issues are raised by this decision? See Crocker 'The Ethics of Moving To Disqualify Opposing Counsel for Conflict Of Interest' (1979) Duke Law Journal 1310-34.

4   Conflict of interest and restrictive settlements

Another situation which can be seen as involving problems of successive conflict of interest can arise during negotiations for the settlement of multi-party litigation. The defendant may offer a settlement conditional on the plaintiffs' lawyers undertaking not to bring further proceedings of this type against the defendants. One impact of such provisions is clearly that other potential claimants are deprived of the know-how developed by the plaintiff's solicitors in the course of bringing the first proceedings. Judicial approval of settlements is not normally required at present and settlements are often subject to confidentiality clauses. Consequently evidence of the use of clauses of this kind and judicial views on their validity are inevitably hard to find. However, their use was exposed to public scrutiny in the Opren litigation. Well over 1,000 plaintiffs claimed damages for negligence based on the side effects they had allegedly suffered as a result of taking an arthritis drug manufactured by Eli Lilley & Co. The proceedings were ultimately settled. Having announced in open court some of the details of the settlement, Hirst J made the following comments:

> I have been asked to clarify the position of various solicitors involved in the settlement. This includes Eli Lilley solicitors, the six leading firms acting for the great majority of Opren Plaintiffs and some 200 other firms who have accepted the terms of the offer on behalf of their clients.
>
> Part of the terms of the offer put forward by Eli Lilley's solicitors have been that the financial details, both globally and in relation to each individual settlement, should be kept confidential. There is nothing unusual in a term of this kind, nor in seeking to ensure that such confidentiality is preserved by imposing limitations on the solicitors acting for persons with a similar claim to whom the settlement does not apply.
>
> I am informed that public criticism has been advanced against the six leading firms and their 200 or so colleagues above referred to for declining to act for potential Opren Plaintiffs who are outside the scope of the settlement.
>
> It is commonplace for solicitors (and indeed other professional persons) to have to decline to represent, or to continue to represent, a potential or actual client. This may arise because of a possible conflict of interest between the two, or alternatively it may arise because of a possible conflict between the duties the solicitor would owe to each if he acted for both. The dangers of a solicitor exposing himself to such conflicts

have frequently been stressed by the court. (See for example the decision of the Court of Appeal in *Moody v Cox and Hatt* [1917] 2 Ch 71.)

In the present case their perception is of a possible conflict between their duty to their existing Opren clients to negotiate and if possible conclude a settlement under the seal of confidentiality and their duty to potential new clients to give them all available information. They are also naturally anxious to maintain their obligation of strict confidentiality relating to documents disclosed by Lilley on discovery solely within the ambit of the actions which fall under the co-ordinated arrangements.

This does not seem to me to be in any way unreasonable, and I am not impressed by the suggestion that has apparently been made that it is somehow in breach of the Solicitors Practice Rules.[11]

Notes

1. This issue recurred in 1999 when Leigh Day & Co and Irwin Mitchell (two of the UK's leading personal injury firms) acted on a conditional fee basis for clients suing two of the leading tobacco companies for smoking-related injuries. The plaintiffs were unable to obtain insurance against their liability for the defendant's costs but nevertheless proceeded (for consideration of the ethics of proceeding on this basis see *Hodgson v Imperial Tobacco* supra chapter 8). When the claims failed, the clients were liable for the defendants' costs. If the defendants had pursued the clients, the clients would clearly have been ruined. However, the defendants offered not to pursue the clients provided their lawyers undertook not to act against them again in tobacco-related litigation. The lawyers reluctantly agreed.[12]

2. Principle 1.01[13] of the LSGPC provides that:

A solicitor shall not do anything ... which compromises or impairs or is likely to compromise or impair ...
(b)   a person's freedom to instruct a solicitor of his or her choice. ...
(f)   the solicitor's duty to the Court

Comment 7 adds that

it would ... be wrong for solicitor X , acting for a defendant in litigation to offer a settlement which included a provision that the plaintiffs solicitor Y refrain from acting for other plaintiffs against the defendant in other future matters. Equally, it would wrong for solicitor Y to accept any such restriction. However a solicitor may nevertheless be unable to act for other potential plaintiffs where information has been disclosed under compulsion and the information has not been referred to in open

11   *Davies* v *Eli Lilley* (unreported, 14 January 1988, Hurst J).
12   See 'Tobacco Firms Avoid Cancer Court Battle' *Times* February 1999.
13   Practice Rule 1 forms part of the Solicitors Practice Rules 1990 made by the Council of the Law Society with the concurrence of the Master of the Rolls under s 31 of the Solicitors Act 1972.

court. In such a case the solicitors duty to the Court (rule 1(f)) would take precedence over the principle of freedom of choice of solicitor (rule 1(b)).

3. On the confidentiality issue see the case of *Distillers v Times Newspapers*[14] discussed in chapter 7 supra.

Questions

1. Was Hirst J correct to regard the issue in this case as being largely a matter of preventing conflicts of interest between successive clients?

2. Is it relevant that subsequent plaintiffs could obtain discovery of all the documents obtained by the current plaintiffs?

14   [1974] 3 WLR 728.

Index

Printed in Great Britain
by Amazon